HUMAN FACTORS IN SIMPLE AND COMPLEX SYSTEMS

ROBERT W. PROCTOR
Purdue University

TRISHA VAN ZANDT
Northwestern University

ALLYN AND BACON
Boston London Toronto Sydney Tokyo Singapore

Editor in Chief—Social Science: Susan Badger
Senior Editor: Laura Pearson
Editorial Assistant: Marnie Greenhut
Production Administrator: Marjorie Payne
Editorial-Production Supervisor: Raeia Maes
Cover Administrator: Linda Dickinson
Composition Buyer: Linda Cox
Manufacturing Buyer: Louise Richardson

 Copyright © 1994 by Allyn and Bacon
A Division of Simon & Schuster, Inc.
160 Gould Street
Needham Heights, MA 02194

Library of Congress Cataloging-in-Publication Data

Proctor, Robert W.
   Human factors in simple and complex systems / Robert W. Proctor and Trisha Van Zandt.
      p.   cm.
   Includes bibliographical references and index.
   ISBN 0-205-13999-X
   1. Human engineering.   2. Systems engineering.   I. Van Zandt, Trisha.   II. Title.
TA166.P75   1994
620.8′2   dc20   93-10148
                                         CIP

ISBN 0-205-13999-X
H39993

Printed in the United States of America

10   9   8   7   6   5   4   3   2   1   99   98   97   96   95   94

CONTENTS

PART FOUR
MOVEMENT FACTORS AND THEIR APPLICATIONS

PREFACE

Whether it's called human factors, ergonomics, usability engineering, or *engineering psychology,* the importance of designing for human use is well documented. Any equipment that is not ergonomically sound, even if it serves the purposes for which it was designed, will always be operated a little more slowly and be a little more prone to error. Although humans are adaptable and quick to learn, there are certain basic limitations to human performance. Anyone who designs equipment for human use must know and respect these limitations.

Our goal in writing this book is to provide a solid foundation in the principles of human performance and a broad overview of the field of human factors for advanced undergraduate and graduate students. Our intent is to emphasize the close relationship between basic and applied research. Recent years have seen considerable growth in the core disciplines from which human factors derive, as well as in the range of problems that have been addressed. Consequently, a wealth of information pertaining to human factors exists that can be brought to bear on specific design issues. This text will provide the reader with an understanding of the variables that influence human performance and the ways in which the human factors expert draws on this knowledge.

We have placed considerable emphasis on basic research and the way in which contemporary views of human performance have been developed. We make no apology for this. The methods and reasoning used by both basic and applied researchers, as presented here, are implemented to solve problems involving human beings. The human, as an object for research, is not the passive and controllable object to which most people trained in science are accustomed. The methods used to study people are unique, developed from years of experience with a subject that did not care to be studied. Human factors researchers work with people, sometimes stubborn and uncooperative, but their methods ensure that meaningful data can be collected in most situations.

Coupled with our emphasis on research and research methods is an emphasis on theory. We offer no apology for this, either. Most scientists regard the development of theory as the ultimate goal of science, because it is theory that provides the understanding that enables prediction in novel circumstances. This is no less true for an applied science, such as human factors, than for basic science. Because human factors requires prediction and generalization to new situations, theory is an indispensable tool.

The organization of the book, *Human Factors in Simple and Complex Systems,* is based on viewing the human as an information-processing system. The information-processing approach provides a common referent for studying both humans and machines. It is the predominant approach to the investigation of human performance in contemporary psychology and related disciplines. The broadest distinction typically made within an information-processing system is between the stages of information input, processing, and output. In the human, this distinction is represented by the stages of perception, cognition, and action, which provide the framework around which most findings can be organized and which define the three major sections of this book.

From our perspective as experimental psychologists, human factors research and design decisions must be based on a thorough understanding of basic principles of human performance. Similarly, the theoretical analysis of human performance requires frequent contact with real-world situations in which people actually perform. To that end, this text provides an integrated approach to the study of human factors, embedding the principles of human factors within a foundation based on contemporary views of human performance.

Part 1 is devoted to the basic material necessary for understanding the rest of the text. Chapter 1 discusses the historical foundations of human factors and the characteristics of the modern human factors profession. Chapter 2 covers the scientific method and behavioral research methods used in many human factors studies. We also present the statistical principles involved in the analysis of data and in many theoretical models. Those well grounded in behavioral research methods and statistics may choose to omit this chapter. Chapter 3 discusses the nature of systems, system reliability analysis, and human error—topics that form the core of human factors. Chapter 4 introduces the human information-processing approach, around which the remainder of the book is organized.

The next three parts in the book reflect the distinctions among perception, cognition, and action. Part 2 discusses basic and applied research involving perceptual processes. Chapter 5 is devoted to the human sensory systems and how physical energy is transformed into input to the human information-processing system. Chapters 6 and 7 discuss basic and higher-level perceptual transformations of sensory input that lead to such things as the perception of color, patterns, motion, and speech. Chapter 8 examines the design of displays for use in human-machine systems and relates the design recommendations to the perceptual issues discussed in the preceding chapters.

Part 3 is concerned with topics involving cognitive processes. Chapter 9 presents models of attention and relates these to the concept of mental workload. Chapter 10 discusses human memory characteristics, with an emphasis on the way in which information is remembered and comprehended. Chapter 11 examines human problem solving and decision making and techniques for improving reasoning skills. Chapter 12 considers the acquisition of cognitive skill, distinctions between experts and novices, and the relevance of expert performance to the design of expert systems.

Part 4 relates psychomotor and response-selection skills to the performance of controlled actions. Chapter 13 is concerned with the cognitive aspects of response selection and factors that influence compatibility between displays and controls. Chapter 14 deals with the speed and accuracy with which movements can be made in a variety of circumstances. Chapter 15 examines the acquisition of perceptual-motor skill, with emphasis on training schedules and the role of feedback. Chapter 16 relates the information in the previous chapters of Part 4 to the design of controls and control panels.

Part 5 considers human factors within the context of the living and working environment. Chapter 17 defines engineering anthropometry and discusses anthropometric considerations in tool design, manual materials handling, and workspace design. Chapter 18 examines the more global aspects of the physical environment, including the effects of lighting, noise, vibration, temperature, and air quality. Chapter 19 discusses macroergonomics, or the social and organizational factors that influence performance in the workplace. Chapter 20 examines the topic of human-computer interaction and brings together a wide range of issues and principles discussed throughout the book. Finally, Chapter 21 discusses the implementation of human factors programs in the system development process, forensic human factors, and the contribution of human factors to society.

A student workbook is available to accompany this text. It contains projects for each chapter that illustrate many of the major concepts and techniques. These projects require students to perform basic computations, contain questions to probe their understanding of these computations and associated concepts, and encourage students to relate their knowledge to specific applied issues. Although the text can be used without the workbook, we think that the projects in the workbook significantly enhance the learning experience.

We would like to acknowledge the contribution of D. J. Weeks in the initiation of this project and his assistance with several chapters. We would also like to thank Addie Dutta for reading drafts of the book and making many helpful recommendations. Julie Smith, the world's greatest secretary, did most of the typing. The book also benefited from the guidance provided by Susan Badger, Diane McOscar, and Laura Pearson of Allyn and Bacon during its development, from the day-to-day attention of Raeia Maes, who ushered our manuscript through the production process, and from the comments of Kitty Campbell, Liz Franz, Gil Reeve, and students who used preliminary copies in Purdue's PSY/IE 577 Human Factors in Engineering. We would like to thank our families and friends for their encouragement and support during the writing of this book.

We extend a note of thanks to the following reviewers: John Lott Brown, University of South Florida; Mark Chignell, University of Toronto; Gregory M. Corso, Georgia Institute of Technology; Marvin J. Dainoff, Miami University-Oxford Campus; Arthur Fisk, Georgia Institute of Technology; Timothy E. Goldsmith, University of New Mexico; Charles O. Hopkins, University of Illinois at Urbana-Champaign; Stephan Konz, Kansas State University; P. E. Patterson, Iowa State University; Richard A. Schmidt, University of California-Los Angeles; and Laura A. Thompson, New Mexico State University.

R. W. P.
T. V. Z.

FOREWORD

Human Factors in Simple and Complex Systems is being published at a very opportune time. Business and industry are experiencing major revolutions in the introduction of advanced technologies that require increased utilization of human cognitive and perceptual abilities. The design and operation of simple and complex systems in industrial, military, and service industries require a firm grounding in the core disciplines on which the field of human factors draws. This book effectively covers the critical areas of perception, cognition, and motor behavior, examining the implications for system development and operation. The theoretical approach that it takes is in contrast to the classical "cookbook" approach frequently seen in human factors, from which students get information about specific functions or attributes that can be applied only to a particular area. Instead, this book demonstrates a general approach to solving a broad range of system problems. It provides a long awaited and much needed coverage of the theoretical foundation on which the discipline of human factors is built. The book will be especially useful for students in engineering, science, and management who may not be familiar with the literature on basic human capabilities. It will become a "must" on the bookshelves of all human factors students and practitioners.

Gavriel Salvendy
NEC Professor of Industrial Engineering
Purdue University
West Lafayette, Indiana

HISTORICAL FOUNDATIONS OF HUMAN FACTORS

Our interest in the design of machines for human use runs the full gamut of machine complexity—from the design of single instruments to the design of complete systems of machines which must be operated with some degree of coordination

—A. Chapanis, W. Garner, and C. Morgan, 1949

INTRODUCTION

In everyday life, we interact constantly with machines and other inanimate systems. These interactions range from turning on and off a light by means of a switch, to the operation of household appliances such as stoves and video-cassette recorders (VCRs), to the control of complex systems such as aircraft and spacecraft. In the simple case of the light switch, the interaction of a person with the switch and those components controlled by the switch forms a system (see Figure 1–1). Every system has a purpose or a goal; evident in the lighting system is the purpose of illuminating a dark room or extinguishing a light when it no longer is needed. The efficiency of the inanimate parts of this system, that is, the power supply, wiring, switch, and light bulb, in part

determines whether the system goal can be met. For example, if the light bulb burns out, illumination is no longer possible.

The abilities of the lighting system and other systems to meet their goals also depend on the human components of the systems. For example, if a small person cannot reach the light switch, the goal of providing illumination will not be met. Thus, the total efficiency of the system depends on both the performance of the inanimate components and the performance of the human component. A failure of any one can lead to failure of the entire system. The probability that any one component does not fail is a measure of its reliability. Total system reliability is a function of the system structure and the reliabilities of the individual components. A system that consistently meets its goal has high reliability.

1

FIGURE 1–1 Diagram of a Lighting System.

The systems and products arising from the increasingly sophisticated technology of the twentieth century have become quite complex, and their performance often is limited by the human component. For example, contemporary VCRs can be complicated to operate. It is estimated that the majority of VCR owners have never used their VCRs to their fullest capabilities (Pollack, 1990). Almost one-third have never even set the clock, which is necessary if the VCR is to be programmed for recording at specific times.

While consumers' struggles with their VCRs may seem amusing, in other cases great amounts of money and many human lives rely on the successful operation of systems. As one example, design flaws, relaxed safety regulations, and a sequence of bad decisions led to the failed launch of the space shuttle, *Challenger*. This resulted in the loss of human lives, crippled the space program, and incurred a substantial cost to the government and private industry. Similarly, poorly designed warning displays and control panels contributed to the Three-Mile Island nuclear incident, in which the reactor system failed. Although the emergency equipment functioned properly, the inadequate display and control designs led to a series of human errors that turned a minor incident into a major disaster. This resulted in considerable bad press for the nuclear power industry, as well as financial loss. The *Challenger* and

Three-Mile Island incidents can be traced to errors in both the machine components and human components of the systems.

What Is Human Factors?

When engineers design machines, systems are evaluated in terms of their properties of reliability, ease of operation, and error-free performance, among other things. Because the efficiency of a system depends on the performance of the operator as well as the adequacy of the machine, the operator and machine must be considered together as a single *human–machine system*. With this view, it then makes sense to analyze the performance capabilities of the human component in terms that are consistent with those used to describe the inanimate components of the system. For example, the reliability of human components can be evaluated in the same way as the reliability of machine components. The variables that govern the efficiency of the operator within a system fall under the topic of *human factors:* the study of those variables that influence the efficiency with which the human performer can interact with the inanimate components of a system to accomplish the system goals. This also is called *ergonomics* and sometimes *engineering psychology*. In fact, the term ergonomics is more familiar than the term human factors outside the United States and to the general population within the United States.

Because of the widespread use of the term ergonomics, the representative organization for human factors in the United States, the Human Factors Society, voted to change its name to the Human Factors and Ergonomics Society beginning in 1993. As described by Laughery (1992), the last straw apparently was an article that appeared in *Computerworld,* May 1991, which incorrectly stated that "there is no professional ergonomists' association and there are only about 300 professional ergonomists in the entire U.S." (Savage, 1991, p. 67).

A more elaborate definition for the human factors profession that captures its primary characteristics and goals has been developed by a committee of the Human Factors Society:

> Human factors is that branch of science and technology that includes what is known and theorized about human behavioral and biological characteristics that can be validly applied to the specification, design, evaluation, operation, and maintenance of products and systems to enhance safe, effective, and satisfying use by individuals, groups, and organizations. (Christensen, Topmiller, & Gill, 1988, p. 7)

The human factors profession depends on basic research from pertinent supporting sciences, applied research that is unique to the profession, and application of the resulting data and principles to specific design problems. Human factors specialists are thus involved in research and application of the data from research to all phases of system development and evaluation.

Embodied in the definition of human factors is the importance of basic human capabilities, such as perceptual abilities, attention span, memory span, and physical limitations. The human factors specialist must be knowledgeable of these capabilities and bring this knowledge to bear on the design of systems. For example, the placement of a light switch at an optimal height requires knowledge of the anthropometric constraints (that is, the physical characteristics) of the population of intended users. If the switch is intended for use by people confined to wheelchairs as well as by people who are not, it should be placed at a height that allows easy operation of the switch by both groups. Similarly, knowledge about operators' perceptual, cognitive, and movement capabilities must be considered in the design of information displays and controls, such as those found in automobiles, computer software packages, and microwave ovens. Only designs that specifically consider basic human capabilities will be able to maximize total system performance. Otherwise, system performance will be reduced and system goals may not be met.

Fortunately, considerable research has been conducted on basic human capabilities. This research spans more than a century and forms the core of the more general study of human performance. Specifically, the study of human performance involves analyses of the processes that underlie the acquisition, maintenance, and transfer of skilled behavior (Fitts & Posner, 1967). The research identifies factors that limit different aspects of performance, analyzes complex tasks into simpler components, and establishes estimates of the human's basic capabilities. This knowledge enables predictions of the human's ability to perform both simple and complex tasks.

Just as engineers analyze the machine component of a complex system in terms of its constituent subsystems (recall the wiring, switch, and light bulb of the lighting system), the human–performance researcher analyzes the human component in terms of its subsystems. Before the light can be turned on, the human must perceive a need for light, decide on the appropriate action, and execute the action necessary to flip the switch. In contrast, the human factors specialist is concerned primarily with the interface between the human and machine components, with the goal of making the exchange of information between these two components as smooth and efficient as possible. In our lighting system example, this interface is embodied in the light switch, and the human factors issues involve the design and placement of the switch for optimal use. Thus, whereas the human performance researcher is interested in characterizing the processes within the human component, the human factors specialist is concerned with designing the human–machine interface to optimize achievement of the system goal.

In designing a system, there is much more freedom in the specification of the operating characteristics of the machine than in the specification of those of the human operator. That is, the machine components can be redesigned and improved, whereas "redesigning" the operator is not possible and improvement is severely limited. Operators can be carefully screened and extensively trained before placing them in the system, but many limitations that characterize human performance cannot be overcome. Because of this relative lack of freedom regarding the operator, it becomes imperative to know the constraints that human limitations impose on machine designs. Thus, the human factors specialist must consider basic human performance capabilities in order to wisely use the freedom that is available in the design of the machine component of the system.

The domains of the design engineer, the human performance researcher, and the human factors specialist are summarized in Figures 1–2 and 1–3. Figure 1–2 depicts an example human–machine system: a human operating a microcomputer. The human–computer interface involves a video screen on which information is displayed visually by the microcomputer to communicate with the operator. This information is received by the operator through the visual sense. The information is processed by the operator, and communication back to the computer is made by responding on the keyboard. The computer then processes this information, and the sequence begins anew. Because of the increasingly widespread use of microcomputers, a branch of human factors has developed specifically to deal with the problems involved in human–computer interaction.

FIGURE 1–2 Human-Computer System.

Figure 1–3 shows a more abstract version of the human–computer system. In this abstraction, the similarity between the human and computer is clear. Both can be conceptualized in terms of subsystems that are responsible for input, processing, and output, respectively. This figure illustrates how the human component can be conceived in terms similar to the machine component. While the human receives input primarily through the visual system, the computer receives its input from the keyboard and other peripheral devices. The central processing unit in the computer is analogous to the cognitive capabilities of

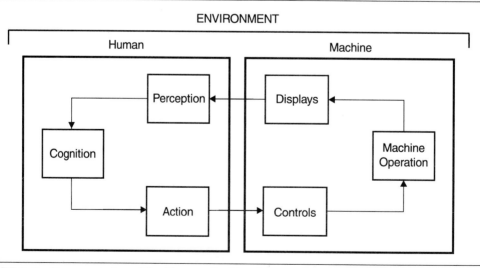

FIGURE 1–3 Representation of the Human–Machine System. The Human and Machine Are Composed of Subsystems Operating Within the Larger Environment.

the human brain. Finally, the human produces output through overt physical responses, such as key presses, whereas the computer exhibits its output on the display screen.

Also indicated in Figure 1–3 are the domains of the design engineer, the human performance researcher, and the human factors specialist. The design engineer is interested primarily in the subsystems of the machine and their interrelations. Similarly, the human performance expert studies the subsystems of the human and their interrelations. Finally, the human factors specialist is most concerned with the relations between the input and output subsystems of the human and machine components or, in other words, with the human–machine interface.

The final point to note from Figure 1–3 is that the entire human–machine system is embedded within the larger context of the work environment. Thus, the environment influences the performance of the system. This influence can be on the machine component or on the human component, as well as on their interface. If the computer is in a very hot and humid environment, some of its components may be damaged and destroyed, leading to system failure. Similarly, extreme heat and humidity can adversely affect the operator's performance, which may likewise lead to system failure. The environment also consists of those social and organizational variables that influence the operator. The term *macroergonomics* is used to describe the interactions between the organizational environment and the design and implementation of a system.

The total system performance depends on the operator, the machine, and the environment in which they are placed. Whereas the design engineer works exclusively in the domain of the machine, and the human performance researcher in the domain of the operator, the human factors specialist is concerned with the interrelations among machine, operator, and environment. In solving a particular problem involving human–machine interaction, the human factors specialist usually starts with a consideration of the capabilities of the operator. Human capabilities began to

receive serious scientific scrutiny in the nineteenth century, well ahead of the technology with which the design engineer is now faced. This early research forms the foundation of contemporary human factors.

HISTORICAL ANTECEDENTS

The major impetus for the establishment of human factors as a discipline came from technological developments related to World War II. As weapon and transport systems became increasingly sophisticated, great technological advances were also being made in factory automation and in equipment for common use. Through the difficulties encountered while operating such sophisticated equipment, the need for human factors analyses became evident. Human factors research was preceded by research in the areas of human performance psychology and industrial engineering. Thus, the historical overview presented here will begin by establishing the groundwork within these areas that relates to human factors.

The Psychology of Human Performance

The study of human performance dates to the early nineteenth century (Boring, 1942). Two major figures were Ernst Weber and Gustav Fechner. Both Weber and Fechner performed investigations on the basic sensory and perceptual capabilities of humans. Weber (1846/1978) examined people's ability to tell that two stimuli, such as two weights, differ in magnitude. The relation that he discovered has come to be known to as *Weber's law*. This law can be expressed quantitatively as

$$\frac{\Delta I}{I} = K$$

where I is the intensity of a stimulus, ΔI is the amount of change between it and another stimulus needed to tell that the two stimuli differ in magnitude, and K is a constant. What Weber's law indicates is that the absolute amount of change needed to perceive a difference in magnitude increases with intensity, whereas the relative amount remains constant. In other words, the heavier a weight is, the greater the absolute increase must be to perceive another weight as heavier. Weber's law is still described today in textbooks on sensation and perception (for example, Goldstein, 1989) and provides a reasonable description for the detection of differences with many types of stimuli, except at extremely high or low physical intensities.

Fechner (1860/1966) formalized methods of the type used by Weber and constructed the first scales intended to relate psychological magnitude (for example, loudness) to physical magnitude (for example, amplitude). Fechner assumed that the amount of change needed to perceive a difference (the just noticeable difference) evokes a constant increment in the magnitude of the psychological sensation. He then integrated Weber's law and obtained the psychophysical function

$$S = K \log(I)$$

where S is the magnitude of sensation, I is physical intensity, K is a constant, and log is to any base. This function, relating physical intensity to the psychological sensation, is called *Fechner's law*. The term *psychophysics* has been used to describe such research that examines the basic sensory sensitivities. Like Weber's law, Fechner's law is presented in contemporary textbooks on sensation and perception and still provokes theoretical inquiry concerning the measurement of psychological magnitude (Krueger, 1989).

The work of Fechner and Weber supplied evidence that characteristics of human performance could be revealed through controlled experimentation and, consequently, provided the impetus for the broad range of research on humans that followed. At approximately the same historical period, considerable advances were being made in sensory physiology. One of the most notable investigators was Hermann von Helmholtz, who made many contributions that remain as central theoretical principles today. One of Helmholtz's most important contributions was establishing a method by which the time for

transmission of a nerve impulse could be estimated. His method involved measuring the difference in time between application of a stimulus to a frog's nerve and the resulting muscle contraction for two different points on the nerve. The measures indicated that the speed of transmission was approximately 27 m/s (Boring, 1942). The importance of this finding was to demonstrate that neural transmission is not instantaneous but takes measurable time.

Helmholtz's finding served as the basis for early research by Donders (1868/1969) using procedures that are referred to as chronometric methods. Donders reasoned that, when performing a speeded reaction task, observers must make a series of judgments. A stimulus is first detected (is something there?) and is then identified (what is there?). Subsequently, the stimulus can be discriminated from other stimuli (is this the stimulus to which I am to react?). At this point the observer selects the appropriate response to the stimulus (what response am I to make?). Donders designed several tasks for humans to perform that differed in terms of the combination of judgments required for each task. By using a subtractive logic, in which the time to perform one task was subtracted from the time to perform another task that required one additional judgment, Donders estimated the time for the respective component judgments.

The importance of the subtractive logic is that it provided the foundation for the notion that mental processes can be isolated. This notion is the central tenet of *human information processing,* the approach that underlies most contemporary research on human performance. This approach assumes that cognition occurs through a series of operations performed on information originating from the senses. The conception of the human as an information-processing system is invaluable for the investigation of human factors issues, because it meets the requirement of allowing human and machine performance to be analyzed in terms of the same basic functions. As shown in Figure 1–4, both humans and machines perform a sequence of operations on input from

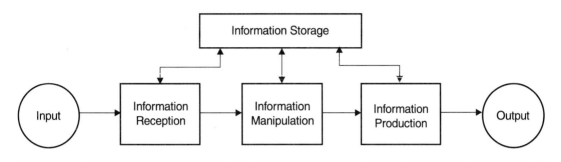

FIGURE 1–4   Information Processing in Humans and Machines.
Adapted with permission from M. S. Sanders & E. J. McCormick, *Human Factors in Engineering and Design* (6th ed.). Copyright © 1987 by McGraw-Hill, Inc.

the environment that leads to an output of new information. Given this parallel between human and machine systems, it makes sense to organize our knowledge of human performance around the basic information-processing functions.

Both the psychophysical methods developed by Fechner and the chronometric methods developed by Donders were used extensively in the early years of experimental psychology. The founding of psychology as a distinct discipline usually is dated from the establishment of the first laboratory devoted exclusively to psychological research, by Wilhelm Wundt in 1879. Wundt was a prolific researcher and teacher. Consequently, his views largely defined the field of psychology and the study of human performance in the late 1800s.

With respect to contemporary human-performance psychology, Wundt's primary legacy is in the orientation that he took. Specifically, Wundt promoted a deterministic approach to the study of mental life. He advocated the view that mental events play a causal role in human behavior. Wundt held that our mental representation of the world is a function of experience and the manner in which the mind organizes that experience. As such, he proposed that the workings of the mind could be understood by a decomposition of sensory and perceptual experience into basic elements. Although Weber, Fechner, Donders, and Wundt conducted research that differed in

many respects, they all shared the view that mental activity is composed of a series of mental events having distinct properties.

Whereas Wundt and the others had tackled the experimental problem of isolating mental events, Hermann Ebbinghaus (1885/1964) was the first to successfully apply experimental rigor to the study of learning and memory. This contribution was important because previously it had been thought that the quantitative study of such higher-level mental processes was not possible (Herbart, 1816/1891). In a lengthy series of experiments conducted on himself, Ebbinghaus examined his ability to learn and retain lists of nonsense syllables. The procedures developed by Ebbinghaus, the quantitative methods of analysis that he employed, and the theoretical issues that he investigated provided the basis for a scientific investigation of higher mental function.

In a landmark study in the history of human performance psychology, Bryan and Harter (1899) extended the topic of learning and memory to the investigation of skill acquisition. In their study of the learning of Morse code in telegraphy, Bryan and Harter determined many of the factors involved in the acquisition of what would later come to be called perceptual–motor skills. Using procedures and methods of analysis similar to those provided by Ebbinghaus, Bryan and Harter were able to contribute both to our basic understanding of skill learning and to our applied understanding of telegraphic skill. By examining learning curves (plots of performance as a function of practice), Bryan and Harter proposed that learning proceeds in a series of phases. Contemporary models of skill acquisition still rely on this notion of phases (for example, Anderson, 1983).

Another topic of central concern for the study of human performance, as well as for human factors, is that of attention. Of the early psychologists, perhaps the most influential views on the topic were those of William James. In his classic book, *Principles of Psychology,* published in 1890, James devoted an entire chapter to attention. James states:

> Everyone knows what attention is. It is the taking possession by the mind, in clear and vivid form, of one out of what seems several simultaneously possible objects or trains of thought. Focalization, concentration, of consciousness are of its essence. It implies withdrawal from some things in order to deal effectively with others. (James, 1890/ 1950, pp. 403–404)

This quote captures many of the properties of attention that are still addressed in modern research, such as different types of attention, limitations in processing capacity, and the role of consciousness (for example, Shiffrin, 1988).

Human Performance in Applied Settings

Although we have dated the founding of human factors as a discipline from World War II, considerable applied work important to modern human factors was conducted prior to that time. Charles W. Babbage wrote the book *Economy of Machinery and Manufactures* in 1832, in which he proposed methods for increasing the efficiency by which workers could perform their jobs. In the spirit of the modern factory assembly line, Babbage advocated job specialization, with the idea that this would enable a worker to become skilled and proficient at a limited range of tasks.

Among the first work to systematically investigate human performance in applied settings was that of Frederick W. Taylor. Taylor, who was an industrial engineer, examined worker productivity in industrial settings. He conducted one of the earliest human factors studies. As described by Gies (1991), Taylor was concerned that the workers at a steel plant used the same shovel for all shoveling tasks. Through careful scientific scrutiny, he designed several different shovels and several different methods of shoveling that were appropriate for different materials.

Taylor is best remembered for developing a school of thought that is referred to as scientific management (Taylor, 1911/1967). He made three contributions to the enhancement of productivity in the workplace. The first contribution is known as *task analysis,* in which the components of a task are determined. One technique of task analysis is *time-and-motion study.* With this technique, a worker's movements are analyzed across time to determine the best way to perform a task. Taylor's second contribution was the concept of *pay for performance.* He suggested a piecework method of production, for which the amount of compensation to the worker is a function of the number of pieces completed. Taylor's third contribution involved *personnel selection,* or fitting the worker to the task. While personnel selection is still important, human factors emphasizes fitting the task to the worker. Although dehumanizing, Taylor's techniques were effective in improving human performance (that is, increasing productivity), and time-and-motion study is still used in contemporary human factors.

One of the earliest and best-known examples of applied time-and-motion study is F. B. Gilbreth's (1909) investigations of bricklaying and of operating-room procedures. Gilbreth, a former bricklayer, examined the number of movements made by bricklayers as a function of the locations of the workers' tools, the raw materials, and the structure being built. Similarly, he examined the interactions among members of surgical teams. The changes instituted by Gilbreth for bricklaying resulted in an impressive increase in productivity; his analysis of operating-room procedures led to the development of contemporary surgical protocols.

Productivity was examined in a classic study of applied human performance conducted at the Hawthorne plant of the Western Electric Company from 1924 to 1933. The most widely known investigation was one relating illumination to productivity. To determine whether production would increase under higher intensity lighting, illumination levels were raised for one group of workers and kept at the normal level for another group. Surprisingly, both groups showed increased productivity. The apparent reason for this finding was that the workers knew that their performance was being monitored by the researchers. This effect, which came to be called the *Hawthorne effect,* was given prominence in the fields of basic and applied human performance, although its validity can be questioned (for example, Bramel & Friend, 1981).

Personnel selection grew from work on individual differences in abilities developed during World War I, with the use of intelligence tests to select personnel. Subsequently, numerous other tests involving performance, interests, and so on, were developed to select personnel to operate machines and to perform other jobs. Personnel selection can increase the quality of system performance. However, there are limits to how much performance can be improved through selection. A poorly designed system will not perform well even if the best personnel are selected. Thus, a major impetus to the development of the discipline of human factors was the need to improve the design of systems for human use.

Biomechanics and Physiology of Human Performance

Human performance has also been studied from the perspective of biomechanics and physiology (Cooper & Glassow, 1972). The biomechanical analysis of human performance has its roots in the early theoretical work of Galileo and Newton, who helped to establish the laws of physics and mechanics. Giovanni Alphonso Borelli (1679/1989), a student of Galileo, brought together the disciplines of mathematics, physics, and anatomy

in one of the earliest works on the mechanics of human performance.

Probably the most important contribution to biomechanical analysis in the area of work efficiency was made by Jules Amar. In his book *The Human Motor,* Amar (1920) provided a comprehensive synthesis of the physiological and biomechanical principles related to industrial work. Amar's research initiated investigations into the application of biomechanical principles to work performance. The ideas of Amar and others were adopted by and applied to the emerging field of human factors.

Another major accomplishment was the development of procedures that allowed for a dynamic assessment of human performance. In the latter part of the nineteenth century, Eadweard Muybridge constructed an apparatus comprised of banks of cameras that allowed him to take pictures of animals and humans in action (for example, Muybridge, 1955). Each series of pictures captured the biomechanical characteristics of a complex action (see Figure 1–5). The pictures also could be viewed at a rapid presentation rate, with the result being a simulation of the actual movement.

Muybridge's work opened the door for a range of biomechanical analyses of dynamic human performances. In particular, Etienne-Jules Marey (1902) exploited related photographic techniques to decompose time and motion. Today, such analyses involve videotaping performances of human action that can then be evaluated. Modern camera-based systems, such as WATSMART (see Figure 1–6), are able to provide definitive assessment of movement kinematics in three dimensions.

THE EMERGENCE OF THE HUMAN FACTORS PROFESSION

Although interest in basic human performance and applied human factors goes back to before the turn of the century, a trend toward systematic investigation of human factors did not begin in earnest until the 1940s. The technological ad-

FIGURE 1–5   An Example of Muybridge's Photographs of Human Motion.
From E. A. Muybridge, *Complete Human and Animal Locomotion, Volume 1.* Copyright © 1979
by Dover Publications, Inc. Reprinted with permission.

vances brought about by World War II created a need for more practical research from the academic community. Moreover, basic research psychologists became involved in applied projects, along with industrial and communications engineers. By the close of the war, psychologists were collaborating with engineers on the design of aircraft cockpits, radar scopes, and underwater sound detection devices, among other things. Similarly, some industries began to research human factors, with Bell Laboratories establishing a laboratory devoted specifically to human factors

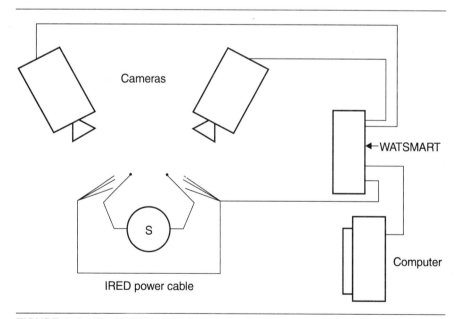

FIGURE 1–6   The WATSMART System for Recording Movement Trajectories.
The Cameras Pick Up Infrared Light from the Infrared Light Emitting Diodes
(IRED) Attached to the Human Subject (S). Computer Analysis Provides a
Three-dimensional Account of Each IRED at Each Sampling Interval.
Courtesy of Howard N. Zelaznik.

in the late 1940s. The interdisciplinary efforts that were stimulated during and immediately after the years of the war provided the basis for the development of the human factors profession.

The profession was formalized in England with the founding of the Human Research Group in 1949. In 1950, the group changed its name to the Ergonomics Research Society, and the term ergonomics came to be used in the European community to characterize the study of human–machine interactions. More recently, the name of the society has been shortened to the Ergonomics Society. The year 1949 also marked the publication of the first text on human factors, *Applied Experimental Psychology: Human Factors in Engineering Design* (Chapanis, Garner, & Morgan, 1949). This text was responsible for the designation of the discipline as "human factors" in the United States.

Several years later, in 1957, the Ergonomics Society began publication of the first journal devoted to human factors, *Ergonomics.* In that same year, the Human Factors Society was formed in the United States, and publication of their journal, *Human Factors,* began one year later. Also, the American Psychological Association established Division 21, Engineering Psychology, and in 1959 the International Ergonomics Association was established.

From 1960 to 1991 the profession of human factors grew immensely (see Figure 1–7). The current composition of the Technological Groups of the Human Factors and Ergonomics Society is shown in Table 1–1. The topics covered by these groups are indicative of the broad range of issues now addressed by human factors specialists. Professional societies have been established in numerous other countries, and more specialized societies have developed. Human–computer interaction alone is the focus of the Association for Computing Machinery's Special Interest Group on Computer Human Interaction, the Software

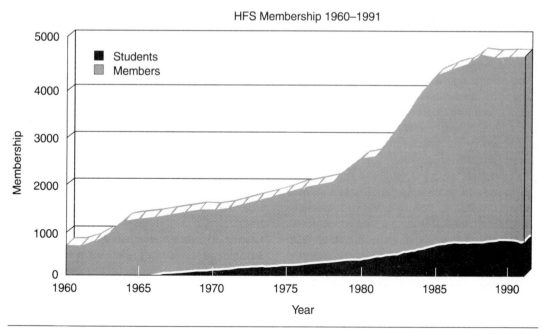

FIGURE 1–7 Membership of the Human Factors Society, 1960–91.

TABLE 1-1 Technical Groups of the Human Factors and Ergonomics Society

Aerospace Systems: Development, design, and operation of human–machine systems in the aviation and space environments.

Aging: Meeting the needs of older people and other special populations in a wide variety of life settings.

Communications: Human factors as applied to communication systems, from initial determination of user needs through design, installation, maintenance, operation, field evaluation, personnel selection, and training.

Computer Systems: The human factors aspects of interactive computer systems, the data-processing environment, and software development.

Consumer Products: The development and design of publicly sold consumer goods, office equipment, and related items.

Educators' Professional: Education and training of human factors specialists.

Environmental Design: The constructed physical environment, including architectural and interior design aspects of home, office, and industrial settings.

Forensics Professional: "Standards of care" and accountability established within the legislative, regulatory, and judicial systems.

Industrial Ergonomics: Application of ergonomic data in the service and manufacturing process.

Organizational Design and Management: Improving productivity and the quality of work life by an integration of psychosocial, cultural, and technological factors with user interface factors in the design of jobs, work stations, organizations, and related management systems.

Personality and Individual Differences in Human Performance: Investigating the personality and individual difference characteristics that influence the understanding and prediction of performance in any area of human factors research or application.

Safety: Research and applications concerning human factors for safety in all settings, including transportation, industry, military, office, public building, recreation, and home environments.

System Development: Identifying and integrating the role of human factors in the acquisition of major systems.

Test and Evaluation: Methodologies and techniques of testing and evaluation that have been developed in all areas of human factors.

Training: Training and training research in human factors.

Visual Performance: All aspects of vision as it affects performance in human–machine systems. Areas of concern include the nature and content of visual information and the context in which it is displayed; the physics and psychophysics of information display; perceptual and cognitive representation and interpretation of displayed information; effects of workload; and actions and behaviors that are consequences of visually displayed information.

Adapted from *The Human Factors Society Directory and Yearbook,* 1992.

Psychology Society, and the IEEE Technical Committee on Computer and Display Ergonomics, as well as many others. Outside of computer science, the rapid growth of technology has made the human factors profession a key component in the development and design of equipment and machinery.

CONTEMPORARY HUMAN FACTORS

The profession of human factors has close historic ties with the military. These ties continue today. The U.S. military incorporates human factors analyses into the design and evaluation of all military systems. All branches of the military have human factors research programs. These programs are administered by the Air Force Office of Scientific Research, the Office of Naval Research, the Army Research Institute, and Army Engineering Laboratories. Additionally, the military branches have special programs to ensure that human factors principles are incorporated into the development of weapons and other military systems and equipment. For the Army, the development program is MANPRINT (Manpower and Personnel Integration); for the Air Force, it is IMPACTS (Integrated Manpower, Personnel and Comprehensive Training and Safety); and for the Navy, it is HARDMAN (Hardware/Manpower Integration).

Although the approaches of these programs differ, they all have the goal of satisfying the U.S. Department of Defense Directive 5000.53, "Manpower, Personnel, Training and Safety in the Defense System Acquisition Process," which requires all services to demonstrate planning in these areas. For example, the *MANPRINT Bulletin* states:

> The *MANPRINT* program is a comprehensive management and technical initiative to enhance human performance and reliability during weapons system and equipment design, development, and production. *MANPRINT* encompasses the six domains of manpower, personnel, training, human factors engineering, system safety, and health hazard assessment. The focus of *MANPRINT* is to integrate technology, people, and force structure to meet mission objectives under all environmental conditions at the lowest possible life-cycle cost.

Recent years have seen an expanded influence of human factors into other aspects of society. Nowhere has this been more evident than in the design of nuclear power facilities. Prior to the Three-Mile Island incident, in which a major nuclear disaster was barely averted, the involvement of human factors in the nuclear industry was minimal. However, this incident brought to light the fact that the design of control rooms violated many basic principles of optimal human performance, with a consequent increase in the probability of human error and system failure. Subsequent to this event, the U.S. Nuclear Regulatory Commission instituted a human factors review of all nuclear power facilities so that design deficiencies could be identified and corrected.

More recent examples of the ramifications of human error in a complex system are incidents involving the warship *Vincennes* and the oil tanker *Exxon Valdez*. The crew of the *Vincennes* mistakenly downed a commercial air liner; the *Exxon Valdez* ran aground, resulting in the largest oil spill in U.S. history and a threat to the environment of Alaska. In both cases, less than optimal human performance led to action of a complex system that had disastrous consequences.

The value of human factors analyses is also apparent in our everyday lives. During the past decade, the automotive industry has devoted considerably more attention than previously to human factors in the design of automobiles. This attention has extended from the design of the automobile itself to the machinery used to make it. Similarly, modern office furniture has benefited significantly from human factors evaluations. Still, we often encounter equipment that is poorly designed for human use. The problem noted previously regarding VCRs is but one example. The need for good human factors has become sufficiently obvious that manufacturers and advertising agencies now realize that it can become a selling point for their products. The makers of automobiles, furniture and the like advertise their products in terms of the specific ergonomic advantages that their products have over those of their competitors. If the present is any indication, the role of human factors will only increase in the future.

Among the more exotic challenges for human factors specialists is to bring their profession to bear on the issues that arise as humans begin to colonize extraterrestrial environments. The nature of the extraterrestrial environment demands that human factors concerns be addressed in the initial design phase of the system development process, because oversights will be difficult to correct without the easily available resources of the earthbound environment. Although many human factors principles will hold regardless of environmental conditions, the unique conditions of extraterrestrial environments will pose new constraints (Lewis, 1990). In recognition of the need to consider human factors in the design of space equipment, NASA recently published the first human factors design guide, the *Man–Systems Integration Standards* (1987), to be used by developers and designers to promote the integration of humans and equipment in space (Tillman, 1987).

The construction of the first permanent manned space station provides one opportunity for the design of an extraterrestrial environment. NASA has acknowledged the need to incorporate human factors into the design of all aspects of the space station (*Space-station Human Productivity Study,* 1985). Human factors research and engineering will play a role in designing the station to optimize the crew's quality of life, or habitability (Wise, 1986), as well as to optimize the crew's quality of work, or productivity (Gillan, et al., 1986). Consequently, the reliability of the space-station system will be maximized and crew safety increased.

In sum, the profession of human factors has come to play a major role in the design and evaluation of both simple and complex systems. The importance of the contribution of human factors to industry, engineering, psychology, and the military cannot be overemphasized. When design decisions are made, failure to consider human factors can lead to waste of personnel and money, as well as danger to human life. Consequently, consideration of human factors concerns at all phases of system development is of utmost importance.

RECOMMENDED READING

Boring, E. G. (1950). *A History of Experimental Psychology,* 2nd ed. New York: Appleton-Century.

Chapanis, A., Garner, W. R., & Morgan, C. T. (1949). *Applied Engineering Psychology: Human Factors in Engineering Design.* New York: Wiley.

Hanson, B. L. (1983). A brief history of applied behavioral science at Bell Laboratories. *Bell System Technical Journal, 62,* 1571–1590.

Hilgard, E. R. (1987). *Psychology in America: A Historical Survey.* New York: Harcourt Brace Jovanovich.

Rabinbach, A. (1990). *The Human Motor.* New York: Basic Books.

Taylor, F. W. (1911/1967). *The Principles of Scientific Management.* New York: W. W. Norton.

RESEARCH METHODS IN HUMAN FACTORS

It may be said, fairly enough, that science progresses by the exposure of error and that in so far as an endeavor is scientific it is as ready to look for error within its own contentions as in those opposing it. In particular, it has to be stressed that observation, which plays so special a role in science, is not regarded as error-free.

—W. M. O'Neil, 1957

INTRODUCTION

Human factors is an applied science. It relies on measurement of behavioral and physical properties in settings ranging from the laboratory to working human–machine systems. The human factors researcher must know the scientific method and the specific research methods that are available for conducting human factors research.

The applied human factors specialist likewise must understand these methods and their strengths and limitations to be an effective consumer of the available information and to be able to make wise decisions at all phases of the system-development process.

Because it is an applied science, human factors involves a mix of basic and applied research. Basic research focuses on knowledge and principles of human performance that are independent of any particular application, whereas applied research is concerned primarily with resolving specific real-world problems. The emphasis on specific problems restricts the contributions of applied research to these problems and to existing technology. However, obsolescence is an ongoing concern in any technological society, and new problems continually arise. Thus, basic knowledge that transcends particular applications is needed to effectively address the new problems as they arise.

Consistent with this point, Adams (1972) has noted that the time courses for the influence of basic and applied research on system development are quite distinct. If we look at the important research events leading to a system innovation, the immediately preceding events come primarily from applied research, whereas the longer-term contributions arise from basic research. In other words, basic research provides the conceptual and methodological tools that can subsequently be used to resolve specific applied problems. Applied research is also of value to basic researchers in indicating issues of human performance that need to be addressed and in providing a criterion for meaningful research. This interplay between basic and applied research is the foundation of the science of human factors.

It should be clear that to understand human factors research requires an understanding of the scientific method, research methods, and measurement. The purpose of this chapter is to outline the primary features of the scientific method and to present the general research and statistical methods used in the investigation of human performance. This outline should provide the basic tools needed to evaluate critically the information available to human factors specialists. It should also provide different perspectives on how to think about problems unique to human factors. Techniques specific to particular areas of human factors, which are discussed in later chapters, build from the concepts introduced in this chapter.

THE DISTINGUISHING FEATURES OF SCIENCE

What is science? Any definition of science will always fall short, because science is not a thing. Rather, it is a process—a way of gathering knowledge about the world. This process involves making hypotheses about the nature of things and testing these hypotheses empirically. Science is not the only way of acquiring such knowledge. For example, as a student of human factors, you might undertake the task of designing a keyboard entry device for a new computer system. In designing the keyboard, you could appeal to a number of sources for knowledge regarding the most effective design. You could consult an established authority, perhaps the instructor of your course. Or you could examine various keyboards already available to determine the traditional wisdom. You might even design the keyboard on the basis of your own personal ideas regarding an optimal design. Each of these sources can provide valuable information.

If you were to take a scientific approach, these sources of knowledge would serve as the starting points of your search, rather than as ends in themselves. Why are these sources of information insufficient for designing a keyboard entry device? Imagine that a fellow classmate has been given the same assignment. Although you both may consult the same sources of knowledge to complete the project, you may not interpret each of these sources in the same way. Therefore, it is quite likely that you would arrive at different keyboard designs.

The problem then arises of determining which keyboard is best. This is where the scientific method takes over. It provides a systematic way to objectively resolve this question. In fact, not only could you test to determine which keyboard is best and whether either is better than existing keyboards, but those specific attributes that make one design better than another could be discovered. In this way, you could resolve this specific design issue and also contribute to the knowledge pertaining to human factors in keyboard design.

Foundations of Science

The primary principle on which science is based is *empiricism*. Empiricism means verification by observation. This observation can range from uncontrolled, direct observations within natural settings to tightly controlled experiments in artificial settings. For example, if we are interested in the performance of operators in the control room of a nuclear power plant, their activities during work can be recorded and analyzed, specific exercises can be conducted on a simulator, the ability to identify alternative displays can be tested, and so on. The important point behind the principle of empiricism is that statements are restricted to observable events and the inferences that can be drawn from them. Thus, science provides objective criteria for evaluating the truth value of alternative statements.

Science is distinguished from other ways of acquiring knowledge because it is self-correcting. The reliance on empiricism provides the mechanism for self-correction. Scientific statements are continually tested with observations. When reliable observations deviate systematically from predictions, the scientific statements are revised.

Thus, the observations provide feedback that allows correction of error. In other words, science operates as a closed-loop system of the type described in Chapter 3, with feedback provided regarding the adequacy of scientific statements for predicting empirical observations.

It is this self-correcting characteristic of science that ensures that the knowledge gained will be dependable and that advances in understanding will occur. Consequently, scientists accept any statement only tentatively, no matter how strong the evidence is in support of it. They constantly test the validity of scientific statements, and such tests are open to public observation and scrutiny. These self-correcting aspects of science are embodied in what is called the *scientific method*. What scientists do, then, is to systematically apply the scientific method.

Scientific Method

The scientific method is a logical approach to obtaining answers to questions. This approach requires a succession of steps, beginning from general observations in the world and ending with a detailed, documented statement of the factors that give rise to the observed phenomena. Figure 2–1 shows the steps involved in the scientific method.

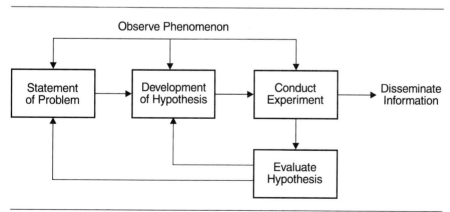

FIGURE 2–1   Steps in the Scientific Method.

The scientific enterprise begins with curiosity regarding the cause of some observed phenomenon (that is, why does this phenomenon occur?). The next step is to phrase the question in a manner that allows it to become a problem that can be investigated. Once you have articulated the problem, further observations are made regarding the factors involved in the phenomenon. You then arrive at a provisional solution to the problem. This solution constitutes a *hypothesis*, which is a tentative causal statement about the relations among the factors involved in the occurrence of the phenomenon. The hypothesis serves as the statement that is to be assessed by research.

The hypothesis is tested by conducting experiments designed to confirm or disconfirm its predictions. The hypothesis is not tested directly; rather, it is the relations predicted by the hypothesis that are tested. The viability of the hypothesis is determined by how appropriately it captures the relations among the factors of interest. The information about the viability of the hypothesis is then applied back to the original problem. The new information pertaining to the problem is distributed to the scientific community by means of books, articles, technical reports, and conference presentations. It is at this point that the new information becomes part of the scientific knowledge base.

Goals of Science

From reading the previous section, you might assume that science is basically a fact-gathering activity. However, this is far from the case. The goals of science typically are described as understanding, prediction, and control. The vehicle for achieving these goals is *theory*. According to Kerlinger (1973, p. 9),

> A theory is a set of interrelated constructs (concepts), definitions, and propositions that present a systematic view of phenomena by specifying relations among variables, with the purpose of explaining and predicting the phenomena.

A scientific theory is closely related to the pertinent empirical evidence. Thus, whereas the layperson tends to conceive of a theory as an armchair speculation, a scientific theory provides instead a detailed, specific organization of existing knowledge. The theory not only needs to be consistent with the existing data base, but it must also allow the derivation of new relations that can be subjected to empirical tests. These new predictions play an important role in the advancement of science. Finally, the theory allows specification of the conditions in which the relations among the factors will be observed. Consequently, it enables control over the phenomenon by understanding the conditions under which it occurs.

Theory is not only important to the basic researcher who seeks to understand the underlying nature of things, but also to the applied researcher and practitioner. Theory offers at least four benefits to the practitioner (Kantowitz, 1989): (1) Theory enables sensible interpolation to a specific real-world problem when data are lacking. (2) Theory can produce quantitative predictions of the type demanded by engineers and designers. (3) Theory allows the practitioner to recognize relations between problems that seem unrelated on the surface. (4) Theory can be used cheaply and efficiently to aid system design. Thus, a theoretical understanding of human performance is necessary for the effective application of existing knowledge to human factors problems.

Perhaps the most important point to realize about science is that it is an approach to thinking about problems and acquiring knowledge. This point is captured clearly by the noted astronomer and popularizer of science, Carl Sagan (1990, p. 265):

> Science is much more than a body of knowledge. It is a way of thinking. This is central to its success. Science invites us to let the facts in even when they don't conform to our preconceptions. It counsels us to carry alternative hypotheses in our heads and see which ones best match the facts. It urges on us a fine balance between no-

holds-barred openness to new ideas, however heretical, and the most rigorous skeptical scrutiny of everything—new ideas *and* established wisdom. We need wide appreciation of this kind of thinking. It works.

MEASUREMENT

The initial question that leads a researcher to conduct a study on a topic has two consequences. First, it defines the domain of interest. The objects or events under study in this domain are *operationally defined* in terms of the physical characteristics that will be measured. Second, it defines the conditions under which the characteristics of the domain can be observed. In human factors, the domain of research is usually human performance within a system environment. Because the performance itself and the conditions under which it is observed can vary, they are referred to as *variables*. That is, a variable is any event that can change. Refining the initial question into a researchable form establishes the primary variables of interest and begins to structure the types of research designs that can be used.

Variables can be classified in a number of different ways. *Behavioral variables* are any overt, observable behaviors. Most research in human factors involves the measurement of behavioral variables. These variables can range from simple key presses to the complex responses required to pilot a jet aircraft. Behavior never occurs in isolation, but always in the context of preceding stimulus events. Stimuli that can have an effect on the behavior of an organism are referred to as *stimulus variables*. Stimulus variables can range from a simple buzzer indicating a desired response to the complex auditory and visual messages received by an air-traffic controller. Most research in human factors is concerned with the influence of stimulus variables on behavioral variables.

Because human factors research is concerned with the role of the operator in both simple and complex systems, the characteristics of the human are of particular importance. People differ along many dimensions, some of which can be directly observed and some of which cannot. Observed *subject variables,* such as height, weight, and physical disabilities, obviously must be taken into account in many design situations. One example that has received considerable emphasis has been the design of public places for accessibility to people in wheelchairs. This is a specific case in which a subject variable has been incorporated into designs to benefit a particular group of people. Unobservable subject variables, such as attitudes and intelligence, also are of concern to the human factors specialist. For offshore oil-rig diving, applicants are subjected to rigorous psychological screening to evaluate their abilities to perform in highly stressful situations.

Another way to classify variables is in terms of whether they are manipulated or measured. An *independent variable* is one that is manipulated by the researcher. Most often, the manipulation is made for stimulus variables, such as the level of illumination. When an independent variable is manipulated, the primary concern is whether it has an effect on another variable, which is referred to as a *dependent variable.* Dependent variables usually are behavioral variables. These are sometimes called criterion variables (Sanders & McCormick, 1987) and can be grouped into measures that reflect performance (such as speed and force of responding), physiological indexes (such as heart rate and EEG recordings), or subjective responses (such as preferences and estimates of effort). The question of interest is the manner in which the dependent or criterion variable changes as a function of the independent variable. In other words, does the independent variable have an effect on the dependent variable? The distinction between independent and dependent variables forms a cornerstone of the true experiment, because it allows causal relations to be established.

In nonexperimental or descriptive research, the distinction between independent and dependent variables does not apply, and causal relations can be established only tentatively. For example, uncontrolled observation of consumer behavior in a grocery store is nonexperimental. Independent variables need not be identified or manipulated, and there may not be a dependent variable either. The distinction between independent and dependent variables sometimes is used in research on individual differences, for which a subject variable is of interest. However, because the subject variable is not actually manipulated, the results should not be interpreted in a causal manner.

Validity and Control

One of the most important concepts in research is that of *validity*. The idea of validity is complex, and many different types are often distinguished. Basically, validity refers to the degree to which an experiment, a procedure, or a measurement does what it is supposed to do. One basic task of a researcher is to optimize validity.

Remember that empirical observations are the central facet of scientific research. In human factors these typically are observations of behavior. This observed behavior can be influenced by a multitude of variables, not all of which are known to the researcher. Moreover, some of the variables may be of interest to the researcher, whereas others are extraneous. If the extraneous variables have a sufficiently great effect, they can cloud the effects of the variables of interest. For example, investigating the performance of workers under new arrangements of assembly line stations may be confounded by wage reductions instituted at the time the study began. In short, extraneous variables threaten the validity of the research, because the observed effects may not be due to what we think. Consequently, an important aspect of research is the reduction of the influence of these variables.

Control procedures are the systematic methods that a researcher uses to reduce the influence of extraneous variables that threaten the validity of the research. The primary means by which the researcher gains control over the situation is through the use of experimental procedures. It is important to realize that extraneous variables

may exert their influence on both the subjects and the researcher. That is, the way that the experimenter records and classifies behavioral events can be affected by bias and other variables. If the research is to be valid, the measurement of the dependent variable must be an accurate reflection of the influence of the independent variable.

Measurement Scales

In scientific research, variables must be measured. Such measurement involves the assignment of a number system to represent values of the variable of interest. When subjects are measured with respect to the variable, the measured values become data. The task for the researcher is to organize and interpret the data. Different number systems exist that have unique properties, and these unique properties must be matched to the characteristics of the variable of interest. If the number system and variable are not matched appropriately, the data may be misinterpreted.

The real number system possesses the following general properties: identity, magnitude, equal intervals, and a true zero. Identity means that each number in the system has a unique meaning. Magnitude means that the numbers possess the property of order, for example, the number 5 is greater than the number 2. Equal intervals mean that the difference between units is the same everywhere along the scale. A true zero reflects an absence of magnitude. These characteristics of the real number system allow us to use the power of mathematics to express lawful relationships between the variables.

Not all variables possess the four properties embodied in the real number system. Thus, the match between it and a given variable will not always be appropriate. For example, consider the values that are assigned to measures of intelligence. Such scores have both identity and magnitude. That is, a score of 100 means something and is greater than a score of 90. However, the intelligence variable does not possess equal intervals nor a true zero. Therefore, you cannot say that the level of intelligence represented by a score of 110 is as far from that represented by a score of 100 as the level of 100 is from the level of 90. Likewise, a person with a score of 100 is not twice as intelligent as a person with a score of 50. Consequently, some mathematical transformations cannot be applied meaningfully to intelligence scores; the relationships between the transformed scores may not reflect true relationships among the variables.

Some variables used in human factors, such as the intensity of illumination, closely match the characteristics of the real number system. Others, such as estimates of task difficulty, do not. The human factors specialist must be able to distinguish between four scales of measurement that differ in the extent to which the properties of the real number system are represented in the variable (Stevens, 1951; see Table 2–1). Nominal scales are those for which only identity holds. We may wish to investigate flight performance with different scenes in a simulator. If five possible scenes can occur, we may assign these the numbers 1 through 5. Thus, a particular number (for example, 3) designates the presentation of a particular scene (for example, night flying). However, these numbers do not have the properties of magnitude, equal interval, or true zero. Ordinal scales are those for which the values have the order property, as well as identity. An example

would be rank in a graduating class. The magnitude of a particular value tells you whether the person's grade-point average was higher or lower than someone else's, but it does not tell you by how much. Ordinal measures, such as any rank order, do not convey information regarding amounts of difference between two scores.

For values to convey information about amounts of difference, they must come from an interval scale. An interval scale possesses all the properties of the real number system except a true zero, so meaningful statements can be made about the relative amounts of difference between values. A common example of an interval scale is the Fahrenheit temperature scale. Not only can you say that 30 degrees is warmer than 20 degrees, but you can say that the difference between 30 and 20 degrees is equal to the difference between 20 and 10 degrees. When the property of a true zero (that is, an absence of the property being measured) is added, the scale is said to be a ratio scale. An example would be the Kelvin temperature scale, for which an absolute zero is defined. In human factors, anthropometric measures, such as arm length, have ratio properties. For variables that fit the properties of a ratio scale, all mathematical operations are appropriate and meaningful.

TABLE 2–1   Measurement Scales

	SCALE			
	Nominal	*Ordinal*	*Interval*	*Ratio*
Mathematical properties	Identity	Identity Magnitude	Identity Magnitude Equal intervals	Identity Magnitude Equal intervals True zero point
Permissible mathematical operations	Any (1:1) transformation that preserves unique identities	Any (strictly increasing) transformation that preserves rank order	Any transformation of the form $x' = mx + b$	Any transformation of the form $x' = ax$
Examples	Accident categories	Ranks of skill Perceptibility	Temperature	Frequency of responses

RESEARCH METHODS

Because of the wide range of issues investigated in the study of human factors, no single research method is preferred. Fortunately, there exists a broad range of research techniques in the behavioral sciences, each suited for a different type of investigation. These techniques allow you to ask various questions, and they differ in the degree to which confidence can be given to the answers. The degree of confidence depends on the relative control that you have over the various factors involved in the situation being investigated. Thus, procedures range from the simple observation and reporting of phenomena in natural settings to tightly controlled laboratory experiments. No single method will be most appropriate for answering all types of questions.

This section outlines some of the more generally accepted methods. In each case, we will describe the strengths and weaknesses of each procedure, including when and where it can be used, the nature of questions that can be asked and the answers that will be provided, and the type of statistical rigor that can be applied.

Descriptive Methods

We can use a scientific approach to asking questions about the world, even for situations in which true experiments are not possible. Such situations typically arise when you are not able to exercise any control over the events under investigation. Some experts in human factors (for example, Meister, 1985) place considerable emphasis on these descriptive methods, because the primary concern of human factors is the operational system, which by its nature is complex and not subject to precisely controlled investigation. When aspects of these systems are studied in controlled laboratory situations, the research often loses its relevance to the original system. This is because the constraints imposed by tight experimental control will make the task environment differ in potentially significant ways from the real-world

setting. The extent to which a research setting emulates the real-world setting is called *ecological validity*. In this section, we summarize descriptive methods that preserve ecological validity.

Naturalistic Observation. The least amount of control and the most ecological validity afforded a researcher is when he or she observes behaviors in naturalistic settings. When conducting *naturalistic research,* the researcher serves as a passive observer of behavior. The intent usually is to have a nonreactive and nonintrusive situation, in which the individuals under observation are free to behave with virtually no constraints. In human factors, one role of observational research is to characterize the way that people perform their work in real-world, functioning systems. For example, a human factors analysis of task performance could begin with observation of the task within the work environment itself. Sometimes a complete narrative record (that is, a faithful reproduction of the behavior as it originally occurred) will be made. Often this will be in the form of a videotaped or audiotaped record that can be examined subsequently for behaviors of interest.

When only certain behaviors are of interest, the observer typically will record just the behaviors (or other events) that correspond to predetermined categories. A checklist can be used to record the presence or absence of these specific behaviors. Measures of the frequency or duration of the behaviors then can be derived. Also, rather than just indicating the presence or absence of a behavior, each incident can be rated on a scale in terms of the amount or quality of the behavior.

Observational measurement methods also vary in several other ways (Meister, 1985): (1) The observations can be recorded at the time the performance occurs or later. (2) The content and amount of detail in the observations can vary. (3) The length of time during which observations are made can be short or long. (4) Observations can vary in terms of the amount of inference, or degree of interpretation, that is required to classify events into the measurement categories.

In conducting observational research, the investigator must develop a taxonomy of the behaviors that are to be observed, decide on a strategy for observation, establish the reliability and validity of the taxonomy and strategy, and organize the resulting data in a meaningful manner (Sackett, Ruppenthal, & Gluck, 1978). In deciding on a behavioral taxonomy, the investigator determines whether the measurement categories are to be molecular or molar. Molecular categories are defined in terms of specific actions, such as the number of times a particular control is used, whereas molar categories are more abstract and are defined according to function or outcome. The number of products completed on an assembly line would be a molar category.

Three sampling strategies have been used in observational research (Meister, 1985). With continuous measurement, every occurrence or duration of a behavior during a session is recorded. With discontinuous measurement, responses are recorded only during discrete time intervals. A final measurement procedure uses discrete sample intervals but scores responses only once per interval. In other words, a record is made of whether any response of a particular type occurred during the interval. The strength of continuous measurement is that a complete record is maintained. However, the observer may become overloaded, thus lowering the reliability of the measurement. Sampling during discrete time intervals has the advantage of being simpler, but a misleading picture may result, particularly for low-frequency behaviors.

One of the most important considerations in observational research is observer reliability. If an observer is unreliable, unreliable data will be produced. Reliable observations require well-constructed measurement scales and well-trained observers. Typically, reliability is established in observational research by using more than one observer. Some measure of the agreement between the observers, such as the percentage agreement between two observers,

$$\frac{\text{number of times two observers agree}}{\text{number of opportunities to agree}} \times 100$$

is then calculated. High interobserver reliability provides assurance that the measurements are accurate, but not necessarily that they are valid. Videotape can be used to check the reliability of observers, as well as to provide a permanent record of the behavior for future reference.

Observational procedures are good to use when few data are available on a topic. This kind of research often serves as a basis for hypotheses that can be tested later with experimental methods. It is probably the most efficient way of doing research if we are interested in behavior in real-world settings. The general weakness of observational methods is that they do not provide a firm basis for drawing inferences about the cause of the observed behavior, because no systematic control is exerted.

Surveys and Questionnaires. Sometimes the best way to begin addressing a problem is by asking the people at work what they think. This information is invaluable, because the operators of a particular system will be familiar with it in a way that an outsider could not be. The questioning can be done informally, but often more formal surveys need to be constructed or questionnaires administered. By using a carefully designed set of questions, it is possible to obtain a succinct summary of the issues, and probable relations among variables may be determined.

A questionnaire must be well constructed. As with any other measurements, the data that are obtained will only be as good as the measurement device. Six steps are involved in preparing a questionnaire (Shaughnessy & Zechmeister, 1985). The first of these is to decide on the information that you want the questionnaire to provide. One way of making this decision is to talk with the operators themselves. The second step is to decide what type of questionnaire should be used. Do you need to write your own new questionnaire, or is one already available? Should the questionnaire be self-administered or administered by a trained interviewer? If you decide to write your own questionnaire, the third step is to write a first draft. The questions should be unambiguous, and leading or loaded questions should be avoided.

After the first draft is finished, the fourth step is to revise the questionnaire. Often it is helpful to have someone else read your questionnaire to find ambiguous or biased questions that you may have missed. The fifth step is to pretest the questionnaire. This is done by administering the questionnaire to a small sample from the population for which it is intended. This will allow further evaluation of the fitness of the questions and provide the basis for the sixth step, the final revision, in which problems are eliminated and the questions fine-tuned.

Something else to be considered is the form of the responses. Multiple-choice questions provide a limited number of distinct options and are easy to analyze. On the other hand, open-ended questions that allow the respondent to answer freely provide a lot of unstructured data. Another common response format is the rating scale. This allows the respondent to indicate a strength of preference or agreement with the statement being rated. For example, if asked to rate the amount of workload imposed by a particular task, the possible responses could be *very low, low, moderate, high,* and *very high.*

The results of surveys and questionnaires can be summarized by descriptive statistics of the type presented later in the chapter. As with all nonexperimental methods, we should be hesitant about inferring causal relations from questionnaire data.

Differential Research.   Research on differences between people is called *differential research.* Differential research provides an additional increment in control by examining the relations among factors for groups of people that share a common characteristic, for example, high versus low intelligence. Often the distinction between groups serves as the basis for the choice of independent variables. For example, the performance of a group of young adults may be compared to that of a group of elderly people. The distinction between these two groups (age) can be referred to as a subject variable. Subject variables are not true experimental variables because, by their very nature, they preclude the random assignment of people to groups. Thus, many uncontrolled variables may covary along with the designated subject variable.

How well a differential study provides insight into a phenomenon depends on the strength of the relation between the subject variable and the phenomenon of interest. Differential research has the additional benefit of allowing the use of more sophisticated statistical methods than are possible with the other research methods. But as with the other nonexperimental designs described thus far, causal inferences are risky. Therefore, even if a phenomenon does covary with the subject variable, you cannot make a causal statement.

Correlational Research.   The next increment in control occurs when correlational research is conducted. In correlational designs, an a priori decision is made regarding the behavioral variables of interest. Typically, the variables are chosen on the basis of some hypothesis about their relation. After the measurements have been made, statistical procedures are then used to evaluate how the variables change together, or covary.

In the simplest case, two variables are measured to determine the degree of relationship between them. We can determine the extent of this relationship by calculating a correlation coefficient, as described in the statistical methods section. Correlational research can be conducted with any of the descriptive methods discussed in the present section.

The value of correlational procedures is that they enable the prediction of future events based on the strength of the observed relations. That is, if we establish that a reliable relationship exists between two variables, we can predict with some accuracy the value of one when we know the value of the other. Suppose, for example, that the number of accidents attributable to operator error increases as the total number of hours on duty increases. This correlation can then be used to predict the likelihood of an operator making an error given the amount of time spent on duty. This information could be used to determine the optimal shift length.

Finding that factors covary does not allow you to make a causal inference. This restriction is due in part to the fact that uncontrolled, intervening variables may influence the correlation. Thus, while these procedures have predictive power, they contribute relatively little to an understanding of the causal factors involved in the phenomena. For example, we cannot say that the time spent on duty causes mistakes, because some other variable, such as boredom or fatigue, may be involved.

Experimental Methods

True experiments have three defining features: (1) They test a hypothesis that makes a causal statement about the relation among variables. (2) A comparison of the dependent measure is made for at least two levels of an independent variable. (3) True experiments offer the highest level of control, primarily by randomly assigning people to experimental conditions. With a random assignment, each person has an equal probability of being assigned to any condition. Random assignment ensures that there can be no systematic influence from extraneous factors, such as education or socioeconomic status, on the dependent variables. Consequently, differences among treatment conditions can be attributed solely to the manipulation of the independent variable. As such, a causal statement about the relation between the independent and dependent variables can be made.

Because of the restricted nature of laboratory experiments, a well-designed experiment is considered to have high *internal validity*. That is, the

relations observed in the study can be attributed with a high degree of confidence to the variables of interest. Typically, the strict control results in low ecological validity, because the controlled experimental situation is far removed from the real-world environment. Ecological validity can be increased by performing experiments in simulated environments or real-world settings, although usually at the cost of a decrease in internal validity.

Between-subject Designs. In between-subject designs, two or more groups of people are tested, and each group receives only one of the treatment conditions of the independent variable. Subjects in such experiments are usually assigned to each condition randomly. Because subjects are randomly assigned, the groups are equivalent (within chance limits) on the basis of preexisting variables. Thus, any reliable performance difference should be a function of the independent variable.

In cases where a subject variable is known to be correlated with the dependent measure, a matching design can be used. There are several alternative matching procedures, but the general idea behind all of them is to equate the groups in terms of the subject variable. For example, suppose two methods for loading crates onto a truck are to be compared. The company for which you are employed has 20% female dock workers and 80% male. Half the workers are to be assigned to one method and the other half to the other method. Because physical strength is strongly correlated with sex, it would be best to match the groups in terms of the percentages of males and females. If this was not done, one group might contain more females than the other and thus be less strong on the average. Consequently, any differences in performance between the two groups might not be due to the loading methods.

The rationale behind the use of matching designs is to allow for the systematic distribution of subject variables across treatment conditions. Whereas random assignment ensures that there is no systematic difference in the makeup of the groups prior to the experiment, the matching procedure gives you the added confidence that you have spread a known extraneous factor equally across the treatment conditions.

Within-subject Designs. Both random assignment and matching are means by which we try to make groups equivalent. At the extreme, the groups can be made most equivalent by using the same subjects. That is, each person is tested in all conditions and serves as his or her own control. This increases the sensitivity of the design, making it more likely that small differences in the treatment conditions will be detected. It also substantially reduces the number of people that must be tested.

Within-subject designs have two major drawbacks. First, *carryover effects* may occur, in which previously received treatment conditions influence performance on subsequent conditions. Second, *practice* or *fatigue effects* may occur, regardless of the particular treatment orders. Various *counterbalancing procedures* can be used to minimize these problems. Such procedures equate and/or distribute order of treatments in various ways so as to minimize their impact. For example, if subjects are tested under both conditions A and B, order can be counterbalanced by testing half with condition A followed by condition B and half in the reverse order. Again, random assignment would be used, this time involving the assignment of people to the two orders. Although within-subject designs are useful for many situations, they cannot be used when a person's participation in one condition precludes participation in another.

Complex Designs. In most cases, more than one independent variable will be manipulated in an experiment. Also, any combination of between-, matched-, and within-subject designs can be used for these manipulations. The importance of such complex experiments is that they enable the researcher to determine whether the variables have interactive effects on the dependent measure.

That is, does the manipulation of one variable exert the same effect regardless of the presence of the other variable? If so, the effects of the variables are independent; if not, the variables are said to interact. We will discuss examples of such interactions later in the chapter. Examination of interactions among variables is important because many variables operate simultaneously in the real world. Moreover, patterns of interaction and noninteraction can be used to infer the structure of the processes that underlie the performance of a task.

Summary

Whenever possible, experimental designs should be used to answer scientific questions. That is, if we desire a precise understanding of the causal nature of phenomena, experimental designs are necessary. However, this is not to deny the importance of descriptive methods for the human factors specialist. Such methods provide important information about real-world systems that cannot be obtained from controlled experiments. Also, in situations for which the specialist needs only to predict behavior, without understanding of the causal mechanisms, the descriptive procedures are useful. In short, because of the distinct strengths and weaknesses of the experimental and descriptive methods, a blend of both is necessary in human factors research. This point will be illustrated by an example in the last section of the chapter.

STATISTICAL METHODS

The results obtained from both descriptive and experimental research typically consist of many numerical measurements for the variables of interest. These results must be organized and analyzed if they are to make sense to the researcher and to others who wish to make use of the information. Statistical methods are used to perform these functions. Typically, two types of statistics are distinguished: descriptive and inferential.

Frequency
Polygon

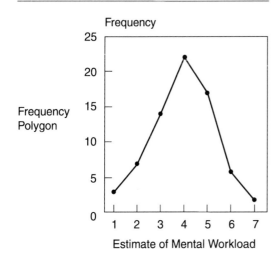

Relative
Frequency
Polygon

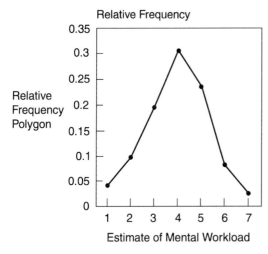

FIGURE 2–2   Frequency and Relative Frequency Polygons.

Descriptive Statistics

As implied by the name, *descriptive statistics* are used to describe or summarize the results of research. One concept that is fundamental to descriptive statistics is that of the *frequency distribution*. When numerous measurements of a variable are taken, they can be organized and plotted in terms of the frequencies of the ob-

served values. For example, if we have a group of people estimate the mental workload imposed by a task on a scale of 1 to 7, we can record the number of people who responded with each value. This record of the frequency with which each score occurred comprises a frequency distribution. A frequency distribution often is plotted in the form of a frequency polygon, as is shown in Figure 2–2. A *relative frequency distribution,* also shown in the figure, displays the same plot on the scale of the proportion (or percentage) of times that each score was observed. A score can be described in terms of its *percentile rank* in the distribution. A percentile is a point on a measurement scale below which a specified percentage of scores falls. The percentile rank is the percentage of scores that falls below that percentile. Percentile ranks are used for, among other things, creating tables of anthropometric data and applying these data in the design of equipment for human use.

Central Tendency and Variability.   Although a distribution helps to organize the data from research, other summary values may convey the crucial information more succinctly. Typically, measures of central tendency and variability are the primary descriptive statistics reported in research articles. Measures of central tendency indicate the representative score for the distribution. Most studies present their results in the form of measures of central tendency, such as means or medians. The *arithmetic mean* is obtained by adding up all of the score values and dividing by the total number of scores. If X represents the variable of interest, then the mean $\overline{X}$ is given by

$$\overline{X} = \frac{\sum_{i=1}^{n} X_i}{n}$$

where X_i refers to the ith of n scores. The mean is an estimate of the population mean μ. The *median* is the score for which 50% of the distribution falls below and 50% above or, in other words, the score with the percentile rank of 50%. The mean and median values are equivalent for a symmetric distribution, but not otherwise. If there are extremely low or high scores, the median may be a better estimate of central tendency because it is sensitive only to the ordinal properties of the scores and not their magnitudes.

One other measure of central tendency is the *mode*, the most frequently occurring score. In most cases, the mode will not be very useful. However, for nominal data it is the only meaningful measure of central tendency. The mode is also used to classify the shapes of distributions. For example, a distribution is said to be unimodal if it has only one mode and bimodal if it has two.

Measures of variability provide indications of the dispersion of the individual scores about the measure of central tendency. In other words, most scores may be close to the most typical score, or they may be widely dispersed. Measures of variability increase as the amount of dispersion increases. The most widely used measures of variability are the *variance* and the *standard deviation*. The formula for the variance of a sample of scores is

$$s_X^2 = \frac{\sum\limits_{i=1}^{n} (X_i - \overline{X})^2}{n-1}$$

where s_X^2 represents the sample variance, X_i an individual score, $\overline{X}$ the mean, and n the number of scores or observations in the sample. This statistic is an estimate of the population variance σ^2. Another name for the variance is mean squared deviation, which emphasizes that the variance reflects the average of the squared deviations of each individual score from the mean.

The sample standard deviation is obtained by taking the square root of the sample variance:

$$s_X = \sqrt{\frac{\sum\limits_{i=1}^{n} (X_i - \overline{X})^2}{n-1}}$$

The advantage of the standard deviation for descriptive purposes is that it exists in the same scale as the original measurements and thus reflects the average absolute deviation of the individual scores from the mean.

In many situations, when the sample size is sufficiently large, distributions will approximate a normal (Gaussian) curve (unimodal, bell shaped, and symmetric; see Figure 2–3). Normal distributions can be described well by their mean and standard deviation. It is often useful to transform such distributions into the standard normal distribution. The standard normal distribution expresses the value of the variable in terms of standard deviation units from the mean, or z-scores:

$$z_i = \frac{X_i - \overline{X}}{s_X}$$

The score z_i is the z-score corresponding to the ith observation in the original scale of the variable. Z-scores are useful because it is more informative to know that $z_i = 1.0$, meaning one standard deviation above the mean, than to know that $X_i = 80$. Note that the variable X need not be normally distributed to make the transformation into z-scores. However, if z is to represent a standard normal deviate, then X must be normally distributed. The standard normal distribution is called standard because its mean is 0.0 and its standard deviation is 1.0. Because any normally distributed variable X can be transformed into z-scores, the relative frequencies and percentile ranks of normally distributed variables are presented in z tables (see Appendix 1).

As an example, in 1985, the thumb-tip reach, or distance from thumb to shoulder, for women was found to have a mean of 74.30 cm and a standard deviation of 4.01 cm. For an individual found to have a thumb-tip reach of 70.00 cm, the z-score would be

$$\frac{70.00 - 74.30}{4.01} = -1.07$$

or 1.07 standard deviation units below the mean. Using the table in Appendix 1, it can be deter-

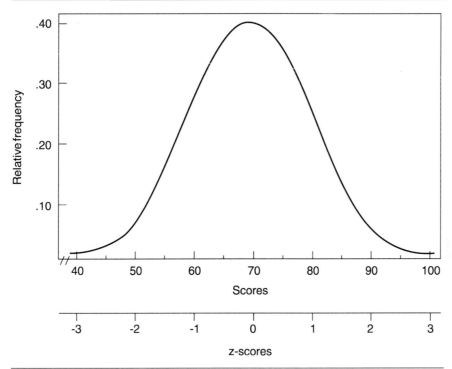

FIGURE 2–3   A Normal Distribution with $\overline{X} = 70$ and $S = 10$, and Corresponding z-scores.

mined that this individual has a percentile rank of 14%. In other words, 14% of women have a shorter thumb-tip reach than this person.

Correlation Coefficient. In correlational research, a common descriptive statistic is the Pearson product–moment correlation r:

$$r = \frac{s_{XY}}{s_X s_Y}$$

where X and Y are the two variables and

$$s_{XY} = \sum_{i=1}^{n} \frac{(X_i - \overline{X})(Y_i - \overline{Y})}{n - 1}$$

is the covariance between X and Y. The covariance between two variables is a measure of the degree to which changes in one variable correspond to changes in another. The correlation coefficient is an indicator of the linear relationship between two variables.

The coefficient r is always between -1.0 and $+1.0$. When X and Y are uncorrelated, r will equal 0. This means that there is no linear relationship between X and Y. When they are perfectly correlated, r will equal $+1.0$ or -1.0, and the values of one variable can be related to the values of the other variable by a straight line. A positive correlation means that, as values of X increase, so do values of Y; a negative correlation means that, as values of X increase, those of Y decrease. Figure 2–4 provides illustrations of data for several values of r. Another useful statistic is r^2, which gives the proportion of total variance that can be traced to the covariance of the two variables. It is often

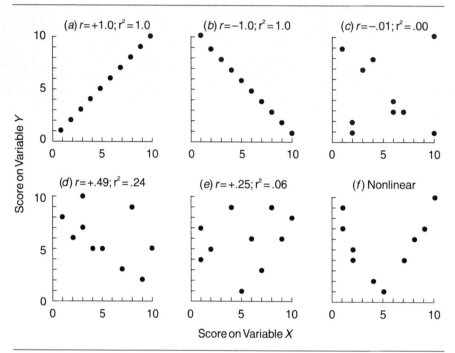

FIGURE 2–4   Scatterplots for Different Correlations Between *X* and *Y* Variables.

said that r^2 reflects the amount of variance "explained" by the linear relationship.

Use of the correlation coefficient, as well as means and standard deviations, can be illustrated with an example. Lovasik, Matthews, and Kergoat (1989) investigated the effect of foreground and background color on performance of a visual detection task, in which subjects were required to search a computer display for a target symbol during a 4-hr period. The response time to find the target in each display was measured as a function of the amount of time already spent on the task and the foreground and background colors of the display. Table 2–2 presents the search times under all time-on-task and color conditions for each subject. Search times are presented as the percentage of the search time after $\frac{1}{2}$ hr on the task.

The mean percent search times for each of the three color conditions is computed in Table 2–2. Note that a mean of 100 would indicate no

improvement from the initial search time and that the smaller the mean is, the greater the improvement. The red/green condition showed virtually no improvement, whereas the blue/black condition showed the most improvement. The variance of the target search time is computed in Table 2–3, as well as the correlation between search time and time-on-task. The least variance is shown for the red/green condition. The correlations between time-on-task and search time are negative for all display conditions, indicating that as time-on-task increased search time decreased.

Inferential Statistics

Probability.   Inferential statistics rely on the concepts of probability theory. We speak of events as having some probability of occurring when we are uncertain of the outcome. Probabilities are measurements that assign a number from 0.0 to 1.0 to an event, according to how likely that event is to occur. Probability represents the proportion of times that the event occurs relative to all other possible events. Thus, a *probability distribution* is a relative frequency distribution over the entire set of possible events. For an event to have a probability of 0.0 means that it has no chance of occurring. If an event has a probability of 1.0, then we know with absolute certainty that it will occur. If an event has probability 0.5, then approximately half of the outcomes will consist of that event. For example, the event *heads* that could be observed on the toss of a fair coin has the probability of 0.5. Thus, if we flip the coin many times, we would expect to observe heads approximately half of the time.

The combined outcome of two separate events can be considered a joint event. For example, if two die were rolled, with two dots observed on the first die, event 2, and four dots observed on the second die, event 4, the outcome could be considered the joint event (2, 4). Just as a relative frequency distribution can be observed over all possible outcomes of a single event, a joint rela-

tive frequency distribution can be observed over all possible outcomes of a joint event. In other words, the proportion of times that each possible joint event occurs can be calculated.

The two events that make up the joint event may or may not depend on each other. If knowing the outcome of the first event provides no information about what might happen for the second event, then the two events are independent. For independent events A and B, the probability of the joint event A and B, written $A \cap B$, is

$$\Pr(A \cap B) = \Pr(A)\,\Pr(B)$$

That is, the joint probability can be written as the product of the marginal probabilities of the individual events. It is possible, however, that the outcome of the first event influences the outcome of the second, in which case the two events are dependent. For dependent events, the probability that event B occurs given that event A occurred is

$$\Pr(B \mid A) = \frac{\Pr(A \cap B)}{\Pr(A)}$$

TABLE 2–2   Percent Target Search Time Relative to the First Half-Hour of Time-on-Task (in Hours)

OBSERVATION (N)	TIME ON TASK (T)	RED/BLACK (R)	BLUE/BLACK (B)	RED/GREEN (RG)
1	0.5	100	100	100
2	1.0	97	93	102
3	1.5	95	94	98
4	2.0	90	89	99
5	2.5	91	88	100
6	3.0	94	90	98
7	3.5	91	87	97
8	4.0	90	83	98
$\sum_{N=1}^{8}$	18.0	748	734	792
	$\overline{T} = \dfrac{18.0}{8}$	$\overline{R} = \dfrac{748}{8}$	$\overline{B} = \dfrac{734}{8}$	$\overline{RG} = \dfrac{792}{8}$
	$= 2.25$	$= 93.50$	$= 91.75$	$= 99.00$

Estimated from Lovasik, Matthews, and Kergoat, 1989, Figure 10.

TABLE 2–3 Computations of Variance and Correlation Coefficients for the Data in Table 2–2

N	$T - \bar{T}$	$(T - \bar{T})^2$	$R - \bar{R}$	$(R - \bar{R})^2$	$B - \bar{B}$	$(B - \bar{B})^2$	$RG - \overline{RG}$	$(RG - \overline{RG})^2$
1	−1.75	3.06	6.50	42.25	8.25	68.06	1.00	1.00
2	−1.25	1.56	3.50	12.25	1.25	1.56	3.00	9.00
3	−0.75	0.56	0.50	0.25	2.25	5.06	−1.00	1.00
4	−0.25	0.06	−4.50	20.25	−2.75	7.56	0.00	0.00
5	0.25	0.06	−5.50	30.25	−3.75	14.06	1.00	1.00
6	0.75	0.56	−3.50	12.25	−1.75	3.06	−1.00	1.00
7	1.25	1.56	−6.50	42.25	−4.75	22.56	−2.00	4.00
8	1.75	3.06	−0.50	0.25	1.25	1.56	−1.00	1.00
$\sum\limits_{N=1}^{8}$		10.48		160.00		123.48		18.00
s^2		$\dfrac{10.48}{7} = 1.50$		$\dfrac{160.00}{7} = 22.22$		$\dfrac{123.48}{7} = 17.64$		$\dfrac{18.00}{7} = 2.57$

N	$(T - \bar{T})(R - \bar{R})$	$(T - \bar{T})(B - \bar{B})$	$(T - \bar{T})(RG - \overline{RG})$
1	−11.38	−14.44	−1.75
2	−4.38	−1.56	−3.75
3	−0.38	−1.69	0.75
4	1.12	0.69	0
5	−1.38	−0.94	0.25
6	−2.62	−1.31	−0.75
7	−8.12	−5.94	−2.50
8	−0.88	2.19	−1.75
$\sum\limits_{N=1}^{8}$	−28.02	−23.00	−9.50
r	$\dfrac{-28.02}{(10.48)(160.00)} = -0.68$	$\dfrac{-23.00}{(10.48)(123.48)} = -0.64$	$\dfrac{-9.50}{(10.48)(18.00)} = -0.69$

Probabilities are important because a researcher tests a sample selected from a larger population. However, the researcher is not interested in reaching conclusions about the specific sample, but about the population from which it was drawn. Yet, because the entire population was not measured, there is a probability of some measurement error. For example, if you are interested in determining the mean height of adult males for a particular population, you might measure the height for a sample of 200 males.

Each height that you observe has some probability of occurring in the population, which has an average around 5 ft 10 in. A sample mean could be computed and used as an estimate of this population mean. However, it is only an estimate. It is possible, although not likely, that all 200 men in the sample would be taller than 6 ft. Thus, the sample mean would be greater than 6 ft, although the population mean is closer to 5 ft 10 in. This is an instance of sampling error. Generally, increases in the sample size will lead to more precise estimates of the population characteristic of interest.

Probability theory will be important in later chapters. The concepts of probability theory are central to reliability analysis (Chapter 3), signal-detection theory (Chapter 4), and decision theory (Chapter 11). They also are central to simulations of human and system performance.

Hypothesis Testing. Typically, in conducting experiments or other types of research, the researcher wants to test hypotheses. In the simplest type of experiment, two groups of subjects may be tested. One group receives the experimental treatment and the other, referred to as the control group, does not. The concern is whether the two groups differ on a particular dependent variable. Typically, sample means are computed. We can compare these means to determine whether they differ. However, because these sample means are only estimates of the population means and are subject to sampling error, just examining these values will not tell us whether the treatment had an effect. In other words, how much of a difference between the sample means do we need to see before concluding that the difference reflects a "real" difference in the population means?

Inferential statistics provide a way to answer this question. In our two-group experiment, we begin by formulating a *null hypothesis.* The null hypothesis is that the treatment had no effect or, in other words, that the population means for the two conditions do not differ. The inferential test determines the probability that the observed mean difference could have been due solely to chance, given some estimate of error variance and a population mean difference that is specified by the null hypothesis. It is important to note that the researcher does not know whether or not the null hypothesis is true. Based on the probabilistic evidence provided by the statistical test, the researcher must decide whether to accept or reject the null hypothesis. The combination of two possible states of the world (null hypothesis true or false) with two possible decisions (null hypothe-sis true or false) yields a 2 by 2 matrix of outcomes, two of which are correct (see Table 2–4).

As shown in the table, two distinct types of errors can occur when trying to infer characteristics of the population from the sample. The first of these is called a type I error. This type of error occurs when the sample mean difference is sufficiently large that the null hypothesis is rejected, yet the population mean difference is zero. The second, called a type II error (β), occurs when the population means are different, but the observed sample means are sufficiently similar that the null hypothesis is accepted. The researcher, given some knowledge about the distribution of the population means, must select an acceptable probability for a type I error by deciding the point at which the null hypothesis will be rejected. This probability is called the α-level.

Traditionally, the rule has been to conclude that the experimental manipulation had a reliable or *significant* effect if the difference between the sample means is so large that the probability of obtaining a difference that large or larger is less than 0.05, if the null hypothesis were true. The null hypothesis is provisionally accepted if this probability is greater than 0.05. If a 0.01 α-level were used instead, the probability of a type I error would be less, but the probability of a type II error would increase. In other words, the criterion level adopted by the researcher affects the relative likelihood of each error occurring.

TABLE 2–4   Statistical Decision Making

Decision	NULL HYPOTHESIS	
	True	False
True	Correct acceptance $(1 - \alpha)$	Type I error (α)
False	Type II error (β)	Correct rejection $(1 - \beta)$

Whenever differences between conditions are reported for experiments described in this book, it can be assumed that the difference was significant at the 0.05 level. Remember that a significant difference is meaningful only in a well-designed study. That is, a significant inferential test tells you that something other than chance apparently was operating to distinguish the two groups, not what that something was. Also, accepting the null hypothesis does not necessarily mean that the independent variable had no effect. The failure to show a reliable difference could reflect only large measurement error or, in other words, low experimental power.

One widely used inferential test that is important to issues discussed later in the text is the analysis of variance (ANOVA). One strength of the ANOVA is that it can be applied to experiments with complex designs. The ANOVA allows us to evaluate the interactions between different independent variables. In the two-variable case, an ANOVA will tell not only whether each variable had an overall effect on the dependent variable (that is, a main effect), but also whether the two independent variables together had an interactive effect. Figure 2–5 shows some example patterns of interaction and noninteraction. Nonparallel lines indicate interactive effects, whereas parallel lines indicate independent effects. When an experiment includes more than two independent variables, complex interaction patterns among all the variables can be evaluated similarly.

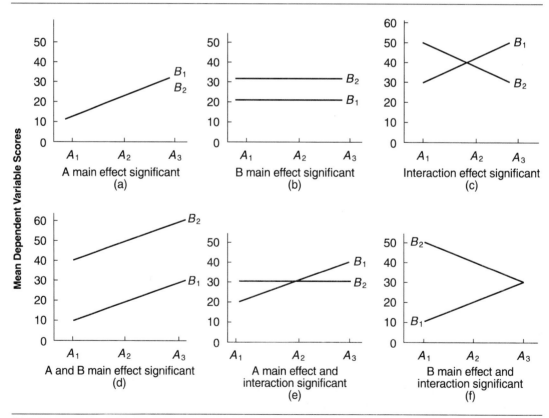

FIGURE 2–5   Example Patterns of Interaction and Noninteraction.

As an example, alcohol and barbituates are known to have interactive effects on behavior. If A and B represent the level of alcohol and barbituates consumed, respectively, let A_0 indicate no alcohol and B_0 no barbituates and A_1 and B_1, some fixed amounts of each. An interaction of these variables on driving performance is shown in Figure 2–6, where the dependent variable is the variance of the distance from the center of the lane in feet squared. As you can see, performance under the combined effect of both drugs is considerably worse than with either drug alone.

A STUDY EVALUATING HUMAN FACTORS DESIGN

To make some of the issues regarding research and statistical issues concrete, we will discuss in detail a specific study. Marras and Kroemer (1980) conducted a laboratory and field study on design factors crucial to the efficient operation of boating distress signals. To begin, Marras and Kroemer surveyed the distress signals that were available on the market and categorized them according to the steps that were required to identify, unpack, and operate them. After the signals were categorized, a preliminary study was conducted in which naive and experienced boaters were videotaped while operating the signals. The performance of these individuals with the various

signals was used to identify the design variables of interest, such as form, labeling, size, and so on.

The next stage in the study was a series of laboratory tests in which each identified design variable was used as an independent variable in an experiment. For example, one test investigated how different shapes affected the identification of the distress-signal device. Three differently shaped flares (one that fully complied with proposed human factors regulations, one that partially complied, and one that did not comply) were painted red and left unlabeled. The person's task was to pick up the flare from among five other devices, and the time to do so was measured as the dependent variable. The primary finding was that people selected the flare that complied with the human factors guidelines faster than the flare that did not.

The final stage of the study took place in a natural environment. Participants were taken by boat to an island where they boarded a rubber raft that was rigged to deflate. The boaters were told that the purpose of the study was to rate the visibility of a display shown from shore. One of two types of hand-held flares was placed on board the raft. These flares are shown in Figure 2–7. The raft was pushed onto the lake, and within two minutes began to deflate, prompting the boater to use the distress signal. After being pulled back to shore, the procedure was repeated with the second device. The total times to unpack and operate the two types of flares for 20 people are shown in Table 2–5.

For flare A, which had a handle that clearly distinguished the grip end of the flare, the mean performance time was 0.289 min. For flare B, which did not have a clearly distinguished grip, the mean performance time was 1.376 min. An analysis of variance showed that the difference was significant. In other words, the grip reliably reduced total performance time.

One nice characteristic of this study is the systematic progression from descriptive survey and observational methods, to controlled laboratory experiments, and back to a field experiment conducted in an ecologically valid setting. Thus,

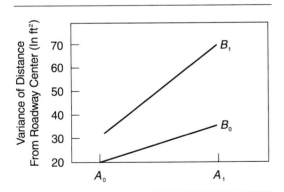

FIGURE 2–6   Interactive Effects of Alcohol (A) and Barbituates (B) on Driving Performance.

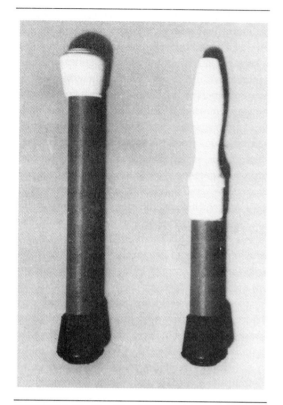

FIGURE 2–7 The Two Types of Hand-held Flares Tested by Marras and Kroemer.

From W. S. Marras & K. H. E. Kroemer, A method to evaluate human factors/ergonomics design variables of distress signals. Reprinted by permission from *Human Factors*, Vol. 22, No. 4, pp. 389–399, 1980. Copyright 1980 by The Human Factors Society, Inc. All rights reserved.

the research coupled the ecological strengths of the observational and field methods with the internal strengths of the experimental method. In this way, the study provides an ideal example of how different research methods can be combined to address a specific human factors problem.

You should be able to determine from the description of the field experiment that it used a within-subjects design, because each person was tested in both flare conditions. Therefore, the order in which the flares were used is an extraneous variable that could potentially confound the re-

sults. For example, if flare A had been tested first and flare B second for all people, then the disadvantage for flare B could have been due to fatigue or some other order effect, such as the absence of fear in the second test. To control for such order effects, Marras and Kroemer (1980) counterbalanced the order in which the two devices were tested. Half of the people were tested with flare A first, and half were tested with flare B first.

Even though order was counterbalanced, you still might question the appropriateness of the within-subject design. One reason for conducting the field experiment was for boaters to perform in a real emergency. After the test with the first flare, it is very likely that the boaters became aware of the true purpose of the experiment. No evidence is apparent in the data that performance

TABLE 2–5 Results of On-water Experiments: Performance Times in Minutes

SUBJECT	FLARE A	FLARE B
1	0.21	1.46[a]
2	0.29[a]	0.87
3	0.10	0.64[a]
4	0.23[a]	0.92
5	0.24	0.81[a]
6	0.43[a]	0.36
7	0.42	1.42[a]
8	0.16	2.32[a]
9	0.11	0.80[a]
10	0.10[a]	2.23
11	0.25[a]	0.72
12	0.22	0.98[a]
13	0.57[a]	1.39
14	0.44	2.53[a]
15	0.35[a]	0.73
16	0.67[a]	1.84
17	0.20	1.87[a]
18	0.27[a]	2.45
19	0.26	2.14[a]
20	0.26[a]	1.04
Mean	0.289	1.376
Standard deviation	0.152	0.687

From Marras and Kroemer, 1980.

[a] = first trial

was affected greatly by any such awareness, so it may not be a problem. This potential drawback of the within-subject design was offset by the benefits that fewer people had to be tested and extraneous variables, such as boating experience, were equated for the two conditions. This example of the relative merits of within- and between-subject designs indicates that there are no hard and fast rules for making research design decisions.

The changes in smoke signal and flare design that Marras and Kroemer (1980) recommended on the basis of their study have since been instituted. Kroemer remarks,

> But nowadays, if you go into the store and buy those marine emergency signals, they are of different colors, they are of different designs, and they work fine. Nobody ever said anything but I have always considered this one of the very satisfying results. We may have saved some people this way. This really made me happy. We never got any formal reply but we know it was being used—*that's the best.* (Quoted in Rogers, 1987, p. 3)

SUMMARY

The present chapter has provided an outline of the basics needed to understand research in human factors. Human factors is an applied science. Thus, scientific reasoning guides the activities of the researcher and the designer. Because science relies on empirical observation, the methods by which these observations are made are of fundamental importance. Furthermore, the statistics used to summarize and evaluate these observations also must be understood.

The scientific method requires the continuous development and refinement of theory based on our observations. The observations provide the basic facts, and the theory helps to explain why they are so. Good theories not only explain but also make predictions about new situations and allow us to optimize performance in those situations.

The research methods used to obtain data vary according to how tightly controlled the setting is and to how much the setting approximates the environment of interest. Laboratory experiments typically are highly controlled but have low ecological validity, whereas descriptive methods tend to be relatively uncontrolled but have high ecological validity. Thus, the choice between the various experimental and descriptive methods depends on the goals of the study, and often some combination of methods provides the best understanding of an issue.

RECOMMENDED READING

Christensen, L. B. (1988). *Experimental Methodology,* 4th ed. Boston: Allyn and Bacon.

Kiess, H. O. (1989). *Statistical Concepts for the Behavioral Sciences.* Boston: Allyn and Bacon.

Martin, D. W. (1985). *Doing Psychology Experiments,* 2nd ed. Monterey, CA: Brooks/Cole.

McCain, G., & Segal, E. M. (1982). *The Game of Science,* 4th ed. Monterey, CA: Brooks/Cole.

Meister, D. (1985). *Behavioral Analysis and Measurement Methods.* New York: Wiley.

RELIABILITY AND HUMAN ERROR IN SYSTEMS

It is evident that human reliability is too often (some would argue always) the weak link in the chain of events which leads to loss of safety and catastrophic failure of even the most advanced technological systems.

—B. A. Sayers, 1988

INTRODUCTION

Everyone has had the experience of making errors that lead to the failure of a system. When driving a car, you may be distracted, fail to see that the car in front has stopped, and collide with it. Alternatively, you may see that the car has stopped but fail to execute a braking action in sufficient time to prevent a collison. As with this example, errors often have adverse consequences. Many commercial airline accidents, at least 50% of which are attributable to pilot error (Jensen, 1982), may leave few survivors. Similarly, 50% to 70% of offshore petroleum drilling accidents and nuclear power plant accidents, which can be environmentally devasting, arise from erroneous human action or inaction (Dougherty & Fragola, 1988).

A primary goal of the human factors specialist is to minimize human error and so to maximize system performance. This requires that the tasks performed by the operator be identified and possible sources of error be determined. This information must then be incorporated into the design of the system, if performance is to be optimized. Before considering ways in which the likelihood of human error can be evaluated, we must first consider the system concept and its role in human factors.

THE CENTRAL CONCEPT IN HUMAN FACTORS: THE SYSTEM

In the context of human factors, a *system* can be defined as a grouping of machines, people, and other parts that operate together to achieve a common goal. As emphasized in Chapter 1, the system approach is fundamental to the field of human factors. The belief is that application of behavioral principles to the design of systems will lead to improved functioning of the systems. System analyses provide the basis for evaluating reliability and error, as well as for the design recommendations intended to minimize errors. Several implications of the system concept are important in this regard (e.g., Bailey, 1982).

Implications of the System Concept

The operator is part of a human–machine system. For human factors, one implication of the system concept is that human performance in applied settings should be evaluated in terms of the whole human–machine system. That is, the specific system performing in the operational environment must be considered, and human performance should be studied in relation to the system.

The system goals are superordinate. Systems are developed with specific goals in mind that need to be achieved for acceptable system performance. Evaluations of all aspects of a system, including human performance, must occur with respect to the system goals.

Systems usually are hierarchical. The system can be broken down into components. This hierarchy involves the human and machine subsystems. These subsystems can be characterized as having subgoals that must be satisfied for the

superordinate system goals to be met. This hierarchical analysis can proceed further, distinguishing between components within both the human and machine subsystems. Consequently, each part of a system can be evaluated relative to a specific subgoal, as well as to the higher-level goals within the system.

Systems and their components have inputs and outputs. At each level of a system, the nature of input and output can be specified. The human factors specialist is particularly concerned with the input to the human from the machine and the actions of the human performed on the machine. Because the human subsystem can be broken down into its constituent processes, we are also interested in the nature of the inputs and outputs from these processes and how errors can occur among them.

A system has structure. The components of a system are organized and structured in a particular manner. This structure provides the system with its own special properties. In other words, the whole operating system has properties that emerge from those of its parts. By analyzing the performance of each component within the context of the system structure, the performance of the overall system can be predicted and/or specified.

Deficiencies in system performance are due to inadequacies of system components. The total performance of a system is determined by the nature of the system components and their interactions with each other. Consequently, when a system fails to perform accurately and reliably, this failure can be attributed to one or more components.

A system operates within a larger environment. The system itself cannot be understood without reference to the larger environment in which it is embedded. A failure to consider this environment in system design and evaluation will lead to an inadequate assessment of the system. Although it is easy to say that there is a distinction between the system and its environment, the boundary between them is not clearly defined, just as the boundaries between subsystems are not always clearly defined. The boundaries can be very broad or very narrow. The broader the boundary is the more variables that are taken into account and the more control that can be exerted over the performance of the system.

System Variables

Systems consist of all the machinery, procedures, and operators carrying out these procedures that work to fulfill the system goal. It is possible to distinguish between mission-oriented and service-oriented systems (Meister, 1991). Mission-oriented systems subordinate the needs of their personnel to the goal of the mission. These systems are common in the military, as with weapon and transport systems. Service-oriented systems are characterized by the goal of catering to the personnel, clients, or users. Such systems include supermarkets and offices. Most systems fall between these two extremes, involving components of both. For example, the manufacturing of automobiles has a mission component, that is, building a functional vehicle. However, it also has a service component in that the vehicle is being built for a consumer. Furthermore, the vehicle is built by assembly line workers, whose welfare is of concern to the system designers.

The variables that define the system properties, such as the size, speed, and complexity of the system, determine the requirements of the operator necessary for efficient operation of the system. According to Meister (1989), system variables are of two types. One type describes the functioning of the physical system and its components, whereas the other type describes the performance of individual and team operators. Table 3–1 lists variables of the respective types.

Physical System Variables. Physical systems can be distinguished by their organization and complexity. Complexity is determined by the number and arrangement of subsystems. The number of subsystems operating at any one time, which subsystems receive inputs from and direct outputs to the other subsystems, and the way in which the components are connected all contribute to system complexity.

The organization and complexity of the system determine interdependencies among subsystems. Subsystems that depend on others for their input and those that must make use of a common resource pool to operate are interdependent. The performance of a subsystem depends on the availability of resources and the inputs needed to produce output. The individual functions performed by a system are intended to accomplish some goal or goals. The system performs functions and tasks within the requirements imposed on it to produce system output that is as close to the original goals as possible. The number and specificity of these goals differ across systems.

An important characteristic is the number and nature of information feedback mechanisms. Feedback refers to input or information flow traveling backward in the system. This information usually gives some indication of the difference between the actual and desired state of the system. Positive feedback is added to the system input, keeping the state of the system changing in its present direction. Such systems are usually unstable, because positive information flow amplifies error instead of correcting it. It is generally beneficial for a system to include negative feedback mechanisms, in which the information is subtracted from the system input. Suppose that a system's goal is to produce premixed concrete. A certain amount of concrete requires some amount of water for mixing. If too much water is added, sand can be introduced to the mixture to dry it. A negative feedback loop would monitor the water content of the mixture, and this information would be used to direct the addition of more water or more sand until the appropriate texture had been achieved.

Such systems, which make use of feedback, are called *closed-loop systems* (see Figure 3–1b). In contrast, systems that do not use feedback are referred to as *open-loop systems* (see Figure 3–1a). Closed-loop systems that use negative feedback are error correcting because the output is continuously monitored. In contrast, open-loop

TABLE 3–1   System Variables

Physical System Variables
1. The number of subsystems.
2. The organization of the system.
3. The complexity of the system.
4. The number and type of interdependencies within the system.
5. The nature and availability of resources required by the system.
6. The functions and tasks performed by the system.
7. The requirements imposed on the system.
8. The number and specificity of goals and missions.
9. The nature of system terminal output or mission effects.
10. The number and nature of information feedback mechanisms.
11. System attributes, for example, determinate/indeterminate, sensitive/insensitive.
12. The nature of the operational environment in which the system functions.

Operator Variables
1. The functions and tasks performed.
2. Personnel aptitude for tasks performed.
3. The amount and appropriateness of training.
4. The amount of personnel experience and skill.
5. The presence or absence of reward and motivation.
6. Fatigue or stress condition.
7. The physical environment for individual or team functioning.
8. Requirements imposed on the individual or team.
9. The size of the team.
10. The number and type of interdependencies within the team.
11. The relationship between individual/team and other subsystems.

Adapted by permission from Meister (1989) Tables 1.2 and 1.3, p. 29. Meister, David. *Conceptual Aspects of Human Factors.* The Johns Hopkins University Press, Baltimore/London, 1989.

systems have no such error-detection mechanisms. In complex systems, there may be numerous feedback loops at the different hierarchical levels of the system.

The goals, functions, organization, and complexity of a system determine its attributes. As one example, a system can be relatively sensitive or insensitive to deviations in inputs and outputs. Determinate systems are highly proceduralized. Operators follow specific protocols and have little flexibility in their actions. Indeterminate systems are not as highly proceduralized, and there is a wide range of activities in which the operators can engage. Also, the operator's response must often be based on ambiguous input, with little feedback.

Systems operate in environments that may be friendly or unfriendly. Adverse conditions, such as heat, wind, and sand, take their toll on system components. For the system to operate effectively, the components must be able to withstand the environmental conditions.

Operator Variables.   The requirements for system operators depend on the functions and tasks that must be performed for effective operation of the system. To perform these tasks, operators must meet certain aptitude and training requirements. For example, fighter pilots should be selected according to aptitude profiles and physical requirements, and they also must receive extensive training.

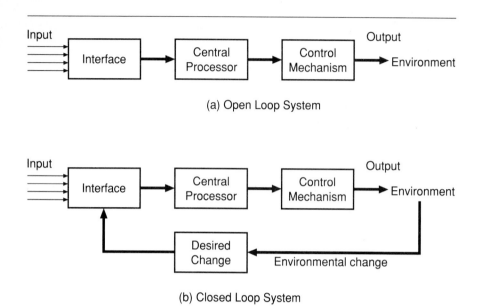

FIGURE 3–1   (a) Open-loop and (b) Closed-loop Systems.

Performance can also be affected by motivation, fatigue, and stress. Depending on the levels of these factors, the performance of the same individual can vary from good to bad. Recently, there has been considerable concern with fatigue factors in the performance of medical internists. The purpose of an internship is to provide hands-on training for new doctors. The traditional school of medical education requires duty shifts of up to 36 hours so that young doctors can observe the course of an illness or other emergency from start to finish. Unfortunately, a doctor's judgment concerning diagnoses and courses of action severely deteriorates by the end of the shift. Combining this level of fatigue with the high level of stress that a doctor experiences while on shift makes it likely that life-threatening mistakes of judgment will occur. Such mistakes have been amply documented in malpractice suits to the extent that some hospitals are now changing to less demanding on-duty schedules.

The demands that can be placed on an individual operator will vary across different physical environments. Variables to be considered include temperature, humidity, noise level, illumination, and so on. When more than one operator is required, team factors become important. The size of the team and the interrelations among the various team members influence the efficiency with which the team operates and, hence, the efficiency with which the system operates.

Summary

The system concept is fundamental to the discipline of human factors. A system must be considered in terms of both the physical and mechanical variables and the individual and team operator variables. The performance of the operators must be evaluated with respect to the functioning of the entire system. The assumptions and implications of the system concept dictate the way that researchers and designers approach applied problems. The system concept is the basis for reliability analysis, which we consider later in the chapter, and for the information-processing approach to human performance, which is discussed in Chapter 4.

HUMAN ERROR

A human error occurs when an action is taken that was "not intended by the actor; not desired by a set of rules or an external observer; or that led the task or system outside its acceptable limits" (Senders & Moray, 1991, p. 25). The important point here is that an error is a function of the goals of the operator and of the system. Whereas in certain situations imprecise control actions may not qualify as errors, performance must be quite accurate in other situations.

During normal flight, displacements of a few meters above or below an intended altitude are not crucial and would not be classified as errors. However, in stunt flying and when several planes are flying in formation, slight deviations in altitude and timing can be fatal. In 1988, three Italian Air Force jets collided in the worst-ever aerobatics show disaster involving spectators. Over 40 people, including the three pilots, were killed. The collision occurred when the jets were executing a crossing maneuver in which one jet was to cross immediately above five jets flying in formation. A former member of the flying team concluded,

> Either the soloist was too low or the group was too high. . . . In these situations a difference of a meter can upset calculations. . . . [This deviation could have been caused by] a sudden turbulence, illness or so many other things. (1988, UPI wire story)

In this case, the system failed because of a very slight altitude error.

The principal consideration of the human factors specialist is with system malfunctions that involve the operator. Although such errors typically are referred to as human errors, they most often are due to the design of the human–machine interface and/or the training provided the operator. Thus, the failure of a technological system often begins with its design. The system design can put the user in situations for which a high probability of success cannot be expected. The term *operator error* can be restricted to those system failures that are due entirely to the human,

and the term *design error,* to those human errors that are due to the system design. The primary objective of the human factors specialist is to make recommendations concerning system design to minimize all human errors that lead to system failure.

Why Human Error Occurs

Human error usually arises from inadequacies of the system design. These inadequacies fall into three groups (Park, 1987). The first type involves task complexity. As illustrated in subsequent chapters, humans have limited capacities for perceiving, attending, remembering, calculating, and so on. Errors are likely to occur when the task requirements exceed these capacity limitations. The second type of inadequacy includes error-likely situations. This category refers to more general situational characteristics that predispose operators to make errors. It includes factors such as inadequate workspace, inadequate training procedures, and poor supervision. Finally, errors can also reflect individual differences. These differences are human attributes of the worker, such as abilities and attitudes. Among the individual factors that are important are susceptibility to stress and inexperience, which can produce as much as a tenfold increase in human error probability (Miller & Swain, 1987).

Error Taxonomies

Numerous taxonomies exist for classifying human errors into categories. Some refer to the type of action taken or not taken, others to particular operational procedures, and others to the locus in the human information-processing system. We will describe several of these taxonomies.

Action Classification. Human error occurs when the actions taken by the operator lead to performance of the system that is outside of tolerance limits. Such errors can be categorized according to the nature of the action that was or was not taken (Meister & Rabideau, 1965). An *error of omission* is made when the operator fails to perform a required action. For example, a worker in a chemical waste disposal plant may omit the step of opening a valve in the response sequence to a specific emergency. An *error of commission* occurs when an incorrect action is performed. In this case, the worker may set the valve, but incorrectly. Commissions can be subdivided further into *timing errors* that occur when actions are performed at the wrong time, *sequence errors* that arise when a step is performed out of the proper order, *selection errors* for which an incorrect control is manipulated, and *quantitative errors* in which too little or too much of the appropriate control manipulation is made.

Failure Classification. A distinction can be made between recoverable and nonrecoverable errors. Recoverable errors can be corrected and their consequences minimized. In contrast, nonrecoverable errors will automatically affect system performance. Human errors are of most concern when they are unrecoverable and lead to system failure.

Human-initiated system failures can arise in several ways (Meister, 1971). An *operating error* refers to situations when the machine is not operated according to the correct procedures. A *design error* occurs when the system designer does not incorporate human factors principles into the system design. An *assembly* or *manufacturing error* arises when a worker does not assemble a product in accordance with the design. An *installation* or *maintenance error* occurs when machines are either installed or maintained improperly.

An example of the latter types of errors involves the wiring on Boeing aircraft. In 1988, a Boeing 737 crashed in England after the pilots reported that smoke and fumes from a malfunctioning engine were filling the cabin and cockpit. The crash occurred because the functioning engine was inadvertently shut off, rather than the malfunctioning engine. One cause of this error was speculated to be miswiring of the fire warning panel to indicate that the wrong engine was on

fire. Although this turned out not to be the case, the tragedy led to inspections of other Boeing aircraft, which revealed 78 instances on 74 aircraft of miswiring in the systems designed to indicate and extinguish fires (Fitzgerald, 1989). To avoid future wiring errors during assembly and maintenance, plans were made to redesign the connectors so that each would be a unique size.

Processing Classification. Errors can also be classified according to their locus within the human information-processing system (Payne & Altman, 1962). *Input errors* are those attributable to sensory and perceptual processes. *Mediation errors* reflect the cognitive processes that translate between perception and action. Finally, *output errors* are those due to the selection and execution of physical responses.

A more detailed classification of this nature developed by Berliner, Angell, and Shearer (1964) is shown in Table 3–2. The terms *perceptual* and *motor* are substituted for *input* and *output,* respectively, in this classification. Moreover, an additional type of error, referred to as *communication error,* is included. These communication errors reflect failures to accurately transmit information among team members. Table 3–2 lists specific behaviors for which errors of each type can occur. In subsequent chapters, the details of the human information-processing system will be elaborated on and the specific sources of errors within it spelled out in more detail.

Intentional Classification. Human errors can also be classified according to whether or not the action was performed as intended. More technically, *slips* occur through a failure in execution of action, and *mistakes* arise from errors in planning of action. One example of a slip is that of an operator of a nuclear power plant who intended to close pump discharge valves A and E, but also closed valves B and C inadvertently. Another incident, in which the operators used an incorrect strategy to depressurize the coolant system, illustrates a mistake (Reason, 1990).

TABLE 3–2   Berliner's Processing Classification of Tasks

PROCESSES	ACTIVITIES	SPECIFIC BEHAVIORS	
Perceptual	Searching for and receiving information	Detect Inspect Observe Read	Receive Scan Survey
	Identifying objects, actions, and events	Discriminate Identify	Locate
Mediational	Information processing	Calculate Categorize Compute Encode	Interpolate Itemize Tabulate Transfer
	Problem solving and decision making	Analyze Calculate Choose Compare	Compute Estimate Predict Plan
Communication		Advise Answer Communicate Direct Indicate	Inform Instruct Request Transmit
Motor	Simple, discrete tasks	Activate Close Connect Disconnect Hold Join	Lower Move Press Raise Set
	Complex, continuous tasks	Align Regulate Synchronize	Track Transport

For a slip, the deviation from the intended action often provides immediate feedback about the error. This is not true in the case of the mistake, because the immediate feedback is that the intended action was executed correctly. It is this intended action that is incorrect, and so the error is more difficult to detect. Consequently, mistakes are regarded as more serious than slips.

Norman (1981) developed a model of action that distinguishes three major categories of slips.

The first category is errors in the formation of intention. Such slips include mode errors in which the situation is erroneously classified and description errors for which the intention is ambiguous or incomplete. An example of this first category of errors occurs when instruments (such as a digital watch) have several display modes. The person may misinterpret the display and make an erroneous response that would be correct under a different mode.

Slips can also result from a second category, faulty activation of action schemas (organized bodies of knowledge that can direct the flow of motor activity). Inaccurate schema activations are responsible for such errors as failing to make an intended stop at the grocery store while driving home from work. The highly overlearned responses that take you home are activated in place of the less common responses that take you to the grocery store. The third category of slips includes those that result from faulty triggering of one of several activated schemas. Such slips are attributable to a schema being triggered at the incorrect time or not at all. Common forms of such errors are "Spoonerisms" in which words or syllables are interchanged. These are statements such as "You have tasted the whole worm" instead of "You have wasted the whole term."

In contrast to Norman's (1981) model of slips, Reason (1987) presents a model of mistakes. This model attributes mistakes to the basic processes involved in planning. First, the appropriate information may not be part of the information being used in the planning processes. The planning data base will include only a small amount of the potentially relevant information, and the information selected for inclusion will be influenced by a variety of factors, such as attention. Second, the mental operations involved in planning are subject to biases, such as overweighting of vivid information, a simplified view of causality, and so on. Third, once a plan, or sequence of action schemas, is formulated, it will be resistant to modification or change. Various sources of bias can lead to an inadequate data base, unrealistic goals, inadequate assessment of consequences, and overconfidence in the formulated plan.

Summary. The respective error taxonomies capture different aspects of human performance, and each has its uses. The action and failure classifications have been used with success to analyze human reliability in complex systems, but they categorize errors at only a superficial level. That is, errors that are considered to be instances of the same action category may have quite different cognitive bases. The processing and intentional classifications are at a deeper level in the sense that they identify underlying causal mechanisms. However, these taxonomies involve more assumptions than do the surface categories. Because the processing and intentional classifications focus on the root causes of the errors, they have the potential to be of greater ultimate use than classifications based on surface error properties.

RELIABILITY ANALYSIS

When a system performs reliably, it completes its intended function satisfactorily. The discipline of reliability engineering began to develop in the 1950s. The central tenet of reliability engineering is that the total system reliability can be determined from the reliabilities of the individual components and their configuration in the system. Early texts (for example, Bazovsky, 1961) and comprehensive works (for example, Barlow & Proschan, 1965) provided quantitative bases for reliability analysis by combining the mathematical tools of probability analysis with the organizational tools of system analysis. The successful application of reliability analyses to hardware systems led human factors specialists to apply similar logic to human reliability.

System Reliability

Although we would like for constructed systems to function well indefinitely, they do not. The term *reliability* is used to characterize the dependability of performance for a system, subsystem, or component. Reliability can be defined as "the probability that an item will operate adequately for a specified period of time in its intended application" (Park, 1987, p. 149). Performance that constitutes adequate operation must be specified clearly for the resulting probability estimate to be meaningful. The intended application of the item must also be considered when evaluating reliability.

There are three categories of failure for hardware systems (Dougherty & Fragola, 1988). Failures of equipment can occur while operating. For example, a fan may cease turning. Failures also can arise while in standby. Such a classification would be made for the fan if a failure occurred when it was not activated, but the failure prevented the fan from operating when needed. Finally, failures can occur on demand, that is, at the specific time that the equipment is needed to operate.

For an analysis of system reliability to be successful, a taxonomy of component failures must first be determined. Table 3–3 shows an example of such a taxonomy. After this determination, the reliabilities for each of the components must be estimated. Reliability of a component is the probability that it does not fail. Thus, the reliability r is equal to $1 - p$, where p is the probability of component failure. When the reliabilities of individual components are known or can be estimated, the system reliability can be derived by the application of principles of probability.

When determining system reliability, a distinction between components in *series* and *parallel* becomes important. In many systems, components are arranged such that they all must operate appropriately if the system is to satisfy its function. In such systems, the components can be characterized as being in series (see Figure 3–2). When independent components are arranged in series, the system reliability is the product of the

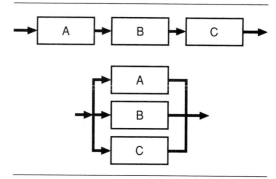

FIGURE 3–2   Examples of Serial (top) and Parallel (bottom) Systems.

individual probabilities. For example, if two components, each with a reliability of 0.9, must both operate for successful system performance, then the reliability of the system is $0.9 \times 0.9 = 0.81$. More generally,

$$R = (r_1) \times (r_2) \times \cdots (r_n) = \prod_{i=1}^{n} r_i$$

where r_i is the reliability of the ith component and R is the system reliability.

Two points are important regarding the reliability of a series of components. First, adding another component in series always decreases the system reliability unless the component reliability is 1.0 (see Figure 3–3). Second, a single component with low reliability will lower the system reliability considerably. For example, if three components in series each have a reliability of

TABLE 3–3   A Component Failure Taxonomy for an Example System

FAILURE:	MODES	MECHANISMS	CAUSES
	Fail to operate	Motor failures	Too high temperature
	Fail to start	Bearing failure	Lack of lubricant
	Fail to run	Seal failure	Oxidation
	Fail to change state	Contact failure	Misalignment
	Spurious operation	Command fault	Contamination
		Control instrument failure	

0.95, the system reliability is 0.90. However, if one of these components is replaced with a component whose reliability is 0.20, the system reliability drops to 0.18. More generally, in a serial system, the reliability can only be as great as that of the least reliable component.

Another way to arrange components is to have two or more perform the same function. Successful performance of the system requires that only one of the components operate appropriately. In other words, the additional components provide redundancy to guard against system failure. When components are arranged in this manner, they are said to be parallel (see Figure 3–2). For a simple parallel system in which all components are equally reliable,

$$R = [1 - (1 - r)^n]$$

where r is the reliability of each individual component and n is the number of components arranged in parallel. In this case, system reliability

is found by calculating the probability that at least one component remains functional.

The formula for the reliability of a parallel system can be generalized to situations in which the components do not have equal reliabilities. In this case,

$$R = 1 - [(1 - r_1)(1 - r_2) \dots (1 - r_n)] = 1 - \prod_{i=1}^{n} (1 - r_i)$$

When i groups of n parallel components with equal reliabilities are arranged in series,

$$R = [1 - (1 - r)^n]^i$$

More generally, the number of components within each group need not be the same, and the reliabilities for each component within a group need not be equal. Total system reliability can be found by considering each of n subsystems of parallel components in turn. Let c_i be the number of components operating in parallel in the ith group, and let r_{ji} be the reliability of the jth component in the ith group (see Figure 3–4). The reliability for the ith subsystem is

$$R_i = 1 - \prod_{j=1}^{c_i} (1 - r_{ji})$$

Total system reliability, then, is the reliability of the series of parallel subsystems:

$$R = \prod_{k=1}^{n} R_k$$

Whereas in serial systems the addition of another component dramatically decreases system reliability, in parallel systems it increases system reliability. It is clear from the expression for R_i that, as the number of parallel components increases, the reliability tends to 1.0. As an illustration, the system reliability for five parallel components each with a reliability of 0.20 is 0.67. When ten components each with a reliability of 0.20 are arranged in parallel, the system reliability is 0.89.

Some environmental processes, such as the heat caused by a fire, are sudden. Other environ-

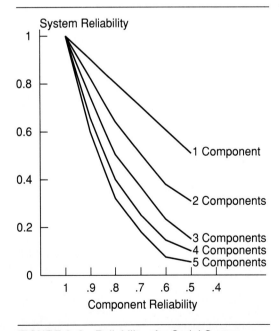

FIGURE 3–3   Reliability of a Serial System as a Function of Number of Task Components and the Reliability of Each Component.

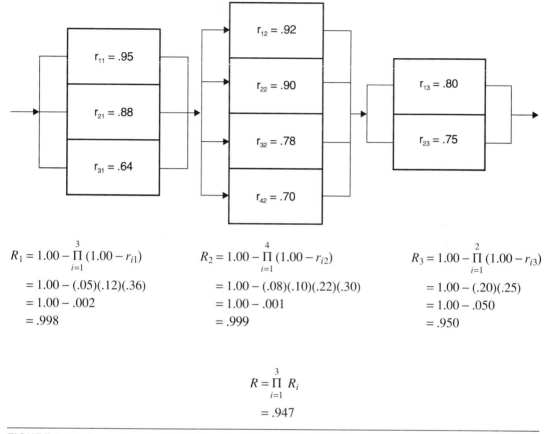

$$R_1 = 1.00 - \prod_{i=1}^{3} (1.00 - r_{i1})$$

$$= 1.00 - (.05)(.12)(.36)$$
$$= 1.00 - .002$$
$$= .998$$

$$R_2 = 1.00 - \prod_{i=1}^{4} (1.00 - r_{i2})$$

$$= 1.00 - (.08)(.10)(.22)(.30)$$
$$= 1.00 - .001$$
$$= .999$$

$$R_3 = 1.00 - \prod_{i=1}^{2} (1.00 - r_{i3})$$

$$= 1.00 - (.20)(.25)$$
$$= 1.00 - .050$$
$$= .950$$

$$R = \prod_{i=1}^{3} R_i$$

$$= .947$$

FIGURE 3–4 Computing the Reliability of a Series of Parallel Subsystems.

mental processes, such as the effect of water on underwater equipment, affect the reliability of the system continuously over time. Consequently, two types of reliability measures are used. For demand or shock-dependent failures, $r = \Pr[\mathbf{S} <$ capacity of the object]. That is, reliability is defined as the probability that the level of shock **S** does not exceed the capacity of the equipment to withstand the shock during the equipment's operation. For time-dependent failures, $r(t) = \Pr[\mathbf{T} > t]$, where **T** is the time of the first failure. In other words, reliability for time-dependent processes is defined as the probability that the first failure occurs after time t.

Whereas the random variable of interest in shock-dependent failure is discrete (failure or no failure), the random variable of interest in time-dependent failures is continuous (time to first failure). For continuous random variables such as time, the probability that an event occurs, say, 2.3 min after the machine is turned on cannot be expressed. This is because the probability of a failure occurring at precisely that instant in time is infinitesimally small. Instead, we can describe the behavior of time-dependent failures in terms of their *probability density functions* (pdfs). The pdf of a random variable **T** representing the time to failure can be used to determine the probability that the failure occurs between times $\mathbf{T} = t_1$ and $\mathbf{T} = t_2$ (see Figure 3–5). This probability is defined as the area under the pdf between points t_1 and t_2. In Figure 3–5, the pdf of $\mathbf{T}$ is exponentially distributed.

Often it is more convenient to discuss $\mathbf{T}$ in terms of its *cumulative distribution function* (cdf) rather than its pdf. The cdf of $\mathbf{T}$ gives the probability that $\mathbf{T}$ is less than some value t_0 for all possible values of t_0. The table of standard normal scores presented in Appendix I, used in Chapter 2 to compute percentiles, is a table of the values of the cdf of $\mathbf{T}$ when $\mathbf{T}$ is normally distributed. More generally, when the pdf of $\mathbf{T}$ is known to be $f(t)$, the cdf of $\mathbf{T}$ is

$$\Pr(\mathbf{T} < t) = F(t) = \int_{-\infty}^{t} f(u)\,du$$

Thus, $F(t)$ represents all the area under the curve $f(t)$ up to the point t.

For time-dependent failures, we are interested in the probability that failures occur after some time t, or the *survivor function* $1 - F(t)$. The

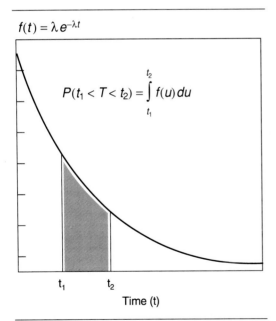

$f(t) = \lambda e^{-\lambda t}$

$$P(t_1 < T < t_2) = \int_{t_1}^{t_2} f(u)\,du$$

$t_1 \qquad t_2$

Time (t)

FIGURE 3–5   Exponential Probability Density Function.

survivor function of a component determines the component's reliability over time. If $f(t)$ is known for a particular component and can be integrated, the survivor function can be easily computed.

One of the most common pdf's arising in reliability analysis is that of the exponential distribution pictured in Figure 3–5:

$$f(t) = \lambda e^{-\lambda t}, \qquad t \geq 0$$

where λ is a parameter representing the rate of failure. The exponential cdf is

$$F(t) = 1 - e^{-\lambda t}, \qquad t \geq 0$$

and its survivor function is

$$1 - F(t) = e^{-\lambda t}, \qquad t \geq 0$$

Thus, the reliability of a component whose lifetime follows an exponential distribution decays exponentially as soon as the component is turned on. The average time to failure for this component is λ^{-1}. It is interesting to note that, although the pdf of the time to failure is known and although the reliability of the component decays exponentially with use, the probability that the component fails at any instant in time is independent of the length of time that the component has been in service. That is, the probability that the component fails given that it has been operating for five minutes is exactly equal to the probability that the component fails given that it has been operating for five days. This is called the memoryless property of the exponential pdf. It is reflected in a constant *hazard function* $h(t)$, where

$$h(t) = \frac{f(t)}{1 - F(t)}$$

is the likelihood that a component fails in the instant t given that it has not failed up to that point.

The significance of the memoryless property is that the length of time that a component has been in service tells us nothing about when it should be replaced. There are costs associated with replacing a component before it has failed and costs associated with replacing a component when it fails while operating. The goal of a maintenance strategy is to minimize these costs. If the failure time for a component has an exponential pdf, the best maintenance strategy is to replace the component when it fails in service.

When many components must be considered together, as within the context of a large system, time-dependent reliability analysis can be extremely difficult. Often these calculations are based on theories of stochastic processes. A stochastic process is a sequence of events, or many sequences of events, that are governed by probabilistic laws. Further discussion of these processes is beyond the scope of this book, but there are many excellent books on the topic (for example, Barlow & Proschan, 1965; Karlin & Taylor, 1975).

Human Reliability

Procedures similar to those used to determine the reliability of inanimate systems can be applied to the evaluation of human reliability in human–machine systems. Human reliability analysis thus involves quantitative predictions of operator error probability and of successful system performance. Operator error probability is defined as the number of errors made divided by the number of opportunities for such errors. *Human reliability* thus is 1 − (operator error probability). Just as hardware failures can be classified as time dependent or time independent, so can operator errors.

Human reliability analysis can be carried out for both normal and abnormal operating conditions. During normal operation, the following activities are important (Whittingham, 1988): routine control (maintaining a system variable, such as temperature, within an acceptable range of values); preventive and corrective maintenance; calibration and testing; restoration after maintenance; and inspection. In such situations, errors of omission and commission occur as discrete events within the sequence of activity. These errors may not be noticed or have any

consequence until abnormal operating conditions arise. Under abnormal operating conditions, the operator recognizes and detects the fault condition, diagnoses the problem and makes decisions, and takes actions to recover the system. Although action-oriented errors of omission and commission can still occur, perceptual and cognitive errors become more likely.

Human reliability analyses can be based on either *Monte Carlo methods* that simulate performance on the basis of a system model or on *computational methods* that analyze errors and their probabilities (Boff & Lincoln, 1988). The steps for performing such analyses are shown in Figure 3–6. As in any system analysis, the first step for both methods involves a description of the system, that is, its components and their functions. For the Monte Carlo method, the next step is to model the system in terms of task interrelations. On a probabilistic basis, input distributions of task times and success probabilities are selected to simulate the operations of the human and the system. The simulation is repeated many times; each time, it either succeeds or fails in accomplishing its task. The reliability of the human or system is the proportion of times that the task is completed in these simulations.

For the computational method, the next step is to identify potential errors for each task that must be performed and to estimate their likelihoods and consequences. These error probabilities are then used to compute the likelihood that the operator accomplishes her or his tasks appropriately and the probability of success for the entire system. The error probabilities can be obtained from several sources, described later; they must be accurate if the computed probabilities for successful performance of the operator and the system are to be meaningful.

The Monte Carlo and computational methods are similar in many respects, but each has its strengths and weaknesses. For example, if the computational method is to be accurate, detailed analyses of the types of errors, as well as their probabilities and consequences, must be performed. The Monte Carlo method, in turn, re-

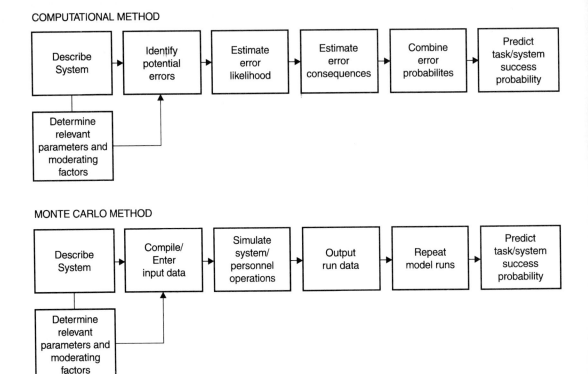

FIGURE 3–6 Computational and Monte Carlo Methods of Conducting Human Reliability Analysis.
Figure from K. R. Boff and J. E. Lincoln, (Eds.), *Engineering Data Compendium: Human Perception and Performance,* 1988. Reprinted with permission.

quires the development of accurate models of the system.

The *Human Reliability Assessor's Guide* provides a review of eight major techniques that are available for the quantification of human error probabilities (Humphreys, 1988). It also includes guidelines for the selection of techniques. We will provide detailed examples of one specific Monte Carlo method and two different types of computational methods.

Stochastic Modeling Technique. An example of the Monte Carlo method of human reliability analysis is the stochastic modeling technique developed by Siegel and Wolf (1969). The tech-

nique is intended to determine if the average person can complete all tasks in the allotted time and the points in the processing sequence at which the system may overload the personnel (Park, 1987). It has been applied in complex systems, such as landing an aircraft on a carrier, in which there are numerous subtasks that the operator must execute properly. The model uses estimates of the following information:

1. The mean time to perform a particular subtask; the average variability (standard deviation) in performance time for a representative operator.
2. The probability that the subtask will be performed successfully.

3. An indication of how essential successful performance of the subtask is to completion of the task.
4. The subtask that is to be performed next, which may differ as a function of whether or not the initial subtask is performed successfully.

Three calculations are derived from these data for each subtask (Park, 1987). Urgency and stress conditions are calculated from the subtasks to be performed by the operator in the remaining time. A specific execution time for the subtask is selected by randomly sampling from the distribution of response times. Similarly, whether the subtask was performed correctly is determined from random sampling of the probabilities for successful and unsuccessful performance.

The stochastic modeling technique is used to predict the efficiency of the operator within the entire system based on the simulated performance of each subtask. This technique has been applied with reasonable success to a variety of systems. Moreover, it has been incorporated into measures of total system performance.

Technique for Human Error Rate Prediction.
The technique for human error rate prediction (THERP), developed in the early 1960s, is one of the oldest and most widely used of the computational methods for human reliability analysis (Swain & Guttman, 1983). It was designed initially to determine human reliability in the assembly of bombs at a military facility, and it subsequently has been the basis of reliability analyses for industry and nuclear facilities.

The reliability analyst using THERP proceeds through a series of steps (Miller & Swain, 1987): (1) The system failures that could arise from human errors are determined. (2) The tasks performed by the personnel in relation to the system functions of interest are analyzed and identified. (3) The relevant human error probabilities are estimated. (4) The human reliability analysis is integrated with a system reliability analysis to determine the effects of human errors on the sys-

tem performance. (5) Changes to the system are recommended to increase the reliability, and then these changes are evaluated.

The most important steps in THERP are the third and fourth. These involve determining the probability that an operation will result in an error and the probability that a human error will lead to system failure. Such probabilities can be estimated from a THERP data base (Swain & Guttmann, 1983) or from any other data, such as simulator data, that are considered to be pertinent. Figure 3–7 depicts these probabilities in an event-tree diagram. In this figure, a is the probability of successful performance of task 1, and A is the probability of unsuccessful performance. Similarly, b and B are the probabilities for successful and unsuccessful performance of task 2. The first branch of the tree thus distinguishes the probability of performing or not performing task 1. The second level of branches involves the probabilities of performing or not performing task 2 successfully, conditioned on the performance of task 1. If the two tasks are independent (see Chapter 2), then the probability of completing task 2 is b, and B is the probability of not completing it. The general point is that, if the

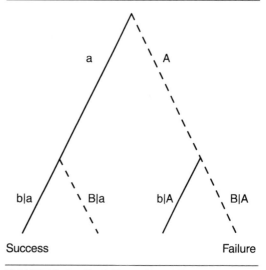

FIGURE 3–7   Task/Event Tree Diagram.

probability values for the individual component tasks are known, the probability of any particular combination of performance or nonperformance of the tasks can be generated, as well as the overall likelihood for total system failure resulting from human error.

As an example, suppose that a THERP analysis is to be performed for a worker's tasks at one station on an assembly line for portable radios. The final assembly of the radio requires that the electronic components be placed in a plastic case. To do this successfully, the worker must bend a wire for the volume control to the underside of the circuit board and snap the two halves of the case together. If the wire is not wrapped around the board, it can be damaged by the process of closing the case. The case itself can be cracked during assembly. The probability that the wire is positioned correctly is 0.85, and the probability that the case does not crack is 0.90. Figure 3–8 illustrates the event tree for these tasks. The probability that the radio is assembled correctly at this stage is 0.765.

The THERP error categorization procedure is based primarily on the action classification described earlier, that is, on errors of omission and commission. This error categorization is independent of the human information processes that produce the specific errors. More recent techniques, such as the model discussed next, place more emphasis on the processing basis of errors. However, THERP still compares favorably with other methods for quantifying errors, as indicated in a recent evaluation comparing it with four other human reliability assessment techniques (Kirwan, 1988).

Human Cognitive Reliability Model. This model, developed by Hannaman, Spurgin, and Lukic (1985), emphasizes human cognitive processes. The approach was developed to model the performance of a crew during an accident sequence. Because the time to respond with appropriate control actions is limited in such situations, the model provides a time-dependent human failure (nonresponse) probability. The input parame-

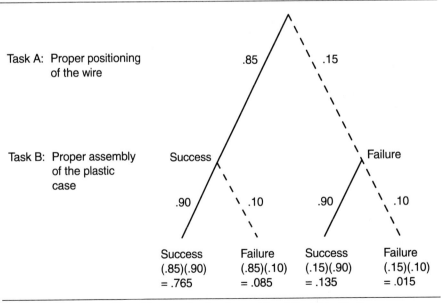

FIGURE 3–8 Event Tree Diagram for the Assembly of Portable Radios.

ters to the model are of three types: category of cognitive behavior, median response time, and performance-shaping factors (environmental influences on human performance).

The categories of cognitive behavior are skill based, rule based, and knowledge based. These categories are derived from a *skill–rule–knowledge framework* proposed by Rasmussen (1986, 1987). Skill-based behavior represents performance of activities in an automatic manner. Rule-based behavior is guided by a rule or procedure that has been communicated to or learned by the performer. Knowledge-based behavior is the level involved when the situation is unfamiliar. At this level, a goal is explicitly formulated to guide behavior.

The median response time for a task is estimated from a human-performance data source. The performance-shaping factors are incorporated into the model through modification of the median times to perform tasks. These factors involve level of stress, arrangement of equipment, and so on.

The most important part of the human cognitive reliability (HCR) model is a set of normalized time–reliability curves, one for each mode of cognitive processing (see Figure 3–9). These curves must be based on an assumed pdf describing the probability of a nonresponse at any point in time. The normalized time T_N is obtained as follows:

$$T_N = \frac{T_A}{T_M}$$

where T_A is the actual time and T_M is the median time to perform the task. Thus, these normalized curves can be used to generate nonresponse probabilities within various amounts of time after an emergency in the system develops.

The HCR model has been developed and evaluated within the context of operation of nuclear power plants. Although testing of the model is not complete, many of its fundamental hypotheses have been at least partially verified (Worledge, Joksimovich, & Spurgin, 1988).

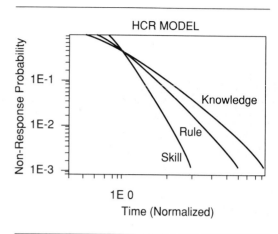

FIGURE 3–9   Normalized Crew Non-response Curves for Skill-, Rule-, and Knowledge-based Cognitive Processing.

Reprinted by permission from G. W. Hannaman, A. J. Spurgin, & Y. Lukic, A model for assessing human cognitive reliability in PRA studies. In *1985 IEEE third conference on human factors and nuclear safety* (pp. 343–353). Copyright © 1985 IEEE.

Whittingham (1988) has proposed that a combination of the THERP and HCR models may provide the most accurate predictor of human reliability. According to him, THERP most adequately captures the errors that occur during normal operation, whereas HCR is best for abnormal operating conditions.

Human Performance Data Sources.   Human reliability analysis requires that estimates of human performance for various tasks and subtasks be specified in quantitative form. Such estimates include the probability of correct performance, reaction time, and so on. Figure 3–10 shows several possible sources for the estimates. As in any science, it is best if the estimates are based on empirical data. Such data may come from laboratory studies, from research conducted on trainers and simulators, or from actual system operation. The empirical data are summarized in data banks (such as *Human Reliability Data Bank for Nuclear Power Plant Operators*, Topmiller,

Eckel, & Kozinsky, 1982) and handbooks (such as the *Handbook of Human Factors,* Salvendy, 1987), with more detailed descriptions presented in the original research reports. The primary limitations at this time are that the most commonly used data come from laboratory studies that are typically conducted under restricted, artificial conditions; generalization to more complex systems thus should be made with caution. Moreover, the amount of data from any of the sources that has been organized into data banks is limited.

Simulators provide a growing source of data for complex systems, such as chemical waste disposal plants, for which a failure can be hazardous.

The simulator can create specific accident sequences to analyze the performance of the personnel in such circumstances. A simulator exercise involves five steps (Dougherty & Fragola, 1988, p. 50):

1. Identify the sequences to be modeled, including the initiating incident and the equipment status.
2. Choose one or more trained crews to perform the exercises.
3. Run the exercise, recording the times when prechosen events occur, as well as the crews' responses to them.

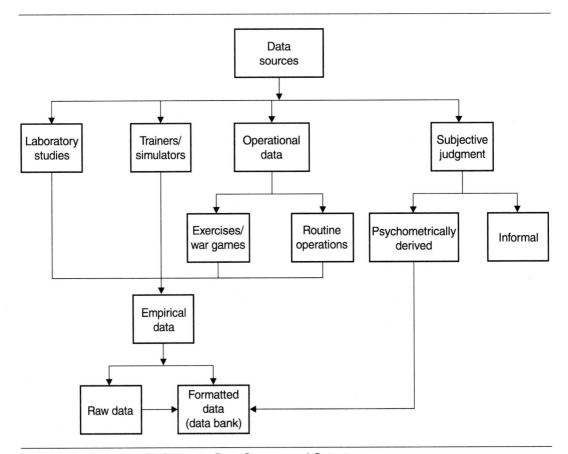

FIGURE 3–10   Human Performance Data Sources and Outputs.
Figure from K. R. Boff and J. E. Lincoln (Eds.), *Engineering Data Compendium: Human Perception and Performance,* 1988. Reprinted with permission.

4. Conduct postexercise interviews to obtain information about such things as which indicators were used and how decisions were made.
5. Analyze the data.

When the pertinent empirical data are not available, expert opinion often is used. In most cases, these subjective assessments are made informally. Clearly, estimates of performance based on objective, empirical data are to be preferred when available.

Risk Analysis

To this point, we have discussed reliability analysis. In such an analysis, the interest is in specifying the overall performance of a system in terms of the performance of its components. In human reliability analysis, the performance of the operators is determined from the performance of the component tasks. To be most beneficial, this human reliability analysis must be incorporated into the analysis of overall system reliability.

In complex systems, it is important to assess the risks associated with various system failures as part of a reliability analysis. Risk refers to events that can be harmful, such as a nuclear power plant releasing radioactive steam into the atmosphere. A *risk analysis,* therefore, considers not only the reliability of the system, but also the risks that accompany specific failures, such as monetary loss and loss of life. Probabilistic risk analysis involves decomposing the risk of concern into smaller elements for which the probabilities of failure can be quantified. These probabilities are then used to estimate the overall risk.

When analyzing a complex system like a nuclear plant, the human risk analysis includes the following goals:

1. Representing the plant's risk contribution due to its people and their supporting materials, such as procedures.
2. Providing a basis from which plant managers may make modifications to the plant while optimizing risk reduction and enhancing human factors.
3. Assisting the training of plant operators and maintenance personnel, particularly in contingencies, emergency response, and risk prevention. (Dougherty & Fragola, 1988, p. 74)

In sum, the focus of a reliability analysis is on successful operation of the system, and concerns about the environment are in terms of its influence on system performance. In contrast, for risk analysis, the emphasis is primarily on the influence of system failures on the environment. To maximize system reliability while minimizing system risk, these concerns must be addressed at all phases of system development and implementation.

SUMMARY

The operator is part of a human–machine system. Consequently, the system concept plays a central role in human factors. The contribution of the operator must be examined from within the context of the system. The performance of a system depends on a multitude of variables, some unique to the mechanical aspects of the system and some unique to the human aspects.

Errors by the operator can result in system failure. A basic goal of human factors is to analyze the sources of potential human errors and evaluate their consequences for overall system performance. Several alternative classifications for types of errors can be used for this purpose.

System reliability can be estimated from the reliabilities of the system's components and the structure of the system. Reliability analysis has been successful in predicting the reliability of machines. Human reliability analysis is based on the assumption that the performance of the operator can be analyzed using the same methods. Human and machine reliability analyses can be combined to predict the overall performance of the human–machine system.

For a system to be optimized, different types of human errors and their likelihoods must be considered at all phases of the system development process. Through the incorporation of known behavioral principles into system design and the evaluation of design alternatives, the human factors specialist ensures that the system can be operated safely and efficiently.

RECOMMENDED READING

Dhillon, B. S. (1986). *Human Reliability.* Elmsford, NY: Pergamon Press.

Park, K. S. (1987). *Human Reliability: Analysis, Prediction, and Prevention of Human Errors.* Amsterdam: Elsevier.

Rasmussen, J., Duncan, K., & Leplat, J. (1987). *New Technology and Human Error.* New York: Wiley.

Reason, J. (1990). *Human Error.* New York: Cambridge University Press.

Senders, J. W., & Moray, N. P. (1991). *Human Error: Cause, Prediction, and Reduction.* Hillsdale, NJ: Lawrence Erlbaum.

HUMAN INFORMATION PROCESSING

Because the language of information processing provides an objective and quantitative way of describing the basis of human performance, it has proven useful in applications. Indeed much of the impetus for the development of this kind of empirical study stemmed from the desire to integrate description of the human within overall systems.

—M. I. Posner, 1986

INTRODUCTION

The human information-processing approach characterizes the human as a communication system that receives input from the environment, acts on that information, and then outputs a response back to the environment. The information-processing approach is used to develop models that depict the flow of information in the human, in much the same way that system engineers use models to depict information flow in nonhuman systems. This fact is not coincidental, in that the human information-processing approach arose from the contact that psychologists had with industrial and communication engineers during World War II.

Information-processing concepts have been influenced by information theory, control theory, and computer science (Posner, 1986). However, experimental studies of human performance provide the empirical base for the approach (Fitts & Posner, 1967). An information-processing account of performance describes the encoding of perceptual information, how different codes are used within internal psychological subsystems, and the organization of these subsystems. The information flow for particular tasks is captured by diagrams of hypothesized processing subsystems. These diagrams in turn assist in identifying the mental operations that take place in the processing of various types of information from input to output.

An example of an information-processing model is shown in Figure 4–1. This model was proposed by Townsend and Roos (1973) to explain human performance in a variety of tasks in which responses are made to visually presented stimuli. The model consists of a set of distinct subsystems that intervene between the presentation of an array of visual symbols and the execution of a physical response to the array. The model includes perceptual subsystems (the visual form system), cognitive subsystems (the long-term memory components, the limited-capacity translator, and the acoustic form system), and action subsystems (the response–selection and response–execution systems). Flow of information through the system is indicated by the arrows. In this example, information is passed between stages and subsystems.

Engineers can look inside a machine to determine its internal structure. However, the behavioral scientist cannot look inside the head to examine the various subsystems that underlie human performance. Instead, they must be inferred on the basis of behavioral and physiological data. Alternative models are proposed that differ in terms of the number and arrangement of subsystems. The subsystems can be arranged serially, so that information flows through them one at a time, or in parallel, so that they can operate simultaneously. Complex models can be hybrids that are composed of both serial and parallel subsystems. In addition to the arrangement and nature of

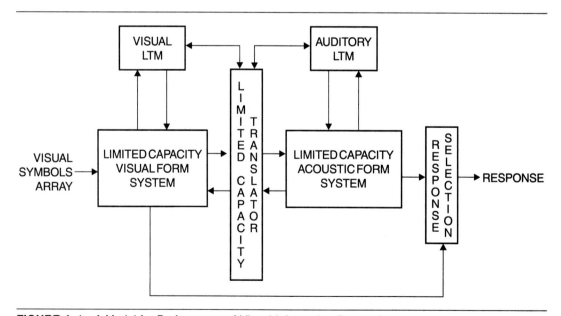

FIGURE 4–1   A Model for Performance of Visual Information Processing

From J. T. Townsend & R. N. Roos (1973), *Memory & Cognition, 1,* 319–332. Reprinted by permission of Psychonomic Society, Inc.

the proposed subsystems, the models also must address the processing cost associated with each subsystem.

Predictions are derived from the alternative models and evaluated by experimental data. The models that are most consistent with the data are accepted as more credible than alternative models. However, good models must do more than simply explain a limited set of behavioral data. They are also required to be consistent with other behavioral phenomena and with the knowledge of human neurophysiology. In keeping with the scientific method, models are revised and re-placed as additional data are gathered.

The importance of the information-processing approach for human factors is that it describes the operator in the same terms as the machine. The advantage of doing so is that an integrated treatment of the human–machine system can be realized. For example, Rasmussen (1986) stresses that models of human information processing are prerequisites for the conceptual design of computerized industrial control systems, which are used to support decision making during supervisory control tasks and management of emergencies. This is because optimal communication between the machine and the operators requires that information be presented in a way that is useful to the human processor. Information-processing models have also been applied successfully to other issues in human–computer interaction (Card, Moran, & Newell, 1983), as well as to a variety of human factors concerns (for example, Elkind, et al., 1989).

The information-processing approach provides a convenient framework for understanding and organizing a wide range of human–performance results. Additionally, it provides a basis for analyzing the task components in terms of their demands on perceptual, cognitive, and action processes. In this chapter, we will introduce the basic concepts and tools of analysis that are used in the study of human performance.

A THREE-STAGE MODEL

Figure 4–2 presents a general model of information processing that distinguishes three stages intervening between the presentation of a stimulus and the execution of a subsequent response. Early processes associated with perception and stimulus identification can be classified as the perceptual stage. Following this stage are intermediate processes involved with decision making and thought, classified as the cognitive stage. Information from this cognitive stage is used in the final action stage to select, prepare, and control the movements necessary to effect a response.

The three-stage model provides an effective organizational tool that we will use in this book. However, you should keep in mind that the boundaries between perception, cognition and ac-

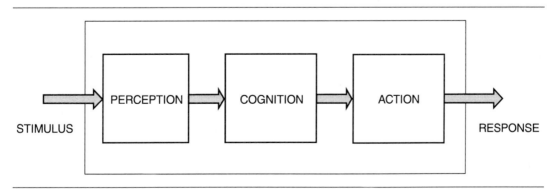

FIGURE 4–2   Three stages of Human Information Processing.

tion are not as clearly defined as implied by the model. Researchers who study human performance are interested in determining to which processing stage experimental findings should be attributed and in characterizing information flow within the system. It is not always clear whether a change in performance should be attributed to the perceptual, cognitive, or action stage. Once a specific change in performance can be clearly attributed to a stage, detailed models of the processing within that stage can be developed.

Perceptual Stage

The perceptual stage includes processes that operate from the stimulation of the sensory organs through the identification of that stimulation. These processes are involved in the detection, discrimination, and identification of displayed information. For example, a visual display produces or reflects patterns of light energy that are absorbed by photoreceptors in the eye. This triggers a neural signal that travels to areas of the brain devoted to filtering the signal and extracting the pertinent information contained in it. The ability of the brain to extract information from the signal depends on the quality of the sensory input. This quality is determined by, among other things, the clarity and duration of the display.

If the display is not clear, much of the information will be lost. When a film projector is focused improperly, you cannot see the details of the picture. Similarly, a poorly tuned television picture can be snowy and blurred. Displays that are presented very briefly or that must be examined very quickly, such as road signs, do not allow for the extraction of much information during the time that they are available. Such degradations of input to the sensory system restrict the amount of information that can be extracted and, thus, will restrict performance.

Cognitive Stage

After enough information has been extracted from a display to allow the identification or clas-

sification of the stimuli, processes begin to operate with the goal of determining the appropriate action or response. These processes can include the retrieval of information from memory, comparisons among displayed items, comparison between these items and the information in memory, arithmetic operations, and decision making. The cognitive stage imposes constraints on performance. For example, people have limited abilities to attend to multiple sources of information, to retrieve information from memory, and to perform complicated mental calculations.

Errors in performance may arise from these and other cognitive limitations. Performance can be less than optimal because of limitations in cognitive resources. Major advances in understanding these cognitive limitations and how people adapt to them have been made in the recent past.

Action Stage

Following the perceptual and cognitive stages of processing, an overt response (if required) needs to be selected, programmed, and executed. After a response is selected, it must then be translated into a set of neuromuscular commands. These commands control the specific limbs or effectors that are involved, including their direction, velocity, and relative timing. Because selection of the appropriate response and specification of the movement parameters take time, the latency to initiate a movement will increase with increased difficulty of response selection and movement complexity (Henry & Rogers, 1960). Errors in performance, such as the failure of a movement to terminate accurately at its intended destination, can arise from limitations of the action stage.

Human Information Processing and the Three-stage Model

The three-stage model is a general framework that we are using to organize many of the findings regarding human capabilities. It enables us to examine performance in terms of the characteristics and limitations of the three stages. This simple classification of human information processing allows for a more detailed examination of the processing subsystems within each stage. For example, as shown in Figure 4–3, each of the stages can be further partitioned into subsystems whose properties can then be analyzed.

Performance at each stage can suffer from different kinds of limitations (Norman & Bo-

brow, 1975). *Data-limited processing* takes place when the information input to the stage is degraded or imperfect, such as when a visual stimulus is only briefly flashed. *Resource-limited processing* occurs if the system is not powerful enough to perform the required operations efficiently, such as when a long-distance phone number has to be remembered until dialed. *Structurally limited processing* arises from an in-

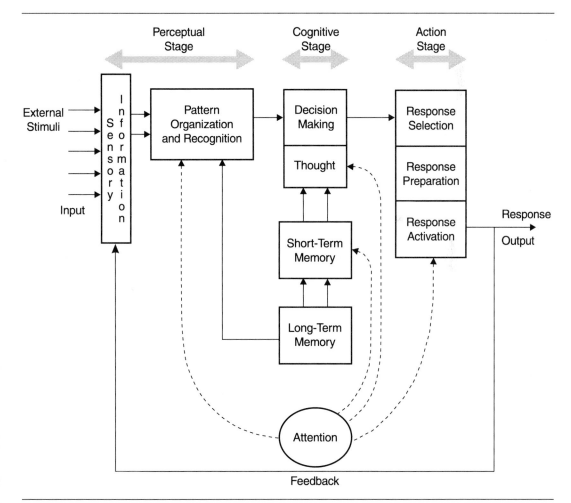

FIGURE 4–3   An Elaborated Model of Human Information Processing.

Adapted from B. H. Kantowitz, The role of human information processing models in system development. Adapted with permission from *Proceedings of the Human Factors Society 33rd Annual Meeting,* 1989, pp. 979–983. Copyright 1989 by The Human Factors Society, Inc. All rights reserved.

ability of one system to perform simultaneous operations. Although structural limitations can appear at any stage of processing, the most obvious effects occur in the action stage when two competing movements must be performed simultaneously with a single limb.

THE PSYCHOLOGICAL REPRESENTATION OF THE PHYSICAL WORLD

Although the view of humans as information-processing systems is relatively recent, it is consistent with the historical tradition surrounding the study of sensation and perception. As summarized in Chapter 1, since the 1800s, researchers such as Weber and Fechner have been concerned with the relation between physical stimuli and their sensory experience. Research in this tradition has emphasized the use of frequencies of responses, such as the number of times that an observer reports perceiving the presence of a stimulus. These frequencies are used to derive psychophysical measures of sensory experience.

Two questions about the senses are fundamental in psychophysics: (1) what are the limits of the senses to sensory stimulation, and (2) how do changes in stimulus intensity relate to changes in sensory experience? Psychophysical methods exist that provide answers to questions about detectability, discriminability, and perceived magnitude. *Detectability* refers to the absolute limits of the sensory systems to provide information that a stimulus is present. *Discriminability* involves the ability to determine that two stimuli differ from each other. The relation between perceived magnitude and physical magnitude is referred to as *psychophysical scaling.*

Most of what we know about the limits of the human sensory system have been discovered using psychophysical techniques. These techniques are also used to investigate applied issues in many areas. Moreover, knowledge of the basic theoretical principles that underlie the methods can be used by the human factors specialist in

solving specific problems relating to optimal design.

Classical Methods for Detection and Discrimination

The most important concept in classical psychophysics is that of the threshold. An *absolute threshold* refers to the minimal amount of energy necessary for a stimulus to be detected. A *difference threshold* is the minimal amount of difference necessary for two stimuli to be perceived as different. The goal of the classical psychophysical methods is to measure thresholds accurately.

The definition of threshold suggests fixed values below which stimuli cannot be detected or differences discriminated and above which stimuli are always perfectly detected. That is, the relation between physical intensity and detectability would be a step function (illustrated by the dashed line in Figure 4–4). However, psychophysical studies have determined that a range of stimulus values exists over which an observer will detect a stimulus or discriminate between two stimuli only some percentage of the time.

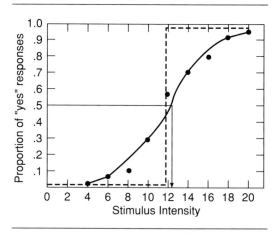

FIGURE 4–4 Proportion of Detection Responses as a Function of Stimulus Intensity for Idealized (Dashed) and Actual (Points) Observers.

Thus, the typical psychophysical function is an S-shaped curve (as shown by the points in Figure 4–4). Because such a function does not show a distinct threshold, the threshold value must be defined statistically by examining responses across many stimulus presentations.

The classical methods for measuring thresholds were developed by Fechner. Although numerous modifications to the procedures have been made over the ensuing years, the methods in this tradition still follow closely the procedures that he outlined. The methods involve multiple measurements under formalized procedures, with the threshold estimated from the resulting distribution of responses.

One method for determining thresholds is the *method of limits*. To find an absolute threshold with this method, stimulus intensities that bracket the threshold are presented in a succession of small increments. For an ascending order, the initial stimulus is below threshold, that is, it is one that the observer will not detect. The intensity of the stimulus is incremented, and another judgment is then made. This procedure is repeated until the observer responds *yes*. The mean of the intensities for that trial and for the immediately preceding trial is taken as the threshold for the series. The procedure is then repeated several times, with half of the series involving a descending order in which the initial stimulus is above threshold and then is decremented until the observer no longer detects it. The mean of the individual threshold measurements for each series defines the observer's absolute threshold.

To find difference thresholds with the method of limits, two stimuli are presented on each trial. The comparison stimulus varies in intensity, while the standard stimulus remains constant. The observer must indicate whether the comparison stimulus is less than, greater than, or equal to the standard stimulus. Intensities for the comparison stimulus are incremented and decremented as described previously. Two thresholds can be obtained, a lower threshold at which response changes from *less than* to *equal* and an upper threshold at which the response changes from *equal* to *greater than*.

A second widely used method is the *method of constant stimuli*. To obtain an absolute threshold with this method, the different stimulus magnitudes are presented randomly, with the observer again responding either *yes* or *no*. For each magnitude, the percentage of times that the stimulus was detected is calculated, and the threshold is defined as the magnitude of the stimulus that was detected on 50% of the trials. Difference thresholds are found similarly by randomly varying the magnitude of the variable stimulus from trial to trial.

These and other related methods have been used successfully since Fechner's work to obtain basic, empirical information regarding the senses. It is important to understand that the measurement of a threshold in an isolated condition is not very informative. Rather, it is the changes in the threshold under varying conditions that provide critical information about sensory limitations. For example, the absolute threshold for auditory stimuli is a function of the stimulus frequency (see Chapter 6). It is not as easy to detect stimuli that are of very high or very low frequency. These findings not only reveal basic characteristics of the auditory system, but they also indicate that there is an optimal range of frequencies within which auditory signals should be presented if detectability is a concern.

Although the threshold concept and accompanying psychophysical methods are of considerable value, there are several potential problems. Most serious is the fact that the measured value for the threshold, which is assumed to reflect sensory sensitivity, may be affected by the observer's desire to say *yes* or *no*. As an extreme case, a person might decide to respond *yes* on all trials. If so, the researcher would not know whether the person actually detected any stimuli. This problem can be addressed by inserting some catch trials on which no stimulus is presented. If the observer responded *yes* on those trials, his or her data could be excluded from consideration.

However, catch trials will not pick up response biases that are less extreme.

Signal Detection

Another way to characterize the problem with the classical methods is that the tests of sensitivity are subjective. That is, we have to take the observer's word that the stimulus has been detected. This is much like taking an exam that consists of the instructor asking you whether you know the material but not verifying it. Instead of testing you in this manner, an objective test, such as a true–false test, is used that requires you to distinguish between true and false statements. In this case, the instructor can evaluate your knowledge of the material by the extent to which you correctly respond *yes* to true statements and *no* to false statements. The signal-detection methods are much like an objective test, in that the observer is required to discriminate trials on which the stimulus is present from trials on which it is not.

Methods. In the terminology of signal detection (Green & Swets, 1966), noise trials refer to those on which the stimulus is not present and signal-plus-noise trials (or signal trials) refer to those on which the stimulus is present. In a typical signal-detection experiment, a single stimulus value is selected and used for a series of trials. For example, the signal may be a tone of a particular frequency and intensity presented in a background of auditory noise. On some trials, only the noise is presented, whereas on other trials both the signal and noise are presented. The observer must respond *yes* or *no* regarding whether the signal occurred. The crucial distinction between the signal-detection methods and the classical methods is that the observer's sensitivity to the stimulus can be calibrated by taking into account the responses made when the stimulus is not present.

The four combinations made up of the two possible states of the world (signal, noise) and two responses (yes, no) are shown in Table 4–1.

TABLE 4–1 Classifications of Signal and Response Combinations in a Signal-detection Experiment

Response	STATE OF THE WORLD	
	Signal	Noise
Yes (present)	Hit	False alarm
No (absent)	Miss	Correct rejection

A *hit* is said to have occurred when the observer responds *yes* on signal trials, a *false alarm* when the response is *yes* on noise trials, a *miss* when the response is *no* on signal trials, and a *correct rejection* when the response is *no* on noise trials. Because the proportions of the latter two response categories are redundant with those of the first two, signal-detection analyses typically focus only on the hit and false-alarm rates. You should note that this 2 by 2 classification of states of the world and responses is equivalent to the classification of true and false states in inferential statistics (see Table 2–4); the emphasis on optimizing human performance in terms of hits and false alarms can be regarded as minimization of type I and type II errors, respectively. The key to understanding signal-detection theory is to realize that it is just a variant of the statistical model for hypothesis testing.

It should be clear that sensitivity is good if the hit rate is high and the false-alarm rate low. This means that *yes* responses predominate when the signal is present and *no* responses when it is not. Conversely, sensitivity is poor if the hit and false-alarm rates are similar, indicating that the response *yes* is being given approximately equally often when the signal is present and when it is not. Several measures of sensitivity can be derived from the hit and false-alarm rates, but they are all based on this general logic.

Similarly, if a person tends to make many more responses of one type or the other, regardless of whether the signal is present, a *response bias* exists. If signal trials and noise trials are

equally likely, an unbiased observer should respond *yes* and *no* equally often. If the observer
responds *yes* on 75% of the trials, this would
indicate a bias to respond *yes*. If *no* responses
predominate, it would indicate the opposite bias.
As with sensitivity, there are numerous measures
of response bias based on this general logic.

Theory. Signal-detection theory provides a
theoretical framework for interpreting the results
from detection experiments. In contrast with the
notion of a fixed threshold, signal-detection theory assumes that the sensory evidence regarding
the presence of the signal can be represented on a
continuum. Even when the noise alone is presented, a certain amount of evidence will be registered to suggest the presence of the signal.
Moreover, the amount will vary from trial to trial,
meaning that there will be more evidence at some
times than at others to suggest the presence of the
signal. For example, when detecting an auditory
signal in noise, the amount of energy contained in
the frequencies around that of the signal frequency will vary from trial to trial due to the
statistical properties of the noise-generation process. Even when no physical noise is present, variability is introduced by the sensory registration
process, neural transmission, and so on. Often the
effects of the noise can be characterized by a
normal distribution because of the many different
sources of variation; consequently, it is only the
normal distribution that we will consider here.

The noise will have similar effects when the
signal is present and when it is not. However, if
the signal is detectable beyond chance, the distribution for the signal trials will be shifted in the
direction of greater evidence. Because detection
experiments typically involve situations in which
the signal trials and noise trials are not perfectly
distinguishable, the two distributions will overlap. Thus, when the sensory evidence for a given
trial falls within the region of overlap (see Figure
4–5), it could have been produced either by a
signal trial or by a noise trial. Whether the ob-

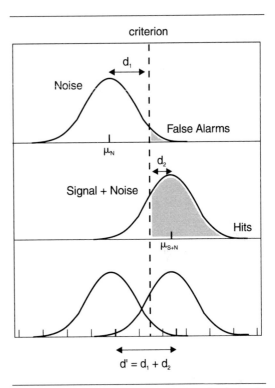

FIGURE 4–5   Signal and Noise Distributions of
Sensory Evidence Illustrating Determination of
d'.

server will make a *yes* or *no* response will depend
on the criterion value that the observer adopts. If
the evidence for the presence of the signal exceeds this criterion value, then the response is
yes; if not, the response is *no.*

Detectability and Bias.   In signal-detection theory, the detectability of the stimulus is reflected
in the difference between the means of the signal
and noise distributions. When the means are identical, the signal is not detectable. As the mean for
the signal distribution shifts away from the mean
of the noise distribution in the direction of more
evidence, the signal becomes increasingly detectable. Thus, the most commonly used measure of
detectability is

$$d' = \frac{\mu_S - \mu_N}{\sigma}$$

where d' is detectability, μ_S is the mean of the signal distribution, μ_N is the mean of the noise distribution, and σ is the standard deviation of both distributions. The d' statistic is the standardized distance between the means of the two distributions.

The setting of the criterion reflects the observer's bias to say *yes* or *no*. If the signal trials and noise trials are equally likely, an unbiased criterion setting would be at the evidence value for which the two distributions are equal in height (that is, the value for which the likelihood of the evidence coming from the signal distribution is equal to that of it coming from the noise distribution). A biased, conservative criterion would be shifted in the direction of more evidence (that is, respond *yes* only if the evidence is strong); a biased, liberal criterion would be shifted in the direction of less evidence. The bias is designated by the Greek letter β. This value is defined as

$$\beta = \frac{f_S(C)}{f_N(C)}$$

where C is the criterion, and f_S and f_N are the heights of the signal and noise distributions, respectively. If $\beta = 1.0$, then the observer is unbiased. If β is greater than 1.0, the observer is conservative, and if it is less than 1.0, the observer is liberal.

It is easy to compute both d' and β from the standard normal table (Appendix 1). To compute d', we must find the distances of μ_S and μ_N from the criterion. The location of the criterion with respect to the noise distribution is conveyed by the false-alarm rate, which reflects the proportion of the distribution that falls beyond the criterion (see Figure 4–5). Likewise, the location of the criterion with respect to the signal distribution is conveyed by the hit rate. We can use the standard normal table to find the z-scores corresponding to different hit and false-alarm rates. The distance from the mean of the noise distribution to the criterion is given by the z-score of $1 - $ (false-alarm rate), and the distance from the mean of the signal distribution is given by the z-score of the hit rate. The distance between the means of the two distributions, or d', is the sum of these scores:

$$d' = z(H) + z(1 - FA)$$

where H is the proportion of hits and FA is the proportion of false alarms.

Suppose a detection experiment is performed, and it is observed that the proportion of hits is 0.80 and the proportion of false alarms is 0.10. Referring to the standard normal table, the point on the abscissa corresponding to an area of 0.80 is $z(0.80) = 0.84$, and the point on the abscissa corresponding to an area of $1.0 - 0.10 = 0.90$ is $z(0.90) = 1.28$. Thus, d' is equal to $0.84 + 1.28$, or 2.12. Because a d' of 0.0 corresponds to chance performance (that is, hits and false alarms are equally likely) and a d' of 2.33 to nearly perfect performance (that is, the probability of a hit is very close to 1, and the probability of a false alarm is very close to 0), the value of 2.12 can be interpreted as good discriminability.

The bias in the criterion setting can be found by obtaining the height of the signal distribution at the criterion and dividing it by the height of the noise distribution. This is simply expressed by the formula

$$\beta = e^{-(z(H)^2 - z(1 - FA)^2)/2}$$

For this example, β is equal to 1.59. The observer in this example shows a conservative criterion because β is greater than 1.0.

Changes in Criteria. The importance of signal-detection methods and theory is that they allow measurement of detectability independent from the response criterion. In other words, d' should not be influenced by whether the observer is biased or unbiased. This aspect is captured in plots of *receiver operating characteristic* (ROC) curves (see Figure 4–6). For such curves, the hit rate is plotted as a function of the false-alarm rate. If performance is at chance ($d' = 0.0$), the ROC

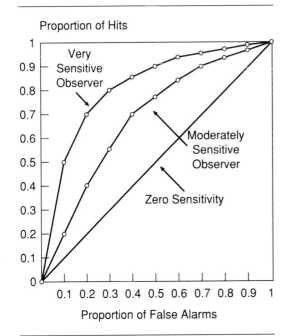

Proportion of Hits

FIGURE 4–6 ROC Curves Showing the Possible Hit and False-alarm Rates for Different Discriminabilities.

curve is a straight line along the positive diagonal. As d' increases, the curve pulls up and to the left. A given ROC curve thus represents a single detectability value, and the different points along it reflect possible combinations of hit and false-alarm rates that can occur as the response criterion varies.

How can the response criterion be varied? One way is through instructions. Observers will adopt a higher criterion if they are instructed to respond *yes* only when sure that the signal was present than if they are told to respond *yes* when they think that there is any chance that the signal was present. Similarly, if payoffs are introduced that differentially favor particular outcomes over others, the criterion will be adjusted accordingly. Finally, the probabilities of signal trials $p(S)$ and noise trials $p(N)$ can be varied. Making the signal more likely will cause a lowering of the response criterion, whereas making the signal less likely will raise the criterion. As predicted by signal-detection theory, manipulations of these variables

typically have little or no effect on measures of detectability.

When the signal and noise are equally likely, and payoffs do not favor a particular response, the optimal strategy is to set β equal to 1.0. When the relative frequencies of the signal and noise trials are different, or when the payoff matrix is asymmetric, the optimal criterion will not necessarily equal 1.0. To maximize the payoff, the ideal observer should set the criterion at the point where $\beta = \beta_{opt}$, and

$$\beta_{opt} = \frac{p(N)}{p(S)} \times \frac{\text{value } (CR) - \text{cost } (FA)}{\text{value } (H) - \text{cost } (M)}$$

where CR and M indicate correct rejections and misses, respectively, and value and cost indicate the amount the observer gains for a correct response or loses for an incorrect response (Gescheider, 1985). The criterion set by the observer can be compared to that of the ideal observer to determine the extent to which performance deviates from optimal.

Applications. Although signal-detection theory was developed from basic, sensory detection experiments, it is applicable to virtually any situation in which a person must make binary classifications based on stimulus situations that are not perfectly discriminable. As one example, signal-detection theory has been applied to problems in radiology. Radiologists are required to determine if shadows on X-ray films are indicative of disease (signal) or merely reflect differences in human physiology (noise). The accuracy of a radiologist's judgment rarely exceeds 70% (Lusted, 1971), so the development of superior imaging systems is of great concern. By examining changes in d' or other measures of sensitivity (called *figures of merit*), different imaging systems can be evaluated in terms of the improvement in detectability of different pathologies (Barrett & Swindell, 1981; Swets & Pickett, 1982).

With some thought, you may be able to extend signal-detection techniques to other situations in which we are interested in people's sensitivity to whether two stimuli differ. These techniques have been applied to such problems as pain perception, recognition memory, vigilance, fault diagnosis, and allocation of mental resources (Gescheider, 1985).

Psychophysical Scaling

The concept of measurement scales, that is, rules by which we assign numbers to events, was introduced in Chapter 2. In psychophysical scaling, the concern is with developing scales of psychological quantities that, in many cases, can be mapped to physical scales. A distinction is made between prothetic and metathetic continua (Stevens & Galanter, 1957). A prothetic continuum is a dimension of sensory experience that has the aspect of intensity. For example, a sound may vary from being barely audible to being annoyingly loud. For a prothetic continuum, the question of "How much?" makes sense. In contrast, a metathetic continuum is one in which the differences are qualitative rather than quantitative. For example, sounds may also differ in the pitch that is perceived. Thus, for dimensions of this type, questions of "How much?" are meaningless. Instead, only questions of "What kind?" can be asked.

Two general categories of scaling procedures for examining prothetic continua can be distinguished. Indirect scaling procedures derive the quantitative scale indirectly from an observer's performance at discriminating stimuli. For developing a scale of loudness, the observer never would be asked to judge loudness. Instead, the task would be to discriminate stimuli of different intensities. In contrast, with direct scaling procedures, the judgments involve the perceived magnitude of the stimulation. A direct scale for loudness would be based on the observer's reported numerical estimation of loudness.

The initial use of indirect scales is attributed to Fechner. Remember from Chapter 1 that he constructed scales from absolute and difference thresholds. The absolute threshold provided the zero point on the psychological scale. This stimu-

lus was then used as a standard to determine a difference threshold. This new stimulus was used as a standard to find the next difference threshold, and so on. By assuming that the change in perceived magnitude was equivalent for each of the successive difference thresholds, the resulting function relating stimulus intensities to perceived change can be taken to be a scale of magnitude relations. As described in Chapter 1, such functions are typically logarithmic.

Direct scaling procedures have a history of use roughly equivalent to that of indirect procedures. As early as 1872, scales were derived by Plateau (1872) from direct measurements. However, the major impetus for direct procedures came from Stevens (1975) in this century. Stevens popularized the procedure of magnitude estimation, in which observers rate stimuli on the basis of their apparent intensity. The experimenter assigns a value to a standard stimulus, for example, the number 10, and the observers then rate the magnitude of other stimuli in proportion to the standard. So, if a stimulus seems twice as intense as the standard, it would be given the number 20.

With these and other direct methods, the resulting magnitude scales are not logarithmic. Instead, the scales appear to follow the power function

$$S = aI^n$$

where S is sensory intensity, a is a constant, I is physical intensity, and n is an exponent that varies for different sensory continua. This relation often is called *Stevens's law*.

Figure 4–7 shows the functions for three prothetic dimensions. It should be noted that when the exponent is 1.0 the function relating perceived to physical magnitude is linear. For values greater than 1.0, the function is convex (perceived magnitude increases at a more rapid rate than physical magnitude), whereas for values less than 1.0 it is concave (perceived magnitude increases less rapidly than physical magnitude). The exponents for a variety of sensory continua

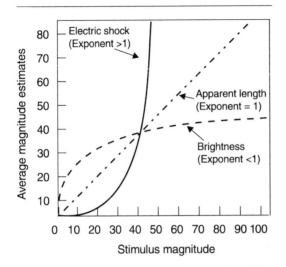

FIGURE 4–7   Power-function Scales for Three Prothetic Dimensions.

The evaluation of psychological magnitude is of particular relevance for applied problems involving noxious stimuli such as high noise levels or odorous pollution. Environmental psychophysics uses modified psychophysical techniques to measure the perceived magnitude of stimuli occurring in the living environment. Berglund (1991) and her colleagues have developed a master-scale procedure that enables scale values for environmental stimuli to be obtained from magnitude estimation judgments. With this procedure, estimates obtained in the laboratory for controlled intensities of a stimulus are used to standardize the judgments made to environmental stimuli. For example, Berglund, Berglund, and Lindvall (1974) investigated the odor problems associated with hog farms. Wet manure was spread on a field using various spreading techniques. The time intervening between the spreading of the manure and the judgment of odor magnitude was also varied, as was the distance of observers from the source. The same observers provided magnitude estimates for several concen-

are shown in Table 4–2. Power functions are very flexible and describe the widest range of data for magnitude scales.

TABLE 4–2   Representative Exponents of the Power Functions Relating Sensation Magnitude to Stimulus Magnitude

CONTINUUM	EXPONENT	STIMULUS CONDITIONS
Loudness	0.6	Both ears
Brightness	0.33	5° target (dark adapted eye)
Brightness	0.5	Point source (dark adapted eye)
Lightness	1.2	Gray papers
Smell	0.55	Coffee odor
Taste	0.8	Saccharine
Taste	1.3	Sucrose
Taste	1.3	Salt
Temperature	1.0	Cold (on arm)
Temperature	1.6	Warmth (on arm)
Vibration	0.95	60 Hz (on finger)
Duration	1.1	White-noise stimulus
Finger span	1.3	Thickness of wood blocks
Pressure on palm	1.1	Static force on skin
Heaviness	1.45	Lifted weights
Force of handgrip	1.7	Precision hand dynamometer
Electric shock	3.5	60 Hz (through fingers)

Based on Stevens, 1961.

trations of pyridine (which has a pungent odor), and these latter estimates were used to convert the estimates of odor strength for the manure to a standardized master scale on which the scale values for the individual subjects were comparable. Techniques such as these can provide valuable information regarding factors that reduce the perceived magnitude of noxious environmental stimuli.

INFORMATION THEORY

Another methodological tool that played an important role in the rise of the human information-processing approach is *information theory* (Garner, 1962). Information theory was developed by communication engineers to characterize the flow of information through communication channels. In the 1950s, contemporaneous with the development of signal-detection theory, psychologists began to apply the concepts of information theory to human performance (Fitts & Posner, 1967). Information theory does not play the prominant role today that it once did, but it is still useful in many circumstances.

Information theory is not a scientific theory. It is a system of measurement for quantifying information. The amount of information conveyed by an event (a stimulus, response, or the like) is a function of the number of possible events and their probabilities of occurring. If an event is certain, then its occurrence conveys no information. For example, if I know that the motor in an automobile is not working, then I gain no information by turning the key in the ignition and observing that the car will not start. On the other hand, if I am uncertain about the operating status of the engine, then I gain information from the same event. The uncertainty of the event is the amount of information that we gain by observing it.

The general idea behind information theory is that the most efficient way to uniquely identify one of a set of events is to ask a series of binary questions. For example, if I told you that I was thinking of a number between 1 and 16, and you were to identify that number by asking me questions, you could proceed in several ways. One way would be to guess randomly each of the numbers until I said *yes.* While you occasionally might guess the number the first time, on the average it would take eight questions to determine the correct number.

It would make more sense to systematically restrict the number of possibilites by asking *yes–no* questions. There are many ways that you could do this, but the most efficient would be to ask the questions in such a way that each reduced the number of possible alternatives by half. For identifying one of 16 numbers, the first question thus should be, "Is it between 1 and 8?" If my answer is *yes,* the next question should be, "Is it between 1 and 4?" Proceeding in this manner, you always would identify the correct number with four questions. In fact, of all possible guessing strategies you could use, four is the minimum number of questions that would have to be asked on average to correctly identify the number.

This idea of binary questions underlies the information theory definition of information. The number of binary questions required to decode a message provides the measure of information.

When all alternatives are equally likely, the amount of information (*H*) is given by

$$H = \log_2 N$$

where N is the number of alternative events. The basic unit of information is the bit, or binary digit. Thus, an event conveys 1 bit of information when there are two equally likely possibilities, 2 bits when there are four possibilities, 3 bits when there are eight possibilities, and, as we have demonstrated, 4 bits when there are sixteen possibilities. In other words, each item in a set of sixteen can be represented by a unique 4-digit binary code.

The amount of uncertainty, and thus the average information conveyed by the occurrence of one of N possible events, is a function of the probability for each event. The maximum amount of information is conveyed when the N events are equally likely. The average amount of information is less when the events are not equally likely. The uncertainty of a single event i that occurs with probability p_i is $-\log_2 p_i$; thus, the average uncertainty over all possible events is

$$H = -\sum_{i=1}^{N} p_i \log_2 p_i$$

The equation for H when all events are equally likely, that is, $p_i = 1/N$, can be easily derived from the more general equation by noting that $-\log_2 p_i = \log_2(1/p_i)$.

The importance of information theory is in analyzing the amount of information transmitted through a system. Because the human can be regarded as a communication system, an examination of the information input $H(S)$ (stimulus information) and the information output $H(R)$ (response information) will tell us about the properties of the human system. If four equally likely stimuli can occur (say, the letters A, B, C, and D), then there are 2 bits of stimulus information. If there are four response categories, again A, B, C, and D, each used equally often, then there are 2 bits of response information.

In studying a communication system, we are interested in the output that results from a particular input. Given that, say, the stimulus A is input into the system, we can record the number of times that the responses A, B, C, and D are output. The frequency of each stimulus–response pair can be counted, thus forming a bivariate frequency distribution (see Table 4–3). From such a table, the joint information can be computed by the equation

$$H(S,R) = -\sum_{i=1}^{N} \sum_{j=1}^{N} p_{ij} \log_2 p_{ij}$$

where p_{ij} equals the relative frequency of response j to stimulus i.

Of most importance is the amount of *transmitted information*. If the responses correlate per-

TABLE 4–3   Stimulus–Response Matrices for Three Amounts of Information Transmission

PERFECT INFORMATION TRANSMISSION

	Response			
Stimulus	A	B	C	D
A	24	—	—	—
B	—	24	—	—
C	—	—	24	—
D	—	—	—	24

NO INFORMATION TRANSMISSION

	Response			
Stimulus	A	B	C	D
A	6	6	6	6
B	6	6	6	6
C	6	6	6	6
D	6	6	6	6

PARTIAL INFORMATION TRANSMISSION

	Response			
Stimulus	A	B	C	D
A	9	8	3	4
B	3	15	2	4
C	4	4	8	8
D	0	5	3	16

fectly with the stimuli, for example if the stimulus A is classified as A every time, then all the information in the stimuli is maintained in the responses, and the information transmitted is 2 bits (see top panel of Table 4–3). Although the example in the table shows all the responses as correct, note that the responses only have to be consistent. In other words, if stimulus A were always identified as B, and vice versa, the information transmitted would be unaffected. If the responses are distributed equally across the four stimuli, as in the center panel of Table 4–3, then no information is transmitted. When there is a less than perfect, nonzero correlation, as in the bottom panel of Table 4–3, then the information transmitted is between 0 and 2 bits. To determine the amount of information transmitted, the stimulus information, response information, and joint information must be calculated. Transmitted information is then given by

$$T(S,R) = H(S) + H(R) - H(S,R).$$

For the data in the bottom panel of Table 4–3, the amount of transmitted information is computed as follows (see Table 4–4). By summing across the frequencies of the responses to each stimulus, we can determine that each stimulus was presented 24 times. Because the four stimuli were equally likely, the stimulus information is equal to $\log_2 4$ or 2.00 bits. By summing

TABLE 4–4 Calculating Transmitted Information

	RESPONSE				
Stimulus	A	B	C	D	Stimulus Frequency
A	9	8	3	4	24
B	3	15	2	4	24
C	4	4	8	8	24
D	0	5	3	16	24
Response frequency	16	32	16	32	

Stimulus information

$H(S) = \log_2 4 = 2.00$ bits

Response information

$$H(R) = -\sum_{i=1}^{4} p_i \log_2 p_i$$

$$= \left(\frac{16}{96} \log_2 \frac{96}{16} + \frac{32}{96} \log_2 \frac{96}{32} \right) \times 2$$

$$= 1.92 \text{ bits}$$

Joint information

$$H(S, R) = -\sum_{j=1}^{4} \sum_{i=1}^{4} p_{ij} \log_2 p_{ij}$$

$$= \frac{9}{96} \log_2 \frac{96}{9} + \frac{8}{96} \log_2 \frac{96}{8} + \cdots + \frac{16}{96} \log_2 \frac{96}{16}$$

$$= 3.64 \text{ bits}$$

Transmitted information

$T(S, R) = H(S) + H(R) - H(S, R)$

$= 2.00 \text{ bits} + 1.92 \text{ bits} - 3.64 \text{ bits}$

$= 0.28 \text{ bit}$

across the stimuli, we can determine that the responses were not made equally often. Thus, we can use the general equation, with the relative frequency of each response, to calculate the response information. When that is done, the response information is found to be 1.92 bits. Similarly, the joint information is found by using relative frequencies for each stimulus–response combination. The joint information thus is 3.64 bits. The information transmitted then can be found by adding the stimulus information and response information (2.00 + 1.92 = 3.92) and subtracting the joint information (3.92 - 3.64 = 0.28). Thus, in this example, the transmitted information is 0.28 bit.

Among other things, information theory has been applied to the measurement of the human's ability to make absolute judgments. This ability is relevant to situations in which an operator needs to be able to identify displayed signals accurately. Numerous studies have found that as the amount of stimulus information increases the amount of information transmitted increases and then levels off. This asymptotic value of information transmitted can be regarded as the channel capacity of the human information-processing system. For example, the channel capacity for discriminating distinct pitches of tones is approximately 2.3 bits, or five pitches (Pollack, 1952). Thus, when there are six or more pitches, observers will make classification errors. Across a variety of sensory dimensions, the channel capacity is approximately 2.5 bits of information. This point was stressed in a classic article by George Miller (1956) on limitations in perception and memory called "The Magical Number Seven, Plus or Minus Two."

Perhaps of most concern to human factors specialists is the fact that this limit in the number of stimuli that can be identified accurately applies only to unidimensional stimuli. When two dimensions, for example, pitch and loudness, are varied simultaneously, the capacity for transmitting information increases. Thus, multidimensional stimuli should be used for situations in which more than just a few potential signals can occur.

As we will discuss in later chapters, information theory has been shown to accurately describe the relationship between uncertainty and reaction time, as well as movement time (Schmidt, 1988). However, in recent years, research in human information processing has become less concerned with information theory and more concerned with information flow. The emphasis is on developing models of the processes that intervene between stimuli and responses, rather than just looking at the correspondences between them. Nevertheless, information theory's emphasis on uncertainty continues to play an important role in contemporary human performance.

UNCOVERING PSYCHOLOGICAL STRUCTURE WITH CHRONOMETRIC METHODS

The rise of the information processing approach has coincided with increased use of reaction time and related chronometric measures to determine the underlying processes. The characteristic of a reaction-time task is that the person is to respond as quickly as possible. The reaction times, in conjunction with the accuracy of the responses, provide the primary dependent measures.

Three types of reaction-time tasks can be distinguished. In *simple reaction time,* a single response is made whenever any stimulus event occurs. That is, the response can be executed as soon as a stimulus event (for example, the appearance of a letter) is detected. A *go-no go reaction time* is obtained for situations in which only one response is to be executed to some subset of the possible stimulus events. For example, the task may involve responding when the letter *A* occurs but not when the letter *B* occurs. Thus, the go–no go task requires discrimination among possible stimuli. Finally, *choice reaction time* refers to situations in which more than one response can be made, and the correct response depends on the stimulus that occurs. Using the preceding example, this would correspond to designating one response for the letter *A* and another response for the letter *B*. Thus, the choice task requires not only discrimination among stimuli, but that they be related to the assigned responses.

Subtractive Logic

Donders (1868/1969) used the preceding distinctions among reaction tasks in what has come to be called *subtractive logic*. This logic is illustrated in Figure 4–8. Donders assumed that the simple reaction (a type *A* reaction in his terminology) involved only the time to detect the stimulus and execute the response. The go–no go reaction (type *C*) required an additional process of identification of the stimulus, and the choice reaction (type *B*) included still another process, response selection. Donders argued that the time for the identification process could be found by subtract-

ing the type *A* reaction time from the type *C*. Similarly, the difference between *B* and *C* should be the time for the response–selection process.

Subtractive logic, particularly as applied by Donders, can be questioned (Pachella, 1974). However, it has been used in numerous situations during the past 25 years to estimate the time required for particular mental operations. The general idea is that whenever a task variation can be conceived of as involving all the processes of another task, plus something else, the difference in reaction time for the two tasks can be taken to reflect the time to perform the "something else."

One of the clearest applications of subtractive logic involves studies of mental rotation. In such tasks, two forms are presented that must be judged as *same* or *different*. One form can be

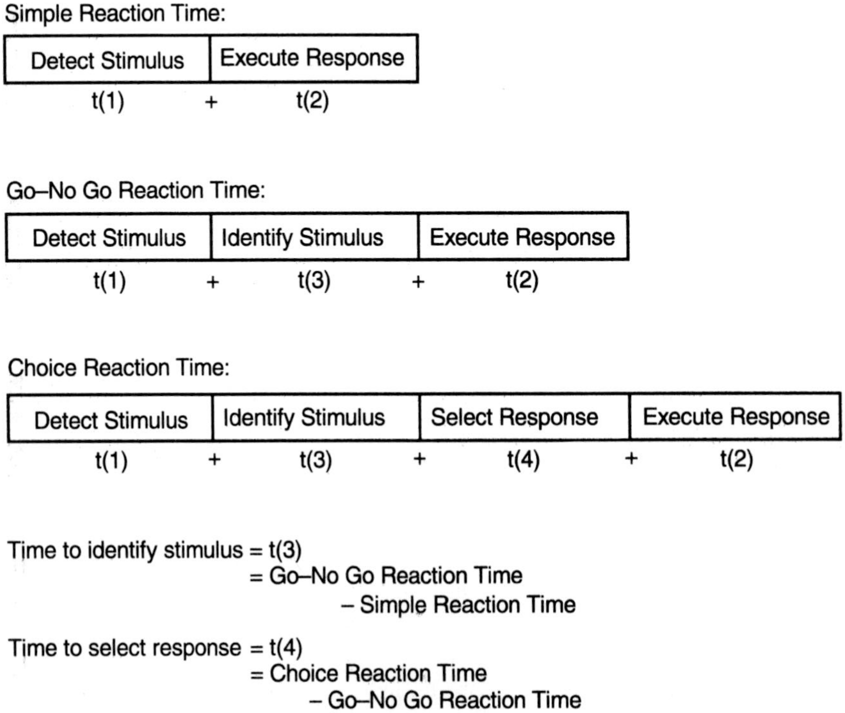

Simple Reaction Time:

Detect Stimulus	Execute Response
t(1) +	t(2)

Go–No Go Reaction Time:

Detect Stimulus	Identify Stimulus	Execute Response
t(1) +	t(3) +	t(2)

Choice Reaction Time:

Detect Stimulus	Identify Stimulus	Select Response	Execute Response
t(1) +	t(3) +	t(4) +	t(2)

Time to identify stimulus = t(3)
  = Go–No Go Reaction Time
    – Simple Reaction Time

Time to select response = t(4)
  = Choice Reaction Time
    – Go–No Go Reaction Time

FIGURE 4–8   The Subtractive Logic Applied to Simple (A Reaction), Go-No Go (C Reaction), and Choice (B Reaction) Reaction Times.

rotated relative to the other, either in depth or in the picture plane (see Figure 4–9). For *same* responses, reaction time is a linearly increasing function of the amount of rotation. This linear function has been interpreted as indicating that people mentally rotate one of the stimuli into the same orientation as the other before making the *same–different* judgment. The rate of mental rota-

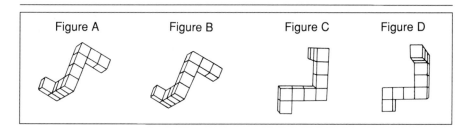

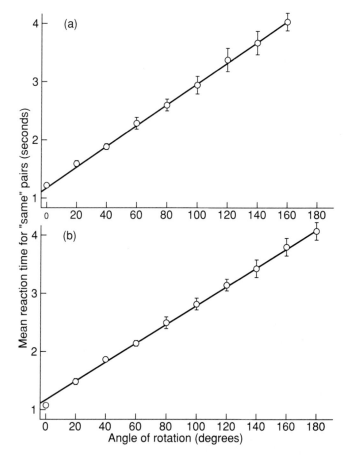

FIGURE 4–9   Mental Rotation Stimuli (upper panel) and Results (lower panel) for Rotation (a) in the Picture Plane and (b) in Depth.

Reprinted with permission from R. N. Shepard & J. Metzler (1971). Mental rotation of three-dimensional objects. *Science, 171,* 701–703. Copyright 1971 by the AAAS.

tion can then be estimated from the slope of the function. For the situations shown in Figure 4–9, each additional deviation of 20° between the orientations of the two stimuli adds approximately 400 ms to the reaction time, and the rotation time is roughly 20 ms/deg. This is an example of subtractive logic in that the judgments are assumed to involve the same processes except for rotation. Thus, the difference between the reaction times to pairs rotated 20° and pairs with no rotation is assumed to reflect the time to rotate the forms into alignment.

Additive-factors Logic

Even more influential in recent years is the *additive-factors logic* developed by Sternberg (1969). His work was presented at the centennial symposium in honor of Donders's first analyses of reaction times. The importance of the additive-factors logic is that it is a technique for identifying the underlying processing stages. Thus, whereas the subtractive logic requires that you assume what the processes are and then estimate their times, additive-factors logic provides evidence about how these processes are organized.

In the additive-factors approach, processing is conceived as a series of discrete stages. Each stage runs to completion before providing input to the next stage. If a variable affects the duration of one processing stage, differences in reaction time will reflect the relative duration of this stage. For example, if a stimulus-encoding stage is slowed by degrading the stimulus, then the time for this processing stage will increase, but the durations of the other stages will be unaffected. Importantly, if a second variable is manipulated that affects a different stage, such as response selection, that variable will influence only the duration of this stage. Because the two variables independently affect different stages, their effects on reaction time should be additive. That is, when an analysis of variance is performed, there should not be an interaction between the two variables. If the variables interact, then they must be affecting the same stage.

The basic idea behind additive-factors logic is that through careful selection of variables it should be possible to determine the underlying processing stages from the patterns of interactions and additive effects that are obtained. Sternberg (1969) applied this logic to examinations of memory-search tasks, in which people are given a memory set of items (letters, digits, or the like), followed by a target. The task is to indicate whether or not the target is in the memory set. Sternberg was able to show that the size of the memory set has additive effects with variables that should influence target identification, response selection, and response execution. Thus, he proposed a *search* stage of performance in this task that is independent from the other processing stages.

Continuous Information Accumulation

An assumption underlying both the subtractive and additive-factors logics is that human information processing occurs in a series of discrete stages. Because of the highly parallel nature of the brain, this assumption is an oversimplification. In recent years, researchers have advocated more continuous models of information processing in which many operations are performed simultaneously and possible responses receive priming continuously on the basis of partial information (Eriksen & Schultz, 1979; McClelland, 1979; Miller, 1988). Among the findings that support these ideas is that, in at least some situations, responses show partial activation during processing of the stimulus information (Coles, et al., 1985).

In reaction-time tasks, people typically make errors. Therefore, you cannot study reaction time in isolation from accuracy. Both reaction time and accuracy can be described by models of information accumulation that assume that the state of the system changes continuously over time (Luce, 1986). Such models account for the relation between speed and accuracy through changes in response criteria and rates of accumulation. The major distinctions between alternative models of this type are in the nature of the time scale and the nature of the information changes. Time can be defined as a discrete or a continuous variable; likewise, information can accumulate in constant increments or in variable amounts.

One example of an accumulation model is the *random walk* (see Figure 4–10, top panel). When one of two possible stimuli (*A* or *B*) is displayed at time 0, evidence begins to accumulate toward one response or the other. When this evidence reaches a criterial level, the corresponding response is initiated. The time required to accumulate a sufficient amount of evidence determines the reaction time, and the level to which the evidence accumulates determines the response and the accuracy. This model can account for response biases by varying the relative levels of the criteria for *A* and *B* and the relation between speed and accuracy by varying the overall levels of the criteria. By setting the response criteria to low levels, it will take less time to accumulate that amount of information, but chance variations in the accumulation process make it more likely that an error will occur (see Figure 4–10, bottom panel).

Accumulation models are the only ones that readily account for the relation between speed and accuracy. Because the models explain a wide range of phenomena involving both speed and accuracy, they provide the most complete accounts of human performance. One mechanism that is well suited for modeling information accumulation assumes simultaneous activation of many processes. This mechanism is the currently popular neural network (Rumelhart & McClelland, 1986).

In such networks, information processing takes place through the interactions of many elementary units. Units are arranged in layers, with excitatory and inhibitory connections extending to other layers. The information pertinent to the task at hand is distributed across the network in the form of a pattern of activation. Network models have been useful in robotics and machine pattern recognition. In psychology, they can provide an intriguing, possibly more neurologically

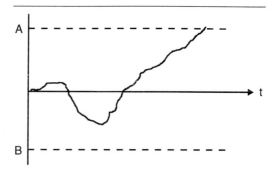

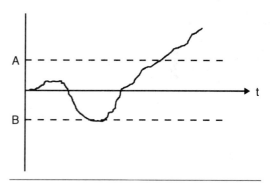

FIGURE 4–10 The Random Walk Model and Its Relation to Speed and Accuracy. Information Accumulates to the Criterion Level for Response *A* or *B*. The Relation Between the Top and Bottom Panels Demonstrates a Tradeoff Between Speed and Accuracy.

valid, alternative to traditional information-processing models. However, they are difficult to test. Presently, it is not clear what basic and applied human-performance researchers can gain from models directed at the level of neurophysiological implementation rather than at the level of cognitive functioning (Uttal, 1990).

SUMMARY

The human information-processing approach views the human as a system. As with any other system, human performance can thus be analyzed in terms of subsystems and component performance. The nature and organization of these subsystems are inferred from behavioral measures such as accuracy and latency of performance. General distinctions among perceptual, cognitive, and action subsystems provide a framework for organizing our basic knowledge of human performance and relating this knowledge to applied human factors issues.

Many specific methods are used to analyze the human information-processing system. Response accuracy can be examined using classical threshold techniques and signal-detection methods to evaluate basic sensory sensitivities. Response latencies can be examined using additive and subtractive logics to clarify the nature of the underlying processing stages. Information theory can provide a useful metric of uncertainty.

Techniques of the type described in this chapter provide the primary means by which the findings discussed in the subsequent chapters have been obtained. The details of the techniques will not usually be given, but you should be able to determine such things as whether the reported data are thresholds, whether a conclusion is based on additive-factors logic, and so on. Because the distinctions among perception, cognition, and action subsystems provide a convenient way to organize our knowledge of human performance, the next three parts of the book will examine each of these subsystems in turn. In the final part, the influence of the physical and social environment on human information processing will be considered.

RECOMMENDED READING

Baird, J. C., & Noma, E. (1978). *Fundamentals of Scaling and Psychophysics.* New York: Wiley.

Gescheider, G. A. (1985). *Psychophysics: Method, Theory, and Application,* 2nd ed. Hillsdale, NJ: Lawrence Erlbaum.

Lachman, R., Lachman, J. L., & Butterfield, E. C. (1979). *Cognitive Psychology and Information Processing: An Introduction.* Hillsdale, NJ: Lawrence Erlbaum.

Lindsay, P. H., & Norman, D. A. (1977). *Human Information Processing,* 2nd ed. New York: Academic Press.

MacMillan, N. A., & Creelman, C. D. (1991). *Detection Theory: A User's Guide.* New York: Cambridge University Press.

SENSORY INPUT

> *The sensory system is designed . . . to pick up patterns of information*
> *from the external world, transduce this information from any of a*
> *number of physical forms of energy to the electrochemical forces of*
> *neural activity, and transmit that pattern toward the complex portions*
> *of the central nervous system.*
>
> —W. R. Uttal, 1973

INTRODUCTION

For an organism to operate effectively within any environment, natural or artificial, information must be transferred from that environment to the organism. Likewise, the organism must be able to act on that information and to perceive the effect of its action on the environment. Because the performance of the operator in any human–machine system will be limited by the quality of the information perceived, a primary concern in human factors is how to display information in forms that are easily perceptible.

Any information from the environment is input to the human through the senses. Consequently, consideration of the factors involved in display design must begin with an understanding of the basic principles of sensory processing and characteristics of the specific sensory systems. A good display will take advantage of those features of stimulation that the sensory systems can most readily transmit to higher-level brain processes.

This chapter gives an overview of sensory anatomy and physiology, with an emphasis on characteristics that directly pertain to human factors. Chapter 6 will explore perceptual phenomena that have their basis in the structure of the sensory systems. Much of the present chapter is devoted to vision, because it is the most important and widely studied sensory system. Vision provides immediate and precise information about the physical properties of the environment from afar. Audition will also be covered in some detail because it supplies precise omnidirectional environmental information. Whereas vision is predominantly a spatial system, audition is predominantly temporal. These two senses provide the most dependable information about the environment over the widest range of space. The remaining senses, somasthesis, the vestibular sense, taste, and smell will be discussed in less detail.

Before describing the specific senses, we will consider some general properties of sensory systems. Much of our knowledge of these properties comes from comparative studies of infrahuman species, although this point is not stressed throughout the chapter.

Properties of Sensory Systems

The following properties are common to all sensory systems. First, *sensory receptors* are sensitive to some aspect of the physical environment, such as light energy or air-pressure changes. These receptors transform physical energy into neural signals. Second, highly structured neural pathways carry the information from the receptors to the brain. These pathways sort the incoming information according to specific features, as opposed to passively transmitting it. Third, the pathways typically pass through distinct nuclei within a region of the brain called the thalamus, which serves as a switching station, and then project to distinct receiving areas in the cortex.

These cortical areas are also highly structured and sensitive to specific kinds of stimulation. The structured nature of the sensory pathways and receiving areas enables analysis of the sensory input for features that are important to perception. Consequently, the information available to higher-level brain processes is very refined.

The sensory pathways and the brain are composed of complex networks of nerve cells called neurons. A *neuron* has three parts: dendrites, a cell body, and an axon (see Figure 5–1). The inside of a neuron has a negative resting potential with respect to its outside. When the neuron is stimulated sufficiently, an electrical charge travels down the axon, away from the cell body, to deliver stimulation to subsequent neurons. This all-or-none electrical charge is called an *action potential.* Immediately following an action potential, the neuron enters a refractory period during which it is less likely to "fire." The greater the stimulation to the neuron, the sooner it will fire again. Thus, the firing rate, or number of action potentials per unit time, will increase as the level of excitation increases. The limit on maximum firing rate is 1,000 impulses per second but frequencies higher than 400 to 500 impulses per second are relatively uncommon.

The transmission of sensory signals is initiated by the receptors, which use unique methods of transduction for each of the senses (Barlow & Mollon, 1982). For neurons stimulated by other neurons, the method for initiating an action potential is independent of the particular sensory system involved. The axonal endings of a neuron come close to the dendritic beginnings of another neuron. Activity of the initiating neuron releases a transmitter substance at the *synapse,* a narrow gap that separates the neurons (see Figure 5–2). This transmitter substance affects receptor sites on the receiving neuron. A transmitter substance can be either excitatory or inhibitory. An excitatory transmitter tends to increase the firing rate of the neuron that it affects, whereas an inhibitory transmitter tends to decrease the firing rate. In the absence of stimulation, most neurons fire at a rate called the maintained discharge. The firing rate of

stimulation to which the neuron is sensitive. As we will see, neurons can be sensitive to very complex features through the inputs they receive from other neurons responsive to simpler features.

THE VISUAL SYSTEM

The visual system provides precise spatial information about objects that are not in direct contact with our bodies. This is the basis for our ability to guide moving vehicles, as well as our own movement. Vision also is used for the communication of written information. The primary means by which we acquire knowledge is the reading of books. Moreover, visual displays are most often used to communicate information from machines to humans. In all cases, the visual information is conveyed by light energy that is projected or reflected into the eye.

The human eye is sensitive to energy from a small region of the electromagnetic spectrum.

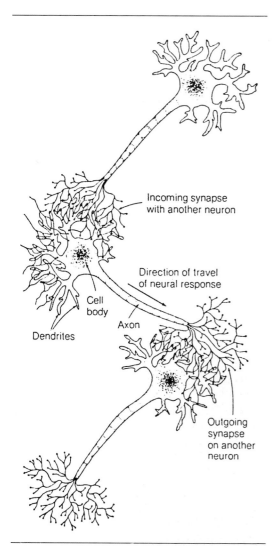

FIGURE 5–1 Neurons and Their Primary Parts.
Figure from *Sensation and Perception,* Second Edition, by Stanley Coren, Clare Porac, and Lawrence M. Ward, copyright © 1984 by Harcourt Brace Jovanovich, Inc., reprinted by permission of the publisher.

a neuron can be either increased or decreased relative to this discharge when stimulation is applied.

Any single neuron receives input from many other neurons, some excitatory and some inhibitory. These inputs determine the features of

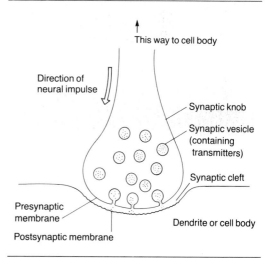

FIGURE 5–2 A Typical Synapse.
Figure from *Sensation & Perception,* Third Edition, by Stanley Coren and Lawrence M. Ward, copyright © 1989 by Harcourt Brace Jovanovich, Inc., reprinted by permission of the publisher.

Light can be characterized as waves of particles (photons) that are emitted from a source and reflected by objects in the world. The intensity of light is determined by the number of photons. The light waves can vary in length, resulting in the perception of different colors. The range of wavelengths to which humans are sensitive runs from approximately 380- to 760-billionths of a meter, or nanometers (nm). The long wavelengths are perceived as red, whereas short wavelengths are perceived as violet (see Figure 5–3). White light is composed of a mixture of equal amounts of many different wavelengths.

Within the environment, light is generated by and reflected from many sources. The resulting pattern of waves must be focused by the lens system within the eye onto a two-dimensional matrix of photoreceptors. The photoreceptors contain photopigments that convert the different light energies into neural signals, which are then transmitted to the brain. The signals received from the eye provide the basis for visual perception.

The Focusing System

A schematic diagram of the eye is shown in Figure 5–4. Light is projected by a source or reflected from a surface into the eye. It enters the eye through the transparent front covering, called the cornea, and passes through the pupil, which varies in size. The light is then directed through

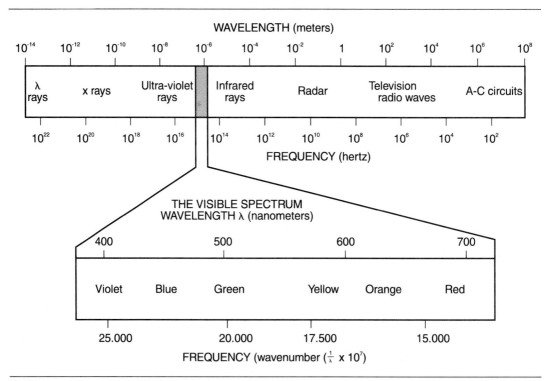

FIGURE 5–3 The Visual Spectrum, as Located Within the Electromagnetic Spectrum.

From I. Abramov & J. Gordon, Vision. In E. C. Carterette & M. P. Friedman (Eds.), *Handbook of Perception,* Vol. 3, pp. 327–357. Copyright © 1973 by Academic Press, Inc. Reprinted with permission.

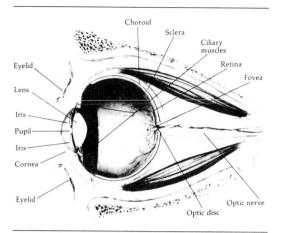

FIGURE 5–4   The Human Eye and Optic Nerve.
From M. W. Matlin, *Sensation and Perception,* Second
Edition. Copyright 1988 by Allyn and Bacon. Reprinted
with permission.

the lens and focused on the receptors that line the
back wall of the eye.

Cornea and Lens.   The cornea is part of a lens
system that focuses, or converges, the light rays
onto the photoreceptors. The other part of the lens
system is the structure referred to as the lens,
through which the light passes after entering the
eye through the pupil. To most people's surprise,
the cornea actually provides most of the focusing
power. The lens serves primarily to make fine
adjustments, depending on the distance of the
object that is being fixated and brought into
focus.

Due to the optical properties of the eye, more
power is needed to focus the image on the sensory
receptors when an object is close than when it is
far away. Consequently, through the process of
accommodation, the lens changes its shape to
keep objects focused on the retina (see Figure
5–5). When the fixated object is approximately
3 m or farther away, the lens is relatively flat.
This distance can be regarded as the *far point,*
where the lens does not change shape significantly as the distance to a fixated object is in-

creased further. As the distance to the object decreases from the far point, ciliary muscles attached to the lens reflexively relax, allowing the
lens to become progressively more spherical and
thus increasing its optical power. Accommodation breaks down as objects move closer than the
near point, which is approximately 20 cm in
young adults. Changes of accommodation in
young adults typically are completed within approximately 900 ms after the onset of a stimulus
(Campbell & Westheimer, 1960).

For years, the assumption was made that the
resting state of the lens corresponded to the setting of minimal focusing power, or fixation at the
far point. However, recent research has established that the resting focus in the absence of light
(dark focus) is intermediate to the far and near
points (Leibowitz & Owens, 1975; Miller, 1990).
This dark-focus setting differs across individuals
and is affected by such factors as the distance of
a prior sustained focus (Cline, Hofstetter, & Griffin, 1989). On average, the dark focus is less than
1 m in young adults. The findings regarding dark
focus have played a significant role in the design
of visual displays.

Pupil.   Whereas the cornea and lens have the
primary purpose of focusing the light, the pupillary opening, or pupil, controls how much light
enters the eye. The size of the pupil is determined
in part by a light reflex. In dim light, it may
reflexively dilate to 8 mm in diameter, whereas in
bright light, it may contract to as small as 2 mm.
Thus, there is an approximately 16-fold increase
in the area of the pupil at its largest relative to its
smallest size and, consequently, in the amount of
light that enters the eye. The size of the pupil also
varies with the state of accommodation and
arousal. A change in fixation from far to near
causes a contraction of the pupil (Bartleson,
1968), whereas an increase in arousal level results in dilation (Kahneman, 1973).

The size of the pupillary opening determines
the *depth of field* of a fixated image. Suppose that
an object some distance away is fixated, and so its

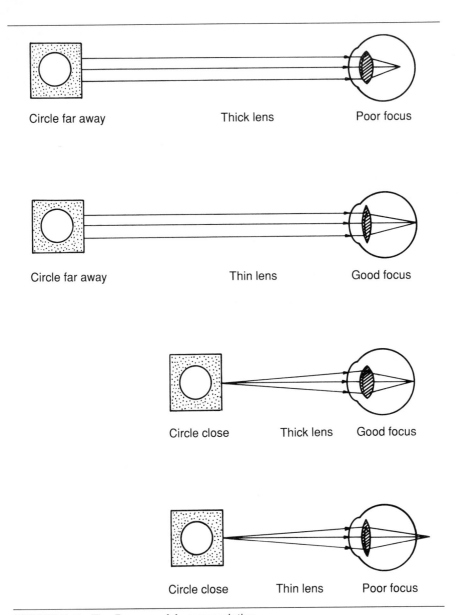

FIGURE 5–5 The Process of Accommodation.
From M. W. Matlin, *Sensation and Perception*, Third Edition. Copyright 1992 by Allyn and Bacon. Reprinted with permission.

image is clearly in focus. For some distance in front of the object and for some distance behind it, other objects in the image will also be clearly in focus. The total distance in depth for which objects in a scene are in clear focus is the depth of field. When the pupillary opening is small, depth of field is greater than when the pupillary opening is large. Consequently, for situations in which the pupil size is large, such as when illumination is low, accommodation must be more precise (Randle, 1988), and it can be fatiguing to maintain focus.

Vergence.   A final change that occurs as a function of the distance of a fixated object is the degree of *vergence* of the two eyes. Vergence refers to the rotation of the eyes inward or outward that is necessary to cause the images from a fixated object to fall on the central regions of the left and right eyes. This process allows the images to be fused and seen as a single object. When the point of fixation changes from far to near, the eyes turn inward and the lines of sight converge. Conversely, when the point of fixation changes from near to far, the eyes diverge and the lines of sight become more parallel. Beyond fixated distances of approximately 6 m, the lines of sight remain parallel and make no further change. The near point of convergence is approximately 5 cm; at this distance, objects become blurred if they are moved any closer.

Changes in vergence are closely coupled with changes in accommodation and are controlled reflexively through muscles that position the eyes. As with accommodation, the vergence resting state in the absence of illumination (dark vergence) is at an angle that corresponds to an intermediate distance (Owens & Leibowitz, 1983). Dark vergence also shows large individual differences and shifts as a function of the angle of prior sustained vergence (Owens & Leibowitz, 1980).

Focusing Problems.   The focusing system that includes the cornea, pupil, and lens must function properly if it is to fulfill its purpose of presenting light to the photoreceptors in a manner that will allow accurate perception of the world. One common flaw in this system is that the shape of the eye prevents the focal point from falling on the receptors. In other words, the receptors are not at the appropriate position for the image to be in focus on them (see Figure 5–6). For nearsighted-

ness, or *myopia,* the focal point is in front of the receptors, and the image is blurred. For farsightedness, or *hyperopia,* the focal point is behind the receptors. Both of these conditions are customarily corrected by additional compensatory lenses in glasses or contact lenses.

As people become older, both the speed and extent of accommodation decrease continually. The loss of accommodative ability is called *presbyopia,* or old-sightedness. The near point increases from as near as 10 cm for 20-year-olds to approximately 100 cm by age 60. Presbyopia can be corrected with reading glasses or bifocals, which typically are not prescribed until age 45 years or older. A person can have perfect vision in all other respects but still need reading glasses to compensate for the decreased accommodative ability of the lens.

People often report discomfort when they engage in close work, such as reading computer displays. Such visual fatigue seems to be associated with the amount of vergence effort that is required to fixate at short distances for long periods of time (Owens & Wolf-Kelly, 1987; Tyrrell & Leibowitz, 1990). People whose dark vergence posture is farther than others show more visual fatigue during close work. For example, Jaschinski-Kruza (1991) found that the more distant a person's dark vergence posture is, the more visual fatigue they experience when viewing a visual display screen from 50 cm. However, at a viewing distance of 100 cm, no such correlation was evident. As would be expected if vergence effort causes visual fatigue, people with far dark vergence postures tend to position themselves farther from a visual display screen than do people with near dark vergence postures (Heuer, et al., 1989).

Another focusing problem that can occur is *astigmatism,* which arises from a misshapen cornea. The consequence of an astigmatism is that contours in certain orientations will be in focus on the retina, and hence clear, whereas those in other orientations will not be in focus. Thus, no matter how much the eye accommodates, some

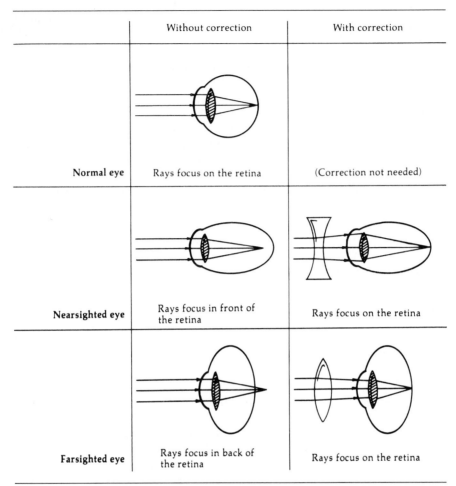

	Without correction	With correction
Normal eye	Rays focus on the retina	(Correction not needed)
Nearsighted eye	Rays focus in front of the retina	Rays focus on the retina
Farsighted eye	Rays focus in back of the retina	Rays focus on the retina

FIGURE 5–6   Focusing for Normal, Nearsighted, and Farsighted eyes.
From M. W. Matlin, *Sensation and Perception,* Third Edition. Copyright 1992 by Allyn and Bacon. Reprinted with permission.

parts of the image will always be blurred. As with the previous problems, an astigmatism can be corrected by glasses.

Because the cornea and lens need to be transparent, anything that reduces their transparencies will interfere with vision. Corneal disease or injury can result in the formation of scar tissue, causing decreased acuity and making lights appear as though they are surrounded by halos. More common are cataracts, which involve clouding of the lens. Cataracts can happen for a number of reasons, but most commonly they occur in the elderly. Seventy-five percent of people over 65 have cataracts, although in most cases the cataracts are not serious enough to interfere with the person's activities. Surgical procedures are necessary to correct major corneal and lens problems.

It should be clear from the preceding examples that research on accommodation, vergence, and other aspects of the focusing system plays an important role in human factors. The focusing system determines such things as the quality of the sensory input, which limits the level of detail that can be resolved, and visual fatigue, which limits the performance of the operator. Moreover, because accommodation and vergence vary systematically with the distance of fixated objects, they provide information about depth and size. Consequently, when accurate depth perception is necessary, such as when operating a vehicle, the factors that influence accommodation and vergence must be taken into account (see Chapter 7).

The Retina

In a properly functioning eye, the image is focused on the *retina,* which is a screen of sensory receptors that lines the back wall of the eye (Fein & Szuts, 1982). The location of an image on the retina is the reverse of its environmental location (see Figure 5-10). That is, an object located in the right visual field will be focused on the left half of the retina, an object in the upper visual field will be focused on the lower half of the retina, and so on. The location on the retina in turn determines where the visual signals are sent for further processing.

The retina itself consists of three major layers: the photoreceptor layer, the bipolar cell layer, and the ganglion cell layer (see Figure 5–7), thus allowing for considerable processing of the sensory information before it leaves the eye. Perhaps of most interest is that the retina is inverted, such that the photoreceptors form the farthest layer from the pupillary opening. Thus, photons must pass through the layers of neurons and supporting blood vessels to reach the receptors.

Photoreceptors. The retina contains two types of receptors, *rods* and *cones.* The receptors of both types contain photosensitive pigments in their outer segments. These photopigments absorb photons of light energy and so initiate neural signals. All rods have a single photopigment, whereas there are three types of cones, each with distinct photopigments. The four photopigments

are maximally sensitive to light of different wavelengths (rods, 500 nm; short wavelength cones, 440 nm; middle wavelength cones, 540 nm; and long wavelength cones, 565 nm), but they have some sensitivity to broad ranges of light energy. When light is absorbed by photopigment molecules, the pigment is said to be bleached. The photopigment is then insensitive to light energy for a period of time until it regenerates to its initial state.

There are many more rods (approximately 1.2×10^8) than cones (approximately 6.0×10^6). However, only cones occur in the *fovea,* one of the landmark areas on the retina. The fovea is a region about the size of a pinhead that falls directly in the line of sight. Outside the fovea, both rods and cones occur, with the rods greatly outnumbering the cones. As will be discussed in more detail later, the rod system is involved primarily in vision under dim light (*scotopic vision*), whereas the cone system is involved in vision under bright light (*photopic vision*). The cone system is responsible for color vision and perception of detail; the rod system provides no color discrimination or perception of detail, but is highly sensitive to small amounts of light energy.

Another landmark of the retina is the *blind spot.* The blind spot is a region located on the nasal side of the retina that is approximately two to three times as large as the fovea. It is the point at which the fibers that make up the optic nerve leave the eye; thus, it contains no receptor cells. As a consequence, any visual stimulus that falls entirely on the blind spot will not be seen. It is interesting to note that we do not notice the blind spot as a hole in the visual field, even when we look with just one eye. Rather, patterns displayed across the blind spot are perceived as complete, as long as certain conditions are fulfilled (Kawabata, 1984, 1990). This is the first example of an important principle that will recur in our discussion of perception: *the perceptual system fills in missing information.*

Neural Layers.   After the receptors convert light energy to neural energy, the signals pass through

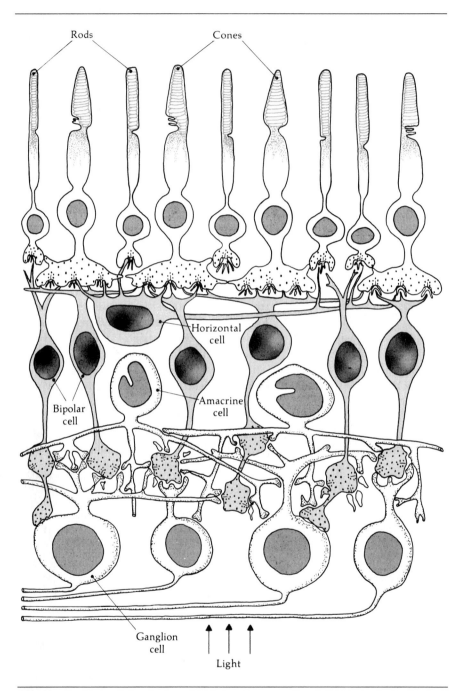

FIGURE 5–7   The Three Layers of the Retina.

Reprinted with permission from J. E. Dowling & B. B. Boycott (1966). Organization of the primate retina: Electron microscopy. *Proceedings of the Royal Society,* Series B, *166,* 80–111.

two layers of neurons, the bipolar and ganglion layers, before leaving the eye via the optic nerve. Specialized neurons called horizontal and amacrine cells provide lateral connections across the retina. Thus, stimulation at one location on the retina can affect the neural signal produced by stimulation in adjacent regions.

Whereas there are approximately 10^8 rods and cones on the retina, there are only approximately 10^6 ganglion cells. Consequently, considerable convergence occurs; that is, the signals from many receptors are pooled onto a single ganglion cell. This convergence is much greater for rods (an average of 120:1) than for cones (an average of 6:1), with many foveal cones showing no convergence.

The difference in convergence for rods and cones has two opposing implications. First, the relatively small amount of convergence in the cone system allows for the accurate perception of details. That is, when there is little convergence, the spatial details of the retinal image are faithfully reproduced in the neurons that convey this information. Second, the relatively large amount of convergence in the rod system enables greater sensitivity to light energy. Although details are lost by convergence, the effects of light energy are magnified by summing the activity of many receptors.

The properties of the ganglion cells have been studied in detail. Almost all these cells have distinct center-surround receptive fields of the type shown in Figure 5–8. The term *receptive field* refers to the region on the retina that, when stimulated, will affect the activity of the neuron. The center and surround regions are antagonistic, in that one is excitatory and the other inhibitory. If the center is excitatory and the surround inhibitory, then illumination falling on the center region increases the firing rate of the ganglion cell and illumination falling on the surround decreases the firing rate. When both regions are stimulated equally, the neuron shows little response. Thus, the majority of ganglion cells will respond primarily when discontinuities of intensity, such as those produced by contours, occur within their receptive fields.

Some ganglion cells exhibit a sustained response; that is, they continue to fire as long as the excitatory area is illuminated. Other ganglion cells show a transient response. These neurons produce an initial burst of firing when the excitatory area is illuminated, but the rate decreases as the light remains on. The two types of ganglion cells, called X-cells and Y-cells, respectively, differ in several other ways. The X-cells are concentrated around the fovea, whereas the Y-cells are distributed evenly across the retina. Also, Y-cells have larger receptive fields, respond better to movement, and show a faster speed of transmission. These findings have led some researchers to speculate that the X-cells are important for the perception of pattern, whereas the Y-cells are important for the perception of motion (Barlow & Mollon, 1982).

Retinal Structure and Acuity. The structure of the retina determines many characteristics of perception. One of the most important of these is the ability to perceive detail as a function of retinal location. This ability to resolve detail is called *acuity*. As shown in Figure 5–9, acuity is highest at the fovea and decreases sharply as the image is moved farther into the periphery. The acuity function is similar to the distributions of cone receptors and X-cells across the retina, suggesting that it may be determined by the X-cell system, which has small receptive fields. In other words, the less pooling of information that occurs in the pathway, the better the acuity. As would be expected from the greater amount of pooling that occurs for the rods, acuity is worse under scotopic viewing conditions than under photopic conditions.

The acuity function is relevant to many human factors problems. For example, in determining the design of instrument faces and where instruments should be located on an instrument panel, the human factors specialist must take into account where images will fall on the retina and

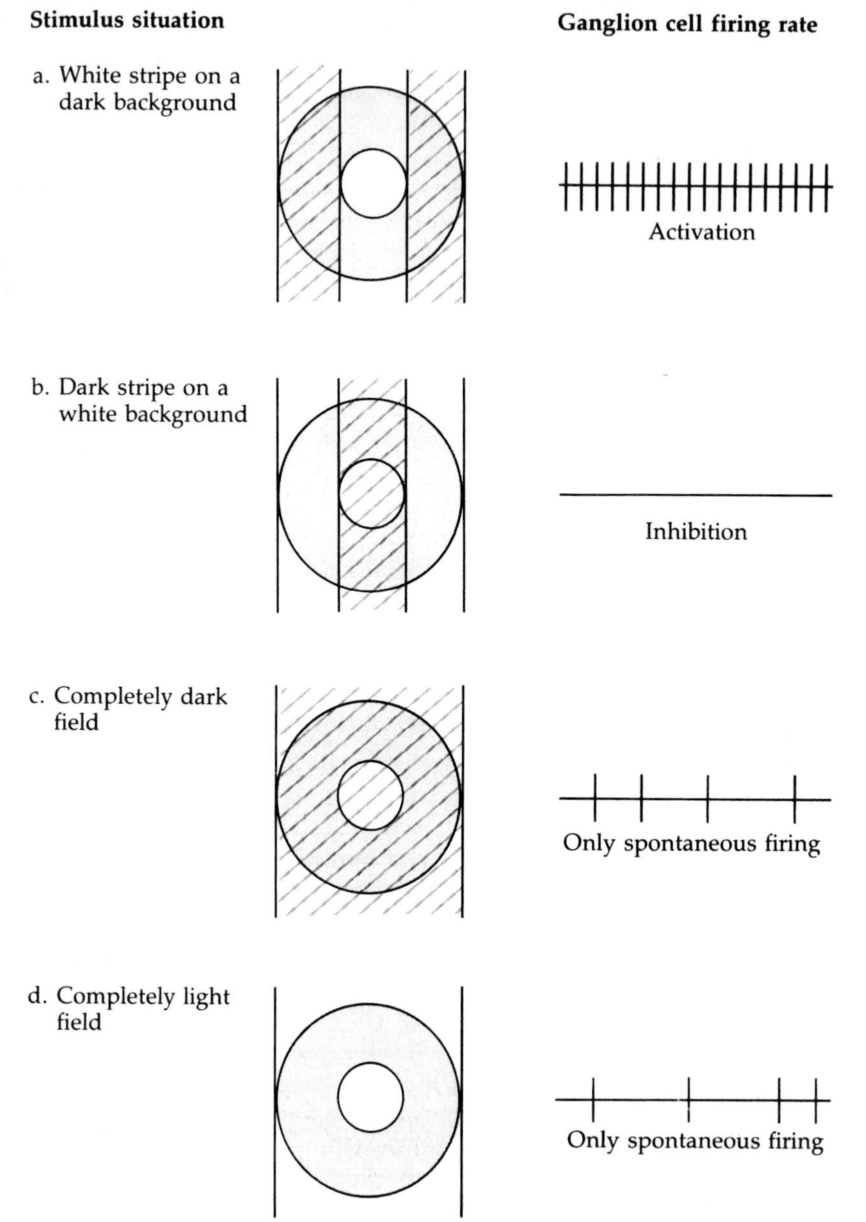

Stimulus situation   **Ganglion cell firing rate**

a. White stripe on a
   dark background

Activation

b. Dark stripe on a
   white background

Inhibition

c. Completely dark
   field

Only spontaneous firing

d. Completely light
   field

Only spontaneous firing

FIGURE 5–8   Ganglion Cell Receptive Fields and Firing Rates for Different
Stimulus Situations.

From M. W. Matlin & H. J. Foley, *Sensation and Perception,* Third Edition. Copyright 1992 by
Allyn and Bacon. Reprinted with permission.

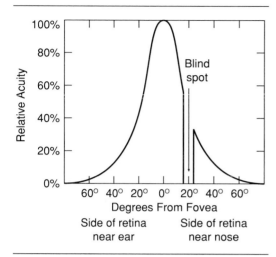

FIGURE 5–9   Acuity as a Function of Retinal Location.

From M. W. Matlin, *Sensation and Perception,* Third Edition. Copyright 1992 by Allyn and Bacon. Reprinted with permission.

the level of detail that must be resolved by the operator. We will discuss additional factors that affect acuity, as well as other aspects of perception that are influenced by the retinal structure, in Chapter 6.

Visual Pathways

The axonal fibers of the ganglion cells leave the eye at the blind spot and make up the optic nerve. An interesting relation exists between the optic nerve and the left and right halves of the brain. At the optic chiasm, the optic nerve from each eye splits (see Figure 5–10). Fibers that carry information from the left hemiretina (half retina) of each eye go to the left half of the brain, and fibers that carry information from the right hemiretina go to the right half of the brain. Because the left hemiretina receives images from the right visual field, and the right hemiretina receives images from the left visual field, information about objects located in the right visual field goes initially to the left half of the brain, and vice versa.

Geniculostriate and Tectopulvinar Systems.
Beyond the optic chiasm, two pathways are taken

to the visual cortex. The primary pathway, the geniculostriate system, passes through a region of the thalamus called the lateral geniculate nucleus (LGN). Here the fibers synapse in six layers, each of which receives input from only one eye. Each layer contains a retinotopic map of the visual field, in that light falling on receptors close together on the retina tends to activate neurons that are close together in the LGN. The receptive fields of the LGN neurons are similar to those of the ganglion cells in that they have center-surround organizations. Moreover, the distinction between X-cells and Y-cells is retained, with the axonal fibers from the X and Y ganglion cells having input to different layers of the LGN. From the LGN, the fibers go to the visual cortex.

The second pathway is called the tectopulvinar system. These fibers split off from the main pathway and go to structures in the brain stem. One of these structures is the tectum, which is a primitive visual center. Y-cells project into this

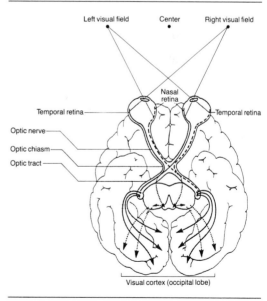

FIGURE 5–10   The Visual Pathways.

Figure from *Sensation and Perception,* Third Edition, by Stanley Coren & Lawrence M. Ward. Copyright © 1989 by Harcourt Brace Jovanovich, Inc. Reprinted by permission of the publisher.

system, but X- cells do not. From the tectum, the pathway proceeds through regions in the thalamus to the visual cortex. Researchers have proposed that the tectopulvinar and geniculostriate systems have different functions. The former seems to be involved in spatial localization of objects and control of eye movements (Sparks, 1991), whereas the latter is involved in fine-grained pattern perception.

Visual Cortex. The *visual cortex* is highly structured (Hubel & Wiesel, 1979). It consists of six layers that contain approximately 10^8 neurons. The fibers from the LGN enter at layer 4, where the neurons have circular center-surround receptive fields. However, the receptive fields in other layers are more complex (see Figure 5–11). Simple cells have receptive fields that respond best to bars or lines of specific orientations. That is, the receptive fields are composed of linear excitatory and inhibitory regions located side by side. Complex cells also respond optimally to bars of a given orientation, but primarily when the bar moves across the visual field in a particular direction. Hypercomplex cells likewise respond best to moving bars, but they will not fire if the stimulus is too long. Therefore, the cortical cells may be responsible for signaling the presence or absence of specific features in visual scenes.

The visual cortex is organized into columns and hypercolumns. Within a column, all cells (except for those in layer 4) have the same preferred orientation (see Figure 5–12). The preferred orientation from an adjacent column of cells is about 10° different. As we proceed through adjacent columns, the sequence of preferred orientations will pass through a complete rotation of 180°. A group of approximately 20 adjacent columns is called hypercolumn. As we move from one hypercolumn to the next, the same organization for orientational selectivity will occur, but corresponding to an adjacent location on the retina. Thus, the visual cortex is a spatiotopic map of hypercolumns.

The cells in the visual cortex are sensitive to additional features of stimulation. Most impor-

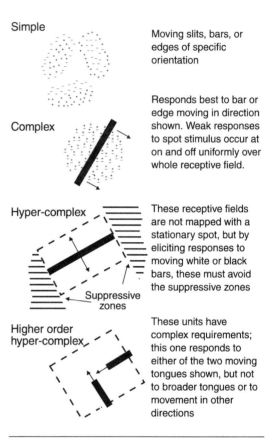

FIGURE 5–11   Receptive Fields for Simple, Complex, Hypercomplex, and Higher-order Cells.

From H. B. Barlow, General principles: The senses considered as physical instruments. In H. B. Barlow & J. D. Mollon (Eds.), *The Senses* (pp. 1–33). Copyright © 1982 Cambridge University Press. Reprinted by permission of Cambridge University Press.

tant are the attributes of binocularity and velocity of motion. The velocity-sensitive cells respond optimally to a specific rate of movement across the retina and likely play a role in motion perception. The binocular cells can be excited by stimulation from both eyes and are sensitive to disparities in the image received by each eye. These cells provide information that is used in depth perception. In sum, the visual cortex ana-

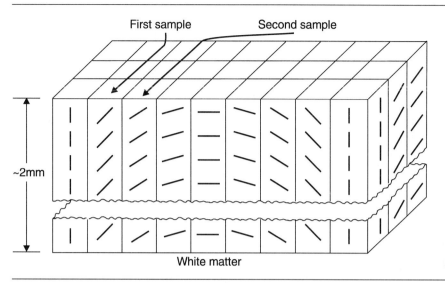

FIGURE 5–12   Columnar Organization of the Visual Cortex.
Figure from R. Sekuler & R. Blake, *Perception,* Second Edition. Copyright 1990 by McGraw-Hill, Inc. Reprinted with permission.

lyzes the visual input for several specific features that are fundamental to perception.

Although it is convenient to refer to the cortical cells as "feature detectors," the activity of any single cell cannot signal the presence of a feature. The reason for this is that multiple factors determine the firing rate. It is the pattern of activity across groups of neurons that provides unambiguous information about the nature of the stimulus. For example, when a vertical line is presented, not only will neurons whose peak sensitivity is vertical respond, but so will neurons whose peak sensitivity is nonvertical. The extent of firing for these other neurons depends on how close their preferred orientations are to vertical. The presence of the vertical line is thus signaled by the pattern of activity across the entire group of orientation-sensitive neurons.

The visual cortex is assumed to be the locus for perceptual effects involving orientation. Vertical lines will appear to be tilted in the opposite direction of tilted surrounding lines (see Figure 5–13a), a phenomenon called tilt contrast (Tolhurst & Thompson, 1975). Similarly, if you fixate for a while on lines that are tilted slightly from vertical (see Figure 5–13b) and then look at vertical lines, the vertical lines will appear to be tilted in the opposite direction (Magnussen & Kurtenbach, 1980). This tilt aftereffect and tilt contrast typically are attributed to adaptation or inhibition of orientation-sensitive neurons in the visual cortex. The tilt aftereffect can be explained by a shift in the pattern of activity across the neurons that occurs when those sensitive to the initial tilted line have been adapted and are not as responsive as normal (Carpenter & Blakemore, 1973).

People show greater sensitivity at detecting and resolving lines that are oriented vertically or horizontally rather than obliquely (Appelle, 1972), a phenomenon that is called the oblique effect. Evidence indicates that the proportion of neurons in the visual cortex devoted to vertical and horizontal orientations is greater than the proportion devoted to oblique orientations (Mansfield, 1974). Thus, the oblique effect seems to be a function of the relative amount of cortical neurons devoted to the respective orientations.

Relation of Pathway Structure to Human Performance. The neurophysiological evidence

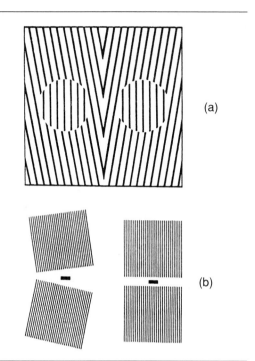

FIGURE 5–13 (a) Tilt Contrast and (b) the Tilt Aftereffect.

From I. P. Howard, The perception of posture, self-motion, and the visual vertical. In K. R. Boff, L. Kaufman & J. P. Thomas (Eds.), *Handbook of Perception and Human Performance.* Copyright © 1986 by John Wiley & Sons, Inc. Reprinted with permission.

implicates two separate visual channels (Livingston & Hubel, 1987), with a third subsystem integrating the information from these channels. The three subsystems are called the magnocellular, parvocellular, and interlaminar pathways (see Table 5–1). The parvo channel is organized around the cones and the X-cells and seems to be involved in the perception of spatial detail and color at photopic illumination levels. The magno system is organized around the rods, cones, and both the X- and Y-cells and is specialized for monochromatic temporal detail, such as detection of brief flashes of light. The interlaminar pathway receives inputs from both of the other pathways and is specialized for stereoscopic perception and accommodation.

Each of these systems seems to make distinct contributions to the performance of perceptual tasks. For example, Barber (1990) examined predictors of performance of short-range air defense weapon operators in simulated combat. The combat task involved detection of aircraft, identification of the aircraft as friendly or hostile, acquisition of the target aircraft with the gunnery system, and the tracking of the aircraft with the system once an initial fix was obtained. A correlational analysis of these performance components with measures of basic visual abilities was performed. This analysis suggested that the magno system helps to control detection and acquisition, the parvo system helps to control detection and identification, and the interlaminar pathway helps to control identification and tracking. Barber's study illustrates that the performance of complex visual information-processing tasks appears to depend on contributions from each of these three systems.

Summary

The most obvious characteristic of the visual sensory system is that it is designed to analyze and sort the visual input on the basis of features that provide information about the environment. These features are processed and transmitted through many separate parallel channels. The sensory analysis includes emphasis of contours, onsets and offsets, and movement. Additionally, the location of objects is preserved and seems to be analyzed separately from the analysis of their identity. Binocular relations that are important to the perception of a three-dimensional world are extracted as well. As we have shown, the way that the visual system processes information influences the ease and accuracy with which various aspects of the physical world will be perceived.

THE AUDITORY SYSTEM

The sense of hearing plays an important role in the communication of information. Sound provides us with information about such things as the speed and direction of travel of an approaching object or whether an engine is functioning cor-

TABLE 5–1   Visual Pathways and Their Attributes

VISUAL PATHWAY	ABILITIES OR ATTRIBUTES
Magnocellular	Broadband (no color)
Rods and cones	Scotopic (low luminance)
Transient cells	Contrast sensitivity
Peripheral vision	High temporal resolution
Large receptive fields	Low spatial resolution
	Fast decay/rapid rebound
	Resting state of the eyes
Parvocellular	Color selectivity
Cones	Photopic (high luminance)
Sustained cells	Contrast sensitivity
Foveal vision	Low temporal resolution
Small receptive fields	High spatial resolution
	Slow decay/delayed rebound
	Acuity and range of focus
Interlaminar	Accommodation flexibility
Inputs from magno and parvo	Stereoscopic capabilities
	Blur interpretation
	Properties of magno, parvo

From A. V. Barber, Visual mechanisms and predictors of far field visual task performance, p. 218. Adapted with permission from *Human Factors,* Vol. *32,* No. 2, 1990. Copyright 1990 by the Human Factors Society, Inc. All rights reserved.

rectly. Auditory stimulation is often used for warning signals, such as smoke alarms. Even more important is speech communication. Virtually all our direct communications with other people are conveyed through speech by way of the sense of hearing. Moreover, speech messages are being used more frequently in human–machine systems to convey information, as, for example, the messages used in people-movers at airports to warn passengers that the doors are closing and the vehicle is about to move. To understand the nature of the auditory input that the human brain receives, we need to know how the sense of hearing operates.

Sound begins with a mechanical disturbance that produces vibrations. These vibrations are transmitted outward from the sound source, through collisions among molecules in the air, at a speed of 340 m/s. The nature of sound waves is understood most easily by considering simple waves of the type produced by tuning forks. Striking a tuning fork produces an oscillating motion of the prongs. When moving in one direction, the prongs push the air molecules before them. This produces a small increase in pressure that reaches a peak when the prongs attain their maximal displacement. As the prongs move back in the opposite direction, the pressure decreases and reaches a minimum when they attain the opposite extreme displacement. These repeated cycles of compression and rarefaction produce the sound wave.

If we plot the changes in air pressure across time that occur at a single location, we see that they follow a cyclical, sinusoidal pattern (see Figure 5–14). This pattern can be characterized in several ways. Its frequency is defined as the number of complete cycles that occur in 1 second, or hertz (Hz). For example, a 1-kHz tone goes through 1000 cycles per second. The period of the waveform, T, is the duration of a single cycle and is the inverse of the frequency, F:

$$T = \frac{1}{F}$$

The sound's wavelength, λ, is the distance between two adjacent peaks. It can be calculated from the frequency and the speed of sound, c, as follows:

$$\lambda = \frac{c}{F}$$

Amplitude can be specified in terms of pressure or intensity. The sound pressure is a function of the difference between the maximal and minimal pressures that occur. It usually is specified as the root mean square (rms) deviation from the static pressure, or the square root of the mean of the squared instantaneous deviations over some time interval. Intensity is closely related to rms pressure and is specified in units of watts per square meter (W/m^2). For the tuning fork, amplitude is determined by the distance over which the fork moves. Striking the fork forcefully produces high-amplitude movement and high-amplitude sound waves, whereas striking it less forcefully results in lower amplitudes. The intensity of the sound also decreases the farther the point of measurement is from the source, following an *inverse square law:* the intensity is proportional to 1 over the square of the distance.

Rarely do we encounter pure tones. Typically, sound waves are much more complex. However, any sound wave, from that corresponding to the noise produced by a jet when taking off to the voice of a singer, can be characterized in terms of a weighted sum of pure tones. The procedure by which a complex tone is decomposed into pure tones is called *Fourier analysis.*

Waveforms that repeat themselves, such as the simple sinusoid, are called periodic. A complex, periodic tone, such as produced by musical instruments, has a fundamental frequency, f_0, that is the inverse of the period, T_0:

$$f_0 = \frac{1}{T_0}$$

Such waveforms also contain *harmonics* that are integer multiples of the fundamental frequency.

The Outer and Middle Ear

The human ear serves as a receiver for the sound waves (see Figure 5–15). Sound is collected by the *pinna,* the outer part of the ear. The complex form of the pinna will amplify or attenuate sounds, depending on their frequency and direction. The pinna funnels the sound into the *auditory canal,* which isolates the sensitive structures of the middle and inner ears from the outside, thus reducing the likelihood of injury. This canal has a resonant frequency of 3 kHz, which means

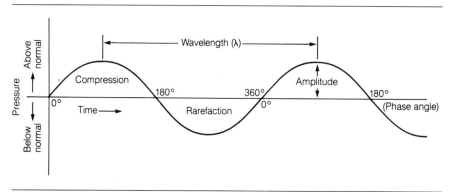

FIGURE 5–14   Simple Sound Wave.

From *Sensation and Perception,* Third Edition, by Stanley Coren & Lawrence M. Ward. Copyright © 1989 by Harcourt Brace Jovanovich, Inc. Reprinted by permission of the publisher.

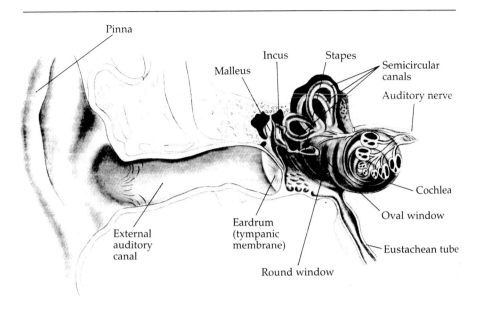

FIGURE 5–15   The Ear.
From M. W. Matlin, *Sensation and Perception,* Third Edition. Copyright 1992 by Allyn and Bacon. Reprinted with permission.

that sounds with frequencies in this range, such as normal speech, receive a boost in amplitude. At the inner end of the auditory canal is the eardrum or *tympanic membrane.* This membrane vibrates when sound-pressure waves strike it. In other words, if the sound wave is a 1-kHz tone, then the eardrum vibrates at 1,000 cycles per second. Perforation of the eardrum results in increased thresholds for detection, particularly at low and middle frequencies (Anthony & Harrison, 1972).

The eardrum is the division between the outer ear and the middle ear. The middle ear passes the vibrations of the eardrum on to a much smaller membrane, the *oval window,* which provides entry into the inner ear. Transmission between these two membranes occurs by means of three bones, which collectively are called the *ossicles.* Individually, these bones are the malleus (hammer), incus (anvil), and stapes (stirrup), in reference to their appearance. The malleus is attached to the center of the eardrum, and the footplate of the stapes lies on the oval window, with the incus connecting the two. Movement of the

eardrum thus causes movement of the three bones, which ultimately results in the oval window vibrating in a pattern similar to that of the eardrum. Typically, the role of the ossicles is described as one of impedance matching. If the eardrum were directly responsible for movement of the fluid in the inner ear, the change in density from air to fluid would damp the incoming sound waves. Transmission of the waves through the eardrum and ossicles to the oval window amplifies the wave so that the change in medium from air to fluid occurs efficiently.

The middle ear is connected to the throat by the Eustachian tube. This tube maintains the air pressure within the middle ear at the level of the outside atmospheric pressure, which is necessary for the middle-ear system to function properly. Discomfort and difficulty in hearing are often experienced when a plane changes altitudes, because the air pressure of the middle ear has yet to adjust to the new atmospheric pressure.

Finally, the middle ear includes muscles connected to the eardrum and to the stapes that together produce the *acoustic reflex* in the presence of loud sounds (Fletcher & Riopelle, 1960). This reflex reduces the sound vibrations sent from the outer ear to the inner ear by making the eardrum and ossicles difficult to move; thus, the inner ear is protected from potentially damaging sounds. However, the acoustic reflex takes approximately 20 ms to exert any influence, and it attenuates primarily low-frequency sounds. Thus, the reflex does not provide protection from sound with rapid onsets (for example, a gunshot) or from intense high-frequency sounds.

Another function of the acoustic reflex may be to reduce a person's sensitivity to his or her own voice, because the reflex is triggered prior to and during speech. Because the low-frequency components of speech tend to mask the high-frequency components, selective attenuation of the low-frequency components probably improves speech perception.

The Inner Ear

The inner ear contains several structures, but the one of importance to hearing is the *cochlea*. The cochlea is a fluid-filled, coiled cavity that contains the sensory receptors (see Figure 5–16). It is partitioned into three chambers: the vestibular canal, the cochlear duct, and the tympanic canal.

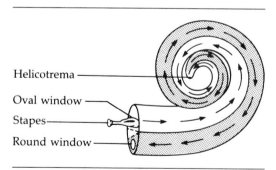

Helicotrema
Oval window
Stapes
Round window

FIGURE 5–16   Schematic Diagram of the Cochlea.

From M. W. Matlin, *Sensation and Perception,* Second Edition. Copyright 1988 by Allyn and Bacon. Reprinted with permission.

All three of the chambers are filled with fluid. The cochlear duct is completely separate from the vestibular and tympanic canals and contains a different fluid. The latter two canals are connected by a pinhead-sized opening at the apex of the cochlea, allowing fluid to pass between them. The oval window, which receives pressure from the stapes, is at the base of the vestibular canal, and the round window is at the base of the tympanic canal. Together, these two windows allow pressure to be distributed within the cochlea.

The membrane that separates the cochlear duct from the tympanic canal, the *basilar membrane,* is important for hearing. The receptor organ that transforms the pressure changes to neural signals sits on the basilar membrane in the cochlear duct (see Figure 5–17). This organ is called the organ of Corti. The sensory receptors are rows of hair cells on the organ that have cilia sticking up into the fluid in the cochlear duct, with the tops of some of the cilia touching the tectorial membrane.

Two groups of hair cells can be distinguished. Approximately 3,500 inner hair cells in a single row run the length of the basilar membrane. In contrast, approximately 12,000 outer hair cells are lined up in three to five rows. The bending of the cilia for both types of hair cells is the event that initiates a neural signal. This bending is produced in the following manner. The presence of a sound wave in the ear ultimately leads to motion (waves) within the fluid of the inner ear. Because the basilar membrane is flexible, it shows a wave motion consistent with the waves in the fluid. However, the tectorial membrane moves only slightly and in directions opposite to that of the basilar membrane. These two opposing actions cause the cilia of the hair cells to bend, triggering an electrical change within them.

The occurrence of a sound causes movement at the base of the basilar membrane that spreads to the apex (Bekesy, 1960). However, because the width and thickness of the basilar membrane varies along its length, the magnitude of vibration

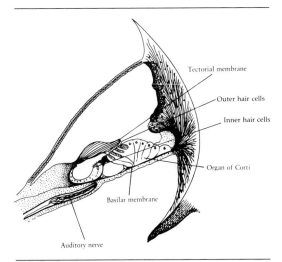

FIGURE 5–17 Cross-section of the Cochlea.
From M. W. Matlin, *Sensation and Perception*, Second Edition. Copyright 1988 by Allyn and Bacon. Reprinted with permission.

of the membrane will not be equal across its entire extent. Low-frequency tones produce the greatest movement at the end away from the oval window. As the tone increases in frequency, the peak displacement shifts progressively toward the oval window.

Auditory Pathways

The electrical activity of the hair cells in the cochlea causes the release of transmitter substances at their bases. These substances act on the receptor sites of neurons whose axonal fibers make up the auditory nerve. There are approximately 30,000 neurons in the auditory nerve, 90% of which are devoted to the inner hair cells. Thus, although there are many more outer hair cells than inner hair cells, fewer neurons are devoted to the outer hair cells in the auditory nerve. This indicates that there is considerably more convergence of the outer hair cells; this distinction between the pathways for the outer and inner hair cells is similar to that between pathways for rods and cones in vision. It suggests that the inner hair cells provide the detailed information about the nature of the auditory stimulus.

The neurons that make up the auditory nerve have preferred or characteristic frequencies. Each neuron fires maximally to a particular frequency and less so to frequencies that deviate from it. The characteristic frequency is presumed to result from the neuron innervating the spot of maximal displacement on the basilar membrane caused by that particular frequency. The entire sensitivity curve for the neuron is called a frequency tuning curve (see Figure 5–18). Thus, the auditory nerve is composed of a set of neurons that have frequency tuning curves with distinct characteristic frequencies. As for color vision, the specific frequency of an auditory stimulus must be conveyed by the pattern of activity within the set of neurons. One important feature of auditory nerve fibers is their response to continuous stimulation. As the sound remains on, the level of neural activity declines, a phenomenon that is known as adaptation.

One finding for auditory nerve responses is that the activity of a fiber in response to a tone can be suppressed by the presence of a second tone. This phenomenon, called two-tone suppression, occurs when the frequency of the second tone falls just outside the tuning curve for the fiber. This suppression is thought to reflect the responsiveness of the basilar membrane (Pickles, 1988) and likely plays a role in the psychological phenomenon of auditory masking (see Chapter 6).

The auditory nerve projects to the cochlear nucleus (see Figure 5–19). Fibers from the front of this nucleus go to the superior olive, half to the same side of the brain and half to the opposite side, and then to the inferior colliculus. This pathway extracts spatial information, among other things. In contrast, fibers from the back of the cochlear nucleus have input directly to the inferior colliculus on the opposite side of the brain. This pathway performs complex frequency analyses of the auditory input. Most of the cells from both pathways project to the medial genicu-

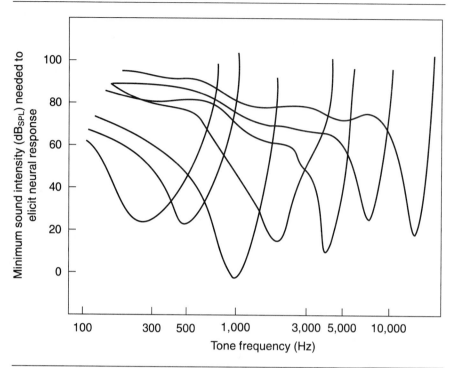

FIGURE 5–18   Frequency Tuning Curves for Auditory Neurons.
From M. W. Matlin, *Sensation and Perception,* Second Edition. Copyright 1988 by Allyn and Bacon. Reprinted with permission.

late, located in the thalamus, and then to the auditory cortex.

All the nuclei subsequent to the auditory nerve have neurons that show frequency tuning (Pickles, 1988). Additionally, some complex patterns of sensitivity emerge. The cochlear nucleus contains onset neurons that respond to tone onsets, pauser neurons that respond initially and then at a lower rate after a brief pause, and chopper neurons that respond with repeated bursts, interspersed with pauses. The medial geniculate contains cells analogous to the center-surround cells in vision. These cells respond optimally to energy in a certain frequency range; energy in surrounding ranges decreases the firing rate. All the nuclei seem to show tonotopic coding similar to the spatiotopic coding shown for vision. A

neuron that responds optimally to a given frequency will be located in close proximity to neurons that respond optimally to similar frequencies.

The auditory cortex also exhibits a tonotopic organization. Furthermore, many cortical cells respond to relatively simple features of stimulation. They show on responses, off responses, or on–off responses. Other cells respond to more complex sounds, such as bursts of noise or clicks. One type of cell is called a frequency sweep detector. It responds only to changes in frequency that occur in specific directions (higher or lower) within a limited frequency range. In short, as in the visual cortex, the neurons of the auditory cortex are specialized for extracting important features of stimulation.

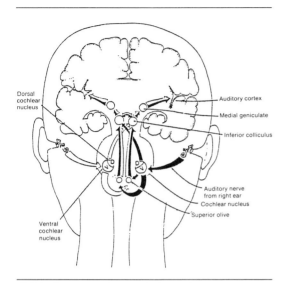

FIGURE 5–19   The Auditory Pathway.

From *Sensation and Perception,* Third Edition, by Stanley Coren & Lawrence M. Ward. Copyright © 1989 by Harcourt Brace Jovanovich, Inc. Reprinted by permission of the publisher.

Summary

An auditory stimulus, experienced as changes in air pressure, initiates a complex sequence of events that leads to the perception of sound. Physical vibrations of the eardrum and ossicles produce a wave motion in the fluid of the inner ear. This wave motion causes neural signals through the bending of cilia on the basilar membrane. Auditory information is transmitted along pathways in which the neurons respond to different frequencies and other acoustic features. As with vision, coding performed by the auditory system provides the basis for auditory perception.

THE SOMESTHETIC SYSTEM

When driving your car, you may reach for the gearshift without looking in its direction. By the sensation provided when your hand comes in contact with the knob, you can tell when you have grasped the shift. Also, you can operate the gearshift by moving it through the various settings without looking at it. The information that allows you to identify the gearshift and its settings is provided by the *somesthetic senses.* These include the senses of touch, pressure, vibration, temperature, pain, and proprioception.

Most sensory receptors of the somesthetic system are located in the skin, which consists of two parts. The epidermis is formed by layers of dead cells on top of a single layer of living cells. The dermis is an inner layer in which most of the nerve endings reside. These nerve endings are of a variety of types. A distinction can be made between fibers with corpuscular endings, such as the Pacinian corpuscle, and ones without. Those with corpuscles are responsive primarily to pressure stimuli; those without are particularly responsive to pain stimuli. Both types of endings respond to mechanical, thermal, or electrical stimulation by generating an action potential that is transmitted along axonal fibers to the brain.

The nerve pathways can be organized according to two major principles (Coren & Ward, 1989): the type of nerve fiber and the place of termination of the pathway in the cortex. Fibers differ in terms of the stimulus type to which they are most responsive, whether they are slow or fast adapting, and whether their receptive fields are small or large. The receptive fields have the same center-surround type of organization as in the visual system.

The nerve fibers follow two major pathways. The first is called the medial lemniscus. The fibers in it conduct information quickly and receive their inputs primarily from fibers with corpuscles. This pathway ascends the back portion of the spinal cord on the same side of the body as the receptors that feed into it. At the brainstem, most of the fibers cross to the other side of the body. The pathway continues until it reaches the somatosensory cortex. The fibers in this system respond primarily to touch and movement. The second pathway is the spinothalamic pathway. The fibers in it conduct information slowly compared to the lemniscal fibers. This pathway ascends to the brain on the opposite side of the body from which the fibers terminate, passes through several areas in the brain, and ends up in the somatosensory cortex. The spinothalamic pathway carries information about pain, temperature, and touch.

The somatosensory cortex is organized much like the visual cortex. It consists of two main parts, each with distinct layers. The organization is spatiotopic, in that the relation between the location of a stimulus on the skin and activity in the cortex is regular. Areas of the skin to which we are more sensitive have relatively larger areas of representation in the somatosensory cortex (see Figure 5–20). Cells respond to features of stimulation, such as movement of ridges across the skin.

Information about the position of our limbs is provided by receptors located within muscle tendons and joints, as well as the skin. This information is called *proprioception* and, when related to movement, *kinesthesis*. It plays a fundamental role in the coordination and control of bodily movement. The input for proprioception comes from several types of receptors. Touch receptors lie deep in layers of tissue beneath the skin. Stretch receptors attached to muscle spindles respond to the stretching of the muscles. Golgi tendon organs are attached to the tendons that connect the muscles to bones. These receptors are sensitive to muscle tension. Joint receptors are located in joints and provide information about joint angle. The neurons that carry the information for proprioception travel to the brain by way of the same two pathways as for touch. They also project into the same general area of the somatosensory cortex.

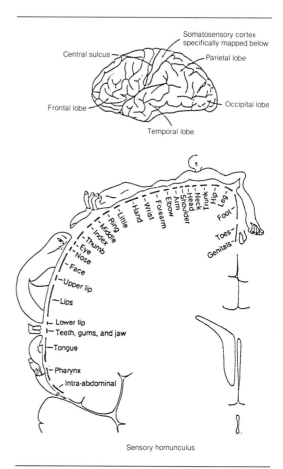

FIGURE 5–20   The Somatosensory Cortex.
Reprinted with the permission of Macmillan Publishing Company from *The Cerebral Cortex of Man* by W. Penfield & T. Rasmussen. Copyright 1950 Macmillan Publishing Company; copyright renewed © 1978 Theodore Rasmussen.

THE VESTIBULAR SYSTEM

The sensory receptors for the *vestibular sense* are located within the membranous labyrinth of the inner ear. This sense is concerned with the perception of bodily motion. It also helps to control eye position when the head is moved and to maintain an upright posture. The vestibular organ is comprised of three structures: the utricle and sacule (collectively called the otolith organs) and the semicircular canals (see Figure 5–15).

The otolith organs are lined with hair cells whose cilia are embedded in a gelatinous liquid that contains ear stones. When the head is tilted, a shearing action is produced on the cilia by the movement of the stones through the liquid. These organs provide information about the direction of gravity and linear acceleration and are involved in controlling posture. The semicircular canals are located in three orthogonal planes. When the head rotates, a relative motion between the fluid and the canal is created. This results in a shearing action on hair cells contained within the canal. Consequently, these receptors respond primarily to angular acceleration.

Responses made on the basis of the information provided by the vestibular system typically occur automatically. The system functions along with vision and proprioception to assist in the control of movements. When subjected to unfamiliar motion or vibration patterns, the vestibular sense responds by inducing motion sickness. The vestibular system eventually adapts to the motion by recalibrating, at which point the motion sickness disappears. Individuals with defective vestibular systems are less susceptible to motion sickness (Cheung, Howard, & Money, 1991).

THE TASTE AND SMELL SYSTEMS

Taste and smell are referred to as chemical senses, because molecules of substances in the mouth and nose serve as stimuli. Taste and smell are important for esthetics and for survival. Things that taste or smell bad are often harmful. Thus, taste and smell can provide naturally occurring information about the environment. In some situations, substances can be added artificially to other potentially harmful substances to convey warnings. One example involves mercaptans, a family of strong-smelling chemical compounds, that are added to natural gas. Mercaptans are produced naturally by skunks to ward off potential predators.

The physical stimulus for taste is a substance dissolved in saliva. The dissolved substance affects receptors that are located on the tongue and throat. The receptors for taste are groups of cells called *taste buds*. Each taste bud is made up of several receptor cells arranged close together. The individual cells are continually developing, having a life span of only a few days. The receptor mechanisms for taste are thought to be contained in projections from the top end of each cell that lie near an opening on the surface of the tongue called a taste pore.

There seem to be at least four basic taste qualities: sweet, salty, sour, and bitter. These tastes are related to the molecular structure of the substances that produce them. Sensitivity for the basic tastes varies as a function of location on the tongue. At present, not much is known about how the molecules affect the sensory receptors to initiate a neural signal. Fibers from the taste buds make up three large nerves that go to several nuclei, including a thalamic center, before projecting to a primary area near the somatosensory cortex. A secondary cortical area is located in the anterior temporal lobe.

We are able to smell substances that are volatile, that is, that can evaporate. Air currents carry the molecules to our nose where they affect smell receptors. The receptor cells are located in a region of the nasal cavity called the *olfactory epithelium*. Each receptor cell has an extension, called an olfactory rod, that goes to the surface of the epithelium. The olfactory rod contains a knob near its end, from which hairlike structures, *olfactory cilia*, protrude. These cilia are most likely the receptor elements. As with the receptors for taste, smell receptors have a limited lifespan. They function for about four to eight weeks. The axons from the smell receptors make up the olfactory nerve, which goes to the olfactory bulb at the front of the brain. The primary route from the olfactory bulb to the cortex is called the lateral olfactory tract.

Smell and taste are closely related. You can demonstrate this for yourself by holding your nose and tasting various foods. This interaction between smell and taste explains in part why food tastes "off" when you have a cold. The activity of tasters for products such as alcoholic beverages emphasizes the relation between taste and smell. One company that makes whiskey uses tasters in the sensory evaluation department and the quality control department (Associated Press wire story, 1990a). In the first department, expert tasters oversee the progress of aged whiskey during the three- to five-year aging process. Tasters in the quality control department perform tests during the blending process and after bottling. Although the tasters sample the whiskey in their mouths, their judgments are based primarily on the smell of the whiskey.

SUMMARY

Machines in the environment communicate with humans by displaying information in at least one sensory modality. The first step toward the optimization of information displays is to understand the sensitivities and characteristics of these sensory input processes. Because the senses are not equally sensitive to all aspects of stimulation, a good display must be based on those aspects that will be readily perceived. For example, if a display is intended for use under low levels of illumination, it makes no sense to use color coding because the cones will not be responsive.

The human factors specialist needs to know the properties of the physical environment to which the sensory receptors are sensitive, the nature of the process involved in the conversion of the physical energy into a neural signal, and the way in which the signal is analyzed in the sensory pathways. It is also important to be aware of how the senses are limited so that displays can be designed to compensate for those limitations.

Although the sensory systems constrain what can be perceived, perception involves more than a passive registration of the results of the sensory analyses. Perception is often characterized as a highly constructive process in which the sensory input serves as the basis for the construction of our perceptual experience. In the next two chapters, we will examine the relation between the physical components of stimulation and their psychological effects.

RECOMMENDED READING

Barlow, H. B., & Mollon, J. D. (eds.) (1982). *The Senses*. New York: Cambridge University Press.

Boff, K. R., Kaufman, L., & Thomas, J. P. (eds.) (1986). *Handbook of Perception and Human Performance: Volume 1, Sensory Processes and Perception*. New York: Wiley.

Coren, S., & Ward, L. M. (1989). *Sensation & Perception,* 3rd ed. New York: Harcourt Brace Jovanovich.

Goldstein, E. R. (1989). *Sensation and Perception,* 3rd ed. Belmont, CA: Wadsworth.

Matlin, M. W., & Foley, H. J. (1992). *Sensation and Perception,* 3rd ed. Boston: Allyn and Bacon.

PERCEPTION OF BASIC PROPERTIES

Physics, optics, anatomy, and physiology describe facts, but not facts at a level appropriate for the study of perception.

—James J. Gibson, 1979

INTRODUCTION

A physical stimulus is transduced into neurophysiological activity by sensory receptors, and this activity ultimately leads to the perception of some aspect of the environment. The material about the structure of the sensory systems presented in the previous chapter is important for human factors, because it provides the basis for understanding how this structure influences what is perceived.

As an example, consider a phenomenon called Mach bands, which can be seen in Figure 6–1. The figure shows a graduated sequence of gray bars ranging in lightness from light to dark.

Although the bars themselves are of uniform intensity, darker and lighter bands are perceived at the boundaries of transition from one region to another. These Mach bands arise from lateral interactions between the neurons in the retina that carry information about intensity at the different locations. Thus, the light and dark bands that are perceived are not present in the physical stimulus but are induced by interactions between retinal neurons.

While some aspects of perception are reducible to the input provided by the sensory systems to the brain, others are not. The present chapter examines some basic perceptual phenomena, such as the Mach bands, that have their origin in

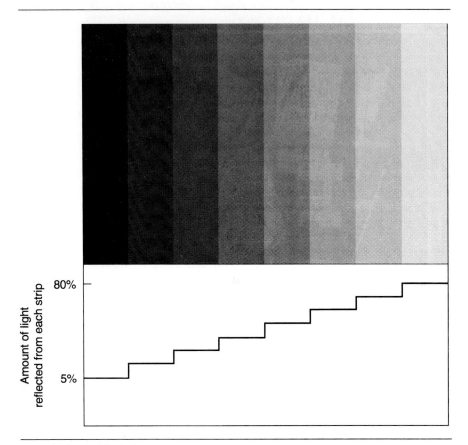

FIGURE 6–1 Mach Bands.
From R. Sekuler & R. Blake, *Perception,* Second Edition. Copyright © 1990 by McGraw-Hill, Inc. Reprinted with permission.

the structure of the sensory systems. In addition, contributions from higher-level brain processes will be discussed. Chapter 7 will be devoted primarily to perceptual phenomena that are not linked as closely to sensory activity.

VISUAL PERCEPTION

The receptor cells in the visual system are sensitive to changes in the intensity and wavelength of light. Therefore, it should not be surprising to learn that visual stimuli are perceived in terms of their psychological properties of brightness and color. Because these aspects of perception are linked closely to the properties of the sensory receptors, many of the phenomena of brightness

and color perception can be traced to the structure of the visual sensory system. The coding performed by retinal cells also determines the detail with which an image can be perceived, and thus properties of visual acuity can be attributed to these same structures.

Brightness

The primary physical determinant of *brightness* is the intensity of the energy produced by a light source (*luminance*). However, you should keep in mind that brightness is the psychological experience, whereas luminance is a physical property. Perceived brightness does not increase linearly with luminance level. Rather, as luminance increases, greater changes are needed to produce equivalent changes in brightness. When measured by a direct scaling technique (see Chapter 4), the relation between brightness and light intensity is described by a power function

$$B = aI^{0.33}$$

where B is brightness, I is the physical intensity of the light, and a is a constant. A scale for brightness called the bril scale has been developed by Stevens (1975). One bril is the brightness of a white light that is 40 decibels above the absolute threshold. A decibel (dB) is a unit of physical intensity that is defined as

$$\log_{10} \frac{I}{S}$$

where S is the intensity of a standard stimulus. For 1 bril, S is the intensity of a white light at absolute threshold.

Although brightness is primarily a function of stimulus intensity, it is influenced by several other factors, such as the state of adaptation of the observer and the wavelength of the light. The influence of many of these factors can also be attributed to the structure of the sensory system.

Dark and Light Adaptation. Differences between the rod and cone photopigments are one important factor contributing to the perception of brightness. Rods are much more sensitive to light overall than are cones. The fovea contains only cones. Therefore, light stimuli presented in peripheral vision should appear brighter. You can verify this prediction by looking at a dim star both directly and out of the corner of your eye. Sometimes you can even see a star peripherally that you cannot detect when looking straight at it.

The phenomenon of *dark adaptation* is due to differences in the rod and cone photopigments. When you first enter a dark room, you are insensitive to light energy; that is, it is very difficult to see anything at all. However, during the first few minutes in the dark, your sensitivity improves substantially and then levels off (see Figure 6–2). After about 8 min, sensitivity again starts improving and continues to do so until approximately 45 min have passed since dark adaptation began. At

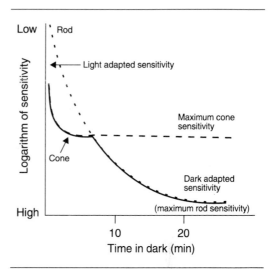

FIGURE 6–2 Dark Adaptation Function, Which Shows Sensitivity to Light as a Function of Time in The Dark.

From E. B. Goldstein, *Sensation and Perception*, Third Edition. Copyright © 1989 by Wadsworth, Inc. Reprinted with permission.

the end of this period, sensitivity is close to 100,000 times greater than it was when you entered the room.

Immediately upon entering the dark, sensitivity is determined by the amount of unsaturated cone photopigments. As these photopigments regenerate during a 3-min period, sensitivity progressively improves. While the cone photopigments regenerate, the rod photopigment is also regenerating. However, it does so across a much longer time period. After about 8 min in the dark, enough rod photopigment has regenerated for sensitivity to again improve. The remainder of the increase in sensitivity as time progresses is due to the continued regeneration of the rod photopigment. The rod segment of the dark adaptation function is not obtained when the stimuli are restricted to the fovea, which contains only cones. Similarly, the dark adaptation curve is a single, continuous function for individuals who have only rod photoreceptors.

In contrast to dark adaptation, light adaptation occurs when the intensity of visual stimulation is increased. When the visual field to which an observer adapts is of low intensity, sensitivity to a target stimulus is determined by the rods, whereas when the adapting field is of higher intensity, sensitivity is determined by the cones. Thresholds for detecting the presence of a target stimulus are an increasing function of the intensity of the adapting stimulus. Moreover, the threshold is highest immediately after the onset of an adapting stimulus and then decreases to a stable level over the next 10 min for photopic intensity levels and 1 min for scotopic levels (Hood & Finkelstein, 1986). Several mechanisms, including a decrease in the number of photopigment molecules capable of absorbing light, contribute to the decrease in sensitivity with increasing adapting field intensity.

The level of adaptation is a concern in situations where the light intensity changes abruptly. For example, Oyama (1987) noted that rapid changes of intensity occur at the entrances and exits of roadway tunnels. Consequently, the roadway appears very dark at the entrance to a tunnel and very bright at its exit. Oyama suggests that brighter lights placed at the beginning and end of a tunnel would provide a more gradual change of illumination and less visual impairment.

Spectral Sensitivity and the Purkinje Shift. A second important property of the rods and cones is their different pigment absorption spectra. As shown in Figure 6–3, the photopigments for both rods and cones are broadly tuned, stretching between 100 and 200 nm, depending on the photopigment. The peak for the combined absorption spectra of the three cone photopigments is around 560 nm, whereas the peak rod absorbance is approximately 500 nm. These absorption properties of the photopigments determine perceptual sensitivity to light of different wavelengths.

This point is illustrated by the fact that the different absorption properties of the rod and cone photopigments are mirrored in spectral sensitivity curves (see Figure 6–4). These curves are the absolute thresholds for the detection of a visual stimulus as a function of its wavelength. The sensitivity curve for photopic vision is similar to that of the combined cone photopigment absorp-

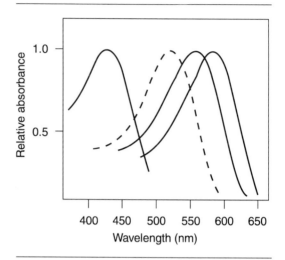

FIGURE 6–3   Pigment Absorption Spectra for Rod (Dotted Line) and Cone (Solid Lines) Photopigments.
Adapted from Barlow & Mollon (1982).

tion curve, and the sensitivity curve for scotopic vision is similar to that of the rod photopigment absorption curve. These curves indicate that, at either photopic or scotopic levels of illumination, sensitivity to light energy varies across the spectrum. Rods are not sensitive to long-wavelength (red) light. Thus, for situations in which a person needs to remain dark adapted, such as for pilots about to fly at night, high-intensity red light can be used to illuminate an environment without significantly reducing the level of dark adaptation.

The shift in the sensitivity curve for scotopic vision toward the short-wavelength (blue) end of the spectrum relative to the curve for photopic vision is evidenced in a phenomenon called the *Purkinje shift*. This shift refers to the fact that, when two light sources, one short and one long wavelength, appear equally bright under photopic levels of illumination, they will not appear so under scotopic levels. The short-wavelength light will look relatively brighter than the long-wavelength light under conditions of dark adaptation because of the contribution of the rods. The Purkinje shift can be experienced at dawn or dusk, when blue and green objects tend to appear brighter than red and yellow objects.

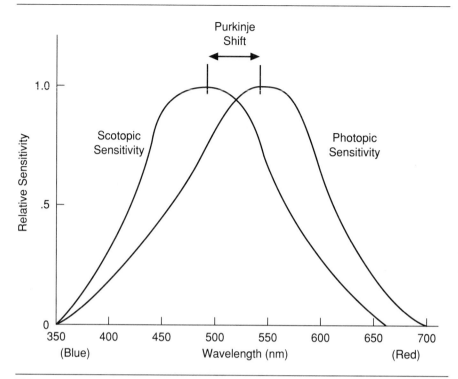

FIGURE 6–4   Scotopic and Photopic Spectral Sensitivity Functions Illustrating the Purkinje Shift.

The fact that observers are not equally sensitive to light of all wavelengths is important when specifying the effective intensity of a light for perception. The physical measurement of light energy is called *radiometry,* with radiant intensity being the measure of total energy. The measurement process that specifies light energy in terms of its effectiveness for vision is called *photometry.* Photometry involves a conversion of radiant intensity to units of luminance by weighting a light's radiance according to the visual system's sensitivity to it. Different conversion functions, corresponding to the distinct spectral sensitivity curves, are used to specify luminance in candelas per square meter.

Temporal and Spatial Summation.   Brightness is also influenced by exposure time and size of the stimulus. For stimuli of approximately 100-ms duration or less, brightness is a function of both the intensity and the exposure time. This relation, known as Bloch's law, is

$$T \times I = C$$

where T is the exposure time, I is stimulus intensity, and C is a constant brightness. Bloch's law indicates temporal summation of light energy. In other words, a 100-ms stimulus that is half the intensity of a 50-ms stimulus will appear equally bright because the energy of both stimuli over a 100-ms period is equal. Thus, it is the total amount of light energy during the interval that is crucial in determining brightness. The critical period over which temporal summation occurs is less than 100 ms in the fovea (Gottlieb, Kietzman, & Berenhaus, 1985) and is influenced by several other factors, such as level of adaptation and wavelength.

The area or size of a stimulus also affects its detectability and brightness. For very small areas of approximately $10'$ of visual angle (discussed later in this chapter), the relation

$$A \times I = C$$

holds, where A is area and I and C are as before. This is referred to as Ricco's law. For larger stimuli, the relation is

$$\sqrt{A \times I} = C$$

which is known as Piper's law. These two laws indicate that there is also spatial summation of energy across retinal areas of limited size. Spatial summation is thought to be due to the neural responses from several receptors feeding into a single ganglion cell. The degree of spatial summation in the perception of brightness is less in the fovea than in the periphery (Lie, 1980), because the degree of convergence is much greater in the periphery.

Lightness Constancy and Contrast. The total amount of light reflected from an illuminated surface is a function of both the level of illumination and the percentage of the illumination that the surface reflects. Brightness is the perceptual attribute associated with the overall light intensity, whereas the term *lightness* refers to the perceptual attribute associated with reflectance. Lightness is how dark or light an object appears on a scale from black to white. Black surfaces have low reflectance and absorb most of the light that falls on them, whereas white surfaces have high reflectance and reflect most of the light that falls on them.

Over a broad range of levels of illumination, objects retain their relative lightness (Jacobsen & Gilchrist, 1988). This phenomenon is called *lightness constancy*. For example, pieces of white and black paper will look white and black whether viewed inside or outside in the sun. Because the intensity of illumination outside typically is greater than inside, the black paper may actually be reflecting more light energy outside than the white paper does inside. Thus, the perception of lightness follows the reflectance properties of the objects rather than the absolute amount of light reflected from them.

Lightness contrast refers to the fact that the perceived lightness of an object is affected by the intensity of surrounding areas. The key difference to note between lightness contrast and lightness constancy is that the former occurs when only the intensity from surrounding regions is changed, whereas the latter occurs when the intensity of illumination across the entire visual field is changed. Lightness contrast is illustrated in Figure 6–5, in which the center squares of constant intensity appear progressively darker as the surround becomes lighter. This phenomenon illustrates a spatial interaction between stimuli. At least part of it may be due to *lateral inhibition,* in which some visual neurons are inhibited by the

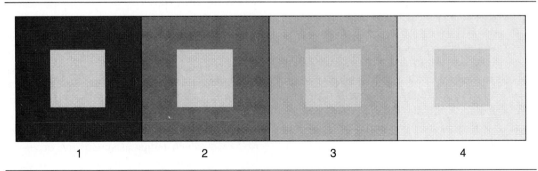

activity of other neighboring neurons. However, lateral inhibition is a relatively localized process; for example the Mach bands discussed earlier are attributed to such inhibition and appear only at intensity boundaries. Because lightness contrast occurs over a large area, higher-level brain processes also seem to be involved.

Wallach (1972) and others have proposed a constant-ratio rule to explain lightness constancy. They have presented evidence that two stimuli will appear equally light when the ratio of each stimulus to its respective surround is the same. Lightness contrast arises from changing the ratio, because only the intensity of the surround is changed. Evidence that lightness constancy follows from the contrast ratio comes from a classic experiment by Gelb (1929). A black disc was suspended in black surroundings. A hidden light source projected light only on the disc. In this situation, the black disc looked white. In terms of the constant-ratio rule, the conditions for constancy were violated because the disc had a source of illumination that its background did not. However, when a small piece of white paper was placed so that it also was illuminated by the hidden light source, the black disc then looked black.

The constant-ratio rule could be implemented by lateral inhibition of cells at the retina. However, findings such as those of Gelb suggest that this is not the whole story, because just a very small region of high illumination was sufficient to drastically alter the perceived lightness of the disc. Other evidence indicates even more clearly that lightness is due at least in part to higher-level brain processes that operate on the basis of cues, such as visible shadows and the location of an object relative to a light source.

One of the most compelling demonstrations of this type was that by Gilchrist (1977). He arranged a situation in which a white card was seen as white or dark gray, depending on the card's apparent position in space. As shown in Figure 6–6, the observer looked at three cards through a peephole. Two of the cards (a white test card and a black card) were in a front chamber that was dimly illuminated, while the third card

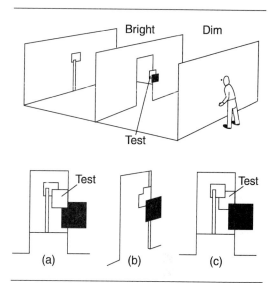

FIGURE 6–6   Gilchrist's Apparatus with the Test Stimulus Constructed to Appear in the Front Room (a) or in the Back Room (b and c).

From E. B. Goldstein, *Sensation and Perception,* Third Edition. Copyright © 1989 by Wadsworth, Inc. Reprinted with permission.

(also white) was in a back chamber that was brightly illuminated. By manipulating the depth cue of interposition (see Chapter 7), Gilchrist was able to cause the third card to be perceived as being either behind (panel a in Figure 6–6) or in front of (panel c) the other two cards.

Observers judged the lightness of the test card (the white card in the front room). When the test card was correctly perceived as in the front chamber, it was seen as white. However, when the depth cues caused the card to be incorrectly perceived as in the back chamber, it was seen as almost black. This phenomenon suggests that the perception of illumination is important to lightness. If the test card really was in the back chamber that had high illumination and was reflecting less light than the white card, then it would have relatively low reflectance and so appear dark. Apparently, the perceptual system uses logic like this to compute lightness. Thus, even the basic aspects of sensory experience of the type covered in this chapter are subject to computations performed by higher-level brain processes.

Spatial and Temporal Resolution

Acuity. To discriminate forms, differences between regions of different intensity in the visual field must be resolved. Acuity can be specified by finding the minimum *visual angle* for a detail that can be resolved. Visual angle is a measure of stimulus size that does not depend on distance. Because of this property, it is the most commonly used measure of stimulus size. As shown in Figure 6–7, the image that reaches the eye is a function of the size of the object and its distance from the observer. Visual angle is a way of specifying the size of the image that the eye is receiving. The visual angle is given by

$$\alpha = \tan^{-1} \frac{S}{D}$$

where S is the size of the object and D is the viewing distance, in equivalent units.

There are several types of acuity. *Identification acuity* can be measured by use of a Snellen eye chart consisting of rows of letters that become progressively smaller. Acuity is determined by the smallest size for which the observer can

identify the letters. Identification acuity is often specified in terms of the distance at which the person could identify letters that an observer with normal vision could identify at a standard distance. In the United States, this standard distance usually is 20 ft (6.1 m); thus, a person with 20/20 vision can identify letters at 20 ft that a normal observer could from 20 ft away, whereas a person with 20/40 vision can only identify letters that a normal observer could from as far as 40 ft away. *Vernier acuity* is based on a person's ability to discriminate between a broken line and an unbroken line. *Resolution acuity* is a measure of the person's ability to distinguish multiple bars (or gratings) from a single area of the same average intensity.

Acuity varies as a function of many of the factors that influence brightness. As we discussed in Chapter 5, acuity decreases as the location of a stimulus is moved out from the fovea to the periphery. This decrease is even more drastic if irrelevant visual noise stimuli are presented in relatively close spatial proximity to the target (Mackworth, 1965) or if a difficult decision must be made about a simultaneously presented foveal stimulus (Williams, 1985).

Acuity is also better under photopic viewing conditions than under scotopic conditions. It

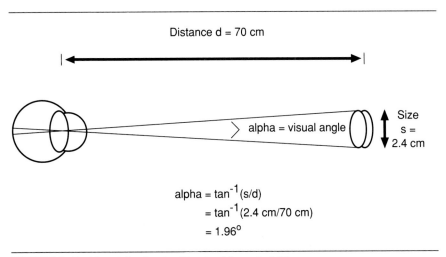

Distance d = 70 cm

alpha = visual angle

Size
s =
2.4 cm

alpha = tan^{-1}(s/d)

= tan^{-1}(2.4 cm/70 cm)

= 1.96°

FIGURE 6–7   Visual Angle of a Quarter Viewed at 70 cm.

shows a time–intensity relation similar to Bloch's law, but for durations of up to 300 ms (Kahneman, Norman, & Kubovy, 1967). In other words, within this duration, the probability of discriminating a detail can be increased by increasing the contrast (difference in intensity between light and dark regions) or by increasing exposure duration.

Acuity can be measured not only for static displays, as described above, but also for displays in motion. *Dynamic acuity* is determined by the performance when there is relative motion between the stimulus and the observer. Typically, dynamic acuity is poorer than static acuity (Morgan, Watt, & McKee, 1983; Scialfa et al., 1988), but they are highly correlated. That is, a person with good static acuity will probably have good dynamic acuity. Both types of acuity decline with age, although the decline is greater for dynamic acuity.

Acuity is an important consideration for any task that requires processing of detailed visual information. One such task is driving. All states in the United States require that applicants for driver's licenses pass acuity examinations. These examinations are tests of static acuity under high levels of illumination, and typically a minimum acuity of 20/40 is required for an unrestricted license. Given that driving involves dynamic vision, and night driving occurs under low levels of illumination the standard static acuity test does not correspond closely to actual driving conditions.

The standard acuity test seems particularly inappropriate for older drivers. People over the age of 65 show little deficiency on the standard acuity test, but show significant impairment relative to younger drivers when static acuity is measured under low illumination (Sturr, Kline, & Taub, 1990). Moreover, the elderly report specific problems with dynamic vision, such as difficulty reading signs on passing buses (Kosnik, Sekuler, & Kline, 1990), which correlate with the larger problem of reduced dynamic acuity (Scialfa et al., 1988). To provide assessment of visual ability for driving, Sturr, Kline, and Taub (1990) have recommended a battery of acuity tests involving static and dynamic situations under high and low levels of illumination.

Spatial Sensitivity.   An alternative way to view acuity is in terms of spatial contrast sensitivity. Remember that any complex waveform can be described in terms of component sine waves by Fourier analysis. The spatial distribution of light is a complex pattern that can be analyzed in this manner. Many studies have suggested that the human visual system analyzes the light array through spatial frequencies, because the appearance of complex patterns can be predicted from their sine-wave components.

The starting point for such studies is the human *contrast sensitivity function*. This function reflects the sensitivity with which a person can discriminate between a sine-wave grating and a homogeneous field of equal average illumination. A sine-wave grating is a series of alternating light and dark bars that, in contrast to a square-wave grating, are fuzzy at the edges (see Figure 6–8). The luminance at a point on the surface of a vertical sine-wave grating is equal to the sine of the horizontal distance of that point from the edge of the grating. High-frequency gratings are composed of many fine bars per unit area, whereas low-frequency gratings are composed of few wide bars per unit area. A threshold for contrast detection can be obtained by finding the least amount of contrast between the light and dark bars for the observer to discriminate a grating from a homogeneous field.

The contrast sensitivity function for an adult (see Figure 6–9) shows that we are sensitive to spatial frequencies as high as 40 cycles/degree. Sensitivity is greatest in the region of 3 to 5 cycles/degree and decreases sharply as spatial frequencies become lower or higher. In other words, the visual system is less sensitive to very low spatial frequencies and high spatial frequencies than to intermediate ones. Because the high frequencies convey the details of an image, this means that under low levels of illumination, such as those involved in driving at night, we will not be able to see details well.

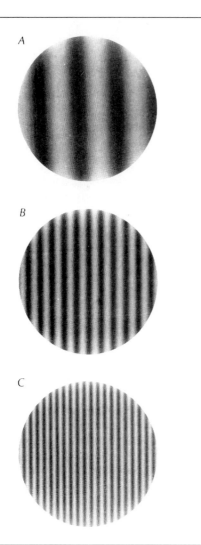

ties to the component frequencies. They showed that, as the contrast of the complex grating was increased, it first looked like the sine-wave component for which sensitivity was highest and then progressively changed appearance as additional components reached their threshold levels. Thus, the appearance of the compound stimulus was a function of the independent effects of the components on the visual system. These and other findings have been interpreted as indicating that the visual system contains distinct channels of neurons tuned to different spatial frequencies.

The contrast sensitivity function specifies how both size and contrast limit perception, whereas standard visual acuity tests measure only size factors. Ginsburg et al. (1982) compared the ability of standard acuity measures and contrast sensitivity functions to predict how well pilots could see objects under conditions of reduced visibility (like twilight or fog). Pilots flew simu-

FIGURE 6–8 Sine-wave Gratings of (A) Low, (B) Medium, and (C) High Spatial Frequencies.

Figure from R. Sekuler & R. Blake, *Perception,* Second Edition. Copyright 1990 by McGraw-Hill, Inc. Reprinted with permission.

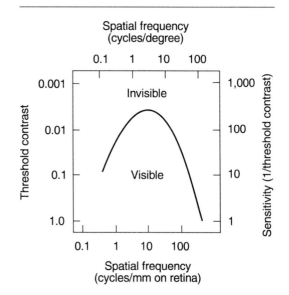

FIGURE 6–9 Spatial Contrast Sensitivity Function for an Adult.

Figure from R. Sekuler & R. Blake, *Perception,* Second Edition. Copyright 1990 by McGraw-Hill, Inc. Reprinted with permission.

In a classic experiment, Campbell and Robson (1968) found the minimum contrast necessary to see each of several sine-wave gratings. They then made predictions about the appearance of complex gratings, constructed from superimposed sine-wave gratings, based on the sensitivi-

lated missions and then landed. On half of the landings, an object blocked the runway and the landing had to be aborted. Pilots who saw the object at the greatest distance were those with the highest contrast sensitivity. Contrast sensitivity to intermediate and low spatial frequencies has also been shown to predict the detectability of stop signs at night (Evans & Ginsburg, 1982) and recognition of faces (Harmon & Julesz, 1973). Such results suggest that measurement of contrast sensitivity may be useful in screening applicants for visually demanding jobs. However, the utility of contrast sensitivity measures is limited because such measurements are expensive and time consuming to make relative to measurements of static acuity.

Temporal Sensitivity. Lights that flicker and flash are present throughout our environment. In some cases, as with train-crossing signals, it is desired that the flicker be perceived. In other cases, such as video display screens, it is not. To determine whether flicker will be visible, we need to know the *critical flicker frequency* (CFF), or the highest rate at which flicker can be perceived (Brown, 1965; Landis, 1954). With high-luminance stimuli of relatively large size, the CFF can be as high as 60 Hz. It is less for stimuli of lower luminance and smaller size. Numerous other factors, such as retinal location, influence the CFF. Video displays or sources of illumination that are intended to be seen as continuous should be well above the CFF, whereas displays intended to be seen as intermittent should be well below it. As an example, the flicker rate of 120 Hz for fluorescent lamps is sufficiently high that they can be used as continuous light sources.

More recent research on temporal sensitivity has closely paralleled that on contrast sensitivity (Watson, 1986). Whereas previous experiments on the CFF used only dark backgrounds, backgrounds of different intensities have been used. Also, the temporal changes in stimulation have been sinusoidal, rather than abrupt onsets and offsets. Sufficiently small sinusoidal changes in amplitude will be invisible, but as the amplitude

is increased, the oscillation may become visible. Contrast sensitivity can be determined in this manner for different temporal frequencies and plotted as a temporal contrast sensitivity function (see Figure 6–10). As with spatial contrast sensitivity, temporal contrast sensitivity increases with temporal frequency to an intermediate value (around 8 Hz for a bright light) and then decreases with further increases in temporal frequency up to the CFF of about 60 Hz (de Lange, 1958). The form of the function is influenced by

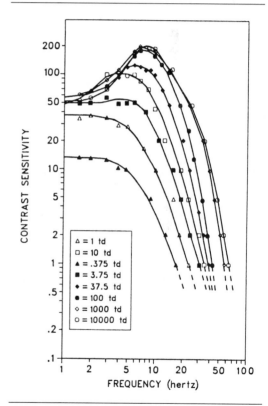

FIGURE 6–10 Temporal Contrast Sensitivity Functions for an Adult at Several Background Intensities. Trolands (td) is a measure of retinal luminance.

From A. B. Watson, Temporal sensitivity. In K. R. Boff, L. Kaufman, & P. Thomas (Eds.), *Handbook of Perception and Human Peformance.* Copyright © 1986 by John Wiley & Sons, Inc. Reprinted with permission.

factors such as the background intensity and the spatial configuration of the target and surround.

Masking. The presentation of one visual stimulus (the mask) can interfere with the perception of another (the target) when the two are presented in close temporal and spatial proximity. Such interference, called *masking,* occurs in a variety of situations. The term simultaneous masking is used when the target and mask occur simultaneously, while the terms forward and backward masking refer to situations in which the mask precedes or follows the target, respectively. With forward and backward masking, the length of the interval between the onsets of the two stimuli will determine the degree of masking.

At least three broad categories of masking situations can be distinguished (Fox, 1978). For homogeneous light masking, the mask is a light flash, and for visual noise masking, the mask consists of random contours. In both cases, the mask overlaps the location of the target stimulus. Homogeneous light masking and visual noise masking typically are greatest with simultaneous presentation of the target and mask. Such masking occurs, for example, in conditions of glare in which the light energy from a glare source decreases the contrast of an image. The magnitude of forward and backward masking decreases as the interval between the two stimuli increases, up to durations of 100 ms. This masking function appears to be attributable to temporal integration. That is, even when presented successively, the energy of the target and mask is at least partially summed, reducing the visibility of the target.

Homogeneous light and visual noise masking involve spatial overlap of the target and mask. The third type of masking occurs when one contour is masked by an adjacent contour; the target and mask do not overlap spatially. This is called metacontrast or lateral masking. The magnitude of metacontrast masking decreases as the spatial separation between the stimuli increases. Moreover, when the target and mask are of approximately equal intensity, the maximum masking occurs when the target precedes the mask by 50

to 100 ms. Theories of metacontrast focus on lateral inhibition in the visual system, possibly due to the different properties of the X-cell and Y-cell systems (for example, Breitmeyer & Ganz, 1976). However, it is also possible that metacontrast reflects the information components available to higher-level decision processes (for example, Bernstein, et al., 1973). Regardless of the causes for visual masking, the human factors specialist needs to be aware that masking can occur when an operator must process multiple visual stimuli in close spatial and temporal proximity.

Color Vision

Except under scotopic levels of illumination, we do not see objects as just varying along a white–black dimension. We see a world that consists of objects in a range of colors. In art, color is used to convey many emotions. More importantly, color plays a crucial role in our acquisition of knowledge about the world. Among other things, it aids in localizing and identifying objects.

Color is determined primarily by the wavelength of the light energy. Long-wavelength stimuli tend to be seen as red, short-wavelength stimuli as blue, and so on. However, as with brightness, it should be kept in mind that the perception of color is psychological, whereas wavelength distinctions are physical. Thus, other factors such as ambient lighting and background color influence the perception of color.

Color Mixing. Most colors that we see in the environment are not spectral colors. That is, they do not come from monochromatic stimuli. Rather, they are determined by mixtures of light of different wavelengths. Nonspectral colors differ from spectral colors in their degree of saturation, or color purity. Whereas spectral colors are completely saturated, nonspectral colors are less so. When light of two or more wavelengths is mixed, the mixture is called additive, as opposed to the subtractive mixture that occurs when combining pigments.

What happens when light of two wave-lengths is mixed additively? It depends on the specific wavelengths and the relative amounts of each. In some cases, colors are seen that differ from the components. For example, if a long-wavelength (red) light and middle-wavelength (yellow) light are mixed in approximately equal amounts, the color of the combination will be orange. If the middle-wavelength component is increased, the mixture will appear more yel-lowish. Combinations of other monochromatic light sources may yield no color. For example, if a short-wavelength (blue) light and an upper-middle-wavelength (yellow) light are mixed in approximately equal amounts, the resulting com-bination will have no hue. More generally, using three primary colors (one long, one middle, and one short wavelength), any hue and saturation values can be created from some combination of the three primaries.

A color appearance system that captures the dimensions of hue and saturation is the *color circle* (see Figure 6–11). Isaac Newton created the color circle by curving the visual spectrum. The circle was completed by connecting the short and long wavelength ends with nonspectral pur-ples. Thus, the outer boundary of the color circle corresponds to the monochromatic or spectral colors (plus the purples), which are highly satu-rated. The center of the circle is neutral (white or gray). If a diagonal is drawn from the center to a point on the rim, the hue for any point on this line corresponds to the hue at the rim. The saturation increases as the point shifts from the center to the rim.

The appearance of any mixture of two spec-tral colors can be estimated from the color circle by first drawing the chord that connects the points for the spectral colors. The point corresponding to the mixture falls on this chord, with the spe-cific location determined by the relative amounts of the two colors. If the two are mixed in equal percentages, the mixture will be located at the midpoint of the chord. The hue that corresponds to this mixture will be the one at the rim at that particular angle, and the saturation will be indi-cated by the distance from the rim.

Additive color mixture occurs when the im-ages from two projectors are overlapped. People are more familiar with subtractive color mixture, which applies to the mixing of pigments, such as paints. Subtractive color mixture follows differ-ent rules than additive color mixture and is not as predictable. The reason is that the pigments have complex reflectance properties, and the color per-ceived will be determined by the reflectance of the combination. Although the rules for additive and subtractive mixing are different, the general principle for both is that the wavelength proper-ties of the combination determine the color that will be seen.

Trichromatic Theory.   The fact that any hue can be matched with a combination of three primary colors was taken as evidence, as early as the 1800s, for the view that human color vision is trichromatic (Helmholtz, 1852; Young, 1802). *Trichromatic color theory* proposes that there are three types of photoreceptors, corresponding to

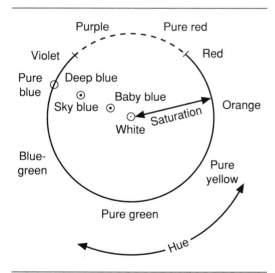

FIGURE 6–11   The Color Circle.

From M. W. Matlin, *Sensation and Perception.* Second Edition. Copyright 1988 Allyn and Bacon. Reprinted with permission.

blue, green, and red, that determine our color perception. According to trichromatic theory, the relative activity of the three photoreceptors determines the color that is perceived.

There are three types of cones with distinct photopigments, as predicted by trichromatic theory. Color information is coded by the cones in terms of the relative sensitivities of the pigments. For example, a light source of 500 nm will affect all three cone types, with the middle-wavelength cones being affected the most, the short-wavelength cones the least, and the long-wavelength cones an intermediate amount (see Figure 6–3). Because each color is signaled by the relative levels of activity in the three cone systems, any spectral color can be matched with a combination of three primary colors.

There are several schemes for specifying color stimuli, but the most widely used is that developed by the Commission Internationale de l'Eclairage (CIE). The CIE system uses a triangular space based on trichromatic theory that is a more sophisticated version of the color circle (see Figure 6–12). In this system, a color is specified by its location in the space according to its values on three imaginary primaries, called X, Y, and Z, under the restriction that $X + Y + Z = 1.0$. These primaries correspond to long-, medium-, and short-wavelength light, respectively. Z is determined when X and Y are known; so the space can be diagramed in terms of the X and Y values.

Because there is only one rod photopigment sensitive to a range of wavelengths across the visual spectrum, color is not seen under scotopic viewing conditions. Because only the single system exists, there is no way to determine whether a high level of activity in it is being caused by high-intensity light of a wavelength to which the photopigment is not very sensitive or by a lower-intensity light of a wavelength to which the photopigment is more sensitive. Thus, the relative levels of activity within the three cone subsystems under photopic viewing conditions enable the perception of color.

Most people know someone, often a male, who is color-blind. Color-blind individuals typically have *dichromatic vision*. That is, they can match any spectral hue with a combination of just two primaries. In other words, two colors may look the same to a color blind individual that look different to a person with normal trichromatic vision. Such individuals typically are missing one of the three types of cone photopigments, although the total number of cones is similar to that of a normal trichromat (Cicerone & Nerger, 1989). The most common form of dichromatic color vision is deuteranopia, which is attributed to a malfunction of the green cone system. Deuteranopes have difficulty distinguishing between red and green. Some individuals show only partial color blindness, in the sense that they do not perform like either normal trichromats or dichromats. Such individuals are presumed to have deficiencies in one of the three photopigments and are said to have anomalous trichromatism. Moreover, there are rare individuals with no cones or only one type of cone who have *monochromatic vision.*

Opponent Process Theory. Although human color vision is based on trichromatic physiology, some phenomena do not fit well with trichromatic theory. As mentioned previously, adding equal amounts of blue and yellow light leads to an elimination of hue, as does adding red and green. Moreover, no colors appear to be combinations of these pairings. That is, orange seems to be a combination of red and yellow, but no such combination exists for red and green. The relations of red with green and blue with yellow show up in other ways, too. If you fixate on an image of one of these colors for a brief period (a procedure known as adaptation), you will see an afterimage of the complementary hue when the image is removed. For example, if you adapt to red, you will see a green afterimage. Similarly, if a neutral gray region is surrounded by a region of one of the colors, the gray region will take on the hue of the complementary color. A gray square surrounded by blue will take on a yellow hue. Therefore, yellow appears to be a fourth basic color.

These phenomena led Ewald Hering to develop the *opponent process theory* of color vision, also in the 1800s. He proposed neural

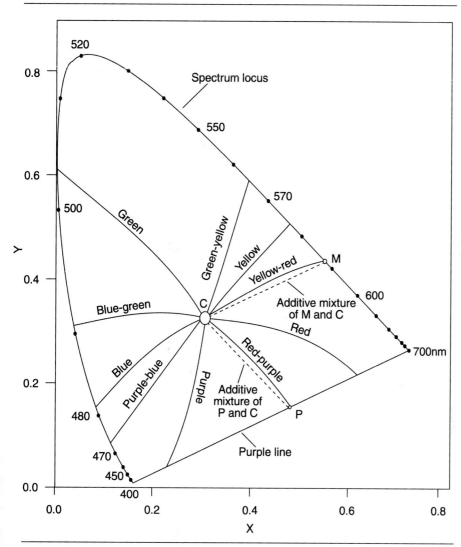

FIGURE 6–12   The CIE Color Space.
From G. Wyszecki, Color appearance. In K. R. Boff, L. Kaufman, & J. P. Thomas (Eds.),
Handbook of Perception and Human Performance. Vol I: Sensory Processes and Perception
(pp. 9-1–9-57). Copyright © 1986 John Wiley & Sons, Inc. Reprinted by permission of John
Wiley & Sons, Inc.

mechanisms that code blue and yellow together and red and green together. Within each of these mechanisms, one or the other color could be signaled, but not both at the same time. Neurophysiological evidence for such opponent coding was obtained initially from the retina of a goldfish (Svaetchin, 1956) and later in the ganglion cells and lateral geniculate cells of rhesus monkeys (DeMonasterio, 1978; De Valois & De Valois, 1980). The receptive fields for these cells are such that, if the neuron has a red excitatory center and a green inhibitory surround, red light presented in the center or over the whole receptive field will increase the firing rate, whereas green light presented in the surround or over the whole field will have the opposite effect.

A well-known phenomenon called the McCollough effect, after its discoverer (McCollough, 1965), shows that color coding is orientation contingent. This effect is demonstrated by preadapting to a grating of red and black bars in one orientation (for example, vertical) and a grating of green and black bars in another orientation (for example, horizontal). When a subsequent display of white and black bars is viewed, a green afterimage is seen in the white areas if the bars are oriented vertically and a red afterimage if they are oriented horizontally. The most commonly accepted account of the McCollough effect is that it is due to adaptation of cortical neurons that are sensitive both to color and orientation. Other related types of color aftereffects are contingent on direction of motion, the spatial frequency of gratings, and other basic aspects of visual stimulation.

To summarize, the majority of the phenomena of human color vision are explainable by the view that the initial sensory transduction is trichromatic. The output from these receptors is then wired into an opponent-process arrangement of the type just described. At the visual cortex, color is evidently coded along with some of the other features described in Chapter 5.

AUDITORY PERCEPTION

The basic properties of auditory stimulation corresponding to those of brightness and color in vision are loudness and pitch. The receptor cells in the auditory system are sensitive to the amplitude and frequency of sound. Consequently, the perception of loudness and pitch is closely linked to the structure of the auditory sensory system. We will examine these properties, as well as some other qualitative characteristics of auditory perception, in the present section.

Loudness

The quantitative dimension of auditory perception is loudness. As with brightness, loudness is psychological and is only correlated with the physical dimension of intensity. Using magnitude estimation procedures, Stevens (1975) found that the perception of loudness is best described by the power function

$$L = aI^{0.6}$$

where L is the loudness, I is the physical intensity of the sound, and a is a constant. On the basis of this function, Stevens derived a scale for measuring loudness in which the unit is called the sone. One sone is the loudness of a 1,000-Hz stimulus at 40-dB intensity. The sone scale and some representative sounds are shown in Figure 6–13.

The loudness of a tone can also be influenced by its frequency (Fletcher & Munson, 1933). This fact is captured by *equal loudness contours,* which are shown in Figure 6–14. These contours are obtained by presenting a standard, 1,000-Hz tone at a given intensity level and then adjusting tones of other frequencies so that they sound

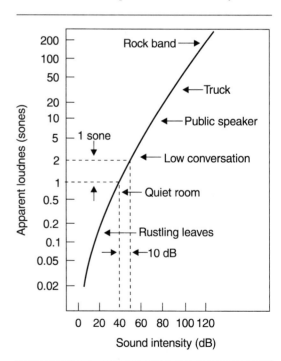

FIGURE 6–13 The Sone Scale of Loudness.

From Stanley Coren and Lawrence M. Ward, *Sensation and Perception,* Third Edition. Copyright © 1989 by Harcourt Brace Jovanovich, Inc. Reprinted with permission.

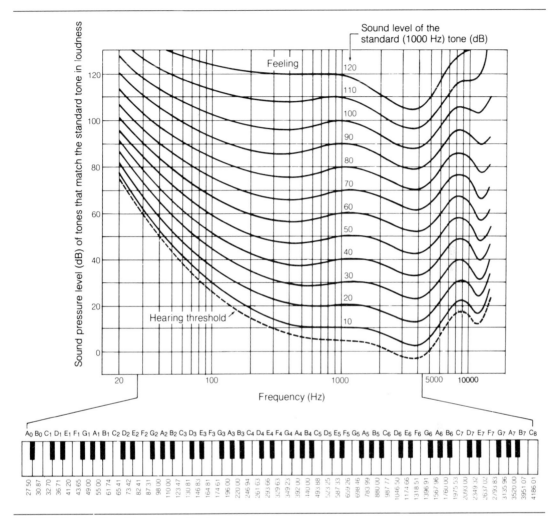

FIGURE 6–14 Equal Loudness Contours.
From P. H. Lindsay & D. A. Norman, *Human Information Processing,* Second Edition.
Copyright © 1977 by Academic Press, Inc. Reprinted by permission.

equally loud. The equal loudness contours illustrate several important points: (1) To sound equally loud, different frequencies must be adjusted to different intensity levels. An alternative way of stating this relation is that, if different frequencies are presented at identical intensities, they will have different loudnesses. (2) Maximal sensitivity is to tones in the range of 3 to 4 kHz. (3) Sensitivity is poor to low-frequency tones below approximately 200 Hz. (4) These differ-

ences in loudness across the frequencies progressively diminish as intensity increases.

One consequence of these relations is that music recorded at high-intensity levels will sound different when played back at low levels. Most obviously, the bass will drop out. Although it is present to the same relative extent in the sound wave, we are less sensitive to the low-frequency energy. Many high-fidelity amplifiers have a "loudness" switch to compensate for this change.

When switched on, the low frequencies are increased in intensity, making the recording sound more normal if played at a low-intensity level.

As with visual intensity, the measurement of sound intensity for purposes of human hearing must be calibrated according to the human's sensitivity to different frequencies. Sound-pressure level is typically specified in decibels as

$$L_p = 20 \log_{10} \frac{p}{p_r}$$

where p_r is a reference pressure of 20 micropascals (μp). (One pascal is equal to one newton of force per square meter.) Measurement is made with reference to the 40-dB equal loudness contour. The resulting measure in decibels is a good characterization of the effective intensity of the sound at moderate energy levels.

Temporal summation occurs for loudness. The energy from sounds over approximately 200 ms is summed to determine the loudness. Adaptation occurs when a tone is played continuously, resulting in the phenomenon that the loudness of the tone diminishes over time. Finally, the loudness of complex tones is affected by the bandwidth, which is the range of frequencies (for example, 950 to 1050 Hz) that is included in the tone. As the bandwidth is increased, with the overall intensity held constant, loudness is not affected until a *critical bandwidth* is reached. Beyond this point, loudness increases as higher and lower frequencies are added to the complex tone.

Whether a sound can be heard depends on other sounds in the environment. If a sound is audible by itself but not in the presence of other sounds, the other sounds are said to mask it. As for vision, simultaneous masking refers to such effects when the stimulus tone and the mask occur simultaneously. As the intensity of a mask is increased, the greater the stimulus intensity must be for it to be detected. The greatest masking effect occurs when the stimulus and mask are of the same or similar frequencies. The thresholds for tones of lower frequency than the mask tend not to be influenced much by its presence (Zwicker,

1958). The masking effect is much greater on tones of higher frequency (see Figure 6–15). This asymmetric effect of the masking tones is thought to be due to the pattern of movement on the basilar membrane. Human factors specialists need to remember that low-frequency tones will be less susceptible to masking in most environments, but that low-frequency masks may affect the perceptibility of a wide range of tones of higher frequency.

Hearing is also subject to individual differences. For instance, cigarette smokers are less sensitive to high-frequency tones than nonsmokers (Zelman, 1973), and people who regularly take large doses of aspirin can suffer temporary decreases in sensitivity of from 10 to 40 dB, often accompanied by tinnitus, a high pitched ringing in the ears (McCabe & Dey, 1965). These effects arise from changes in blood flow to the inner ear induced by nicotine and aspirin.

The frequency range for hearing decreases progressively across a person's life. A young per-

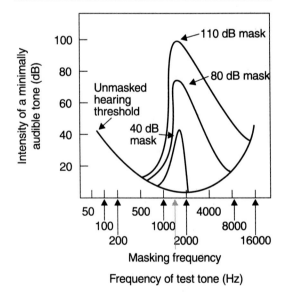

FIGURE 6–15 Thresholds for a Tone Stimulus in the Presence of a Narrow Band of Masking Noise Centered at 1200 Hz.
Based on Zwicker (1958).

son can hear tones as low as 20 Hz and as high as 20 kHz. As a person ages, the ability to hear high-frequency tones is lost. By age 30, most people are unable to hear frequencies above 15 kHz. By age 50, the upper limit is 12 kHz, and by age 70, it is 6 kHz. Substantial loss also occurs for frequencies as low as 2 kHz.

The hearing loss at high frequencies for the elderly means that they will not perform well when perception of high-frequency tones is required. Many modern telephones use electronic bell or beeper ringers, in comparison to the old-style mechanical bell. The frequency spectrum of the electronic bell ringer spans 315 Hz to 20 kHz and that of the electronic beeper ringer, 1.6 kHz to 20 kHz. In contrast, the mechanical bell covers a range of 80 Hz to 20 kHz. Berkowitz and Casali (1990) presented people of various ages with these three ringer types. The electronic beeper was virtually inaudible for older people and was easily masked by noise. This outcome is hardly surprising, given that the beeper includes virtually no acoustic energy in the range at which the elderly are most sensitive. The electronic bell actually was more audible to the elderly than the mechanical bell, apparently because it has a concentration of energy around 1 kHz.

Pitch

Pitch is the qualitative attribute of hearing that is the equivalent of hue in vision. It is determined primarily by the frequency of the auditory stimulus. However, just as the loudness of a sound can be affected by variables other than intensity, pitch can be influenced by variables other than frequency. For example, *equal pitch contours* can be constructed by varying the intensity of stimuli of a given frequency and judging their pitches. As shown in Figure 6–16, below approximately 3 kHz, pitch decreases with increasing intensity, whereas above 3 kHz it increases.

Pitch can also be influenced by the duration of a tone. At durations of less than 10 ms, any pure tone will be heard as a click. Moreover, as

duration is increased up to approximately 250 ms, tone quality is improved. Also, people are better able to discriminate the pitches of longer-duration tones.

Two theories of pitch perception were developed in the 1800s, and contemporary research indicates that both are needed to explain pitch-perception phenomena. The first theory, proposed by Rutherford, is called *frequency theory.* This theory suggests that the basilar membrane vibrates at the frequency of the auditory stimulus. This frequency of vibration of the basilar membrane is then transformed into a pattern of neural firing at the same frequency. Thus, a 1-kHz tone would cause the basilar membrane to vibrate at a 1-kHz rate, which in turn would cause neurons to respond at this frequency.

The alternative theory is *place theory,* which was first proposed by Helmholtz. He noticed that the basilar membrane had a triangular shape and suggested that it consisted of a series of resonators of decreasing length that respond to different frequencies. Thus, the frequency of the tone would affect a particular place on the basilar membrane; the activity of the receptors at this location would then send a signal along the particular neurons that received input from that place.

Considerable research in the present century has been conducted to clarify these two types of theories. One problem with frequency theory is that the maximal possible firing rate of neurons is 1 kHz. Thus, an individual neuron could not signal frequencies greater than this. A major advance was made by Wever (1970) when he provided evidence that frequencies greater than 1 kHz can be signaled by groups of neurons that operate according to the volley principle. This principle is that nerve fibers cooperate so that they fire in groups, or volleys. As shown in Figure 6–17, this is accomplished through phase locking, such that each neuron fires at the same phase of the audiory stimulus but not on every cycle. The result is that the volleys of firing for the groups of neurons correspond to the frequency of the tone. However, phase locking breaks down at frequencies between 4 and 5 kHz,

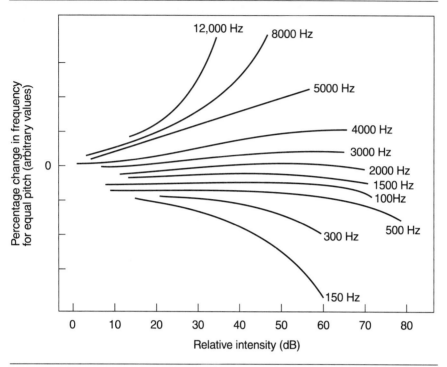

FIGURE 6–16   Equal Pitch Contours.

Reprinted with permission from S. S. Stevens (1935). The relation of pitch to intensity. *Journal of the Acoustical Society of America, 6,* 150–154.

meaning that frequency theory still cannot account for the coding of frequencies that exceed this range.

Place theory received new life from the work of George von Békésy (1960). Physiological investigations revealed that the basilar membrane does not act as a series of resonators, as Helmholtz had proposed. However, by observing the action of the basilar membrane in the ears of guinea pigs and by constructing models, von Bekesy established that different frequency tones produce traveling waves that have maximal displacement at distinct locations on the basilar membrane. The displacement for low-frequency tones is at the wide end of the basilar membrane, away from the oval window. As the frequency of the tone is increased, the location of peak displacement shifts progressively toward the oval window. The term *traveling wave* comes from the fact that the action of the basilar membrane corresponds to the action of a rope that is secured at one end and shaken at the other; a wave ripples down the basilar membrane (see Figure 6–18).

A major problem with traveling wave theory is that the peak displacement for all tones below approximately 500 Hz is at the far end of the basilar membrane. Thus, place coding does not seem possible for these frequencies. Because tones below 4 kHz can be accommodated by frequency theory, the widely accepted view is that place coding holds for tones that exceed 500 Hz, whereas frequency coding holds for tones of less than 4 kHz. Thus, between 500 Hz and 4 kHz, both mechanisms are operating.

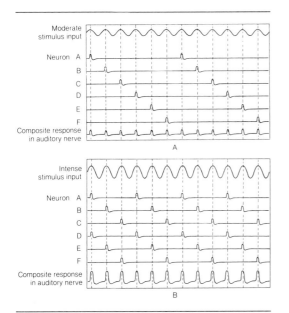

FIGURE 6–17   An Illustration of Phase Locking and the Volley Principle.

Figure from *Sensation & Perception,* Third Edition, by Stanley Coren and Lawrence M. Ward, copyright © 1989 by Harcourt Brace Jovanovich, Inc., reprinted by permission of the publisher.

Timbre, Consonance, and Dissonance

When the same musical note is played by different instruments, it does not sound identical. This qualitative aspect of auditory perception that can occur even for sounds of equivalent loudness and pitch is called *timbre*. Timbre is determined by many factors, with one being the relative strengths of the harmonics. Figure 6–19 shows the frequency spectra for a note with a fundamental frequency of 196 Hz played on a bassoon, guitar, alto saxophone, and violin. The pitch, which is determined by the fundamental frequency, sounds the same. However, the relative amounts of energy at the different harmonic frequencies vary across the instruments; these different spectral patterns are one reason why the tones have distinct timbres. Timbre is also influenced by the time course of the buildup and decay of sound at the beginning and end of the tone.

Consonance and dissonance refer to the degree of pleasantness of combinations of two or more tones. When combining pure tones, the relative dissonance is a function of the critical bandwidth. The relation to consonance and dissonance is that tones within the critical band sound dissonant, whereas tones separated by more than the critical band sound consonant. Within the critical band, a small separation in frequencies leads to the perception of beats, or oscillations of loudness, with the pitch corresponding to that of a frequency intermediate to the two component frequencies. Outside the range that produces beats, the perception is one of roughness. For more complex musical tones, the relation between harmonics is important in determining whether a combination is heard as consonant or dissonant.

PERCEPTION OF TOUCH, TEMPERATURE, AND PAIN

A sensation of touch can be evoked from anywhere on the body. Absolute thresholds for touch vary across the body, with the lowest thresholds being in the facial region (see Figure 6–20). When vibrating rather than punctate stimuli are used, the absolute threshold typically is lowered.

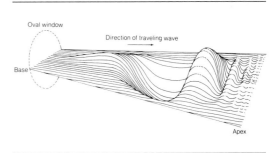

FIGURE 6–18   Traveling Wave Motion of the Basilar Membrane

Reprinted with permission from J. Tonndorf (1960). Shearing motion in scala media of cochlear models. *Journal of the Acoustical Society of America, 32,* 238–244.

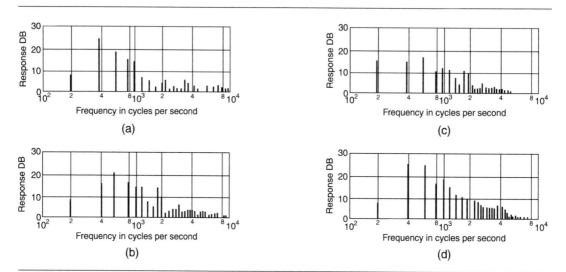

FIGURE 6–19   The Harmonic Structure of a Tone with a Fundamental Frequency of 196 Hz, Played by a (a) Bassoon, (b) Guitar, (c) Alto Saxophone, and (d) Violin. Adapted with permission from H. F. Olson (1967), *Music, Physics, and Engineering* (2nd ed.). Dover Publications.

Two-point thresholds are obtained by requiring observers to determine how far apart two simultaneous points of stimulation must be for two distinct points to be perceived. This threshold measure provides an indication of the accuracy with which points on the skin can be localized. The relative two-point thresholds across the body show a function similar to the absolute thresholds, with the primary difference being that the fingers show the lowest thresholds instead of the face.

For vibratory stimuli, threshold and above-threshold magnitudes can be measured as a function of the frequency of vibration. As shown in Figure 6–21, equal sensation contours are obtained that are of the same general nature as the equal loudness contours found for different auditory frequencies. Maximum sensitivity to vibration is in the region of 200 to 400 Hz.

In addition to receiving direct tactile stimulation, it is possible to receive stimulation indirectly by using tools, through wearing gloves, or with other interposing materials. Operators can use tools to detect faults in manufactured goods

in situations for which direct touch might be injurious. Kleiner, Drury, and Christopher (1987) investigated factors that influence the ease with which such indirect fault detection can be performed. They found that the probability of detecting a fault increased as the size of the fault increased and that sensitivity decreased as the instrument tip increased in diameter.

Temperature sensitivity is measured by the application of thermal stimuli. Temperature thresholds show nearly perfect summation for 0.5 to 1.0 s (Stevens, Okulicz, & Marks, 1973), and spatial summation occurs over large areas (Kenshalo, 1972). Hence, pressing a heated flat surface on the skin will feel hotter than just pressing the edge. Adaptation to thermal stimuli will occur over a period of several minutes. Both hot and cold stimuli also can be localized to some extent, but not very precisely.

Many devices have been used to apply extreme mechanical, thermal, chemical, and electrocutaneous stimuli to all parts of the body. As Sherrick and Cholewiak (1986) describe, "The full array of devices and bodily loci em-

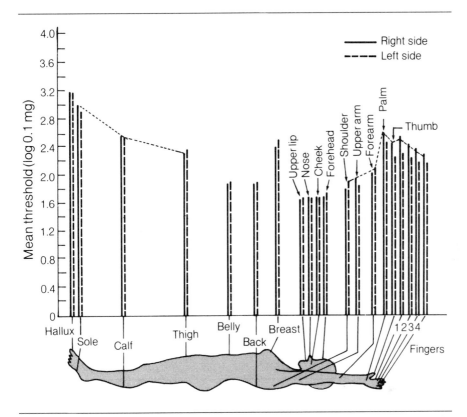

FIGURE 6–20   Absolute Thresholds Across the Body.

From S. Weinstein (1968), in D. R. Kenshalo (Ed.), *The skin senses.* Reprinted with permission of Charles C. Thomas Publisher.

ployed would bring a smile to the lips of the Marquis de Sade and a shudder of anticipation to the Graf van Sacher-Masoch" (p. 12–39). In contrast to touch and temperature, pain thresholds show little temporal or spatial summation. Pain perception does, however, show adaptation during prolonged stimulation.

SUMMARY

The basic quantitative and qualitative aspects of vision, audition, and touch show many similarities. Brightness, loudness and perceived pressure are determined primarily by physical intensity. However, they are influenced by numerous other factors. For these senses, increased intensity results in greater responses of the sensory receptors and, consequently, in higher rates of neural firing, both within single neurons and among groups. The qualitative properties of color and pitch similarly are determined primarily by the wavelength (frequency) properties of the stimuli, with other factors also entering into play.

To ensure that displayed information can be perceived, the designer must take into account the basic perceptual characteristics of the observer. For example, if comprehension of a display requires the resolution of fine detail, the display should not be located in peripheral vision, but rather in the direct line of sight. Similarly, auditory stimuli must be of an intensity and frequency

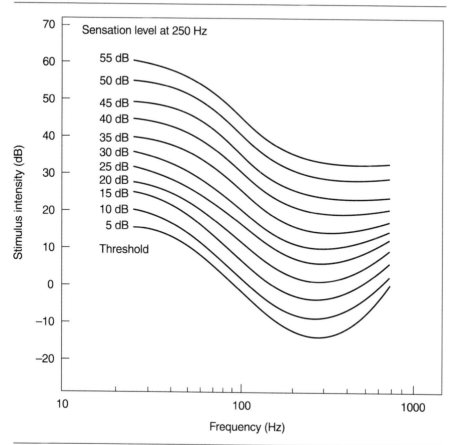

FIGURE 6–21   Equal-sensation Contours for Vibratory Stimuli.
From T. R. Verrillo, A. J. Fraioli, & R. L. Smith (1969). *Perception & Psychophysics, 6,* 366–372. Reprinted by permission of Psychonomic Society, Inc.

that will not prevent masking by environmental noise. The involvement of higher-level brain processes in perception has already been illustrated for some of the phenomena described in this chapter. This involvement will be more apparent when the perception of complex dimensions is considered in Chapter 7.

RECOMMENDED READING

Coren, S., & Ward, L. M. (1989). *Sensation & Perception,* 3rd ed. New York: Harcourt Brace Jovanovich.

Goldstein, E. R. (1989). *Sensation and Perception,* 3rd ed. Belmont, CA: Wadsworth.

Hurvich, L. M. (1981). *Color Vision.* Sunderland, MA: Sinauer.

Marr, D. (1982). *Vision.* San Francisco, CA: W. H. Freeman.

Moore, B. C. J. (1989). *An Introduction to the Psychology of Hearing,* 3rd ed. New York: Academic Press.

PERCEPTION OF OBJECTS IN THE WORLD

The important and salient characteristics of perception are tridimensionality, curvatures, movement, slants, groupings, shapes of all kinds, contours, the various constancies, chords, melodies, speech, rhythm, diminuendos and crescendos, etc.

—C. C. Pratt, 1969

INTRODUCTION

We not only perceive the basic quantitative and qualitative aspects of stimulation of the type emphasized in the previous chapters, but we perceive objects and forms. In fact, one obvious phenomenal characteristic of perception is the automatic and effortless way in which a meaningful, organized world is perceived. The ease with which perception occurs belies the complexity of the problem that is faced by the perceptual system. The immediate, or proximal, stimulus is that of physical energy impinging on sensory receptors. In vision, the proximal stimulus is a two-dimensional array of light energy. Yet, somehow we are able to determine how its pieces go together to form objects, where those objects are located in three dimensions, and whether changes in position of the image on the retina are due to movements of objects in the environment or of ourselves.

The operator of a human–machine system often has to accurately perceive the locations of objects in either two- or three-dimensional space. The displayed information must not only be detected, but it must also be identified and interpreted correctly. Consequently, principles of perceptual organization, depth perception, and pattern recognition become important.

In the present chapter, we will consider the problems that must be surmounted by the perceptual system to perceive accurately the identities and locations of objects in the environment. It should become clear that perception involves much more than just the passive registration of sensory information. As in Chapter 6, we will begin with a detailed examination of visual perception and then consider auditory perception and tactile perception to lesser extents.

VISUAL PERCEPTION

Most psychologists hold that the perceptual world we experience is *constructed*. This means that the senses provide cues that are used to evaluate hypotheses about the state of the world, but it is these hypotheses or constructions themselves that constitute perception. A good example involves the blind spot, which was discussed in Chapter 5. Sensory input is not received from the part of the image that falls on the blind spot, yet no hole is perceived in the visual field. Rather, the field is perceived as complete. The blind spot is filled in on the basis of sensory evidence provided by other parts of the image. The present chapter will provide a better understanding of how the perceptual system operates to construct a percept.

Perceptual Organization

The topic of perceptual organization involves how the perceptual system determines what pieces in the visual field go together. A widely held view around the beginning of the twentieth century was that complex perceptions are simply additive combinations of basic sensory elements. However, a group of German psychologists, known as the Gestalt psychologists, provided convincing demonstrations that such is not the case. The creed usually associated with these psychologists is that the whole is more than the sum

of its parts. Complex patterns of elementary features show properties that emerge from the configuration of features that could not be predicted from the features alone (Koffka, 1935).

One of the clearest demonstrations of this point is that made by Max Wertheimer in 1912 with a phenomenon of apparent movement that is called *stroboscopic motion*. Two lights were arranged in a row. If the left light alone was presented briefly, the perceptual experience was of a single light turning on and off in the left location. Similarly, if the right light alone was presented briefly, then it appeared as a single light turning on and off in the right location. Based on these elementary features, when the left and right lights were presented in succession, the perception should have been one of the left light coming on and going off, followed by the right light coming on and going off. Yet, with a short time interval between the presentations, the perception was of a single light moving from left to right. This apparent movement is the emergent property that cannot be predicted on the basis of the elementary features.

The example of apparent movement clearly illustrates what is meant by *perceptual organization:* "the process by which we apprehend particular relationships among potentially separate stimulus elements (e.g., parts, features, dimensions)" (Boff & Lincoln, 1988, p. 1238). Perhaps most basic is *figure–ground organization.* Typically, a scene is effortlessly perceived in terms of objects against a background. In the case of ambiguous figure–ground arrangements, like those shown in Figure 7–1, each part of the display can be seen as either figure or ground. Such examples illustrate the major distinctions between figure and ground. Contours are seen as belonging to the figure; the figure appears to be in front of the background; and the figure seems to be an object, whereas the ground does not. Six principles of figure–ground organization are summarized in Table 7–1 and illustrated in Figure 7–1. Displays that violate these principles will have ambiguous figure–ground organizations and may be misperceived.

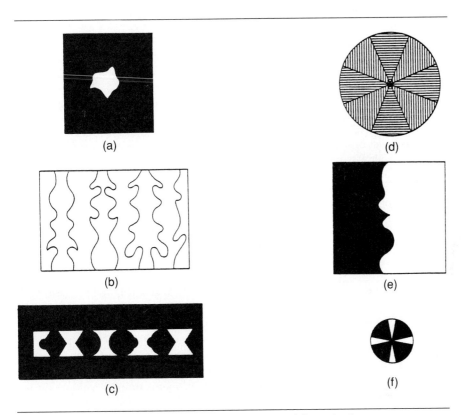

FIGURE 7–1   Factors That Determine Figure-ground Organization:
(a) Surroundedness; (b) Symmetry; (c) Convexity; (d) Orientation; (e) Lightness
or Contrast; and (f) Area.
Based on Boff and Lincoln (1988)

Probably more important for display design are the principles of *Gestalt grouping,* which are illustrated in Figure 7–2. The principle of proximity is that elements close together in space tend to be perceived as a group. Similarity refers to the fact that similar elements (in terms of color, form, or orientation) tend to be grouped together perceptually. The principle of continuity is embodied in the phenomenon that points connected in straight or smoothly curving lines tend to be seen as belonging together. Closure refers to a tendency for open curves to be perceived as complete forms. Finally, for common fate, which is not shown in the figure, elements that are moving in a common direction at a common speed are grouped together.

According to Gestalt psychologists, the overriding determinant of perceptual organization is the minimum principle (sometimes called the law of Prägnanz). This principle states that stimuli will be organized in the simplest possible manner consistent with the physical stimulus. Although the Gestalt psychologists did not specify unambiguously what was meant by simplest, they related it to properties such as regularity and symmetry. An alternative proposed by Helmholtz is the likelihood principle, which states that sensory elements will be organized into the most probable environmental object that is consistent with the sensory evidence. The likelihood principle suggests that the simplest organization is not always the one that will be perceived, and it has a closer

TABLE 7–1 Principles of Figure–Ground Organization

PRINCIPLE	DESCRIPTION
Surroundedness	A surrounded region tends to be seen as figure, while the surrounding region is seen as ground.
Symmetry	A region with symmetry is perceived as figure in preference to a region that is not symmetric.
Convexity	Convex contours are seen as figure in preference to concave contours.
Orientation	A region oriented horizontally or vertically is seen as figure in preference to one that is not.
Lightness or contrast	A region that contrasts more with the overall surround is preferred as figure over one that does not.
Area	A region that occupies less area is preferred as figure.

From K. R. Boff & J. E. Lincoln (Eds.), *Engineering Data Compendium: Human Perception and Performance,* 1988. Reprinted with permission.

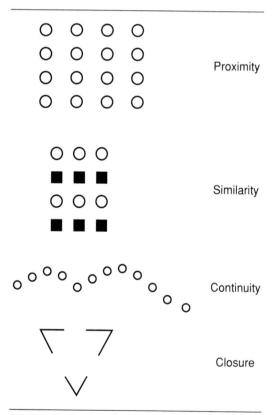

FIGURE 7–2 The Gestalt Organizational Principles of Proximity, Similarity, Continuity, and Closure.

affinity to the view that perception is constructed. According to Pomerantz and Kubovy (1986), the likelihood principle fares better than the minimum principle in explaining known results.

Pattern organization is one of the areas in which information theory has made a substantial contribution. The metric of information (H) from this theory is based on the uncertainty inherent in sets of items. Garner (1974) applied this notion to pattern organization and conducted a series of experiments in which the inferred set for a dot pattern was composed of those patterns produced by all combinations of rotation in 90° increments and reflection (see Figure 7–3). He found that the fewer the unique items in the set were, the more easily a pattern could be classified. Thus, "good" patterns are highly redundant in the information-theoretic sense.

Research on Gestalt organizational principles has shown people to be particularly sensitive to the orientation of stimuli (for example, Beck, 1966). When forms must be discriminated that are the same except for orientation (for example, upright Ts from tilted Ts), responses are faster and more accurate than when the discrimination is between two different forms made from the same features in the same orientations (for example, upright Ts from backward Ls; see Figure 7–4). Sensitivity to orientation as a grouping fea-

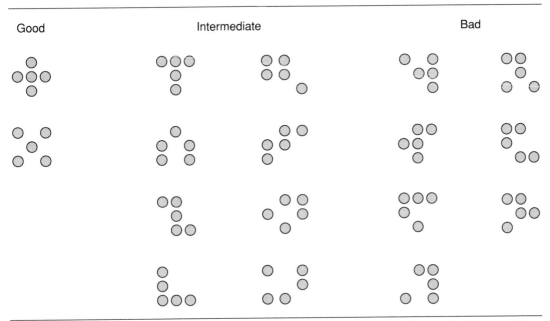

| Good | Intermediate | | Bad | |

FIGURE 7–3   Examples of 5-dot Patterns That Range from Good (Leftmost Column) to Intermediate (Next Two Columns) to Bad (Two Rightmost Columns) in Terms of Redundancy.
Based on Garner, 1974.

ture likely arises from the orientation-sensitive neurons in the visual cortex.

More generally, the identification of information in displays will be faster and more accu-

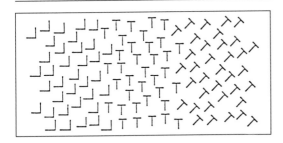

FIGURE 7–4   Example of Orientation as an Organizing Feature.
From J. Beck (1966). Effect of orientation and of shape similarity on perceptual grouping. *Perception & Psychophysics, 1,* 300–302. Reprinted by permission of Psychonomic Society, Inc.

rate when the organization of the display is such that the critical stimulus is segregated from the distracting elements. For example, when observers must indicate whether an F or T is included in a display that has noise elements composed of features from both letters (see Figure 7–5), they are slower at responding if the critical letter is hidden among the distractors by good continuity, as in Figure 7–5b, or proximity (Banks & Prinzmetal, 1976; Prinzmetal & Banks, 1977).

The Gestalt organizational principles determine how visual displays will be perceived and the ease with which specific information can be extracted. A good display design will use these principles to cause the necessary information to stand out. Similarly, if we wish to obscure an object, as in camouflage, the object can be colored or patterned in such a manner that the parts will blend into the background.

The Gestalt organizational factors are important for display panels that contain multiple in-

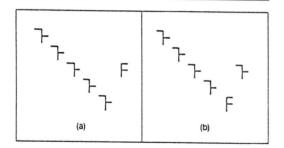

FIGURE 7–5   Example Stimuli Used To Illustrate How Good Continuation Influences Target (F) Identification When It Is Grouped (a) Separately from and (b) Together with Distractors.

From W. Prinzmetal & W. P. Banks (1977). Good continuation affects visual detection. *Perception & Psychophysics, 21,* 389–395. Reprinted by permission of Psychonomic Society, Inc.

of grouping common region and connectedness, respectively. They seem to be particularly useful means for human factors specialists to ensure that dials are grouped by the observer in the intended manner.

Task requirements can influence which display designs will be most appropriate. Wickens struments. Dials with common functions can be grouped together by varying factors such as proximity and similarity (see Figure 7–6(a)). Figure 7–6 also illustrates another aspect of organization that is useful for *check reading,* when dials must be checked to determine whether they all register normal operating values. The bottom of Figure 7–6(b) shows a configuration in which the normal settings are indicated by pointers at the same orientation, whereas the top shows a configuration in which they differ. Because orientation is a fundamental organizing feature, it would be much easier to tell from the bottom display than the top that one dial was deviating from normal, as has been found in several studies (Mital & Ramanan, 1985; White, Warrick, & Grether, 1953). With the bottom arrangement, the dial that deviated from the vertical setting would stand out.

Rock and Palmer (1990) have shown two ways in which grouping can be artificially induced by the inclusion of extra contours. Dials or gauges that share a common function can be grouped within an explicit boundary on the display panel or connected by explicit lines (see Figure 7–7). Rock and Palmer call these methods

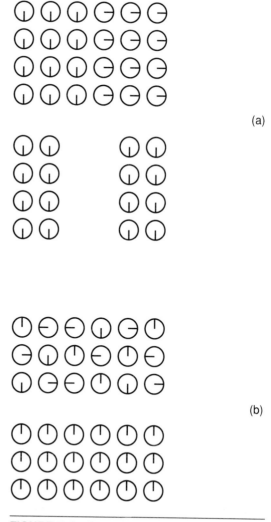

FIGURE 7–6   Displays Grouped by Proximity and Similarity (a) and Display Groups with Similar and Dissimilar Orientations (b).

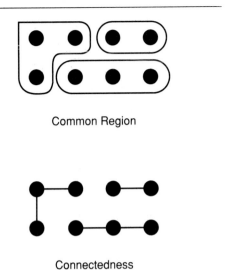

Common Region

Connectedness

FIGURE 7–7   Displays Grouped by Common Region and Connectedness.

and Andre (1990) have demonstrated that, when the task requires integration across display elements, organizational factors have different effects on performance than when the task requires focused attention on a single display element. The task that they used involved three dials that might be found in an aircraft cockpit, indicating air speed, bank, and flaps. Observers either estimated the likelihood of a stall (the integration task) or indicated the reading from one of the three dials (the focused attention task).

Although spatial proximity had no effect in Wickens and Andre's (1990) experiments, they found that performance for focused attention was better when display elements were of different colors than when they were all the same color. In contrast, integration performance was best when all display elements were the same color. Wickens and Andre also experimented with displays that combined the information given by the three elements into a single rectangular object, the position and area of which were determined by air speed, bank, and flaps. They concluded that the usefulness of such displays depends on how well

the emergent feature (the rectangle) conveys task-relevant information.

Depth Perception

Philosophers and psychologists have been concerned for centuries with the question of how we perceive a three-dimensional world from a two-dimensional image. As a first guess, you might think that our ability to see depth is a function of *binocular depth cues* associated with having two eyes. This is in fact part of the story. However, by closing one eye you can see that it is not the entire story. Depth can still be perceived using *monocular depth cues* when the world is viewed with only a single eye.

There are many sources of depth information, as summarized in Figure 7–8. The majority of these come from visual stimulation, with many being monocular. The large number of monocular cues explains why a person can see depth with a single eye. In fact, depth perception from these cues is sufficiently accurate that the ability of pilots to land aircraft is not degraded by patching one eye (Grosslight et al., 1978) and driving practices are no less safe for monocular truck drivers than for binocular truck drivers (McKnight, Shinar, & Hilburn, 1991). The relative contributions of depth cues to three-dimensional perception are of concern in the design of simulator displays (Mazur & Reising, 1990).

Oculomotor Cues. *Oculomotor depth cues* are provided proprioceptively by the muscles of the eye. There are two oculomotor cues to depth, accommodation and vergence. Recall that accommodation refers to automatic adjustments of the lens that occur to maintain a focused image on the retina, and vergence refers to the degree to which the eyes are turned inward to maintain fixation on an object (see Chapter 5). Both accommodation and vergence could act as depth cues through the feedback provided by the muscles that control the setting of the lens and the vergence angle, respectively. The extent of both accommodation and vergence depends on the dis-

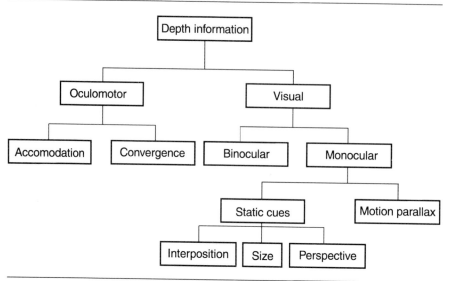

FIGURE 7–8   A Hierarchical Arrangement of the Cues to Depth.
Figure from R. Sekuler & R. Blake, *Perception,* Second Edition. Copyright 1990 by McGraw-Hill, Inc. Reprinted with permission.

tance of the fixed object from the observer. Accommodation only varies for stimuli that are between approximately 20 and 300 cm from the observer. Thus, at most it can serve as a cue for relatively close objects. Vergence varies for objects up to 600 cm from the observer, so it is potentially useful over a wider range of distances than accommodation.

Morrison and Whiteside (1984) evaluated distance estimates for a point source of light when vergence was held constant and accommodation varied, or vice versa. They found that vergence cues enabled relatively accurate distance estimates over a range of several meters, but accommodation cues did not. Surprisingly, the accurate estimates were made with stimulus exposures that were too brief to allow actual vergence changes and hence proprioceptive feedback. Morrison and Whiteside proposed instead that the accuracy arises from observers adopting a constant dark vergence posture. With this constant posture, binocular disparity (see later) could provide accurate depth information. Thus, the

oculomotor cues may enter both directly and indirectly into computations of depth.

Monocular Visual Cues.   Monocular visual cues are sometimes called pictorial cues because they convey impressions of depth in a still photograph. Similarly, artists use these cues to portray depth in paintings. Several of the cues are illustrated in Figure 7–9. The cue of interposition is based on the fact that a near object will block the view of a more distant one if they are in the same line of vision. Depth can be inferred when one image seems to block part of another. The painting shown in Figure 7–10 relies heavily on interposition to portray a collage of three-dimensional objects.

Both retinal and familiar size also provide cues to depth. For an object of constant size, the closer it is to you, the larger is the size of the retinal image. Thus, the relative size of images within the visual field is correlated with distance. Familiar size refers to the fact that, if the size of the object is known, then the absolute size of the

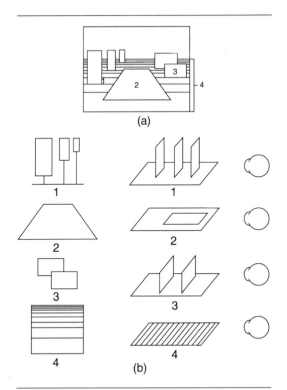

(a)

(b)

FIGURE 7–9   The Depth Cues of Relative Size (1), Linear Perspective (2), Interposition (3), and Texture Gradient (4) in the Complete Image (a) and in Isolation (b).

From Julian E. Hochberg, *Perception*, 2e, © 1978, p. 140. Reprinted by permission of Prentice Hall, Englewood Cliffs, New Jersey.

image can provide information about how far away the object is. Beginning around the late 1970s, the size of the average car began to decrease. In 1985, when larger cars perhaps were still more familiar than small cars, Eberts and MacMillan (1985) noted that small cars were overrepresented in accidents. They proposed that one reason for this is that the smaller visual angle made a less familiar small car look like a more familiar large car far away.

Perspective can also provide depth cues. Usually, two types of perspective are distinguished, aerial perspective and linear perspective. The former refers to interference produced by particles in the air. The farther an object is from you, the more opportunity there is for some of the light from it to be scattered and absorbed. This causes the image from a faraway object to be bluer than images from nearby objects and not as sharply defined. The blue coloration comes from the increased scattering of short-wavelength light compared to long-wavelength light. Linear perspective refers to the fact that parallel lines receding into depth converge to a point in an image. This is true not only for visible lines, but also for the relations among objects that can be captured by invisible lines (see Figure 7–11).

Linear perspective and relative size are combined in what Gibson (1950) calls texture gradients (see Figure 7–12). These gradients refer to the fact that parts of a texture's surface become smaller and more densely packed as they recede in depth. Thus, a systematic texture gradient specifies the depth relations of the surface. If the texture is constant, it is from an object facing the observer directly in the frontal plane. If the texture changes systematically, it indicates a surface that recedes in depth. The rate of change specifies the tilt of the surface.

The attached shadow cue is based on the location of shadows in a picture (Ramachandran, 1988; see Figure 7–13). Regions with shadows at the bottom tend to be perceived as elevated. Regions with shadows at the top tend to be perceived as depressed into the surface. These relations hold when the light source projects from above, as is typically the case. When the light source projects from below, the attached shadow cue can be misleading.

The monocular cues described to this point are available to a stationary observer. However, they become less ambiguous when the observer moves. Additional information about depth relations is provided to a moving observer. If you are riding in a car and fixating on an object at the side, objects in the foreground will appear to move in the direction opposite your movement, whereas objects in the background will seem to move in your direction. This relation is called motion parallax. Also, the closer an object is to

FIGURE 7–10   Edward Collier, Quod Libet (1701). Victoria and Albert Museum, London.

you, the faster its position in the visual field will change. Similar movement cues can be produced by turning your head.

Motion also provides depth information when you move straight ahead. The optical flow of the visual image conveys information about how fast you are moving and how your position is changing relative to those of environmental objects. As you drive down the road, trees on the roadside expand and move outward to the edges of the image (see Figure 7–14). When the typical relation between the speed of your movement and the rate of the optical flow pattern changes, the perception of speed is altered. This is apparent from the window of an airplane taking off. As the plane leaves the ground and altitude increases, the speed at which it is moving seems to decrease.

Binocular Visual Cues.   Although you can see depth relatively well with only one eye, you can perceive depth relations more accurately with

two. This is most obvious when comparing the depth impression that results from a normal picture or movie to that provided by three-dimensional, or stereoscopic, pictures and movies. Stereoscopic pictures mimic the binocular depth information that would be available from a real three-dimensional scene. People can perform most tasks that involve depth information much more rapidly and accurately when using both eyes (Sheedy et al., 1986).

The cues for binocular depth perception arise from *binocular disparity:* each eye receives a slightly different image of the world because of the eyes' different locations. The two images are merged through the process of fusion. When you fixate on an object, the image from the fixated area falls on the fovea of each eye. An imaginary curved plane can be drawn through the fixated object, and the images from any objects located on this plane will fall at the same locations on each retina. This curved plane is called the horop-

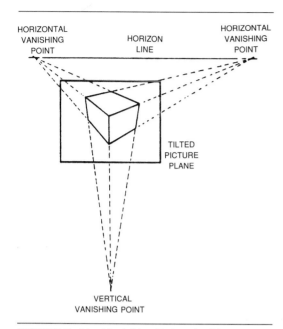

HORIZONTAL VANISHING POINT

HORIZON LINE

HORIZONTAL VANISHING POINT

TILTED PICTURE PLANE

VERTICAL VANISHING POINT

FIGURE 7–11   Vanishing Points for Linear Perspective.

From M. Kubovy, *The Psychology of Perspective and Renaissance Art.* Copyright © 1988 Cambridge University Press. Reprinted by permission of Cambridge University Press.

ter (see Figure 7–15). For objects in front of or behind the horopter, the images will fall on disparate points. Those from objects farther away than the point of fixation will have uncrossed disparity, whereas those closer than fixation will have crossed disparity. The amount of disparity depends on the distance of the object from the horopter, and the direction of disparity indicates whether an object is in front of or behind the horopter. Thus, disparity provides accurate information about depth relative to the fixated object.

Stereoscopic pictures take advantage of binocular disparity to create an impression of depth. A camera takes two pictures at a separation that corresponds to the distance between the eyes. These disparate images then are presented to the respective eyes in a stereoscope. The red and green or polarized lenses used for 3-D movies

accomplish the same purpose. The lenses allow each eye to see a different image.

The process underlying stereopsis is not fully understood. As discussed in Chapter 5, some cortical cells are disparity sensitive; that is, they fire maximally when lines at the two eyes are at a given disparity. These neurons likely play a role in extracting the basic disparity information. However, you can see three-dimensional forms from random-dot stereograms (Julesz, 1971), in which the right stereogram is created by shifting a pattern of dots slightly from the locations in the left stereogram (see Figure 7–16). This perception of objects in depth takes place in the absence of visible contours. The problem, then, is how the visual system determines what dots go together so that depth relations can be computed.

Size and Shape Constancy.   Depth perception is closely related to the phenomena of *size constancy* and *shape constancy*. These refer to the fact that we tend to see an object as having a constant size and shape, regardless of the size (which changes with distance) and shape (which changes with slant) of the retinal image. The relation of these constancies to depth perception is captured by the size–distance and shape–slant invariance hypotheses (Epstein, Park, & Casey, 1961). The former states that perceived size depends on estimated distance; the latter states that perceived shape is a function of estimated slant. The strongest evidence supporting these relations is that size and shape constancy decrease with reduction of depth cues, which provide the basis for estimating distance and slant (Holway & Boring, 1941).

Illusions of Size and Direction.   In most situations, the organizational principles and depth cues produce an unambiguous, accurate percept of objects in three-dimensional space. However, many illusions occur that attest to the fallibility of perception. Several such illusions of size and direction are shown in Figures 7–17 and 7–18.

The illusions of size include lines that are the same physical length or forms that are the same

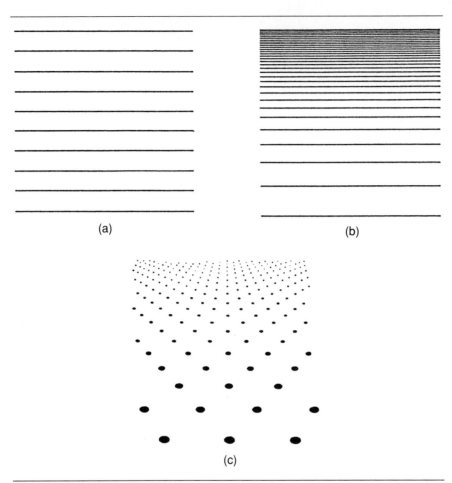

FIGURE 7–12 Texture Gradients for Surfaces (a) Parallel to the Frontal Plane and (b and c) Receding in Depth.

physical size. However, in the context of the illusion, the lines or forms appear to be different. The illusions of direction involve distortions of linearity and shape. Many accounts have been proposed for the various illusions, and several mechanisms are likely involved (Coren & Girgus, 1978). These include misapplied depth processing, displacement of contours, and inaccurate eye movements, among others. As one example, we will examine the depth-processing account of the Ponzo illusion (see Figure 7–17b). The defining feature of this illusion is the two vertical lines with positive and negative slopes that converge

toward the top. Converging lines of this type provide the depth cue of linear perspective, with the convergence indicating parallel lines extending into the distance. Thus, according to this cue, the horizontal line located higher in the display is farther away than the one located lower in the display. Applying the relation between perceived distance and size, the line that is "farther away" must be longer because the image at the retina is the same size as the image for the "closer" line. Hence, the top line is perceived as longer.

Although the illusions are illustrated with two-dimensional line drawings, they can create

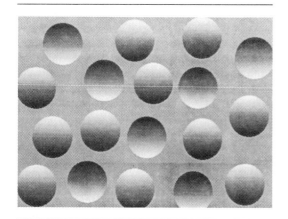

FIGURE 7–13   The Attached Shadow Cue.

From D. A. Kleffner & V. S. Ramachandran (1992). On the perception of shape from shading. *Perception & Psycophysics, 52,* 18–36. Reprinted by permission of Psychonomic Society, Inc.

real-world problems. Coren and Girgus (1978) describe a collision between two commercial aircraft that were approaching the New York city area at 11,000 and 10,000 ft, respectively. At the time, clouds were protruding above a height of 10,000 ft, forming an upward sloping bar of white against the blue sky. The crew of the lower aircraft misperceived the planes to be on a collision course and increased its altitude quickly. The two aircraft then collided at approximately 11,000 ft. The U.S. Civil Aeronautics Board attributed the misjudgment of altitude to a naturally occurring variant of the Poggendorff illusion (see Figure 7–18a) created by the upward-sloping contours of the cloud tops. In the Poggendorff illusion, the two oblique lines do not appear aligned even though they are. The clouds gave the illusion that the two flight paths were aligned even though they were not, and the altitude correction brought

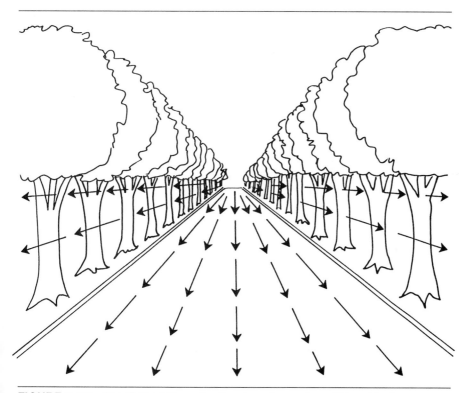

FIGURE 7–14   The Optical Flow of a Roadway Image for a Driver Moving Straight Ahead.

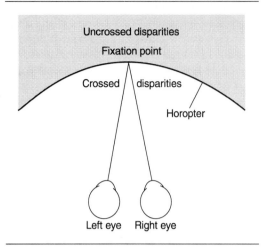

FIGURE 7–15   The Horopter, with Crossed and Uncrossed Disparity Regions Indicated.

the lower plane into a collision course with the upper plane.

A recurring problem for night visual landing approaches is that of landing under "black-hole"

conditions in which only runway lights are visible. In such situations, pilots tend to fly lower approaches than normal, with the consequence that a relatively large number of night-flying accidents involve crashes short of the runway. Experiments have shown that the low approaches arise from overestimates of approach angles due to the insufficiency of the available depth cues (Mertens & Lewis, 1981, 1982). The runway lights provide only relative information regarding such cues as motion parallax and linear perspective, and so the cues must be evaluated according to some familiar standard. Hence, the tendency for low approaches is exacerbated when the runway has a larger ratio of length to width than that of a familiar runway with which the pilot has had recent experience (Mertens & Lewis, 1981).

Perception of Motion

Not only do we perceive a structured, meaningful world, but we see it composed of distinct objects,

FIGURE 7–16   A Random-dot Stereogram in Which the Left and Right Images Are Identical Except for a Central Square Region That Is Displaced Slightly in One Image.

From B. Julesz (1971), *Foundations of Cyclopean Perception,* University of Chicago Press. Reprinted by permission.

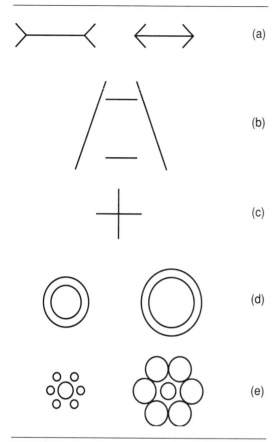

FIGURE 7–17   Illusions of Size: (a) the Müller–Lyer Illusion; (b) the Ponzo Illusion; (c) The Vertical–Horizontal Illusion; (d) a Variation of the Delboeuf Illusion; and (e) the Ebbinghaus Illusion.

Based on Boff and Lincoln (1988).

movement. How the perceptual system resolves the locus of movement constitutes the primary problem in studies of motion perception.

Object Motion.   It is convenient to regard motion perception as involving two systems (Gregory, 1966). The image–retina system responds to changes in retinal position, whereas the eye–head system takes into account the motion from our eye and head movements. Several characteristics of the image–retina system have been

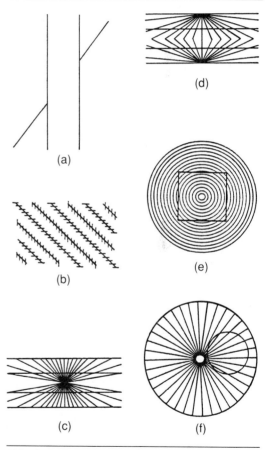

FIGURE 7–18   Illusions of Direction: (a) the Poggendorf Illusion; (b) the Zöllner Illusion; (c) the Hering Illusion; (d) the Wundt Illusion; (e) the Ehrenstein Illusion; and (f) the Orbison Illusion.

Based on Boff and Lincoln (1988).

some stationary and others moving in various directions at different rates of speed. How is motion perceived? An initial answer that you might think of is that changes in displacement of an image on the retina are detected. In fact, many cortical cells are sensitive to motion across the retina and thus could detect such changes (see Chapter 5). However, a problem arises with this simple account if you consider the motion of the observer in the environment. Changes in retinal location can be due either to the movement of objects in the environment or to the observer's

discovered. People are good at discriminating movement as a function of changes in retinal position. Movement can be seen if a small dot moves against a stationary background at speeds as low as 0.2° of visual angle per second. Sensitivity to movement is even greater if a stationary visual reference point is present (Palmer, 1986). In such situations, changes of as little as 0.03° of visual angle per second produce a perception of movement.

Displacement of position on the retina is not sufficient to specify that an object is moving, because the displacement may be due to movement of the observer. Moving objects can be tracked through smooth-pursuit movements of the eyes. Even though the image remains at a foveal location, movement of the object is perceived. Such effects involve the eye–head movement system.

Two theories have been proposed to explain how the eye–head system distinguishes an observer's own movements from movement in the world. Sherrington (1906) proposed what is often called inflow theory. According to this theory, feedback from the muscles that control eye movements is monitored by the brain. The change due to the eye movements is then subtracted from the shift in location of the image on the retina. In contrast, outflow theory, proposed by Helmholtz (1867), states that the motor signal sent to the eyes is monitored. A copy of this outgoing signal, which is called a corollary discharge, is used to cancel the resulting movement of the image on the retina.

Research on motion perception has tended to favor outflow theory over inflow theory. The initial evidence for outflow theory provided by Helmholtz was that the visual world appears to move when you press on the lid of the eye with a finger. Helmholtz proposed that movement is incorrectly seen because there is no corollary discharge associated with commands to the eye muscles to indicate that the eye moved. More recent work has shown that such apparent movement can occur when the eye actually remains

stable on a fixated target, with the eye muscles providing force to prevent the finger pressure from moving the eye (Bridgeman & Delgado, 1984; Stark & Bridgeman, 1983). In this situation, the false movement is seen because there is a corollary discharge but no movement of the eye. Further evidence supporting the outflow theory comes from studies in which curare was used to temporarily paralyze an observer. When the observer tries to move his or her eyes (which do not actually move), the scene appears to move to a new position (Matin et al., 1982; Stevens et al., 1976).

Induced Motion. Although a stationary visual context increases sensitivity to movement, it also can lead to illusions of movement. In such illusions, movement is attributed to the wrong part of the visual display. This phenomenon can be observed when the clouds pass over the moon at night, yet it is the moon that appears to be moving. This also occurs when a test patch of stationary texture appears to move upward when it is surrounded by a downward-drifting inducing texture. When the test and inducing objects are in close spatial proximity, the effect is called *motion contrast*. Motion contrast may be due to lateral inhibitory interactions among motion detectors (Anstis, 1986).

When the test and inducing objects are spatially separated, the phenomenon is called *induced motion*. It can be demonstrated when one of two stimuli is larger than and encloses another. If the larger stimulus moves, at least part of the movement is attributed to the smaller, enclosed stimulus. The enclosing figure is presumed to serve as a frame of reference relative to which the smaller stimulus is displaced (Mack, 1986).

Apparent Motion. Discrete changes in position on the retina can produce *apparent motion*. That is, continuous motion will be perceived. We introduced this phenomenon when discussing Gestalt psychology. It is the basis for the perceived movement of lights on a theater marquee, as well as for the movement perceived in motion pictures and on television. The fact that we perceive smooth movement from motion pictures conveys the power of apparent movement.

Much work on apparent motion has been conducted with simple displays, such as the two lights used to illustrate stroboscopic motion. Apparent motion can be obtained over separations of 18°, with the interval that produces optimal motion increasing with increasing spatial separation. The current view is that two processes contribute to the perception of apparent motion. A short-range process operates over short spaces (15′ of visual angle or less) over short time periods (100 ms or less). This system probably is a function of the cortical motion-detector cells (Baker & Braddick, 1985). A long-range process operates across large spaces (tens of degrees of separation) and over time intervals of up to 500 ms. This process appears to involve more complex inferential operations.

Pattern Recognition

Whereas perceptual organization is concerned with how organized forms are perceived, pattern recognition involves the question of how we identify the forms. Feature models have been developed to explain pattern recognition. In Chapter 5, it was shown how basic features such as line orientation serve to organize visual information. Treisman (1986) has provided evidence that such features are extracted at a preattentive stage of processing. For example, when you have to search for a target element of one orientation in an array of noise elements of another orientation, the time to determine whether the target is present is not influenced by the number of noise elements in the array (array size). Similar results are obtained when the target differs in color from the noise elements. This lack of influence for array size is in contrast to situations in which the target is defined by a combination of primitive features, such as color and orientation, both of which are present among the noise elements in the array. In

the latter case, reaction times increase linearly as a function of the number of noise elements, suggesting that the decision about whether the target is present requires attention and is effortful.

The visual search findings imply that highlighting a subset of options in a computer display by presenting them in a distinct color should shorten the time for users to search the display. This implication has been confirmed in several studies (Fisher et al., 1989; Fisher & Tan, 1989). Users are faster when a target is in the highlighted set and slower when it is not or when no highlighting is used. Moreover, the benefit of highlighting is greater when the probability is high that the target will be in the highlighted set than when the probability is low.

Another distinction of importance is that of integral and separable dimensions (Garner, 1974). Dimensions are said to be integral if it is not possible to specify a value on one feature dimension without also specifying the value on the other dimension. For example, the hue and brightness of a colored form are integral feature dimensions. If dimensional combinations can exist independently of one another, they are called separable. For example, color and form are separable dimensions. You can attend to each of two separable feature dimensions independently, but you cannot do so for two integral dimensions. Thus, judgments based on the feature of a stimulus can be made faster and more accurately if the dimensions are separable, whereas judgments based on the whole stimulus are easier for integral dimensions that are perfectly correlated. That is, a specific value on one dimension always occurs in the presence of a specific value on the other dimension.

A third type of dimension, called configural, can be distinguished. Configural dimensions interact in such a manner that a new emergent feature is created (Pomerantz, 1981). The emergent feature can either facilitate or interfere with performance, as illustrated in Figure 7–19. In each case, contextual stimuli are added that do not in themselves provide information. However, in

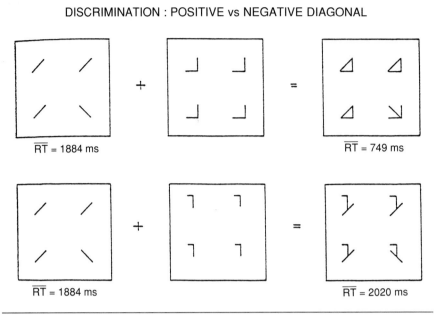

FIGURE 7–19   The Additional Configural Context That Facilitates (Top Row) and Impedes (Bottom Row) Detection of the Negative Diagonal.
Based on Pomerantz (1981).

combination with the original pattern they act to increase (Figure 7–19a) or decrease (Figure 7–19b) the speed with which the odd member can be detected.

Feature models propose that pattern recognition is based on the features that are preattentively analyzed by the visual system. One such model is Selfridge's (1959) Pandemonium, which proposes different levels of "demons" (detectors). As shown in Figure 7–20, the sensory input is signaled by an image demon to feature demons that are sensitive to orientation, curvature, or the like. These feature demons "shout" with an intensity in proportion to the match between the image and the feature for which the demon is sensitive. The feature demons provide input to cognitive demons that are responsive to particular combinations of features. A decision demon then identifies the pattern as the one that corresponds to the "loudest" cognitive demon.

Feature models like Pandemonium can account well for phenomena such as the errors that people make when trying to identify alphabetic characters. When a letter is exposed briefly, the most common identification error is to report a letter that is visually similar to the one that was exposed (Gilmore et al., 1979; Townsend, 1971). The more features two letters share, the more likely that confusions will occur. This relation is predicted by feature models, because the elementary features provide the evidence about what letter was present.

Feature models can also be extended to account for word identification. Figure 7–21 presents three alternative models of the relation between letter detectors and word detectors (Pollatsek & Rayner, 1989). The first alternative is a direct word-recognition model in which word identification proceeds in parallel with letter identification. The general idea is that configural

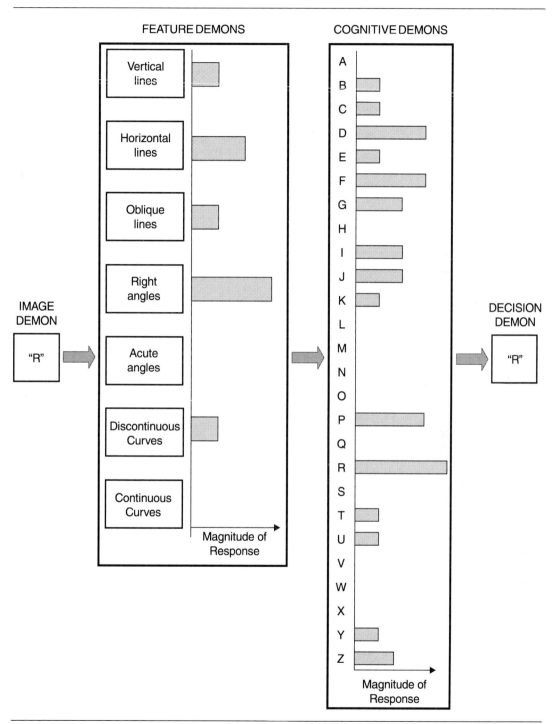

FIGURE 7–20   The Pandemonium Pattern-recognition Model.

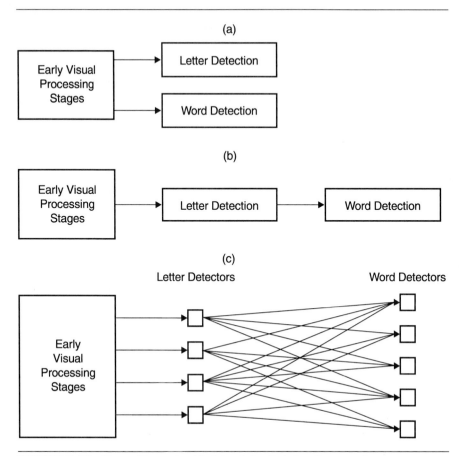

FIGURE 7–21   Three Alternative Models of the Relation Between Letter Identification and Word Identification: (a) Direct Word Recognition Model; (b) Serial Letter Model; and (c) Parallel Letter Model.

From A. Pollatsek & K. Rayner, Reading. In M. I. Posner, *Handbook of Cognitive Science.* Copyright © 1989 by The MIT Press. Reprinted by permission.

properties specific to words allow their identification without the need for identification of the component letters. The second alternative is a serial letter model in which words are identified by a serial scan of previously identified letters. The final alternative is a parallel letter model in which the activation from the letter detectors is sent in parallel to the word detectors. Thus, according to the second and third models, word identification is dependent on letter detectors.

A phenomenon that bears on these models is the word-superiority effect, which is that a letter can be identified better within a word context than without. Reicher (1969) established this effect by briefly presenting a word that differed by one letter from another possible word (for example, WORK versus WORD). At the offset of the word, two letters were presented (K or D), one of which had been in the word. People identified the correct letter with higher accuracy in the word context than when the letter was presented in a nonword context (for example, ORWK) or alone.

The word-superiority effect is inconsistent with the serial letter model because, in this model, word identification occurs only after the letters have been identified. The direct word-recognition model can accommodate the effect because the word-identification route provides a redundant means for identifying the component letters. Similarly, the parallel letter model can explain the word-superiority effect by allowing feedback from the word detectors to the letter detectors. Other evidence favors this latter model (Pollatsek & Rayner, 1989). For example, people can read text in which the letters alternate between uppercase and lowercase almost as well as they can read normal text (Coltheart & Freeman, 1974). This suggests that the configural properties of the whole word are unimportant, contrary to the direct word-recognition model.

To this point, our discussion of pattern recognition has focused on the analysis of elementary features of sensory input. It is generally agreed that such an analysis alone does not determine what we perceive. Expectancies induced by the context also affect what is perceived. We already know from the discussion of signal-detection theory that expectancies influence the criteria for perceiving simple stimuli. Similar mechanisms are presumed to be involved on a larger scale for more complex tasks. For instance, models of word recognition often include a criterion for each word detector so that recognition of a word is a function of both the sensory evidence and the criterion setting (Morton, 1969). As might be expected, word identification under degraded conditions is faster and more accurate when a sentence context is provided than when no context is provided.

Similar expectancy effects occur for objects in the world. Biederman, Glass, and Stacy (1973) presented organized and jumbled pictures and had people search for specific objects within these pictures. They presumed that the jumbled picture would not allow the viewers to use their expectations to aid in searching for the object. Consistent with this hypothesis, search times for coherent scenes were much faster than those for jumbled scenes. Biederman, Glass, and Stacy also examined the influence of probable and improbable objects within the coherent and jumbled scenes. They found that for both kinds of pictures it was much easier to determine that an improbable object was not present than to determine that a probable object was not present. This finding indicates that observers develop expectations about objects that are possible in a scene with a particular theme. What we perceive thus is influenced by our expectancies, as well as by the information provided by the senses.

The influence of expectations is critical when objects fall into the peripheral visual field (Biederman et al., 1981). It is difficult to detect an unexpected object in the periphery, particularly when it is small. Miss rates increase to 70% as the location of an unexpected object shifts from the fovea to 4° in the periphery. The miss rate for a peripheral object is reduced approximately by half when the object is expected.

Biological Motion

You might not think of motion as providing information for pattern recognition, but research on biological motion has shown that it does. The patterns of movement of people and other living organisms are complex and distinct from the patterns of movement shown by inanimate objects. Johansson (1975) demonstrated that little information is required to recognize biological movement. He attached light bulbs to the elbows, wrists, shoulders, hips, knees, and ankles of a person and filmed the person moving in the dark. Whereas the observers perceived a meaningless pattern of lights when the lights were stationary, they immediately perceived a person when the lights started moving. Thus, the complex patterns of movement at the bodily locations marked by the lights were sufficient for the perception of human locomotion. Subsequent research has shown that with presentations of just a brief section of film it is possible to determine how many individuals are present, their genders, and the activities in which they are engaged (for example, dancing).

Runeson and Frykholm (1983) have proposed that the information conveyed by biological motion arises from the biomechanical constraints imposed by the human movement system. They argue that the movement patterns specify the dynamics that underlie them. In a series of experiments, Runeson and Frykholm showed that observers can perceive the distance that an invisible object is thrown and the weight of a box that is being lifted. Moreover, the observers could not be deceived by the actions of the filmed person.

The perception of gender in these displays appears to have such a biomechanical basis (Cutting, 1978). When a person walks, an oscillatory motion of the body is produced. This motion is around a center of movement that is at the intersection of two lines; one connects the left shoulder and the right hip and the other connects the right shoulder and left hip. Because females have broader hips and narrower shoulders than males, the center of movement is relatively higher in females than in males. With computer-generated displays consisting of this information alone, the gender can be easily identified. As would be expected from the biomechanical nature of this information, observers are not easily deceived by someone trying to move like someone of the opposite gender (Runeson & Frykholm, 1983).

Two Visual Systems Concept

Chapter 5 introduced the view that distinct neural systems may mediate different aspects of visual performance. Leibowitz and his associates (Leibowitz & Owens, 1986; Leibowitz & Post, 1982; Leibowitz et al., 1982) have pursued the implications of this view for night driving. Consistent with the parvocellular and magnocellular distinction presented earlier, they have identified a focal mode of processing that is concerned with object recognition and identification and an ambient mode that mediates locomotion and spatial orientation. Focal vision is concerned primarily with the central visual field, whereas the ambient system is based on changes across the entire visual field. For driving, the focal mode is involved in the identification of road signs and objects in the environment, whereas the ambient mode directs guidance of the vehicle.

Night-driving fatality rates are three to four times as great as daytime rates when adjusted for the amount of hours driven. Leibowitz and his associates propose that the high fatality rate arises in part from selective impairment of the focal system. The ease and accuracy with which objects can be recognized decreases greatly under the low levels of illumination present for night driving. However, the ambient system involved in guidance is relatively unaffected. In other words, drivers can steer vehicles as easily at night as during the day. Moreover, most objects that require recognition, for example, road signs and dashboard instruments, are illuminated or highly reflective. Consequently, drivers underestimate the extent to which focal perception is impaired and do not reduce speed accordingly.

The impairment of the focal system becomes critical when a nonilluminated obstacle, such as a pedestrian, appears in the road. By the time the driver recognizes the object, it is too late to stop. In fact, for many cases drivers report not seeing a pedestrian before the accident. Leibowitz and Owens (1986) recommend that drivers be educated about the selective impairment of recognition vision at night as one measure that might reduce night accidents.

AUDITORY PERCEPTION

Our range of auditory perceptions is nearly as rich as that of our visual perceptions. We can perceive complex patterns, determine the locations of stimuli in the environment, and recognize speech with proficiency. Consequently, it is important to know the ways in which auditory perception is influenced by organizational factors, spatial cues, and the features of speech stimuli.

Perceptual Organization

Although the principles of perceptual organization have been studied most thoroughly for vision, they also apply to the other senses. For audition, the principles of proximity and similarity play a major role. In hearing, temporal proximity of tones is more important than spatial proximity. Tones that follow each other close together in time will tend to be perceived as belonging together.

Similarity is determined primarily by the pitch of the tones. Tones with similar pitches tend to be grouped together perceptually. This point was illustrated by Heise and Miller (1951). They played a sequence of tones for which the frequency increased linearly. A tone in the middle was heard as part of the sequence even if its frequency was a bit higher than it should be at that location in the series. However, when the frequency of this tone became too deviant, it was heard as an isolated tone against the background of the increasing sequence.

In music, a rapid alternation between high- and low-frequency notes leads to the perception of two distinct melodies. This effect is called auditory stream segregation. Bregman and Rudnicky (1975) showed that the way that tones are organized can influence performance. They presented listeners with two standard tones, A and B, that differed in frequency (see Figure 7–22). The task was to determine which tone occurred first. When the tones were presented in isolation, performance was good, but when the tones were preceded and followed by a distractor tone of lower frequency, performance was poor. However, if additional captor tones of the same frequency as the distractor tones were presented before and after the distractor tones, performance again was good. Apparently, the captor tones caused the distractor tones to be segregated into one auditory stream and the standard tones into another stream. Consequently, the standard tones did not "get lost" among the distractors, and their order was easy to perceive.

Sound Localization

Although audition is not primarily a spatial sense, we still are able to perceive some information about spatial location. For example, as a train moves toward you and then past, there is a systematic transformation in the frequency of the sound pattern that results in a shift of pitch corresponding to the changes in location (the Doppler

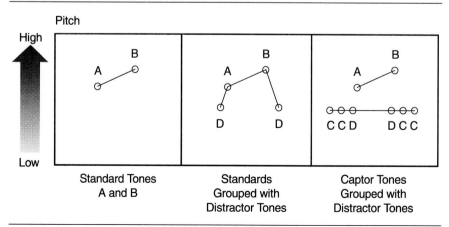

FIGURE 7–22 Auditory Streaming: Standards (Left); Grouped with Distractor Tones (Center); Distractor Tones Grouped with Captor Tones (Right).

effect). Most research on spatial perception in hearing has been on sound localization, which we will consider here.

Our ability to localize briefly presented sounds is relatively good. In a typical experiment on sound localization, the listener will be blind-folded. Sounds are then presented from various locations around the listener. In most cases, the location of the sound can be identified accurately.

Accurate sound localization depends on having two ears. Two different sources of information have been identified: *interaural intensity differences* and *interaural time differences*. The relative intensity at each ear varies systematically as the location of a sound is moved from front to back. When the sound is at the front of the listener, the intensity at each ear is the same. As the location changes progressively toward the right side, the intensity at the right ear relative to the left increases, with the difference reaching a maximum when the sound is directly to the right. As the location is moved behind the observer, the difference shifts back toward zero.

What causes the intensity differences? The answer to this question is that the head produces a sound shadow, much like the way that a large rock produces a dead spot behind it in the flow of a stream. This sound shadow is only significant for frequencies above approximately 4 kHz. The reason for this limitation is that the head is too small relative to the length of the low-frequency sound waves to cause a disturbance.

The interaural time differences show a pattern of change similar to the intensity differences when the origin of a tone is moved. In contrast to the intensity differences, the time differences are most effective for low-frequency tones. The generally accepted view is that interaural time differences are used to localize low-frequency sounds, whereas interaural intensity differences are used to localize high-frequency sounds.

You should note that both cues are ambiguous, in that two different locations on each side (one toward the front, the other toward the back) produce similar time and intensity relations. Some information distinguishing the locations

comes from different coloration of the sounds provided by the pinna. Also, head movements provide dynamic changes that allow a sound to be localized more accurately (Makous & Middle-brooks, 1990). When head movements are precluded, front–back reversals are the most common types of errors.

Anything that decreases the intensity of an auditory signal reaching the ears should decrease the localization accuracy, particularly if it alters the relative timing and intensity relations at the two ears. Caelli and Porter (1980) obtained results consistent with this point. Listeners sat in a car and judged the direction from which a siren sounded. Localization accuracy was poor when all windows were rolled up, with front–back reversals predominating. Accuracy was even worse when the driver-side window was rolled down, as would be expected because of the alteration of the relative-intensity cue.

Speech Perception

Auditory patterns of stimulation must be recognized and identified in order to perceive speech. Speech patterns can be processed quickly and effortlessly. As with most perception, the ease with which speech can be perceived does not reflect the complexity of the processing that must be performed by the speech pattern-recognition system.

The basic unit for speech is the *phoneme,* which is the smallest segment that when changed will alter the meaning of a word. The phonemes for English, which correspond to the vowel and consonant sounds, are shown in Figure 7–23. Because a change in the phoneme results in the perception of a different utterance, people must have the ability to identify phonemes. Much research on auditory perception has concentrated on the way in which this identification occurs.

Figure 7–24 illustrates a *speech spectrogram* for a short speech utterance. The abcissa of the figure indicates time, and the ordinate indicates the frequency of sound. The dark regions at any point in time show that the acoustic signal in-

Major consonants and vowels of English and their phonetic symbols					
Consonants			**Vowels**		
p	pea	θ	thigh	i	beet	o	go
b	beet	ð	thy	ɪ	bit	ɔ	ought
m	man	s	see	e	ate	a	dot
t	toy	ʒ	measure	ɛ	bet	ə	sofa
d	dog	tʃ	chip	æ	bat	ɝ	urn
n	neat	dʒ	jet	u	boot	ai	bite
k	kill	l	lap	ʊ	put	aʊ	out
g	good	r	rope	ʌ	but	ɔɪ	toy
f	foot	y	year	ɒ	odd	ou	own
ç	huge	w	wet				
h	hot	ŋ	sing				
v	vote	z	zip				
ʍ	when	ʃ	show				

FIGURE 7–23   Phonemes of the English Language.

Figure from *Sensation & Perception,* Third Edition, by Stanley Coren and Lawrence M. Ward, copyright © 1989 by Harcourt Brace Jovanovich, Inc., reprinted by permission of publisher.

cludes energy at those frequencies. Most of the energy is contained in distinct, horizontal bands of frequencies, which are called formants. The formants represent the vowel sounds in utter-ances. The initial consonant phonemes correspond to formant transitions (or changes) that occur early in the signal. The problem faced by researchers is to identify the information in the acoustic signal that indicates the presence of specific phonemes.

An obvious starting point is to look for invariant acoustic cues, that is, aspects of the acoustic signal that uniquely accompany particular phonemes in all speech contexts. However, when speech spectrograms are examined, no obvious invariant cues are present. This point is illustrated by a schematic spectrogram used to produce artificial speech corresponding to the utterances *dee* and *do* (see Figure 7–25). Because the vowel phonemes are different, it is not surprising that the formants for the two utterances differ. However, the consonant phoneme is the same in the context of the two vowels, yet the formant transitions are not. Note that the transition for the higher-frequency formant rises in the acoustic signal for *dee* but falls in the signal for *do*. Because of this and other examples of acoustic variability for phonemes in the speech spectrogram, researchers decided that perception must occur by some means other than invariant cues. One group of researchers proposed that this was accomplished by relating the acoustic signal for speech to the way that we produce the sounds (see, for example, Mattingly & Studdert-Kennedy, 1991).

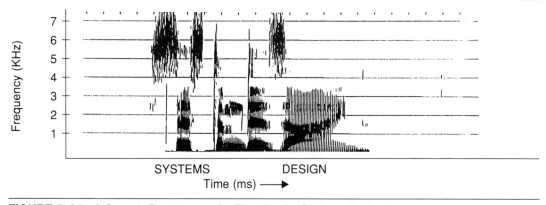

FIGURE 7–24   A Speech Spectrogram for The Words "Systems Design."
Courtesy of David Pisoni.

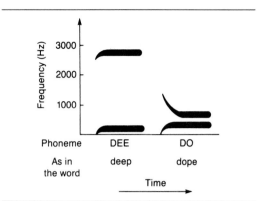

FIGURE 7–25 Artificial Speech Spectrograms for "Dee" and "Do."

Figure from *Sensation & Perception,* Third Edition, by Stanley Coren and Lawrence M. Ward, copyright © 1989 by Harcourt Brace Jovanovich, Inc., reprinted by permission of the publisher.

However, short-term spectra have provided new evidence for invariant acoustic cues (Kewley-Port & Luce, 1984). The short-term spectra provide detailed pictures of the energies that are produced during a brief period of time. They then can be combined into a sequence of running spectral displays. These displays show relatively invariant properties of the signal corresponding to distinct phonemes, as well as variable information. It is now thought that the invariant information, combined with the variable information specific to certain contexts, is sufficient to provide the basis for accurate identification of speech sounds.

One phenomenon in speech perception that has received considerable interest is *categorical perception.* This can be illustrated with the sounds *da* and *ta,* which differ primarily in terms of voice onset time (that is, the delay between when the utterance begins and the vocal cords start vibrating). With artificial speech, the onset time can be varied between the 17-ms value for *da* and the 91-ms value for *ta.* But what do perceivers hear for these intermediate onsets? The answer is that the stimuli are heard as either *da* or *ta,* with a relatively sharp boundary occurring at

an intermediate onset. Moreover, stimuli to the same side of the boundary cannot be distinguished by observers even when their voicing onsets differ. In other words, the physical differences between the stimuli are not heard; the stimuli are strictly categorized as *da* or *ta.*

One finding with categorical perception is that the boundary can be shifted through selective adaptation (Eimas & Corbit, 1973). If a person hears a voiced sound (for example, *ba*) repeatedly for several minutes and then is asked to identify the ambiguous stimulus, the category boundary shifts toward a shorter voice onset time. That is, more of the stimuli are heard as the unvoiced *ta.* Roberts and Summerfield (1981) showed that the adaptation is a function of the acoustic signal. When people see the filmed lip movements of a person saying *ga,* but the auditory signal is *ba,* they hear *da.* Roberts and Summerfield used this situation for adaptation and then presented ambiguous stimuli to be classified. The resulting category shift was consistent with the auditory signal (*ba*), rather than with the sound that had been perceived (*da*). Thus, the evidence suggests that categorization likely occurs on the basis of cortical neurons that respond differentially to voicing delays in the acoustic signal.

Other research on speech perception has focused on conversational speech. When considering such speech, the problem of accurate perception becomes much more complex. In conversational speech, no physical boundaries exist between words. The boundaries that we hear are imposed by the perceptual system. Additionally, words are not enunciated clearly in conversational speech. When individual words are isolated from conversation, they are difficult to identify. If the context in which a word is embedded is insufficient, the word may be confused for one that sounds similar. Such an incident occurred on an interstate bus when a passenger shouted, "There is a bum in the bathroom!" However, the bus driver mistakenly heard the utterance as "There is a bomb in the bathroom." Consequently, the bus was stopped, state troopers were called, the highway was blocked off, and the bus was searched by a bomb-sniffing dog. The transient in the bathroom was charged with misdemeanor theft for avoiding the price of a ticket (Associated Press wire story, 1990b).

Because of the complexity of conversational speech, speech perception depends heavily on *semantic* and *syntactic context*. This is illustrated in a classic experiment by Miller and Isard (1963). They had listeners repeat aloud strings of words as they heard them. The strings were either (1) normal sentences (for example, "Bears steal honey from the hive."), (2) semantically anomalous but grammatically correct sentences (for example, "Bears shoot work on the country."), or (3) ungrammatical strings (for example, "Across bears eyes work the kill."). The percentage of complete strings repeated accurately was lowest for the ungrammatical strings (56%). The semantically anomalous sentences were repeated with higher accuracy (79%), indicating that consistency with grammatical rules benefits perception. Moreover, performance was even better for the meaningful sentences (89%), indicating that semantic context is also beneficial.

One of the more intriguing context effects is the phonemic restoration effect. Warren (1970) had people listen to the passage "The state governors met with their respective legislatures convening in the capital city," with the first *s* in "legislatures" replaced by a cough. No one noticed that the *s* was missing or could identify the location of the cough. This effect also occurred when the context prior to the word was ambiguous, and the phoneme had to be determined from subsequent words. Once again, the phoneme was constructed by the perceptual system on the basis of the sentence context. For restoration of linguistic as well as nonlinguistic auditory stimuli, the context not only must provide suffient cues, but the interpolated sound must also be in the frequency range for which the replaced sound could potentially be masked (Bashford, Riener, & Warren, 1992). The findings obtained with conversational speech indicate that expectancies influence speech perception, much as they do visual pattern recognition.

TACTILE PERCEPTION

We can perceive forms and objects through the sense of touch, as well as through vision. One of the most important distinctions made in tactile perception is between *passive touch* and *active touch*. In passive touch, the skin is stationary and an external pressure stimulus is applied to it. This type of procedure was used to obtain the absolute and two-point thresholds discussed in Chapter 6. In active touch, the person contacts the stimulus by moving the skin. This corresponds more to what we do when we grasp an object and try to identify it.

Gibson (1950) emphasized that passive touch results in the perception of pressure on the skin, whereas active touch results in the perception of the object touched. Although the reasons for these quite distinct perceptual experiences are not fully understood, probably the most important factor is the purposiveness of active touch. That is, an object is manipulated with the purpose of identifying it; expectancies about the object are likely used to encode the relations among the sequence of sensations. The important point for human factors is that movement of stimuli across the skin is required for accurate perception. This is similar to the role of movement in visual perception that was demonstrated by the phenomenon of biological motion.

It is well known that people can read from tactual input, as well as from visual input. Because the tactual sense is not as sensitive to spatial details as vision, the forms must be relatively large and more distinct. The Braille alphabet is one system that meets this requirement. A trained Braille reader can read a maximum of about 100 words per minute, whereas an average visual reader can read at 250 to 300 words per minute. The slower reading speed with Braille reflects the lower tactile acuity and the resulting fact that Braille characters must be sufficiently wide so that only a single letter is perceived at a time.

Research has also examined the tactile presentation of nontext material. Graphical material has been presented in a tangible form, with the components of the graph depicted by raised surfaces. One question is whether the graph should include a grid to aid in localizing points. The answer seems to depend on the information that must be identified from the graph. For questions about position, performance is better with a grid than without, whereas for questions about overall configuration, performance tends to be better without the grid (Aldrich & Parkin, 1987; Lederman & Campbell, 1982).

SUMMARY

Perception involves considerably more than just passive transmission of information from the sensory receptors. The perceived environment is constructed around cues provided by numerous sensory sources. These cues allow for both two- and three-dimensional organization of visual, auditory, and tactile information, as well as for pattern recognition. The cues are comprised of encoded relations among stimulus items, such as orientation, depth, and context.

Because perception is constructed, misperceptions can occur if cues are false or misleading or if the display is inconsistent with what is expected. It is important, therefore, to display information in ways that minimize perceptual ambiguities and conform to the expectancies of the observer. Chapter 8 discusses how information can be displayed to optimize the accuracy of perception.

RECOMMENDED READING

Bregman, A. S. (1990). *Auditory Scene Analysis: The Perceptual Organization of Sound.* Cambridge, MA: MIT Press.

Bruce, V., & Green, P. R. (1990). *Visual Perception: Physiology, Psychology, and Ecology,* 2nd ed. Hillsdale, NJ: Lawrence Erlbaum.

Cutting, J. E. (1986). *Perception with an Eye for Motion.* Cambridge, MA: MIT Press.

Handel, S. (1989). *Listening: An Introduction to the Perception of Auditory Events.* Cambridge, MA: MIT Press.

Kubovy, M., & Pomerantz, J. R. (eds.) (1981). *Perceptual Organization.* Hillsdale, NJ: Lawrence Erlbaum.

CHAPTER 8

THE DISPLAY OF VISUAL, AUDITORY, AND TACTILE INFORMATION

The information was presented in a manner to confuse operators.

—Report of the President's Commission on the Accident at Three Mile Island

INTRODUCTION

From its outset, the discipline of human factors has been concerned with the design of displays for human use. In complex human–machine interfaces, such as the cockpit of an aircraft or the control room of a nuclear power plant, well-designed displays are a necessity. However, display design considerations are equally important in other less complex situations. For example, the increased use of visual display terminals that has accompanied the development of computer workstations and microcomputers has led to concern about the optimal designs for such displays. Moreover, instructional labels and the signs used in public facilities can vary in the efficiency with which they communicate the intended information to the user. The present chapter examines factors to consider in display design, with particular emphasis on relating the design guidelines to the principles of human perception.

Although we have treated the respective sensory systems separately, our perceptual experience is based on a coordinated organization of the information arriving through all the senses. Consequently, complex interactions among the senses occur, such as the influence of lip movements on speech perception described in Chapter 7. One phenomenon evident in a variety of circumstances is *visual dominance*. This refers to the fact that, when conflicting or simultaneous information occurs through different senses, the visual system often determines what we perceive.

An example of visual dominance comes from a study by Colavita (1974). Observers were to respond to a light with one hand and a tone with the other. On most occasions, only a light or tone was presented. Despite the fact that responses were faster to the tone than to the light alone, when both were presented together, observers almost invariably responded to the light. In many cases, they were not even aware that the tone had occurred. Moreover, even when instructed to respond to the tone on conflict trials, more responses were made to the light. Visual stimuli similarly seem to dominate over proprioception and touch (Klein & Posner, 1974).

Posner, Nissen, and Klein (1976) have proposed that visual dominance is related to a relatively poor alerting ability of the visual system. Because stimuli in other modalities can attract attention more readily, perception maintains a bias toward the visual system. Thus, an abrupt auditory stimulus is more useful than a visual stimulus for alerting an operator, but otherwise the auditory modality generally is at a disadvantage when visual events are occurring simultaneously with auditory events.

The majority of displays encountered in human–machine systems are either visual or auditory. Tactile displays are used for limited purposes, such as for controls that must be identified by feel and for conveying spatially distributed information to the blind. Smell and taste displays are rarely used. Thus, the initial decision in display design often is whether to use visual or auditory displays. Table 8–1 presents general guidelines for determining whether the visual or auditory modality is most appropriate for a particular display application. These guidelines are based on the distinct characteristics of the two senses, as well as on characteristics of the environment in which the display will be used.

If the environment is noisy or the auditory system is overburdened by other auditory infor-

TABLE 8–1   When to Use Auditory or Visual Displays

Use auditory presentation if:
1. The message is simple.
2. The message is short.
3. The message will not be referred to later.
4. The message deals with events in time.
5. The message calls for immediate action.
6. The visual system of the person is overburdened.
7. The receiving location is too bright or dark-adaptation integrity is necessary.
8. The person's job requires continual motion.

Use visual presentation if:
1. The message is complex.
2. The message is long.
3. The message will be referred to later.
4. The message deals with location in space.
5. The message does not call for immediate action.
6. The auditory system of the person is overburdened.
7. The receiving location is too noisy.
8. The person's job allows remaining in one position.

From B. H. Deatherage (1972). Auditory and other sensory forms of information presentation. In H. P. Van Cott and R. G. Kinkade (Eds.), *Human Engineering Guide to Equipment Design* (revised edition, pp. 123–160). U.S. Government Printing Office.

mation, auditory messages may be masked and difficult to perceive. In such situations a visual display will usually be most effective. When the visual field is cluttered, visually displayed information may be difficult to perceive, and so auditory displays may be more appropriate. A visual display must be located in the field of view if it is to be seen, whereas the exact location of an auditory display in relation to the person is usually unimportant. Therefore, the position and movements of the operator partially determine the best modality for information presentation.

Because spatial discriminations can be made most accurately with vision, spatial information is best conveyed through visual displays. Likewise, because temporal organization is a primary attribute of auditory perception, temporal information is best conveyed through auditory displays. Auditory information must be integrated over time, which provides the basis for the recommendation that auditory messages should be simple, short, and not needed for later operations. Finally, because auditory signals attract attention more readily than visual signals, auditory signals should be used when immediate action is required.

VISUAL DISPLAYS

One of the first applications of human factors was in the design of aircraft display panels for the military. Considerably more research has been conducted since that early work, resulting in a substantial data base on the optimal design of visual displays. A basic distinction can be made between *static* and *dynamic displays*. Static displays are fixed and do not change, for example, road signs, signs marking exits in buildings, or labels on equipment. Dynamic displays change over time and include such instruments as speedometers, pressure gauges, and altimeters. Dynamic displays usually have many static features, for instance, the tick marks and digits on the dial of a speedometer. Consequently, we will discuss static displays first, followed by dynamic displays.

Static Displays

Effectiveness of Displays.   Several factors must be considered when designing a good static display (Helander, 1987). Principles that enhance the effectiveness of visual displays are shown in Table 8–2. Of primary concern is the *conspicuity* and *visibility* of the display. Conspicuity is how well a sign attracts attention, whereas visibility is how well a sign can be seen. Visual acuity and color sensitivity decrease as a stimulus moves out farther into the periphery of the visual field (see Chapters 5 and 6). Thus, a display or sign should be located where people are likely to be looking, or it should be designed to attract attention so that it will be fixated. Also, the specific environmental conditions under which the display will be viewed should be determined to ensure that it will be visible under those conditions.

One successful human factors analysis involves the centrally mounted brakelight that has been required on automobiles in the United States since 1986. Several studies were conducted in which different configurations of brakelights were field tested on cabs and company vehicles. These studies found that rear-end collisions were reduced by approximately 50% for vehicles that had the high, central brakelight, with less damage when such collisions did occur. The center-mounted brakelight is more conspicuous than brakelights at other locations because it is placed directly in the line of sight (Malone, 1986).

Conspicuity is also of concern in several other aspects of driving. Motorcycles are not very conspicuous under all driving conditions; neither are tractor-trailer rigs at night. Accidents can be decreased by increasing the conspicuity of these vehicles. For motorcycles, daytime conspicuity is better when the headlamp is on and when the cyclist wears a fluorescent vest and helmet cover (Sivak, 1987). At night, the conspicuity of both motorcycles and tractor-trailers can be increased by the use of reflectorized materials and running lights.

Sign conspicuity is a function of the number of other displays in the field of view. Just as with

TABLE 8–2   Principles That Enhance the Effectiveness of Visual Displays

Conspicuity: The sign should attract attention and be located where people will be looking. Three main factors determine the amount of attention people devote to a sign: prominence, novelty, and relevance.

Visibility: The sign or the label should be visible under all expected viewing conditions, including day and night viewing, bright sunlight, and so forth.

Legibility: Legibility may be optimized by enhancing the contrast ratio of the characters against the background and by using type fonts that are easy to read.

Intelligibility: Make clear what the hazard is and what may happen if the warning is ignored. Use as few words as possible, avoiding acronyms and abbreviations. Tell the operator exactly what to do.

Emphasis: The most important words should be emphasized. For example, a sign might emphasize the word *danger* by using larger characters and borderlines.

Standardization: Use standard words and symbols whenever they exist. Although many existing standards may not follow these recommendations, they are usually well established and it might be confusing to introduce new symbols.

Maintainability: Materials must be chosen that resist the aging and wear due to sunlight, rain, cleaning detergents, soil, vandalism, and so forth.

From W. E. Woodson, *Human Factors Design Handbook,* p. 483. Copyright © 1981 McGraw-Hill, Inc. Reprinted with permission.

visual search for simple items in laboratory situations, the more irrelevant or distracting signs there are in a scene, the longer it will take to find the relevant sign. Boersema, Zwaga, and Adams (1989) measured search time for a target word used in a railway station routing sign. They presented observers with photographs of a railway station in which the number of billboard advertisements was varied (see Figure 8–1). As the number of advertisements increased, search time increased. Similar results have been obtained for traffic signs in street scenes (Holahan, Culler, & Wilcox, 1978; Shoptaugh & Whitaker, 1984).

In contrast to conspicuity, *legibility* is the ease with which the symbols and letters that are present in the display can be discerned. Thus, legibility is closely related to visual acuity (see Chapter 7) and so is influenced by such factors as the contrast ratio between the figure and background and the stroke width of the lines comprising letters and other unfilled forms (Woodson, 1981). Generally, the higher the contrast ratio, the higher the legibility. For example, automobile license tags with black characters against a white background, or vice versa, are usually more legible than tags in which characters are red, blue, or green against a white background. The reflectances of red, blue, and green pigments typically are higher than black and less than white, so the contrast ratio of black on white is highest.

As with conspicuity, legibility at night can be increased by the use of reflective materials. Fully reflectorized license plates are more legible than nonreflectorized plates (Sivak, 1987). Such materials can also improve the legibility of street signs. Sivak and Olson (1985) have developed guidelines for the reflectance values needed for highway signs to be legible. Among other things, they recommend that fully reflectorized signs have a figure–ground contrast ratio of 12:1.

Readability is yet another concern that refers to a quality of visual displays allowing the recognition of information, particularly when conveyed by alphanumeric characters. Readability can be considered in terms of intelligibility, emphasis, and standardization. To allow fast and accurate interpretation of the message, it should be simple and direct. Key words, such as WARN-

FIGURE 8–1   Railway Station Scenes with No and Three Advertisements.

From T. Boersema, H. J. G. Zwaga, & A. S. Adams (1989). Conspicuity in realistic scenes: An eye movement measure. *Applied Ergonomics, 204,* 267–273. Reprinted by permission of Butterworth Scientific, Ltd.

ING or DANGER, should be made to stand out by using large letters or a distinct color. Standardized symbols and words should be used when possible, rather than symbols and words that may be unfamiliar or confusing.

The message in the display should be unambiguous, a feature that is related to intelligiblity. For example, signs like the one illustrated in Figure 8–2 should be avoided. In this sign, it is unclear whether the left arrow goes with gates 1–5 or gates 6–10. The sign could be improved by designing it so that the gates and arrows are grouped unambiguously.

In summary, a good sign will be conspicuous, have legible characters, and convey a readable, interpretable message. For practical purposes, maintainability is also important. Signs must be constructed of materials that will withstand soil, mistreatment and weather and maintain high levels of conspicuity, legibility, and readability.

Alphanumeric Displays. Complex alphanumeric displays are used to convey detailed information. For example, in our society, most information is disseminated through text. Simple alphanumeric displays are also used for such things as road signs. Alphanumeric displays are good for many situations, particularly when used in combinations to form words or other meaningful units. One drawback of alphanumeric displays is that some letters and digits share many features and are easily confused. Also, when combined to make words or phrases, the observer for whom the sign is intended must be literate in the language of the text.

Several factors contribute to the ease with which alphanumeric displays can be perceived. Alphanumeric displays will be easier to perceive when the contrast ratio between the foreground and background is high. An important factor to consider is the stroke width of the lines that comprise the alphanumeric forms. For black letters on a white background, under good illumination, the optimal stroke width-to-height ratio is from 1:6 to 1:8. For white letters on a black background, it is from 1:8 to 1:10. The thinner lines for white on black are required because of a phenomenon known as irradiation, or sparkle, in which the features of the white characters tend to bleed together. The preferred size for alphanumeric forms depends on factors such as the viewing distance and the ambient level of illumination. The adverse effects of small character sizes can be overcome partly by increasing the contrast ratio. Similarly, the adverse effects of low contrast ratio can be minimized by increasing the size of the characters (Snyder & Taylor, 1979).

Many thousands of type fonts are available for printed material. These can be classified into four categories: serif, sans serif, script, and those that do not fit into the other three categories. Most serif or sans serif fonts will be acceptable in many conditions, although some will be more legible than others. Serif fonts, which have little embellishments, typically are used for text. The text you are reading now is using a serif font. It is easier to segregate words when the font has serifs, and the letters are easier to identify (Craig, 1980).

Tullis (1983) has identified four basic characteristics of alphanumeric display formats that influence performance. The first of these is the overall density of the display, or the number of characters shown over the total area of the display (compare Figure 8–3a with b and c). The second,

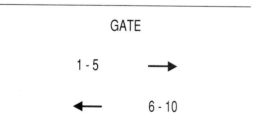

FIGURE 8–2 A Sign for Which the Directions for Gates 1–5 and 6–10 Are Ambiguous. From B. H. Kantowitz, T. J. Triggs & V. E. Barnes, Stimulus–response compatibility and human factors. In R. W. Proctor & T. G. Reeve (Eds.) (1990). *Stimulus–Response Compatibility: An Integrated Perspective.* Reprinted by permission of Elsevier Science Publishers.

and related to the first, is the local density, which is the density in the region immediately surrounding a character (compare Figure 8–3b with c). The third is grouping, which is related to the Gestalt organizational principles (see Figure 8–3d). The fourth is layout complexity, or the extent to which the layout is predictable.

Tullis (1986) developed computer-based methods of analysis to aid in the quantitative evaluation of alternative display formats. He has concluded that overall display density should be as low as possible, with local density at an intermediate level. This will reduce lateral masking and search difficulty. Grouping is beneficial if

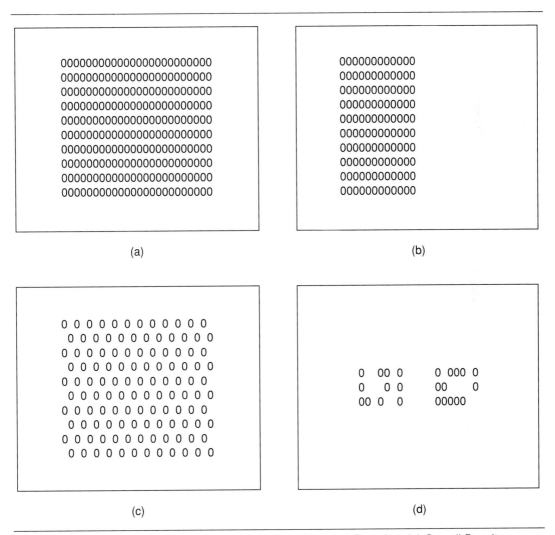

(a)

(b)

(c)

(d)

FIGURE 8–3   Four Examples of Different Display Densities and Grouping: (a) Overall Density = 100%, Local Density = 81%; (b) Overall Density = 50%, Local Density = 72%; (c) Overall Density = 50%, Local Density = 39%; (d) Grouping into Two Sets.
Based on Tullis (1983).

critical characters are segregated into appropriate groups. However, increasing the layout complexity could detrimentally affect performance.

Symbolic Displays. Symbols, sometimes called pictographs, are often effective for conveying information. They are most useful for concrete objects that can be directly depicted. It is more difficult to develop an effective symbol for abstract or complex concepts. For instance, consider how you might design a symbol indicating *exit* without using the word exit or any other text. Because symbols can depict the concepts that they represent, a person does not need to be familiar with the language to comprehend the intended information. Hence, symbolic displays are used extensively for facilities such as airports, in which many people will not be familiar with the local language. For the same reasons, manufacturers of products that will be exported prefer to use symbols.

The primary requirement for a symbolic display is that it be identifiable. People must reliably be able to recognize the depicted object or concept and to determine the referent of the sign. Recognition of the depicted concept does not guarantee comprehension of the referent. Zwaga (1989) examined the comprehensibility of information symbols referring to areas within a hospital, such as orthopedics, dentistry, and so on. He found that certain symbols could be easily recognized, but their referent was misunderstood. Figure 8–4 shows a symbol used to designate the orthopedics clinic. Although the symbol can be recognized as a leg in a plaster cast, most subjects misinterpreted the referent to be the plaster room. In contrast, the tooth symbol for dentistry (see Figure 8–5) was well recognized and well comprehended.

One example of the use of symbols and pictographs involves the process of screening potential blood donors who may have come into contact with the HIV virus that causes acquired immune deficiency syndrome (AIDS). In developing pamphlets to communicate to someone whether they fall into the high-risk category and

therefore should not donate blood, Wicklund and Loring (1990) have proposed that the information be portrayed symbolically to reach people of low literacy. The concepts that need to be communicated, such as "do not give blood if you are a man who has had sex with another man even once since 1977," are abstract. Consequently, Wicklund and Loring examined the effectiveness with which the intended message could be communi-

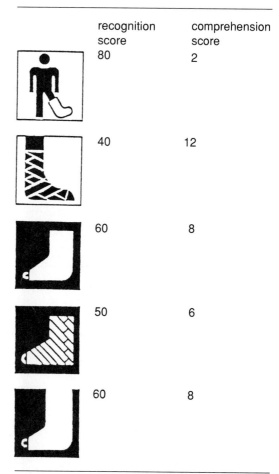

	recognition score	comprehension score
	80	2
	40	12
	60	8
	50	6
	60	8

FIGURE 8–4 Recognition and Comprehension Scores for Orthopedics Symbols.

From H. J. Zwaga, Comprehensibility estimates of public information symbols: Their validity and use. Reprinted with permission from *Proceedings of the Human Factors Society 33rd Annual Meeting*, 1989, pp. 979–983. Copyright 1989 by the Human Factors Society, Inc. All rights reserved.

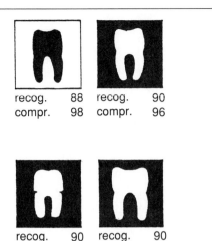

recog.   88   recog.   90
compr.   98   compr.   96

recog.   90   recog.   90
compr.   98   compr.   96

FIGURE 8–5   Recognition and Comprehension Scores for Dentistry Symbols.

From H. J. Zwaga, Comprehensibility estimates of public information symbols: Their validity and use. Reprinted with permission from *Proceedings of the Human Factors Society 33rd Annual Meeting,* 1989, pp. 979–983. Copyright 1989 by the Human Factors Society, Inc. All rights reserved.

cated with alternative symbol designs. The designs that they evaluated for the above concept are shown in Figure 8–6. Of these symbols, the only one that was rated as very effective is D.

The symbols shown in Figure 8–6 are abstract pictographs. For some displays, such as pamphlets, representational pictographs that involve more detailed line drawings can be used. The advantage of representational pictographs is that they are less ambiguous. Wicklund and Loring concluded that information about high-risk behavior is conveyed best by representational pictographs that show interpersonal relationships in an unambiguous manner, accompanied by a limited amount of text (see Figure 8–7).

Wicklund and Loring (1990) relied primarily on the preferences and opinions that they received as feedback from people who read the pamphlets. However, there are other, more objective ways for evaluating symbols. People can be asked to identify the intended meaning of each symbol or to select its meaning from a list of

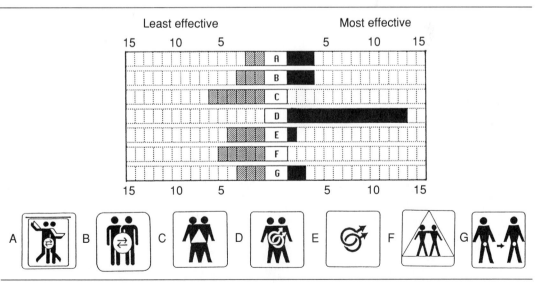

FIGURE 8–6   Effectiveness Ratings for Alternative Pictographs Indicating the Same Concept.

From M. E. Wicklund & B. A. Loring, Human factors design of an AIDS prevention pamphlet. Reprinted with permission from *Proceedings of the Human Factors Society 34th Annual Meeting,* 1990, pp. 988–992. Copyright 1990 by the Human Factors Society, Inc. All rights reserved.

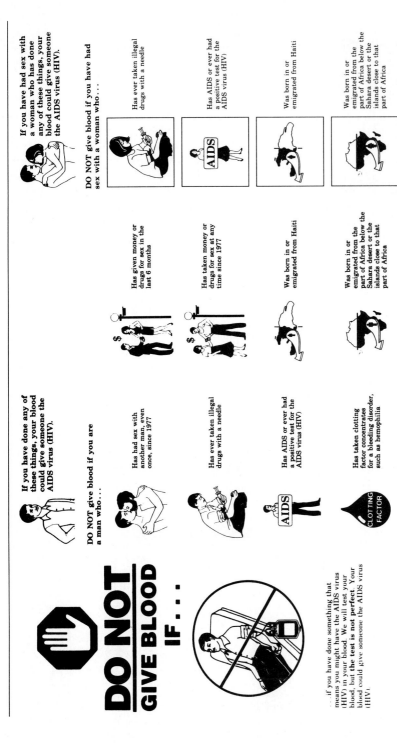

FIGURE 8–7 Prototype AIDS Prevention Pamphlet for Men.

From M. E. Wicklund & B. A. Loring, Human factors design of an AIDS prevention pamphlet. Reprinted with permission from *Proceedings of the Human Factors Society 34th Annual Meeting*, 1990, pp. 988–992. Copyright 1990 by the Human Factors Society, Inc. All rights reserved.

possible alternatives. For example, Mackett-Stout and Dewar (1981) used four different measures to evaluate the adequacy of a number of symbolic public information signs. In addition to preferences, glance legibility, legibility distance, and comprehension were measured. Consistent with Zwaga's (1989) findings regarding orthopedic signs, glance legibility did not significantly correlate with any of the other measures. In other words, the ease with which a sign could be recognized at a glance did not correlate with how readily the message could be comprehended. Preference correlated highly with comprehension and legibility distance, suggesting that preference ratings were valid measures of sign effectiveness.

The speed and accuracy with which symbolic displays can be identified are also influenced by Gestalt organizational principles. Easterby (1967, 1970) provided examples of how symbolic codes can be made more easily interpretable by designing them to be consistent with general organizational principles (see Figure 8–8). The figure–ground distinction should be clear so that there is no ambiguity about what the figure is. The symbols should be as simple and symmetric as possible. It is best for the contours to form a closed and solid figure. The contours should be smooth and continuous, unless discontinuity contributes to the information that is to be conveyed. Easterby's examples illustrate that subtle changes in display design can affect the way in which the display is organized perceptually and, hence, the overall effectiveness of the display.

One issue that confronts the human factors specialist is whether to use an alphanumeric display or a symbolic display. For example, should highway signs be verbal or symbolic? An advantage for verbal signs is that reading is a highly overlearned process for literate people fluent with the language in use, and no new relations need to be learned. However, there are numerous disadvantages as well. Because symbolic displays can depict the intended information directly, less processing should be required than for alphanumeric displays.

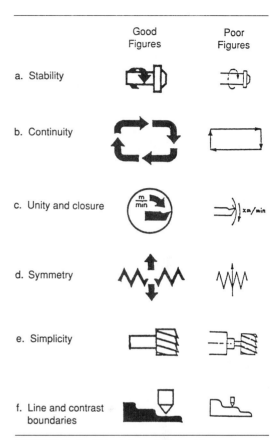

FIGURE 8–8   Principles of Figure/Ground Stability, Continuity, Figure Unity and Closure, Symmetry, Simplicity, and Line and Contrast Boundaries for Symbolic Codes.

Adapted from R. S. Easterby (1970). The perception of symbols for machine displays. *Ergonomics, 13,* 149–158. Adapted with permission of Taylor & Francis.

A study by Ells and Dewar (1979) supports this point. They found that people could determine that a spoken message corresponded to a sign faster when the sign was symbolic than when it was alphanumeric. Most important, this difference was apparent primarily under degraded viewing conditions; when the displays were difficult to see, people were much faster with the symbolic displays. This outcome seems reasonable, since the more complex visual patterns that comprise verbal messages would be expected to be less legible and readable under poor viewing conditions. A good symbolic code should be recognizable; legibility and readability are not as critical as with alphanumeric codes.

Coding Dimensions. The information presented by displays need not be verbal or pictorial. In such cases, features are arbitrarily assigned to code objects or concepts. Such codes can be based on alphanumeric forms, nonalphanumeric forms, colors, sizes, flash rates, and any of a number of other different dimensions. Although the appropriateness of a specific coding dimension depends on the particular task, some general guidelines can be given (see Table 8–3).

The number of unidimensional items that people can discriminate on absolute judgments is limited to between 5 and 7 (see Chapter 4), but varies across dimensions. Thus, the number of values on a particular coding dimension should be kept small if absolute judgments are required. The number of items that can be distinguished accurately is greater when the stimuli are multidimensional or when relative judgments (that is, those in which one item is compared directly to another) are possible.

Color coding is effective in many cases (Christ, 1975), particularly if the color for a target is unique. When the task requires searching for items or counting the number of items of a given type, the benefit of color coding the target increases as the display density increases. This relation holds because the time to search for one colored item among those of other colors is unaffected by the number of extraneous items, as long as all of them can be seen at once (see Chapter 7).

A large number of geometric shapes can be distinguished because they vary along more than one dimension. Some shapes are more discriminable than others, so care must be devoted to the shapes that are used. Discriminability of shapes is influenced by several factors (Easterby, 1970). Triangles and ellipses are best discriminated by their areas, and rectangles and diamonds by their maximum dimensions (for example,

height or width). More complicated shapes, such as stars and crosses, are best discriminated by their perimeters. Other coding dimensions, such as the size of forms, number of forms, angle of inclination, and brightness, have more limited uses (see Grether & Baker, 1972).

Different types of coding have been compared in many studies. For example, Hitt (1961) used five codes, shown in Figure 8–9, including shape, configuration, and color, to represent information in various sections of a map. Observers scanned the display and identified, localized, counted, compared, or verified the locations of different targets. Figure 8–10 presents the number of correct responses made per minute as a function of the code symbol used. Numeral and color codes allowed for the best performance and configuration, the worst. Christ and Corso (1983) obtained similar differences between code sets initially, but found that these differences attenuated with practice. Thus, if the goal is to enhance long-term performance, the choice of code sets probably will not be a significant factor.

Dynamic Displays

Analog and Digital Displays. For dynamic displays, information is conveyed by movement within the display. That is, the operator must be able to perceive changes in the state of the system as the display changes. Several types of dynamic displays are shown in Figure 8–11. The most basic distinction can be made between analog and digital displays. Digital displays, which have become common in recent years, present the information in letters or numerals. Analog displays are those for which the scale varies along a continuum, and the position of a pointer indicates the momentary value on the scale. Analog displays can be categorized further according to two distinctions. The first distinction is between displays with a moving pointer and a fixed scale versus displays with a fixed pointer and a moving scale. The former is exemplified by a typical automobile speedometer, whereas the latter corresponds

TABLE 8–3   Comparison of Coding Methods

Code	NUMBER OF CODE STEPS[a]		Evaluation	Comments
	Maximum	Recommended		
Color				
Lights	10	3	Good	Location time short. Little space required. Good for qualitative coding. Larger alphabets can be achieved by combining saturation and brightness with the color code. Ambient illumination not critical factor.
Surfaces	50	9	Good	Same as above, except ambient illumination must be controlled. Has broad application.
Shapes				
Numerals and letters	Unlimited		Fair	Location time longer than for color or pictorial shapes. Requires good resolution. Useful for quantitative and qualitive coding. Certain symbols easily confused.
Geometric	15	5	Fair	Memory required to decode. Requires good resolution.
Pictorial	30	10	Good	Allows direct association for decoding. Requires good resolution. Good for qualitative coding only.
Magnitude				
Area	6	3	Fair	Requires large symbol space. Location time good.
Length	6	3	Fair	Requires large symbol space. Good for limited applications.
Brightness	4	2	Poor	Interferes with other signals.
Visual number	6	4	Fair	Ambient illumination must be controlled.
Frequency	4	2	Poor	Requires large symbol space. Limited application. Distracting. Has merit when attention is demanded.
Stereo depth	4	2	Poor	Limited population of users. Difficult to instrument.
Angle of inclination	24	12	Good	Good for limited application. Recommended for quantitative code only.
Compound codes	Unlimited		Good	Provides for large alphabets for complex information. Allows compounding of qualitative and quantitative codes.

[a]The maximum number assumes a high training and use level of the code. Also, a 5% error in decoding must be expected. The recommended number assumes operational conditions and a need for high accuracy.

From W. F. Grether and C. A. Baker (1972). Visual presentation of information. In H. A. Van Cott and R. G. Kinkade (Eds.), *Human Engineering Guide to Equipment Design* (rev. ed., pp. 41–121). U.S. Government Printing Office.

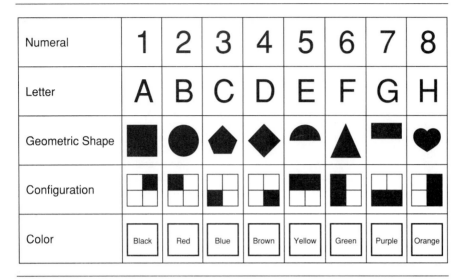

Numeral	1	2	3	4	5	6	7	8
Letter	A	B	C	D	E	F	G	H
Geometric Shape	■	●	⬟	◆	◗	▲	▬	♥
Configuration								
Color	Black	Red	Blue	Brown	Yellow	Green	Purple	Orange

FIGURE 8–9 Code Symbols Used by Hitt.

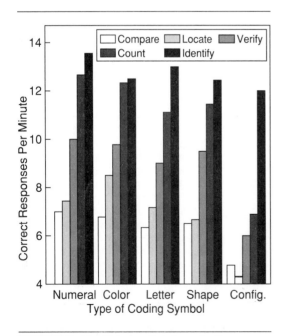

FIGURE 8–10 Relation Between Coding Method and Performance in the Five Tasks Studied by Hitt (1961).

to the displays used on most bathroom scales for measuring weight. The second distinction is whether the display is circular (like a speedometer), linear (like a thermometer), or semicircular (like a voltmeter).

One major issue in the design of a dynamic display is whether the display should be analog or digital (see Table 8–4). The preferred display type will vary across situations, because the two differ in the information that can be transmitted most efficiently. Digital displays convey exact numerical values well. However, they are difficult to read when changing rapidly, and more effort is required to determine trends, such as whether your car is accelerating or decelerating. Analog displays convey spatial information and trends efficiently, but do not provide precise values. Analog displays can also be representational. This means that, rather than a scale and pointer, the display presents a direct depiction of the system state.

Several studies have investigated the use of analog and digital displays in detail. Schwartz

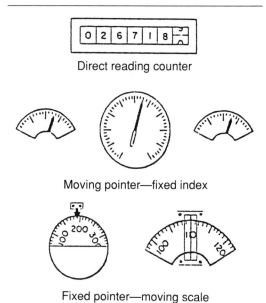

Direct reading counter

Moving pointer—fixed index

Fixed pointer—moving scale

FIGURE 8–11   Digital, Moving Pointer, and Fixed Pointer Dynamic.

From M. G. Helander (1987). Design of visual displays. In G. Salvendy (Ed.), *Handbook of Human Factors* (pp. 507–549). Copyright © 1987 John Wiley & Sons. Reprinted with permission.

and Howell (1985) conducted a simulated hurricane-tracking task in which historical information about the previous and current positions of a hurricane was presented. Observers sampled the information until they were ready to make a decision about whether the hurricane would hit a city. Earlier and better decisions were reached when the position of the hurricane was displayed graphically in a representational, analog display rather than numerically, particularly when time pressure was involved. Similarly, Bauer and Eddy (1986) showed that graphic representations of command language syntax in computer programming were easier to learn, use, and remember than representations based on special metacharacters. Boles and Wickens (1987) found the same advantage for analog indicators in numerical judgment tasks requiring integration of elements. Moreover, regardless of whether the displays were analog, digital, or verbal, integration tasks were performed best when the display elements were in the same format.

For analog dials, a moving pointer–fixed scale display will usually be most efficient. This is in part because the scale markers and labels are

TABLE 8–4   Choice of Display Indicator as a Function of Task

USE OF DISPLAY	TYPE OF TASK	DISPLAY TYPICALLY USED FOR	TYPE OF DISPLAY PREFERRED
Quantitative reading	Exact numerical value	Time from a clock; rpm from tachometer	Counter
Qualitative reading	Trend; rate of change	Rising temperature; ship off course	Moving pointer
Check reading	Verifying numerical value	Process control	Moving pointer
Setting to desired value	Setting target bearing; setting course	Compass	Counter or moving pointer
Tracking	Continuous adjustment of desired value	Following moving target with cross hair	Moving pointer
Spatial orientation	Judging position and movement	Navigation aids	Moving pointer or moving scale

From M. G. Helander, Design of visual displays, p. 508. In G. Salvendy (Ed.), *Handbook of Human Factors* (pp. 507–549). Copyright © 1987 John Wiley & Sons. Used with permission.

stationary and more easily read. A moving pointer display is preferred when the display indicates changes occurring as a function of manual control movements made by the operator. The choice between circular and linear displays is usually arbitrary; there seems to be little difference in the ease with which circular and linear arrays can be read (Adams, 1967). However, circular arrays do not require as much space as linear arrays, and they are simpler to construct.

Additional factors must be considered when designing an analog display. Any labels or symbols used to mark the scales must be legible. Decisions must also be made about the scale units and how they should be marked, as well as the type of pointer that should be used. Scale progressions are easier to read if they are marked in factors of 10 (for example, 10, 20, 30, . . . ; 100, 200, 300, . . .) than by some other set of values (for example, 1, 7, 13; Whitehurst, 1982). On a unit scale, major markers can indicate each 10 units (10, 20, 30, . . .), with minor markers designating each single unit. The major markers should be made distinct, often by being longer than the minor markers. If the display is to be viewed under low illumination, the markers must be wider than if the display is to be viewed under normal illumination. The increased width compensates in part for the decreased acuity of the operator under scotopic viewing conditions. The tip of the pointer should meet the smallest scale markers, and it should be angled or colored so that it is not confused with the marker to which it points.

Display Arrangements. In some situations, a display panel will be a complex arrangement of many dials and signal lights. In such situations, the human factors specialist needs to be sensitive both to the factors that influence the perceptibility of information within each of the individual dials and to the overall organization of the display. As discussed in the previous chapter, Gestalt organizational principles can be used to group dials with related functions.

Another factor that must be considered is the rapid decrease in visual acuity outside the fovea. In other words, the operator can only see a small section of the display panel clearly at any time. The *frequency of use* design principle arises from this limitation. The most frequently used and important displays should be located close to central vision under normal viewing conditions.

The limited acuity across much of the retina means that eye and head movements are required to see several displays clearly. Because eye movements take time, the farther apart two displays are located, the longer it will take to redirect the gaze from one to another. Thus, a second design principle is to locate displays according to their *sequence of use.* That is, if there are fixed sequences in which displays must be scanned, the displays should be arranged in that sequence. Even when there is not a fixed sequence, different displays usually have different functions and should be grouped according to these functions.

A technique that can be used to assist in the design of display configurations is *link analysis.* A link is a connection between a pair of items, in this case display elements, indicating a certain relation between them. For display configurations, links typically represent the percentage of eye movements shifting from one display to another. The general idea is that a display configuration will be designed better if the distance between displays with high-value links is shorter than the distance between displays with low-value links. Also, displays that are examined most frequently should be located close to the line of sight.

There are four steps for performing a link analysis of display arrangements (Cullinane, 1977). First, a diagram should be prepared that shows the interactions between the display components. All relations then should be examined and link values established in terms of the frequency of eye movements between the displays. The next step is to develop an initial link diagram in which the displays are rearranged so that the most frequently used displays are located in close proximity in the central visual field. The initial diagram is refined into the final layout as the last step. Glass, Zaloom, and Gates (1991) have developed a computer-aided method for performing link analysis that incorporates these four steps and allows easy application of link analysis to systems with many elements and links.

Fitts, Jones, and Milton (1950) performed a link analysis of the scanning patterns of pilots during aircraft instrument landings. They recorded the eye movements of each pilot during approaches to the runway, using the standard instrument arrangement shown in Figure 8–12. The highest link value (29%) was between the cross-pointer altitude indicator and the directional gyro. Moreover, the number of fixations per minute was greater for these two display elements. Thus, an improved display arrangement would place the cross-pointer and directional gyro adjacent to each other in the central part of the panel.

Motion Interpretability. Representational displays can be used to convey information about the motion of the system being controlled by the operator. In such situations, the issue arises of

how best to represent the motion information; that is, what frame of reference should be used? Is the external world to be portrayed as moving around a stationary system, or is the system to be portrayed as moving through a stationary world? This issue has been examined for attitude displays used in aircraft, which indicate the orientation of the plane with respect to the horizon.

Figure 8–13 depicts three possible types of attitude displays. The inside-out display shows the plane's attitude by changing the line that marks the horizon. In other words, the horizon marker corresponds to the orientation of the actual horizon that the pilot would see while looking out. In contrast, the outside-in display holds the horizon constant and varies the tilt of the aircraft indicator. This display portrays the relation that an observer from the outside would see.

The inside-out display has the advantage that it is compatible with the view seen by the pilot; the disadvantage is that it is incompatible with the control action that should be taken to return the aircraft to level (see Chapter 13). That is, it looks like the control should be turned counterclockwise to bring the line to horizontal, when in fact

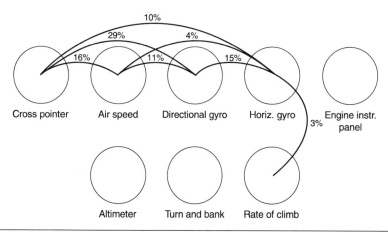

FIGURE 8–12   Links Among Dials in an Airplane Control Panel.

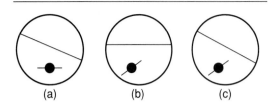

FIGURE 8–13   Inside-out (a), Outside-in (b), and Frequency-Separated (c) Attitude Displays.

the opposite action is required. While the outside-in display has this display–control compatibility, it does not correspond with the view of the world that the pilot sees.

The third type of display, the frequency-separated display, combines the advantages of the inside-out and outside-in displays and has been shown to produce superior performance (Beringer, Williges, & Roscoe, 1975). This display acts like an inside-out display when the control inputs are of low frequency, but changes to an outside-in display during high-frequency control inputs. Thus, when rapid control actions are being performed, the display is compatible with these actions and reduces the number of response reversals; when such actions are not being performed, the display corresponds to the pilot's view of the world.

Advances in Display Technology

Head-up Displays.   Head-up displays are used primarily in aircraft cockpits. A head-up display is a virtual imaging display in which collimated light images are projected onto the windshield in front of the pilot. This type of display is intended to minimize eye movements, shifts of attention, and changes of accommodation and vergence during flight navigation. Because the display is superimposed on the view through the windshield, critical information from the display can be monitored along with the visual information from outside during rapid or delicate maneuvers. The collimated light image is intended to allow

accommodation to be set at optical infinity, as if fixated on a distant object.

In theory, head-up displays offer numerous advantages, the majority of which are due to the reduced attentional shifts required to navigate the aircraft. However, their use has been controversial. Between 1980 and 1985, the U.S. Air Force lost 54 airplanes in clear-weather "controlled flights into the terrain" when using head-up displays (McNaughton, 1985). Many of these crashes seem to be due to problems of accommodation (Roscoe, 1987). The use of a collimated virtual image does not guarantee that the pilot's eyes are accommodated for distant viewing. In fact, it has been observed repeatedly that the eyes tend to fixate at about an arm's length away when such displays are viewed, much as occurs for dark accommodation (see Chapter 5). This *positive misaccommodation* causes objects in the visual field to appear smaller than they actually are. This in turn causes distant objects to appear more distant and items below the line of sight, such as the runway, to appear higher than they really are.

Both these problems in accommodation and problems of image quality contribute to the fact that 30% of tactical pilots report that head-up displays tend to cause disorientation. This is especially true when flying in and out of clouds; cases have been documented where pilots have been unaware that they were flying their planes upside down (McNaughton, 1985).

Despite the problems involved in using head-up displays, they are useful tools. Although pilots report a tendency toward disorientation when using such displays, they do not consider the problem sufficiently severe to warrant discontinuation (Newman, 1987). In fact, the tendency toward disorientation appears to decrease with training and/or better integration of the head-up display into the cockpit. Thus, it is not clear if the problems with the head-up display are due to problems in training or to the display itself (Newman, 1987).

Although head-up displays have been used primarily in tactical aircraft, they also are beginning to be implemented in automobiles and are currently available in some models (Dellis, 1988). The supposed benefit of such displays is that accidents will be reduced because more attention can be devoted to the roadway. The problem of misaccommodation with the automobile displays has been reduced by focusing the display at the edge of the hood, rather than at optical infinity. Because the optical distance of the head-up display is closer to the resting accommodative state than is the standard instrument panel, the time for reaccommodation when the gaze shifts from the display to the roadway is likely less. Although little research has been conducted with head-up automobile displays, it has been shown that salient cues can be responded to more rapidly by people using these displays (Sojourner & Antin, 1990).

Helmet-mounted Displays.   Helmet-mounted displays serve purposes similar to those of head-up displays. The displays are used to present alphanumeric, scenic, and symbolic images that enhance the capability of pilots flying military aircraft. As with head-up displays, they are intended primarily to allow the pilot to obtain critical flight information while continuing to view the scene outside the aircraft (Houck, 1991). The primary barriers to the use of helmet-mounted displays have been their excessive weight and bulk. However, the recent development of miniature cathode-ray tubes, with improved graphics processing, has made the use of helmet-mounted displays more practical (see Figure 8–14).

In a helmet-mounted display, the image on a miniature cathode-ray tube is reflected off a beam splitter into the eye. The display is provided only to the right eye, leaving the left eye with a complete view outside the aircraft. It can provide the pilot with cues to help determine the flight path of his or her own aircraft, as well as the flight path of an adversary.

Helmet-mounted displays can be used with thermal imaging systems (Rash, Verona, & Crowley, 1990). Thermal systems contain sensors that detect infrared radiation emitted by objects in the field of view. They can assist the

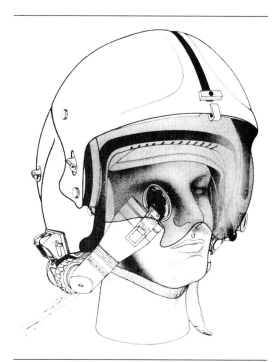

FIGURE 8–14   A Helmet-mounted Display.
From C. E. Rash, R. W. Verona, & J. S. Crowley (1990). Human Factors and Safety Considerations of Night Vision Systems Flight Using Thermal Imaging Systems. USAARL Report No. 90-10. United States Army Aeromedical Research Laboratory, Fort Rucker, Alabama.

pilot's ability to perform effectively at night and during adverse weather. The U.S. Army currently uses a helmet-mounted thermal imaging system on the AH-64 (Apache) attack helicopter. For the pilot, a sensor mounted on the nose of the aircraft provides an image of the external environment. This is coupled with displays indicating speed, heading, altitude, and so on.

Several special problems arise from the helmet-mounted display. The field of view is reduced, thus requiring more head movements by the pilot. Given the weight of the helmet, such movements will produce increased fatigue. Another problem is due to the placement of the sensor at the nose of the aircraft. The optical flow of the display will not correspond to the flow that would occur from the pilot's vantage point, but rather from the vantage of someone sitting at the nose. Consequently, different images of apparent motion, motion parallax, and distance will be presented to each eye. Other possible limitations arise from the elimination of binocular disparity as a depth cue and the potential for binocular rivalry (inattention to the scene at one eye) between the direct view of the environment at the left eye and the thermal-image view at the right eye. It is also important that the helmet be positioned properly and remain stable. Despite these problems, thermal imaging systems can enhance night vision capabilities.

Signal and Warning Lights

Visual displays can be used for general alert or warning signals. Such signals can be classified into three types (Boff & Lincoln, 1988). A warning signal evokes immediate attention and should require an immediate response, a caution signal evokes immediate attention and requires a relatively rapid response, and an advisory signal evokes general awareness of a marginal condition. Alarms can be classified into these categories by considering the consequences of the event being signaled, how rapidly these consequences could occur, the worst outcome that would arise if the signal were ignored, the time required to correct the problem, and how fast the system recovers.

The display design should optimize the detectability of high-priority alerting signals. For visual signals, this means presenting them as near to the operator's line of sight as possible, as well as making them sufficiently large (at least 1° of visual angle) and bright (twice as bright as other displays on the panel). Because flashing stimuli are more readily detected, the signal should flash against a steady-state background. Legends should be sufficiently large to be readable. Because everyone has prior experience with red warning signals and yellow cautionary signals, such as traffic lights, these colors should be used for warning and advisory signals,

respectively. In cases where this relationship is reversed, responses will tend to be slower and less accurate.

In some cases, visual alerting signals must unavoidably be located in the periphery of the visual field. In such situations the use of a centrally located master signal, indicating the onset of one of several alerting signals, improves the time and accuracy of responding to the alerting signal itself (Siegel & Crain, 1960). The readily detectable master signal alerts the operator to the presence of a specific alarm signal, which must then be located. The use of more than one master signal is unnecessary and may cause confusion.

AUDITORY DISPLAYS

Auditory displays are used primarily to convey simple information at low rates of transmission. In fact, one of the foremost uses of auditory displays is as emergency warning signals. When more complicated information needs to be transmitted auditorily, this is done by using speech stimuli.

Warning and Alarm Signals

Auditory warning and alarm signals must be detectable within the normal operating environment, and the information conveyed by the signal should be easily communicated to the operator. For detectability, the concept of the *masked threshold* is important (Sorkin, 1987). The difference between the masked and the absolute thresholds (see Chapter 6) is that the masked threshold is determined relative to some level of background noise, whereas the absolute threshold is determined in the absence of noise. Because warning signals are often presented in noisy environments, our concern must be with the masked threshold in that particular environment. To obtain such a threshold, an observer is presented with two bursts of noise, one of which contains a signal. He or she must then indicate in which noise burst the signal was contained. The masked threshold is defined as the signal intensity level required for 75% correct selection of the noise burst (50% is chance).

Several guidelines can be used to determine the optimal level for auditory signals (Sorkin, 1987). To ensure high detectability, the intensity of the signal should be well above threshold. An intensity 6 to 10 dB above the masked threshold will usually be needed at a minimum. As you might expect from Weber's law (see Chapter 1), the increase above masked threshold will need to be larger for high noise levels than for low noise levels. If a rapid response is required, as is the case for a warning signal, then the intensity should be at least 15 to 16 dB above the masked threshold. An overly loud signal can interfere with speech communication and be generally disruptive, so the intensity of an auditory warning signal in most cases should not exceed 30 dB above the masked threshold (Patterson, 1982).

Antin, Lauretta, and Wolf (1991) investigated levels of intensity for auditory warning tones under different driving conditions. Masked thresholds were obtained relative to three background noise conditions: quiet (56 km/hr on a smooth road), loud (89 km/hr on a rough road), and radio (56 km/hr on a smooth road with the radio on). The tone intensity to allow 95% detection was then determined for each noise condition. For the quiet noise condition, a warning tone 8.70 dB above the masked threshold was required on average. For the loud and radio noise conditions, 17.50 dB and 16.99 dB increases in the warning tone above the respective thresholds were required. Drivers indicated that they preferred even louder tones, perhaps to ensure that they would hear and react quickly to them.

Auditory signals can differ in terms of their distributions of energy across the frequency spectrum, which affects how the signal is perceived (Patterson, 1982). The fundamental frequency of a warning signal should be between 150 and 1,000 Hz, because low-frequency tones are less susceptible to masking. Furthermore, the signal should have at least three other harmonic frequency components. This maximizes the number of distinct signals that can be generated and en-

ables the pitch and sound quality to remain stable under various masking conditions. Signals with harmonically regular frequency components should be used rather than ones with inharmonic components, because their pitches will remain constant in different auditory environments. These additional components should be in the range from 1 to 4 kHz, for which human sensitivity is high. If the signal is dynamic, that is, changing with the state of the environment, then a listener's attention can be "grabbed" by including rapid glides (changes) in its fundamental frequency.

The temporal form and pattern of the auditory signal are also important. Because the auditory system integrates energy across time (see Chapter 6), the minimum duration for a signal should be 100 ms. Brief signals are useful when verbal communication must occur, such as in the cockpit of an aircraft, and when temporal patterning is used to code the information. Rapid onset rates will sound instantaneous to the listener and may produce a startle response. Thus, gradual onsets and offsets over a period of approximately 25 ms are preferred for most situations.

Temporal coding of information can be used for the pattern of the signals. For example, a rapid intermittent signal could be used for high-priority messages and a slower intermittent signal for low-priority messages (Patterson, 1982). A temporal pattern was suggested for a standard national fire-alarm signal (Swets et al., 1975). The proposed code is two short bursts and a long burst, followed by a silent period. The pattern then is repeated as long as necessary. A temporal code was proposed because the pattern would be the same in various auditory environments. This is not true for the pitch of a frequency code signal.

There is some evidence to suggest that performance of information-processing tasks can be improved by the use of *likelihood alarms*. Such alarms convey information about the likelihood of an event, as computed by an automated monitoring system. Sorkin, Kantowitz, and Kantowitz (1988) found that likelihood alarms can improve allocation of attention among multiple tasks and that the information provided by such alarms can be easily integrated into operator decisions.

One concern in the use of auditory warning signals is their number. During the Three-Mile Island incident, over 100 auditory signals were presented during the critical period of system failure. Clearly, this number exceeded the capability of the operators to process the information that was being provided. Similarly, some modern aircraft have as many as 30 auditory signals that can occur. It is more reasonable to restrict the number of high-priority warning signals to 5 or 6. One of two additional signals, called attensons (Patterson, 1982), can be used to indicate a lower-priority condition that then can be specified by a speech display.

Another problem in the use of auditory alarms is that operators tend to disable them. This has been a contributing factor in several recent air and rail accidents (Sorkin, 1989). The primary reason for disabling alarms is that the signal may be aversive and the false-alarm rate high. In such cases, disruptive sound will occur when there often is no need to take action. One way for the operator to avoid this aversive situation is to turn off the alarm system. Consequently, it seems prudent for designers to avoid the use of disruptive auditory signals when false-alarm rates are high.

Three-dimensional Displays

Although audition is not primarily spatial, auditory cues can be used to provide spatial information. Such cues can direct an operator's attention to a particular location without requiring a change in visual fixation. Most of the applications for these cues involve the improvement of fighter-pilot performance, because knowledge of the locations of threats and targets is necessary for survival. The use of auditory localization cues reduces some of the visual clutter in the cockpit and decreases visual overload.

Cues for localization are provided over headphones by introducing interaural intensity and time differences that mimic those that occur naturally. To present information about location ef-

fectively, intensity and time differences must be adjusted to correspond with the orientation of the pilot's head. For example, if a sound is localized in front of the pilot, the intensity at the left ear relative to the right should increase when the pilot's head turns to the right (Sorkin et al., 1989).

Valencia and Agnew (1990) evaluated listeners' ability to perceive simulated direction, as a function of head movement and stimulus type. Listeners judged the directions of pure tones, speech stimuli, and two types of noise. Localization accuracy was best with the noise stimuli. Front–back reversals were relatively common in all conditions, as is typical in studies of auditory localization, but occurred less often with the noise stimuli (approximately 15% of the time) than with the tone and speech stimuli (approximately 20% of the time). One implication of this study is that it is best to use broad-band stimuli when accurate auditory localization is desired.

Speech Displays

Speech messages are being used more frequently for the transmission of auditory information. When designing a speech display, the designer has a choice between natural and artificially generated speech. When using speech displays, the voice must be intelligible. For natural speech, intelligibility depends primarily on the frequencies between about 750 and 3,000 Hz. Intelligibility is affected by several other factors (Boff & Lincoln, 1988): the type of material, speech filtering, the presence of visual cues, and the presence of noise. Speech intelligibility is better for structured material, such as sentences, than for unstructured material, primarily because of the redundancy provided by the structure. Evidence was presented in Chapter 7 that grammatically and semantically correct sentences are perceived more accurately than strings of unrelated words. Similarly, identification thresholds for single words vary as a function of the number of syllables, the phonetic content, and the stress pattern.

Redundancy can be provided not only through structure in the speech signal but also by visual information. The lip-reading cues provided by simultaneously displaying a visual image of a person speaking with the speech signal can increase intelligibility. It is even possible to combine auditory and visual displays that are unintelligible when presented alone so that the speech is intelligible for the combined displays.

For reproducing speech, it is important to know what frequencies can be filtered, or deleted, from the auditory signal without degrading intelligibility. Because most acoustic energy for speech is in the range of 750 to 3,000 Hz, intelligibility decreases most when frequencies within that range are filtered. Frequencies lower or higher than this range can be deleted without having much effect. The ability to perceive speech accurately declines with age, particularly after age 60; this effect of aging is much greater for speech that has been degraded than for speech under optimal conditions (Bergman et al., 1976).

As with nonspeech auditory signals, the human factors specialist must be concerned with the intelligibility of speech within the specific environment where a speech display is to be used. When speech is presented over a noisy background, its intelligibility will often be reduced. The extent of this reduction depends on the signal-to-noise intensity ratio, the amount of overlap between the frequency components of speech and noise, and other factors. Table 8–5 lists methods for reducing the masking of speech by noise.

The first two methods, increasing the redundancy of the speech message and increasing the signal-to-noise ratio, should not need elaboration. The recommendation to utter the speech with moderate vocal force arises from the fact that low-intensity speech will be lost in the noise, whereas high-intensity speech is less intelligible than moderate-intensity speech, regardless of the noise level. Peak clipping involves setting a maximal amplitude for the sound wave and then clipping any signal that exceeds that amplitude to the maximal value. Peak clipping the speech signal and then reamplifying it to the original intensity level will produce a relative increase in the intensities for the frequencies of lower amplitude in the original signal (see Figure 8–15). These lower-amplitude frequencies convey the information about consonants and typically are the limiting factors in speech perception. Thus, a reamplified peak-clipped signal will be more intelligible than an unclipped signal of the same average intensity.

Excluding noise at the microphone minimizes noise effects at the point of transmission. Presenting the speech and noise out of phase at the two ears assists the listener in localizing the speech and noise signals, thus improving intelligibility. Ear plugs can contribute to speech intelligibility under conditions of high-intensity noise by reducing the sound intensity to levels at which the ear is not overloaded. The best earplugs for improving speech are ones that do not filter frequencies below 4 kHz. Thus, the intensity of the

TABLE 8–5   Methods for Reducing the Masking of Speech by Noise

1. Increase the redundancy of speech.
2. Increase the level of the speech relative to the level of the noise.
3. Utter the speech with moderate (versus high or low) vocal force.
4. Peak-clip the speech signal and reamplify to original levels.
5. Exclude noise at the microphone by using a throat microphone, pressure-gradient microphone, or noise shield.
6. Provide intra-aural cuing by presenting the speech out of phase in the two ears.
7. Use earplugs when noise levels are high.

Table from K. R. Boff and J. L. Lincoln, *Engineering Data Compendium: Human Perception and Performance*, 1988. Reprinted with permission.

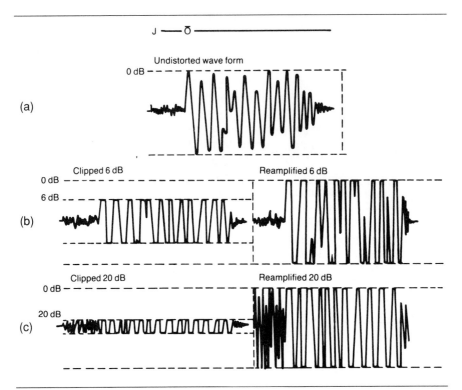

FIGURE 8–15 Reamplification of a Peak-clipped Signal for the word "Joe."
From J. C. R. Licklider, D. Bindra, & I. Pollack (1948). The intelligibility of rectangular speech waves. *American Journal of Psychology, 61,* 1–20. Reprinted by permission of University of Illinois Press.

speech signal is not reduced much, whereas that of the noise is.

Several measures have been developed for estimating the intelligibility of speech in noise, with the *articulation index* apparently being the best (Kryter & Williams, 1965; Webster & Klumpp, 1963). There are two methods for calculating this index. For the 20-band method, the intensity levels of speech and noise are measured for each of 20 frequency bands that contribute equally to speech intelligibility. The average of the differences between the speech and noise levels in each band is normalized to yield a value between 0.0 and 1.0. An articulation index of 0.0 indicates that the speech will be unintelligible, whereas an index of 1.0 indicates perfect intelligibility.

The weighted one-third octave band method is easier to compute, but is less precise. A worksheet for computing the articulation index with this method is shown in Table 8–6. The steps of computation are as follows (Kryter, 1972). First, determine the peak intensity level of the speech signal for each of the 15 one-third octave bands shown in Table 8–6. Then, do the same for the steady noise that reaches the ear. The third step is to find the difference between the speech peak and noise levels for each band. Differences of 30 dB or more should be assigned the value of 30, and negative differences (noise more intense than speech peak) should be assigned a value of 0.0. For the fourth step, multiply each difference by the appropriate weighting factors. These weights are based on the relative importance of the respective frequency bands for speech perception. Finally, add these weighted values to obtain the articulation index. This index is interpreted in the same manner as that obtained by the 20-band method.

Wilde and Humes (1990) evaluated the articulation index as a predictor of recognition accuracy under a wide range of conditions. They determined the index value for 21 conditions that differed in the type of noise (wideband nonspeech or speech), type of hearing protection (unprotected, earplugs, or earmuffs), and signal-to-noise ratio (three levels). Under these conditions, the articulation index accurately predicted the percentages of words recognized for both normal listeners and listeners with high-frequency sensorineural hearing loss. Thus, the articulation index is useful for predicting performance under both optimal conditions and conditions in which hearing protection is provided or listeners are hearing impaired.

Additional considerations arise when artificial speech is used. The artificial speech signal is not as redundant as natural speech. Consequently, speech perception is disrupted more by back-ground noise and the removal of context (Luce, Feustal, & Pisoni, 1983; Pisoni, 1982). Low-quality speech synthesis may be sufficient if there is only a small number of messages or if context information is provided in advance (Marics & Williges, 1988), but higher-quality speech generation may be needed when the messages are unrestricted. Because more effort is required to perceive artificial speech, there is poorer retention of the information that is presented (Luce, Feustal, & Pisoni, 1983; Thomas et al., 1989). However, an advantage of artificial speech is that the system designer has considerable control over speech parameters. Thus, the voice can be generated to suit the particular task environment.

Esthetic considerations are as important as performance considerations when evaluating synthesized speech. A voice stimulus evokes a more emotional response than a light or a tone. If the voice is unpleasant or the message is one that the listener does not want to hear, then the voice can have an irritating effect. This point is illustrated most succinctly by the short-lived use of speech messages, such as "Your seatbelt is not fastened," in automobiles in the early 1980s. Rat-

TABLE 8–6   Worksheet for the One-Third Octave Band Method

ONE-THIRD OCTAVE BAND (Hz)	CENTER FREQUENCY (Hz)	SPEECH PEAK TO NOISE PEAK DIFFERENCE (dB)	WEIGHT	PEAK DIFFERENCE × WEIGHT
180–224	200	_____	0.0004	_____
224–280	250	_____	0.0010	_____
280–355	315	_____	0.0010	_____
355–450	400	_____	0.0014	_____
450–560	500	_____	0.0014	_____
560–710	630	_____	0.0020	_____
710–900	800	_____	0.0020	_____
900–1,120	1,000	_____	0.0024	_____
1,120–1,400	1,250	_____	0.0030	_____
1,400–1,790	1,600	_____	0.0037	_____
1,790–2,240	2,000	_____	0.0038	_____
2,240–2,800	2,500	_____	0.0034	_____
2,800–3,530	3,150	_____	0.0034	_____
3,530–4,480	4,000	_____	0.0024	_____
4,480–5,600	5,000	_____	0.0020	_____

ings of the usefulness of a synthetic voice correlate with its perceived pleasantness and not with the person's performance (Rosson & Mellon, 1985).

TACTILE DISPLAYS

The tactile sense is important in situations for which spatial information is required but vision is not possible. Controls often are coded to be distinguishable by touch, because the operator will not be able to look at them. Similarly, tactile information is crucial for people who must work in a dark environment. Finally, blind individuals rely on the tactile sense extensively for communication.

Tactile displays are not recommended as alerting signals because they tend to be disruptive. However, if they are used, the stimulation should be vibratory to maximize detectability. The amplitude of the vibration should be chosen to be detectable on the specific region of the body to which it will be delivered. Sensitivity is greatest on the hands and the soles of the feet.

Tactile stimuli can be coded for identification according to physical dimensions in the same way as visual and auditory stimuli. Most important are the dimensions of shape and texture, although size and location can also be used. Figure 8–16 presents a standard set of controls distinguishable by touch that have been adopted by the military for use in aircraft.

Tactile stimulation can also be used to supplement the visual and auditory systems in conditions where they are overloaded. For example, Jagacinski, Miller, and Gilson (1979) compared performance with a tactile display to that with a visual display in a system control task. The tactile display was a variable-height slide on the control handle, which indicated the direction and magnitude of error between the actual and desired control settings. Performance was poorer overall with the tactile displays, but in some conditions performance approximated that obtained with visual displays.

Tactile displays have been used as a replacement for visual displays for the visually impaired.

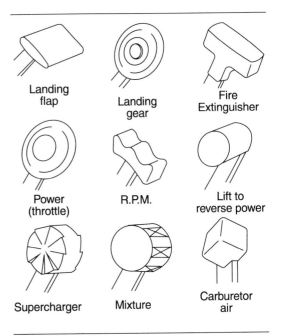

Landing flap

Landing gear

Fire Extinguisher

Power (throttle)

R.P.M.

Lift to reverse power

Supercharger

Mixture

Carburetor air

FIGURE 8–16   A Standard Set of Aircraft Controls Distinguishable by Touch.

The most commonly used tactile displays involve Braille. Visual displays of such things as floor numbers in elevators often appear with Braille characters embossed on their surfaces. Another tactile display that has received widespread use is the Optacon (*optical-to-tactile converter*), which was developed as a reading aid for the blind. To use the Optacon, an individual places an index finger on an array of 6 by 24 vibrotactile stimulators that vibrate at 230 Hz. A light-sensitive probe is passed over the text or other pattern that is to be examined. The scanning of the probe produces a spatially corresponding scanning pattern of activation on the vibrotactile display. Skilled Optacon readers can read text at up to 60 to 80 words per minute.

Another use for tactile displays has been as aids to speech perception for hearing-impaired people. The adequacy of the tactile sense for speech perception is illustrated by a natural method, called Todoma, in which a person with impaired hearing and vision places a hand on the face and neck of the speaker. With this method, individuals can become relatively proficient at recognizing speech (Reed et al., 1985). In recent years, several synthetic devices have been developed for tactile communication of speech. These devices convey characteristics of the speech signal by means of arrays of tactile stimulators. The devices have three characteristics in common (Reed et al., 1989): (1) reliance on variations in location of stimulation to convey information, (2) stimulation of only the skin receptors and not the proprioceptive receptors, and (3) all the elements in the stimulating array are identical.

Several devices are currently available commercially (Lynch, Oller, & Eilers, 1989). The Tactaid II uses two vibrators worn 2 to 4 in. apart. Information for frequencies of less than 2 kHz is transmitted to the left vibrator and that for frequencies greater than 2 kHz to the right vibrator. The Tactaid V is similar, but divides the frequency spectrum into 5 channels. The Tacticon 1600 divides the frequency spectrum even further, into 16 channels. Finally, the Tickle Talker differs from the other three in extracting the fundamental frequency and second formant from the speech signal for presentation on the skin. With this device, electrical pulses are transmitted through eight rings, one on each finger, excluding thumbs. Changes in the fundamental frequency affect the perceived roughness of the stimulation, while second formant frequency is represented by the location stimulated (front or back of different fingers).

Positive results have been obtained from most studies that have used tactile aids to supplement lip reading (Reed et al., 1989). In many studies, users received little training and systematic instruction, so the full potential of tactile aids has yet to be explored (Plant, 1988). Research efforts in the near future likely will lead to the development of the training programs necessary for effective implementation of tactile speech aids.

SUMMARY

All displays are not created equal. Performance in simple and complex human–machine systems can be affected drastically by display design. Choice of an appropriate display involves consideration of the characteristics of the sensory modality for which it is intended. Such characteristics include the temporal, spatial, and absolute sensitivities of the modality. These factors interact with the operating environment, the purpose of the system, the nature of the information that is to be communicated, and the capabilities of the population that will be using the display.

The present chapter has focused primarily on perceptual factors that affect the ease with which a display can be used. However, the ultimate purpose of a display is to convey information to the observer. Therefore, performance will be affected by cognitive factors as well. These factors are the topic of the next part of the book.

RECOMMENDED READING

Easterby, R., & Zwaga, H. (eds.) (1984). *Information Design.* New York: Wiley.

Helander, M. G. (1987). Design of visual displays. In G. Salvendy (ed.), *Handbook of Human Factors* (pp. 507–548). New York: Wiley.

Lehto, M. R., & Miller, J. D. (1986). *Warnings: Vol. 1, Fundamentals, Design, and Evaluation Methodologies.* Ann Arbor, MI: Fuller Technical Publications.

Roscoe, S. N. (1987). VTO control and display design: Principles and methods. In D. J. Oborne (ed.), *International Review of Ergonomics,* Vol. 1 (pp. 135–158). London: Taylor & Francis.

Sorkin, R. D. (1987). Design of auditory and tactile displays. In G. Salvendy (ed.), *Handbook of Human Factors* (pp. 549–576). New York: Wiley.

CHAPTER 9

ATTENTION AND THE ASSESSMENT OF MENTAL WORKLOAD

> *In view of a limited capacity to deal with the available potential stimuli, the organism must somehow select those stimuli which will influence its behavior. It is this process of stimulus selection that constitutes attention.*
>
> —P. Bakan, 1966

INTRODUCTION

The topic of attention was of considerable interest around the turn of the century, as indicated by William James's quote in Chapter 1. Because of attention's reliance on unseen mental events, it fell into disfavor during the first half of the twentieth century. Research by applied psychologists in England, who were interested in such topics as the ability of air traffic controllers to divide attention among multiple inputs and of radar operators to maintain vigilance while monitoring screens for enemy submarines, restored attention as a legitimate topic for research. Much of modern applied research on attention is devoted to studying the performance of operators of land, air, and water vehicles under different cognitive demands. Driving, for example, involves the subtasks of

tracking (steering and maintaining a desired speed), decision making, navigation, adherence to regulations and warnings, tending environmental and mechanical systems (and entertainment systems) within the cab, and communicating, all the while maintaining a watch for various events that may occur inside or outside the vehicle. Like the pilot, [the driver] must keep watch over instrumentation within the car for extremely rare events, such as a low oil pressure indication. (Wiener, 1984, p. 233)

Our ability to attend to stimuli is limited, and the direction of attention will determine how well we perceive, remember, and act on information. Objects or information that do not receive attention usually fall outside our awareness and, hence, have little influence on performance. Thus, a display of information relevant to a task may not be exploited if an operator is not attending to it. However, when a single overlearned response has been executed to a stimulus many times in the past, attention is not needed for the response to be made. In such situations, familiar but irrelevant stimuli outside the focus of attention may interfere with the processing of relevant stimuli that require attention. These and other attentional factors determine an operator's level of performance for any assigned task.

Several basic aspects of attention can be distinguished. The first concerns our ability to focus on certain sources of information and ignore others. This corresponds to situations in which more than one person is talking, yet you can listen to only one speaker. It is known as *selective attention*. Another aspect of attention involves our ability to divide attention among multiple tasks, such as driving a car while carrying on a conversation. This is called *divided attention*. Still another aspect of attention relates to the amount of mental effort required to perform a task. Typically, if a task requires considerable effort it is called attention demanding.

The concept of mental effort is closely related to that of *mental workload:* an estimate of the attentional demands of an operator's duties. Numerous techniques for measuring and predicting workload have been developed based on the methods and concepts derived from basic re-

search on attention. In the present chapter, we will describe alternative models of attention, consider different modes of attention in detail, and examine techniques for assessing mental workload.

MODELS OF ATTENTION

Several models of attention have been proposed. These models have generated much research that has enhanced our knowledge of attention. However, because each model captures a different aspect of human performance, it has not been possible to arrive at a single model upon which all agree.

A hierarchical distinction between attention models is shown in Figure 9–1. The first distinction occurs between bottleneck and resource models. Bottleneck models specify a particular stage in the information-processing sequence at which the amount of information to which we can attend is limited. In contrast, resource models view attention as a limited-capacity resource that can be allocated to one or more tasks, rather than as a fixed bottleneck. Further distinctions can be made within each of these categories. Bottleneck models can be divided into early-selection and late-selection models, depending on where the bottleneck is placed in the information-processing sequence. Resource models can be distinguished by the number of resource pools that are

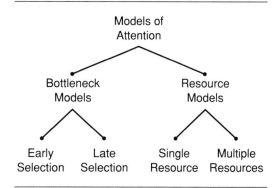

FIGURE 9–1   Hierarchical Classification of Attention Models.

hypothesized: a single resource or multiple resources. We will describe the characteristics of each of these models in turn, along with the pertinent experimental evidence.

Bottleneck Models

Filter Theory.   After the resurgence of interest in the topic of attention, the first detailed model, called *filter theory,* was proposed by Broadbent (1958). The filter theory is an early-selection model in which stimuli enter a central processing channel one at a time to be identified. Thus, filtering of extraneous or unwanted messages must occur early, prior to this identification stage. The filter can be adjusted on the basis of relatively gross physical characteristics, such as spatial location or vocal pitch, to allow information from only one source of input to enter the identification stage (see Figure 9–2).

Broadbent (1958) proposed this particular model because it was consistent with the facts about attention that were known at that time.

Many attentional studies were conducted in the 1950s, primarily with auditory stimuli. Probably the best known of these studies is Cherry's (1953) investigation of the "cocktail party" phenomenon, so called because many different conversations occur simultaneously at a cocktail party. Cherry conducted a study in which listeners had to attend to one auditory message while ignoring others, much like the situation you would encounter at a cocktail party. Listeners were able to shadow (repeat back) one auditory message and ignore another if the messages were physically distinct. For example, when messages were presented through headphones to the left and right ears, listeners could shadow the message in the left ear while ignoring the right, or vice versa.

Not only were listeners able to selectively attend to one of the messages, they also showed little awareness of the unattended message other than its gross physical characteristics (for example, whether the message was spoken by a male or female). In one study, listeners had no memory of words that had been repeated 35 times in the

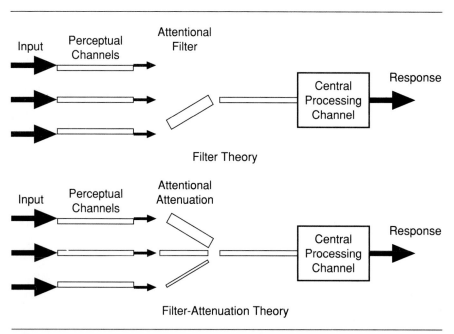

FIGURE 9–2   Filter and Attenuation Theories of Attention.

unattended message (Moray, 1959). Similarly, when the unattended message was switched from English to French after the first few words and then switched back before the end of the message, less than half of the listeners were aware that the language had been changed (Treisman, 1964b). Consistent with the filter theory, these selective-attention experiments suggested that the unattended message is filtered before the stage at which it is identified.

Another critical experiment was performed by Broadbent (1958) using a split-span technique. He presented listeners with pairs of words simultaneously, one to each ear, at a rapid rate. The listeners' task was to report back as many words as possible in any order. This design made a divided-attention experiment in which the messages presented to both ears required attention. Broadbent found that listeners reported the items by ear; that is, all the words presented to the left ear were reported in order of occurrence, followed by any that could be remembered from the right ear, or vice versa. This outcome suggested that the message from one ear was blocked from identification until the items from the other ear had been identified, again consistent with the filter theory.

The filter theory nicely captures the most basic phenomena of attention: it is difficult to attend to more than one message at a time, and little is retained from an unattended message. Consequently, filter theory remains one of the most useful theories of attention to this day. However, filter theory cannot be entirely correct. As usually happens when a theory is sufficiently specific to be falsifiable, evidence has accumulated that is inconsistent with the filter theory. For example, most listeners are aware when their name occurs in the unattended message (Moray, 1959), at least in some circumstances. Also, Treisman (1964a) showed that, when prose passages were switched between the two ears, listeners continued to shadow the same passage after it had been switched to the "wrong ear." So, the context provided by the earlier part of the message was sufficient to direct the listener's attention to the

wrong ear. These and other studies indicate that the content of unattended messages is identified at least in some circumstances, a fact that the filter theory cannot explain.

Attenuation and Late-selection Theories. An attempt to reconcile the filter theory with these conflicting findings was made by Treisman (1964b). She proposed a *filter-attenuation model* in which an early filter served only to attenuate the signal of an unattended message rather than to block it entirely (see Figure 9–2). This could explain why the filter sometimes seemed to "leak," as in the two examples described in the previous paragraph. That is, an attenuated message would not be identified under normal conditions, but the message could be identified if familiarity or context sufficiently lowered the identification threshold. Although the filter-attenuation model is more consistent with the experimental findings than the original filter theory, it is not as easily testable.

An alternative approach to correct the problems of the filter theory was to move the filter to later in the processing sequence, after identification had occurred. Deutsch and Deutsch (1963) and Norman (1968) argued that all messages are identified, but decay rapidly if not selected or attended. The findings cited in support of this *late-selection model* involved evidence that all items were identified. For example, Lewis (1970) presented listeners with a list of five words in one ear at a rapid rate. This list was shadowed, while an unattended word was presented in the other ear. Listeners were not able to recall the unattended word, but its meaning affected reaction times to pronounce the simultaneously presented, attended word. Reaction time was slowed when the unattended word was a synonym of the one being shadowed.

Debate over these and other findings has persisted. For example, Treisman, Squire, and Green (1974) argued that Lewis's findings only occur for short lists or early positions in longer lists, before the filter has been adjusted to exclude the unattended message. The issue has been difficult to resolve, leading Johnston and Heinz (1978) to propose that the bottleneck may not be fixed, but may vary as a function of the specific task requirements. They suggested that as the information-processing system shifts from an early- to a late-selection mode, more information is gathered from irrelevant sources, requiring a greater amount of effort to focus on a relevant source.

Resource Models

The difficulty of pinpointing the locus of a single bottleneck led some researchers to take a different approach and develop resource models of attention. Instead of focusing on a specific location in the information-processing sequence where attentional limitations arise, resource models view attentional limitations as arising from a limited capacity of resources for mental activity. Performance suffers when resource demand exceeds the supply.

Unitary-resource Models.   *Unitary-resource models* were proposed by several authors in the early 1970s. The best known is that of Kahneman (1973), which is illustrated in Figure 9–3. According to Kahneman's model, attention is viewed as a limited-capacity resource that can be applied to a variety of processes and tasks. The execution of multiple tasks is not difficult unless the available capacity of attentional resources is exceeded. Available capacity fluctuates with the level of arousal and the demands of the task that the person must perform. When capacity is exceeded performance will suffer, and a policy for allocating the resources to different possible activities will have to be put into effect. This allocation policy depends on momentary intentions and evaluations of the demands being placed on these resources.

One consequence of the unitary-resource model was that researchers began trying to measure the attentional requirements of various mental subprocesses of tasks. Posner and Boies (1971) used what is called a dual-task procedure in

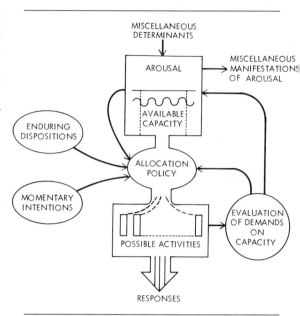

FIGURE 9–3   Unitary Resource Model of Attention.

From Daniel Kahneman, *Attention and Effort,* © 1973. Reprinted by permission of Prentice Hall, Englewood Cliffs, New Jersey.

which a person is required to perform two tasks at once. They classified one task as primary and the other as secondary, with people instructed to perform the primary task as well as possible. Under the hypothesis that attention is a single pool of processing resources, all resources necessary should be devoted to the primary task. Any spare resources will be devoted to the secondary task. If the attentional resources have been depleted by the primary task, performance of the secondary task should suffer. Posner and Boies's procedure is sometimes called the probe technique from the fact that the secondary task is usually a brief tone or visual stimulus that can be presented at any time during an extended primary task. Thus, it is a probe of the momentary attentional demands of the primary task. By looking at the responses to probes throughout the task sequence, a profile of its attentional requirements can be determined.

For their primary task, Posner and Boies (1971) displayed a letter, followed by another letter 1 second later, and the pair was to be judged as *same* or *different*. Reaction times to an auditory probe were slowed only when the tone occurred late in the task sequence (see Figure 9–4), leading Posner and Boies to conclude that it was the late processes of comparison and response selection that required attention. However, subsequent studies have suggested that even the process of encoding the initial letter requires a small amount of attentional resources (Johnson, Forester et al., 1983; Paap & Ogden, 1981). These studies illustrate that dual-task procedures provide sensitive measures of the momentary attentional demands on a person. Such procedures can be used to determine the difficulty of different tasks and to predict when operator performance will suffer.

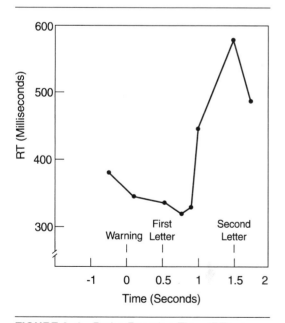

FIGURE 9–4   Probe Reaction Time (RT) at Various Times During a Letter-matching Task.
From M. I. Posner & S. J. Boies (1971). Components of attention. *Psychological Review, 78,* 391–408. Reprinted by permission of the American Psychological Association.

Multiple-resource Models.   An alternative view that has been prominent, particularly in human factors, is multiple-resource theory (Navon & Gopher, 1979). *Multiple-resource models* propose that there is no single attentional resource. Rather, several distinct subsystems each have their own limited pool of resources. Wickens (1980, 1984) proposed a three-dimensional system of resources consisting of distinct stages of processing (encoding, central processing, and responding), codes (verbal and spatial), and input (visual and auditory), plus output (manual and vocal) modalities (see Figure 9–5). The model assumes that two tasks can be performed together more efficiently to the extent that they require separate pools of resources. Changes in the difficulty of one task should not influence performance of the other if the tasks draw on different resources.

Multiple-resource models were developed because the amount of performance decrement for multiple tasks often depends on the stimulus modalities and the responses required for each task. For example, Wickens (1976) had observers perform a manual tracking task in which a cursor was to be kept aligned with a stationary target. At the same time, another task was performed involving either the maintenance of a constant pressure on a stick or the detection of auditory signals. Although the auditory-detection task was judged to be more difficult, it produced less interference with tracking than did the constant-pressure task. This is presumably because the tracking task and the constant-pressure task both require resources from the same output modality pool. The general principle captured by multiple-resource models is that performance of multiple tasks typically will be better if the task dimensions (stages of processing, codes, and modalities) do not overlap.

MODES OF ATTENTION

Selective Attention

Selective attention is a component of many tasks. For example, when reading an instruction man-

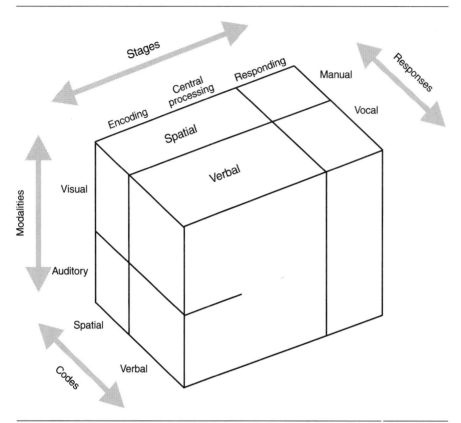

FIGURE 9–5   Multiple-resource Model of Attention.
From C. D. Wickens (1984). Processing resources in attention. In R. Parasuraman & R. Davies (Eds.), *Varieties of Attention* (pp. 63–102). Reprinted by permission of Academic Press, Inc.

ual, the operator needs to attend selectively to the written information and ignore extraneous auditory and visual information. One task used to study selective attention is the selective-listening task, in which an auditory target message that is to be attended to is presented simultaneously with another auditory signal that serves as a distractor. The distractor can interfere with the target message by masking it or by producing confusion about the target's identity. Selective listening is relatively easy when the target message is physically distinct from the distractor. Spatial separation of the target and distractor, either by presenting the signals from distinct loudspeakers or to separate ears through headphones, makes it easier to attend to the target message (Spieth, Curtis, & Webster, 1954; Treisman, 1964a). Similarly, selective listening is easier when the target and distractor are of different intensities (Egan, Carterette & Thwing, 1954) or from different frequency regions within the auditory spectrum (Egan, Carterette, & Thwing, 1954; Spieth, Curtis, & Webster, 1954). These findings are consistent with filter theory's early selection of information to be attended based on gross physical characteristics.

In addition to the importance of the physical relation between the target and distracting signals, semantic and syntactic context affect selective listening performance when both signals are speech messages. Fewer errors are made if the target and distractor are of different languages, if the target message is prose rather than random words, or if the target and distractor are distinctly different types of prose, for example, a novel and a technical report (Treisman, 1964a, 1964b). Moreover, expectancies induced by context can lead to misperception of words to make them consistent with the context (Marslen-Wilson, 1975).

When performing a selective-listening task in which the distractor message is distinguished physically from the target message, say by spatial location, listeners can remember little about the distractor (for example, Cherry, 1953; Cherry & Taylor, 1954). However, if the distractor stimuli are presented visually, subsequent recognition of them is high. Recognition is better when the distractors are pictures or visually presented musical scores than when they are visually presented words, indicating that retention of the distractor information decreases as the tasks become more similar (Allport, Antonis, & Reynolds, 1972).

Selective attention for visual stimuli has been studied by presenting multiple visual signals. Studies have shown that irrelevant stimuli produce minimal interference with the processing of a target stimulus if they are at least one degree of visual angle away (Eriksen & Eriksen, 1974). If the spatial separation is sufficiently great, the distractor stimuli can be excluded from processing. If the letters are not spatially separated, the distractor is identified along with the target, making it difficult to perform the task. Such results have led investigators to characterize the focus of attention as a spotlight of varying width that can be directed to different locations in the visual field (Eriksen & St. James, 1986; Treisman, Sykes, & Gelade, 1977).

One way of selectively attending to visual stimuli is through the positioning of the eyes. Objects that are fixated will be seen clearly, whereas those in the visual periphery will not. However, the spotlight metaphor suggests that it should be possible to dissociate the focus of attention from the direction of gaze. Posner, Nis-

sen, and Ogden (1978) conducted an experiment in which observers responded to an X appearing 0.5° to the left or right of fixation. Prior to presentation of the target, a cue occurred. The cue was either a neutral plus sign or an arrow pointing to the left or right. The arrow cues were valid indicators of the target location on 80% of the trials and invalid indicators on 20%; in other words, the X occurred to the cued side on 80% of the trials. Simple reaction time (the time to execute a response to the onset of a stimulus regardless of location) was facilitated when the stimulus appeared at the cued location and slowed when it occurred at the uncued location (see Figure 9–6). Subsequent studies have shown that a benefit is obtained for stimuli at locations that are intermediate to the fixated and cued locations if the interval between cue and target is short (Shulman, Remington, & McLean, 1979). In other words, it

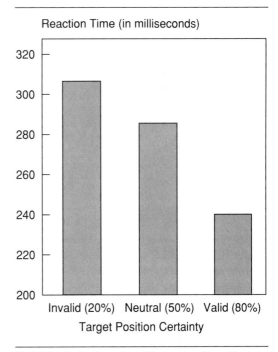

FIGURE 9–6   Reaction Times as a Function of Target Position Certainty.

Data from Posner, Nissen, & Ogden (1978).

is much as if the spotlight of attention is moved gradually from the fixated to the cued location.

It has also been shown that people can focus attention on a narrow band of the auditory spectrum. Scharf et al., (1987) required listeners to decide which of two time intervals contained a tone. The frequency of the tone was either expected or not. Tones within the critical band around the expected frequency were detected well, whereas tones outside the critical band were detected at chance levels. Thus, under at least some conditions, focused attention alters sensitivity to auditory stimuli.

Many tasks, such as driving, require rapid switching of attention between sources of information. Drivers differ in their ability to switch attention from one input to another. Kahneman and his colleagues (Gopher & Kahneman, 1971; Kahneman, Ben-Ishai, & Lotan, 1973) evaluated the attention switching ability of fighter-pilot candidates and bus drivers using a dichotic listening task. After selectively attending to information in one ear while ignoring information in the other, a tone signaled the ear that would contain the target information for the subsequent portion of the task. The number of errors made after the attention-switching signal was negatively correlated with the success of cadets in the Israeli Air Force flight school; successful cadets made few errors. Number of errors was positively correlated with the accident rates of the bus drivers; accident-prone drivers made more errors. Parasuraman and Nestor (1991) note that the shifting of attention is a cognitive skill that deteriorates for older drivers with various types of age-related dementia. Because of these individual differences in attention-shifting ability, driving competence should be determined in part by tests of attention.

Divided Attention

In divided-attention tasks, people are required to attend to several sources of input simultaneously. For many situations, performance is degraded relative to when attention to only a single source is required. This performance decrement appears as decreased accuracy of perception of the message, slower responding to the message, or higher thresholds for detection and identification.

For many applied settings, operators must perform divided-attention tasks by monitoring several sources of input, each potentially carrying a target signal. If attention is divided among many sources involving one or more sensory modalities, detection of the target is only slightly degraded when it is presented in one source (Duncan, 1980; Ostry, Moray, & Marks, 1976; Pohlman & Sorkin, 1976). If multiple targets occur, the probability of detecting at least one increases, whereas the probability that each specific target will be detected decreases. The likelihood of detecting a target from any single source diminishes further as the number of simultaneous targets from other sources increases. In other words, multiple sources can be monitored relatively efficiently. The limitation arises when two or more target stimuli, each of which must be categorized and identified, occur simultaneously. Although the decrement in performance for multiple, simultaneous targets can be reduced with practice (Ostry, Moray, & Marks, 1976), performance never attains the level possible when attending to only one input source. In applied situations, if simultaneous targets are very probable, then each source should be monitored by a separate operator.

For situations in which attention is divided among sources or tasks, it is not necessary that each task be given the same priority. For example, the probe technique, which has already been described, designates one of two tasks as primary and the other as secondary. More generally, any combination of relative weightings can be given to the two tasks. That is, performance on the respective tasks can be traded off.

This trade-off in dual-task performance can be described with a *performance operating characteristic* (POC) curve, which is similar in certain respects to the ROC curve presented in Chapter 4. A hypothetical POC curve is shown in Figure 9–7. The abscissa represents performance on task *A*, and the ordinate represents performance on

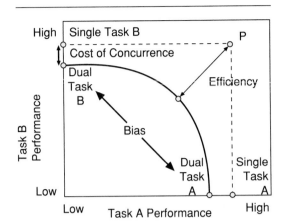

FIGURE 9–7   Performance Operating Characteristic.

task *B*. Base-line performance for each task alone is designated on the respective axes. If the two tasks could be performed together as efficiently as when performed alone, performance would fall on the *independence point P*. This point shows performance when no attentional limitations arise from doing the two tasks together.

The box formed by drawing lines from point *P* to the axes defines the POC space. It represents all possible combinations of joint performance that could occur when the tasks are done simultaneously. The actual performance of the two tasks will fall along a curve within the space. *Performance efficiency,* the distance between the POC curve and the independence point, is an indicator of how efficiently the two tasks can be performed together. The closer the POC curve comes to *P*, the more efficient is performance. Like an ROC curve, the different points along the POC curve reflect only differences in bias induced by changing task priorities. The point on the positive diagonal reflects unbiased performance, whereas the points toward the ordinate or abscissa represent biases toward task *B* or task *A*, respectively. Finally, the *cost of concurrence* is shown by the difference between performance for one task alone and for dual-task performance in which all resources are devoted to that task.

A POC curve is obtained by testing people under different conditions in which only the relative emphasis on the two tasks is varied. Performance on a given task can approximate performance when the task is performed alone or be substantially worse, depending on the relative bias that is adopted in the dual-task situation. POC analyses can be applied to the control of complex systems, such as radar or aircraft, in which operators must perform two or more tasks concurrently.

To illustrate the use of POC curves, we will describe a study by Ponds, Brouwer, and van Wolffelaar (1988) that evaluated dual-task performance for young, middle-aged, and elderly people. One task involved simulated driving, whereas the other required counting a number of dots, which were presented at a location on the simulated windshield that did not occlude the visual information necessary for driving. Performance was normalized for each age group, so that the mean single-task performance for each group was given a score of 100%. POC curves were obtained for each age group by plotting the normalized performance scores obtained for dual-task performance under three different emphases on driving versus counting (see Figure 9–8). For the normalized curves, the independence point is (100, 100). The elderly show a deficit in divided attention, as evidenced by the POC curve for the older adults being farther from the independence point than the POC curves for the middle-aged and young adults. This divided attention deficit for the elderly corroborates Parasuraman and Nestor's (1991) work, among others, and this deficit does not go away with practice (McDowd, 1986).

Arousal and Vigilance

A person's attentional ability is influenced by her or his level of arousal. The arousal level may influence the amount of attentional resources that are available, as well as the policy by which attention is allocated. This relation between attention and arousal underlies a fundamental law

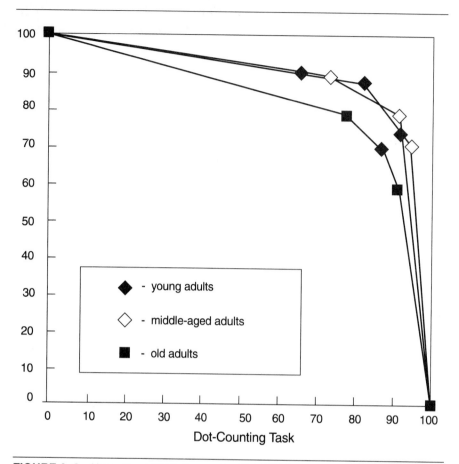

FIGURE 9–8 Normalized POC Curves for Old, Middle-aged, and Young Adults in a Divided-attention Task.

From R. W. H. M. Ponds, W. B. Brouwer, & P. C. van Wolffelaar (1988). Age differences in divided attention in a simulated driving task. *Journal of Gerontology, 43,* P151–P156. Copyright © The Gerontological Society of America. Reprinted with permission.

of performance, the *Yerkes-Dodson* law (Yerkes & Dodson, 1908). According to this law, performance is an inverted U-shaped function of arousal level, with the peak performance occurring at a higher level for simple tasks than for complex tasks (see Figure 9–9). It is not surprising that performance is poor at low arousal levels. Extremely low arousal may lead to failure to adopt a task set (that is, to be prepared to perform the task) or failure to monitor performance and

sufficiently adjust the commitment of attentional resources to the task demands.

It is more surprising that performance deteriorates at high arousal levels. Several factors contribute to this decrement, but it is primarily due to a decrease in attentional control. At high arousal levels, attention becomes more focused and the range of cues used to guide attention becomes more restricted (Easterbrook, 1959). Also, the ability to discriminate between relevant

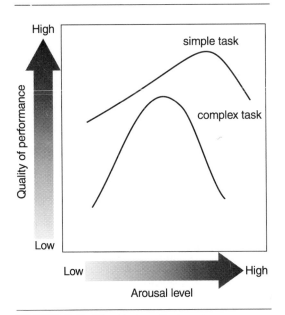

FIGURE 9–9   The Yerkes-Dodson Law.

and irrelevant cues decreases. Thus, at high arousal levels the allocation of attention is controlled by fewer and often less appropriate features of the situation. In fact, Näätänen (1973) has proposed that performance efficiency does not decline at high levels of arousal if attention remains directed toward the task at hand. The number of features to consider in difficult tasks typically is greater and the coordination of control more crucial. This explains why difficult tasks show more of a performance decrement at lower arousal levels than do simple tasks.

The restriction of attention that occurs under high arousal has been called perceptual narrowing (Kahneman, 1973). Weltman and Egstrom (1966) used a dual task to examine perceptual narrowing in the performance of novice SCUBA divers. The primary task involved arithmetic and detection of a dial, and the secondary task required the detection of a light presented peripherally. The level of arousal was manipulated by observing the divers in normal surroundings (low stress), in a tank (intermediate stress), and in the ocean (high stress). As stress increased, the time

to detect the peripheral light increased, although performance on the primary task was unaffected. This is consistent with a narrowing of attentional focus under increased stress.

A low level of arousal can result from having to perform a boring task for a long period of time. This aspect of attention has been investigated in *vigilance tasks*. Vigilance tasks involve detecting relatively infrequent signals that occur at unpredictable times. Research on vigilance began in World War II to determine why radar operators were failing to detect a significant number of submarine targets. As systems have become more automated, the operator's role has become primarily one of passively monitoring displays for critical signals, so vigilance research is still important. Vigilance in part determines the reliability of human performance in such operations as industrial quality control, air traffic control, jet and space flight, and the operation of agricultural machinery (Warm, 1984).

Mackworth (1950) devised a display in which observers had to monitor the movements of a pointer along the circumference of a blank-faced clock. Every second, the pointer would move 0.3 in. to a new position. Occasionally, it would take a jump of 0.6 in. Observers were required to execute a key-press response when a target movement of 0.6 in. was detected. The monitoring session lasted 2 hrs.

Mackworth (1950) found that the hit rate for detecting the target movement decreased over time, a finding that has since been replicated with many tasks. This decline is called the *vigilance decrement*. Figure 9–10 shows the decrement for three tasks over a 2-hr. period. The maximal decrement in accuracy occurs within the first 30 min. Not only does accuracy decrease, but reaction times for hits (as well as for false alarms) become slower as the time spent at the task increases (Parasuraman & Davies, 1976).

The decrease in hit rate could reflect either a decrease in sensitivity to the signals or a shift to a more conservative criterion for responding. To determine which of these is responsible for the decreased hit rate, a signal detection analysis can

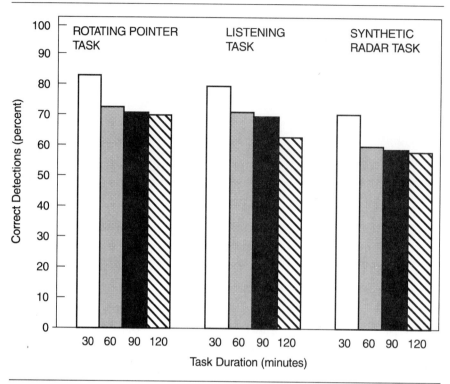

FIGURE 9–10   The Vigilance Decrement for Three Tasks.
Figure from K. R. Boff and J. E. Lincoln (Eds.), *Engineering Data Compendium: Human Perception and Performance*, 1988. Reprinted with permission.

be performed that incorporates the false-alarm rate as well. When such analyses are performed on the vigilance decrement, the primary shift often involves an increase in the criterion (β), with sensitivity (d') remaining relatively constant (for example, Broadbent & Gregory, 1965; Murrell, 1975). The criterion can be maintained at a more optimal, lower level by using artificial signals to increase the frequency of events.

Sensitivity declines in vigilance tasks that require discrimination based on a standard held in memory, particularly if the event rate is high (for example, Parasuraman, 1979). This may be because of the cognitive resources necessary to make a comparison between each event and the memorized standard. For such situations, sensitivity can be improved by having a physical standard present for comparison. High event rates can also produce a decrement in sensitivity when the task involves discrimination of simultaneous stimuli if the stimuli are degraded (Parasuraman & Mouloua, 1987).

Performance in vigilance tasks is affected by other characteristics of the signal, as well as by the motivation of the observer. Stronger signals tend to produce greater sensitivity and reduce the vigilance decrement (Baker, 1963; Wiener, 1964). Sensitivity improves when the signals are auditory rather than visual and is better when auditory and visual modalities are alternated for short blocks of time (for example, 5-min periods; Galinsky et al., 1990). Performance can also be improved by rest periods of 5 to 10 min or by financial incentives (Davies & Tune, 1969).

The typical vigilance task requires detection of only a single target event from a single source. However, in most industrial inspection and monitoring tasks, multiple target events and/or multiple sources must be monitored. Craig (1991) reviewed the literature on vigilance for multiple signals and concluded that, although increasing the monitoring load in this manner tends to decrease performance overall, it has no consistent effect on the vigilance decrement. The vigilance decrement is present for complex as well as simple tasks.

MENTAL WORKLOAD ASSESSMENT

Models of attention have been profitably applied to the solution of human factors problems. One area in which this application is evident is the measurement of mental workload. Workload refers to the total amount of work that a person or group of persons is to perform over a given period of time. Mental workload is the amount of mental work or effort necessary to perform a task. As task demands increase, so does the mental workload. According to Gopher and Donchin (1986), "Mental workload may be viewed as the difference between the capacities of the information-processing system that are required for task performance to satisfy expectations and the capacity available at any given time" (p. 41–3).

In work settings, performance may suffer if the mental workload is too high or too low. At the upper extreme, it is clear that performance will be poor if there are too many task demands. However, an undemanding task may also lead to a deterioration in performance by lowering the operator's level of alertness. Figure 9–11 illustrates the resulting inverted U-shaped function between mental workload and performance.

The purpose of mental workload assessment is to maintain the workload at a level that will allow acceptable performance of the operator's tasks. The workload imposed on an operator varies as a function of several factors. Most important are the tasks that the operator must perform. Workload will increase as required accuracy lev-

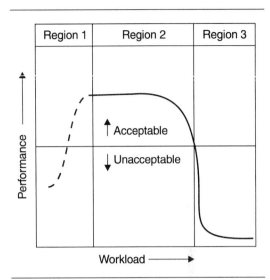

FIGURE 9–11   The Hypothetical Relation Between Workload and Performance.

From R. J. Lysaght et al. (1989). *Operator Workload: Comprehensive review and evaluation of operator workload methodologies.* Technical Report 851, United States Army Research Institute for the Behavioral and Social Sciences.

els increase, as time demands become stricter, as the number of tasks to be performed increases, and so on. Workload will also be affected by aspects of the environment in which the tasks must be performed. For example, extreme heat or noise will increase the workload. Also, because the cognitive capacities and skills of individuals vary, the workload demands imposed by a given task may be excessive for some people but not for others.

The mental workload concept comes directly from the unitary-resource model of attention, in which the human is believed to have a limited capacity for processing information (Kantowitz, 1987). This model lends itself nicely to the concept of spare capacity, or the amount of attentional resources available for use in additional tasks. However, most current workload techniques are more closely linked to the multiple-resources model, for which different task components are assumed to draw on resources from distinct pools of limited capacity. The primary benefit of the multiple-resources view is that it allows the human factors specialist to evaluate the extent to which specific processes are being overloaded.

The many workload-assessment techniques differ in several ways. A useful taxonomy distinguishes between empirical and analytical techniques (Lysaght et al., 1989; see Figure 9–12). Empirical techniques are used to measure workload directly in an operational system or simulated environment, whereas analytical techniques are used to predict workload demands early in the system development process.

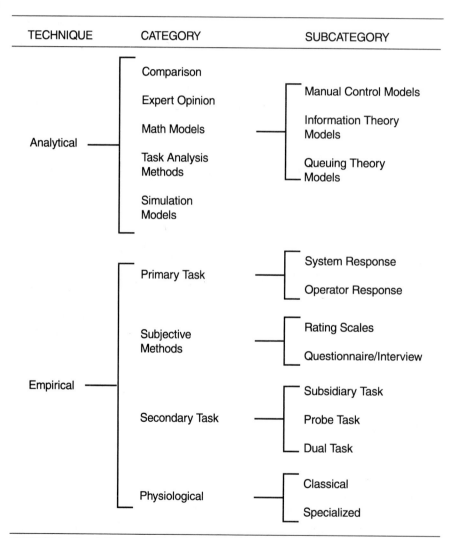

FIGURE 9–12 A Taxonomy of Mental Workload Techniques.

From R. J. Lysaght et al. (1989). *Operator workload: Comprehensive review and evaluation of operator workload methodologies*. Technical Report 851, United States Army Research Institute for the Behavioral and Social Sciences.

Empirical Techniques

Empirical techniques include performance measures of the primary task, performance measures of a secondary task, psychophysiological measures, and subjective scales. Several criteria can be applied to the selection of a workload-assessment technique for a given situation (Boff & Lincoln, 1988; see Table 9–1). A technique should be sensitive to changes in the workload imposed by the primary task, particularly once overload levels are reached. It should be diagnostic to the extent that the assessment can isolate particular processing resources being overloaded. On the basis of multiple-resource theory, this requires discriminating between capacities from the three dimensions of processing stages (perceptual–cognitive versus motor), codes (spatial–manual versus verbal–vocal), and modalities (auditory versus visual).

The remaining three criteria arise from pragmatic considerations. The assessment technique should not be intrusive, because an intrusive technique will cause performance of the primary task to be degraded. In such cases, workload estimates are difficult to interpret because any observed decrement in performance may be due to the measurement technique and not the task. Imple-

mentation requirements are of concern, because some techniques require sophisticated equipment. Techniques should be implemented that involve the fewest problems in doing so. Finally, it is important that the technique be accepted by the operators who are being evaluated. Their compliance with the assessment procedure is necessary to obtain meaningful measures.

Primary-task Measures. Primary-task measures evaluate the mental workload requirements of a task by directly examining the performance of the operator or of the overall system. As task difficulty increases, the assumption is that additional processing resources will be required. Performance should deteriorate when the workload requirements exceed the capacity of the available resources.

Many primary-task measures of workload should be used. If only one performance measure is used, that measure may show no effect of workload, whereas other measures would. For example, in a study evaluating differences between situation displays for air-traffic control, Kreifeldt et al. (1976) obtained 16 measures of control performance, including final air speed, heading, and communications. If a pilot is adjusting both air speed and heading, air speed may show no

TABLE 9–1 Criteria for Selection of Workload Assessment Techniques

CRITERION	EXPLANATION
Sensitivity	Capability of a technique to discriminate significant variations in the workload imposed by a task or group of tasks.
Diagnosticity	Capability of a technique to discriminate the amount of workload imposed on different operator capacities or resources (for example, perceptual versus central processing versus motor resources).
Intrusiveness	The tendency for a technique to cause degradations in ongoing primary task performance.
Implementation requirements	Factors related to the ease of implementing a particular technique. Examples include instrumentation requirements and any operator training that might be required.
Operator acceptance	Degree of willingness on the part of operators to follow instructions and actually utilize a particular technique.

Adapted from K. R. Boff and J. E. Lincoln (Eds.), *Engineering Data Compendium: Human Perception and Performance,* 1988. Reprinted with permission.

decrement as workload is increased, while the control of heading may suffer. If only air speed were measured, then the conclusion might be reached that workload was slight. With multiple measures, a more accurate picture of workload emerges.

Primary-task measures are sensitive at discriminating overload from nonoverload conditions. However, they are relatively insensitive to differences in mental workload when performance is not impaired. One promising approach for minimizing this problem of sensitivity is to examine changes in strategies that operators employ as task demands are varied (Eggemeier, 1988). Such strategy changes can be indicators of increased workload. Primary-task measures are also relatively nondiagnostic of the loads imposed on different types of operator resources. Although they are relatively nonintrusive, they may require sophisticated instrumentation that renders them difficult to implement in many operational settings.

Secondary-task Measures. Another objective method for measuring workload involves the use of secondary tasks. Secondary-task measures are based on the logic of dual-task performance described earlier in the chapter. The operator is required to perform a task in addition to the primary task of interest. Workload is assessed by the degree to which performance deteriorates in the dual-task situation relative to when each task is performed alone. Thus, dual-task interference provides an index of the demands placed on the operator's attentional resources by the two tasks.

Secondary-task measures are more sensitive than primary-task measures. In nonoverload situations for which the primary task can be performed efficiently, secondary-task measures can assess differences in spare capacity. Secondary-task measures are also diagnostic in that specific sources of workload can be determined through the use of multiple measures. Possible drawbacks of secondary-task measures are that they can be intrusive and may introduce artificiality by altering the task environment. Also, some operator

training may be necessary to stabilize dual-task performance.

The demands placed on the operator can be assessed either by manipulating primary-task difficulty and observing variations in secondary-task performance or by manipulating secondary-task difficulty and observing variations in primary-task performance. In the *loading task paradigm,* operators are told to maintain performance on the secondary task even if primary-task performance suffers (Ogden, Levine, & Eisner, 1979). In this paradigm, performance deteriorates more rapidly on difficult than on easy primary tasks. For example, Dougherty, Emery, and Curtin (1964) examined the workload requirements of two displays for helicopter pilots: a standard helicopter display and a pictorial display. The primary task involved flying at a prescribed altitude, heading, course, and air speed. The secondary, or loading, task was reading displayed digits. Primary-task performance did not differ for the two display conditions when flying was performed alone or when the digits for the secondary task were presented at a slow rate. However, at fast rates of digit presentation, the pictorial display produced better flying performance than the standard display. Thus, the mental workload requirements apparently were less with the pictorial display.

In the *subsidiary task paradigm,* operators are instructed to maintain performance on the primary task at the expense of the secondary task. Differences in the difficulty of the primary task will then show up as decrements in performance of the secondary task. This paradigm is illustrated in a study by Bell (1978) that examined the effects of noise and heat stress. For the primary task, performers had to keep a stylus on a moving target. The secondary task involved pressing a telegraph key once if an auditorily displayed number was less than the previous number and twice if the displayed number was greater than the previous number. Secondary-task performance was degraded by both high noise levels and high temperature, although primary-task performance was unaffected.

The human factors specialist must decide which of several types of secondary tasks to use for measuring workload. The task should be one that draws on the processing resources required by the primary task. If not, the measure will be insensitive to the workload associated with that task. Moreover, several distinct dual tasks can be selected to provide a profile of the various resource requirements of the primary task. Some commonly used secondary tasks are simple reaction time, which involves perceptual and response–execution resources; choice reaction time, which also imposes central-processing and response–selection demands; monitoring for the occurrence of a stimulus, which emphasizes perceptual processes; and mental arithmetic, which requires central-processing resources.

To minimize potential problems of artificiality in the assessment procedure, an embedded secondary task can be used (Shingledecker, 1980). This is a task that is part of the normal operator duties but is of lower priority than the primary task. As one example, workload can be measured for pilots using radio communication activities as an embedded secondary task. Intrusiveness is minimized in this way, as is the need for special instrumentation, but the information about workload demands that can be obtained may be restricted.

Psychophysiological Measures. Recent years have seen a rapid increase in instrumentation and applications of psychophysiological indexes of cognition. Some of these psychophysiological indexes can be used to measure workload. Such measures avoid the intrusion problems that come from introducing a secondary task to be performed with the primary task. However, psychophysiological measures have the drawback of requiring sophisticated instrumentation. Moreover, the possibility exists that the procedures necessary to perform the measurements may interfere with primary-task performance.

Several types of psychophysiological measures have been used. One is *pupillometry,* or the measurement of pupil diameter. Pupil diameter provides an indicator of the amount of attentional resources that is expended to perform a task (Beatty, 1982; Kahneman, 1973). The greater the workload demands are, the larger the pupil size. The changes that occur are small but reliable and require a pupillometer to allow sufficiently sensitive measurements. While useful as a general measure of workload, pupil diameter is not a good diagnostic for the specific resources used to perform a task.

A second psychophysiological measure is heart rate. Increased heart rates generally are correlated with increased workloads (Wilson & O'Donnell, 1988). However, because the primary determinants of heart rate are physical workload and arousal level, heart rate is not a consistent indicator of mental workload. A better measure seems to be heart rate variability (Meshkati, 1988). A component of this variability has been isolated that decreases as mental effort increases (Vicente, Thornton, & Moray, 1987).

The most promising psychophysiological measures involve event-related potentials. Presentation of a discrete stimulus event causes a transient evoked response from the brain, which is a series of voltage oscillations that originates in the cortex. These transient responses can be measured by electrodes attached to the scalp; many trials must be averaged to determine the waveform of the event-related potential for a particular situation. Components of the evoked response are either positive (P) or negative (N). They can also be identified in terms of their minimal latencies from the onset of the stimulus event (see Figure 9–13). The P300 (a positive component that occurs approximately 300 ms after the event onset) shows amplitude and latency effects that can be interpreted as reflecting workload. The latency of the P300 peak is regarded as an index of stimulus-evaluation difficulty (Donchin, 1981). The amplitude decreases as a stimulus is repeated but then increases when an unexpected stimulus occurs (Duncan-Johnson & Donchin, 1977). Thus, the P300 seems to reflect the amount of cognitive processing performed on a stimulus.

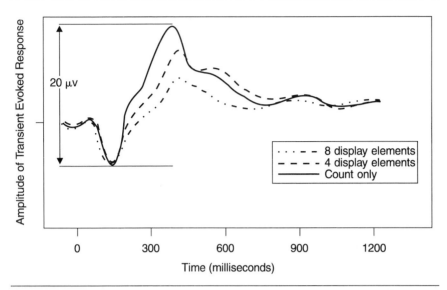

FIGURE 9–13 Amplitude of Transient Evoked Response (P300) Elicited by Infrequent Counted Tones When Presented Alone or Concurrently with a Visual Detection Task of Varying Workload.

From J. B. Isreal et al., The event-related brain potential as an index of display-monitoring workload. Adapted from *Human Factors,* Vol. 22, No. 2, pp. 211–224, 1980. Copyright 1980 by The Human Factors Society, Inc. All rights reserved.

The P300 has been shown to be sensitive to the workload demands of real-world tasks. Kramer, Sirevaag, and Braune (1987) had student pilots fly a series of missions on a flight simulator. The flight was the primary task in a dual-task paradigm. The difficulty of the primary task was manipulated by varying wind conditions, turbulence, and the probability of a system failure. For the secondary task, the pilot pressed a button whenever one of two tones occurred. The P300 latency to the tones increased and the amplitude decreased with increasing difficulty of the mission, indicating that the tones were receiving less processing as the workload of the primary task increased.

The P300 is considered diagnostic of the type of resource on which a workload is imposed, because it is sensitive only to stimulus-evaluation processes. Other components of the event-related potentials are more closely linked to perceptual-identification and response-initiation processes.

The P300 measure is useful when workload must be assessed in a manner that does not disrupt performance of the primary task. However, it requires sophisticated instrumentation and control procedures.

Subjective Measures. *Subjective assessment techniques* evaluate workload through the use of the operators' judgments. These techniques are relatively easy to implement and tend to be accepted by operators. Typically, operators are asked to rate such things as the perceived mental effort, time load, and stress load of particular tasks (Moray, 1982). Although useful, there are some limitations to the subjective assessment techniques (Boff & Lincoln, 1988): (1) They may not be sensitive to aspects of the task environment that affect primary-task performance and hence, it may be best to couple their use with primary-task measures. (2) They lack diagnosticity. (3) Operators may confuse perceived difficulty with perceived expenditure of effort. (4) Many factors that determine workload are inaccessible to conscious evaluation.

Cooper and Harper (1969) developed a rating scale to measure the mental workload involved in piloting aircraft with various handling characteristics. The scale has since been modified by Wierwille and Casali (1983) to be applicable to a variety of settings. As shown in Figure 9–14, the scale involves traversal of a decision tree, yielding a rating between 1 (low workload) and 10 (high workload). These numbers are best conceived as ordinal indicators of the degree of mental workload. The modified Cooper–Harper scale has been shown to be sensitive to differences in workload and to be consistent across tasks (Skipper, Rieger, & Wierwille, 1986), despite the fact that it was not derived psychometrically.

The Subjective Workload Assessment Technique (SWAT) was designed initially for use with a variety of tasks and systems (Reid, Shingledecker, & Eggemeier, 1981). In contrast to the Cooper–Harper scale, it was developed from psychometric principles. The procedure requires operators to make only simple, ordinal judgments of mental workload. Three subcategories of workload (time load, mental effort load, and stress load) are distinguished, with three classifications for each (see Table 9–2). Time load refers to the extent to which a task must be performed within a limited amount of time and the extent to which multiple tasks must be performed at the same time. Mental effort load involves inherent attentional demands of tasks, such as attending to multiple sources of information and performing calculations. Stress load encompasses operator variables, such as fatigue, level of training, and emotional state, that contribute to an operator's anxiety level.

Operators are asked to order all 27 possible combinations of the three descriptions according to their amount of workload. Typically, operators seem to add the difficulty of the separate task descriptions to arrive at estimates for the difficulty of the combinations. A process called conjoint scaling is then applied to the data to derive a scale of mental workload. Once the scale has been derived, workload estimates for various situations can be determined from simple ratings of the individual dimensions. The SWAT procedure is sensitive to workload increases induced by increases in task difficulty, as well as to those caused by sleep deprivation or increased time-on-task (Hankey & Dingus, 1990).

A final widely used subjective technique is the NASA-Task Load Index (NASA-TLX; Hart & Staveland, 1988). This index consists of six scales on which operators rate the workload demands (see Table 9–3). The scales evaluate mental demand, physical demand, temporal demand, performance, effort, and frustration level. These scales were selected from a larger set on the basis of research that showed each to make a relatively unique contribution to the subjective impression of workload. An overall measure of workload can be obtained by assigning a weight to each scale according to its importance for the specific task and then calculating the mean of the weighted values of each scale.

Both the SWAT and NASA-TLX indexes seem to be valid measures of workload, but their predictive validity is uncertain and their use as psychological models of workload is questionable (Nygren, 1991). Based on the characteristics of the scales, the NASA-TLX seems best as a predictor of subjective workload, whereas SWAT is better as a cognitive model. An example of the use to which the NASA-TLX can be put comes from recent studies of vigilance. Whereas previously it was thought that vigilance was relatively undemanding, observers rate the mental workload as high on the NASA-TLX, with mental demand and frustration being the primary contributors (Becker et al., 1991). Such results suggest that the vigilance decrement does not reflect simply a decrease in arousal and that vigilance performance requires considerable effort.

Analytical Techniques

In contrast to empirical techniques, analytical techniques do not require the interaction of an

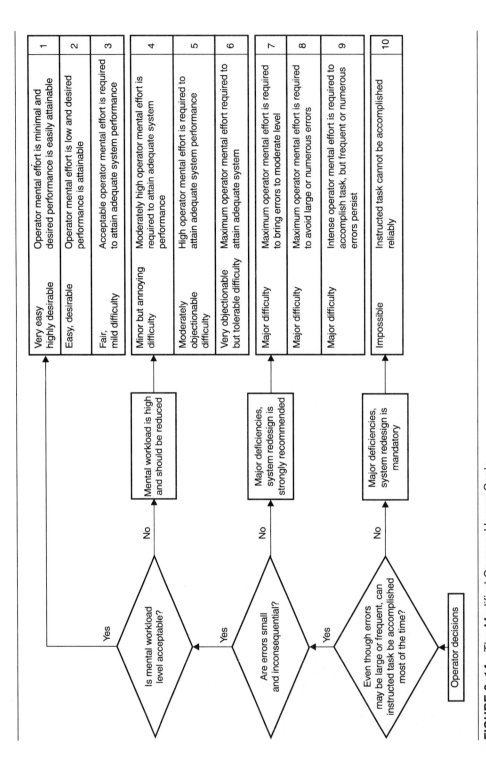

FIGURE 9–14 The Modified Cooper–Harper Scale.

From W. W. Wierwille & J. G. Casali, A validated rating scale for global mental workload measurement applications. Reprinted with permission from *Proceedings of the Human Factors Society 27th Annual Meeting*, 1983, pp. 129–133. Copyright 1990 by the Human Factors Society, Inc. All rights reserved.

TABLE 9–2   Three-Point Rating Scales for the Time, Mental Effort, and Stress Load Dimensions of the Subjective Workload Assessment Technique (SWAT)

TIME LOAD	MENTAL EFFORT LOAD	STRESS LOAD
1. Often have spare time. Interruptions or overlap among activities occur infrequently or not at all.	1. Very little conscious mental effort or concentration required. Activity is almost automatic, requiring little or no attention.	1. Little confusion, risk, frustration, or anxiety exists and can be easily accommodated.
2. Occasionally have spare time. Interruptions or overlap among activities occur frequently.	2. Moderate conscious mental effort or concentration required. Complexity of activity is moderately high due to uncertainty, unpredictability, or unfamiliarity. Considerable attention required.	2. Moderate stress due to confusion, frustration, or anxiety noticeably adds to workload. Significant compensation is required to maintain adequate performance.
3. Almost never have spare time. Interruptions or overlap among activities are very frequent or occur all the time.	3. Extensive mental effort and concentration are necessary. Very complex activity requiring total attention.	3. High to very intense stress due to confusion, frustration, or anxiety. High to extreme determination and self-control required.

From G. B. Reid, C. A. Shingledecker, and F. T. Eggemeir, Application of conjoint measurement in workload scale development. In *Proceedings of the Human Factors Society 25th Annual Meetings* (pp. 522–526). Copyright © 1981 by the Human Factors Society, Inc. All rights reserved.

operator with an operational system or simulator. Hence, they are used to estimate workload at early stages of system development. Many measurement techniques rely on different estimators of workload. Consequently, it is best to use a battery of techniques to assess the workload demands of any specific system. In the following sections, we discuss five categories of analytical techniques (Lysaght et al., 1989): comparison, expert opinion, mathematical models, task analysis methods, and simulation models.

Comparison. The basic idea behind the comparison technique is to use workload data from a predecessor system to estimate the workload for the system under development. Thus, this technique is useful only if such data exist, which often is not the case. One of the first systematic uses of the comparison technique was reported by Shaf-

fer, Shafer, and Kutch (1986). They estimated the mission workload for a single-crew member helicopter, based on data from an empirical workload analysis of missions conducted with a two-crew member helicopter. The application of comparison techniques to workload assessment is in its infancy, and more formal procedures need to be developed.

Expert Opinion. One of the easiest and most extensively employed analytical techniques is expert opinion. Either users or developers of similar systems are provided a description of the proposed system and asked to predict workload, among other things. The opinions often are obtained informally, although it is better to use more formal methods. For example, SWAT has been modified for prospective evaluations from experts. The major modification is that the ratings are based on a description of the system and particular scenarios, rather than on actual operation of the system. Prospective ratings using SWAT or other methods have been shown to correlate highly with workload estimates made on the basis of performance for military aircraft (Eggleston & Quinn, 1984; Vidulich, Ward, & Schueren, 1991).

Mathematical Models. Numerous attempts have been made to develop mathematical models of mental workload. Models based on information theory were popular in the 1960s. One model by Senders (1964) assumed that an operator with limited attentional capacity samples information from a number of displays. The channel capacity for each display and processing rate of the operator determine how often a display must be examined for the information in it to be communicated accurately. The amount of time that an operator devotes to any particular display can thus be used as a measure of visual workload.

In the 1970s, models based on manual control theory and queuing theory became popular. Manual control models apply to situations where continuous tasks, such as the tracking of a target, must be performed. These rely on minimization of error via various analytical and theoretical methods. Queuing models view the operator as a server that processes a variety of tasks. The number of times that the server is called on provides a measure of workload. Although development of these mathematical models has continued, their use for workload estimation has diminished in recent years as computerized task analyses and simulations have been developed.

TABLE 9–3   NASA-TLX Rating Scale Definitions

TITLE	END POINTS	DESCRIPTION
Mental demand	Low/High	How much mental and perceptual activity was required (e.g., thinking, deciding, calculating, remembering, looking, searching, etc.)? Was the task easy or demanding, simple or complex, exacting or forgiving?
Physical demand	Low/High	How much physical activity was required (e.g., pushing, pulling, turning, controlling, activating, etc.)? Was the task easy or demanding, slow or brisk, slack or strenuous, restful or laborious?
Temporal demand	Low/High	How much time pressure did you feel due to the rate or pace at which the tasks or task elements occurred? Was the pace slow and leisurely or rapid and frantic?
Performance	Low/High	How successful do you think you were in accomplishing the goals of the task set by the experimenter (or yourself)? How satisfied were you with your performance in accomplishing these goals?
Effort	Low/High	How hard did you have to work (mentally and physically) to accomplish your level of performance?
Frustration level	Low/High	How insecure, discouraged, irritated, stressed, and annoyed versus secure, gratified, content, relaxed, and complacent did you feel during the task?

From S. G. Hart and L. E. Staveland, Development of NASA-TLX (Task Load Index): Results of empirical and theoretical research. In P. A. Hancock and N. Meshkati (Eds.), *Human Mental Workload,* 1988. Reprinted with permission of Elsevier Science Publishers.

Task Analysis. A task analysis decomposes the overall system goal into segments and operator tasks and, ultimately, into elemental task requirements. The analysis provides a time-based breakdown of demands on the operator. Consequently, most task-analytic measures of mental workload focus on estimation of time stress, which is the amount of mental resources required per unit time relative to those that are available. One exception is the McCracken–Aldrich technique (Aldrich & Szabo, 1986; McCracken & Aldrich, 1984), which distinguishes five workload dimensions: visual, auditory, kinesthetic, cognitive, and psychomotor. For each task element, ratings are made on a scale from 1 (low workload) to 7 (high workload) for each pertinent dimension. Estimates of the workload on each dimension are made during half-second intervals by summing the workload estimates for all active task components. If the sum exceeds 7, it is assumed that an overload exists for that component.

Simulation Models. A simulation model is probabilistic and, hence, will not yield the same result each time it is run. Several simulation models exist that can be used to provide workload estimates. Most are variants of the Siegel and Wolf (1969) stochastic model discussed in Chapter 3. In that model, workload is indicated by a variable called *stress* that is affected by both the time to perform tasks and the quantity of tasks that must be performed. Stress is the sum of the average task execution times divided by the total time available. Several recent extensions of this technique have been developed that allow for greater flexibility in the prediction of workload (Lysaght et al., 1989).

SUMMARY

Research on attention exemplifies the ideal of a close relationship between basic and applied concerns in human factors. The resurgence of interest in attention arose from applied problems, but it has led to much basic, theoretical work on the nature of attentional control. This basic work, in turn, has led to better measures of the attentional requirements in applied settings.

Often operators must perform tasks that require selectively attending to specific sources of information, distributing attention across multiple sources of information, or maintaining attention on a single display for long periods of time. Many principles of attention are now known that can be applied to the design of systems for effective performance under each situation. For example, it is known that presentation of information in distinct modalities avoids decrements in performance due to competition for perceptual resources and improves memory for unattended information. More generally, assessment of mental workload can help determine the tasks that can be performed simultaneously with little or no decrement. Because mental workload varies as a function of the perceptual, cognitive, and motoric requirements imposed on an operator, the structure of a task and the environment in which it is performed can significantly affect workload and performance.

RECOMMENDED READING

Gopher, D., & Donchin, E. (1986). Workload: An examination of the concept. In K. R. Boff, L. Kaufman, & J. P. Thomas (eds.), *Handbook of Perception and Human Performance, Vol. II: Cognitive Processes and Performance* (pp. 41–1 to 41–49). New York: Wiley.

Hancock, P. A., & Meshkati, N. (eds.). (1988). *Human Mental Workload*. Amsterdam: North-Holland.

Kahneman, D. (1973). *Attention and Effort*. Englewood Cliffs, NJ: Prentice Hall.

Parasuraman, R., & Davies, D. R. (eds.). (1984). *Varieties of Attention*. New York: Academic Press.

Shiffrin, R. M. (1989). Attention. In R. C. Atkinson et al, (eds.), *Stevens' Handbook of Experimental Psychology*, Vol. 2, 2nd ed. (pp. 739–811). New York: Wiley.

RETENTION AND COMPREHENSION OF INFORMATION

*Human memory is a system for storing and retrieving information,
information that is, of course, acquired through our senses.*

—A. Baddeley, 1990

INTRODUCTION

Human memory is intricate and diverse. Over a lifetime, vast amounts of information are learned and retained for various amounts of time. However, memories can be distorted, and the ability to retrieve them depends on many environmental and contextual conditions. How well an operator learns and remembers plays an important role in his or her ability to perform within a human–machine system. In most circumstances, successful performance of the system depends on the operator's ability to retrieve the appropriate information from memory.

It has been convenient to conceive of the memory system as composed of three distinct memory stores (Atkinson & Shiffrin, 1968): the *sensory store,* the *short-term store,* and the *long-term store.* Figure 10–1 depicts the relationship between the three stores. When information is first presented, it is retained almost intact for a brief period in the sensory store. Information is read from the sensory store into the short-term store. Material in the short-term store decays very rapidly unless it is kept active through rehearsal, or covert repetition, of the items read from the sensory store. Rehearsal can also enter the information into the long-term store, where it is retained for an indefinite duration.

The present chapter organizes our knowledge of human memory around the memory-store distinctions. Each store has different properties

210

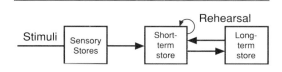

FIGURE 10–1   The Three-store Memory Model.

that affect human performance in a wide variety of situations. These properties are described, as well as pertinent findings regarding factors that affect the acquisition, retention, and retrieval of information in each. The comprehension and retention of written and spoken information are then examined.

SENSORY STORE

The sensory effects of briefly presented stimuli persist for a short period of time after their occurrence. For example, when a visual display is flashed briefly, its perceived duration exceeds its physical duration. This phenomenon is called visible persistence or, more generally, sensory persistence. From persisting sensory effects, it is possible to selectively retrieve information from an immediately preceding display. These and related findings have been taken as evidence for the existence of sensory stores that act as buffer systems to hold information for immediate processing. These stores are typically thought to be of relatively unlimited capacity, and the transfer of information from them is thought to be under voluntary control.

Visual Sensory Store

The first evidence for the existence of a sensory store came from research using visual stimuli. Research on the visual sensory store was inspired by a memory limitation called the *span of apprehension,* known since the 1800s (Cattell, 1886). This span refers to the number of simultaneous, briefly displayed visual stimuli that can be recalled without error. For example, an array of letters may be presented briefly, and the task is to

report as many of the letters as possible. This is known as a whole-report task. Typically, all the letters can be reported correctly as long as no more than four or five are displayed. However, when the arrays are larger, only a subset consisting of four or five letters will be reported.

Although large arrays of stimuli cannot be identified with complete accuracy, observers often claim that they can see the whole display at first but it "disappears" before all the stimuli can be identified (Gill & Dallenbach, 1926). Ingenious experiments by Sperling (1960) and Averbach and Coriell (1961) established that these subjective reports are indeed accurate. They used a procedure known as partial report, in which only a subset of the items is to be reported. Sperling displayed three rows of four letters using a device called a tachistoscope. A tachistoscope is an arrangement of lights and half-silvered mirrors that allows precise control over the duration of visual displays. At the offset of the display, Sperling presented a high-, medium-, or low-frequency tone as a cue, indicating whether the top, middle, or bottom row should be reported. The critical finding was that when the tone occurred immediately at the offset of the array the cued row could be reported with virtually perfect accuracy. Because the observer could not know in advance which row would be cued, this finding suggests that initially all stimuli from the display must be available for report.

If the tone was delayed by as little as one-third of a second, report accuracy dropped to the level of the span of apprehension (see Figure 10–2). That is, report accuracy was at the level that would be expected if only four or five items were available. Between no delay and a delay of the cue by one-third second after the array, partial-report performance gradually decreased. This rapid loss of partial-report superiority was evident only if the field following the display was light. If it was dark, the superiority remained for several seconds. In either situation, when a visual pattern mask (an array of random contours) immediately followed the display and so interfered with any visual memory of the display, partial-re-

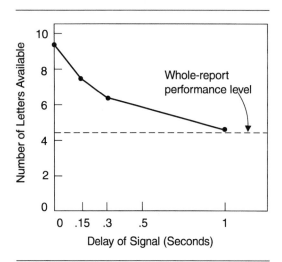

FIGURE 10–2   Partial Report Accuracy as a Function of Delay.

port accuracy remained at the whole-report level of four to five items even when the cue was not delayed.

These and other results led to the conclusion that visual stimuli persist briefly in a sensory store that can be disrupted by subsequent visual stimulation. Considerable research has been conducted on the properties of the visual sensory store, sometimes called *iconic memory,* examining issues such as whether it is postcategorical or precategorical (that is, whether or not it contains identified, meaningful representations of the stimuli) and its locus in the visual system (Coltheart, 1980). Furthermore, the appropriateness of considering visual persistence as a distinct memory store has been questioned (Eriksen & Schultz, 1978). Despite these issues, the major point is that, for a very brief period of time after seeing a visual display, an observer can report virtually any item in the display (within the resoluton limits of the visual system).

Tactile and Auditory Sensory Stores

Sensory stores with properties similar to those of iconic memory seem to exist for the other senses. Bliss et al., (1966) examined an analog of the Sperling task that used tactile stimulators placed on each of the three interjoint regions of the four fingers of both hands. Several locations were stimulated simultaneously, and observers were to report preassigned letters corresponding to the locations. On partial-report trials, only one of the three rows of locations was cued for report. A partial-report benefit for the stimulated locations was obtained if the cue occurred less than 800 ms after the tactile stimuli.

Analogs of the Sperling task also have been used with auditory stimuli, producing estimates for the duration of *echoic memory* of 2 s or longer (for example, Darwin, Turvey, & Crowder, 1972). However, considerably more research has been conducted with the modality effect. When a short list of items (words, numbers, and so on) is presented auditorily, the last one or two are recalled at much higher accuracy than when the same list is presented visually. This modality effect has been attributed to echoic memory (for example, Crowder & Morton, 1969).

Evidence for the auditory sensory store was also given by the finding of a suffix effect. When the last item in an auditory list is followed by an auditory suffix (a speech sound), such as the word *zero* or *one,* recall of the items in the list is disrupted, particularly at the last position (see Figure 10–3). This suffix effect varies as a function of physical differences between the suffix and list items, such as pitch or loudness, but not as a function of variables that influence meaning. There has been considerable debate over whether the suffix effect is due to an auditory sensory store (for example, Battacchi, Pelamatti, & Umiltà, 1990). Regardless of its basis, human factors specialists must consider that at short retention intervals there is a memorial advantage for information presented auditorily, but this advantage may be disrupted by subsequent auditory stimuli.

Multiple Stores within Each Modality

Recent theoretical views suggest that the nature of the sensory stores is more complex than at first envisioned. Evidence indicates that multiple

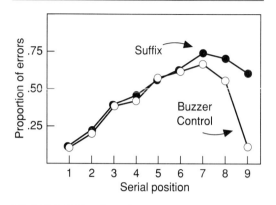

FIGURE 10–3   The Suffix Effect, as Shown by Poorer Recall at the Final Positions When a Suffix Occurs.

stores with different properties may exist for both the visual and auditory systems. Coltheart (1980) concluded that the partial-report benefit in vision is not due to the same memory store as that responsible for visible persistence. Whereas visible persistence is inversely related to stimulus duration and luminance, partial-report accuracy is an increasing function of these variables. Visible persistence apparently results from a process that is initiated by stimulus onset and can be modified by subsequent stimulus events (Clark & Hogben, 1991). The store that underlies partial-report superiority may be postcategorical rather than precategorical. Moreover, it seems to be more dynamic and likely plays a role in the integration of intermittent stimuli and stabilization of percepts across saccadic eye movements. Cowan (1984) reached similar conclusions about echoic memory. He concluded that the partial-report benefit and the suffix effect are due to a postcategorical store that has a duration of 2 to 20 s; a precategorical store of shorter duration (150 to 350 ms) is presumed to be the basis for audible persistence.

SHORT-TERM STORE

Everyone has experienced the situation in which you look up a phone number to call someone. You usually repeat the number to yourself until making the phone call. However, if you are distracted momentarily, the number is forgotten and you must then look it up again. Such experiences suggest that there is a limited-capacity short-term store for which items must be rehearsed if they are to be retained.

Short-term memory is a major limiting factor of many tasks that must be performed by operators in a variety of situations. An air-traffic controller must remember such things as the locations and headings of many different aircraft and the instructions given to each. Similarly, radio dispatchers for a taxi company must remember the taxis that are available and their locations. For jobs that rely on short-term memory, performance can be affected greatly by the manner in which the information is presented and the ways in which the operator's tasks are structured.

Basic Characteristics

Experiments conducted on short-term memory provided evidence of a memory store of longer duration and with different properties than those of the sensory stores. Two studies conducted in different laboratories by Brown (1958) and Peterson and Peterson (1959) provided similar findings. In the latter study, people were presented with a single consonant trigram (for example, BZX) to remember on a trial. This trigram can be recalled easily not just seconds later but minutes later if you are not distracted. However, following the trigram, the people in this experiment were required to count backward by threes from a 3-digit number until signaled to recall. Peterson and Peterson assumed that the mental activity required to count backward would prevent rehearsal, thus causing the trigram to decay from memory. Recall accuracy decreased to about 50% after 6 s and decreased still further to less than 10% after 18 s (see Figure 10–4). This suggested that the trigrams were retained in a short-term store for only a few seconds if rehearsal was prevented.

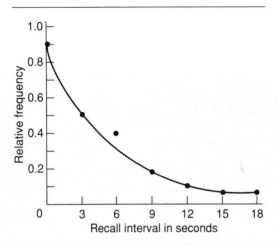

FIGURE 10–4   Recall Performance as a Function of a Filled Retention Interval in a Short-term Memory Task.
Based on data from Peterson & Peterson (1959).

The rapid forgetting that occurs when rehearsal is prevented reflects primarily two types of errors (Estes, 1972). A transposition or order error occurs when the correct items are recalled but in the wrong order. An intrusion or item error occurs when an item that was not in the list is recalled. Transposition errors predominate at short retention intervals, with the relative frequency of intrusion errors increasing as the interval increases. Thus, memory for the order in which items occur decays faster than memory for the items themselves. In other words, if an operator's task does not require remembering the exact order in which information occurred, actions based on that information will not suffer as much from delays in responding.

Although prevention of rehearsal is necessary for the rapid forgetting observed by Peterson and Peterson (1959), it is not sufficient. Keppel and Underwood (1962) demonstrated that recall is virtually perfect after an 18-s retention interval on the first trial that a person receives. However, by the third or fourth trial, forgetting to chance levels is evident. This finding indicates that short-term forgetting does not occur by decay alone.

Proactive interference, or interference from previous material, must also be present. This interference does not build up, and hence short-term forgetting does not occur, if intervals of a few minutes separate successive trials (Peterson & Gentile, 1963). Proactive interference also can be minimized by changing the semantic characteristics of the items to be remembered from those of previous items (for example, changing word categories from fruits to flowers) or, to a lesser extent, by changing physical characteristics (Wickens, 1972). This is often called release from proactive interference. The accuracy of short-term retention can be improved by increasing the intervals between successive messages or by making each message distinctive.

Early work on the short-term store suggested that its contents were coded acoustically, that is, by their sounds. Conrad (1964) presented people with lists of six letters, shown visually at a rate of 0.75 s per letter. Immediately after the last letter had been presented, the people attempted to write the six letters down in the order in which they had appeared. Errors in recall were found to be primarily acoustic confusions. For example, B was often written instead of the acoustically similar letter V, even though the two letters share little visual similarity. This and other evidence suggested that even visual stimuli are coded in terms of acoustic representations in the short-term store. Subsequent findings have demonstrated that codes can also be semantic or visual (Shulman, 1970; Tversky, 1969). However, because acoustic coding predominates for alphanumeric material, sets of items that are acoustically confusable will produce more short-term retention errors than sets that are not.

The capacity of the short-term store is typically described as seven plus or minus two *chunks,* or units, of information (Miller, 1956). If you try to remember isolated digits or letters, this capacity represents the maximum number that you can recall correctly. However, recall can be improved by grouping or recoding the information into larger chunks. For example, lists of digits are easier to remember if they are organized into groups of a maximum of four (Wickelgren, 1964). This principle is exploited for commonly used multidigit numbers, such as postal codes, telephone numbers, and social security numbers. Recoding can also be accomplished by relating the items in meaningful groups. This is particularly easy for letters or words.

Improving Short-term Retention

The limited capacity of the short-term store has implications for any situation in which successful operation of a system requires the operator to encode and retain information accurately for brief periods of time. Research indicates that the accuracy of retention can be increased by such techniques as minimizing the activities that intervene between presentation of the information and action on it, using sets of stimuli that are not acoustically confusable, increasing the interval between successive messages, making the material to be remembered distinct from preceding material, and chunking the information into optimal groups.

Several of these factors are illustrated in a study by Loftus, Dark, and Williams (1979) that examined communication errors between ground control and student pilots in a short-term memory task. Memory was tested for two types of messages: (1) place for the pilot to contact plus a radio frequency (for example, "contact Seattle center on 1.829") and (2) a transponder code (for example, "squawk 4273," which means set the transponder code to 4273). The codes were presented in two-digit chunks (for example, "forty-two, seventy-three") or as unchunked single digits (for example, "four, two, seven, three"). In a low-load condition, only one of the two message types was presented, whereas in a high-load condition both were presented. The message was followed by a variable retention interval during which the subject had to report rapidly presented letters. Following the retention interval, the relevant information from the message was to be filled out on an answer sheet.

The primary finding was that recall was worse overall and forgetting rate higher in the high-load condition than in the low-load condition. In other words, the more information that was to be retained, the worse was performance. Moreover, recall of the radio frequency was better when the transponder code was chunked, suggesting that chunking made more short-term memory capacity available for other information. Loftus, Dark, and Williams (1979) concluded that as little information as possible should be conveyed to a pilot at one time. They also proposed that a delay of at least 10 s should intervene between successive messages, because performance on a trial was an increasing function of the retention interval for the immediately preceding trial. Additionally, their results indicate that the response to a message should be made as quickly as possible to avoid error, and the information should be chunked whenever possible.

Not only does the size of the chunks influence the accuracy of short-term retention, but so does the nature of the chunks. Preczewski and Fisher (1990) examined the format of call signs used by the military in secured radio communications. The U.S. Army currently uses two-syllable codes of the sequence letter–digit–letter (LDL), followed by the sequence digit–digit (DD). These codes make radio communication very difficult, and they change at least once a day. Preczewski and Fisher compared the memorability of the current code format (LDL–DD) to that of three other formats: DD–LDL, DD–LLL, and LL–LLL. Operators were presented with a call sign, which they were to recall later. During a 10-s delay between presentation and recall, the operators read aloud strings of letters and digits. Performance was best when one syllable was composed only of digits and the other of letters (DD–LLL) and worst on the current code. Thus, mixing letters and digits within chunks seems harmful, whereas mixing them between chunks is beneficial.

Specific alphanumeric characters differ in their memorability. Few confusions will occur for letters that do not sound similar to other letters (Conrad, 1964). Chapanis and Moulden (1990) investigated the memorability of individual digits, as well as of doublets and triplets, within 8-digit strings. People viewed a string for 5 s and then immediately entered the string by means of a numeric keyboard. Many errors were made, as would be expected, since the length was beyond the normal memory span. Recall accuracy was a decreasing function of serial position, with a slight increase at the last position. The rank order of the memorability of the single digits was 0, 1, 7, 8, 2, 6, 5, 3, 9, 4. Doublets were generally easier to recall if they contained a zero or if the digit was duplicated. A similar pattern of results was found for triplets. Based on these findings, the authors provide tables that designers can use to construct numeric codes for maximal memorability.

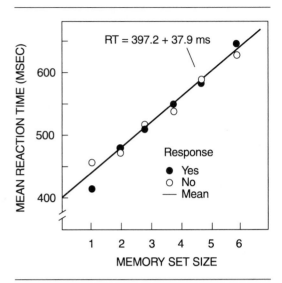

FIGURE 10–5 Memory-search Time as a Function of Set Size and Response.
Based on data from Sternberg (1966).

Memory Search

For many tasks, accurate performance requires not only that pertinent information be retained in the short-term store, but also that the information be acted on quickly. Search and retrieval from the short-term store have been investigated extensively with a memory-search task (Sternberg, 1966). In this task, introduced briefly in Chapter 4, observers are presented a memory set of one or more items (such as digits, letters, or words) to be held in short-term memory. Shortly thereafter, a single target item is presented. The observer is to respond as quickly as possible whether the target is in the memory set, usually by making one of two key presses indicating its presence or absence.

In Sternberg's (1966) study, the memory set was composed of 1 to 6 digits, followed by a single target digit. Reaction time increased as a linear function of the memory set size, and the slopes of the *yes* and *no* reaction-time functions were similar (see Figure 10–5). The rate of increase was approximately 38 ms per item in the memory set. These linear functions were inter-

preted by Sternberg as indicating that a rapid, serial scan was performed on the memory set. This is because, assuming that each comparison takes the same amount of time, the functions will be linear and the slope will reflect the comparison time per item. The intercept of the line represents the time taken by all other processes not involved in the comparison, such as perceptual and response processes.

The fact that the *no* function was parallel to the *yes* function led Sternberg (1966) to conclude that the search was exhaustive. That is, rather than terminating the search when a match was discovered, observers apparently compared the target to each item remaining in the memory set. For the target-absent trials, the target must be compared to all items in the memory set if a *no* response is to be made with certainty. So, for a memory set of size *n*, *n* comparisons must be performed. However, for a trial on which a target is present, it is possible that the *yes* response could be made after the match is found. When performing a serial scan, sometimes the match would be for the first item that was compared, sometimes for the second, and so on. On average, the response could be made after $\frac{n+1}{2}$ comparisons. This predicts that the slope for the *yes* reaction-time function should be one-half that of the *no* function. Because the slopes obtained were equal, Sternberg concluded that the search was not terminated when a match occurred.

Sternberg's findings are consistent with those expected from a serial, exhaustive scan of the memory set. However, this interpretation relies on other assumptions, such as a constant 38-ms comparison time for each item in the memory set. Nonserial, terminating processes can be devised that will also predict linear, parallel reaction-time functions when other assumptions, such as variable comparison rates, are made (Atkinson, Holmgren, & Juola, 1969; Townsend, 1974). Thus, Sternberg's findings are not conclusive evidence for serial, exhaustive comparison processes. Moreover, other experiments have shown findings, such as faster reponses to terminal or repeated items in the memory set (Baddeley & Ecob, 1973; Corballis, Kirby, & Miller, 1972), that are inconsistent with the basic assumptions of the serial exhaustive model.

Regardless of the exact nature of the comparison process, the slope of the function relating reaction time to memory-set size is an indicator of short-term memory capacity. Items such as digits, for which the memory span is large, show a slope that is considerably less than that for items such as nonsense syllables, for which the span is smaller (Cavanagh, 1972). The slope can be used as an indicator of the demands placed on short-term memory capacity. Moreover, this measure of memory capacity can be isolated from perceptual and motoric factors that affect only the intercept. Consequently, the memory-search task has frequently been used as a secondary-task measure to assess mental workload.

The memory search task is particularly relevant to the investigation of pilot workload, because it is similar to the monitoring of messages

that a pilot must perform and because flying a plane places heavy demands on all aspects of processing. Its use was illustrated by Wickens et al. (1986), who studied performance of instrument-rated pilots. An instrument-rated pilot is one who is qualified to fly on instrument readings alone, without visual contact outside the cockpit window. Wickens et al. required the pilots to fly an instrument holding pattern and instrument landing approach in a flight simulator, while performing a memory-search task. The intercepts of the search functions were greater during the approach phase than during the holding phase, but the slopes of the functions did not differ.

The intercept reflects the time to perform perceptual and motor processes, and so Wickens et al. (1986) concluded that the approach phase increases perceptual and response loads. Because there was no change in the slope of the search function, they concluded that short-term memory load was not any greater during approach than during holding. Additional tasks that require perceptual–motor processing should not be performed during the approach phase.

Working Memory

Recent work on the short-term store has focused on its function. This function is considered to be primarily one of temporarily storing and manipulating the information or calculations necessary for performing mental arithmetic, comprehending the meaning of a sentence, elaborating the meaning of material, and so on. Consequently, the term *working memory* has come to be used with increasing frequency. If a unitary store is assumed, that is, if working memory and short-term store are one and the same, then the capacity for mental manipulations should be closely related to that for retaining alphanumeric stimuli for recall.

However, several findings suggest that working memory and short-term store are not the same. Individual differences in memory span do not correlate highly with measures of intellectual ability, as would be expected if a larger span reflected a greater capacity to reason (Klapp, 1988). Also, when people are required to retain a memory load (for example, a set of digits) to be recalled after another task is performed, the memory load often has little effect on the performance of the embedded task. For example, Baddeley (1986) varied the number of digits that were to be retained while performing a reasoning or learning task. Maintaining a memory load of up to eight items produced only small amounts of interference with performance of the reasoning or learning task. The rehearsal process needed to maintain the digits does not seem to use the same capacity that is needed to reason and learn.

Figure 10–6 shows a diagram of the working-memory model proposed by Baddeley (1986) to explain results from studies of this type. Acoustic or phonological coding is represented by the phonological loop, which Baddeley has suggested plays a role in vocabulary acquisition, learning to read, and language comprehension. The model also includes visual coding, in the form of the visuospatial "sketch pad." This sketch pad is assumed to be responsible for visual imagery. Another feature of the model is its emphasis on the central executive, an attentional control system that supervises and coordinates the visuospatial and phonological subsystems. This emphasis on attentional control suggests that the

| Visuo-spatial sketch pad | Central executive | Phonological loop |

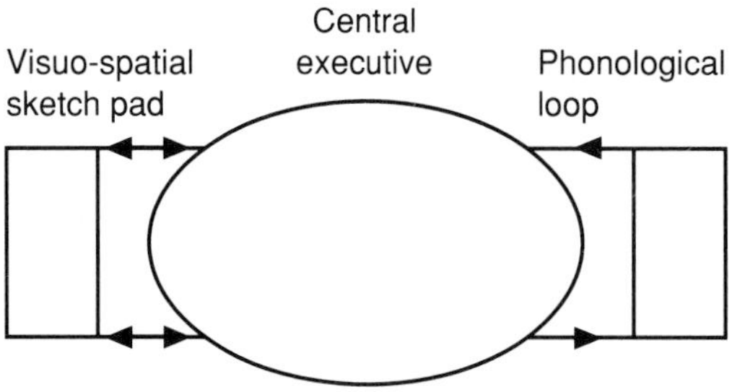

FIGURE 10–6 Working-memory Model.

From Alan Baddeley, *Human Memory: Theory and Practice*. Copyright © 1990 by Allyn and Bacon. Reprinted with permission.

short-term store is closely related to attentional processes. Moreover, the distinction between multiple stores is in agreement with the multiple-resource models of attention discussed in Chapter 9.

According to Baddeley's working-memory model, tasks should not interfere if they use different subsystems. In his experiments described above, the absence of interference between the memory load task and the reasoning and learning tasks implies that the tasks did not share the same processing subsystem. Retention of digits likely occupied the phonological loop, while the reasoning and learning tasks used the central executive. Another prediction from the model is that tasks sharing the same subsystem, such as scanning a visual image in short-term memory while performing a visuospatial task, should interfere.

Brooks (1968) reported evidence of such interference. Observers were asked to image a block letter, for example, the letter F (see Figure 10–7). They were told to mentally trace around the letter, starting from a designated corner and proceeding around the perimeter, responding to each successive corner with *yes* if it was either at the top or bottom of the figure or *no* if it was at an intermediate location. One group of observers responded vocally, and a second group tapped either of their index fingers. A third group had to point to a column on a sheet of paper that contained either Y's or N's in a sequence of staggered pairs (see Figure 10–7). It took much longer to respond in the third group, presumably because the task required visually perceiving the locations of the Y's and N's while at the same time visualizing the locations on the letter. These results are not due to the pointing responses being more difficult than the other modes of responding, because pointing did not cause difficulty for a similar task that involved verbal judgments.

Imagery

The nature of visual imagery has been the subject of many recent experiments. We reviewed in Chapter 4 some studies showing that observers

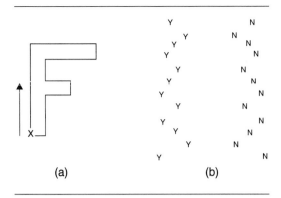

(a)   (b)

FIGURE 10–7 Block-letter Stimulus and "Yes"–"No" Response Display.

Reprinted by permission from L. R. Brooks (1968). Spatial and verbal components of the act of recall. *Canadian Journal of Psychology, 22,* 349–368.

can mentally rotate objects into similar orientations to determine whether the objects are the same. Other researchers, most notably Kosslyn (1980) and his colleagues, have supported the view that imagery is very much like perception. Several of their studies have suggested that images are mentally scanned in a manner similar to visually scanning a picture. For example, Kosslyn, Ball, and Reiser (1978) had observers memorize a map of a fictional island (see Figure 10–8). The experimenter then read the name of one of the objects on the island. The observer was to image the entire map, but focus on the specific object. Five seconds later, the experimenter named a second object. The observer was to mentally scan to the object and press a response key as soon as it was reached. The farther apart the two locations were, the longer it took to mentally scan from the first to the second.

Similarly, Kosslyn (1975) provided evidence that it is more difficult to make judgments about components of small images than of large images. A particular animal was visualized next to either a fly or an elephant. The reasoning was that it would be imaged as larger in the former situation than in the latter. When asked to verify whether a certain property, such as fur, was part of the imaged animal, responses were faster if the animal was imaged as large than if it was imaged as small.

The concept of an imagery component in working memory has been extended to the notion of a *mental model:* a dynamic representation or simulation of the world (Johnson-Laird, 1983, 1989). Johnson-Laird has argued that mental models are a form of representation in working memory providing the basis for many aspects of language comprehension and reasoning. He conceives of images as two-dimensional representations projected from a three-dimensional model. The key element in the mental model concept is that thinking about events occurs through mentally simulating specific instances. The general idea is that, if an operator possesses

FIGURE 10–8 Map of a Fictional Island Used by Kosslyn, Ball, and Reiser (1978).

From S. M. Kosslyn, T. M. Ball, & B. J. Reiser (1978). Visual images preserve metric spatial information: Evidence from studies of image scanning. *Journal of Experimental Psychology: Human Perception and Performance, 4,* 47–60. Reprinted by permission of the American Psychological Association.

an accurate mental model of a task or system, she or he may be able to solve problems through visualizing a simulation of the task.

To summarize, the view of short-term memory that has emerged is considerably more complex than that proposed in the 1960s. Short-term memory is not merely a repository for recent events, but it plays a crucial role in many aspects of cognition. It is used to temporarily represent and retain information in forms that are useful for problem solving and comprehension. Through carefully controlling the short-term memory demands placed on operators, the overall performance of many human–machine systems can be improved.

LONG-TERM STORE

Clearly, information can be remembered for more than a few seconds without rehearsing it continuously. Thus, in addition to the short-term store, there must exist a long-term memory store. An operator is often required to retrieve information from the long-term store to comprehend current system information and to determine an appropriate response. Failure to remember such things as previous instructions may have catastrophic consequences.

The Japanese air raid at Pearl Harbor on December 7, 1941, which was the worst disaster in U.S. naval history, provides an example. Several factors contributed to the lack of preparation of the U.S. Navy for the attack, with one being forgotten information that would have allowed a preceding event to be interpreted as signaling imminent attack (Janis & Mann, 1977). Five hours before the attack, two U.S. mine sweepers spotted a submarine that they presumed to be Japanese just outside Pearl Harbor. The sighting was not reported, presumably because the officers had forgotten an explicit warning given two months earlier. The warning was that a single submarine sighting should be regarded as extremely dangerous because an accompanying aircraft carrier might be nearby. Had the officers remembered the warning, the naval forces could

have been put on alert and been prepared for the attack that followed. By presenting information in a manner that will enhance long-term retention, it is possible to increase the likelihood that critical information will be retrieved when needed.

In discussing long-term store, it is useful to distinguish between episodic and semantic memory. *Episodic memory* refers to memory for specific events or episodes (for example, remembering that your dog chased a car this morning), whereas *semantic memory* refers to general knowledge (for example, remembering that dogs chase cars). The present section considers only episodic memory; semantic memory is discussed subsequently, along with comprehension of verbal material.

Basic Characteristics

Until the 1970s, the vast majority of research on long-term memory concerned individual episodes, and much effort continues to be devoted to this topic. An early view of long-term memory was that long-term codes are semantic and reflect the meanings of items. For example, in a test of recognition memory you are given a long list of words to remember; you are then tested a few minutes later with a second list in which those words that were in the first list must be distinguished from those that were not. In such situations, the false recognitions are primarily synonyms (that is, a word with a similar meaning to a word in the original list; Grossman & Eagle, 1970). More generally, when remembering passages or events, the gist or meaning will be remembered rather than the specific wordings.

As with research on the short-term store, coding in long-term memory is now seen as flexible and not restricted to semantic codes. Evidence for visual codes has come from several findings. For example, when people must decide whether an object indicated by a drawing is one that has been seen previously, they respond more quickly if the test version is identical to the drawing seen initially (Frost, 1972). Similar evidence for acoustic coding has been obtained (for example, Nelson & Rothbart, 1972). Considerable evidence exists that concrete and imageable words are remembered better than are abstract words, apparently because dual codes (verbal and visual) are stored for the former and only a single code (verbal) for the latter (Paivio, 1986).

One way that information is entered into long-term memory is through rehearsal. A view popular with advocates of the three-store model was that rehearsal not only maintains information in the short-term store, but it also transfers the information to long-term store (Atkinson & Shiffrin, 1968; Waugh & Norman, 1965). According to this view, the longer an item is maintained in the short-term store, the greater the probability of it being transferred to the long-term store. Many studies have in fact shown long-term retention to be a positive function of the number of times that items are rehearsed (for example, Hebb, 1961). However, the nature of the rehearsal has been shown to be of much more importance than the amount of rehearsal. It is possible to distinguish between *maintenance rehearsal,* which involves repeating material to yourself (done when trying to retain a phone number until the call is placed), and *elaborative rehearsal,* which involves relating material together in new ways. Numerous studies have shown that there is relatively little benefit of maintenance rehearsal on long-term retention. Simply repeating information over and over is not sufficient to ensure registration in long-term store.

Questions about the capacity and duration of the long-term store are difficult to answer. No limits are known to exist on the capacity for acquiring new information. Psychologists have debated whether long-term memory is permanent (for example, Loftus & Loftus, 1980). This is probably an unanswerable question. For many years, forgetting was assumed to reflect the loss of information from memory. Questions focused on whether the loss was due simply to time (decay theory) or to similar events that occurred either before (proactive) or after (retroactive) the events that were to be remembered (interference

theory). The results of many experiments were consistent with predictions of interference theory (Postman & Underwood, 1973). However, forgetting in many circumstances is not due to information loss but to a failure to retrieve information that is still available in memory.

Tulving and Pearlstone (1966) had people learn lists of 48 words, 4 from each of 12 categories. During the acquisition phase, the appropriate category name was presented with the category members that were to be learned. Subsequently, the people were asked to recall the words; half of them did so with the category names provided and half without. The people provided with the category names recalled significantly more words than those who were not. In Tulving and Pearlstone's terminology, the latter group of people must have had words available in the long-term store that were not accessible without the category cues.

The point of Tulving and Pearlstone's (1966) experiment is that effective retrieval cues enhance the accessibility of items in memory. This is captured by the *encoding specificity principle* (Tulving & Thomson, 1973): "Specific encoding operations performed on what is perceived determine what is stored, and what is stored determines what retrieval cues are effective in providing access to what is stored" (p. 369). In other words, a cue will be effective to the extent that it matches the encoding performed initially. Appropriate use of retrieval cues is a way to maximize the likelihood that an operator will remember information when it is needed at a later time.

Processing Strategies

In recent years, considerable emphasis has been placed on the influence of processing strategies on long-term retention. The seminal work of this type was a paper by Craik and Lockhart (1972), in which they introduced the concept of *levels of processing.* The levels-of-processing framework makes three basic assumptions about memory (Zechmeister & Nyberg, 1982): (1) Memory arises from a succession of analyses of increasing depth performed on stimuli. (2) The greater the depth of processing is, the stronger the memory trace and the better the retention. (3) Memory improves only by increasing the depth of processing and not through the repetition of processing that has already been performed. The levels-of-processing view leads to the prediction that long-term retention will be a function of the depth of the processing performed during the initial presentation of items.

The approach taken by researchers within this area is to vary the nature of the orienting tasks that are performed by the people, usually in an incidental learning situation. In other words, people perform a particular task on a set of items, unaware that they will receive a subsequent memory test on those items. For example, Hyde and Jenkins (1973) used five types of orienting tasks, two of which apparently required *deep-level* semantic processing of words' meanings (rating the pleasantness or unpleasantness of the words, estimating frequency of usage) and three that did not (checking words for the letters E and G, determining the part of speech for a word; and judging in which of two sentence frames a word fit best). On a subsequent free recall test in which the words were to be reported in any order, recall was better for those who performed the semantic-orienting tasks than for those who performed the surface-orienting tasks. Moreover, recall of those who performed the semantic-orienting tasks was equivalent to that of a group who received standard intentional memory instructions and studied the list without an orienting task. Thus, this study and others indicate that whether a person intends to remember the presented information is unimportant. What matters is that the information receive the requisite deep level of processing.

Although the levels-of-processing framework was instrumental in broadening the types of situations studied by memory researchers, it has some limitations. One is that there is no independent designation of the depth required for specific orienting tasks, so the interpretation

becomes circular (that is, this task led to better recall than another; therefore, it involves a deeper level of processing). Also, another factor, elaboration, has been found to influence retention. Craik and Tulving (1975) showed that retention was better for words judged relative to complex sentence frames (for example, "The great bird swooped down and carried off the struggling – – –") rather than to simpler frames ("He cooked the – – –"), where the word *chicken* could be used to complete either frame. This finding lead to the proposal that the degree of semantic elaboration performed on items to be remembered is important.

The perspective that has developed from the work on elaboration is that the *distinctiveness* of encoding is important for retention (Eysenck, 1979; Jacoby & Craik, 1979). According to this view, elaborative processing improves retention to the extent that it produces a representation of an item distinct from those representations for other items to be remembered. Einstein and Hunt (1980) have referred to information based on the distinctive features of items as item-specific information. They have proposed that, whereas the quality of item-specific information is important for recognition performance, another type, called relational information, is important for recall. Relational information concerns the common features among items and is crucial to generating the items in recall when few retrieval cues are available. The type of information that is emphasized by particular materials and strategies will determine the level of performance on subsequent retention tests.

Because of these differences between recall and recognition, it is possible to selectively influence recall performance without affecting recognition performance. Philp, Fields, and Roberts (1989) obtained such a difference between recall and recognition for divers. The divers were presented lists of words and later performed free recall and recognition tests. These tests were performed at the surface and in a hyperbaric chamber after 35 min of bottom time in 36 m of seawater. The divers showed a 28% total decrement in recall during the dive over performance at the surface, but no such effect was observed for recognition. Thus, although the information was intact in the long-term store, the divers had difficulty recalling it. Because free recall is so impaired, an accurate assessment of divers' memories may require that they be provided retrieval cues during debriefing.

Consistent with the encoding specificity principle, research has also indicated that the relationship between the type of processing and the type of retention test is important. Morris, Bransford, and Franks (1977) had people perform either a shallow orienting task (deciding whether a word rhymed with another in a sentence frame) or a deep orienting task (deciding whether a word made sense in a particular sentence frame). The deep orienting task produced better performance on a recognition test for which the distractors were semantically similar to the targets. However, when the distractors were auditorily similar, the shallow orienting task led to better performance. In other words, it is better to process sounds

than meanings when the recognition test requires discriminations based on sound. Such relations between processing activities and retention illustrate the principle of *transfer-appropriate processing:* the processing performed initially is effective for retention to the extent that the resulting knowledge will transfer to the retention test.

Long-term retention can also benefit from the use of organizational strategies. Recall is better from categorized lists than from uncategorized lists, and members from a given category tend to be recalled in clusters (Bousfield, 1953). Moreover, presentation of words in explicit categorical hierarchies produces considerably better recall performance than does random presentation of the words from the categories. Bower et al. (1969) had observers study pages on which categories of words were presented in either a hierarchically organized manner (see Figure 10–9) or randomly. More than twice as many words were recalled with the organized list. The hierarchy apparently was used as a retrieval plan for cueing subsequent recall.

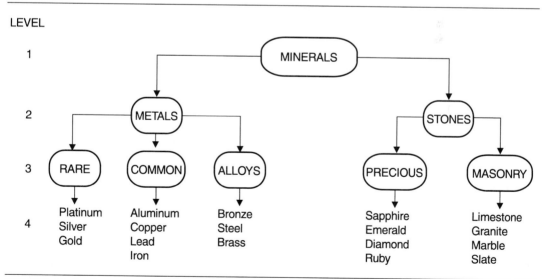

FIGURE 10–9   Conceptual Hierarchy for Minerals.
From G. H. Bower et al. (1969). Hierarchical retrieval schemes in recall of categorized word lists. *Journal of Verbal Learning and Verbal Behavior, 8,* 323–343. Reprinted by permission of Academic Press.

Specific organizational strategies to improve long-term retention have been investigated. *Mnemonics* refer to the use of encoding strategies that organize material in memorable ways. In addition to providing organization, mnemonic strategies make the material more distinctive. This distinctiveness may arise in part from the generation of the novel relationships between items to be remembered that is induced by the mnemonic strategy.

Two classes of mnemonic techniques can be distinguished: visual and verbal. For imagery mnemonics, visual images are formed that relate the items that must be remembered. An example is the method of loci, for which items to be remembered are imaged at various locations in a familiar environment, such as your home. When the items need to be retrieved later, you mentally walk to the locations and "find" the stored items. Visual mnemonics can significantly improve the learning of foreign language vocabulary (Raugh & Atkinson, 1975) and face–name associations (Geiselman et al., 1984), as well as the performance of the elderly on memory tasks (Poon, Walsh-Sweeney, & Fozard, 1980). For most verbal mnemonics, either the items to be learned are combined into sentences or stories, or the first letters are combined into new words or phrases (acronyms) or are used as first letters of new words in a meaningful sentence (acrostics). Verbal mnemonics have also been shown to be effective, whether used by themselves or as components in more complex techniques (Cook, 1989). One problem regarding the use of mnemonics that is particularly severe in the elderly and mentally handicapped is the failure to spontaneously use them.

In addition to using internal aids, people use external memory aids. These include such things as tying a string around a finger, making notes for reminders, and so on. External memory aids tend to be used more often to (1) assist future remembering rather than to remember past events, (2) remember spatial tasks rather than verbal tasks, and (3) remember to do things rather than to remember information (Intons-Peterson & Fournier, 1986).

Commercial memory aids, such as alarm settings on watches, are also marketed. Herrmann and Petros (1990) assessed the available commercial aids and noted that virtually all are designed and advertised for specific memory tasks. Because an aid is intended to assist the performance of a particular task performed in a specific context, the effectiveness of an aid depends on the extent to which it corresponds to the situation for which it is being used. In the future, more general memory aids will likely be developed. Already, a software package is marketed that includes alarms, a calendar, a phone book, automatic dialing of phone numbers, category organizers for personal tasks and events of interest, and a memory jogger that reminds the user of unfinished tasks.

COMPREHENDING AND REMEMBERING VERBAL MATERIAL

Without memory, our ability to comprehend environmental events would be limited. Objects and events are recognized by accessing knowledge in the long-term store, with continuity among events provided by maintaining knowledge representations in working memory. Actions that will be taken in a situation, as well as memory for the events that occur, depend on what is comprehended.

These relationships between memory and comprehension are most obvious for language, that is, reading and listening. Language presented visually can be as simple as the word *stop* on a sign or as complex as a technical manual providing instructions for operating a system. Similarly, language presented auditorily can be a single utterance (the word *go*) or a complex narrative. Comprehension and retention of the intended meaning of presented information is of utmost importance for any situation involving verbal material. In this section, we examine the nature of our general semantic knowledge and the processes involved in the comprehension and retention of sentences, text, and structured discourse.

Semantic Memory

Comprehension begins by accessing knowledge in semantic memory. This is the part of the long-term store that contains everything known about a stimulus, including its relation to other stimuli. Until publication of the book *Organization of Memory,* edited by Tulving and Donaldson (1972), very little semantic memory research had been conducted. Since then, considerable research has examined the representation of semantic knowledge and the way that this knowledge is accessed.

Most research on semantic memory has used the sentence verification technique. People are presented simple sentences, such as "A beagle is a dog," that must be classified as true or false. Several reliable phenomena are obtained with this task. Decisions are made faster when an item is a member of a small category rather than a large category, the category-size effect. For example, the decision that a beagle is a dog can be made faster than the decision that a beagle is an animal. Also, responses are faster if an item is a typical member of a category, the typicality effect. For example, the decision that a canary is a bird can be made faster than the decision that a buzzard is a bird.

Two general types of semantic memory models have been proposed to account for these and related effects. *Network models* assume that concepts are interconnected within an organized network (for example, Collins & Loftus, 1975). In such models, the time to verify a sentence is a function of the distance between the concepts and the strengths of the connecting links in the network. *Feature-comparison models* propose that concepts are stored as lists of features (for example, Smith, Shoben, & Rips, 1974). According to these models, faster responses can be made when a comparison of features between concepts yields an unambiguous decision. When it does not, more extensive search and evaluation processes must be performed, taking more time. Both network and feature representations have provided adequate explanations of the category size and typi-

cality effects and are used to represent knowledge in many simulated memory stores, such as those used for expert systems.

Written Communication

Whereas studies of semantic memory are concerned primarily with the comprehension of individual words, normal reading requires integration of information across sentences and passages. Reading efficiency is affected by many factors. These include the purpose for reading, the nature of the materials, the educational background of the reader, and the characteristics of the environment. Given that so many factors affect reading efficiency, it should come as no surprise that the operation of human–machine systems can be improved by considering these factors.

An operator must read the technical manuals, instructions, and information provided with a system if it is to be controlled effectively. Also, training programs often involve large reading components; the education system stresses written language, and the ability to read is a requirement for most occupations. Consequently, although the topics of reading and writing are not typically included in courses on ergonomics, they should be. In the words of Wright (1988, p. 265),

> As working life becomes more information intensive, so a better understanding of how to design and manage written information becomes more urgent. In this sense reading and writing may become core topics in future ergonomics courses, a functional literacy requirement for human factors specialists.

In reading, the primary goal is to comprehend as quickly and accurately as possible the information that is being conveyed. Reading speed is influenced by several factors. Sentences can be decomposed into basic ideas or propositions. The more propositions there are in a sentence, the longer it takes to read, even when the length of the sentence is held constant (Kintsch & Keenan, 1973). Reading speed is also a function of the type of reading task. Reading a sentence with word-for-word recall in mind takes longer than reading it for comprehension and produces different patterns of relative reading times across the sentence (Aaronson & Scarborough, 1976). Thus, reading strategies vary as a function of the intent of the reading task.

The efficiency of perception and accuracy of memory for sentences can be influenced by the syntactic structure of the material. For example, comprehension is better when relative pronouns (for example, *that, which, whom*) are used to signal the start of a phrase than when they are omitted (Fodor & Garrett, 1967). Additionally, sentences containing nested clauses are difficult to comprehend (Schwartz, Sparkman, & Deese, 1970). Semantic structure is also important. Sentences are recalled better when the order of events in the sentence is consistent with the actual temporal order of events (Clark & Clark, 1968).

A related finding occurs for the order in which information is presented in instructions. Dixon (1982) measured the time to read each sentence as people followed multistep directions for operating an electronic device. Reading was faster when the action to be performed (for example, "turn the left knob") preceded condition information ("the alpha meter should read 20") rather than followed it, regardless of whether the action was performed immediately or from memory or whether the condition information was an antecedent to or consequent of the action. This finding suggests that the conditions in procedural directions are organized with respect to the actions, so comprehension is easier when the action is specified first.

Most communication involves more than just the comprehension of an isolated sentence. Usually, information must be integrated across many sentences. A novel or instruction manual may be several hundred pages long, and information late in the text will have to be integrated with information that came earlier if the events are to be comprehended. Because the purpose of reading is comprehension, successful readers construct an abstract, rather than literal, representation of what is read. Inferences are made about relations and

events that are implied but not directly stated. These inferences will later be remembered as part of the material that was read (Johnson, Bransford, & Solomon, 1973).

Most models of text comprehension assume that working memory plays an important role in comprehension, because comprehension requires that new information be interpreted in terms of and integrated with information already in memory (for example, Just & Carpenter, 1980; Kintsch & van Dijk, 1978). Evidence for this assumption is that the comprehension of sentences correlates with *working memory span:* the number of words remembered from the sentences that are being comprehended (Baddeley et al., 1985; Daneman & Carpenter, 1980). The function of working memory for text comprehension seems to be to maintain a representation of earlier information into which the new information can be integrated. Poor readers differ from good readers primarily in the efficiency with which the integration of new propositions into the working representation can be performed (Petros et al., 1990).

Many authors have reached the conclusion that the nature of the working representation takes the form of organized structures called *schemas* or, alternatively, scripts or frames (Rumelhart & Norman, 1988; Thorndyke, 1984). Schemas are frameworks organizing our generalized conceptual knowledge regarding objects, situations, events, actions, and sequences of events and actions. They are prototypical frameworks, representing the concepts of interest, that are used to organize specific events related to the concept. They enable the development of expectancies about what should occur. These expectancies aid in the interpretation of specific information and in determining its relative importance. Violations of schemas tend to draw attention and, consequently, to be remembered well (Brewer & Lichtenstein, 1981).

The importance of an appropriate activated schema for comprehension is illustrated in a study by Bransford and Johnson (1972). Students read the passage shown in Table 10–1 and then

TABLE 10–1   Passage about the topic of washing clothes

The procedure is actually quite simple. First you arrange things into different groups. Of course, one pile may be sufficient depending on how much there is to do. If you have to go somewhere else due to lack of facilities, this is the next step; otherwise you are pretty well set. It is important not to overdo things. That is, it is better to do too few things at once than too many. In the short run this may not seem important, but complications can easily arise. A mistake can be expensive as well. At first the whole procedure will seem complicated. Soon, however, it will become just another facet of life. It is difficult to foresee any end to the necessity for this task in the immediate future, but then one can never tell. After this procedure is completed, one arranges the material into different groups again. Then they can be put into their more appropriate places. Eventually they will be used once more and the whole cycle will then have to be repeated. However, that is part of life.

From J. D. Bransford and M. K. Johnson (1972). Contextual prerequisites for understanding: Some investigations of comprehension and recall. *Journal of Verbal Learning and Verbal Behavior, 11,* 722.

rated its comprehensibility and tried to recall the ideas contained in it. Both comprehensibility and recall were substantially higher for students who were told prior to reading the passage that the topic was "washing clothes" than for students who either were never told this or were told the topic after reading the passage. Schematic knowledge appropriate to the activities involved in washing clothes had to be active in working memory for the passage to be comprehended easily.

Schemas for stories, called story grammars, that are independent of the content of the story have also been shown to be important for comprehension (Rumelhart, 1975; Thorndyke, 1977). Every story has a structure in which each sentence contributes to an episode that moves the story toward resolution of the plot. The story grammar analyzes stories into goals and episodes that contain subgoals. The relationships among the various story components must be comprehended if the story is to be understood. Similarly, schemas for technical documents can aid in the comprehension and retention of technical material.

Johnson-Laird (1983, 1989) has argued that schematic knowledge is applied in the comprehension process through the use of mental models. He states that, "Discourse models make explicit the structure *not* of sentences, but of situ-

ations as we perceive or imagine them" (1989, p. 471). The theory of discourse models is based on three principal ideas (Johnson-Laird, 1989, p. 475):

1. A mental model represents the *reference* of a discourse; that is, the situation that the discourse describes.
2. The initial linguistic representation of a discourse, together with the machinery for constructing and revising discourse models from it, captures the *meaning* of the discourse; that is, the set of all possible situations that it could describe.
3. A discourse is judged to be true if there is at least one model of it that can be embedded in [is consistent with] the real world.

Evidence for the use of mental models in discourse comprehension arises from studies in which the inferences that are drawn would be explicit only in a representational model. When readers are presented with the sentence, "Three turtles rested on a floating log and a fish swam beneath them," they later confuse it with the sentence, "Three turtles rested on a floating log and a fish swam beneath it." This confusion arises because the second sentence corresponds with the mental model implied by the first sentence (Bransford, Barclay, & Franks, 1972). The second sentence is not confused when the first is, "Three turtles rested beside a floating log and a fish swam beneath them," for which the mental model differs.

One area in human factors for which comprehension and memory of textual material are important is that of instruction manual warnings. Because failure to heed warnings may lead to injury, manuals should be designed to enhance the comprehensibility and memorability of such warnings. Young and Wogalter (1990) noted that comprehension and memory could be improved by increasing the likelihood that the warning is read in the first place and then by providing visual information to accompany the verbal information. They conducted two experiments, one using instruction manuals for a gas-powered generator and the other using instruction manuals for a natural-gas oven/range, in which the printed message was either plain or salient (larger type, orange shading) and was either accompanied by an icon or not (see Figure 10–10). Comprehension and memory were significantly better when the warnings had both salient print and a pictorial icon than for the other three conditions. The authors suggest that this effectiveness of the salient print and icon combination may arise from better integration of the verbal and visual codes.

Spoken Communication

Communication by spoken language plays a prominent role in most operational settings. In many organizations, briefings are provided at the beginning of the work shift. Also, members of an organization must communicate effectively with each other if the organizational and system goals are to be achieved. The comprehensibility and memorability of spoken communication can be increased by considering the limitations in human cognition (Jones, Morris, & Quayle, 1987).

The points made about syntax, semantics, and mental models for reading comprehension also apply to the comprehension of spoken language. Much of the research on such comprehension has been conducted on conversation, in which a listener tries to comprehend the information that a speaker wants to convey. Conse-

quently, the listener assumes that the utterance of the speaker is sensible and constructs an interpretation that he or she hopes is the one intended by the speaker. As part of this construction process, the listener develops models about what the speaker knows and believes and why.

Several components of a speech act can be distinguished (Miller & Glucksberg, 1988). These include the utterance act itself, the literal meaning of the utterance, and the meaning intended by the speaker. Comprehension requires more than just establishing the literal meaning; the speaker's intention must also be inferred. Mistaking a speaker's intentions will likely produce more communication errors than any other factor.

A speaker follows rules in selecting utterances to convey particular meanings and that, consequently, a listener can use to infer the speaker's intentions. According to Grice (1975), the most important rule is the *cooperative principle:* the assumption that the speaker is being cooperative and sincere. The speaker can be assumed to be trying to do what is required to further the purpose of the conversation. The cooperative principle involves maxims of quantity, quality, relation, and manner (see Table 10–2). Basically, these maxims require that the speaker be informative and truthful and that the statements made be relevant and unambiguous.

Haviland and Clark (1974) proposed what they called the *given-new strategy.* This strategy refers to the fact that sentences include two types of information: given and new. The given information is assumed to be already known by the listener, whereas the new information is to be added to the old. By syntactically arranging sentences to distinguish between given and new information, the listener's task can be made easier. In general, a sentence will be comprehended more rapidly when there is a direct reference to information that was given previously.

Of particular concern in speech comprehension is how we understand utterances for which the literal meaning does not coincide with the meaning intended by the speaker. This occurs for

Plain Print, Icons Absent

Warning: Operate generator only in well ventilated areas. The exhaust from the generator contains poisonous carbon monoxide gas. Prolonged exposure to this gas can cause severe health problems and even death.

Plain Print, Icons Present

Warning: Operate generator only in well ventilated areas. The exhaust from the generator contains poisonous carbon monoxide gas. Prolonged exposure to this gas can cause severe health problems and even death.

Salient Print, Icons Absent

Warning: Operate generator only in well ventilated areas. The exhaust from the generator contains poisonous carbon monoxide gas. Prolonged exposure to this gas can cause severe health problems and even death.

Salient Print, Icons Present

Warning: Operate generator only in well ventilated areas. The exhaust from the generator contains poisonous carbon monoxide gas. Prolonged exposure to this gas can cause severe health problems and even death.

Note: Shading represents orange highlighting.

FIGURE 10–10   Warnings Differing in Conspicuousness of Print and the Presence of an Icon.

From S. L. Young & M. S. Wogalter, Comprehension and memory of instruction manual warnings: Conspicuous print and pictorial icons. Reprinted with permission from *Human Factors*, Vol. *32*, No. 6, pp. 637–649, 1990. Copyright 1990 by The Human Factors Society, Inc. All rights reserved.

indirect requests, in which a request for some action on the listener's part is not stated directly, as well as for figurative language, such as irony, metaphor, and idiomatic expressions. In all these cases, both literal and nonliteral meanings of the utterance are constructed, with the nonliteral meanings being derived as quickly as the literal meanings only when strongly supported by the

TABLE 10–2 Grice's Conversational Maxims

1. Maxims of quantity:
   Make your contribution as informative as is required.
   Do not make your contribution more informative than is required.
2. Maxims of quality:
   Try to make your contribution one that is true.
   Do not say what you believe to be false.
   Do not say that for which you lack adequate evidence.
3. Maxim of relation:
   Be relevant.
4. Maxims of manner:
   Be clear.
   Avoid obscurity of expression.
   Avoid ambiguity.
   Be brief.
   Be orderly.

context (Miller & Glucksberg, 1988). One implication of this research is that nonliteral meanings should be avoided in communication with an operator for situations in which they are not clearly dictated by the context.

Speech communication seems to be a particularly effective way to solve problems. Chapanis et al. (1977) had two-person teams solve problems, such as equipment assembly, under one of four communication modes: typewriting, handwriting, voice, and natural unrestricted communication. The problems were solved approximately twice as fast in the latter two oral modes as in the former two written modes, although the communications were much more verbose. One reason for the better performance in the oral modes was that the teams could engage in more than one activity at a time, whereas they could not do so in the written modes.

In summary, as with reading, the listener must bring to bear several different types of knowledge on the utterances of a speaker if the intended meaning is to be comprehended and remembered. Discourse will be most comprehensible when it is consistent with the knowledge and rules used by the listener.

SUMMARY

Successful performance of virtually any task depends on memory. If accurate information is not retrieved at the appropriate time, errors may occur. Three general categories of memory stores can be distinguished. The sensory stores retain information in a modality-specific format for brief periods of time. The short-term store retains a limited amount of information in an active state and provides a mental workspace for reasoning and comprehension. The long-term store retains unlimited amounts of information over extended periods of time. As our knowledge about memory has progressed, the views of these stores have evolved into more flexible, dynamic systems with multiple coding formats. The characteristics of the stores and the processes in which they are involved have predictable effects on human performance that need to be remembered while designing human–machine systems.

Memory is intimately involved in the comprehension and communication of information. Verbal materials and environmental events are identified by activating knowledge in semantic memory. Comprehension of both written and spoken language is based on mental representations. These representations are constructed from the individual's perception of the material and the context in which it is perceived. To the extent that information is consistent with the ob-server's mental representation, language comprehension will be facilitated. Memory and comprehension play pivotal roles in thought and decision making, the topics of Chapter 11.

RECOMMENDED READING

Baddeley, A. (1986). *Working Memory.* New York: Oxford University Press.

———(1990). *Human Memory: Theory and Practice.* Boston: Allyn and Bacon.

Cohen, G. (1989). *Memory in the Real World.* Hillsdale, NJ: Lawrence Erlbaum.

Just, M. A., & Carpenter, P. A. (1987). *The Psychology of Reading Comprehension and Language.* Boston: Allyn and Bacon.

Klatzky, R. L. (1980). *Human Memory: Structures and Processes.* San Francisco: W. H. Freeman.

CHAPTER 11

SOLVING PROBLEMS AND MAKING DECISIONS

Like any goal-directed activity, thinking can be done well or badly.
Thinking that is done well is thinking of the sort that achieves its goals.

—J. Baron, 1988

INTRODUCTION

Complicated problem-solving and decision-making processes occur at all levels of human activity. Decisions must be made for things as simple as what clothes to wear in the morning and as complex as how to raise your children. The actions that we take as a result of our decisions can have long-lasting consequences. A management decision to expand a company based on an overestimate of the company's financial strength may result in bankruptcy. This in turn can cost the jobs of many employees and have devastating consequences on the local economy. Similarly, a government's decision to enter into war will result in loss of lives, disruption of personal life, economic

hardship, and aftereffects of varying types that carry far into the future. Clearly, it is important for human thought and decision-making processes to be understood so that poor decisions can be prevented.

In many situations, an operator of a human–machine system must reason about the information with which he or she is provided and decide on the appropriate action to take. A problem arises for the operator when displayed information indicates that system failure will result unless a corrective controlling action is taken. The necessary action may be obvious, or the problem may be complex and require a novel solution based on an assessment of many sources of information. For example, the many visual and auditory displays in the cockpit of a space shuttle provide multiple sources of information that must be considered when diagnosing the nature of an emergency and deciding on the actions that should be taken in response. Yet, as has been documented in previous chapters, the human's capacity for processing such information is limited, and a less than optimal decision may be made by a well-intentioned operator.

The present chapter examines the way that people reason about and decide among alternative choices. *Normative models* will be described that specify the choices that should be made by a rational person. However, as Johnson-Laird (1983, p. 133) states, "Human reasoners often fail to be rational. Their limited working memories constrain their performance. They lack guidelines for systematic searches for counterexamples; they lack secure principles for deriving conclusions; they lack a logic." In other words, reasoning and decisions often deviate from those prescribed by normative models, primarily because of the human's limited capacity for processing information. Thus, *descriptive models* of reasoning and decision making try to capture the procedures by which people actually think. By understanding how and why people deviate from normative rationality, the human factors specialist is in a position to present information in such a way as to maximize the likelihood that an operator arrives at an optimal problem solution.

PROBLEM SOLVING

Virtually any task involving thought can be viewed as problem solving. In psychology, problem solving has been studied most thoroughly for situations in which a person confronts a problem that has a clear goal. Most research has examined multistep tasks that take minutes or hours to perform, with many observable actions required of a person during the task. An example problem of this type is the Tower of Hanoi (see Figure 11–1). The task is to move all the discs from peg A to peg C, with the restrictions that only one disc can be moved at a time and a larger disc cannot be put

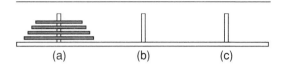

(a)   (b)   (c)

FIGURE 11–1   The Tower of Hanoi Problem.

on top of a smaller disc. Problem solving in such tasks is studied by recording the specific moves made by the person, as well as the accuracy and time to solution.

In addition to the measurement of observable actions, verbal reports or protocols of the steps toward problem solution can often be obtained (Ericsson & Simon, 1980, 1984). Such reports are especially useful for tasks in which the intermediate steps are not observable. These reports are typically generated while the task is being performed, because forgetting and fabrication can occur if the reports are obtained retrospectively (Russo, Johnson, & Stephens, 1989). Moreover, since the protocols are intended to reflect the information and hypotheses being attended to in working memory, they usually are reports of the thoughts that are occurring and not explanations of them (Ericsson & Simon, 1980).

When verbal protocols are collected systematically, they can provide valuable information about the cognitive processes required for a given task. However, concurrent verbalization may change the way that the primary task is processed, due to such things as resource competition (Biehal & Chakravarti, 1989; Russo, Johnson, & Stephens, 1989). This is called *reactivity*. It should also be kept in mind that the information supplied by a verbal report is a function of what the investigator has requested. So, poor instructions about what to verbalize will lead to useless protocols.

A Production System Framework

Problem solving is proposed to take place within an abstract mental problem space. The representation of the problem space can be regarded as *declarative knowledge,* which is the knowledge about facts and relations that we are able to verbalize. The allowable actions or operators defined by the rules of the problem are classified as *procedural knowledge.* This knowledge refers to processes for performing particular mental or physical actions; it is usually more difficult to verbalize than declarative knowledge. Finally, *control knowledge* refers to the strategies used to coordinate the overall problem-solving process.

In artificial intelligence, problem solving is often modeled by *production systems.* A production system includes a global data base, which is the central data structure used by the system, production rules that operate on the global data base, and a control system that determines which rules to apply (Nilsson, 1980). The heart of any production system is formed by the production rules, or productions, which consist of "if–then" pairings of the form "if a certain situation occurs, then a particular action should be taken." These rules are applied to modify the data base when their preconditions are met. Using various strategies, the control system resolves conflicts when the conditions satisfy more than one rule and ends computation when the goal state is reached.

Newell and Simon (1972) proposed a framework based on production systems for describing human problem-solving performance. Within this framework, different problems are distinguished in terms of their *task environments,* or the objects and actions that are relevant for the solution of the problem. These environments can be characterized by a set of states and a set of operators (production rules) that produce allowable changes between states. A problem is specified by its starting state and its goal state. Newell and Simon portrayed problem solving as a series of movements between states that lead from the starting state to the goal state. For the Tower of Hanoi problem, the starting state is the initial tower on peg A, the goal state is a tower on peg C, and the operators are the allowable movements of discs among the three pegs.

Two aspects of Newell and Simon's (1972) portrayal are important in determining performance. The first is how to represent the problem mentally, that is, the structure of the problem space, which is based on the task environment and other knowledge. It must include the initial situation, the desired goal, any intermediate states, and the operators. Because the problem space is a mental representation of the task environment, it may differ from the task environment in certain respects. For example, some moves that are legitimate within the task environment may not be included as part of the problem space.

A commonly used illustration of this point is the nine-dots problem shown in Figure 11–2. The goal is to connect the dots in the figure by drawing four straight lines, without lifting the pencil from the paper. Most people find the nine-dots problem difficult. The reason for this is that the solution requires the lines to go outside the boundaries of the square (see Figure 11–3). This alternative typically is not included in the problem space and, thus, it is not considered as an allowable move. Yet the problem description does not exclude such moves. As in this example, an incomplete or inaccurate problem representation is a common source of problem-solving difficulty. Hence, one way to improve problem solving is to spend more time constructing a mental representation before seeking a solution (Rubinstein, 1986).

The second important aspect of problem solving in Newell and Simon's (1972) framework is the search of the problem space. The allowable moves within the problem space must be consid-

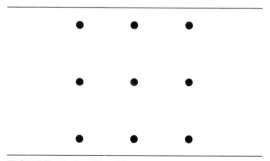

FIGURE 11–2 The Nine-dots Problem.

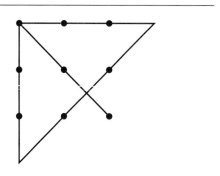

FIGURE 11–3   The Solution to the Nine-dots Problem.

ered and evaluated. The limited capacity of short-term memory provides a major constraint on the number of moves that can be considered. For complex problems, only a part of the problem space can be held in memory and searched at any one time. Thus, a limited number of moves can be examined, and the evaluation of other alternatives will be difficult.

Several different strategies can be used to search the problem space. A few distinct *weak methods* are used by people when they must resolve a problem in a domain about which they know little. These methods are used for unfamiliar problems in which the correct way to proceed is unknown; in contrast, *strong methods* are used for familiar problems. The weakest of the weak methods, trial and error, consists of unsystematic or random selections of moves between states to attain the goal. Two general, more systematic strategies are forward chaining (working forward) and backward chaining (working backward). Forward chaining involves starting from the initial state, considering the possible actions, selecting the best one, receiving feedback, and then repeating the process. Backward chaining involves starting from the goal state and constructing a solution path to the initial state. A third general strategy is operator subgoaling. An operator is selected without regard to whether the preconditions for applying it to the current state

have been met. If the operator is inapplicable, a subgoal is formed to determine how to change the current state so that the preconditions for the operator's application are satisfied.

These strategies all incorporate heuristics, similar to those used in artificial intelligence, to narrow the search for possible moves. Heuristics are rules of thumb that increase the probability of finding a correct solution. One such heuristic is called hill climbing. This method is based on an evaluation of whether the goal is closer after a move. Much like climbing to the top of a hill while blindfolded, each step in solving the problem is evaluated according to whether it brings you "higher" or closer to the goal state (the top of the hill). Any step that leads downhill is retraced. Because only the direction of each local move is considered, hill climbing methods may leave the problem solver "stranded on a small knoll"; that is, every possible move may lead downhill although the goal state has not yet been reached. Consequently, the best solution will not be found.

Means–ends analysis is a widely used method that is also based on minimizing the distance between the current location in the problem space and the goal state. The distinction between means–ends analysis and hill climbing is that in means–ends analysis the move needed to reach the goal can be seen, allowing an appropriate move to be selected to reduce the distance. Means–ends analysis is a heuristic based on identifying the difference between the current state and the goal state and trying to reduce it. When using this heuristic, solution paths that require increasing the distance from the goal by taking steps away from it are particularly difficult.

One benefit of the production-system approach to problem solving is that human performance can be described using the same terminology as machine performance. Consequently, insight into how human problem solving occurs can be used to further the advancement of artificial intelligence, and vice versa. This interaction lays the foundation for the design of cognitively engineered computer programs to assist human problem solving.

Analogy

Analogy is a potentially powerful heuristic in problem solving and reasoning. It involves a comparison between a novel problem and a similar problem for which the steps to a solution are known. An appropriate analogy can provide a structured representation for the novel problem, indicate the operations that likely will lead to a solution, and suggest potential mistakes. Analogies tend to be goal centered (Holland et al., 1986). That is, detection and application of analogies may occur when the goal characterizations are similar, even though the problems are structurally quite different. Thus, the use of an analogy requires that some similarity be recognized between the novel problem and the familiar analogous problem.

In general, people are adept at using analogies to solve problems, but they often fail to retrieve analogies from memory. These points are illustrated by the research of Gick and Holyoak (1980, 1983), who investigated the use of analogies in solving the radiation problem originated by Duncker (1945). The problem is stated as follows:

> Suppose you are a doctor faced with a patient who has a malignant tumor in his stomach. It is impossible to operate on the patient, but unless the tumor is destroyed the patient will die. There is a kind of ray that at a sufficiently high intensity can destroy the tumor. If the rays reach the tumor all at once at a sufficiently high intensity, the tumor will be destroyed. Unfortunately, at this intensity the healthy tissue that the rays pass through on the way to the tumor will also be destroyed. At lower intensities the rays are harmless to healthy tissue, but they will not affect the tumor either. What type of procedure might be used to destroy the tumor with the rays, and at the same time avoid destroying the healthy tissue? (Gick & Holyoak, 1983, p. 3).

Because the problem operators are ill defined, the problem must be transformed. An analogy could be used to transform the problem into a representation with more specific operators. Gick and Holyoak (1980) preceded the X-ray problem with a military story in which a general divided his army to converge on a single location, analogous to the solution of splitting the ray into several of lower intensity converging on the tumor. They found that approximately 75% of the people tested following the military story generated the convergence solution to the X-ray problem, but only if directed to use the analogy between the story and the problem. When a hint to use the story was not given, only 10% of the people solved the problem. In short, the analogical relation was difficult to recognize, but it could be applied when it was.

Use of the analogy is better if people receive two different stories using the convergence solution. Gick and Holyoak (1983) attribute this enhanced performance to the acquisition of an abstract convergence schema. Specifically, when two stories with similar structure are presented, an abstract schema of the structure is generated. This schema benefits recognition of the analogy because it is directly applicable within the subsequent problem space. These findings suggest that several different applications of a new problem-solving procedure should be provided during training to ensure the appropriate use of the procedure in later circumstances.

Given the spatial nature of the solution to the radiation problem, it would seem that a visual analog should also promote solution of the problem. Gick and Holyoak (1983) found that the diagram for the convergence solution shown in Figure 11–4a did not facilitate performance. However, Beveridge and Parkins (1987) noted that this diagram does not capture one of the essential features of the solution: several relatively weak beams have a summative effect at the point of intersection. Showing people the diagram in Figure 11–4b or colored strips of plastic arranged to intersect as in Figure 11–4c, both of which show summation, did increase the number of problem solutions. Thus, the visual cue must be an appropriate representation of the task features. Holyoak and Koh (1987) reached a similar conclusion about verbal analogies, for which

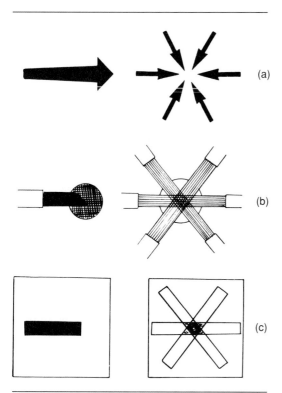

FIGURE 11–4 The Visual Analogs of the Radiation Problem Used (a) by Gick and Holyoak (1983) and (b and c) by Beveridge and Parkins (1987).

From M. Beveridge & E. Parkins. Visual representation in analogical problem solving. *Memory & Cognition, 15,* 230–234. Reprinted by permission of Psychonomic Society, Inc.

their spontaneous use was an increasing function of the number of salient structural and surface features shared by the two problems. By exploiting the variables that increase the probability that an analogy is recognized as relevant, the human factors specialist can optimize the likelihood that previously learned solutions will be applied to novel problems.

Learning to Use a Device

One type of problem of concern in human factors is that of learning to use a device. Kieras and Polson (1985) distinguish two components of knowledge involved in device operation: the user's task representation and the user's device representation. The task representation is all the procedural knowledge needed to perform a task with the device. This knowledge can be either device dependent or device independent. For example, the use of manual and electric can openers requires the device-independent procedures of snapping the opener into the top of the can and rotating the opener around the rim. However, device-dependent knowledge is involved in the specific ways that the rotation is performed. A new device should be relatively easy to learn to use if its operation requires primarily device independent knowledge.

The device representation is knowledge about the device itself. "How-it-works" knowledge is most important. This is related to the internal workings of the device. It forms the basis of the person's device model, or mental model of the device, and reflects how deeply it is understood. The knowledge embodied in this mental model conceivably could facilitate use of the device by allowing the user to infer its operating procedures.

The complexity of a device, then, will be a function of the complexity of the knowledge representations needed to operate the device. In terms of the preceding distinctions, device complexity involves:

1. The complexity of the user's task representation, and the learning, memory, and processing capacity demands implied by the task representation;
2. The number of device-dependent functions, which are not part of the user's initial task representation, and the difficulty of learning them;
3. The ease with which a user can acquire how-it-works knowledge. (Kieras & Polson, 1985, p. 367)

The roles played by these various knowledge types have been the subject of many experiments. Dixon and Gabrys (1991) distinguished between operational knowledge, which refers to the step by step procedures for operating a device at the structural level, and conceptual knowledge, which refers to an understanding of how the device works. Operators learned to use one of several simulated devices for landing an airplane, shutting down a nuclear reactor, controlling a robot arm, or sending a message on a spy radio. They then learned to use either another version of the same device or a new device. The second version of the same device was both conceptually and operationally similar to the first version. In other words, it involved the same task (for example, landing the plane), and the steps for performing the task were similar. A new device could be either conceptually or operationally similar to the first. The results showed a substantial benefit of operational similarity, but conceptual similarity did not significantly enhance performance.

The Dixon and Gabrys (1991) study suggests that familiarity with the operating procedures is what facilitates the use of a new device. This procedural knowledge can be represented as production rules. Kieras and Bovair (1986) demonstrated that the amount of benefit of prior training on the learning of a subsequent device can be predicted by the number of production rules that transfer from the first task to the second. People in their experiments had to learn to operate a device consisting of a toggle switch, a three-position rotary switch, two push buttons, and four indicator lights mounted on a control panel (see Figure 11–5). Ten different procedural tasks were learned, in different training orders, by each person. The goal of each task was to get the PF indicator light on the panel to flash. Each task could be characterized in terms of a series of production rules. Thus, for each task, it was possible to determine the number of rules known from tasks already performed and the number of rules that were new. The number of new production rules required for a task closely predicted the amount of training time required to learn the task.

In another study, Kieras and Bovair (1984) demonstrated that conceptual knowledge can have a positive influence on learning to use a device. Two groups of students learned to use the

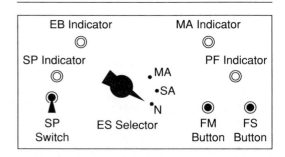

FIGURE 11–5 The Control Panel Used by Kieras and Bovair.

From D. E. Kieras & S. Bovair (1984). The role of a mental model in learning to operate a device. *Cognitive Science, 8,* 255–273. Reprinted with permission of Ablex Publishing Corporation.

previously described control panel. One group learned the procedures by rote, whereas another group received conceptual knowledge prior to the rote learning. For this latter group, the device was described as the control panel for a "phaser bank" on the "Starship Enterprise," and its processes were explained accordingly. After learning the procedures, both groups were tested immediately and one week later. The group trained with the conceptual knowledge learned the procedures faster and retained them better than the rote group. They also simplified inefficient procedures more often, suggesting that they understood how the device worked. Kieras and Bovair concluded that conceptual knowledge produces a benefit to performance when the procedures for operating a new device can be inferred from this knowledge. A procedural inference of this type was not possible in the Dixon and Gabrys (1991) study.

LOGIC AND REASONING

Problem solving requires logic and reasoning. Two types of reasoning are usually distinguished: deductive and inductive. *Deduction* refers to reasoning in which the conclusion about particular conditions follows necessarily from general premises about the problem. Deduction is the type of reasoning for which formal rules of logic determine which conclusions are valid. *Induction* is reasoning in which a generalized conclusion is drawn from particular conditions. It involves inferential processes that expand knowledge under uncertainty (Holland et al., 1986). For both types of reasoning, systematic errors occur that produce deviations from the correct or optimal conclusion.

Deduction

One issue of concern in the research on deduction is how the performance of humans compares with the prescriptions of formal logic. Formal logic involves arguments in the form of a list of premises and a conclusion. Such arguments are called *syllogisms;* a syllogism is valid if the conclusion follows from the premises and invalid if it does not. Rules of inference determine when it is permissible to infer a conclusion from the premises. Two inference rules are modus ponens and modus tollens. Modus ponens states that, given the major premise that *A implies B* and the minor premise that *A is true,* then it can be inferred that *B is true.* Modus tollens states that given the major premise that *A implies B* and the minor premise that *B is false,* it is valid to infer that *A is* also *false.*

Conditional Reasoning. Deductive reasoning with conditional statements of an "if–then" form is called conditional reasoning. For example:

> If the system was shut down, then there was a system failure.

Conditional syllogisms are of the form:

> If the red light appears, then the engine is overheating.
> The red light appeared.
> Therefore, the engine is overheating.

In a typical experiment, observers judge whether or not the conclusion of a syllogism is valid. The modus ponens rule can be applied successfully to conditional syllogisms (Rips &

Marcus, 1977); valid inferences by this rule typically are judged as true, whereas invalid inferences are judged as false. However, a fallacy called denial of the antecedent often occurs. Many people judge incorrectly that the conclusion "the engine is not overheating" is valid when the premises are "if the red light appears, the engine is overheating" and "the red light did not appear." A fallacy called affirmation of the consequent also occurs. A significant number of people believe that it is valid to conclude that "the red light appeared" from the premises "if the red light appears, the engine is overheating" and "the engine is overheating." These invalid conclusions are due in part to misinterpretations of conditional statements as biconditional statements instead. That is, "if" is treated as meaning "if and only if": the light always appears if the engine is overheating and never when it is not.

Modus tollens is a particularly difficult concept to grasp. This has been vividly illustrated with Wason's (1969) four-card problem. Four cards, two with letters showing and two with digits showing, are presented as in Figure 11–6. The following rule is stated:

> *If a card has a vowel on one side, then it has an even number on the other side.*

The task is to name the cards that need to be turned over to determine whether the rule is true or false.

Most people turn over the E and possibly the 4. However, the two cards that must be turned over are the E and the 7. The reason is that the statement is false either if the E has an odd number on the other side or if the 7 has a vowel on the

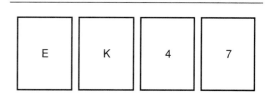

FIGURE 11–6 The Four Card Problem.

other side. Whether the number behind the K is odd or even, or whether the letter behind the 4 is a vowel or consonant, is irrelevant to the validity of the rule.

The failure to turn over the 7 reflects a failure to use modus tollens to determine if the antecedent is disconfirmed when the consequent is. This failure arises primarily from an insufficient search of the problem space. A bias exists to choose the cards that match those in the rule statement (that is, the vowel and even number; Evans, 1989). Consequently, the subgoal of determining the relevance of each card or the relevance of each possible result from turning over a card is not considered. Surprisingly, college students who have taken a course in formal logic do no better at this task than students who have not (Cheng et al., 1986), suggesting that this bias is fundamental to human reasoning.

Although the four-card problem is difficult, performance is much better when the task is framed within a familiar context. Johnson-Laird, Legrenzi, and Legrenzi (1972) found that people selected the correct choices more often when the problem was described as a rule relating amount of postage to whether or not a letter was sealed. Similarly, Griggs and Cox (1982) found that when asked to test the rule, "If a person is drinking beer, then the person must be over 19 years of age," students correctly examined those drinking beer and those under 19. Such effects of the content of the premises on reasoning have been interpreted by many authors as indicating that people do not use general-purpose inference rules (Evans, 1989). For example, Cheng and Holyoak (1985) have argued that performance on the four-card task is accurate when a permission schema is invoked. In other words, from experience we can reason about rules of permission, such as the drinking age. Reasoning seems to be context specific.

The bias to look for confirming rather than disconfirming evidence in the four-card problem is apparent in many other situations. Rouse (1979) noted that maintenance trainees had difficulty diagnosing a fault within a network of inter-connected nodes because they looked for failures and ignored information about which nodes had not failed. Fault diagnosis was improved by the use of a computer-aided display that kept track of the tested nodes that had not failed. As expected from the view that the development of appropriate schemas facilitates problem solving, people trained with the display performed better even after it was removed.

Categorical Reasoning.   Categorical syllogisms are statements that include the quantifiers *some, all, no,* and *some–not.* For example, a valid categorical syllogism is

All *A*'s are *B*'s.
All *B*'s are *C*'s.
Therefore, all *A*'s are *C*'s.

As with conditional syllogisms, judgments about the validity of a categorical syllogism can be influenced by irrelevant features of the situation and by incorrect representations of the premises.

A common error made with such syllogisms is to accept false conclusions as true. For example, the syllogism

Some *A*'s are *B*'s.
Some *B*'s are *C*'s.
Therefore, some *A*'s are *C*'s.

will be incorrectly accepted as valid. These types of errors have been explained in part by the atmosphere hypothesis (Woodworth & Sells, 1935). This hypothesis states that the quantifiers in the premises set an atmosphere. People tend to accept conclusions consistent with that atmosphere. In the second of the two syllogisms above, the presence of the term *some* in the premises creates a bias to accept the conclusion as valid because it contains the same term.

Many errors on categorical syllogisms may also be a consequence of an inappropriate conversion of the premises. For example, the premise *some A's are B's* could be incorrectly converted by a person to mean *all B's are A's,* among other things. The accuracy of syllogistic reasoning is also affected by the figure of the premises. This refers to the spatial arrangement of the objects (A, B, C) in the premises. For example, when the figure is of the form A–B, B–C, as in the syllogisms above, people have a bias to accept conclusions of the form A–C, which is correct for the first syllogism but incorrect for the second. For syllogisms with the form B–A, C–B, there is a bias to accept conclusions of the form C–A. This may be a function of people inverting the order in which the premises are encoded so that the two instances of the B term occur in close proximity (Johnson-Laird, 1983).

Johnson-Laird (1983) proposes that reasoning occurs through the construction of a mental model of the relations described in the syllogism. For example, given the premises

All the artists are beekeepers.
All the beekeepers are chemists.

a mental tableau would be constructed. The first premise designates every artist as a beekeeper but allows for some beekeepers who are not artists. The tableau for this would be of the following type:

artist = beekeeper
artist = beekeeper
artist = beekeeper
        (beekeeper)
        (beekeeper)

The parentheses indicate that the latter may or may not exist. The tableau can be expanded to accommodate the second premise for which all beekeepers are chemists, but some chemists may not be beekeepers. It leads to the following model:

artist = beekeeper = chemist
artist = beekeeper = chemist
artist = beekeeper = chemist
        (beekeeper) = (chemist)
        (beekeeper) = (chemist)
                      (chemist)

When asked whether a conclusion such as *All the artists are chemists* is valid, the mental model is consulted to determine whether the premise is true.

According to Johnson-Laird (1983), two factors affect the difficulty of a syllogism. The first factor is the number of different mental models consistent with the premises. Because all such models must be considered, this factor imposes a heavy load on working memory resources. The second factor is the figural arrangement of the terms, as discussed above. The arrangement dictates the ease with which the second premise can be related to the first to form an integrated mental model. The point to understand is that Johnson-Laird's account, as well as most alternative theories, proposes that reasoning does not occur through the use of formal rules, such as those developed by logicians.

Induction

Induction requires generating a general conclusion from particular conditions. It differs from deduction in that the conclusion does not necessarily follow if the premises are true, as is the case with valid deductions. Induction typically involves categorization, reasoning about rules and events, and problem solving (Holyoak & Nisbett, 1988).

Two types of knowledge are modified by induction: procedural knowledge of the type previously emphasized and conceptual knowledge, which involves representations of both general and specific categories. Concepts and procedures can be encoded in production rules and are often represented by interrelated clusters of rules (schemas). Rules and rule clusters operate as mental models that can simulate the effects of possible actions.

Adaptive Heuristics. Human induction is constrained by adaptive heuristics that favor certain classes of hypotheses over others and by cognitive limitations (Kahneman, Slovic, & Tversky, 1982). One such heuristic is *availability,* which refers to estimating probabilities or frequencies of events on the basis of the ease with which these events can be retrieved from memory. More easily remembered events are judged as more likely than less memorable events. For example, if asked to judge whether the letter R is more likely to occur in the first or third position of words in the English language, most people pick the first position as most likely. In reality, R occurs more often in the third position. Tversky and Kahneman (1973) argue that this happens because it is easier to retrieve words from memory on the basis of the first letter. Availability also biases people to overestimate the probability of dying from accidents relative to routine illnesses (Lichtenstein et al., 1978). Violent accidents such as plane crashes are much more available because they receive more media coverage than most illnesses, so their incidence tends to be overestimated.

Another heuristic is *representativeness,* which refers to the degree of resemblance between different events. More representative outcomes will be judged as more likely to occur than less representative ones. The following example from Kahneman and Tversky (1972) illustrates this point:

> All families of six children in a city were surveyed. In 72 families the *exact order* of births of boys (B) and girls (G) was GBGBBG.

> What is your estimate of the number of families surveyed in which the *exact order* of births was BGBBBB?

Although these two sequences are equally probable, the latter sequence is often judged to be less likely than the first. The apparent reason is that the sequence with five boys and one girl is less representative of the proportion of boys and girls in the population.

Representativeness is closely related to the gambler's fallacy, which is the belief that a continuing run of one of two or more possible events is increasingly likely to be followed by an occurrence of the other event. For example, suppose the births in the second sequence above were presented sequentially to a person who made a probability judgment for each successive event. The predicted probability that the subsequent birth is a girl would become larger through the run of four boys, even though the probability is always 0.5. The gambler's fallacy occurs because people fail to treat the occurrence of random events as independent.

The failure to perceive independent events as independent has also been demonstrated in a simulated tactical situation. Fleming (1970) required observers to estimate the overall probability of an enemy attack on each of three ships, given the altitude, bearing, and type (for example, size and armament) of an enemy plane. The goal was to protect the ship that was most likely to be attacked. Although each aspect of the plane was independent and of equal importance, the observers tended to add the different probabilities together rather than to multiply them, as was appropriate. Thus, high probabilities were underestimated and low probabilities overestimated, even when full feedback was given. Decision makers apparently experience considerable difficulty in aggregating probabilities from multiple sources, suggesting that such estimates should be automated when possible.

When base rates or prior probabilities of events are known, the information from the current events must be integrated with the base rate information. The formal principle for such integration is Bayes's theorem, which gives the conditional probability of event B given the occurrence of event A:

$$Pr(B|A) = \frac{Pr(A|B)Pr(B)}{Pr(A)}$$

Bayes's theorem indicates that base rate probabilities need to be considered and modified on the basis of the new information. In the previous example, if the prior probabilities of each of the three ships being attacked were not equal, then this information would need to be integrated with the altitude, bearing, and type information.

Decision makers deviate from both aspects of Bayes's theorem. Base rates typically are not considered. For example, Kahneman and Tversky (1973) gave people descriptions of several individuals supposedly drawn at random from a pool of 100 engineers and lawyers. One group was told that the pool contained 70 engineers and 30 lawyers, whereas the other group was told the reverse. These prior probabilities did not affect the judgments. If a person was assigned a 0.5 probability of being an engineer by one group, she was also assigned a 0.5 probability by the other group. The probability judgments appeared to be determined almost exclusively through representativeness.

Decision makers do modify probabilities on the basis of new information, but the revision tends to be conservative. Moreover, an *anchoring heuristic* is used that weights the initial instances too heavily (Tversky & Kahneman, 1974). This initial evidence is used to form a preliminary judgment, which leads to the final judgment being disproportionately influenced by the initial evidence. The importance of anchors is demonstrated by Lichtenstein et al. (1978), who had people estimate the frequencies of death in the United States for 40 causes. They were given an initial anchor of either "50,000 people die annually from motor vehicle accidents" or "1,000 deaths each year are caused by electrocution," and then they estimated the frequencies of death due to other causes. The frequency estimates were considerably higher with the former anchor than with the latter.

In summary, when performing complex reasoning tasks, people often use heuristics that reduce the mental workload. These heuristics will produce accurate judgments in many cases, particularly when the reasoner is knowledgeable of the domain in question. The benefit of heuristics is that they render complex tasks workable by drawing on previous knowledge. The cost is that these heuristics are the source of many mistakes made by operators and decision makers.

Concepts. A concept is an abstract representation derived from particular instances. The study of how concepts are learned and used is closely related to the investigation of inductive reasoning. Concepts have at least three functions (Smith, 1989). First, they minimize the amount of information that must be stored, a function called cognitive economy. Second, concepts enable past experience from related situations to be brought to bear on the current problem. Third, classifying a particular event as an instance of a certain conceptual category permits the formulation of inductive inferences.

Induction is subject to constraints that prevent or curtail inferences. Inferences are made only when there is a triggering condition that activates the appropriate conceptual knowledge. Similarly, if a property of the input is not coded as part of the mental representation of the concept, inductive reasoning about that property cannot occur. An increasingly popular view in recent years is that inductive reasoning occurs by using mental models to simulate possible outcomes of actions (Gentner & Stevens, 1983). These models and their associated concepts are acquired by interacting with a system or through other experiences. They work, but are not necessarily technically correct. The accuracy of the mental models is one factor that allows experts to reason better than novices in a particular domain (see Chapter 12).

As one example, McCloskey (1983) examined naive theories of motion acquired from everyday interactions with the world. People were required to solve problems of the type shown in Figure 11–7. For the spiral tube problem, they were told to imagine a metal ball put into the end of the spiral tube marked by the arrow. For the ball and string problem, they were to imagine the ball being swung at high speed above them. The person was to draw the path of the ball, when exiting the tube in the first case and when the string broke in the second case. The correct path in each case is a straight line, but many people responded that the balls continue in curved paths. These and other findings led McCloskey to propose that people used a "naive impetus theory": the movement of an object sets up an impetus for it to continue in the same motion. Simulation of a

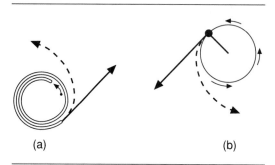

(a)   (b)

FIGURE 11–7 The Spiral Tube (a) and Ball-and-string (b) Problems with Correct (Solid Lines) and Incorrect (Dashed Lines) Solutions.

mental model based on the theory leads to the inferred paths in specific situations.

In many field studies, Klein (1989) observed the decision making of fireground commanders (leaders of teams of firefighters), platoon leaders, and design engineers. He concluded that mental simulation is a major component of their decisions. This is captured in the following example:

> The head of a rescue unit arrived at the scene of a car crash. The victim had smashed into a concrete post supporting an overpass, and was trapped unconscious inside his car. In inspecting the car to see if any doors would open (none would), the decision maker noted that all of the roof posts were severed. He wondered what would happen if his crew slid the roof off and lifted the victim out, rather than having to waste time prying open a door. He reported to us that he imagined the rescue. He imagined how the victim would be supported, lifted, and turned. He imagined how the victim's neck and back would be protected. He said that he ran his imagining through at least twice before ordering the rescue, which was successful. (Klein, 1989, pp. 58–59)

Such mental simulations allow possible consequences of alternative courses of action to be evaluated quickly.

The classic view of concepts is that an item is classified as belonging to a particular category if and only if it contains the features that define the category (Smith & Medin, 1981). However, the classic view has been criticized for not providing a general account of concepts. These criticisms center on the fact that defining features do not exist for many categories. For example, no single feature is shared by all instances of the concept *games*. Moreover, typicality effects, such as those observed in semantic-memory research (see Chapter 10), show that all instances of a category are not equal members of that category. Judgments in many tasks can be made faster and more accurately if the instance is typical of the category than if it is atypical.

Shafir, Smith, and Osherson (1990) have shown that typicality is closely involved with reasoning fallacies. One consequence of the representativeness heuristic is that people will often make conjunction errors in which the probability of a person being from a conjunctive category (for example, female bank teller) is estimated to be greater than the probability that the person is from one of the component categories (for example, bank teller). Shafir et al. had people make typicality judgments and probability judgments and found that the magnitude of the conjunction error was larger when an instance was judged as more typical of the conjunctive category. Thus, the representativeness heuristic seems to rely on estimates of the typicality of a member of a particular conceptual category.

Concepts have also been viewed in terms of prototypes. A prototype is a collection of the salient properties of instances that occur in many, but not all, cases. The prototype does not contain defining features. Category membership is determined instead by the similarity of an instance to the prototype. An alternative to the prototype view is exemplar models, which predict many of the same results without assuming that a prototype is computed (for example, Estes, 1986; Nosofsky, 1987). The exemplar view is supported by the fact that similarity does not seem to be the only basis for deciding category membership.

Osherson, Smith, and Shafir (1986) propose other ways to determine category membership that are based on converting an inductive problem into one of deduction through the use of additional knowledge. For example, when given a diameter for an object and asked to decide whether it is a pizza or a quarter, objects that are closer in size to the quarter than to the average pizza will be classified as a pizza (Rips, 1989). Apparently, the knowledge that quarters are of a fixed size is incorporated into the categorical judgment, changing the problem into one of deduction.

DECISION MAKING

Studies of decision making examine the way that different outcomes of a decision affect both the decision maker and others. Decisions can be made under conditions of certainty, in which the outcomes or consequences are known, or under conditions of uncertainty. Decision making under uncertainty has been of most concern to researchers. The problems considered are ones such as whether it is feasible to include an air bag as standard equipment on a line of automobiles, given the estimated cost, prevailing market conditions, effectiveness of the air bag, and so on. Decisions based on both certain and uncertain conditions are faced regularly by operators of human–machine systems, as well as by human factors specialists. Therefore, it is important to understand the ways in which decisions are made and the factors that influence them.

Normative Theory

Normative theories of decision making concern how we should choose between possible actions under ideal conditions. Normative theories rely on the notion of *utility,* or how much particular outcomes are worth to the decision maker. The option that provides the greatest total utility should be selected. If outcomes are uncertain, both the probabilities of the various alternatives and their utilities must be figured into the decision-making process.

The relation between probabilities and utilities is fundamental to *expected-utility theory.*

This theory prescribes actions for choice problems that can be analyzed as gambles. For monetary gambles, the expected value $E(v)$ of the gamble can be found by multiplying the probability of each possible outcome by its value. That is,

$$E(v) = \sum_{i=1}^{n} p(i)\, v(i)$$

where $p(i)$ is the probability of the ith outcome and $v(i)$ is the value of the ith outcome. In choosing between two gambles, the rational choice would be the one with the highest expected value.

As a concrete example, consider the following two hypothetical gambles:

(A) 0.10 chance to win $10; 0.90 chance to lose $1.
(B) 0.90 chance to win $1; 0.10 chance to lose $10.

The expected value for gamble A is

$$0.10(\$10) - 0.90(\$1) = \$1 - \$0.90 = \$0.10$$

The expected value for gamble B is

$$0.90(\$1) - 0.10(\$10) = \$0.90 - \$1 = -(\$0.10)$$

Thus, gamble A should be chosen because it has the highest expected value.

When dealing with nonmonetary outcomes, each outcome can be assigned a utility based on the extent to which it achieves the decision maker's goals. Substituting utility for value, the expected utility is defined by the relation

$$E(u) = \sum_{i=1}^{n} p(i)\, u(i)$$

Again, in a choice situation the alternative with the highest expected utility should be chosen. Expected-utility theory provides a yardstick for rational action, because the most rational decisions are consistent with those that yield the greatest utility.

Expected-utility theory is based on several axioms (Wright, 1984). Outcomes unrelated to the choice should not influence it. Thus, extraneous information should not affect the decision. Also, transitivity among preferences should be shown: if A is preferred to B, and B to C, then A should be preferred to C. Finally, the preferences among alternatives should not be influenced by the manner in which they are described or the context in which they are presented. As we shall see, these axioms do not always hold in real decision-making tasks.

Descriptive Theory

Do people perform optimally in the way proposed by expected-utility theory? The answer is no. Numerous factors lead to violations of expected-utility theory and its axioms. Such violations led Simon (1957) to introduce the concept of *bounded rationality*. This concept is that a decision maker bases decisions on a simplified model of the world. The decision maker

> behaves rationally with respect to this (simplified) model, and such behavior is not even approximately optimal with respect to the real world. To predict his behavior, we must understand the way in which this simplified model is constructed, and its construction will certainly be related to his psychological properties as a perceiving, thinking, and learning animal. (Simon, 1957, p. 198)

Many biases have been demonstrated for decisions made under certainty. For example, one axiom of utility theory is that preferences should show transitivity; if A is chosen over B, and B over C, A should be chosen over C. Yet violations of transitivity occur (Tversky, 1969), in part because small differences between alternatives are ignored in some situations but not in others.

When decisions are difficult, all possible features of the alternatives are seldom considered. For example, in buying a new car, you cannot compare all cars on all possible features that dif-

ferentiate them. Tversky (1972) has proposed that such decisions are made on the basis of an *elimination by aspects* heuristic. This heuristic is to consider aspects of features that distinguish the alternatives one at a time, usually beginning with the most important. All alternatives that are favorable on this aspect are retained. For you, price may be the most important aspect of a new car. You decide to eliminate all cars that cost more than $10,000. Size may be next important; from the cars of $10,000 or less, you eliminate any compact cars. This procedure continues until only a few alternatives remain that can be compared in more detail. While this procedure reduces the processing load, it can also lead to the elimination of the optimal choice.

Decision makers generally pay attention to a single dominant attribute and are less willing to make trade-offs on other dimensions than they should be. In a study of proposals for coastline development in California, Gardiner and Edwards (1975) found that people fell into either a prodevelopment or a proenvironment group. Members of each group attended only to the dimension important to them. However, when people were forced to rate each proposal on several major dimensions, they gave some weight to alternative dimensions.

The tendency to base decisions on only salient dimensions is even greater under stress. Stress increases the level of arousal and, as discussed in Chapter 9, at high levels of arousal attentional focus becomes narrowed and less controlled. Wright (1976) found evidence for both of these effects in the decisions of people who rated how likely they would be to purchase each of several automobiles. In one experiment, task-relevant time stress was increased by reducing the time for making the decisions. In another, task-irrelevant noise stress was induced by playing a radio talk show at high volume. Under both types of stress, the consistency of the decision makers' judgments decreased. Moreover, under time stress, the decision makers focused on the negative characteristics of the cars. The studies on attentional focus suggest that the tendency to focus on only a limited number of dimensions when making a decision can be minimized by eliminating unnecessary stressors and by structuring the decision process in such a way that the alternative dimensions must be considered.

Under uncertainty, violations of expected-utility theory are more systematic. One such violation involves *preference reversals*. Lichtenstein and Slovic (1971) found that, when choosing between a bet with a high probability of winning a modest amount of money and one with a low probability of winning a large amount of money, most people chose the high-probability bet. However, when asked the lowest amount of money for which they would sell the bet and allow the buyer to perform the gamble, most people gave a higher selling price for the low-probability event than for the high-probability event. This is a preference reversal. Tversky, Sattath, and Slovic (1988) conclude that such reversals occur because the choice version focuses attention on probability, whereas the selling version focuses attention on the dollar amounts.

Several models have been developed to address the failures of utility theory as a descriptive theory of human decision making. All the models assume that the internal representation of the decision situation is not an exact copy of the information pertinent to the problem. Some features are attended, while others are ignored. One of the more successful models is prospect theory (Kahneman & Tversky, 1979), which is so named because gambles can be viewed as risky prospects. Prospect theory is based on three pervasive phenomena. The *certainty effect* refers to the fact that highly probable outcomes are overweighted. In other words, people tend to choose certain outcomes of relatively low expected value over uncertain alternatives of higher value. The *reflection effect* is that preferences among positive prospects tend to reverse when the gains are changed to losses. This effect suggests that people are risk averse when choosing between gains and risk seeking when choosing between losses. The *isolation effect* is a tendency to focus only on the component features that dis-

tinguish alternatives and not those features that they share.

Prospect theory suggests that the choice process consists of two phases. The first is an editing phase, involving reformulation of the problem by using editing operations to simplify the choice. After editing, the second phase is a determination of the overall value for a prospect. This is done by obtaining subjective values for each outcome and multiplying each by a weighting of the subjective probability of obtaining that outcome. The subjective probabilities can be seen as estimates of the subjective importance of each outcome. The prospect with the highest value is chosen. The value function is S-shaped, but steeper for losses than for gains (see Figure 11–8).

One finding consistent with prospect theory is that of *framing*. This refers to changes in choice behavior that depend on how the decision problem is presented. Tversky and Kahneman (1981) showed that with formally identical problems reversals in the choice of outcomes could be obtained by simply changing the context of the

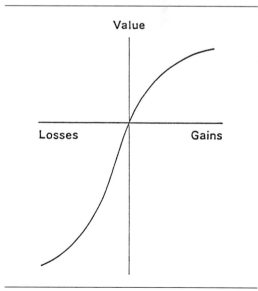

FIGURE 11–8   Asymmetric S-shaped Value Function.

problems to emphasize gains over losses. As one example, the following problem was administered in two forms.

> Imagine that the U.S. is preparing for the outbreak of an unusual Asian disease, which is expected to kill 600 people. Two alternative programs to combat the disease have been proposed. Assume that the consequences of the programs are as follows.

One description of the programs was

> If Program A is adopted, 200 people will be saved. If Program B is adopted there is a 1/3 probability that 600 people will be saved, and 2/3 probability that no people will be saved. Which of the two programs would you favor?

Another description was

> If Program C is adopted, 400 people will die. If Program D is adopted, there is 1/3 probability that nobody will die, and 2/3 probability that 600 people will die. Which of the two programs would you favor?

Despite the fact that the two descriptions are formally identical, most people who received the first description chose Program A over Program B, whereas most who received the second version chose Program D over Program C. The apparent basis for this framing effect is that the first description provides a positive frame for "saving lives," whereas the second provides a negative frame for "lives that will be lost." In short, a person's decision may be affected greatly by the way in which the pertinent information is presented, primarily through influencing how attention is paid to various attributes of the situation.

IMPROVING DECISIONS

In many situations, individuals in an organization and operators of human–machine systems are faced with complex decisions that often must be made under stress. Given the tendency for humans to make less than optimal decisions because of their limited capacity for attending to and

working with information, the human factors expert must be concerned with the improvement of decision making. Three approaches can be taken for improving the quality of decisions: education and training, improving the design of the task environment, and the development of decision aids (Evans, 1989).

Training and Task Environment

A common finding in research on reasoning and decision making is that people with formal training in logic make the same types of errors as people without such training. For example, Cheng et al.'s (1986) experiments found that people performed no better on Wason's four-card problem after a semester course in logic than before the course. Reasoning bias thus is relatively unaffected by instruction. Performance-based training in specific contexts is likely to be more beneficial, since much reasoning seems to be based on context-specific knowledge.

One deficiency in reasoning and decision making that seems amenable to instructional training is the judgment of probability. Such training might be beneficial for probability judgments, but not for reasoning in general, because statistical principles are not well understood by most people. Fong, Krantz, and Nisbett (1986) showed that people could be taught to reason accurately according to the law of large numbers. Generally, this law states that the larger a sample is, the better the sample is as an estimate of the population from which it was drawn. People received brief training sessions on the law of large numbers, using either rules, examples or both. The frequency and quality of reasoning with this law on a range of problems were increased by all of the types of training.

Gebotys and Claxton-Oldfield (1989) performed a similar experiment in which students were classified as experts and novices in statistical knowledge. Following a 15-minute training session or no training on how to apply the basic rules of probability, a probability test containing questions from Kahneman, Slovic, and Tversky (1982) was administered. Training improved the performance of both novices and experts on the probability test, eliminating performance differences that were observed without training. This improved performance was maintained for at least five weeks. Thus, minimal training on the application of probability rules is sufficient to allow application of probability concepts.

The importance of the way in which information is presented should not be underestimated. If it is not presented in a way that allows decision makers to apply their knowledge, then performance will suffer. We have already seen the influence of framing, in which the same problem presented in two different ways can lead to very different decisions. Information should usually be framed in a way that important attributes can be encoded positively rather than negatively in the mental representation (for example, Griggs & Newstead, 1982).

Many errors of inference and bias can be attributed to complicated and unclear presentation of information (Evans, 1989). Although the necessary information may have been presented, it can be obscured by the display. Russo (1977) demonstrated how display format can influence the decision maker's ability to use the information presented. Unit price information for several products was presented either on shelf tags under each product or on a single posted list. When the list was used, comparisons across brands were easier, and consumers purchased the less expensive brand more often.

Decision Aids

Given that many deficiencies in reasoning and decision making arise from cognitive limitations, performance should be improved by providing decision makers with decision aids that circumvent such limitations. One such aid, *decision analysis,* is a set of techniques for structuring complex decision problems and decomposing them into simpler components. The structuring process usually involves construction of a decision tree specifying alternative possible actions, along with their associated outcomes. Then normative theory is used to recommend an optimal choice from estimates of utilities and probabilities of outcomes (von Winterfeldt & Edwards, 1986). Decision analysis has been applied with success to problems like suicide prevention and landslide risks. This success is due in large part to adequate structuring of the complex problem.

Decision analysis must be used with care. Because probabilities and utilities are estimated by the decision analyst, biases can still arise in the assessment of uncertainty and preference. Moreover, it is important that all relevant aspects of the problem be considered. One of the more spectacular failures of decision analysis involved the decision to place the Ford Pinto gas tank behind the rear axle (von Winterfeldt & Edwards, 1986). When the Pinto was hit from behind, there was a chance that the gas tank would explode. A decision analysis was performed in which the cost of relocating the tank in front of the axle was compared to the expected dollar value of lives saved by tank relocation. The cost of tank relocation was greater, so the gas tank was left behind the rear axle. Not considered in this analysis were the cost of punitive damages awarded in liability suits and the cost of the negative publicity resulting from publication of the analysis.

Another way to aid the decision-making process is with *decision-support systems.* A decision-support system is a computer-based tool used to guide operators through the decision-making process (Liebowitz, 1990). Decision-support systems do not replace decision makers, but provide them with pertinent information in such a way that the best choices can be made. This presentation of information may involve retrieval of data, filtering of the retrieved data, computer simulations or projections, and useful models (Keen & Scott-Morton, 1978). Decision-support systems should be flexible, use scientific methods when possible, and allow fast access to data and models.

A decision-support system has three major components: a *user interface, control structure,* and *fact base*. The interface is involved in presenting the output of the system to the user and receiving input from the user. As with all human–computer interfaces, this interface should allow for effective dialogue between the operator and the computer. The control structure consists of a data-base management system and a model-management system. The former is a set of programs for creating data files organized according to the needs of the user. The latter is used to model the decision situation using information from the data base. The fact base includes not only the data base, but also the models that can be applied to the data. Pertinent models need to be available upon the user's request.

An example decision-support system is MAUD (Multi-Attribute Utility Decomposition; Humphreys & McFadden, 1980). MAUD is a computer aid that structures problems and then recommends decisions. It contains no domain-specific knowledge but elicits information from the decision maker by asking how alternatives differ from each other. It then uses normative decision theory to reason out a solution to the problem. In addition to aiding the structuring of the problem, MAUD makes biasing of attributes more difficult.

An alternative to support systems based on decision theory is case-based aiding. Case-based aiding uses knowledge about specific cases to support the decision maker. Kolodner (1991) argues that such an approach should be beneficial in many circumstances because it fits well with the way that humans solve problems. Humans do not think in an abstract, normative manner, but in terms of prior knowledge that can be brought to bear on the current decision. Because people find it natural to reason using analogies, but have difficulty retrieving analogies from memory, the role of the case-based support system is to store and retrieve appropriate analogies.

For example, an architect might be given the following problem:

> Design a geriatric hospital: The site is a 4-acre wooded sloping square; the hospital will serve 150 inpatients and 50 outpatients daily; offices for 40 doctors are needed. Both long-term and short-term facilities are needed. It should be more like a home than an institution, and it should allow easy visitation by family members. (Kolodner, 1991, p. 58)

The architect could highlight the key words in the problem specification, and the computer would retrieve cases of geriatric hospitals that are similar to the design criteria. The architect could then evaluate the successes and failures of one or more of those cases and borrow large portions of the designs.

The primary benefit of decision-support systems is improved and faster decisions. This saves time for the decision maker and gives a better understanding about the system that is being simulated. In contrast to expert systems, discussed in Chapter 12, decision-support systems are intended to assist experts in their decisions, rather than to allow a naive user to perform at the level of experts.

SUMMARY

Human problem solving, reasoning, and decision making are notoriously fallible. When normative prescriptions are applicable, human performance deviates systematically from that defined as correct or optimal. However, these deviations do not imply that humans are irrational. Rather, they reflect characteristics of the human information-processing system. Decision-making performance is constrained by an operator's limited ability to attend to multiple sources of information, to retain information in working memory, and to retrieve information from long-term memory. Consequently, many heuristics are used to solve problems and make decisions. These heuristics have the benefit of rendering complex situations manageable, but at the expense of increasing the likelihood of errors. In virtually all situations, performance depends on the accuracy of the mental representation or model of the problem. To the extent that the representation is inappropriate, errors will occur.

The procedures that people use to solve problems and make decisions can be modeled with production systems. The models must specify the knowledge base needed by the problem solver, the productions that operate on this knowledge base, and the control system that directs these operations toward a goal state. Decision-support systems can also be developed around the pro-

duction system framework or other ways of structuring and representing a problem. Such systems can be used by a decision maker to minimize many of the shortcomings of human decision making. Limited training in the application of statistical concepts can also improve the quality of judgments. However, other aspects of reasoning benefit primarily from training in specific domains. The knowledge possessed by an expert in a domain differs substantially from that of a novice. These differences and how expertise is incorporated into expert systems are topics of Chapter 12.

RECOMMENDED READING

Baron, J. (1988). *Thinking and Deciding*. New York: Cambridge University Press.

Bell, D. W., Raiffa, H., & Tversky, A. (eds.) (1988). *Decision Making: Descriptive, Normative, and Prescriptive Interactions*. New York: Cambridge University Press.

Kahneman, D., Slovic, P., & Tversky, A. (eds.) (1983). *Judgment Under Uncertainty: Heuristics and Biases*. New York: Cambridge University Press.

Sternberg, R. J., & Smith, E. E (eds.) (1988). *The Psychology of Human Thought*. New York: Cambridge University Press.

Yates, J. F. (1990). *Judgment and Decision Making*. Englewood Cliffs, NJ: Prentice Hall.

EXPERTS AND EXPERT SYSTEMS

In recent years, research has examined knowledge-rich tasks—tasks that require hundreds and thousands of hours of learning and experience. These studies of expertise, together with theories of competent performance and attempts at the design of expert systems, have sharpened this focus by contrasting novice and expert performances.

—R. Glaser and M. T. H. Chi, 1988

INTRODUCTION

The previous chapters in this section have discussed the basic processes involved in attention, memory, and thought. In Chapter 9, we discussed the limited capacity that observers have for attending to multiple sources of information. Chapter 10 emphasized that similar capacity limitations are present for the ability to retain and perform computations on information in working memory and that information available in long-term memory is often not retrieved when it is needed. Chapter 11 showed that the ability to perform abstract reasoning is also limited. Because of these information-processing limita-

tions, human reasoning relies heavily on simplifying heuristics and past experience. For novice performers who lack specialized knowledge about the domain in which they are reasoning, errors may often occur due to improper simplifications and a lack of experience.

Despite the limitations of the human information-processing system, people can become highly skilled in specific domains. An expert in a domain solves problems much faster, more accurately, and more consistently than does a novice. The question of how experts differ from novices is thus a central concern for human engineering. Differences in performance do not seem to arise from differences in general ability, but more from the knowledge that the expert has about the particular domain. This knowledge enables the expert to see problems differently from the novice and to use different strategies to obtain solutions. Because at least some degree of skill is required to perform virtually any task or job, the human factors specialist needs to know how expert knowledge is acquired and used.

The present chapter focuses on the acquisition of specialized knowledge and how this knowledge affects information processing and performance. The way that speed and accuracy of performance vary as a function of practice is examined, and several taxonomies and models of cognitive skill acquisition are described. Expert and novice performers are compared to provide evidence about the characteristics of expertise. These comparisons reveal some of the reasons why experts are able to think efficiently and how novices may best be trained.

Research on the skilled performance of experts is also of importance to the design of expert systems, which are computer systems that are intended to function as experts. As Eberts, Lang, and Gabel (1987, p. 985) note, "To design more effective expert systems, we must understand the cognitive abilities and functioning of human experts." In this chapter, we will also discuss expert systems and the role that human factors plays in their development.

ACQUISITION OF COGNITIVE SKILL

The acquisition of skill has been a central topic since the earliest research on human performance (for example, see Bryan & Harter's 1899 study of telegraph skill described in Chapter 1). However, until recently, most research dealt with the development of perceptual–motor skills (see Chapter 15). As technology has progressed, jobs have tended to become increasingly specialized and dependent on information. Consequently, in the recent past the acquisition of cognitive skills has been examined in more detail, and studies comparing the performances of experts and novices have been conducted. This research has led to the

formulation of models devoted to explaining the changes in cognitive processing that occur as knowledge of a specialized domain is acquired (for example, Anderson, 1983).

A person is said to be skilled in a particular domain when her or his performance is relatively precise and effortless. Cognitive tasks at which a person can become skilled vary along several dimensions (Colley & Beech, 1989). A task can be as simple as pressing a key when a stimulus event occurs or as complex as air-traffic control. Tasks are said to be convergent if there is only one acceptable, predetermined response, whereas divergent tasks require novel responses. Some tasks are algorithmic, in the sense that a sequence of steps can be learned that infallibly lead to a correct response, and so no deeper understanding of the task requirements is necessary. Tasks that are not algorithmic require an understanding of the principles that underlie the problem to be solved. Skills can involve deductive reasoning or inductive reasoning, and they can be performed in closed (predictable) or open (unpredictable) environments. Finally, there are highly specialized cognitive skills such as chess playing or universal skills such as reading. Given these distinctions, it should be clear that general principles of skill acquisition must always be qualified according to the particular task requirements.

Power Law of Practice

Both speed and accuracy of performance improve with practice. Across a wide variety of perceptual, cognitive, and motor tasks, the change in speed is characterized by a power function (Newell & Rosenbloom, 1981). This function has been called the *power law of practice*. The simple form of the function is

$$T = BN^{-\alpha}$$

where T represents the time to perform the task, N the amount of practice or the number of times the task has been performed, and B and α are positive constants. One characteristic of the power law is that the improvement in performance between two successive trials decreases as the number of trials increases. The rapidity with which improvement decreases is a function of the rate parameter α. For power law curves, the amount of improvement on each trial is a constant proportion of what remains to be learned.

An illustration of the power law is provided in a study by Neves and Anderson (1981) in which students practiced geometry-like proofs. Over 100 proofs were constructed from a set of eight postulates, with each proof being 10 statements long. It took approximately 25 min to solve the first proof, with the solution time being a decreasing function of practice. By the one-hundredth proof, the time to solution was only about 3 min. Figure 12–1a shows the practice function plotted on a linear scale. Two characteristics of the power law are apparent. First, the benefits of practice continue indefinitely. Second, the greatest benefits occur early in practice. Figure 12–1b shows the same data plotted on a log–log scale. The function should be linear if it follows the power law, because

$$\ln(T) = \ln(B) - \alpha \ln(N)$$

As shown by the straight-line fit to the data, the effect of practice on the geometry-like proofs closely approximates a power function.

The power law can be generalized to include a nonzero asymptote and to take into account previous experience with the task. Because the level of "best" performance is never zero, and most operators bring some potentially useful information to the task, both of these factors are important. The generalized form of the power law is

$$T = A + B(N + E)^{-\alpha}$$

where A is the asymptote for performance as N increases indefinitely, and E is the number of trials of learning that occur prior to the first trial tested, that is, the amount of previous experience. This generalized function still yields a straight line with slope $-\alpha$ when plotted on a log–log scale. The family of generalized power functions fits almost all the data on skill acquisition.

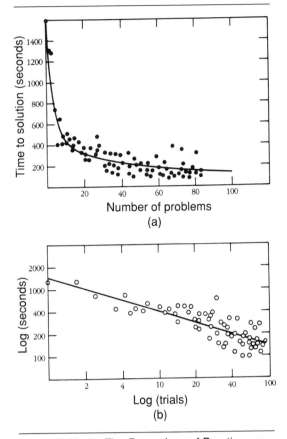

FIGURE 12–1   The Power Law of Practice, as Illustrated by the Time to Generate Geometry-like Proofs, on (a) a Linear Scale and (b) a Log-log Scale.

From *Cognitive Psychology and Its Implications,* 3rd edition, by John R. Anderson. Copyright © 1980, 1985, 1990 by W. H. Freeman and Company. Reprinted by permission.

One final point to note is that the power law not only holds for individual improvement with practice, but it also describes increasing productivity in a production process that occurs as a result of a group of operators' increasing experience with the system (Lane, 1987; Nanda & Adler, 1977). Such manufacturing process functions apply directly to the entire system of production and only secondarily to the performance of individual operators.

Taxonomies of Skill

Although the power law of practice suggests that improvement occurs continuously across time, there appear to be qualitative changes in performance as well. Several taxonomies have been developed to capture these qualitative changes. Two complementary and influential taxonomies are Fitts's phases of skill acquisition and Rasmussen's levels of behavior.

Phases of Skill Acquisition. Fitts (1964; Fitts & Posner, 1967) developed a widely used taxonomy that distinguishes three phases of skill acquisition: *cognitive, associative,* and *autonomous.* Levels of performance in the initial cognitive phase are determined by instructions and demonstrations. The term *cognitive* refers to the fact that the novice is trying to understand the task requirements and must attend to cues and events that do not require attention in later phases. The subsequent associative phase is an intermediate level of skill acquisition, during which the distinct pieces of knowledge that have been learned in the cognitive phase begin to be related to each other. This is accomplished by combining these elements into single, unitized procedures. The final autonomous phase is characterized by the procedures becoming progressively more automatic and less subject to cognitive control.

Automatic processes are those that do not require limited-capacity attentional resources for their performance. Three characteristics are typically attributed to automaticity (Schneider & Fisk, 1983; Shiffrin, 1988). (1) Automatic processes are mandatory and occur without intention. (2) They do not interfere with other mental activity, regardless of whether this activity requires attentional resources. (3) Automatic processes may occur without awareness.

The acquisition of automatic procedures can be illustrated by a study conducted by Kristofferson (1972) that used a hybrid visual/memory search task. In this task, observers were asked to determine if a number of items displayed visually contained one of several previously memorized

targets. The number of targets held in memory was varied. Initially, search times and errors were increasing functions of the memory set size. Kristofferson found that when the task was practiced with a consistent mapping procedure, in which the targets for which the person searched remained constant from trial to trial, the increase in search times and errors as a function of set size was virtually eliminated with sufficient practice (see Figure 12–2). In contrast, Schneider and

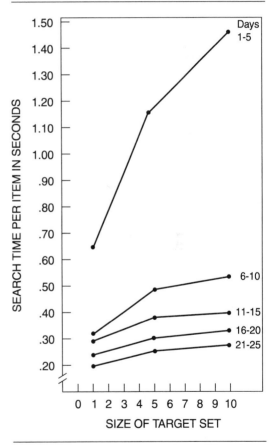

FIGURE 12–2   Set-size Functions of Search Time under Different Levels of Practice with a Consistent-mapping Task.

From M. W. Kristofferson (1972). When item recognition and visual search functions are similar. *Perception & Psychophysics, 12,* 379–384. Reprinted by permission of Psychonomic Society, Inc.

Shiffrin (1977) later observed that when a similar task was practiced with a varied mapping procedure, in which targets on some trials appeared as nontargets on others, and vice versa, there was little change in performance with practice. Schneider and Shiffrin concluded that practice with a consistent mapping leads to automatic search, which they distinguished from the controlled, attentional processing that is required otherwise.

The power of automaticity is illustrated in an experiment conducted by Shiffrin and Schneider (1977) in which people first practiced with a consistent mapping for 2,100 trials. At this point, the stimuli were reversed so that former distractors became targets, and vice versa. Nine hundred trials with the reversed task were required to achieve the level of performance obtained on the initial task without any practice at all (see Figure 12–3). Performance on the reversed task (as measured by the percentage of targets detected)

remained worse than that on the initial task until 1,500 trials after the reversal. Thus, the automatic procedures for target identification developed during the initial training apparently continued to "fire" when their stimulus conditions were present, even though the task was then defined differently.

Skill–Rule–Knowledge Framework. Whereas Fitts's taxonomy focuses on different phases of skill acquisition, Rasmussen's (1986) taxonomy focuses on three levels of behavioral control that interact in determining performance in specific situations. These levels correspond to Fitts's phases of skill acquisition, with the assumption that specific environmental conditions differ in terms of the extent to which an individual will have had experience with them. Skill-based behavior involves relatively simple relations between stimuli and responses, with the behavior performed by automatic, highly integrated ac-

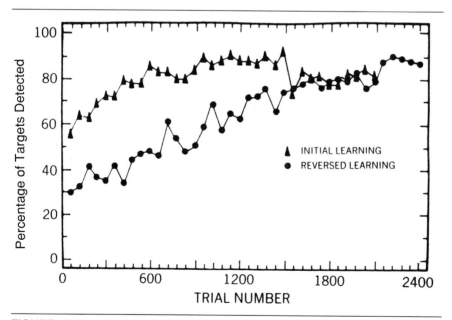

FIGURE 12–3 Learning with Initial and Reversed Consistent Mappings.

From R. M. Shiffrin & W. Schneider (1977). Controlled and automatic human information processing: II. Perceptual learning, automatic attending, and a general theory. *Psychological Review, 84,* 127–190. Reprinted by permission of the American Psychological Association.

tions that do not require conscious control. Performance of routine activities in familiar circumstances would fall within this category, as would the visual search skill established by Shiffrin and Schneider (1977). For some skills, such as simple assembly and repetitive drill operations, training is intended to produce highly integrated, automatic routines (Singleton, 1978). However, for most skills the purpose of training is to develop high flexibility, as well as fast and accurate performance. Flexibility arises from being able to organize many elemental skilled routines through the conscious intention of accomplishing a specific goal.

Rule-based behavior is controlled by a stored rule or procedure derived from previous experiences or learned through instructions. This level of behavioral control occurs when automatic performance is not possible and is often invoked by a deviation from the planned or expected conditions. Rule-based performance is goal oriented and typically under conscious control. Consequently, the rule being used can often be explicitly described by the person who is using it.

Knowledge-based behavior occurs in situations for which no known rules are applicable. It will often be engaged in after an attempt to find a rule-based solution to a problem has failed. Knowledge-based behavior relies on a conceptual model of the domain or system of interest. A concrete goal is formulated, and then a useful plan is developed through functional reasoning. Knowledge-based behavior involves problem solving, reasoning, and decision making of the type described in Chapter 11. Consequently, performance depends on the adequacy of the mental model of the operator and can be influenced by the numerous heuristics that people use to solve problems and make decisions.

According to Reason (1990), distinct types of failures can be attributed to each different performance level. For skill-based performance, most errors involve misdirected attention. Failures due to inattention often occur when there is an intent to deviate from a normal course of action. These errors typically arise when attention is

momentarily diverted and automatic habits intrude. Conversely, errors of overattention occur when an attentional check is made inappropriately during performance of an automatized sequence. At the rule-based level, failures can result from either the misapplication of good rules or the application of bad rules. At the knowledge-based level, errors arise primarily from fallibilities of the strategies and heuristics that problem solvers use to circumvent their limited capacities for reasoning and representing the problem. To minimize failures, most skills require that routine procedures become automatized and also that enough appropriate knowledge be learned for efficient rule-based and knowledge-based reasoning.

Theories of Skill Acquisition

Two types of theories have recently been applied to cognitive skill acquisition: production-system models and connectionist models. *Production-system models* view skill acquisition as similar to problem solving and describe the changes in production rules and their use that occur with practice. *Connectionist models* are based on networks of connections between representational units, with activation patterns within networks determining performance. These models are supposed to more closely mimic the neural networks of the brain; skill acquisition is characterized by changes in the connections within the network. We will describe one example of each in some detail.

Anderson (1983) developed a production-system model, ACT* (pronounced ACT-star; ACT stands for Adaptive Control of Thought and star designates a particular instantiation within the class of ACT models) that distinguishes three phases of skill acquisition similar to those proposed by Fitts (1964). Anderson's model includes a procedural memory that contains the productions used to perform tasks, a declarative memory that contains facts in a semantic network, and a working memory that is used to relate the declarative and procedural knowledge. The first phase of skill acquisition is called the declarative stage, because it relies on declarative knowledge. In this stage, performance depends on general problem-solving productions that use weak heuristic methods of the type described in Chapter 11. The set of facts necessary to perform the task are encoded declaratively by the problem solver. These facts, often rehearsed verbally, must be retained in working memory to be interpreted by the general productions.

Errors are gradually detected and eliminated in the second associative phase. Domain-specific productions begin to develop that no longer require declarative codings for their operation. The process that leads to the acquisition of domain-specific productions, called knowledge compilation, has two subprocesses. The subprocess of composition collapses several productions into a single production that produces the same outcome. The proceduralization subprocess removes from the productions those conditions that require declarative knowledge for their execution.

The productions acquired in the associative phase become increasingly specific and automatic in the third phase, which Anderson calls the procedural stage, as performance becomes more skilled. The domain-specific productions are further tuned through subprocesses of generalization (development of more widely applicable productions), discrimination (narrowing the conditions in which a production is used to only those situations for which the production is successful), and strengthening through repeated application.

One example of a connectionist model of skill acquisition is that proposed by Gluck and Bower (1988). They developed a connectionist model to describe the performance of students who learned to make medical diagnoses based on descriptions of patients' symptoms. The symptoms were imperfect indicators that had only probabilistic relations to the diseases. Students had to make a decision about which of two diseases each patient had, and the decision was followed by feedback regarding the correct diagnosis.

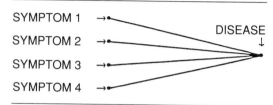

FIGURE 12–4   Gluck and Bower's (1988) Network Model.

The medical symptoms are represented in Gluck and Bower's (1988) model by a network of input nodes (see Figure 12–4). Each symptom produces input activation, which is multiplied by a corresponding weight. These weighted values are then summed at the output node to reflect the extent to which one disease is favored over the other. This sum is used to classify the disease, and feedback regarding the accuracy of the diagnosis is used to modify the weights. This enables the network to adapt to the correlations between symptoms and diseases.

Transfer of Learning

A significant issue in human factors is the extent to which the benefits of practice can transfer to related tasks and domains. The investigation of transfer has a long history in both basic and applied research, although it did not receive as much emphasis as other areas during the 1960s and 1970s (Cormier & Hagman, 1987). More recently, there has been renewed interest in the topic (Singley & Anderson, 1989).

An early extreme view of transfer is the doctrine of formal discipline, originated by John Locke (Higginson, 1931). This doctrine attributes thinking to general skills. Thus, the particular domain of study should be of little concern. Extended practice at solving problems within a specific area should allow the acquisition of procedures related to reasoning and problem solving. Transfer should occur across a broad range of domains because of the general nature of the procedures that are acquired.

At the opposite extreme is the theory of identical elements, advocated by Thorndike (1906), the first scientist to systematically investigate transfer. This theory states that transfer should occur only if two tasks share common stimulus–response elements. Practice at solving problems within a specific area should benefit problem-solving performance within a different area to the extent that the two areas share common features. Thus, transfer should be restricted and highly dependent on the nature of the specific domains of the initial and final tasks.

Studies of transfer indicate that neither of these extreme views is completely correct. The evidence for transfer of general problem-solving skills has been primarily negative. For example, students who received several weeks of training on a general procedure for solving algebraic word problems did no better at solving such problems than students who had not received training (Post & Brennan, 1976). The lack of evidence for transfer of general skills may be due to the fact that the weak methods applicable to a range of tasks are already highly practiced for most adults (Singley & Anderson, 1989). Other evidence indicates that transfer is not as specific as envisioned by Thorndike. Studies such as those interpreted in terms of a permission schema (see Chapter 11) show that transfer can occur when the stimulus and response elements are not identical (Cheng et al., 1986). However, skill acquisition seems to occur more like the processes suggested by Thorndike's identical-elements view than those suggested by the formal discipline view.

As a solution to the issue of transfer, Singley and Anderson (1989) have proposed an account of skill acquisition related to the identical-elements view but applied to mental representations. Singley and Anderson's account is based on the distinction made in ACT* between a declarative phase of performance and a procedural phase. They argue that the specific productions developed with practice are the elements of cognitive skill. Transfer will occur to the extent that the productions acquired to perform one task overlap with those required to perform a second task. In other words, the specific stimulus and response elements do not have to be identical for positive transfer to be obtained; rather, the acquired productions must be applicable to the new situation.

This point is emphasized by an experiment on use specificity in calculus problems conducted by Singley and Anderson (1989). Students who were unfamiliar with freshman calculus learned to translate word problems into equations and select operations to perform on those equations. These operations included differentiation and integration, among others. When problems stated as applications in economics were changed to applications in geometry, and vice versa, there was total transfer of the acquired skill of translating the problem into equations. Transfer in operator selection was also observed between problems that required integration and differentiation, but only to the extent that the operators were shared. In short, transfer occurred only when the productions required for integrating and differentiating economics and geometry problems were similar.

EXPERT PERFORMANCE

Typically, the amount of practice given in a laboratory experiment will be limited relative to that experienced by a skilled performer outside of the laboratory. Consequently, studies have been conducted that compare what experts do to what novices do. These studies have enhanced our understanding of cognitive skill and have provided a foundation for the development of expert systems.

Distinctions between Experts and Novices

Research has produced relatively robust and generalizable findings concerning the differences between experts and novices (Glaser & Chi, 1988). Some discriminating characteristics are summarized in Table 12–1. These characteristics reflect the expert's possession of a readily accessible, organized body of facts and procedures that can be applied to problems concerning his or her area. That is, the special abilities of experts arise from

TABLE 12–1 Characteristics of Experts' Performances

1. Experts excel mainly in their domains.
2. Experts perceive large meaningful patterns in their domain.
3. Experts are fast; they are faster than novices at performing the skills of their domain, and they quickly solve problems with little error.
4. Experts have superior short-term and long-term memory for material in their domain.
5. Experts see and represent a problem in their domain at a deeper (more principled) level than novices; novices tend to represent a problem at a superficial level.
6. Experts spend a great deal of time analyzing a problem qualitatively.
7. Experts have strong self-monitoring skills.

Adapted from Glaser & Chi, 1988.

the substantial amount of knowledge that they have about a particular area and not from a more efficient general ability to think. For example, expert taxi drivers can generate many more secondary, lesser-known routes than can novice taxi drivers (Chase, 1983). Also, experts in chemistry appear to solve problems in physics much like novices (Voss & Post, 1988), although both chemists and physicists are presumed to be of equal scientific sophistication.

The most influential research on expertise compared the performance of chess masters to that of less skilled players (Chase & Simon, 1973; de Groot, 1966). De Groot presented chess masters with a chess board for five seconds, on which the pieces were configured in a legitimate chess arrangement. The masters could reconstruct the positions of more than 20 pieces in this condition. In contrast, nonexperts could recontruct only approximately five positions. However, when the pieces were arranged randomly, no differences existed between the reconstruction performance of the experts and nonexperts. Chase and Simon examined how the masters "chunked" the pieces together in memory and found that the chunks involved meaningful game relations among the pieces. It has been estimated that chess masters can recognize approximately 50,000 board patterns (Simon & Gilmartin, 1973). Each of these patterns likely has specific procedures associated with it that determine the appropriate moves to make. This large number of patterns and procedures that chess experts have learned allows

them to respond faster and more accurately than nonexperts.

Chase and Ericsson (1981) examined skilled memory in more detail for a single person (S.F.). He practiced a standard digit-span task for over 250 hours during the course of two years. Initially, his digit span was the normal seven digits. However, by the end of the two-year period, his span was approximately 80 digits. How did S.F. accomplish this more than tenfold increase in memory span? Verbal protocols and performance analyses indicated that he did so by using mnemonics. S.F. began, as most people would, by coding each digit phonemically. However, on day 5, he started using a mnemonic of running times, based on his experience as a long-distance runner. S.F. first used three-digit codes, switching in later sessions to four-digit running times and decimal times. Much later in practice, he developed additional mnemonics for digit groups that could not be converted into running times.

Based on the performance of S.F. and other people, Chase and Ericsson (1981) developed a model of skilled memory. According to this model, the improvement beyond normal memory span does not reflect an increase in the capacity of short-term store, but more efficient use of long-term store. The model attributes five characteristics to skilled memory: (1) the information is encoded efficiently using existing conceptual knowledge; (2) the stored information is rapidly accessed through retrieval cues; (3) the encoded information is stored in long-term memory; (4)

the speed of encoding can be constantly improved; and (5) the acquired memory skill is specific to the stimulus domain that was practiced.

Ericsson and Polson (1988) used this model as a framework to investigate the memory skills of a particular headwaiter at a restaurant who could remember complete dinner orders from more than 20 people at several tables. As expected, he used a highly organized mnemonic scheme. Orders were organized in groups of four and represented in a two-dimensional matrix for the dimensions of order (by person) and food category (for example, entrée). In addition, he used imagery to relate each person's face to her or his order and special encoding schemes for the different food categories.

The headwaiter's memory showed all the characteristics predicted by the skilled memory model, with the exception that his skills transferred to other stimulus materials. Ericsson and Polson (1988) attribute the relatively broad generality of the headwaiter's memory skills to the wide range of situations that he had to remember. Consequently, he had developed not only considerable flexibility in encoding dinners, but also a more general understanding of his own memory structure, of long-term memory properties, and of broadly applicable "metacognitive" strategies. Skilled memory apparently plays a major role in the skilled performance of other tasks, such as mental calculation (Staszewski, 1988).

Another way in which experts are thought to differ from novices is in the quality of their mental models. Because the models are more adequate, performance is better. Hanisch, Kramer, and Hulin (1991) evaluated the mental models of novice users of a business phone system. These models were determined from analyses of similarity ratings that the users made for nine standard features of the phone. The mental models of the novice users were compared to those for system trainers, who were highly knowledgeable about the system features. The users' mental models were found to be quite different from those of the trainers, with the trainers' models corresponding closely to documentation about the system features. In other words, the novice users' mental models contained deficiencies and inaccuracies. Assuming that a user's performance will be better if his or her mental model is like that of an expert, training programs could be instituted that would highlight and explain clusters of features of the phone system that correspond to those features treated as similar by the trainers.

Although experts are faster overall than novices, they take longer to analyze a problem qualitatively before beginning to find a solution. This qualitative analysis may be used to construct a mental model that allows for the inference of relationships from the problem situation. The extra time spent on qualitative analysis may also be used to add constraints to the problem. These analyses, while time consuming, allow for the efficient generation of solutions.

One reason why experts spend more time analyzing the problem is that they are better able to recognize the conceptual structure of the problem and its correspondence to related problems. Experts are also better able to determine when they have made an error, failed to comprehend material, or need to check a solution. They can more accurately judge the difficulty of problems and the time it will take to solve them. This allows experts to allocate time among problems more efficiently. Chi, Feltovich, and Glaser (1981) found that physics experts sorted problems into categories according to the physical principles upon which they were based, whereas novices were more likely to sort the problems in terms of the similarities among the literal objects described in the problems. However, Hardiman, Dufresne, and Mestre (1989) have shown that it is possible to distinguish between good and poor novices, in that good novices tend to organize the problems by fundamental principles whereas poor novices do not.

Acquisition of Programming Skill

Computer programming is a prototypical problem-solving task. The programmer solves a specific problem by generating a functioning program. As with other problem-solving tasks, the programmer must form an initial mental representation of the problem, which includes a goal structure and operators, and proceed through the resulting problem space to the goal. Explicit strategies and hypotheses are developed that can be verbalized, and a record of the problem-solving process can be obtained through the attempts and partial solutions made by the programmer. Objective measures, such as the accuracy of a solution and the time taken to reach it, can be obtained. Given the problem-solving nature of programming, as well as the fact that many researchers in problem solving also have training in artificial intelligence, it should come as no surprise that considerable effort has been devoted to investigating the acquisition of programming skills.

Experts differ significantly from novices in the ways that they write and read programs. Specifically, skilled programmers show many of the characteristics exhibited by experts in other domains. They can recall several times as many lines of program as novices, but do no better than novices if the program is scrambled (Adelson, 1981; McKeithen et al., 1981). Thus, experts seem to chunk program code into functionally meaningful groups of commands, which are then mapped to chunks of action to be retrieved when the appropriate code is present (Ehrlich & Soloway, 1984). These findings indicate that the expertise of computer programmers is largely a function of domain-specific, skilled memory that bypasses working-memory limitations.

Experts also show better automatization of syntactic knowledge. They can classify lines of code as correct or incorrect approximately 25% faster than novices, with 40% fewer errors (Wiedenbeck, 1985). Similarly, experts demonstrate a better understanding of the higher-level organization of a command system (Mayer, 1988), enabling them to solve problems from a more global perspective. They also exhibit better planning and self-monitoring than novices. When given a program to debug, experts examine the high-level modules and take more time to familiarize themselves with the program than do novices (Vessey, 1986).

The differences between experts and novices indicate that expert programmers have at least two types of knowledge that novices do not (Soloway, Adelson, & Ehrlich, 1988). One type is the knowledge of programming plans representing stereotypic action sequences. The other is the knowledge of programming discourse rules specifying programming conventions (see Figure 12–5). Analogous to conversational rules, these programming rules can generate expectancies about the structure of a particular program.

Soloway, Adelson, and Ehrlich (1988) obtained evidence for programming discourse rules using pairs of executable programs that differed only in whether they did (alpha version) or did not (beta version) conform to the discourse rules (see Figure 12–6). Programmers had to complete a blank line in each program. More programs were completed correctly when they conformed

---

(1)	Variable names should reflect function.
(2)	Do not include code that will not be used.
(3)	A variable that is initialized via an assignment statement should be updated via an assignment statement.
(4)	Do not do double duty with code in a nonobvious way.
(5)	An IF statement should be used when a statement body is guaranteed to be executed only once, and a WHILE statement used when a statement body may need to be repeatedly executed.

FIGURE 12–5   Rules of Programming Discourse.
Adapted from Soloway, Adelson, & Ehrlich (1988).

Program Type

Basic plan:	search plan (max, min)
Discourse rule:	A variable's name should reflect its function
Version Alpha:	variable name agrees with search function
Version Béta:	variable name does NOT agree with search function (i.e., the discourse rule is violated)

Version Alpha

```
PROGRAM Magenta (input, output):
VAR Max, 1, Num : INTEGER;
BEGIN
    Max := 0;
    FOR I := 1 TO 10 DO
        BEGIN
            READLN(Num);
            IF Num > Max THEN Max := Num
        END
    WRITELN(Max):
END
```

Version Beta

```
PROGRAM Purple (input, output):
VAR Max, 1, Num : INTEGER;
BEGIN
    Max := 999999;
    FOR I := 1 TO 10 DO
        BEGIN
            READLN(Num);
            IF Num < Max THEN Max := Num
        END
    WRITELN(Max):
END
```

FIGURE 12–6 Programs That Conform to Discourse Rules (Alpha Version) or Do Not (Beta Version).
Adapted from Soloway, Adelson, & Ehrlich (1988).

to the discourse rules than when they did not, and expert programmers performed better than novices. However, the difference between experts and novices was reliable only for the alpha version programs (see Figure 12–7). In other words, experts were better than novices only when they could use their knowledge of discourse rules.

Among experts, those who have used the most programming languages perform the best (Connelly, 1984; Holt, Boehm-Davis, & Schultz, 1987). Consistent with the view that experts have acquired knowledge of programming plans and discourse rules that are independent from a particular language, Petre (1991) concluded that this correlation occurs because experts do not initially develop a program in the target programming language. Rather, experts first develop an abstract model of the solution and then express it in the particular programming language being used.

Petre found that, having settled on an algorithm, programmers preferred distorting the programming language into conformance rather than changing the algorithm. Conversely, they were willing to change programming languages.

Studies of the acquisition of programming skill can provide basic knowledge regarding the underlying processes, as well as applied benefits for teaching the skill. Anderson and his colleagues have investigated the process of learning to program in LISP, the most widely used language in artificial intelligence, from the perspective of ACT*. Anderson, Farell, and Sauers (1984) analyzed protocols of programmers during their first 30 hours of learning LISP. According to ACT*, performance is initially mediated through the declarative knowledge provided by instructions. Consistent with this view, the programmers initially relied on structural analogy

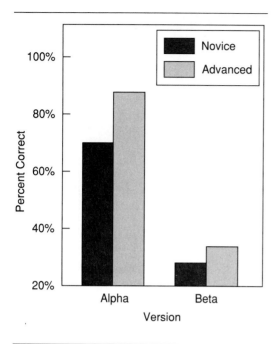

FIGURE 12–7   Interaction: Expertise and Program Type.

Based on data from Soloway, Adelson, & Ehrlich (1988).

(the structure of definitions and examples) to guide their programming. As they practiced, procedures were developed that directly reflected the language structure rather than the form of the instructions. Anderson et al. concluded that the rate at which LISP is learned is determined initially by the knowledge of the language and subsequently by working-memory limitations.

Based on these and other findings, Anderson and his colleagues developed a LISP tutor that has been used at Carnegie–Mellon University since 1984 (Anderson, Conrad, & Corbett, 1989). This tutor provides the student with a series of programming exercises and, concurrently, runs an expert model for the solution of these exercises. Each step taken by the student is evaluated, with feedback provided when needed. The model is based on ACT* and includes 500 production rules that represent knowledge about LISP. The goal is to teach the student these 500 rules. The

applied benefit of the tutor is that learning occurs faster with the tutor than without.

The LISP tutor also has been used to collect additional data on skill acquisition that confirm some of the assumptions of ACT*. The most basic assumption is that the initial declarative knowledge is compiled into productions, which form the basic units of skill. Analysis of the errors made by students indicates that production rules are learned individually. The initial acquisition is followed by more gradual refinement in the use of the productions as they are "tuned" with further practice.

EXPERT SYSTEMS

Given that the efficiency of experts is due primarily to their domain-specific knowledge, it makes sense to develop artificial systems based on this knowledge to aid nonexperts. As the role of specialized knowledge in expert performance has become better understood, this understanding has been applied to the development of *expert systems:* computer programs or software intended to perform like expert consultants. More specifically,

> An expert system is a program that relies on a body of knowledge to perform a somewhat difficult task usually performed by only a human expert. The principal power of an expert system is derived from the knowledge the system embodies rather than from search algorithms and specific reasoning methods. An expert system successfully deals with problems for which clear algorithmic solutions do not exist. (Parsaye & Chignell, 1987, p. 1)

In many cases, the expert system is designed to mimic the information processing of an expert, a characteristic that is called cognitive emulation (Slatter, 1987). The system is applied to problems of a recurring nature within a specific knowledge domain. Unlike decision-support systems, which are intended to provide information to assist experts, expert systems are designed largely to replace the experts (Liebowitz, 1990).

Because the primary goal of an expert system is to represent and use the knowledge of a human expert and to provide its expertise to the user in a form that will enhance performance in the pertinent domain, numerous human factors issues are involved. It is not sufficient for a system to be only technically acceptable; it also must be ergonomically acceptable and organizationally acceptable (that is, compatible with the organization in which it will be used; Preece, 1990). Hence, human factors considerations are vital to the development of expert systems (Madni, 1988; Wheeler, 1989). The potential benefits of expert systems will be fully realized only if they are designed well from a human factors perspective. In this section, we will review the characteristics of expert systems and discuss the contributions that can be made by human factors.

Characteristics of Expert Systems

Most expert systems have several features (Gallant, 1988; Liebowitz, 1990). First, there is an explanation facility that outlines the system's reasoning processes to the operator. Second, the program includes a mechanism for dealing with uncertainty among the facts that are input to the system and the heuristics that are to be used; it should be able to reach conclusions on the basis of partial information. Third, the system typically is interactive; it should efficiently direct the acquisition of facts relevant to the case being evaluated. Fourth, the system has a modular structure consisting of a knowledge or fact base that contains the domain-specific knowledge on which decisions are based, an inference engine that controls the system and is knowledge independent, and a user interface through which the system and the user communicate.

Knowledge can be represented in an expert system in several distinct ways (Ramsey & Schultz, 1989; Tseng, Law, & Cerva, 1992), which correspond to the alternative ways of representing knowledge in models of human information processing. Rule-based representations use production rules specifying that, if some condition is true, then some action is performed. A semantic network system is a connected group of elements called nodes and links. Each node represents basic data elements and each link a relation between them. Frame-based systems represent knowledge in abstract schemas called frames or scripts. A frame contains information about one particular genre of events and describes the stereotyped or prototypical information for the category. Scripts can be used to represent organized sequences of events.

Knowledge representations are selected according to the following three considerations:

> Expressive power: Can experts communicate their knowledge effectively to the system?
> Understandability: Can experts understand what the system knows?
> Accessibility: Can the system use the information it has been given? (Tseng, Law, & Cerva, 1992, p. 185)

None of the methods of representation satisfy these and other criteria perfectly, so the best representation to use will depend on the specific application. Production systems are convenient for representing procedural knowledge, since they are in the form of actions to be taken when conditions are satisfied. They also are relatively easy to modify and understand. Semantic networks are convenient for representing declarative knowledge, such as the properties of an object. Frames and scripts provide useful representations when stereotypic situations are involved. More than one form of knowledge representation can be used in an expert system, and in many cases this will be the most suitable solution.

The role of the inference engine is to generate and evaluate hypotheses from the knowledge base. The type of inference engine used is often closely linked to the type of knowledge base employed, and vice versa. The inference engine generates hypotheses through various search strategies. Forward or backward chaining, or some combination of the two, is often used to search for hypotheses (Liebowitz, 1990). The former is driven by the data that are input, whereas the latter works backward from the goal.

The user interface must have a dialogue structure capable of supporting three modes of interaction that a user has with the expert system. These modes are (1) obtaining solutions to problems, (2) adding to the system's knowledge base, and (3) examining the reasoning process of the system (Liebowitz, 1990). Creation of a useful dialogue structure requires the designer to understand what information is needed by the user and how and when to display it. The dialogue structure should be such that the information requested by the computer is clear to the user and the user entry tasks are of minimal complexity.

Because many decisions are made under situations of uncertainty, the appropriate expert system must be able to represent those uncertainties and operate when they are present (Hamburger & Booker, 1989). As in human decision making, the system must account for preferences of outcomes, costs of actions, and so on, to generate appropriate decisions. There are several specific ways for doing this, with the application of probability theory in belief networks being among the most promising. A belief network is a representation of the interdependencies among different propositions, so that each is not treated as a single, independent unit but as a group of units that systematically interact.

An Example System

A system called DESPLATE (Diagnostic Expert System for Steel Plates) has been developed to diagnose faults in shapes of rolled steel plates (Cung & Ng, 1989). Slabs of reheated steel are rolled into plates of specified thickness and shape. The final products are to be rectangular, but perfect rectangular shapes rarely occur. Figure 12–8 illustrates five examples of faulty shapes. Some plates may be sufficiently deviant that they must be cut into smaller dimensions, which is a costly and time-consuming process. Therefore, DESPLATE is designed to locate the

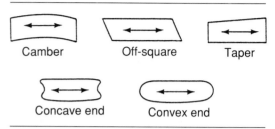

FIGURE 12–8   Examples of Faulty Shapes.
From L. D. Cung & T. S. Ng (1989). DESPLATE: A diagnostic expert system for faulty plan views shapes of steel plates. In J. R. Quinlan (Ed.), *Applications of Expert Systems* (Vol. 2; pp. 156–169). Copyright © 1989 Addison-Wesley. Reprinted by permission.

cause of particular faulty shapes and recommend adjustments to correct the problem.

DESPLATE uses a mixture of forward and backward chaining to reach a conclusion. The user is prompted for a set of facts observed prior to or during the session in which faulty plates were produced. From this set of data, DESPLATE forward chains until the solution space is sufficiently narrow. If a cause can be assumed, backward chaining is then used to prove this cause; otherwise, forward chaining continues.

DESPLATE searches a knowledge base that is arranged hierarchically. The entire knowledge base is organized according to the time required to test for a fault and the frequency of that fault. Observations or tests that are easily performed have priority over those that are more difficult, and faults that rarely occur are only tested when everything else has failed. Information is presented in order of these priorities. There are three kinds of information in the knowledge base: (1) the observations, or symptoms, that are used to identify different types of faults; (2) the tests used to diagnose faults; and (3) the faults themselves, which are hierarchically arranged according to their nature.

DESPLATE was installed in 1987 at the plate mill of the BHP Steel International Group, Slab and Plate Products Division, Port Kembla,

Australia. It has produced satisfactory solutions and recommendations for three faulty shapes: camber, off-square, and taper.

Expert systems have been used successfully in a variety of other domains (Tseng, Law, & Cerva, 1992). The XCON system used by Digital Equipment Corporation configures a computer hardware–software system specific to the customer's needs. The MYCIN system is used for diagnosis and treatment of infectious diseases. The ACE system is used by telephone companies to identify cable problems that may need preventive maintenance. These examples convey the range of applications to which expert systems can be applied. With the success of current systems, it can be expected that widespread use of more sophisticated expert systems will occur in the future.

Human Factors Issues

The development of an expert system usually involves several people (Parsaye & Chignell, 1987). A domain expert provides the knowledge that is collected in the knowledge base. An expert-system developer, or *knowledge engineer*, designs the system and its interface, as well as programs for accessing and manipulating the knowledge base. Users are typically involved from the outset to ensure that the system will be usable by the people for whom it is intended. In other respects, standard procedures for system development and evaluation are followed.

Several human factors concerns must be addressed during the construction of an expert system (Chignell & Peterson, 1988; Nelson, 1988). The first area in which the human factors specialist can play a role is the selection of the task or problem that is to be modeled in the expert system. Deductive problems are more easily implemented than inductive problems (Wheeler, 1989). The task should be easily structured, and it should rely on a focused area of knowledge. Experts must be available who agree on how the task in question is best performed.

A second area involves the representation of knowledge and the accompanying inference engine in the expert system. The objects in the knowledge base must be described in a way that reflects the expert's knowledge structure. This involves defining characteristics that influence the reasoning and decision-making processes. Different objects should be discriminable through these characteristics. There is a continuing need for human factors research determining those forms of knowledge representation and inference engines that will best reflect the knowledge of experts in various domains.

The knowledge and inference rules entered into the system must be acquired from an expert. Most often, the knowledge is extracted through interviews, questionnaires, and verbal protocols collected while the expert performs the tasks to be modeled. It is important that (1) the knowledge engineer and subject-matter expert maintain a common frame of reference, (2) the elicitation procedure be compatible with the expert's mental model, (3) biases and exaggerations in the expert's responses be detected and compensated for, and (4) the end user's expectations be kept in mind (Madni, 1988). Because much of the procedures that distinguish the expert from a novice are highly automatized, verbal reports may not reveal the most important knowledge.

User-friendly expert system shells are available for developing specific expert systems. The shells include domain-independent reasoning mechanisms and various knowledge representation modes for building knowledge bases. One benefit of these shells is that they allow the opportunity for the domain expert to be directly involved in the development of the expert system, rather than just serving as a source of knowledge. This may allow more information about the expert's knowledge to be incorporated into the system, because the input is more direct. Naruo, Lehto, and Salvendy (1990) describe a case study in which this method was used to design an expert system for diagnosing malfunctions of a machine for mounting chips on an integrated-circuit board. A detailed knowledge elicitation process was used to organize the machine designer's knowledge. This process took several weeks, but the implementation as a rule-based expert system using the shell then took only about a week. On-site evaluation showed that the expert system successfully diagnosed 92% of the malfunctions of the chip-mounting machine.

An alternative to basing the knowledge of an expert system on an expert's verbal protocols is to have the system develop the knowledge from experiences of the actions taken by the expert in particular situations. The connectionist approach to modeling is particularly suited to this enterprise, because connectionist systems acquire knowledge through experience (Gallant, 1988). The system is presented with coded input and output, corresponding to the environmental stimuli and the action taken, for a series of specific problems. A learning algorithm adjusts the weights of the connections between nodes to closely match the behavior being simulated.

Hunt (1989) describes the results of several experiments that illustrate the potential for this type of approach. In one, students were instructed to imagine that they were learning how to troubleshoot an internal combustion power plant. Readings of instruments, such as coolant temperature and fuel consumption, were displayed as in Figure 12–9. From the configuration of readings, one of four malfunctions (radiator, air filter, generator, or gasket) had to be diagnosed. In an initial series of such problems, performance of the students began at chance (25%) and increased to 75% by the end. Another series of new configurations was then given, and these malfunctions were also diagnosed with 75% accuracy.

A connectionist model was developed for each student based on their responses for the initial series. These models were then used to classify the configurations of the second series. The models were relatively accurate in approximating the performance of the individual students, with the mean classification accuracy being 72%. In contrast, a rule-based system for which the knowledge was acquired by interviews after the

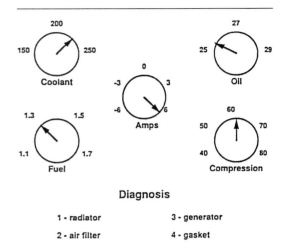

Diagnosis

| 1 - radiator | 3 - generator |
| 2 - air filter | 4 - gasket |

FIGURE 12–9   A Typical Display Shown in the Diagnostic Task.

From E. Hunt (1989). Connectionist and rule-based representations of expert knowledge. *Behavior Research Methods, Instruments, & Computers, 21,* 88–95. Reprinted by permission of Psychonomic Society, Inc.

first series averaged only 55% correct for the second series. These results suggest that more objective methods of knowledge elicitation, coupled with a system that learns from the expert's actions, may ultimately enable the development of better expert systems.

A third human factors concern is the design of the interface. If the interface is poorly designed for the user, the benefit provided by the expert system may be lost. Users may stop using the system, or the interface may lead to operator errors. The human factors specialist can provide input regarding how tasks should be allocated to the expert system and the user and how the two should interact. The specialist can also help determine the way in which the information should be presented to the user to optimize the efficiency of the human–machine interactions. Of particular concern is presentation of the system's reasoning in such a manner that the user will be able to understand it.

Two modes of interaction are commonly used for expert-system interfaces (Hanne &

Hoepelman, 1990). Natural language interfaces, in which the communications are in the user's natural language, are most common. Such interfaces can be used by the widest range of individuals, but they can lead the user to overestimate what the system "understands." Direct graphical presentation of the working environment is an alternative that is being used more often. This type of interface is effective for communicating such things as dynamic changes, paths to solution, and so on. In many situations, a combination of language and graphical dialogue will be most effective. A good design strategy is to have users evaluate prototypes of the intended interface early in the development process so that interface decisions are not made only after the rest of the expert system has already been developed.

Fourth, the performance of the expert system must be validated. The potential for errors in the knowledge base and faulty rules require that the correctness of conclusions be tested. A system can be tested by simulating its performance with historical data and assessed by experts to determine its validity. Because the system ultimately will be used in a work environment by an operator, it is important to also test the performance of the operator. This requires the development of experimental procedures that represent the conditions faced during actual operation and that are sufficiently sensitive to reveal any improved performance for operators using the expert system compared to operators who are not using it. It is difficult to debug a system once it is installed in the field, so these tests of system performance and knowledge validity need to be performed prior to installation.

Unfortunately, the important step of evaluating the operator's performance with the expert system is often not taken. The consequences of omitting this step are apparent from a study by Nelson and Blackman (1987). They evaluated two variations of a prototype expert system developed for operators of nuclear reactors. The expert system used response trees to help operators monitor critical safety functions and to identify a "success path" for implementation when a

safety function became endangered. One variation was operator controlled, requiring the operator to provide input about failed components when they were discovered and to request a recommendation when one was desired. The other variation was automated, automatically registering any failures that occurred, checking to determine whether a new success path recommendation was necessary, and displaying this new recommendation.

As might be expected, the automated system was much more usable than the operator-controlled system. Among other things, wrong information could be entered by the operator for the latter system, resulting in erroneous and confusing recommendations. More important, neither system significantly enhanced performance relative to operators who were not aided by an expert system. The authors discuss many aspects of their experimental procedures that may limit the generalizability of their findings, but the important point is that it cannot be assumed that an expert system always improves operator performance.

If the expert system is to be successful, it must be accepted by the users. Acceptance problems can be minimized by involving users in all phases of the development process. Training programs must be developed to ensure that operators understand how the expert system is to be integrated into the required tasks. Maintenance procedures need to be implemented that will ensure the reliability of the system. Finally, possible extensions of the system into areas for which it was not initially designed can be evaluated.

It should be clear that human factors issues are critical to the implementation of expert systems, as they are for most sophisticated technology. When sound decisions about these issues are made, the benefit of the resulting expert system to the user and to performance of the intended tasks should be optimized.

SUMMARY

The acquisition of skill occurs in an orderly manner across a range of cognitive tasks. Performance is determined initially by the application of generic, weak problem-solving methods. With practice, domain-specific knowledge is acquired that can be brought to bear on the task at hand. It is this knowledge that defines an expert. The domain-specific knowledge possessed by experts enables them to perceive, remember, and solve problems better in that domain than can nonexperts. The transferability of this knowledge is relatively low; positive transfer occurs only for a narrow range of situations in which the acquired procedures apply. When behavior is controlled by such knowledge, it can be characterized as skill based or rule based. Knowledge-based behavior is evoked when a novel solution to a problem is required; such behavior involves the use of general problem-solving strategies and mental models.

Expert systems are computer programs designed to emulate an expert. An expert system has three basic components: a knowledge base, an inference engine, and a user interface (dialogue structure). The potential benefits of expert systems are limited by human performance issues. Human factors specialists can provide input regarding which tasks can be successfully modeled, the most appropriate methods for extracting the pertinent knowledge from domain experts, the best way to represent this knowledge in the knowledge base, the design of an effective dialogue structure for the user interface, evaluations of the performance of the expert system, and integration of the system into the work environment.

RECOMMENDED READING

Berry, D., & Hart, A. (eds.) (1990). *Expert Systems: Human Issues.* Cambridge, MA: MIT Press.

Chi, M. T. H., Glaser, R., & Farr, M. J. (eds.). (1988). *The Nature of Expertise.* Hillsdale, NJ: Lawrence Erlbaum.

Colley, A. M., & Beech, J. R. (eds.) (1989). *Acquisition and Performance of Cognitive Skills.* New York: Wiley.

Liebowitz, J. (1990). *The Dynamics of Decision Support Systems and Expert Systems.* Chicago: Dryden Press.

Parsaye, K., & Chignell, M. (1988). *Expert Systems for Experts.* New York: Wiley.

CHAPTER 13

RESPONSE SELECTION AND PRINCIPLES OF COMPATIBILITY

It's the le. . . . It's the right one.

—David McClelland, copilot of a British Midland flight that crashed
in January 1989, before the crew turned off the wrong engine

INTRODUCTION

Human–machine interaction involves both communication of information from the machine to the operator and communication from the operator back to the machine. The perception of displayed information and the subsequent cognitive processing of that information by the operator ultimately lead to selection and execution of a controlling action. Even if perception and cognition are accomplished flawlessly, inappropriate or inaccurate actions can still be taken. The quotation that begins this chapter illustrates an occasion in which a flight crew turned off the wrong engine, resulting in the crash of a commercial aircraft. Response–selection errors of this type cannot be avoided entirely, but proper design can increase the speed and accuracy with which responses are selected. Response selection has been studied extensively in laboratory experiments in which speeded reactions are required.

Three basic processes can be distinguished in reaction-time tasks, just as can be done more generally for human information processing (see Chapter 4). We will refer to these processes as stimulus identification, response selection, and response programming (see Figure 13–1). They correspond to the more general distinctions between perception, cognition, and action. Whereas stimulus identification is a function of stimulus

271

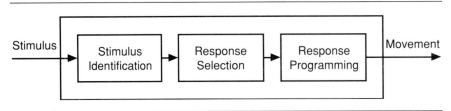

FIGURE 13–1   The Three-stage Model for Reaction-time Tasks.

properties, and response programming a function of response properties, response selection involves translating from stimuli to responses. These translation processes are influenced primarily by the relationship between the stimuli and the responses assigned to each. For a human–machine system to operate effectively, the interface must be designed to optimize the efficiency with which displayed information can be translated into the required controlling responses. Although response selection is generally considered to be a cognitive process, it is critical to our understanding of action. The topic of this chapter concerns the factors that influence the time to translate between stimuli and responses and the factors that determine the controlling actions that will be performed.

SIMPLE REACTIONS

Monitoring tasks sometimes require that an operator react to any signal with a single, predetermined response (Teichner, 1962). Situations in which a single response is made to any stimulus event are called simple reaction tasks. Because only one response is to be made to any event, response–selection processes are presumed to play a minimal role. However, even for a simple reaction, a decision still must be made about the presence or absence of the stimulus. Many results from simple reaction tasks can be characterized in terms of a model in which evidence about the presence of the stimulus accumulates on a cognitive mechanism. This mechanism allows execution of the response when the evidence reaches a criterion level.

The time to make a simple reaction will decrease to a minimum as the stimulus is made more salient. For example, as the luminance of a light flash is increased, reaction time to the onset of the flash will decrease (Mansfield, 1973; Teichner & Krebs, 1972). The fastest that a simple reaction can be is approximately 150 ms for visual stimuli and 120 ms for auditory and tactual stimuli (Boff & Lincoln, 1988). Stimulus factors such as intensity affect primarily the rate at which information about the presence of the stimulus accumulates.

It is possible to influence a person's readiness to respond through the use of warning signals. In a simple reaction-time study, responses are made more slowly if there is no warning and the interval between trials is long and uncertain than if there is a warning. The warning signal thus can be construed as increasing the state of preparation and lowering the criterion amount of evidence for responding. Grice (1968) developed a model (see Figure 13–2) based on the notion that intensity affects the rate of evidence accumulation toward an adjustable criterion. The stronger the stimulus intensity is, the faster the information accumulates; the height of the criterion line corresponds to the criterion level. The point to note from the graphical representation of the model is that it predicts an interaction between intensity and variables that affect the criterion level. Criterion manipulations should have a greater effect for weak stimuli than for strong stimuli.

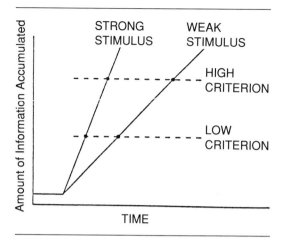

FIGURE 13–2   Grice's Adjustable Criterion Model for Simple Reaction Time.

Several studies have obtained results consistent with this model. For example, to vary the rate of accumulation, Kohfeld (1969) had observers respond to auditory tones of 30, 60, or 90 dB. The stimulus was preceded by an auditory warning signal that also could be 30, 60 or 90 dB. The logic was that the observer adapts to the intensity of the warning signal, so more evidence is needed to respond as the intensity of the warning signal increases. Reaction times were a decreasing function of stimulus intensity, but an increasing function of warning signal intensity. Most importantly, an interaction between warning signal and stimulus intensities of the type predicted by the accumulation model was obtained (see Figure 13–3a). Stimulus intensity had a greater effect on reaction time following a warning signal of high intensity than one of low intensity.

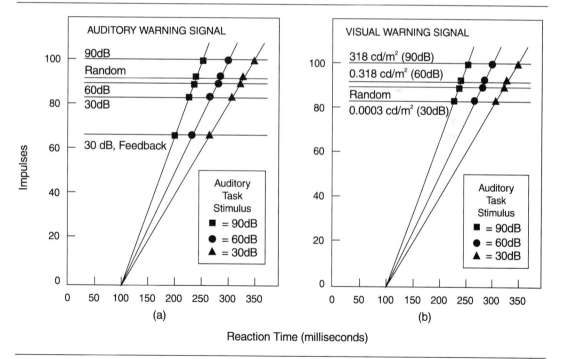

FIGURE 13–3   Reaction Times as a Function of the Intensities of the Auditory Task Stimulus and (a) an Auditory Warning Signal and (b) a Visual Warning Signal.

From D. L. Kohfeld (1969). Effects of the intensity of auditory and visual ready signals on simple reaction time. *Journal of Experimental Psychology, 82,* 88–95. Copyright © 1965 by the American Psychological Association. Reprinted by permission.

The higher-intensity warning signals apparently raised the response criterion. Kohfeld obtained similar results when the warning signal was presented visually (see Figure 13-3b).

Kohfeld's (1969) study and related experiments indicate that performance in simple reaction tasks is influenced by a response-selection factor, that is, the criterion for responding. Observers can directly control the amount of evidence required to respond that a stimulus is present.

CHOICE REACTIONS

Outside the laboratory, the vast majority of reaction tasks require a choice among alternative stimuli and responses. For example, several distinct auditory alarm signals, each with its own assigned response, may be used in a process control room. Response-selection factors become much more important when a person must choose between alternative responses.

Response selection has been investigated most thoroughly for tasks in which one of two or more responses is to be made to one of two or more possible stimuli. Most of the variables that affect simple reaction time, such as stimulus intensity and temporal uncertainty, also influence choice reaction time. However, numerous other factors become important, including the relative emphasis on speed or accuracy, warning interval, amount of information (*H*), compatibility of stimuli and responses, and practice. These additional factors are involved with having to decide which of several stimuli occurred and which of several responses to make.

Speed–Accuracy Trade-off

In a simple reaction task, an incorrect response cannot be selected, because there is only one response. However, in choice reaction tasks, incorrect responses are possible. It should be apparent that response latency in choice tasks will depend on the accuracy of the response-selection process. For example, if accuracy was of no con-

cern, you could make a preselected response whenever the onset of a stimulus was detected (extreme speed emphasis in Figure 13–4). Such guesses would yield fast reaction times, but with chance accuracy. Alternatively, you could wait until you were sure about the identity of the stimulus and its associated response (extreme accuracy emphasis in Figure 13–4). Your responses would be slower, but accuracy would be better.

Between these two extremes, a range of response criteria could be adopted that would vary in their relative emphasis on speed versus accuracy. The function relating speed and accuracy shown in Figure 13–4 is called the speed–accuracy trade-off. The speed–accuracy trade-off function shows different combinations of speed and accuracy that can be obtained for a single-choice situation, much like an ROC curve indicates different hit and false-alarm rates for a given sensitivity (see Chapter 4). As with the ROC curve, the selection of a point on the speed–accuracy function is affected by such things as instructions, payoffs, and prior probabilities. For situations in which the time to choose a response is limited, these factors can be applied to ensure that operators adopt the appropriate speed–accuracy strategy.

One of the easiest ways to account for the speed–accuracy trade-off is through information

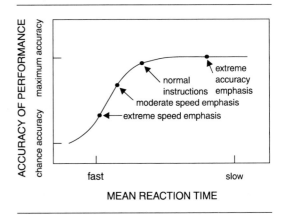

FIGURE 13–4 A Theoretical Speed–Accuracy Trade-off Function.

accumulation models similar to Grice's model for simple RT tasks. Such models have a separate mechanism for each response, and the trade-off is attributed to the settings of the criteria for each response. Responses will be made on the basis of less information if the criteria are lowered, leading to faster but less accurate responses. Moreover, just as the criterion in signal-detection theory reflects an observer's bias to respond *yes* or *no,* the criterion settings across the alternative responses reflect an observer's bias. The lower a criterion is in relation to other criteria, the greater the bias toward that response.

For human factors, the primary implication of the speed–accuracy trade-off is that variables may affect either the efficiency of information accumulation or the criteria settings. This point is illustrated by a study of Rundell and Williams (1979) that examined the effect of alcohol on the speed–accuracy trade-off. People performed a two-choice task in which the stimuli were low- or high-frequency tones and the responses were left and right key presses. No increase in reaction time was apparent for people who had ingested alcohol prior to performing the task, but their error rates did increase. This finding suggests that alcohol impaired the efficiency of the information accumulation, rather than just affecting bias. One implication is that an alcohol-impaired individual would have to make slower responses to avoid increasing the error rate.

Temporal Uncertainty

Another factor influencing reaction time is the knowledge about when a stimulus is going to occur. If you know that a stimulus will be occurring at a particular time, a heightened state of preparation can be achieved. However, in some situations such forewarning is not possible. One example is emergency warning signals. Warrick, Kibler, and Topmiller (1965) had secretaries respond to the sound of a buzzer by reaching to and pressing a button located to the left of their typewriters. The buzzer was sounded once or twice a week, without warning, for six months. Although

their reaction times decreased over the six-month period, they were always approximately 150 ms slower than secretaries who were alerted to the forthcoming stimulus.

The effects of preparation are examined by varying the interval between a warning signal and the stimulus to which an observer is to respond. Typical preparation functions are shown in Figure 13–5. The data come from a study by Posner et al. (1973) in which observers responded with a left or right key to an X that occurred to the left or right of a vertical line. On each trial, there either was no warning or a brief warning tone, followed by the X after a variable delay. Reaction times were a U-shaped function of warning interval, with the fastest responses occurring when the warning tone preceded the stimulus by 200 ms. However, the percentages of errors were the inverse of the reaction-time function. Errors increased and then decreased as foreperiod increased. Slower response times were associated with higher accuracy, demonstrating a speed–accuracy trade-off.

This pattern of results, which is relatively common, again can be attributed to an effect of temporal uncertainty on response criteria. That is, the fact that the slower responses are more accurate than the faster ones suggests that the effect of the warning tone is to vary the response criteria and not the information on which the decision is based. Consequently, although responses are slower when a person is unprepared, they may be based on better information.

When considering whether an alerting signal should be used in an operational environment, it is important to consider the overall time to respond. Simpson and Williams (1980) had airline pilots respond to a synthesized speech message while flying a simulator. Reaction time measured from the onset of the message was faster when an alerting tone occurred 1 second prior to the message than when one did not. However, when the additional time for the alerting tone was taken into account, overall system response time was actually longer (see Figure 13–6). Consequently, Simpson and Williams concluded that

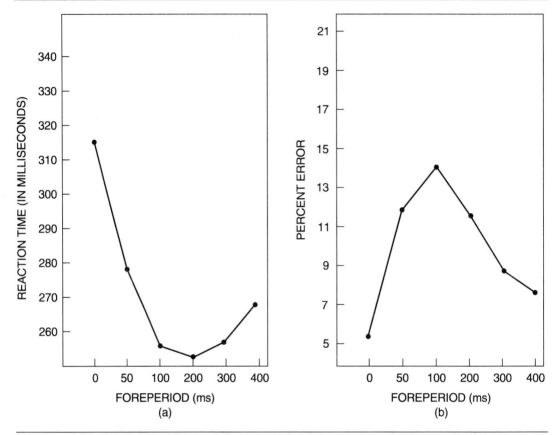

FIGURE 13–5   Reaction Times (a) and Percentages of Error (b) as a Function of Foreperiod in a Two-choice Task.

From M. I. Posner, R. Klein, J. Summers, & S. C. Buggie (1973). On the selection of signals. *Memory & Cognition, 1,* 2–12. Reprinted by permission of Psychonomic Society, Inc.

an alerting tone probably should not be used with synthesized speech displays in the cockpit environment.

Stimulus–Response Uncertainty

Information theory, which was introduced in Chapter 4, expresses the amount of information (*H*) in a set of stimuli or responses as a function of the number of possible alternatives and their probabilities. One reason that information theory became popular was that choice–reaction time is a linear function of the amount of information transmitted, a relation that has come to be known

as Hick's law, or the *Hick–Hyman law,* after the researchers who established this relation.

Hick (1952) used a display of 10 small lamps arranged in an irregular circle and 10 corresponding response keys on which a person's fingers were placed. When one of the lamps came on, the corresponding key-press response to that stimulus was to be made. In different sets of trials, the number of possible stimuli (and responses) was varied from 2 to 10. Reaction time showed a curvilinear increase as a function of the number of alternative stimuli; the function was linear when plotted as a function of $\log_2 N$, or the amount of information in the stimulus set (see

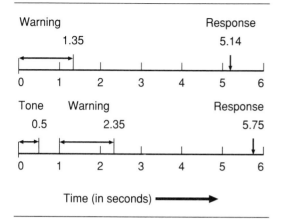

FIGURE 13–6   Mean Times to Respond to a Warning Message Alone or Preceded by an Alerting Tone.

From C. A. Simpson & D. H. Williams, Response time effects of alerting tone and semantic context for synthesized voice cockpit warnings. Adapted with permission from *Human Factors,* Vol. 22, No. 3, pp. 319–330, 1980. Copyright © by The Human Factors Society, Inc. All rights reserved.

Figure 13–7). This relation indicates that the rate of information gain was a constant function of time.

In Hick's (1952) experiment, the stimuli were equally likely, and performance was measured for sets of trials in which no errors were made. However, the amount of information transmitted varies not only as a function of the number of stimuli and responses, but also as a function of accuracy and stimulus probabilities (see Chapter 4). Therefore, in a second experiment, Hick encouraged people to respond faster but less accurately. The decrease in reaction time was consistent with the reduction in information transmitted, as measured by the error rate. Similarly, Hyman (1953) showed that when overall uncertainty was reduced by making some stimuli more probable than others or by introducing sequential dependencies across trials (which altered the probabilities on a trial to trial basis), the mean reaction times could still be expressed as a function of the amount of information.

The results obtained by Hick (1952) and Hyman (1953) are fit well by the equation

$$\text{reaction time} = a + b[T(S, R)]$$

where a is a constant reflecting sensory and motor factors, b is the time to transmit 1 bit of information, and $T(S, R)$ is the information transmitted (see Figure 13–7). This equation is the relation known as the Hick–Hyman law. It has been found to fit data from many other choice–reaction tasks, but the rate of information transmission ($1/b$) varies greatly as a function of the specific task. The general point of the Hick–Hyman law is that in most situations an operator's reaction time will increase a constant amount for each doubling of the number of distinct possible signals and associated responses. The fewer the alternatives are, the faster the operator can respond.

The studies by Hick (1952) and Hyman (1953) led to a resurgence of interest in choice–reaction time, which had been studied extensively in the latter part of the nineteenth century and the early part of the twentieth century. Much of the research following Hick and Hyman placed qualifications on the Hick–Hyman law. For instance, Leonard (1958) tested whether the rela-

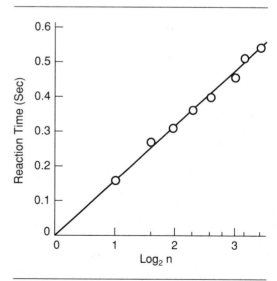

FIGURE 13–7   Reaction Times Plotted as a Function of Number of Alternatives on a Log₂ Scale.

Data from Hick, 1952.

tion between information and reaction time actually arises from making a series of binary decisions. For example, with a linear array of four lights, an initial decision might be that the stimulus was one of the two to the left of center. The second decision would then involve which of the two to the left it actually was. Only the latter decision would be required if an array of two lights was used.

To test this sequential decision hypothesis, Leonard (1958) provided advance information in a variant of the movement-precuing procedure that has since become widely used (see Proctor, Reeve, & Weeks, 1990; Rosenbaum, 1983). Leonard first found the difference in reaction times between a six-choice and a three-choice task to be 45 ms. He then conducted a six-choice task in which the initial six choices were reduced by a precue to three choices. This precue occurred 45 ms before the onset of the stimulus to which the observer was to respond. His logic was that, if the 45-ms difference between the original six-choice and three-choice reaction times reflected the time for the additional binary decision, then reaction times in the precued version of the six-choice task should approximate those in the three-choice task. However, people were slower in the precued condition than in the original three-choice task, providing evidence against the sequential decision hypothesis. The importance of this and related findings was to show that, although the Hick–Hyman law describes the effect of the information on reaction time, it does not provide an explanation of the processes that act on that information.

Despite the fact that advance information does not affect reaction times in a manner consistent with the sequential decision hypothesis, it does usually speed responding (see for example, Proctor, Reeve, & Weeks, 1990). When a precue or priming stimulus is predictive of the subsequent stimulus that will occur, conscious expectancies are developed. Responses to the subsequent target stimulus will be facilitated if it is consistent with the primed expectancies and inhibited if it is not (Neely, 1977). This means

that the speed and accuracy of responding can be increased by providing an operator with predictive contextual information that allows the development of appropriate expectancies about the likely stimulus events.

Although reaction time typically increases as a function of the number of stimulus–response alternatives, the slope of the Hick–Hyman function is not constant and can be reduced to zero with sufficient practice (Mowbray, 1960; Mowbray & Rhoades, 1959; Seibel, 1963). Moreover, for highly compatible stimulus–response mappings, the slope approximates zero even without practice. Leonard (1959) demonstrated this using stimuli that were vibrations to the tip of a finger and responses that were depressions of the stimulated fingers. With these vibrotactile stimuli, there was no systematic increase in reaction time as the number of choices was increased from two to eight. Thus, the number of alternatives has virtually no effect for highly compatible or highly practiced stimulus–response relations, topics to which we turn next.

PRINCIPLES OF COMPATIBILITY

Stimulus–Response Compatibility

About the same time as the work of Hick and Hyman, another classic choice–reaction time study was reported by Fitts and Seeger (1953). They used three different stimulus and response sets, all with eight alternatives. Thus, the sets were equivalent in terms of the amount of stimulus and response information they contained. The stimulus sets differed in the way that the information was signaled (see Figure 13–8). For set *A,* any one of eight lights could come on; for stimulus sets *B* and *C,* any of four lights alone or any four pairs of these lights could occur. The two sets differed in the spatial configuration of the lights. The three response sets corresponded conceptually to the displays. People were required to move a single stylus to a target location for sets *A* and *B,* and two styli to locations for set *C.* For

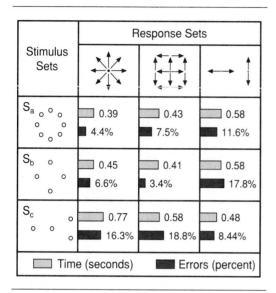

Stimulus Sets	Response Sets		
	(8-spoke)	(4-path T)	(left-right / up-down)
S_a (circle of 8)	0.39 / 4.4%	0.43 / 7.5%	0.58 / 11.6%
S_b (3 diagonal)	0.45 / 6.6%	0.41 / 3.4%	0.58 / 17.8%
S_c (3 horizontal)	0.77 / 16.3%	0.58 / 18.8%	0.48 / 8.44%
Time (seconds)		Errors (percent)	

FIGURE 13–8   Stimulus Sets, Response Sets, and Data (Reaction Time and Error Rates).

From P. M. Fitts & C. M. Seeger (1953). S–R compatibility: Spatial characteristics of stimulus and response codes. *Journal of Experimental Psychology, 46,* 199–210.

response set *A,* there were eight locations in a circular configuration; for response set *B,* there were also eight locations, but responses were made by moving from the start point along one of four pathways, which then branched into T's; for response set *C,* there were left–right locations for the left hand and up–down locations for the right hand, with the eight responses signaled by combinations of the two hand movements.

Responses in this study were faster and more accurate for the pairings of stimulus sets and response sets that corresponded naturally than for those that did not. In other words, with the number of stimulus–response alternatives constant, performance varied as a function of the correspondence of the stimulus and response sets. Fitts and Seeger called this phenomenon *stimulus–response (S–R) compatibility* and attributed it to cognitive representations or codes based on the spatial locations of the stimulus and response sets.

In a second classic study, Fitts and Deininger (1954) manipulated the assignment of stimuli to responses within a single stimulus and response set. People placed a stylus at the intersection of eight pathways that were organized like the spokes of a wheel (see Figure 13–9). The stimulus set was a corresponding set of eight lights arranged around the periphery of a circle. The person's task was to move the stylus to an assigned response location when one of the stimuli was lit. With the direct assignment, each stimulus location was assigned to the corresponding response location. With the mirrored assignment, the left-side stimulus locations were assigned to their right-side counterparts of the response set, and vice versa. For example, if the light occurred in the upper-left location of the display, the stylus was to be moved to the upper-right location. Finally, with the random assignment, no systematic relation existed between the stimuli and their assigned responses. Responses were faster and more accurate with the direct assignment than

FIGURE 13–9   Fitts and Deininger's Experimental Apparatus (1954).

From P. M. Fitts & R. L. Deininger (1954). S–R compatibility: Correspondence among paired elements within stimulus and response codes. *Journal of Experimental Psychology, 48,* 483–491.

with the mirrored assignment. Even more striking, the reaction times and error rates for the random assignment were over twice those for the mirrored assignment.

Morin and Grant (1955) pursued this ordering of relative compatibility further by having people respond to one of ten lights arranged in a row with one of ten fingers placed on response keys. As would be expected, responses were fastest when there was a direct correspondence between stimulus and response locations (see Figure 13–10). However, responding was also fast when the stimulus and response locations were perfectly negatively correlated (that is, the rightmost response would be made if the leftmost stimulus occurred, and so on), and reaction time increased as the correlation decreased to zero. These findings indicate that people can translate quickly between a stimulus and response when a simple rule (for example, respond at the location

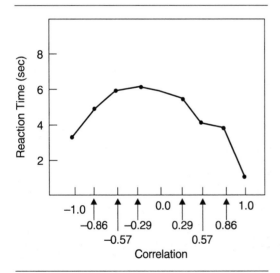

FIGURE 13–10   Reaction Time as a Function of the Correlation Between Stimulus and Response Locations.

From R. E. Morin & D. A. Grant (1955). Learning and performance on a key-pressing task as a function of the degree of spatial stimulus–response correspondence. *Journal of Experimental Psychology, 49*, 39–47.

opposite to the stimulus location) describes the relation (Duncan, 1977). Moreover, it also has been suggested that the correlation coefficient might provide a metric for compatibility in real-world situations for which several stimuli and responses are involved (Kantowitz, Triggs, & Barnes, 1990).

The implication of the spatial compatibility studies for display–control arrangements is clear. The assignment of controls to display elements should be spatially compatible, when possible. The classic applied illustration of this principle comes from studies of four-burner ranges conducted by Chapanis and Lindenbaum (1959) and Shinar and Acton (1978). A common arrangement is to have two back burners located directly behind two front burners, with the controls arranged linearly across the front of the range (see Figure 13–11, panels 2, 3, 4, and 5). For this arrangement, there is no dominant stereotypic mapping of controls to burners, so there is some confusion about which control operates a particular burner. However, by staggering the burners in a sequential left-to-right order (see Figure 13–11, panel 1), each control location corresponds directly to a burner location and confusion about the relation between controls and burners is eliminated.

Relative Location Coding.   The prototypical procedure for studying S–R compatibility is a two-choice task in which visual stimuli are presented to either the left or right of a central fixation point (see Figure 13–12, A and B). In the compatible condition, the observer is to respond to the left stimulus with a key press at a left response location and to the right stimulus with a key press at a right location. In the incompatible condition, the assignment of stimulus locations to response locations is reversed. Responses in the two-choice task are faster and more accurate when they are compatible with the stimulus locations (Umiltà & Nicoletti, 1990). Note that this is not simply a speed–accuracy trade-off because accuracy improves as reaction time decreases.

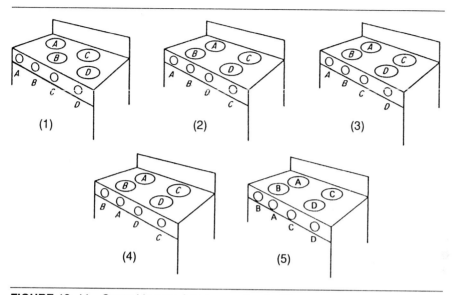

FIGURE 13–11   Control-burner Arrangements of a Stove.

Based on A. Chapanis & L. E. Lindenbaum, A reaction time study of four control-display linkages. Reprinted from *Human Factors,* Vol. 1, No. 4, pp. 1–7, 1959. Copyright © 1959 by The Human Factors Society, Inc. All rights reserved.

When the hands are situated on their anatomical sides (as shown in panels A and B of Figure 13–12), the distinction between left and right response locations is redundant with the distinction between left and right response effectors. To dissociate response locations from effector locations, the left and right hands can be crossed (see Figure 13–12, C and D). With this crossed-hands placement, the left hand is at the right response location and the right hand at the left location. In such situations, responses are still faster when there is a direct correspondence between the stimulus and response locations, even though the opposing hand is used to make the response (for example, Anzola et al., 1977; Brebner, Shephard, & Cairney, 1972). The importance of the response locations, rather than the effectors used to execute the responses, is consistent with the implication of Fitts's earlier discovery that spatial coding underlies S–R compatibility effects.

The dependence of compatibility effects on the spatial relations between stimuli and responses also occurs for unimanual responses (Heister, Schroeder-Heister, & Ehrenstein, 1990) and four-choice tasks (Reeve & Proctor, 1984). Moreover, the standard spatial compatibility effect occurs when both stimuli are located in the same hemispace and when both responses are located to the same side of the body midline (Nicoletti et al., 1982; Umiltà & Liotti, 1987). In other words, it is not the absolute physical locations of the stimuli and responses that determine the degree of compatibility, but their relative locations. These findings are interpreted as indicating that location coding is based on relative position (Umiltà & Nicoletti, 1990). For optimal performance, compatibility of relative locations must be maintained regardless of the absolute locations of the alternative displays and controls.

Not only is correspondence between absolute physical locations unnecessary for the compatibility effect, but the effect also occurs when stimuli and/or responses have no physical spatial dimension. Responses are faster when the words

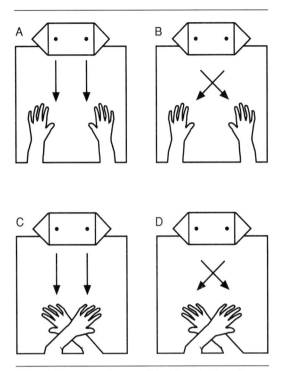

FIGURE 13–12   Compatible (A and C) and Incompatible (B and D) Stimulus–Response Assignments in Two-choice Tasks, with the Hands Uncrossed (A and B) and Crossed (C and D).

left and *right* are assigned directly to left and right physical responses (Magliero et al., 1984; McCarthy & Donchin, 1981) or *left* and *right* vocal responses (Weeks & Proctor, 1990). Similar results are obtained with left- and right-pointing arrow stimuli (Bashore, 1990; Weeks & Proctor, 1990). Compatibility effects can also occur when the stimulus dimension is above–below and the response dimension is left–right, or vice versa (Weeks & Proctor, 1990). For two stimulus-response alternatives, responses tend to be faster when *above* is paired with *right* and *below* with *left* than when the assignment is reversed. Thus, compatibility effects have their basis in the cognitive representations of stimulus and response sets. Such effects are likely to occur for situations in which there is no obvious relation

between stimulus and response sets, as well as for situations in which there are.

Theoretical Interpretations. Taken together, the results indicate that spatial compatibility effects do not depend on physical correspondence, but on what Alluisi and Warm (1990) call conceptual correspondence. These findings led to refinements of Fitts and Seeger's (1953) original spatial coding account of S–R compatibility, with an emphasis on the cognitive codes for spatial relationships used to translate between stimuli and responses. Compatibility effects will occur whenever implicit or explicit spatial relationships exist among stimuli and among responses. A stimulus–response mapping will be compatible if the codes are similar for the stimuli and their assigned responses and incompatible if the codes conflict. The spatial coding hypothesis predicts that compatibility effects will be relatively independent of the means by which the stimulus information is presented and the response information effected.

Perhaps the best evidence for spatial coding as the basis for S–R compatibility is that compatibility effects for symbolic stimuli assigned to spatial responses can be predicted from the correspondence between salient nonspatial features of the stimulus set and the spatial features of the response set (Proctor & Reeve, 1985; Proctor, Reeve, & Weeks, 1990). Coding is flexible and is based on these salient features. For stimuli and responses that are distinguishable only by their locations, spatial coding is usually based on where stimuli and responses are located relative to each other. In situations for which location coding is made difficult or is not a factor, symbolic codes for stimuli and anatomical codes for responses can be used. Thus, coding accounts not only explain spatial compatibility effects, but they also provide a means for integrating a range of compatibility effects that appear dissimilar on the surface (Kornblum, Hasbroucq, & Osman, 1990; Proctor, Reeve, & Weeks, 1990).

To summarize, the ease with which an operator can select a response associated with a given stimulus display largely depends on the spatial configurations of the display and response panel. The operator's performance may be impaired if the stimuli and responses are not related by spatial locations or a simple, easy to remember rule. When space allows, control panels should be designed to mimic the spatial relations between elements of the display. If not, an easily remembered rule should be used that relates salient display and control features.

Formal models can be used to predict performance with different display–control relationships. The most detailed model of S–R compatibility to date is that of Rosenbloom and Newell (1987; see also Laird, Rosenbloom, & Newell, 1986). Their algorithmic model is implemented within a production-system framework. By specifying the nature of the productions that must operate to translate between stimuli and responses in different situations, Rosenbloom and Newell have been able to predict compatibility effects across tasks that range from the standard choice–reaction tasks to computer programming. The predictions are sufficiently accurate for John and Newell (1990) to propose an engineering model for use in systems design. Their model is based on Rosenbloom and Newell's theory of S–R compatibility and the Model Human Processor (Card, Moran, & Newell, 1983). From it, the designer can determine the relative compatibilities for alternative display–control configurations.

S–C–R and R–R Compatibility

Most research on S–R compatibility has focused on situations in which simple rules relate stimuli to responses (Kantowitz, Triggs, & Barnes, 1990). However, by attributing compatibility effects to the cognitive codes used to represent the stimulus and response sets, central cognitive processes must be responsible for the effects. Because the role of cognitive mediation in response selection is likely larger for more complex tasks that do not involve simple rules or response tendencies, Wickens, Sandry, and Vidulich (1983)

have used the term S–C–R compatibility to emphasize the central processes (C). In short, the mediating processes can be conceived more generally as reflecting the operator's mental model of the task. Compatibility will be observed to the extent that stimuli and responses correspond with the features of the mental model.

Wickens, Sandry, and Vidulich (1983) structured their theory of S–C–R compatibility around the multiple-resource view of attention and, hence, stressed the importance of the cognitive code (verbal or visual) used to represent the task. They proposed that this code must be matched with the types of input and output modes for S–C–R compatibility to be maximized. Wickens et al. provided evidence that tasks represented by a verbal code are most compatible with speech stimuli, whereas tasks represented by a spatial code are most compatible with visual stimuli. Similarly, verbal codes are more compatible with speech responses and spatial codes with manual responses.

Robinson and Eberts (1987) obtained evidence consistent with the coding relations proposed by S–C–R compatibility in a simulated cockpit environment. Either a synthesized speech display or a picture display was used to communicate emergency information, with the response activated manually. As predicted by the S–C–R compatibility hypothesis, the manual responses were made faster to the picture display depicting spatial relationships than to the speech display.

S–C–R compatibility has been expanded by Eberts and Posey (1990) to take other aspects of the operator's mental model into account. Specifically, they propose that a good mental model that accurately represents the conceptual relations of the task should enable better and more efficient performance than a poor mental model. Eberts and Schneider (1985) have obtained several results with a difficult control task that indicate better performance when training incorporates an appropriate mental model. Along with John and Newell's (1990) work on compatibility effects in human–computer interaction, this work indicates that the ramifications of compatibility extend to a range of complex tasks.

The time to select a particular response to a stimulus can also be affected by the other members of the response set. Such phenomena are called response–response (R–R) compatibility effects. Responses are slower when the alternatives are mechanically antagonistic (Berlyne, 1957), when the initial elements of alternative response sequences are unique rather than common to both sequences (Rosenbaum, Hindorff, & Munro, 1987), when different movements (for example, tapping versus alternating between keys) are assigned to the left and right hands (Heuer, 1990), and when two alternative finger responses are on the same hand as opposed to different hands (Reeve & Proctor, 1988).

The implication of R–R compatibility effects for the design of human–machine interfaces is that response time and accuracy can be influenced by the particular set of required responses. Therefore, to optimize performance, the members of the response set also need to be of high compatibility.

PRACTICE AND RESPONSE SELECTION

As with virtually everything else, performance on choice–reaction tasks improves with practice. This improvement is characterized by the power law described in Chapter 12 (also see Newell & Rosenbloom, 1981). Thus, although performance continues to improve indefinitely, the additional benefit for a constant amount of practice becomes less and less as the person continues to perform the task. Moreover, because practice effects are greater for tasks that have more stimulus–response alternatives, the slope of the Hick–Hyman law function becomes progressively less as people become more practiced (Teichner & Krebs, 1974).

A classic study that illustrates the extent to which human performance can improve with practice is one by Crossman (1959). He examined the time required for people to make cigars on a hand-operated machine. Operators were tested whose experience ranged up to 6 years. Speed of performance increased as a power function up to 4 years, at which point the minimum machine-cycle time limited performance from improving further. In other words, the machine reached its limits before the operators reached theirs.

Using a more typical choice–reaction task, Seibel (1963) also showed improvement with practice that followed a power function. He performed a 1,023-choice task in which a stimulus subset of 10 lights required the corresponding subset of response keys to be pressed simultaneously. Initially, his reaction times averaged over 1 s, but they reached 450 ms after 70,000 trials of practice. As can be seen in Figure 13–13, his performance improved continuously over the course of the study.

There are several views of how response-selection processes change as a person becomes skilled at a task. The power law suggests a continuous change from unpracticed to practiced states, leading some authors to treat practice effects as quantitative changes in the number of procedures that are incorporated into a single chunk (for example, Laird, Rosenbloom, & Newell, 1986). Alternatively, a qualitative change, in which the role of the translation stage decreases as performers become practiced, is often hypothesized (for example, Teichner & Krebs, 1974).

S–R compatibility effects usually decrease with practice, but they do not typically disappear (Dutta & Proctor, 1992). For example, Fitts and Seeger (1953) found that responses for an incompatible display–control arrangement were still considerably slower than those for a compatible arrangement after 26 sessions of 16 trials for each arrangement. Such findings are consistent with proposals of Eberts and Posey (1990) and Gopher, Karis, and Koenig (1985) that mental representations continue to play an important role in translating between stimuli and responses even for well-practiced performers. Although the best account for the persistence of compatibility effects is not clear, the obvious point for human factors is that the effects are not short term. An

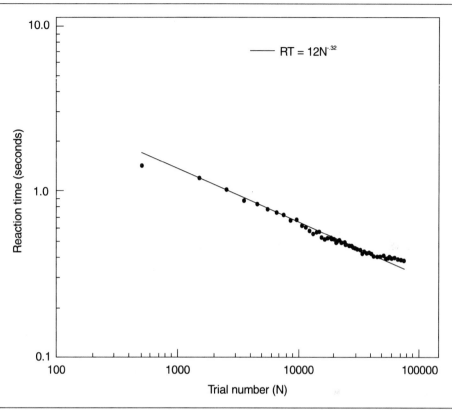

FIGURE 13–13   Reaction Time as a Function of Practice in a 1,023-choice task.
Adapted from R. Seibel, (1963). Discrimination reaction time for a 1,023 alternative task. *Journal of Experimental Psychology, 66,* 215–226. Copyright © 1963 by the American Psychological Association.

incompatible display–control arrangement can result in long-term decrements in performance.

IRRELEVANT STIMULI

Spatial S–R compatibility effects occur not just when stimulus location is relevant for determining the correct response, but also when it is irrelevant (Simon, 1990). For example, if the color of an indicator light is the relevant stimulus dimension to which an operator is to respond, the location in which the light occurs can still influence response selection. Suppose you are to make one response to a red light and another to a green light and that these lights can occur to the left or right

of a central point. If you are to respond to the red light by pressing a key with the right index finger and the green light with the left index finger, your responses will be fastest when the red light occurs to the right side or the green light to the left. This phenomenon is called the Simon effect, after its discoverer, J. R. Simon.

Research has shown that the Simon effect generalizes across sensory modalities and that the effect is determined by the relationship between stimulus locations and response locations (for example, Wallace, 1971), as is the case when stimulus location is relevant. Simon initially proposed that the effect reflects an innate tendency to respond in the direction of the stimulus (Simon,

1969). When this response tendency conflicts with the correct response, it must be inhibited before the correct response can be made. Recent accounts have maintained this response competition view (but see Hasbroucq & Guiard, 1991, for a different view), while linking the competition to activation of conflicting spatial codes (Umiltà & Nicoletti, 1990).

A closely related phenomenon to the Simon effect is the Stroop effect, which is named after its discoverer, J. Ridley Stroop (Stroop, 1935/1992). The standard Stroop task requires naming the ink colors of words that specify conflicting colors. For example, the word *green* could be printed in red ink. The Stroop effect is that responses are considerably slower and less accurate in this conflict situation than when the ink colors are presented as patches of color rather than spelled words. The Stroop task has been thoroughly investigated, and the interference has been found to occur for numerous variations, including picture–word combinations, physical locations and words that spell location names, and auditory stimuli (MacLeod, 1991). The difference between the Stroop and Simon paradigms is that the two stimulus dimensions are closely related for the former, but not for the latter.

Explanations of the Stroop effect have tended to focus on response competition, much like accounts of the Simon effect. Cohen, Dunbar, and McClelland (1990) have provided a neural network model that generates many of the basic findings for the Stroop effect. According to this model, processing occurs through activation along pathways of different strengths. When two pathways are active simultaneously and produce conflicting activation at their intersection, interference occurs. Consequently, interference is not restricted to overt responses but can occur at different processing levels.

A final phenomenon arising from irrelevant stimuli is called the Eriksen effect. Observers are to identify a target stimulus (usually a letter) presented at the point of fixation. On most trials the target is flanked by noise letters. The primary finding is that responses are slower and less accurate when the flanking letters include a letter assigned to the alternative response from that required by the target. Eriksen and his associates have interpreted such results in terms of response competition in a continuous activation model (Eriksen & Schultz, 1979), much like that proposed by Cohen, Dunbar, and McClelland (1990) for the Stroop effect.

All three of these effects illustrate that irrelevant stimulus attributes can interfere with performance when they conflict with the stimulus and response attributes relevant to the task at hand. They reflect people's limited ability to selectively attend to relevant stimulus attributes and to ignore irrelevant ones. The human factors specialist should be aware of such possibilities for interference and minimize potential sources of conflict, such as irrelevant location cues, when designing display panels and other interface devices.

DUAL-TASK AND SEQUENTIAL PERFORMANCE

In most real-world situations, people are required to perform several tasks or task components at once. Often several stimuli must be responded to in rapid succession. In these more complex tasks, issues arise regarding how effectively multiple responses can be selected and coordinated. This effectiveness limits the performance of operators in complex stimulus–response environments.

Psychological Refractory Period

When people respond to two stimuli presented in rapid succession, the reaction time to the second stimulus is slowed. The slowing of the response to the second stimulus is a decreasing function of interstimulus interval (that is, the interval between the two stimuli). This phenomenon, discovered by Telford (1931), was named the *psychological refractory period*, because he thought that it was related to neural refractoriness. However, neural refractory periods are on the order of a few milliseconds, whereas Telford's effects were on the order of hundreds of milliseconds. Subsequent research implicated a response-selection basis for the phenomenon.

Two types of models have been proposed to account for the psychological refractory period (for example, Pashler, 1989): postponement and capacity-sharing models. Postponement models presume that some processing operations for the second task are delayed until the operations for the first task are completed. Capacity-sharing models propose that the two tasks are performed simultaneously, but with reduced efficiency. Experimental results are more consistent with postponement models. Postponement models predict a linear decrease in reaction time to the second stimulus as the interval between stimulus onsets increases. After a critical value is reached, no further decrease should occur. In general, such a relationship is observed. However, responses to the second task are never as fast as when that task is performed alone (Gottsdanker, 1980; Pashler, 1984), and the response to the first stimulus often is slowed as well (for example, Herman & Kantowitz, 1970).

From a postponement perspective, the question is what stage of processing is being postponed. Several experiments conducted by Pashler (1984, 1989) have favored postponement at the response-selection stage (see Figure 13–14). Factors affecting response selection for the second task (for example, repetition of stimuli within a trial) have additive effects with dual-task slowing, whereas the effects of visual intensity are greatly reduced (Pashler, 1984). Moreover, interference with responding to the second stimulus occurs only when a speeded response to it is required.

For example, in two of Pashler's (1989) experiments, the first stimulus was a high- or low-frequency tone that was to be identified by pressing one of two keys with fingers on the left hand. The second stimulus was an array of digits; the response was to indicate whether the highest digit was 6, 7, 8, or 9 by pressing one of four fingers on the right hand. The interval between onset of the tone and onset of the array was var-

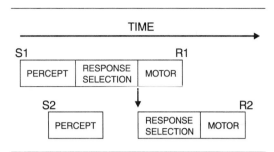

FIGURE 13–14   The Sequence of Stages in Response-selection Postponement.

From H. Pashler (1989). Dissociations and dependencies between speed and accuracy: Evidence for a two-component theory of divided attention in simple tasks. *Cognitive Psychology, 21,* 469–514. Copyright © 1989 by Academic Press, Inc. Reprinted by permission.

ied. In one experiment, the visual array was masked after a brief presentation, and the person could take as long as desired to respond. Under these conditions, no interference was apparent. In the second experiment, the array was not degraded, and a speeded response was required. As shown in Figure 13–15, interference with the response to the second stimulus was obtained. Responses were slower at the two shorter intervals than at the longest interval. Because slower responses tended to be more accurate, this refractoriness in response selection appears to be due at least in part to elevated response criteria.

A similar pattern of reaction times and errors is often obtained when responses and subsequent stimuli occur in close succession. For example, Wilkinson (1990) had people respond to one of four lights by pressing a finger at the corresponding response location. The time between the response and the presentation of the next stimulus was varied in 40-ms steps from 0 to 600 ms. Reaction times decreased as the interval increased up to 320 ms and then leveled off as the duration of the interval increased further. Again, this decrease in reaction times was accompanied by an increase in error rates, suggesting that the slower responses at shorter response–stimulus in-

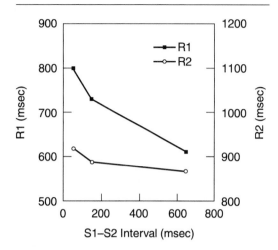

FIGURE 13–15   Mean Reaction Times for the Response on Task 1 (R1) and Task 2 (R2) as a Function of the Interval Between S1 and S2 Onsets.

From H. Pashler (1989). Dissociations and dependencies between speed and accuracy: Evidence for a two-component theory of divided attention in simple tasks. *Cognitive Psychology, 21,* 469–514. Copyright © 1989 by Academic Press, Inc. Reprinted by permission.

tervals are based on better information. One implication of findings such as these is that presenting two signals, each requiring a distinct response, in close succession will not harm performance unless the response to the second signal must be fast.

These findings have led some authors to propose a reconceptualization of attention (Allport, 1989; Neumann, 1987). Rather than attributing attentional limitations to the limited availability of resources, these authors argue that such limitations are based on the same mechanisms involved in the selection and control of action. Neumann distinguishes two types of response–selection problems: effector recruitment (which actions are given access to the effector system?) and parameter specification (which of the possible values for an action parameter is put into effect?). According to this view, interference of the type reported by Pashler (1989) and Wilkinson (1990) is due to

the problem of coordinating actions that must be made in close succession.

Response Inhibition

Another issue of concern is the extent to which an operator can inhibit a response that has already been signaled for execution. In the stop-signal paradigm, a stimulus to which a person is to respond may be followed at unpredictable times by a signal to inhibit the response (Logan & Cowan, 1984). The standard finding is that the longer the stop signal is delayed relative to the reaction stimulus, the less likely it is that the response will be stopped. This result is typically interpreted in terms of a race model. The general idea behind this model is that one set of processes begins when a reaction stimulus is presented. These processes will produce a response to the stimulus unless they are inhibited prior to response initiation. On stop-signal trials, a second set of processes begins with the onset of the stop signal. The race, then, is between the two sets of processes. If the inhibition process wins the race, the response is inhibited. If it loses, the response is executed.

Within the race-model framework the question can be asked as to how late in the processing sequence the response to the reaction stimulus can be stopped. In other words, what is the point of no return? De Jong et al. (1990) tried to determine the point of no return with a procedure that evaluated response-related brain potentials, electromyogram (EMG) recordings of muscle activation, and continuous response measures (dynamometer squeezes). They concluded that there are two inhibitory mechanisms. One mechanism inhibits central activation processes, whereas the other inhibits the transmission of motor commands from the brain to more peripheral structures. This latter mode of inhibition was implicated by the finding that the overt response could be prevented up to the point that it reached a particular amount of pressure.

Although an intended response can be inhibited up to the point that the action is executed, this inhibition may have persisting effects that restrict the processing of subsequent stimulus events. When irrelevant information is presented with a target, such as in the Stroop task or the Eriksen task, responses on the trial that follows are slowed if the relevant stimulus information corresponds to the previously irrelevant information. Such interference suggests that the irrelevant information must be actively inhibited; once inhibited, it is temporarily less available for processing on subsequent trials. Recent findings have suggested that the mechanism for such inhibition involves disconnection of the ignored information from the response system (Neill, Lissner, & Beck, 1990; Tipper, 1985).

Stimulus and Response Repetition

In contrast to the inhibition that occurs when previously irrelevant information must now be processed, facilitation usually occurs when previously relevant information is repeated. In a typical choice–reaction task, reaction times will be faster on a trial in which the stimulus and response are the same as on the preceding trial, with this repetition effect being greatest at short response–stimulus intervals (Kornblum, 1973).

The magnitude of the repetition effect is influenced by several factors (Kornblum, 1973). The benefit of a repetition on reaction time is greater for larger numbers of stimulus–response alternatives than for fewer. Moreover, increases in stimulus–response compatibility decrease the magnitude of the repetition effect. Nonrepetitions show a greater advantage from compatible assignments than do repetitions. Another way of stating the interactions of repetition with number of alternatives and compatibility is that repetition is most beneficial when response selection is difficult.

Pashler and Baylis (1991) have presented evidence that this relation occurs because repetition enables the person to bypass the normal process of response selection when the stimulus–response link is already in an active state. When two stimuli were assigned to each of three key-press responses, a benefit of repetition occurred only when the stimulus was repeated and not just the response. However, if the assignment of responses to stimuli was changed on a trial to trial basis, stimulus repetition produced no benefit. One way to interpret this is that the person has an expectancy for the preceding stimulus and its associated response.

ACTION SELECTION

All the research discussed in this chapter has concerned situations in which assigned responses are to be executed to specific stimuli. This situation relates closely to an operator's interactions with display and control panels, on which particular buttons must be pushed or switches flipped in response to displayed information. More generally, however, we are always faced with the problem of choosing among action alternatives for achieving specific goals. Much less is known about how selection of action is controlled in these circumstances, but research on grip patterns and display–control relationships provides some insight.

Grip Patterns

Grip patterns are the choices of movements and placements of fingers assumed to grasp and manipulate an object. Two factors have been shown to affect the grip pattern that is selected. The first involves the properties of the object for which a person is reaching. Jeannerod (1981) showed that when people reach to grasp a visible object the grip aperture is directly related to the size of the object. Moreover, the maximum aperture and the pattern of change as the hand approaches the object are unaffected by whether the hand is visible to the person.

The second factor affecting grip patterns involves what the person plans to do with the object after it is grabbed. Rosenbaum et al. (1990) examined whether people would pick up a cylindrical bar positioned horizontally, as in Figure 13–16, with an overhand or underhand grip when

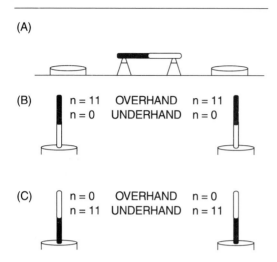

FIGURE 13–16 Apparatus Used by Rosenbaum et al. (1990) (A) with the Number of Right-handed Subjects Who Used the Overhand or Underhand Grip to Bring (B) the White (Right) End of the Bar to Both Target Disks and (C) the Black (Left) End of the Bar to Both Target Disks.

We thank the International Association for study of Attention and Performance for permission to reprint D. A. Rosenbaum et al. (1990). Constraints for action selection: Overhand versus underhand grips. In M. Jeannerod (Ed.), *Attention and performance XIII* (pp. 321–342). Hillsdale, NJ: Lawrence Erlbaum.

one end of the bar was to be placed on a horizontal surface. Of the 11 people who used their right hand, all used the overhand grip to bring the white (right) end of the bar to either target disk and the underhand grip to bring the black (left) end to either disk. The one person who used the left hand showed the reverse relation. The overhand grip was selected when the end of the bar that was to be placed on the disk was closer to the hand that was used, whereas the underhand grip was selected when the end farther from the hand was to be placed on the disk.

Rosenbaum et al.'s (1990) results support the general proposal that selection among alternative actions for achieving specific goals is based on optimization constraints. They proposed that one

such constraint is to minimize the amount of time spent in extreme joint angles, because more force is required to maintain such an angle (see Chapter 14). The apparent reason for the observed pattern of grip selection is that the grip that was not used would result in an awkward final posture using extreme joint angles. People apparently planned the initial grip to minimize the awkwardness of the final position. Thus, grip selection will be influenced both by the object that is to be gripped and by the intended use of the object.

Population Stereotypes

Another situation in which selection among controlling actions has been studied involves display–control relationships. In a typical task, people either are asked to indicate the most natural relation between a control and a visual indicator or are required to align the indicator with a particular dial setting. For many types of displays and controls, certain display–control relationships are preferred over others (Loveless, 1962). In the simplest case, consider a horizontal display whose settings are controlled by movements of a parallel, horizontal control stick (see Figure 13–17). It should be clear from our earlier discussion of S–R compatibility that rightward movement of the control stick should cause rightward movement of the indicator, and so on, rather than having rightward responses associated with leftward movements of the indicator. Because most people would intuitively make this association between the stick and indicator, the association is called a *population stereotype.*

More interesting is the fact that population stereotypes are found when there is no direct relation between the display and control. Often, the settings of linear displays are controlled by rotary knobs, as in many radios. For such situations, several principles act to determine the preferred relationship:

1. *Clockwise to right or up principle:* A clockwise turn of the control is expected to move a pointer to the right for a horizontal display or upward for a vertical display.

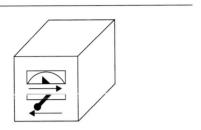

FIGURE 13–17 Horizontal Display and Control Arrangements, with Preferred Movements Indicated.

2. *Warrick's principle:* When the control is at one side of the display (see Figure 13–18), the pointer should move in the same direction as the side of the control nearest the display.
3. *Clockwise to increase principle:* Clockwise rotation is expected to correspond with an increased reading on the display scale.
4. *Clockwise away principle:* When the control is at the top or bottom of the display, clockwise movement tends to be associated with movement of the indicator away from the control.
5. *Scale-side principle:* The indicator is expected to move in the same direction as the

side of the control that is next to the display's scale.

Much as with Gestalt organization, it is possible to vary the extent to which a particular display–control relationship is consistent with these principles. Hoffman (1990) evaluated the relative contribution of each of these principles for horizontal displays. Groups of engineers and psychologists indicated their preferred direction of movement for 64 display–control arrangements composed from eight control locations (see Figure 13–19), two directions of scale increase (left, right), two types of indicator (a neutral line or directional arrow), and two scale sides (top, bottom). For these situations, the dominant principles were the clockwise-to-right and Warrick's principles. For engineers, Warrick's principle was most important, whereas for psychologists, the clockwise-to-right principle was. Hoffman attributed this difference to the engineer's knowledge of the mechanical linkage between control and pointer, with which Warrick's principle is consistent. It may be speculated that the engineers' mental models of the control–display relationship incorporate this knowledge. More generally, the difference between engineers and psychologists illustrates that the population of interest must be considered when evaluating display–control relations.

Another factor that influences expected display–control relations is the orientation of the operator. Worringham and Beringer (1989) had people guide a cursor to one of 16 target locations

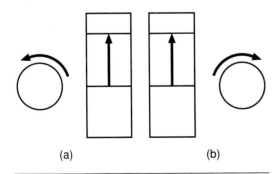

(a)   (b)

FIGURE 13–18 Illustration of Warrick's Principle. The Stereotypic Control Movement to Produce an Upward Movement of the Display Indicator Is Counterclockwise for (a) and Clockwise for (b).

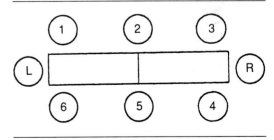

FIGURE 13–19 Locations of the Knobs Tested by Hoffman (1990).

with a joystick. The joystick was always operated with the right hand, but the positioning of the arm, hand, and trunk was varied across 11 experimental conditions (see Figure 13–20). With this procedure, the effects of three types of compatibility could be distinguished. Visual–motor compatibility was defined as display movement in a given direction produced by control movement that would be in the same direction if the person were looking at the control. Control–display compatibility was defined in terms of the actual

CD: Control-Display VM: Visual-Motor VT: Visual-Trunk
N: None

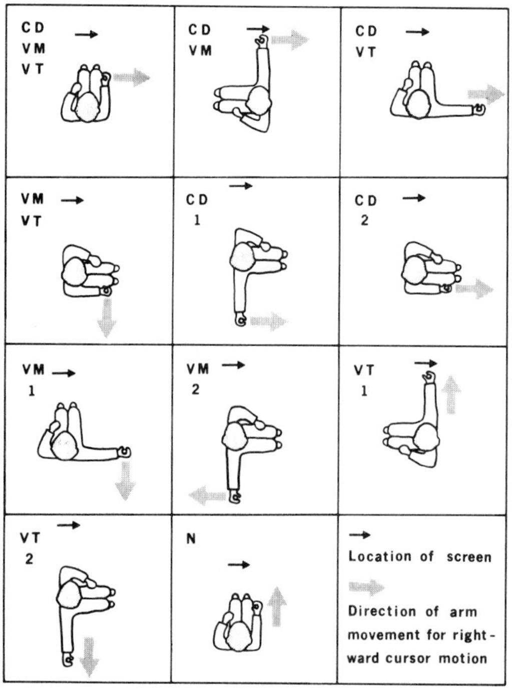

FIGURE 13–20 Relationship Between Direction of Arm Movement and Cursor Movement, and Positions of Hand, Trunk and Arm for Worringham and Beringer's Experimental Conditions.

From Operator orientation and compatibility in visual-motor task performance. *Ergonomics, 32*, 387–399, C. J. Worringham & D. B. Beringer (1989), Taylor & Francis, London. Reproduced with permission.

direction of movement of the control relative to the display. Visual–trunk compatibility indicated whether the control movement was in the same direction as the display movement, relative to the operator's trunk. Visual–motor compatibility was found to be the significant factor, regardless of the person's physical orientation. This suggests that, when possible, it may be best to fix controls relative to the operator when the operator is mobile.

There are population stereotypes for complex, three-dimensional displays. Kaminaka and Egli (1984) showed that for three-dimensional displays, pushing motions were preferred over pulling motions for rightward shifts, backward shifts, and clockwise rotations in the frontal plane. Pulling motions were preferred for upward shifts and rotations toward the operator.

Stereotypic responses have also been demonstrated for controls that are not associated with displays. Hotta et al. (1981) conducted a survey of preferred direction of motion for controls used regularly in daily life. People were shown cubes, each of which had a rotary lever, a slide lever, or a push button on the front, top, bottom, left, or right sides. Given the task of turning a doorknob; turning on water, gas, or electricity, or a more generic "output increase," people selected different preferred movements. Hotta et al. found evidence for the distinct stereotypes shown in Table 13–1. Preferred directions depended on the purpose of a control and the plane in which it was located.

Performance may be degraded under normal operating conditions when display–control relations are incompatible or inconsistent with population stereotypes. Errors can be minimized by assigning control functions to be consistent with the stereotypes. Table 13–2 summarizes some of the recommended relations between control actions and functions. In emergencies, responding is more automatic, and stereotypic response tendencies tend to come to the fore. Loveless (1962) describes a case in which the ram of a heavy hydraulic press was raised by pushing a lever down. When an emergency occurred that re-

TABLE 13–1 Common Direction-of-Motion Stereotypes in Relation to the Control Purpose and the Control Plane

PURPOSE	PLANE	ROTARY KNOB	ROTARY LEVER	BUTTON	SLIDE LEVER	TWO BUTTONS
Door	F		Counterclockwise	Pull		
Water/gas	F	Clockwise	Counterclockwise		Downward	
	T		Counterclockwise		Backward	
	B	Clockwise	Clockwise	Pull	Backward Right	
	R	Clockwise	Clockwise	Pull	Downward Backward	
	L	Counterclockwise	Counterclockwise			
Electricity	F	Clockwise	Counterclockwise	Push	Downward	
	T	Clockwise	Counterclockwise	Push	Backward	
	B	Clockwise	Clockwise		Backward Right	Backward
	R		Clockwise	Push	Downward Backward	Backward
	L		Counterclockwise	Push	Downward	Upward
Increase	F	Clockwise	Counterclockwise		Upward	
	T	Clockwise	Counterclockwise		Forward Right	
	B	Clockwise	Clockwise	Pull	Forward	
	R	Clockwise	Clockwise	Pull	Forward	
	L	Counterclockwise	Counterclockwise		Backward	

From A. Hotta et al. (1981). Relations between direction-of-motion stereotypes for controls in living space. *Journal of Human Ergology, 10,* 73–82. Reprinted by permission.
F, front side; T, top side; B, bottom side; R, right side; L, left side.

TABLE 13–2   Recommended Control Movements

CONTROL FUNCTION	RESPONSE OUTCOME
On	Up, right, forward, pull
Off	Down, left, rearward, push
Right	Clockwise, right
Left	Counterclockwise, left
Up	Up, rearward
Down	Down, forward
Retract	Rearward, pull, counterclockwise, up
Extend	Forward, push, clockwise, down
Increase	Right, up, forward
Decrease	Left, down, rearward

From H. J. Bullinger, P. Kern, & W. F. Muntzinger (1987). Design of controls. In G. Salvendy (Ed.), *Handbook of human factors* (pp. 577–600). Copyright © 1987 by John Wiley & Sons, Inc. Reprinted by permission of John Wiley & Sons, Inc.

quired the ram to be raised, the operator mistakenly made the more stereotypic response of pulling the lever up, which caused the ram to move down and destroy the press. The moral of this story is that it is always best to use display–control relationships that are highly consistent with population stereotypes.

SUMMARY

Response selection is a critical aspect of human performance. The operator of a human–machine system is faced with displays of information that indicate specific actions to be taken. In many systems, the time in which these response-selection decisions are made is crucial, as is their accuracy. The relative speed and accuracy of responding in a particular situation will be influenced by the criterion used to evaluate the accumulating information. With a conservative criterion, responses will be slow but accurate, whereas with a liberal criterion, they will be fast but inaccurate.

The efficiency of response selection is affected by many factors. These include the number of possible stimuli, the number of possible responses, their interrelationship, and the amount of practice. Moreover, many limitations in performance of multiple tasks can be traced to the response-selection stage. Probably the most important factor in response-selection efficiency is the compatibility of stimuli and responses. Principles of compatibility can be applied to ensure that the easiest or most natural control actions are required in response to displayed information.

When manipulating objects in the environment, the operator has a range of alternative actions for accomplishing a goal. Information about the objects to be grasped and the resulting postures for the limbs is involved in the selection of the particular action. In Chapter 14, the way in which the action is controlled will be examined.

RECOMMENDED READING

Newell, A., & Rosenbloom, P. S. (1981). Mechanisms of skill acquisition and the law of practice. In J. R. Anderson (eds.), *Cognitive Skills and Their Acquisition* (pp. 1–55). Hillsdale, NJ: Lawrence Erlbaum.

Pachella, R. G. (1974). The interpretation of reaction time in information-processing research. In B. H. Kantowitz (ed.), *Human Information Processing: Tutorials in Performance and Cognition* (pp. 41–82). Hillsdale, NJ: Lawrence Erlbaum.

Proctor, R. W., & Reeve, T. G. (eds.) (1990). *Stimulus–Response Compatibility: An Integrated Perspective*. Amsterdam: North-Holland.

Rosenbloom, P. S., & Newell, A. (1987). An integrated computational model of stimulus–response compatibility and practice. In G. H. Bower (ed.), *The Psychology of Learning and Motivation*, Vol. 21 (pp. 1–52). New York: Academic Press.

Stroop, J. R. (1935/1992). Studies of interference in serial verbal reaction. *Journal of Experimental Psychology: General, 121*, 15–23.

CHAPTER 14

CONTROL OF MOVEMENT

> *Rather than viewing perceptual–motor behavior as a series of motor*
> *responses made to reach some goal, it is possible, and I believe*
> *considerably more profitable, to view such behavior as an*
> *information-processing activity guided by some general plan or*
> *program.*
>
> —P. M. Fitts, 1964

INTRODUCTION

Any interaction of a human with a machine or with the natural environment ultimately requires the execution of a motor response. This response can be as simple as pushing a button or as complex as the coordinated actions required to perform heart surgery or to operate heavy machinery. In all cases, the operator must perceive the information correctly, make appropriate decisions and select appropriate responses, and successfully carry out the intended actions. Often, the limiting factor in performance will be the speed and accuracy with which these actions can be executed. Because motor control is a major component of many tasks, the human factors specialist must understand the ways that simple and complex movements of various types are executed.

Every movement requires the cooperation of different muscle groups and their neural control mechanisms. An effector must be selected and prepared, sequences of movements timed and coordinated, and the final movements executed with sufficient force and speed to accomplish the goal. This is achieved through the activation of the appropriate muscle groups in a precise order. The nervous system must not only activate the muscles, but also use feedback to coordinate and modify ongoing movements, maintain posture, and plan future actions. For example, the relatively simple act of riding a bicycle requires that balance be maintained, that the legs pedal with sufficient force to attain desired speeds, that steering actions be executed by the arms, and that braking actions be executed with appropriate force when needed. The coordinated performance of all these actions requires constant monitoring of proprioceptive, visual, and vestibular feedback.

Just as an understanding of perception begins with consideration of the sensory structures that provide environmental input, an understanding of motor control begins with consideration of the structures of the nervous system involved in the output of movement. Figure 14–1 shows a model describing the neural mechanisms that underlie information processing in the control of action. Our primary concern is with the way that motor output is coordinated to produce effective patterns of movement. In this chapter, we will first describe the physiological foundations of movement, represented in the bottom portions of each stage in Figure 14–1. We will then discuss the psychological aspects of motor control represented by the upper portions of each stage.

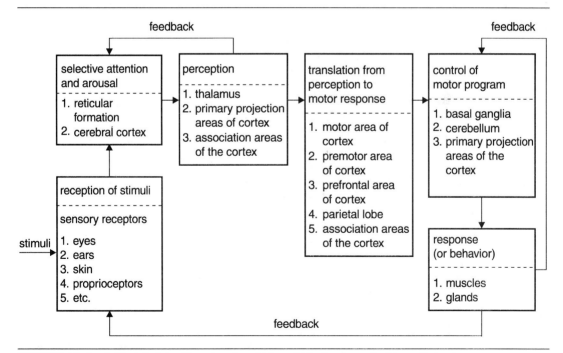

FIGURE 14–1   A Model of the Functional and Neural Mechanisms for Motor Behavior.
Adapted from G. H. Sage, *Motor Learning and Control: A Neuropsychological Approach,* Wm. C. Brown Publisher, 1984.

PHYSIOLOGICAL FOUNDATIONS OF MOVEMENT

The Musculoskeletal System

There are over 200 bones in the human skeletal system that provide support for the body. The bones are joined by connective tissues called ligaments. Similar tissues, called tendons, connect the bones to muscles. Bodily movement results from changes of joint angles, which are accomplished through muscular contractions acting on the bones. The muscles and connective tissues can be damaged by sudden or repetitive movements or external force, resulting in pain, decreased range of motion, and a decrement in performance. One major ergonomic concern in designing for human use is to construct interfaces, tools, and tasks to prevent musculoskeletal damage.

Movements at some joints take place only in two dimensions and are said to involve one degree of freedom (movement in a single plane). The movement of the forearm in relation to the upper arm at the elbow is of this type. Other movements can occur in more dimensions and involve multiple degrees of freedom. For example, movement of the upper arm at the shoulder involves three degrees of freedom. Because of these degrees of freedom, there are an infinite number of trajectories that a limb could take to move from one location to another. Yet, the motor system constrains the degrees of freedom to arrive at a single, smoothly executed trajectory. The question of how this is accomplished has been called the degrees of freedom problem (Bernstein, 1967). Some of the constraints used by the motor system are biomechanical, such as the range of motion of a particular joint or the stiffness of a particular muscle, and others are imposed by higher-level structures that coordinate action.

The range of motion in the body joints is of particular importance in human factors. Figures 14–2, 14–3, and 14–4 show ranges for head movements; wrist, shoulder, and elbow movements; and ankle, knee, and hip movements, respectively. The placement of controls, as well as the actions required to operate them, should not require movements that are at the extremes or outside these ranges.

Muscles are arranged in groups with opposing actions. One muscle or group (the agonist) engages in flexion, and its opposing group (the antagonist) engages in extension. Movement is produced through motion of the joints controlled by the coupled actions of the agonists and antagonists. A muscle will contract when it receives a neural signal from the motor pathways in the nervous system. Excitatory and inhibitory signals from axons that terminate at the muscles produce a depolarizing action on the muscle cells, causing muscle filaments to slide toward each other, with a resulting contraction of the muscle (see Figure 14–5). Subsequently, the filaments return to their resting positions.

Control of Movements

The nervous system controls movements through a hierarchy of mechanisms. At the lowest level are the elastic properties of the muscles themselves. Controlled movement begins with activation of the motor unit: a small clump of sensory receptors and muscle fibers connected to the peripheral nervous system through one or more synapses. At a higher level, the central nervous system is able to control movement through ascending and descending pathways in the spinal cord. We will examine these different levels of control, beginning with the mass–spring properties of muscles and the motor unit, proceeding through the levels of the nervous system, and culminating in the higher-level organization and execution of action mediated by the brain.

Mass–Spring Properties. The physical properties of the muscle alone are believed to play an important role in movement. Every muscle has some degree of elasticity or stiffness. A convenient way to describe the behavior of the muscle is as a mass–spring system (Bernstein, 1967; Bizzi

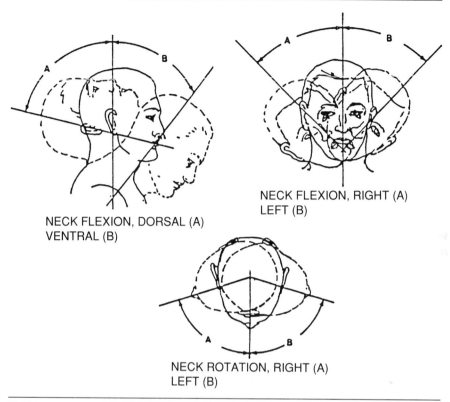

NECK FLEXION, DORSAL (A)
VENTRAL (B)

NECK FLEXION, RIGHT (A)
LEFT (B)

NECK ROTATION, RIGHT (A)
LEFT (B)

FIGURE 14–2   Range of Neck Flexion and Rotation.

From H. T. E. Hertzberg (1972). Engineering anthropology. In H. P. Van Cott & R. G. Kinkade (Eds.), *Human Engineering Guide to Equipment Design* (pp. 467–584). U. S. Government Printing Office.

& Mussa-Ivaldi, 1989; Fel'dman, 1966). The stretchy muscle can be thought of as a spring attached to the bone. The length and tension of this spring are constrained by Hooke's law, which states that the amount of its elongation is directly proportional to the mass attached to it.

The important characteristic of a mass–spring system is that it has a point of equilibrium determined by the mass applied to the system, the stiffness of the spring, and the medium in which the spring is operating. The equilibrium point is the resting length of the spring attached to a particular mass. When moved from the equilibrium point and then released, the spring will bounce up and down a bit, but always return to its resting length. No ongoing control is needed to return to that length, because it is determined by the viscoelastic properties of the mass–spring system.

At a joint, muscles are arranged in groups of agonists and antagonists, with the amount of flexion and extension of each determined by their equilibrium points. When the joint angle is changed by some external force, the muscles in one group will be stretched and the muscles in the other will be compressed. Upon removal of the force, the muscles will return to their equilibrium points, causing the joint angle to return to its original position. This is the most basic level of

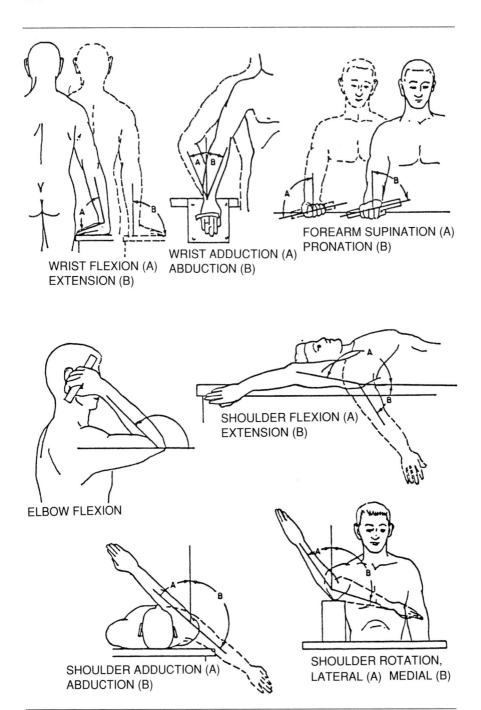

WRIST FLEXION (A)
EXTENSION (B)

WRIST ADDUCTION (A)
ABDUCTION (B)

FOREARM SUPINATION (A)
PRONATION (B)

ELBOW FLEXION

SHOULDER FLEXION (A)
EXTENSION (B)

SHOULDER ADDUCTION (A)
ABDUCTION (B)

SHOULDER ROTATION,
LATERAL (A) MEDIAL (B)

FIGURE 14–3   Range of Wrist, Shoulder, and Elbow Movements.

From H. T. E. Hertzberg (1972). Engineering anthropology. In H. P. Van Cott & R. G. Kinkade (Eds.), *Human Engineering Guide to Equipment Design* (pp. 467–584). U. S. Government Printing Office.

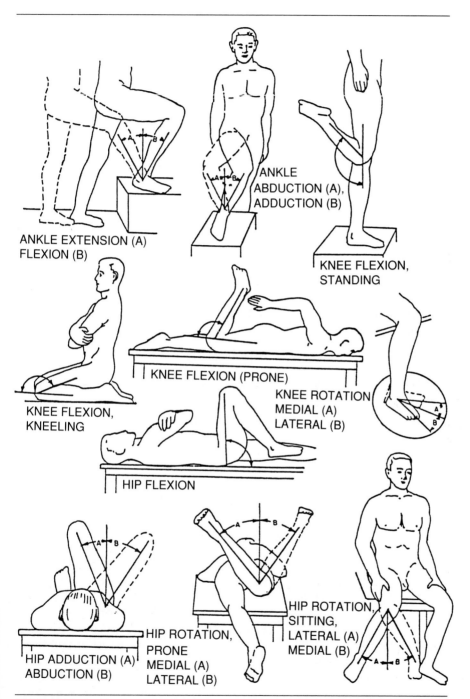

FIGURE 14–4 Range of Ankle, Knee, and Hip Movements.

From H. T. E. Hertzberg (1972). Engineering anthropology. In H. P. Van Cott & R. G. Kinkade (Eds.), *Human Engineering Guide to Equipment Design* (pp. 467–584). U. S. Government Printing Office.

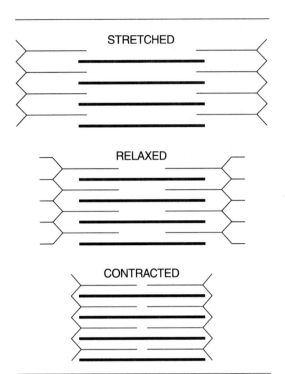

FIGURE 14–5 The Relation of Filaments in Stretched, Relaxed, and Contracted Muscles.

movement, in that it can occur in the absence of any neural signal. However, some movements controlled by higher levels of the central nervous system may rely on the mass–spring properties of muscles. For movements such as elbow flexions, the central nervous system may specify a systematic change in the stiffness, and hence the equilibrium point, of each muscle. The elastic properties of the muscles cause the position of the limb to change in accord with the changing equilibrium points.

The Motor Unit. Each muscle is composed of many muscle fibers innervated by hundreds of nerve fibers in the motor nervous system. An individual motor neuron innervates many muscle fibers; the neuron and fibers together are called a *motor unit.* Because a person must activate all the muscle fibers within the unit, the motor unit is considered the most basic level of motor control.

Several properties of motor units contribute to motor control (Bridgeman, 1988). First, the number of muscle fibers in a motor unit varies from fewer than 100 to as many as 1,000. This number is called the innervation ratio. The lower the innervation ratio is, the more precise are the possible movements. For example, the muscles controlling eye movements have a low innervation ratio, whereas those in the lower leg have high innervation ratios. A second property is that the muscle fibers within a motor unit are spread throughout the muscle. When a motor unit is activated, it produces diffuse contraction throughout the muscle. Third, motor units differ in the contractile properties of their muscle fibers. Some fibers produce long, slow, and weak contractions. Others produce short, fast, and powerful contractions. As the tension exerted by a muscle increases, the weak fibers are activated first, with the powerful fibers activated only when the tension becomes more extreme.

Although all muscles include both weak and powerful fibers, the large muscles, such as those used for walking, have a relatively high percentage of the powerful fibers. In contrast, small muscles have a higher percentage of the weak fibers. In all cases, the contractions of the individual motor units summate over time, meaning that a higher firing rate of the motor neurons results in more continuous contraction. The mechanical force generated by a muscle is determined by the type and number of motor units that are active at any one time.

Muscle strength and fatigue are of central concern in human factors. Tasks and equipment must be designed to accommodate normal strength and endurance. Muscle strength depends primarily on the muscles involved and the regulation of their contractions (Kroemer & Marras, 1981). Muscle fatigue occurs when prolonged, strong contraction of a muscle is required for an extended period of time. The greater the strength required, the shorter is the period for which it can be maintained (see Figure 14–6). The onset of muscle fatigue can be delayed or possibly even eliminated for tasks such as light assembly, in which the arms are usually unsupported, by pro-

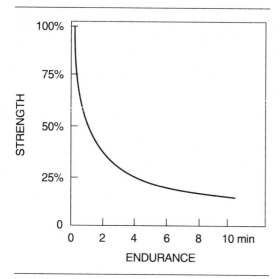

FIGURE 14–6   Muscle Strength and Endurance.

viding physical supports (Kassab, 1974). Once muscles have become fatigued, the fatigue can be eliminated by a period of rest.

Spinal Control.   The spinal system interacts with the central nervous system to control movement. The higher-level brain centers can affect the activity of spinal neurons by biasing circuits between the spinal column and the motor end plates (called reflex loops). However, most actual movement is controlled through the spinal cord. Thus, lower-level spinal systems and higher-level brain centers act together to control our actions.

The spinal cord coordinates and controls certain actions by way of *spinal reflexes* (Bridgeman, 1988). Such reflexes begin with stimulation of the sensory receptors that provide information about limb position. These proprioceptive cells are located within the muscles, tendons, joints, and skin. Their signals are sent to the spinal cord, where a motor signal is quickly evoked and sent to the appropriate muscles. Spinal reflexes allow movements to be made within milliseconds of the initiating stimulus.

One example is the stretch reflex. Stretch receptors (those receptors attached to muscles)

send information about muscle tension to the spinal cord and exert relatively direct effects on the motor system. Some of the stretch receptors have synapses directly on the motor neurons controlling the fibers that produce contractions, forming what is called a monosynaptic reflex arc. When sensory activity in this system indicates that a muscle is being stretched, a contraction is initiated to resist the stretch. The stretch reflex serves to maintain posture by resisting gravity, and it uses feedback about external forces to control the strength of contraction. Other similar reflexes assist in such things as locomotion and response preparation.

The contribution of the spinal cord to motor control extends beyond just the initiation of reflexes. Gait and other movement patterns seem to be initiated by the brain but to be controlled by the spinal cord once initiated (Grillner, 1975). Moreover, the spinal cord seems capable of performing complex controlling operations for which the movements vary as a function of the position of the respective limbs (Schmidt, 1988). The relatively sophisticated information-processing capabilities of the spinal cord free higher levels of the brain to engage in other activities.

Brain Stem, Cerebellum, and Basal Ganglia. Moving up from spinal control, the next three structures critical to motor control are the brain stem, cerebellum, and basal ganglia (see Figure 14–7). The brain stem contains cranial nerve nuclei that serve the same purpose for head movements as the spinal cord serves for the rest of the body. It also controls vital motor activities such as respiration and heart rate, and it can moderate the sensitivity of the stretch reflex loops. In addition, the brainstem contains nuclei involved in the control of the oculomotor system.

The cerebellum is thought to be involved in several aspects of motor control (Rosenbaum, 1991). One region may help maintain muscle tone, and another may be involved in balance. A typical characteristic of patients with cerebellar damage is an inability to maintain balance. The largest part of the cerebellum is specialized for the rapid coordination of action sequences. Dam-

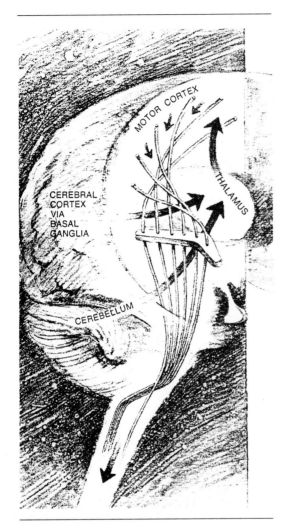

FIGURE 14–7 The Brain Stem, Cerebellum, and Basal Ganglia.

From C. W. Cotman and J. L. McGaugh, *Behavioral Neuroscience: An Introduction.* Copyright © 1980 by Academic Press, Inc. Reprinted by permission.

age to this region results in movement production deficits for sequences and timing. Another region seems to play a role in the planning of movement and still another region in movement execution. Finally, the cerebellum is involved in perceptual–motor learning.

The basal ganglia are structures in the forebrain that play a role in the activation or retrieval of movement plans, the scaling of movement amplitudes, and perceptual–motor integration. They are involved in the control of slow, smooth movements, such as those that occur for postural adjustments, and in the control of force. Huntington's disease and Parkinson's disease, which are attributed to ganglionic damage, are characterized by movement deficits of various types. The symptoms of Parkinson's disease include slowness of movement, rigidity of musculature, and resting tremor. Parkinson's patients also show an impaired ability to control muscle force precisely (Stelmach, 1991).

Motor, Premotor, and Supplementary Motor Cortices. The primary cortical areas devoted to motor control are the motor, premotor, and supplementary motor cortices. These three areas are located in adjacent regions of the frontal lobes (see Figure 14–8). The motor cortex is structured as a topographic map in the form of a homunculus (see Figure 14–9). This topographic arrangement corresponds to the types of maps seen for the sensory areas of the cortex. Moreover, as in the sensory systems, neurons in the motor cortex show directional sensitivity to movement (Georgopoulos, 1990).

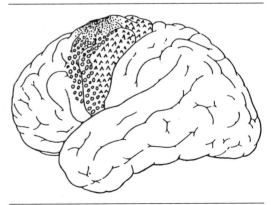

FIGURE 14–8 The Motor (^), Premotor (o), and Supplementary-motor (•) Cortices.

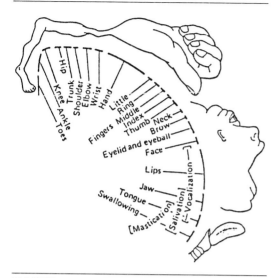

FIGURE 14–9   The Homunculus on the Motor Cortex.

Reprinted with permission of Macmillan Publishing Company from *The Cerebral Cortex of Man* by W. Penfield & T. Rasmussen. Copyright 1950 Macmillan Publishing Company; copyright renewed © 1978 Theodore Rasmussen.

The motor cortex seems to be involved in the triggering of movements, rather than in their planning. Deecke, Scheid, and Kornhuber (1969) instructed people to lift their right index fingers from a switch at irregular, self-determined intervals. They found reliable increases in the brain potentials from the motor cortex 50 ms before the movement. This short delay between activity in the motor cortex and movement initiation suggests that the motor cortex is one of the last sites in the process of movement initiation.

The motor cortex receives projections from the premotor cortex and the supplementary motor cortex (Brinkman & Porter, 1983). The premotor cortex projects primarily to the motor neurons of the trunk and shoulders. It contains one group of neurons whose activity relates to specific aspects of movement performance and another group associated with movements and visual events. The premotor cortex may be involved in visuomotor

integration and likely plays a role in orienting the body and preparing for forthcoming movements.

The supplementary motor cortex has many neurons that show modulation of their discharge in relation to specific movements (Brinkman & Porter, 1983). In contrast to the motor cortex, these modulations often precede the initiation of the movement by up to 1 second (Deecke, Scheid, & Kornhuber, 1969). Moreover, sensory input does not have much effect on the activity of these neurons. Thus, the supplementary motor cortex appears to be involved in the planning and execution of skilled movement sequences.

Summary.   The neurological substrate of movement is hierarchically organized (see Figure 14–10). The brain controls the higher-level aspects of movement, with distinct areas devoted primarily to movement planning and movement execution. The lower-level aspects are controlled by spinal mechanisms, with the properties of individual motor units and of the muscle fibers themselves contributing to control at the lowest

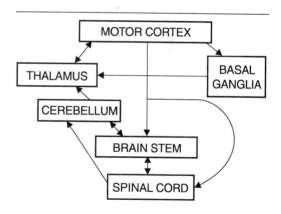

FIGURE 14–10   A Schematic of the Neural Systems Underlying Motor Control.

From E. Armstrong (1989). A comparative review of the primate motor system. *Journal of Motor Behavior, 21,* 493–517. Reprinted with permission of the Helen Dwight Reid Educational Foundation. Published by Heldref Publications, 1319 Eighteenth St., N.W., Washington, D. C. 20036–1802. Copyright © 1991.

levels. It is an oversimplification to consider the organization to be strictly hierarchical, because there are many interconnections and interactions among the structures at all levels (Wiesendanger, 1990). However, the hierarchical nature of the nervous system is apparent in the way that motor behavior is structured.

CONTROL OF ACTION

Motor performance is controlled by cognitive processes. Models of these processes are based primarily on measures of human performance under a variety of conditions. Movement tasks vary in several crucial ways. Of most importance is the discrete–continuous dimension. Some tasks, such as throwing a ball or pressing a key, are discrete because the action has a distinct beginning and ending. In contrast, tasks such as steering a car are continuous. Tasks such as assembly line work that involve a series of discrete actions fall in between. Another distinction is between open and closed skills (Poulton, 1957). Open skills are

those performed in dynamic environments, whereas closed skills involve static environments. Open skills are externally paced by the environment, and closed skills are self-paced. Driving a car requires both open and closed skills. Because they are paced by the environment, open skills require rapid adaptations to the environment that closed skills do not.

Closed-loop Control

The distinction between closed-loop and open-loop systems introduced in Chapter 3 has been influential in the investigation of motor control. Do not confuse it with the closed- and open-skill distinction just discussed, which depends on the environment in which a task is performed. Recall that closed-loop models are characterized by the use of negative feedback to regulate their outputs. Some aspects of movement control can be viewed as closed loop (see Figure 14–11). In such situations, a referent is generated that represents the desired movement goal. Sensory feedback is pro-

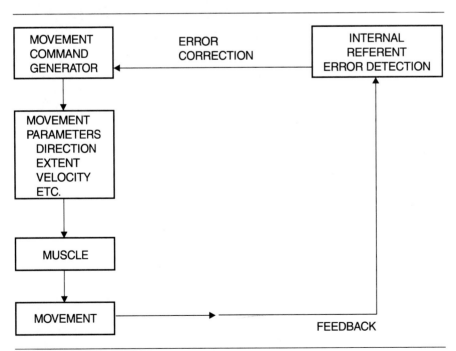

FIGURE 14–11 A Closed-loop System for Motor Control.

vided for comparison to the referent. The difference between the actual position and the desired position of the limb is perceived as error. This error is used to select corrective movements that will bring the desired and actual positions closer together. The decision is then passed along to the effector system, which activates the appropriate muscles for the corrective action. Comparisons are made continuously between the referent and the feedback until the difference between the actual and desired positions is minimized.

Closed-loop control depends on the sensory feedback produced by the system as it acts on the environment. Earlier in this chapter we discussed one source of feedback, the sensory information about position provided by proprioception. Another major source of feedback is vision. As a hand is being moved to an object, visual feedback provides information about the locations of each. Feedback can also be provided by audition, for example, the sounds made by the feet as they touch the floor when walking (Winstein & Schmidt, 1989). Finally, the vestibular sense provides feedback regarding posture and head orientation.

There are three types of mechanisms for the modification of movement based on feedback that differ in their speed and flexibility (Winstein & Schmidt, 1989). First, reflexes such as the stretch reflex provide fast, automatic adjustments to feedback. Second, and at the opposite extreme, voluntary modifications are slow but highly flexible. Finally, triggered reactions are at an intermediate level of speed and automaticity. They differ from reflex responses in that they are influenced by instructions and the number of stimulus–response alternatives. Reflex and triggered reactions allow rapid modification of movement based on momentary feedback, whereas intentional changes are more global and take longer to implement.

Open-loop Control

Open-loop control does not depend on feedback (see Figure 14–12). Performance of movements

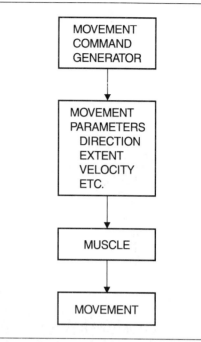

FIGURE 14–12 An Open-loop System for Motor Control.

that occur too rapidly to allow modification from feedback can be characterized as open loop, as can well-learned slower responses. Open-loop control must be achieved by developing a sequence of movement instructions and parameter specifications prior to movement initiation. The structure detailing the movement instructions is usually called a *motor program*.

The concept of a motor program, or plan of action, extends back to James (1890), who proposed that an action is initiated by an "image" of it. Contemporary interest in the concept can be traced to Lashley (1951), who argued that rapid sequential movements cannot be controlled by a serial chain, in which feedback from each component movement serves as the stimulus to initiate the next. Keele (1968) formalized the motor program concept, proposing that a motor program is a set of muscle commands structured before the initiation of a movement sequence. More recently, the view that a program involves specific muscle commands has been replaced with the concept of a generalized motor program (Schmidt, 1975). The program is regarded as an abstract plan for controlling specific classes of movements. To execute a particular movement, such parameters as the muscles to be used, their order, and the force, duration, and timing of their contractions must be specified.

The concept of a generalized motor program has several implications. First, coordinated movement should be possible when feedback is not available. This has been found in monkeys that have been deprived of proprioceptive feedback through the surgical procedure of deafferentation. Deafferented monkeys can still perform some skilled actions, such as grasping, walking, and running (Bizzi & Abend, 1983; Taub & Berman, 1968). Similarly, people who lack feedback from their limbs due to degeneration of the peripheral pathways can perform many manual tasks in the absence of visual input. Rothwell et al. (1982) studied such a patient who was able to perform sequences of fine motor skills such as thumb-to-finger touches. Because movement information cannot be conveyed over sensory pathways in an organism that has been deafferented surgically or pathologically, the movement is likely triggered by motor programs under the control of the central nervous system.

The generalized motor program concept also implies that rapid movements can be made accurately even when the sensory feedback takes more time than the movement itself. Such is the case for keyboarding, in which the interval between keystrokes is less than the time to use proprioceptive or visual feedback (Lashley, 1951). These movements must be programmed in advance, with the program coordinating the complex pattern of muscular activity needed to execute the keystrokes (Wadman et al., 1979).

Another implication is that the more complex a movement is, the longer it should take to program. Initiation of a response to a stimulus (the reaction time) has been shown to take longer as the complexity of the movement to be made increases (Henry & Rogers, 1960; Klapp, 1977). Thus, the speed with which a person can react to a stimulus is directly related to the complexity of the response that must follow.

Generalized motor programs are modular and can be used with various motor systems for execution. Distinct features called invariant characteristics specify critical structural aspects of the class of movements that a particular program controls. Invariant characteristics are independent from the particular muscles used to execute the movement. These general features may be such things as the order of movement components, the relative amount of time that each component takes, and the way that force is distributed to each component. To specify a particular movement, parameters are selected that specify the muscles, the speed, and the overall force with which the movement is to be made.

One example of such modularity is that similar writing samples are produced by different muscle groups (Merton, 1972; see Figure 14–13). This similarity suggests that the sequential representation for writing is independent from the effectors used for execution. Wright (1990) recently has qualified this point, noting that many salient details of the trajectory produced by the dominant hand are absent when the nondominant hand is used. The two hands seem to share only a relatively abstract spatial repre-

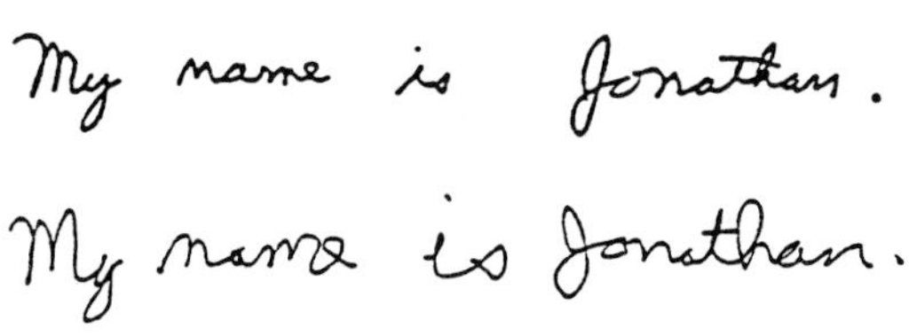

FIGURE 14–13 Writing Samples Produced Using the Hand [on a Piece of Paper (top)] and the Arm [at a Blackboard (bottom)].
We thank Bob Hines for contributing these samples.

sentation at higher levels. There is more similarity between large writing (as on a blackboard) and small writing (as on a piece of paper), suggesting that these two ways of writing share a common lower-level representation.

The timing of movement also seems to involve an independent module or component of control (Keele, Cohen, & Ivry, 1990). Individual differences in the production of movements of regular time intervals are correlated across different effectors. However, timing ability does not correlate with the regulation of force production. Thus, the timing module seems to be used for a variety of different tasks.

Motor programs are typically assumed to be hierarchical, in that high-level program modules pass control to lower-level modules. Evidence for hierarchical control comes from studies that required the execution of tapping sequences. Povel and Collard (1982) had people tap their fingers in response to sequences of six numbers. The sequence 123321 refers to the order for three fingers, labeled 1, 2, and 3, respectively. As a general rule, the first and fourth response latencies were longer than the others (see Figure 14–14). This suggests that a hierarchical program is executed, with the top level passing control to the first response subgroup (123) and then to the second response subgroup (321).

Although the motor program perspective presumes that movement can be executed without feedback, feedback is still assumed to contribute to the control of action in several ways. First, information fed back through the senses specifies the position of the body part that is to be moved and where it is to be moved. Without this information, it would not be possible to select the motor program and adjust its parameters for the desired outcome. Second, for slow movements, feedback can be used to correct the parameters of an ongoing program or a new program can be selected. Third, rapid corrections of movements based on proprioceptive and visual feedback can occur in less than 100 ms in some situations (Carlton, 1992). This rapid feedback allows for the correction of errors in the execution of a movement, but does not drive the pattern of action.

AIMED MOVEMENTS

Aimed movements are those that require an arm or some other part of the body be moved to a target location. The movement made by an operator to bring a finger to a push button is an example, as is moving the foot from the accelerator pedal to the brake pedal in an automobile.

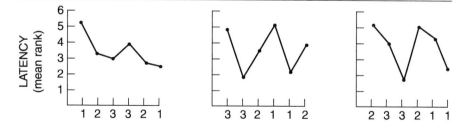

FIGURE 14–14   Mean Latency of Intertap Intervals for the Sequences 123321 (Left panel), 332112 (Center panel), and 233211 (Right Panel).

From D. J. Povel & R. Collard (1982). Structural factors in patterned finger tapping. *Acta Psychologica, 52* 107–123. Reprinted by permission of Elsevier Science Publishers BV.

The speed and accuracy with which such movements can be made are influenced by many factors, including the effector used, the distance of the movement, and the presence or absence of visual feedback. To ensure that an operator's movements will be made within necessary speed and accuracy limits, a designer must consider the way in which aimed movements are controlled.

Aimed movements were first studied by Woodworth (1899). He proposed that rapid aimed movements have two phases that he called initial adjustment and current control. The initial phase transports the body part toward the target location. The second phase uses sensory feedback to correct errors in accuracy and home in on the target. Much of Woodworth's interest was in the amount of time needed to use visual feedback in this second phase.

To investigate this issue, Woodworth (1899) used a task in which people repeatedly drew lines on a roll of paper moving through a vertical slot in a table top. The lines were to be of a specified length, with the rate of movement set by a metronome that beat from 20 to 200 times each minute. One complete movement cycle (up and down) was to be made for each beat. The role of visual feedback was evaluated by having people perform with their eyes open or closed. Movement accuracy was equivalent for the two conditions at rates of 180/min or greater; thus visual feedback had little or no effect on performance. However, at rates of 140/min or less, the eyes-open condition yielded better performance. Consequently, Woodworth concluded that the minimum time required to process visual feedback was 450 ms.

Relatively little research was conducted during the first half of the twentieth century to follow up Woodworth's (1899) work. However, aimed movements have been examined extensively in the last half of this century. In addition to the time-matching task used by Woodworth, a time-minimization task has been widely used (Meyer et al., 1990). In the latter task, people are to minimize their movement times while approximating a specified target accuracy value. For both tasks, single movements as well as repetitive movements have been examined.

Fitts's Law

Fitts (1954) established a fundamental relation between aimed movement time and the variables of distance and precision that has come to be known as *Fitts's law*. He examined performance in a repetitive tapping task, in which a person was required to move a stylus back and fourth between two target locations as quickly as possible. As the distance between the targets increased, movement time increased. Conversely, as the widths of the targets increased, movement time decreased. Because the width of the targets dictates the precision of the movements, this relation can be viewed as a speed–accuracy tradeoff.

From these relations, Fitts (1954) defined an *index of difficulty* (*I*) as

$$I = \log_2 \frac{2D}{W}$$

where D is the center-to-center distance between the targets and W is the width of the targets. Fitts found this index to be related to movement time (MT) by the linear equation

$$MT = a + b(I)$$

where a and b are constants representing base time and channel capacity, respectively (see Figure 14–15). According to Fitts's law, when the distance required for a movement is doubled, the movement time will not change if the target width is also doubled.

Fitts's law is of considerable generality. He obtained similar results with tasks that required washers to be placed onto pegs or pins into holes (Fitts, 1954). Other researchers have found the law to hold in tasks as diverse as angular positioning of the wrist (Crossman & Goodeve, 1963/1983), arm extension (Kerr & Langolf, 1977), positioning a cursor with a joystick or a head-movement controller (Jagacinski & Monk, 1985), working with tweezers under a microscope (Langolf & Hancock, 1975), and making

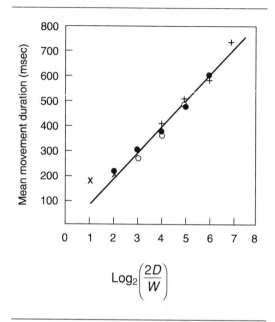

FIGURE 14–15   Movement Time as a Function of the Index of Difficulty.

From P. M. Fitts (1954). The information capacity of the human motor system in controlling the amplitude of movement. *Journal of Experimental Psychology, 47,* 381–391.

aimed movements underwater (Kerr, 1973). Newell (1990, p.3) characterizes this generality as follows:

> "Fitts' law is extremely robust. . . . Indeed, it is so neat, it is surprising that it doesn't show up in every first-year textbook as a paradigm example of a psychological quantitative law."

One possible basis for Fitts's law is the number of adjustments that must be made during the movement to land on the target. This control of the movement could be either continuous or discrete (Crossman & Goodeve, 1963/1983). However, given that Fitts's law conforms to the quantitative metric of information (H), it seems reasonable to try to relate the law to the number of discrete movement decisions that must be made. The *iterative corrections model* (Crossman & Goodeve, 1963/1983; Keele, 1968) proposes

that every movement is actually a series of discrete submovements, each traversing a fixed proportion of the distance to the target. Feedback is used to correct the trajectory as the movement progresses. More difficult movements require more corrections. Crossman and Goodeve (1963/1983) favored this model over a continuous control model, because the trajectories in a wrist-rotation task showed distinct ripples in their velocity profiles (see Figure 14–16). While such evidence for discrete movements was apparent in their task, it is not observed for all tasks. Moreover, Fitts's law still holds when people are deprived of visual feedback (Wallace & Newell, 1983).

An exception to Fitts's law occurs for time-matching tasks, such as those used originally by Woodworth (1899), in which the movement is to be made with a specified duration. For these tasks, accuracy is a linear rather than logarithmic function of the velocity required to complete the movement at the specified duration (Schmidt et al., 1979). This linear relation has been explained by an *impulse variability model* that attributes the relation to the initial impulse that generates the movement, rather than to the use of feedback (Schmidt et al., 1979). According to this model, the total movement can be divided in half. A burst of force is applied for the first half and then damped for the second half. There is assumed to

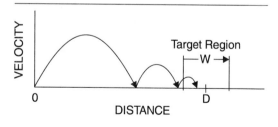

FIGURE 14–16   Movement Trajectories with Distinct Submovements.

From D. E. Meyer et al. (1988). Optimality in human motor performance: Ideal control of rapid aimed movements. *Psychological Review, 95,* 340–370. Copyright © 1988 by American Psychological Association. Reprinted by permission.

be some degree of variability in both the forces themselves and the amount of time for which they are applied. These variabilities are proportional to the total force and total time. According to this model, the linear trade-off arises from the person's attempt to minimize both sources of variability. Thus, the impulse variability model attributes the speed–accuracy function to noise that occurs during the execution of a motor program. Because the model does not rely on feedback, it has difficulty accounting for the situations in which discrete submovements are observed.

A recent model, the *optimized initial impulse model,* combines the characteristics of the iterative corrections and impulse variability models (Meyer et al., 1988). An aimed movement toward a specified target location is presumed to involve a primary submovement and an optional secondary submovement that is made if the initial submovement is off target. The submovements are programmed to minimize the average time for the total movement. Among the evidence supporting the model is that movements rarely show more than two submovements and the time to execute these submovements is constrained by Fitts's law. It is interesting that, although considerably more detailed, the Meyer et al. (1988) model maintains the biphasic view of aimed movements originally proposed by Woodworth (1899).

Because aimed movement tasks are common in work environments, Fitts's law can be used to predict performance for real-world tasks. The rate of information transmission (that is, the inverse of the slope of the function relating movement time to the index of difficulty) can be used to evaluate alternative response modes. As one example, Wiker, Langolf, and Chaffin (1989) noted that many tasks requiring manual assembly or use of hand tools are performed with the hands located above the shoulders. They examined the performance of a stylus-to-hole version of a repetitive movement task with the hand elevated -15° to +60° relative to shoulder level (see Figure 14–17). The slope of the Fitts's law function increased approximately 20% for the highest hand

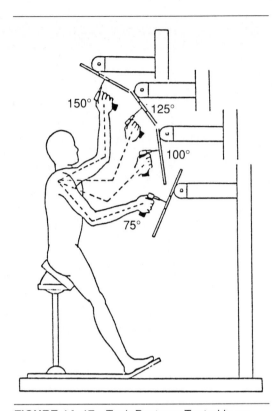

FIGURE 14–17 Task Postures Tested in an Experiment by Wiker, Langolf, and Chaffin.

From S. F. Wiker, G. D. Langolf, D. B. Chaffin, Arm posture and human movement capability. Reprinted with permission from *Human Factors,* Vol. 31, No. 4, pp. 421–441, 1989. Copyright © 1989 by The Human Factors Society, Inc. All rights reserved.

elevation relative to the lowest. Wiker et al. attributed this increase in movement time to the tensing of the musculature required to raise the hand. They recommended that sustained manual activity be restricted to below shoulder level when possible.

Another example involves the use of head positioning devices. For physically challenged workers, such as those whose movements are restricted to turns of the head, a head or chin stick can be used to depress keys on a keyboard. Andres and Hartung (1989) assessed how well Fitts's law could predict the time to bring the stick to a key by turning the head. People tapped a chin stylus between targets that varied in width and separation. Fitts's law fit the data well, with the mean information transmission rate of 7 bits/s being considerably less than is typically found for hand or foot movements. The design of tasks that require head-movement responses must take into account this reduced processing rate.

Visual Feedback

Another issue in the control of aimed movements is the role of visual feedback. Remember that Woodworth (1899) first estimated the time to process visual feedback to be 450 ms, because people benefited from vision in a repetitive movement task only for slower rates of movement. This estimate seems quite long, in that it is twice the minimum choice reaction time that can be obtained to visual stimuli. Moreover, it is too long for visual feedback to play a major role in aiming tasks.

Keele and Posner (1968) proposed that the 450-ms value is an overestimate because, with repetitive movements of the type studied by Woodworth, part of the total time is used for reversing the movement. Consequently, they had people perform a time-matching task with discrete movement of a stylus to a target. In separate pacing conditions, the movement was to be of approximately 150-, 250-, 350-, or 450-ms duration. The lights were turned off at the initiation of the movement on half of the trials without foreknowledge of the performer. A trial was scored as either a hit or a miss depending on whether the stylus landed on the target. For all pacing conditions except the fastest, movement accuracy was better with the lights on than off. Because the actual mean movement times were 190 ms in the fastest condition and 260 ms in the next fastest, Keele and Posner concluded that the minimum duration for processing visual feedback was between 190 and 260 ms.

Although Keele and Posner's (1968) estimate was considerably less than Woodworth's (1899), it also overestimated visual feedback processing time. Zelaznik, Hawkins, and Kissel-burgh (1983) attributed this overestimation to both the uncertainty in Keele and Posner's experiment regarding whether visual feedback would be present and the use of hit or miss scores. Zelaznik et al. examined performance under conditions in which people knew in advance whether feedback would be present. Under these conditions, there was evidence that feedback was used for movements with durations of less than 140 ms.

These findings indicate that the time for visual processing in aimed movements can be quite short. Thus, even rapid movements may benefit from the availability of visual feedback in some situations. However, this benefit for fast movements is inconsistent across task variations, suggesting that there is no single minimal correction latency. Zelaznik et al. propose that shorter feedback estimates may reflect the time to correct errors in the execution of the motor program, whereas the longer feedback estimates may reflect the time to select a new program.

Bimanual Control

In the studies discussed to this point, people were required to make a single aimed hand movement. Yet many work tasks, such as light assembly, require two different aimed movements at once with each hand. Kelso, Southard, and Goodman (1979) had people perform bimanual movements for which the index of difficulty differed. In one condition, the right hand was to move to a close, large target and the left hand to a distant, small target. According to Fitts's law, if the two hands moved independently, the right-hand movement should take less time than the left-hand movement, since the index of difficulty is less. Instead, the two hands reached the targets simultaneously. Although the hands moved at different velocities, the profiles of relative velocity and acceleration were synchronized. The timing for both movements closely approximated that for the more difficult movement when it was performed alone. Thus, the easier movement seemed coupled to the harder movement.

One interpretation of this coupling is that the two hands may be controlled by the same motor program (Schmidt et al., 1979). This program specifies the phase characteristics of the movements for the two limbs. Other characteristics, such as the distance to be traveled, are specified separately for each. Another interpretation of the coupling is that it reflects natural groupings of the muscles called functional synergies (Kelso, Southard, & Goodman, 1979). As would be expected if the hand movements are controlled by a unitary structure, such as the same motor program or a synergistic group, a hurdle placed in the path of one limb produces a perturbation in the movement paths for both limbs (see Figure 14–18; Kelso, Putnam, & Goodman, 1983).

One implication of the research on bimanual aiming is that the index of difficulty does not have to be equal for two controls (for example, push buttons) that must be activated simultaneously. However, although bimanual movements seem to be controlled by a unitary structure, they cannot be completely synchronized. Warrick and Turner (1963) showed that release times for buttons pressed with the left and right hands can vary by as much as 20 ms. They concluded that these differences are sufficiently large to create problems for the operation of equipment or machinery that requires simultaneous activation of left- and right-hand controls. Thus, the designer must allow for some deviation from true simultaneity in all cases.

GRASPING AND INTERCEPTING OBJECTS

More often than not, a person must both aim for a target object and also grasp the target when it is reached. Grasping is basic to actions as diverse as picking up a cup of coffee, grabbing a hammer, opening a door, or operating a selector switch. Two components can be distinguished for movements that require grasping, a transport phase (reaching) and a grasp phase (grasping). The transport component involves moving the hand to the object, whereas the grasp component involves positioning the fingers for grabbing the object when contact is made.

Jeannerod (1981, 1984) proposed that the two components are controlled by distinct visuo-motor channels that are activated in parallel. The

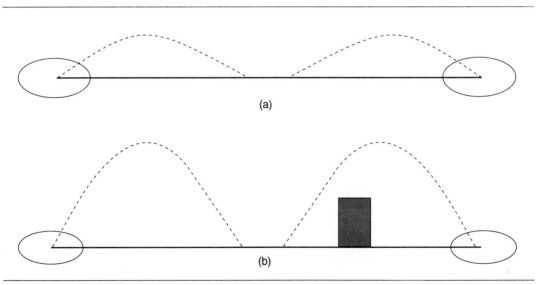

FIGURE 14–18   Bimanual Movement Without (a) and With (b) a Hurdle.

transport component moves the arm to the target location. Consequently, it must be based on perceptual information of spatial location, which is used to activate the muscles at the shoulder joint and elbow that are responsible for such movements. In contrast, the visuomotor channel for the grasp component relates information about intrinsic properties of the object (for example, its size and shape) to more distal muscles (for example, fingers). Jeannerod provided evidence that the two movement components can be dissociated by showing that a change in object size at movement initiation affects the grasp component but not the transport component of the movement.

Considerable research, summarized by Jeannerod and Marteniuk (1992), has since been devoted to examining the characteristics of the transport and grasp components, as well as their interrelation. One way to study the transport component is to introduce perturbations of the target location. When the perturbation occurs after presentation of the initial target and before a movement is initiated, the movement cannot be modified before a substantial delay of several hundred milliseconds (Soechting & Laquaniti, 1983; Van Sonderen, Denier Van der Gon, & Gielen, 1988). However, when such perturbations in target location occur after the onset of movement, the corrections can be executed within approximately 100 ms (for example, Paulignan et al., 1990). The different times for using visual feedback about a change in position conform to Zelaznik, Hawkins, and Kisselburgh's (1983) suggestion that longer times may reflect reprogramming of the movement, whereas shorter times reflect corrections made on-line within a program.

Although the transport component is basically an aimed movement of the type covered in the previous section, it is not identical in aiming and grasping tasks. Marteniuk et al. (1987) had people either hit a target with the index finger or grasp a disk. Movement time was longer when grasping was required. Kinematic analyses showed that the acceleration pattern was similar for the two types of movements, with a higher

percentage of total movement time spent in decelerating when a grasping action was required. Moreover, deceleration took longer when the disk had to be placed in a tightly fitting well than when it was to be thrown into a large container. Thus, the kinematic structure of reaching movements is affected by the goal of the action.

The grasping phase of movement involves a gradual opening of the grip to a maximum aperture, followed by closure until it conforms to the object size (see Figure 14–19). The thumb and index finger reach maximal separation when the deceleration of the movement begins. The amplitude of the grip opening is a function of object size. The larger the object is, the wider the opening (Jeannerod, 1981, 1984). Moreover, as the speed of the movement increases, the maximum separation between the thumb and index finger increases. This change in grasp size accommodates decreased movement accuracy. Regardless of the reach duration, this maximum occurs within the first 60% to 70% of the reach movement (Jeannerod, 1981, 1984). Thus, the transport and grasp phases appear to be coupled within a single motor program.

When a moving object must be intercepted, the actions taken must coincide with the movement of the object. This is characteristic of ball-playing skills, such as baseball. For an outfielder to catch a fly ball requires that the ball be detected and its flight path be determined on the basis of its velocity, trajectory, and position relative to the ballplayer (for example, Whiting, 1969). The point of interception must be calculated, movements must be executed to reach that point, and

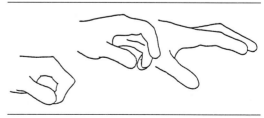

FIGURE 14–19   The Grasping Phase of Movement.

then precise positioning and timing of the limbs and hands must occur to make the catch.

Performance in catching tasks is best with full vision of the ball. However, the visual information early in flight and at the end is most important (Sharp & Whiting, 1974, 1975). During the final 300 ms, vision assists in the positioning of the hand at the correct time to make the catch. Not only must the ball be visible for good catching performance, but so must the hand (Fischman & Schneider, 1985). When the hand cannot be seen, novice catchers show a decline in performance due to improper positioning of the catching arm, whereas experienced ballplayers show more timing errors.

Lee (1976) proposed that the optic variable tau, which is the inverse of the rate of dilation of an object on the retina, is used to determine time-to-contact. Lee et al. (1983) required people to jump and hit balls dropped from different heights. Elbow and knee angles showed constant patterns of change as a function of the value of tau at a short time before contact.

Time-to-contact is a predictor of the regulatory actions taken by a driver in a vehicle that is on a collision course with a stationary or moving obstacle. In a simulated driving situation using film clips, Lee (1976) showed that estimates of time-to-contact were based solely on tau. However, Cavallo and Laurent (1988) found that other factors come into play under actual driving conditions. Experienced and beginning drivers had to indicate when they expected a collision to take place with a mock-up of the rear of a car. While the vehicle was moving at a constant speed, the driver was allowed 3 s of viewing time. This viewing was conducted (1) monocularly versus binocularly, (2) with the normal visual field versus a field restricted to 10°, (3) with a 3- or 6-s time-to-collision following viewing, and (4) at two vehicle speeds. Both speed and distance information were taken into account by beginners, with experienced drivers relying primarily on distance information. These findings indicate that in real-life tasks variables other than tau are used to estimate time-to-contact.

MOVEMENT SEQUENCES

Many activities, such as diving or piano playing, require the execution of complex sequences of movements. Consequently, the control of movement sequences has been investigated since the earliest studies of motor performance. One topic that has been examined is the maximal rate at which repetitive motor activity can occur (Keele, 1986). Keele and Hawkins (1982) found that the maximal tapping rates for the finger, thumb, and foot (each approximately 5 taps per second) were somewhat less than those for the wrist and elbow (both approximately 6 taps per second). The rate for strides in human running is considerably lower, possibly due to biomechanical factors associated with the size of the effectors (Keele, 1986).

The maximal tapping rate for finger movements and forearm movements is only slightly slowed by increasing the amplitude of the tapping movements (Bryan, 1892; Fenn, 1938). The cycle time for leg movements increases as a person goes from walking slowly to running. However, when someone runs, the cycle time remains relatively constant, and speed is increased primarily by increasing stride length (Lee, Lishman, & Thomson, 1982; Shapiro et al., 1981). Thus, the limitation on the rate of repetitive action is relatively independent of the magnitude of the movements. One implication of these studies is that the performance of some skills may be limited by the rate at which repetitive movements can be made. Such may be the case for typing and handwriting, for which skilled performance is at frequencies close to the maximum tapping rates.

Many tasks do not require performance at a maximal rate. Instead, it is the timing between successive responses that is crucial. Experiments have been conducted in which people begin tapping at a fixed rate along with a metronome. After the tapping becomes synchronized with the metronome beats, the metronome goes off and the person is to maintain the tapping rate (Wing & Kristofferson, 1973). The concern is with the person's performance once the pacing stimulus is no longer available. As would be expected, there is variability in the interresponse interval durations around the target duration. This variability shows two systematic characteristics. First, for target intervals exceeding 250 ms (4 taps per second), the variance is a positive function of the mean interval. In other words, the slower the tapping rate is, the more variability there is in tapping. Second, the interresponse times for successive responses are negatively correlated. If the interval between one response and the next is long, the following interval will tend to be short, and vice versa.

Wing and Kristofferson (1973) accounted for these results with a model that attributes the variability in timing to two sources, a central timekeeper and a motor delay. The variability of these two components combines to produce the observed total variability. The model accounts for the negatively correlated intervals by assuming that when the motor delay is long the response will be executed closer in time to the next timing impulse, and vice versa. This correlation is used as a direct estimate of motor delay variance. The positive relation between the variance of the interresponse interval and the mean interval duration is attributed to the timekeeper. The timekeeper variability has been shown to be similar for finger, wrist, and forearm movements (Wing, 1980), suggesting a common central timing mechanism.

Previously in this chapter, it was noted that people synchronized aimed movements for the two hands. A similar relation is found for coordinated tapping of telegraph keys with the left and right index fingers. Klapp (1979) required people to press and release a left telegraph key in synchrony with the onset and offset of a tone presented to the left ear; the same task was performed concurrently by the right hand in synchrony with a tone in the right ear. Performance was better when the left and right presses were perfectly synchronized or had a 2:1 harmonic relation than when they were unsynchronized.

OTHER ASPECTS OF MOTOR CONTROL

To this point, we have discussed general issues in motor control. In this final section, we consider four specific aspects of motor control that are involved in our daily interactions with the environment and are of concern in human factors. Posture is required for maintaining a stable orientation and is critical to basic activities, such as locomotion. Eye and head movements are fundamental to receiving visual and, to a lesser extent, auditory input from our surroundings. Finally, because vocal utterances are the primary form of human communication, the control of speech production has been an important area in the field of motor control.

Posture

Posture and balance are maintained through closed-loop control. The proprioceptive, vestibular, and visual senses provide feedback that serves as the basis for postural adjustments. When this feedback is removed, postural stability decreases. It is also possible to induce postural imbalance through illusions.

Lee and Lishman (1975) had people stand in a room in which the walls could move forward or backward. When the wall approached the person swayed backward, but when the wall receded, the person swayed forward. The visual feedback induced by the moving walls corresponded to the feedback that would be received when falling forward or backward. This demonstrates that visual feedback plays a dominant role in maintaining an upright posture, because the proprioceptive and vestibular information indicated that the posture was upright.

The feedback loops responsible for the control of posture are calibrated according to the earth's gravity (1 G). After prolonged spaceflight, astronauts and cosmonauts often have difficulty maintaining posture. Lackner (1990) has suggested that this occurs because spinal neurons adapt to altered gravity and then must readapt when gravity is returned to normal. To support this point, he had people perform deep knee bends or step onto and off a platform. The experiment took place on a Boeing KC-135 aircraft performing parabolic flight maneuvers, which produced G-forces of 1.8 to 2 G. Early in the flight, people reported illusory movements of themselves and their surroundings while performing the tasks. However, by the fortieth parabola, people reported no illusory movement. When gravity returned to normal, illusory movement was again reported. Lackner suggests that the spinal discharge rate must be retuned after abnormal gravity conditions.

Locomotion

When you arise from bed in the morning, you first establish an upright posture. Throughout the rest of the day, much of your time is spent locomoting through the environment. All the leg movements required for locomotion are comprised from the same four-phase step cycle (see Figure 14–20). During the stance portion of a step, the first phase begins as the heel strikes the ground. While the foot is on the ground, the second phase begins

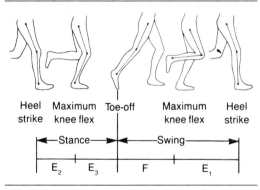

Heel strike	Maximum knee flex	Toe-off	Maximum knee flex	Heel strike
◄—Stance—►		◄—Swing—►		
E_2	E_3	F		E_1

FIGURE 14–20 The Step Cycle.
From D. C. Shapiro et al. (1981). Evidence for generalized motor programs using gait pattern analysis. *Journal of Motor Behavior, 13,* 33–47. Reprinted with permission of the Helen Dwight Reid Educational Foundation. Published by Heldref Publications, 1319 Eighteenth St., N.W., Washington, D. C. 20036–1802. Copyright © 1981.

when the knee reaches its maximal flex. The swing portion of the step begins with the third phase as the foot leaves the ground. The fourth and final phase begins when the knee reaches its maximal flex behind the body. The foot is then returned to the ground, completing the cycle. One difference between walking and running is in the absolute time spent in each phase.

Evidence from spinalized cats suggests that the step cycle is controlled by spinal generators (Grillner, 1975). When stimulation is provided to the cat's midbrain, the step cycle is initiated, and the cat walks. After the stimulation is removed, the cat continues to walk. This suggests that, after the initial signal is received from higher-level brain centers, the step cycle continues with little intervention from these centers.

Although the brain plays a minimal role in generating the step cycle after locomotion is initiated, visual feedback serves two important purposes in locomotor control (Corlett, 1992). Visual cues are used to plan routes from a current position to a desired location and to provide ongoing feedback during locomotion that can be used to modify the plan. This information is not required to be continuously available, but it is particularly important near a target.

Eye and Head Movements

Eye and head movements play an important role in processing visual feedback, because the retina has only a limited region of high visual acuity. Each eye has three pairs of extra-ocular muscles that control its position. These muscles allow both abrupt, saccadic movements and several kinds of smooth movements.

Saccadic movements are under voluntary control. Saccades are quick, short-duration movements in which fixation is shifted from one location to another. In addition to being involved in reading, they are made to scan a scene and to maintain fixation on an object that abruptly changes position. Saccades typically are initiated approximately 200 ms after a target event. However, the latency is affected by several factors, including target characteristics and expectancies.

As with other types of aimed movements, saccades show variability and a speed–accuracy trade-off (Abrams, Meyer, & Kornblum, 1989). As the average distance toward a target point increases, the standard deviations of the end points increase linearly with the saccades' average velocity. Abrams et al. have provided an account of this trade-off in terms of an impulse-variability model originally designed for limb movements.

To track a moving target, smooth pursuit movements must match the velocity of the eye with that of the target. This allows the target to remain fixated. The eye is able to track targets relatively accurately for velocities of up to 30°/s, with accuracy deteriorating at faster rates of movement. Both retinal and extraretinal sources of information are used to control the movements. Anticipated target movements are preceded by initiation of the tracking movement.

Eye movements are coordinated with head movements through the vestibulo-ocular reflex. This reflex is triggered by rotation of the head or body as you try to fixate an object. The eye movement is in the direction opposite the head movement and compensates for it. Compensation is not as accurate at high angular head velocities (Pulaski, Zee, & Robinson, 1981). When someone fixates on a target image that rotates with the head, as in a helmet-mounted display, the vestibulo-ocular reflex is suppressed, degrading the ability to maintain fixation.

Speech Production

When people think of motor control, they typically do not have speech in mind. Yet, precise motor coordination of the articulatory system is required for speech production. As described in Chapter 8, speech stimuli are constructed from phonemes. In speech production, the concern is with the generation of these phonemes. The lungs provide the power supply for speech through exhalation, the larynx provides the sound, and the mouth and nasal cavity filter the sound.

When the vocal cords vibrate, the speech sound is said to be voiced. When it does not, the sound is unvoiced. All vowels are voiced, whereas consonants can be either voiced or unvoiced. Both vowels and consonants can be classified in terms of distinctive articulatory features. For consonants, these are the manner of articulation, or the way in which the airstream is affected by the articulators, and place of articulation, or the location of constriction in the vocal tract. There is considerable variability across contexts for the production of phonemes, so recent theories have focused on the idea that relative positions of articulators are important, rather than absolute positions.

Despite the vast difference in the output for speech and other types of motor activity, many similar results are obtained. As with nonspeech stimuli, it takes longer to initiate a longer utterance than a shorter one (Sternberg et al., 1978), and speech sequences seem to be organized hierarchically (Gordon & Meyer, 1987). Thus, the general views regarding motor control described earlier in the chapter may bear on some aspects of speech production.

A recent application of speech production research is the use of speech analysis to provide evidence for alcohol impairment in situations for which audio recordings are available (Brenner & Cash, 1991). It is well known that alcohol impairs motor performance, as evidenced by the coordination tests of walking a straight line and touching your nose. One consequence of this motor impairment is that speech deteriorates. The speaking rate slows, difficult words are slurred, speech errors occur, and speech quality changes (for example, mumbling). Recordings can be examined for the presence of these characteristics if samples of speech are available for both the period in question and one or more periods in which there was no alcohol impairment.

Speech analysis was used in the investigation of the *Exxon Valdez* accident of 1989, in which the oil tanker ran aground and spilled over 200,000 gallons of crude oil. Recorded radio transmissions from the captain were analyzed for evidence of alcohol consumption by two independent groups of researchers. Transmissions that occurred 33 hr and 1 hr before the ship ran aground were evaluated, as were transmissions that occurred immediately, 1 hr, and 9 hr after the accident. The researchers concluded that the captain's speech immediately before and after the accident showed the four types of speech changes characteristic of alcohol impairment. This evidence was used by the investigatory board to conclude that the captain's judgment had been impaired by alcohol at the time of the accident.

SUMMARY

Without movement, human factors issues would not be issues at all. Therefore, the way in which humans execute and control action is fundamental to an understanding of human factors. Control of action is hierarchical. The motor cortex receives proprioceptive feedback and delivers signals for the control and correction of movement. These signals travel through the spinal cord, which alone can control movement to some degree. It is speculated that the brain develops plans for the execution of complex actions, whereas the spinal cord is involved in control of the fine adjustments. At the lowest level is the muscle itself, whose viscoelastic properties provide for a limited range of movement in the absence of neural input.

The central plans for action typically are called motor programs. Much recent work has been devoted to clarifying the nature of motor programs. Research has indicated that they are hierarchical and modular, just like the central nervous system. Complex actions involving more than one muscle group are often controlled by a single motor program. Most actions can be characterized as involving a mixture of open- and closed-loop control. Sensory feedback can be used to modify some actions as they are being executed, but it plays a lesser role in other actions, such as those executed quickly. Historically, a major concern in the investigation of motor control is how highly skilled behavior is learned. This concern includes issues such as how motor programs are acquired and how the role of sensory feedback changes with practice. These and related topics are addressed in Chapter 15.

RECOMMENDED READINGS

Jeannerod, M. (ed.) (1990). *Attention and Performance XIII: Motor Representation and Control.* Hillsdale, NJ: Lawrence Erlbaum.

———. (1990). *The Neural and Behavioral Organization of Goal-directed Movements.* New York: Oxford University Press.

Kelso, J. A. S. (ed.) (1982). *Human Motor Behavior.* Hillsdale, NJ: Lawrence Erlbaum.

Rosenbaum, D. A. (1991). *Human Motor Control.* New York: Academic Press.

Schmidt, R. A. (1988). *Motor Control and Learning: A Behavioral Emphasis,* 2nd ed. Champaign, IL: Human Kinetics.

THE ACQUISITION OF MOTOR SKILL

*A skilled response . . . means one in which receptor–effector–feedback
processes are highly organized, both spatially and temporally. The
central problem for the study of skill learning is how such organization
or patterning comes about.*

—P. M. Fitts, 1964

INTRODUCTION

In the previous chapter we examined the nature of
motor control. The performance of both simple
and complex movements was seen to depend on
hierarchically organized motor programs that are
selected and executed on the basis of environmental feedback. No mention was made of how
these programs are acquired or how people become highly skilled at perceptual–motor tasks.
Yet, in most human–machine systems, considerable skill is required for the operator to interact
with the machine efficiently and appropriately.

Many hours of training are needed before a typist,
surgeon, or athlete can perform at the required
level of proficiency.

The acquisition of motor skill is studied by
researchers interested in motor learning. Of concern is the way that movements are represented
and retained in memory, the role of feedback in
the acquisition of motor skill, the schedules of
practice and feedback that optimize learning, and
the relation to other types of skill. The findings
from studies in these areas have direct implications for the structuring of training programs and
the design of equipment for use in the workplace

(see Druckman & Swets, 1988, and Druckman & Bjork, 1991).

THEORIES OF MOTOR LEARNING

For the first half of the twentieth century, learning of skills, or procedural learning, was the primary topic of interest in psychology. Much detailed and carefully controlled research, conducted with rats and other laboratory animals, investigated many of the same issues that are of concern in motor learning (see Bower & Hilgard, 1981). This research was conducted from a behavioristic perspective that explained learning and performance in terms of the conditions of stimuli and responses. Some of the concepts from the behavioral theories of people like Edward Thorndike and Clark Hull were incorporated into accounts of motor learning (Adams, 1987; Salmoni, 1989). However, contemporary research in motor learning derives primarily from two information-processing theories proposed in the 1970s: Adams's (1971) *closed-loop theory* and Schmidt's (1975) *schema theory*. Although these theories have since been shown to be wrong in their details, their general features illustrate many of the issues and principles prominent in contemporary research on the learning of motor skills.

The primary contribution of Adams's (1971) closed-loop theory was its treatment of movement control as a closed-loop system in which sensory feedback is compared to a referent, with corrections made when the two deviate significantly. Adams restricted his theory to relatively slow, simple positioning movements of the type for which feedback can be used so that specific predictions could be developed. The theory proposed two types of memory, the memory trace and the perceptual trace, that are involved in motor learning and performance.

The memory trace is a simple motor program used to initiate the movement. The perceptual trace is activated at the beginning of a movement in anticipation of the resulting sensory feedback. It provides the referent for the closed-loop system against which the sensory feedback is compared as the movement is being made. If the feedback differs significantly from the referent, the movement is modified to eliminate the error. The distinction between two aspects of memory, one involved in movement initiation and the other involved in the evaluation of sensory feedback, is fundamental to contemporary views of motor learning.

Adams (1971) distinguished two phases of skill acquisition, called the verbal–motor and motor phases, that are similar to the cognitive and autonomous phases of Fitts's (1964) taxonomy. In the verbal–motor phase, a cognitive representation of the task is formed based on instructions and other situational factors. This representation will include such things as the goal of the task and the possible steps for achieving the goal, and performance of the movements will be mediated by verbal rehearsal. Because the perceptual trace is poorly defined, the performer needs to be provided with information about the success of the movement. This information must be provided by an external source, such as an instructor. The knowledge about the response outcome can be related to the response-produced sensory feedback to refine the perceptual trace. The importance of knowledge of results early in skill acquisition is another fundamental principle of motor learning.

When the task has been practiced to the point of highly accurate performance, the perceptual trace will be sufficiently vivid that the operator now knows what the sensory feedback should feel like. Verbal mediation is no longer required, and the movements can be executed efficiently and smoothly. At this point, learning is said to be in the motor phase. Knowledge of whether the goal of the action was achieved is no longer needed, because the correctness of any given response can be determined without such knowledge.

Closed-loop theory was a major advance in the study of motor learning, but it has several limitations (Schmidt, 1975). Because it was developed primarily for slow positioning movements, it does not make direct predictions for situations in which movements are fast or complicated. Also, because the theory relies on specific memory traces for each movement, it does not specify how a movement would be performed the first time or how a slight variation of a previously learned movement would be performed accurately, as is needed in open skills. Finally, because each movement has its own memory and perceptual traces, the number of traces that would have to be stored would be exceedingly large.

Schmidt (1975) proposed schema theory to overcome the limitations of closed-loop theory. At the heart of schema theory is the concept of the generalized motor program, introduced in Chapter 14. Recall that a generalized motor program is an abstract plan for controlling a specific class of movements. Accurate performance requires that the appropriate motor program be selected and that parameters such as force and timing be specified correctly. Parameter values are determined by motor schemas, or rules. The characteristics of each movement are related to the initial conditions prior to the movement, the sensory feedback during the movement, and the outcome of the movement. Two types of schemas are abstracted from this information when a class of similar movements is performed repeatedly.

When a response is to be produced, the initial conditions and outcome goal are used by a recall schema to select the response parameters for a generalized motor program. In addition, a recognition schema is generated that specifies the expected sensory consequences. The recall schema both initiates and controls a rapid movement. After the movement is completed, the actual sensory consequences can be compared against those expected from the recognition schema, and corrections to the recall schema can be made. For slow movements, comparison of feedback to the recognition schema occurs during the movement, and corrective movements are made when an error is detected. Because the schemas are abstract representations for classes of movements, experience with many movement variations within a class is necessary to produce precise, refined re-

call and recognition schemas. Hence, according to schema theory, practice with many variations of a movement class should lead to better performance of movements within that class than should practice with only a single instance of the class.

Although the closed-loop and schema theories differ in several respects, they share many features (Magill, 1989). They both assign a prominent role to sensory feedback, incorporate motor programs, have two memory traces (one involved in movement initiation and the other in evaluating feedback), consider feedback to be important during learning, and provide a means for error to be detected during or after execution of the movement. These general features are central to contemporary views of motor-skill acquisition.

MOTOR SHORT-TERM MEMORY

Both Adams's (1971) closed-loop theory and Schmidt's (1975) schema theory postulate memory representations that initiate and control movement. This requires that the appropriate movement plan be selected from those available in the long-term store and activated in a working short-term store. Feedback from the resulting movement and knowledge of the outcome must be coded and stored. This information must then be compared to the representation of the intended action and the movement plan revised accordingly. One might expect, then, that the way information is represented, retained, and operated on in working memory is of critical importance for motor learning (Marteniuk, 1976, 1986).

The nature of short-term memory representations has been addressed in research examining the retention of motor responses. The impetus for this research was the extensive study of verbal short-term memory that began in the late 1950s (see Chapter 9). Adams and Dijkstra (1966) were the first to demonstrate that movement information shows short-term forgetting similar to that shown for verbal materials. Blindfolded people made a linear positioning movement to a stop and returned to the starting location. After a variable delay of 5 to 120 s, during which the stop was removed, they were to move to the target position. As shown in Figure 15–1, accuracy decreased for delays of up to 80 s, with the maximum decrease occurring during the first 30 s.

One concern in short-term motor memory tasks has been with what the person remembers. When the start position is the same for each trial, the target location (movement end point) and the distance of the movement (movement extent) are confounded. Consequently, recall could be based on memory of the correct position or of the distance that the limb was programmed to move. Laabs (1973) unconfounded these by changing the starting position for the reproduction after the performance of the movement to be remembered. In one condition, the person was to move to the

final position of the prior movement, whereas in the other condition the person was to move the distance of the prior movement. Location recall was much better than distance recall, suggesting that memory was based on the final location. Other studies have shown that, although location is more memorable, distance may be used when the movement to be remembered is short (30 cm or less; Wrisberg & Winter, 1985).

Forgetting occurs during retention intervals in which no other movements are made (Adams & Dijkstra, 1966). This suggests that the forgetting may be caused by decay and/or proactive interference. Recall that proactive interference is the term used to describe forgetting of new information caused by remembering prior information. Evidence for proactive interference was given by a study that used methods for motor memory similar to those used for verbal short-term memory. Leavitt, Lee, and Romanow (1980) presented people with a target distance or target location in a task that required linear movement of a handle. Recall decreased as the number of prior movements increased from zero to five. However, when the criterion for successful movement was switched from distance to location, or vice versa, on the sixth trial, performance returned to the initial level of accuracy. This is similar to the improved memory performance for verbal materials observed when the categories of items to be remembered are changed (Wickens, 1972).

Retroactive interference (that is, forgetting caused by subsequent information) can be evaluated by requiring the performance of additional movements during the retention interval. Such interference effects are obtained, but they are relatively subtle. The effects show up as a constant biasing away from the target location (constant error), as well as in increased variability around the movement end point (Pepper & Herman, 1970; Stelmach, 1974). Marteniuk (1986) proposed that substantial interference occurs in motor learning when the intervening task requires that an additional action plan, whether motor or nonmotor, be kept active in working memory.

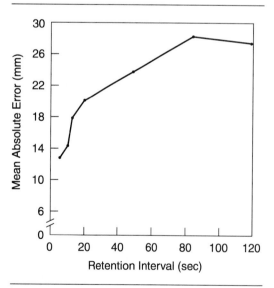

FIGURE 15–1   Short-term Forgetting in a Motor Memory Task.

From J. A. Adams & S. Dijkstra (1966). Short-term memory for motor responses. *Journal of Experimental Psychology, 71,* 314–318. Copyright © 1966 by the American Psychological Association. Reprinted by permission.

This again suggests that considerable cognitive information processing is involved in the early stages of motor-skill acquisition.

PRACTICE AND TRAINING

The goal of training routines for motor skills is to provide more than acquisition of the skill. They also must promote long-term retention and transfer to a range of related situations. There are many ways that specific motor skills can be taught effectively. However, not all these methods will necessarily result in the same amount of learning for the same amount of training. Consequently, a lot of effort has been invested in research to determine how practice should be structured to optimize performance and minimize training time.

Despite the fact that long-term retention of skill is the primary goal of training, training procedures are often evaluated by the amount of practice required to attain a criterion level of performance and not how long that level can be maintained. The level of performance reached during training can be influenced by many other factors and does not always indicate the amount of learning that has occurred. Thus, learning variables, which make a relatively permanent change on behavior, need to be distinguished from performance variables, which only temporarily affect performance. For example, performance may deteriorate toward the end of a long and difficult practice session due to fatigue, but be better once the performer is no longer fatigued.

Learning can be demonstrated by showing improved performance under different training conditions on retention trials, for which performance of the motor skill is tested following a delay. Another dimension of learning is the ability to perform new tasks that are related to but different from the tasks that were practiced. Transfer trials, in which performance is tested under new conditions, can be used to evaluate this dimension of learning. Training programs should be evaluated by the degree of retention and transfer that they engender.

Retention

The rate at which a motor skill is acquired, as indicated by retention tests, is greatly influenced by the amount and distribution of practice. Because the instructor has control over the scheduling and structure of practice in most training environments, it is possible to structure training sessions to optimize retention.

Amount of Practice. The amount of learning typically will increase with the amount of practice. One way to increase the amount of practice, and hence the long-term retention of a skill, is to make the level of acceptable performance more difficult. After the acceptable level has been attained, continued practice (often called overlearning) may lead to better retention of the skill. That is, even though performance may be close to perfect in terms of the level of skill, there is still opportunity for learning.

Schendel and Hagman (1982) illustrated this fact in an experiment in which soldiers were required to disassemble and assemble an M60 machine gun. Three groups of soldiers were required to perform both disassembly and assembly to the criterion of one errorless execution. The control group received no further training and was retested following an 8-week retention interval. The two other groups received overtraining; soldiers in these groups performed additional assemblies equal in number to that required to achieve the first errorless execution. For one group, the overtraining was part of the initial training, whereas for the other group it was received 4 weeks later, midway between the initial learning and the retention test. Regardless of when the overtraining was received, it led to better performance on the first trial of the retention session, as well as to better performance overall in the session. The authors conclude that although overtraining seems excessive and wasteful, it is an effective way to ensure that skills are remembered.

Fatigue and Practice. Practicing motor tasks is physically fatiguing. Consequently, an important issue is whether practice is as effective when the learner is fatigued. Fatigue clearly has a detrimental effect on the performance of a variety of laboratory tasks during motor skill acquisition (Pack, Cotten & Biasiotto, 1974; Williams & Singer, 1975). The effect on learning is not as severe. Several studies in which fatigue was induced prior to practice report no deficit when learning is measured under nonfatigued conditions in a later retention session (Cotten et al., 1972; Heitman, Stockton, & Lambert, 1987). However, other studies have shown some deficit in learning (for example, Carron, 1972; Pack, Cotten, & Biasiotto, 1974).

As one example, Godwin and Schmidt (1971) had people perform a task that involved rotating a handle in a clockwise direction, then rotating it in a counterclockwise direction, and finally knocking down a wooden barrier. On the first day, people in a fatigued group had to turn a hand-crank ergometer for 2 min before each trial on which the task was performed. People in a nonfatigued group performed tapping before each trial. The fatigued group performed the movement task more slowly than the nonfatigued group (see Figure 15–2). However, when both groups were tested after a three-day rest without first performing the fatiguing tasks, there was only a small difference in performance. This difference was eliminated by the fourth retention trial, indicating that fatigue had relatively little effect on learning.

It is likely that the effects of fatigue on learning are greater at higher levels of fatigue. Pack, Cotten, and Biasiotto (1974) demonstrated such an interaction of fatigue level with learning. They had people perform a ladder-climbing task that required maintenance of balance. Three levels of fatigue were induced for different groups by requiring strenuous exercise to maintain the heart rate at 120, 150, or 180 beats/s between trials. The groups with the two highest heart rates showed a performance decrement on a subsequent retention task, while the group with the lowest heart rate did not. One reason why high levels of fatigue may impair learning is that it

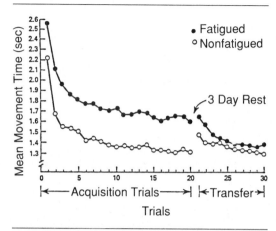

FIGURE 15–2 Effect of Fatigue on Initial Performance and Learning.

From M. A. Godwin & R. A. Schmidt, Muscular fatigue and discrete motor learning. This article is reprinted with permission from the *Research Quarterly for Exercise and Sport,* vol. 42, 1971, pp. 374–383. The *Research Quarterly for Exercise and Sport* is a publication of the American Alliance for Health, Physical Education, Recreation and Dance, 1900 Association Drive, Reston, VA 22091.

becomes difficult to maintain attention on the task at hand.

Distribution of Practice. Distribution of practice refers to the influence that scheduling of practice sessions and work periods has on learning. Beginning in the 1930s, considerable effort has been devoted to determining whether massed or distributed practice produces superior learning of motor skills. With *massed practice,* the performer practices continuously for an extended period, whereas with *distributed practice,* rest intervals are interspersed between trials. A related issue, similar to that examined in the study by Schendel and Hagman (1982) described earlier, is whether it is better to have fewer, longer sessions of practice or more, but shorter sessions.

The research on the distribution of practice illustrates the learning–performance distinction made earlier. Massed practice often produces substantially poorer performance than distributed practice during initial acquisition. For example, Lorge (1930) found that people performed best with distributed practice when learning to trace a star by watching their movements in a mirror. It cannot be determined from performance on the acquisition trials alone whether the difference between distributed and massed practice reflects differences in learning or a temporary degradation in performance during massed practice. Lorge shifted a group of people from distributed to massed practice midway through training, and their performance dropped to the level of the people who had received massed practice all along. This finding suggests that the distribution variable was only temporarily affecting performance.

The issue of whether massed practice results in poorer learning than distributed practice has not yet been settled. One reason for this is that there are several possible measures of learning, and it is difficult to know which is the best to use. Recently, Lee and Genovese (1988) reviewed the literature on distribution of practice using a technique called meta-analysis, which is a statistical evaluation of the combined results of many studies. Their conclusion was that massed practice depresses learning in motor tasks that require continuous movements, although its effect on learning is much less than its effect on performance during practice.

Lee and Genovese (1988) found only one study that used a task with discrete movements. Carron (1969) had people pick a dowel out of a hole, reverse the ends of the dowel, and put it back in the hole. In contrast to the studies using continuous tasks, Carron found that massed practice produced better retention of this task than did distributed practice. Lee and Genovese (1989) replicated this result using a timing task in which a stylus was to be moved between two metal plates in as close to 500 ms as possible. In a continuous version of the task, in which 20 timing estimates were performed in succession (moving back and forth between the plates), they found the opposite result; distributed practice produced better retention. Because movement decisions and

evaluations are made during the performance of continuous tasks, but not until after the performance of discrete tasks, Lee and Genovese (1989) concluded that distributed practice interferes with the decision-making process that occurs between trials of a discrete task.

In short, massed practice often produces substantially poorer performance during acquisition but only slightly poorer retention. Also, whether massed or distributed practice is most beneficial for learning depends on whether the task is continuous or discrete. Distributed practice tends to be better for continuous tasks, whereas massed practice tends to be better for discrete tasks.

Mental Practice.   Since the 1930s, there also has been considerable interest in the question of whether mental practice can facilitate the acquisition of motor skill. Such practice typically is thought to involve mentally imaging the execution of the desired action (for example, putting a golf ball into a hole) and, possibly, rehearsal of strategies for performing the task. In the typical experiment, four conditions of learning are tested (Druckman & Swets, 1988). One group of performers receives physical practice on the task, and a second group is instructed to mentally practice the task for the same amount of time. The remaining two groups are a control group that receives no practice and a group that receives both physical and mental practice. The specific types of skills examined and the conditions under which they are acquired have varied greatly across studies.

Feltz and Landers (1983) reviewed the literature on mental practice using meta-analysis. The analysis showed a reliable benefit of mental practice relative to no practice; performance was usually better when mental practice had been used than when it had not. Hence, they concluded that mental practice does have beneficial effects, as have other authors (Annett, 1985; Druckman & Swets, 1988; Richardson, 1967a & b).

Most motor skills involve a cognitive–symbolic component, as well as a motor component. One theory attributes the benefits of mental practice to rehearsal of the symbolic components of the task (Sackett, 1934). Another theory attributes the benefits to the motor component, by assuming that the same neuromuscular patterns of activity are generated during mental practice as during physical practice; they are just reduced in magnitude (Jacobson, 1932). At least two implications of these theories can be used to test between them. The cognitive theory predicts that mental practice should be more beneficial for motor tasks that have a large cognitive component (for example, card sorting) than for those that do not (for example, a repetitive tapping task), whereas the motor theory predicts no such relation. Feltz and Landers's (1983) meta-analysis showed reliably better performance with mental practice of tasks with larger cognitive components, supporting the cognitive theory.

The second testable implication is that the motor theory predicts that the benefits of mental practice will be restricted to the specific movements practiced, whereas the cognitive theory predicts no such relation. Annett (1985) summarizes results showing that the movements are not crucial. For example, MacKay (1981) had bilingual persons read sentences in German or English as rapidly as possible. Silent reading (mental practice) not only produced a benefit for overt reading time, but it produced significantly greater transfer to translations of the practice sentences than did physical practice. In other words, the benefits of mental practice were not dependent on the specific patterns of muscular activity that would be required to read the sentences. The primary benefit of mental practice apparently is to allow rehearsal of the cognitive components of the practiced task.

Given that the initial phase of skill acquisition is presumed to involve the most cognitive mediation (Fitts, 1964), we might expect that mental practice would be most beneficial early in skill acquisition. Alternatively, there is a possibility that some familiarity with the task is needed, so that the maximal benefit should occur later in practice (Weinberg, 1981). Feltz and Landers's (1983) meta-analysis did not favor either of these

alternatives, showing no significant difference between benefits from early and late mental practice. Although mental practice has an effect both early and late, different processes may be affected.

Performance is best when mental practice is combined with physical practice (Druckman & Swets, 1988). Mental practice apparently assists in the structuring of higher-level movement plans, not in the lower-level components. An optimal training routine will likely use some combination of mental and physical practice. There are several benefits to allocating a portion of training to mental practice, including no need for equipment, no physical fatigue, and no danger.

Transfer

Whenever the performance of a new task is affected by skills that are already established, transfer has occurred. Transfer is of special concern within human factors, because training environments are often not identical to the environments in which the skills must be performed. Also, an operator may perform in several different but related environments, and it is important to know the extent to which transfer will occur. Ideally, training should produce positive transfer, for which performance is facilitated, and no negative transfer, for which performance is inhibited.

The only situations that produce significant negative transfer are ones in which previously learned stimulus–response relations are reassigned so that stimuli that required one response now require another. Lewis, McAllister, and Adams (1951) obtained negative transfer in a complex task where a two-dimensional joystick was manipulated by hand and a rudder was controlled by the feet. A pattern of three stimulus lights indicated the positions to which the controls were to be set. When set properly, a new pattern appeared that required new control settings. People first learned a reversed control–display relation in which the location of the stimulus was opposite the location for the control setting. Performance was considerably poorer when they were then transferred from the reversed to a standard, direct display–control relation, with the amount of negative transfer being an increasing function of the amount of original learning.

One implication of this finding is that changes between stimulus and response sets when a relationship has already been learned should be avoided. You may remember that this same point was evident in the studies showing a need for consistent mapping in search tasks (see Chapter 12; Schneider & Shiffrin, 1977). Yet, significant violations of this principle occur in practice, as in two control rooms at the Dresden Nuclear Power Plant that are mirror reversals of each other (Kantowitz, 1982).

Because negative transfer rarely occurs in most situations, motor skill research has focused primarily on positive transfer. Just as with cognitive skills, positive transfer of motor skills is limited (Schmidt & Young, 1987). When positive transfer occurs, its magnitude is usually small. Moreover, the extent of positive transfer decreases rapidly as the similarity between the original task and the new task decreases. The relatively limited positive transfer that occurs for motor skills is consistent with an identical elements, procedural view of the type described for cognitive skills in Chapter 12, as well as with the view that motor learning is specific to classes of similar actions.

Variability of Practice. One factor that influences transfer is the *variability of practice*. This refers to the extent to which the movements required for each practice trial differ. When the same movement is performed on each trial, there is little variability, as compared to when two or more distinct movements are performed on different trials. Variability of practice has been investigated extensively, because Schmidt's (1975) schema theory predicts that variability should enhance learning. According to schema theory, variable practice produces a stronger recall schema when a new version of the movement task is encountered. This will enable appropriate response specifications to be better determined.

The procedure used to investigate variability can be illustrated by an experiment conducted by Lee, Magill, and Weeks (1985). People performed a two-part timed-movement task in which an arm movement was made from a microswitch pressed by a finger to a barrier that was to be knocked down and then to a second barrier. Desired movement times were specified for each of the two submovements. Four pairs of times were used during practice: 300–700, 400–600, 600–300, and 700–400; the first number in each pair refers to the time to execute the first movement (in milliseconds) and the second number to the time to execute the second movement. People who received variable practice performed 15 trials with each of the four pairs, randomly intermixed (the random group). People who did not receive variable practice performed 60 practice trials with only one of the pairs of movement times (the constant group). Following the acquisition phase, they were tested with new times (500–500 and 800–800).

Schema theory predicts that the persons who received variable practice should perform better on the test movements than those who did not. Lee, Magill, and Weeks's (1985) results supported this prediction (see Figure 15–3). The finding of enhanced performance following variable practice has been obtained for both children and adults with many types of movement tasks (Shapiro & Schmidt, 1982). There are some exceptions, however, particularly for adults.

Lee, Magill, and Weeks (1985) noted that most previous studies that failed to find a benefit for variable practice used a blocked presentation procedure in which the different types of movements were grouped together within a block. Consequently, they also tested people who received variable practice but with blocks in which 15 trials for one set of criterion times were presented, then 15 trials for another, and so on (the blocked group). These people showed no better performance on the test trials than those people who practiced with only one set of criterion times (see Figure 15–3). Thus, variable practice is beneficial primarily when the criterion move-

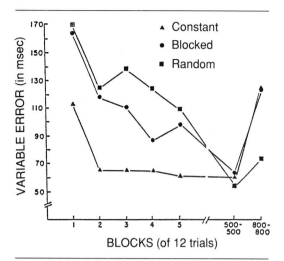

FIGURE 15–3 Accuracy of Movement Time for Constant, Blocked, and Random Practice.

From T. D. Lee, R. A. Magill, & D. J. Weeks (1985). Influence of practice schedule on testing schema theory predictions in adults. *Journal of Motor Behavior, 17,* 283–299. Reprinted with permission of the Helen Dwight Reid Educational Foundation. Published by Heldref Publications, 1319 Eighteenth St., N. W., Washington, D. C. 20036-1802. Copyright © 1985.

Shea and Morgan (1979) were the first to apply this concept to motor learning. At the onset of a stimulus light, performers were required to knock down three of six barriers in a specified order as quickly as possible. Three different versions of the task were performed during acquisition that differed in the barriers that were to be knocked down. Three sets of 18 acquisition trials were administered. For half of the performers, each set contained one of the barrier orders, whereas for the other half the three orders were randomly intermixed within each set. Half of the performers in each group were tested with 18 retention trials after a 10-min delay or a 10-day delay. Nine of the retention trials were administered in a blocked sequence and nine in a random sequence. Although performance during acquisition was consistently faster for the blocked group, performance at both retention intervals was faster for the random group, particularly when the contextual conditions were different from those under which learning occurred (see Figure 15–4).

Shea and Morgan (1979) interpreted the contextual interference effect in terms of an elabora-

ment changes from trial to trial. This influence of the organization of variable practice is not predicted by schema theory.

Performance differences arising from differences with practice schedules are consistent with the concept of *contextual interference* introduced by Battig (1979) to explain verbal learning performance. According to this concept, an item on a to-be-remembered list will be subjected to interference produced by the context of other items on the list. This contextual interference will be minimal when other items do not intervene between repetitions of an item and will be maximal when they do. According to Battig, low contextual interference allows acquisition requirements to be satisfied with little processing, but this processing may not be enough for retention. Conversely, maximal contextual interference should produce difficulty in the acquisition phase, but good retention.

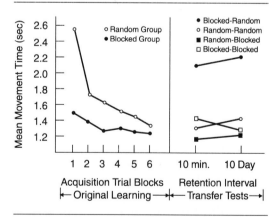

FIGURE 15–4 Performance During Acquisition and Retention in a Barrier Knock-down Task.

From J. B. Shea & R. L. Morgan (1979). Contextual interference effects on acquisition, retention, and transfer of a motor skill. *Journal of Experimental Psychology: Human Learning and Memory, 5,* 179–187. Copyright © 1979 by the American Psychological Association. Reprinted by permission.

tion–distinctiveness theory. According to this account, random practice promotes more elaborative and distinctive processing. Lee and Magill (1985) proposed instead that, when memory for the action is readily available in working memory, the processing activities will not have to be reconstructed. Because this reconstruction process is critical to retention and transfer, practice without reconstruction will not be as beneficial as practice with reconstruction.

Lee and Magill (1983, 1985) replicated the procedure of Shea and Morgan, but added a serial group in which the three different tasks were practiced in a consistently rotating fashion. They reasoned that this group should have moderate contextual interference, if Shea and Morgan's account were correct, because the serial schedule had some predictability but was not simply repetitive. In contrast, the intervening trials in the serial condition should require that the processing activities be reconstructed each time, as does the random schedule. The serial group performed just as fast on the retention test as the random group, supporting the hypothesis that retention will be better when each performance of the movement must be reconstructed from long-term memory.

Traditionally, repetitive drill-type training has been used to teach motor skills. Although such training works, the studies we have reviewed suggest that learning and retention of the skills can be improved significantly by varying the routine. To be most effective, this variability needs to be on a trial to trial basis. The primary principle underlying the effects of variability of practice and contextual interference is that of transfer-appropriate processing (Morris, Bransford, & Franks, 1977), which was introduced in Chapter 10. Randomized conditions of practice induce processing that produces more elaborate mental representations. These representations can then be transferred more readily to situations encountered after training that differ from those in which the original training occurred.

Bilateral Transfer. Bilateral transfer refers to a benefit in performing a task with one hand (or

foot) that occurs from having practiced the task with the other hand (or foot). Bilateral transfer has been demonstrated in numerous studies (Ammons, 1958). For example, although handwriting is typically performed with the dominant hand, considerable transfer is evident when a person is required to write with the nondominant hand.

There are two possible bases for bilateral transfer (Magill, 1989). A cognitive explanation is that the two tasks are the same except for the specific movements that must be made. These identical nonmotoric elements are likely of primary importance in tasks that have a large cognitive component, such as figure reproduction.

An alternative explanation arises from the concept of the generalized motor program. Generalized programs are presumed not to include the specific muscles required to produce an action. Instead, the muscles are parameters that are specified when the action is to be executed with a particular limb. The fact that bilateral transfer also occurs in tasks that are more purely motoric suggests that both cognitive and motoric factors are involved (Schmidt & Young, 1987).

Part–Whole Transfer. The operator of a human–machine system typically has to perform a complex task composed of many subtasks. The issue of *part–whole transfer* involves the question of whether performance of the whole task can be taught by teaching how to perform the subtasks. From a practical standpoint, there are many reasons why part training might be preferable. For example, Adams (1987) notes that (1) whole-task simulators are complex and expensive; (2) subtasks critical to successful performance of the whole task may receive relatively little practice in the whole-task situation; (3) experienced operators could be trained more efficiently on only the new subtasks required for a new machine or task, rather than repeating an extensive training routine; and (4) relatively simple training devices could be used to maintain essential skills.

Part–whole transfer is greatest when a task is composed of a series of movements, each of which is of relatively long duration (Schmidt & Young, 1987). Such tasks can be broken into subtasks in three ways (Wightman & Lintern, 1985). Segmentation can be used for tasks that are composed of successive subtasks. The subtasks can be performed in isolation or in groups and then recombined into the whole task. Fractionation is similar to segmentation, but is applicable to tasks in which two or more subtasks are performed simultaneously. This procedure involves separate performance for each subtask before combining them. Finally, simplification is a procedure used to make a difficult task easier by simplifying some aspect of the task. It is more applicable to tasks for which there are no clear subtasks.

When the use of the part method seems appropriate, it is important to plan how the components will be reassembled into the whole task once they have been individually mastered. Three schedules have been identified for part-task training (Wightman & Lintern, 1985). With a pure-part schedule, all parts are practiced in isolation before being combined in the whole task. With a repetitive-part schedule, subtasks are presented in a predetermined sequence and progressively combined with other components as they are mastered. A progressive-part schedule is similar to the repetitive-part schedule, but each part receives practice in isolation before being added to the preceding subtasks. In certain circumstances, the whole task may be presented initially to identify the difficult components. After identification, the part method is then used to practice those components.

No single method of training is best for all situations. Part-task training is most beneficial for complex tasks composed of a series of subtasks of relatively long duration. For example, Adams and Hufford (1962) found that part-task training on a complex flight maneuver produced positive transfer to the whole flying task. Tasks that are fast and simple or relatively continuous show little part–whole transfer. Segmentation and fractionation tend to be more effective than the simplification method. Regardless of whether part-task training is better than whole-task training, there almost always is at least some positive transfer from the parts to the whole task.

Training with Simulators

The issue of transfer is of particular concern in the design and use of military and industrial simulator training devices (Baudhuin, 1987), such as those used to train pilots. Simulators are used for situations in which it is not feasible to have operators train in the real system. The goal of simulator training is to provide the greatest amount of overlap with, and hence the greatest amount of transfer to, the operational system that is being simulated. If training on a simulator transfers to the operational system, then money can be saved that would have been spent for the operation of the system itself. Moreover, the risk of physical harm and damage to the real system can be minimized. A "crash" in a flight simulator causes no real harm.

A major issue in simulator design involves the fidelity of the simulation to the real operational system. Designers often assume that physical similarity is important and that the physical characteristics of the simulator should closely resemble those of the real system. For example, the Unit Conduct-of-Fire Trainer (UCOFT) used by the U.S. Army is an elaborate tank-gunnery training device. It includes a complete mock-up of the tank interior. The crew is provided with video displays showing the terrain and with complete and functional instrumentation. Flight simulators are similarly designed to be of high fidelity.

However, it was emphasized previously that positive transfer occurs when the functional procedures are the same, even if the specific stimulus and response elements are not identical. Given the cost of high-fidelity simulation, along with the technological limitations that prevent perfect resemblance in certain situations, it is more appropriate to emphasize *functional equivalence* (Baudhuin, 1987). This is the equivalence between the specific tasks that the operator will be required to perform in the simulated and real systems. Because the procedures acquired with practice pertain to specific skills, the important characteristic for good transfer is that the simulator be functionally equivalent to the simulated system.

With the development of relatively low cost computer-generated image systems, it has become easy to present a large number of different displays that are not of extremely high fidelity. There are benefits to using displays of this type for devices such as flight trainers, because a virtually unlimited number of scenarios can be easily created. In contrast, if only high-fidelity films of real-life situations are used, the number of possible scenarios presentable to the operator will be limited. Studies have shown that positive transfer from computer-generated displays to operational systems does occur (for example, Rockway & Nullmeyer, 1984). High fidelity is not a necessary requirement for transfer. The degree of fidelity needed for a simulator will depend on the specific skills that are being trained.

FEEDBACK AND SKILL ACQUISITION

When a person executes an action, many sources of sensory feedback are available both during task performance (concurrent feedback) and on completion (terminal feedback). Such intrinsic sources of feedback can be used for ongoing control of movements, as described in the last chapter; they also provide a basis for the learning of motor skill (for example, Mulder & Hulstijn, 1985). Because learning solely on the basis of intrinsic feedback typically is slow, some form of augmented feedback that provides information not inherent in the performance of the task is often provided. Augmented feedback regarding the success of the action *(knowledge of results)* must be distinguished from augmented feedback regarding the performance itself *(knowledge of performance)*.

Knowledge of Results

Augmented feedback presented at the end of a movement that specifies the degree of success in achieving the desired goal of a performed action is called knowledge of results (KR). Such feedback can be provided by an instructor or by an automated device. For example, a flight instructor may tell a student whether or not the goal of a particular maneuver was accomplished, or a flight simulator may indicate whether a landing was accomplished safely. Virtually any provision of KR facilitates both the initial performance of a motor-learning task and its subsequent retention (Newell, 1976; Salmoni, Schmidt, & Walter, 1984). However, the presentation of KR can be varied in many ways, and some forms of presentation are better than others. Research has focused on the effects of the frequency, delay, and precision of KR.

Frequency of KR. Both Adams's (1971) closed-loop theory and Schmidt's (1975) schema theory predict that KR should be most beneficial when it is given on every trial, with such benefits decreasing as the percentage of trials on which KR is given decreases. This is true for performance during the acquisition phase of tasks (Salmoni, Schmidt, & Walter, 1984). However, more KR results in poorer retention of a skill, suggesting that less KR may produce better learning.

Winstein and Schmidt (1990) had people learn to produce a lever-movement pattern. This pattern consisted of four movement segments (trajectories and reversal points) that were to be produced in 800 ms. KR could be provided on a computer terminal by superimposing the temporal–spatial movement function with that of the goal movement. One group of people (100% condition) received KR after each trial in two acquisition sessions. The other group (50% condition) received KR on only half the trials, and the proportion gradually reduced from 100% early in each session to 25% later in the session. Performance was equivalent for the two conditions during acquisition, but was substantially better for the 50% condition on a delayed retention test. Wulf and Schmidt (1989) obtained comparable results for a task that required learning of classes of actions involving the same temporal structure.

The fact that learning is better when KR is not provided for every trial suggests that it might be effective to provide summary KR for which feedback about sets of trials is not presented until the set is completed. This suggestion has been confirmed in several experiments (Lavery, 1962; Schmidt et al., 1989). Schmidt et al. had people learn a timed lever-movement task similar to that used by Winstein and Schmidt (1990). Summary KR was provided after sets of 1, 5, 10, or 15 trials. All groups improved during the acquisition phase, with performance being a decreasing function of the length of the set (see Figure 15–5). However, a delayed retention test showed an inverse relation between the length of the set and accuracy. Learning was best when summary KR was given every 15 trials and worst when KR was provided every trial.

Delay of KR.   The intertrial interval can be divided into two parts, the delay between comple-

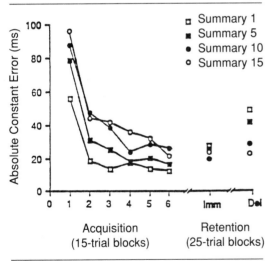

FIGURE 15–5   Effects of Summary Knowledge-of-results.

From R. A. Schmidt et al. (1989). Summary knowledge of results for skill acquisition: Support for the guidance hypothesis. *Journal of Experimental Psychology: Learning, Memory, and Cognition, 15,* 352–359. Copyright © 1989 by the American Psychological Association. Reprinted by permission.

tion of the trial and KR (KR delay) and the post-KR delay until the next trial. Studies generally have shown that the length of the KR delay is of little importance (Salmoni, Schmidt, & Walter, 1984), unless the KR is provided immediately. Swinnen et al. (1990) reported evidence that very short KR delays may interfere with learning. In one experiment, people performed a timing task, with two reversals of direction, for which the goal movement duration was 1 s. The intertrial interval for all people was 13 s, with half of them receiving KR about the actual movement duration instantaneously and half after an 8-s KR delay. A delayed retention test showed that learning was poorer with the instantaneous KR than with the delayed KR. Swinnen et al. interpreted their results as indicating that people actively evaluate intrinsic feedback after performance, resulting in the acquisition of error-detection capabilities. Presenting KR immediately interferes with this process.

The importance of information-processing activities during the KR delay interval is also indicated in findings by Swinnen (1990). He required an attention-demanding secondary task to be performed during the KR delay. This task interfered with learning, because retention performance declined for the primary motor task. Less interference was observed when the secondary task was performed after KR and before the next trial, indicating that processing during the KR delay is critical. Marteniuk (1986) similarly showed that an interpolated movement during the KR delay interval produced interference only when it also had to be remembered. Moreover, an intervening number solving problem produced the same magnitude of interference, indicating that higher-level cognitive activity during the KR delay is crucial.

Precision of KR.   The issue of KR precision involves the extent to which exact feedback enhances learning. A distinction can be made between qualitative KR that provides general information about the quality of performance (for example, correct or incorrect) and quantitative

KR that specifies the direction and magnitude of error. Typically, quantitative KR produces better performance than qualitative KR, but few studies have evaluated learning with a retention test (Salmoni, Schmidt, & Walter, 1984).

Recent experiments by Magill and Wood (1986) and Reeve, Dornier, and Weeks (1990) have included retention tests. In both studies, people who received quantitative KR performed better on the retention trials than people who did not. This result occurred even when both groups performed equally well during acquisition.

Role of KR. There has been considerable debate over the role of KR in motor learning. Three major roles have been proposed (Salmoni, Schmidt, & Walter, 1984). A motivational role of KR may affect performance, with more effort being exerted when KR is present than when it is not. A second role of KR may be to form associations. For example, in schema theory, KR forms associations between stimulus and response features to create recall and recognition schemas. A final role may be that KR provides guidance. In other words, it directs performance during acquisition.

Clearly, to learn a motor skill requires that the learner be engaged in active processing of the information that is contained in KR. Provision of KR during training is more beneficial if the KR is precise and if competing tasks do not have to be performed during the time that it is being evaluated. Moreover, with frequent KR the learner may rely on the guidance provided by KR and fail to engage in the information-processing activities necessary to acquire the skill. Hence, KR should not be provided continuously throughout training. In short, KR will be useful to the extent that it engenders processing appropriate to the enhancement of the skill.

Knowledge of Performance

The second form of augmented feedback is called knowledge of performance, or KP (Gentile, 1972). Whereas KR provides only information about the outcome of the movement, KP provides information about the performance of the movement. Some researchers have proposed that KP should be more potent than KR, because KP provides information about the way in which the movement is controlled and coordinated (Newell, Sparrow, & Quinn, 1985; Newell & Walter, 1981). A distinction can be made between kinematic KP, which describes some aspect of the motions involved in an action, and kinetic KP, which describes the forces that produce those motions. For both types of KP, people are typically shown information pertaining to movements on the preceding trial, with the pattern of a successful movement sometimes presented for comparison.

Kinematic KP involves measures such as the spatial position, velocity, and acceleration of the limbs. One of the earliest studies to use kinematic KP was that of Lindahl (1945). He studied the foot actions of operators who were cutting discs from tungsten rods. The disc cutoff machine was operated through a coordinated pattern of hand and foot actions. Lindahl noted that the foot movements used, in particular, determined the cutting efficiency and the quality of the discs. He recorded the foot actions of skilled machine operators (see Figure 15–6a) and used these records to train new operators. Providing new operators with the knowledge of their own foot actions in relation to those of the skilled operators facilitated learning (see Figure 15–6b) and reduced training time. This kinematic KP also improved the performance of more experienced operators.

Schmidt and Young (1991) emphasized that two difficulties complicate the interpretation of existing research on kinematic feedback. Studies typically fail to separate learning and performance, and the movement goal and kinematic pattern are often the same. Schmidt and Young examined kinematic feedback with a coincident-timing task that allowed separation of the goal from the movements required to produce it. As shown in Figure 15–7, sequentially illuminating a series of light-emitting diodes produces the impression of a moving ball. The performer grasps

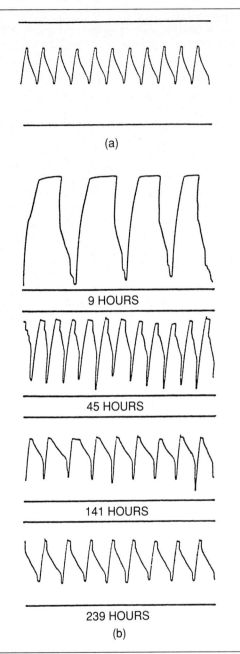

(a)

9 HOURS

45 HOURS

141 HOURS

239 HOURS

(b)

FIGURE 15–6 Foot Action Patterns for (a) an Expert Operator and (b) a New Operator After Various Amounts of Practice with Kinematic KP.

From L. G. Lindahl (1945). Movement analysis as an industrial training method. *Journal of Applied Psychology, 29,* 420–436.

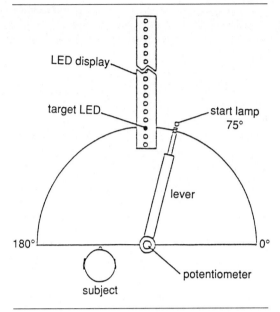

FIGURE 15–7 Schematic Diagram of the Coincident-timing Apparatus Used by Schmidt and Young.

From R. A. Schmidt & D. E. Young (1991). Methodology for motor learning: A paradigm for kinematic feedback. *Journal of Motor Behavior, 23,* 13–24. Reprinted with permission of the Helen Dwight Reid Educational Foundation. Published by Heldref Publications, 1319 Eighteenth St., N. W., Washington, D.C. 20036-1802. Copyright © 1991.

the vertical handle of a horizontally mounted lever. When the light begins to move, a back-swing anywhere to the left of the lights is to be made, followed by a forward swing to intercept the moving object. This task, which is much like batting a ball, only minimally constrains the actions that can be used, because the forward swing can be begun at any time.

Schmidt and Young (1991) determined that the best performance was associated with back-swings to a position of approximately 165°. Hence, they tested people who were provided either only KR about the accuracy of the intercept or the KR plus KP about the maximum amplitude of the backswing. The people who also received KP performed better during acquisition and during a subsequent retention test where kinematic feedback was not provided.

Because muscular forces and their durations are a product of the central mechanisms thought to underlie the control of action, kinetic KP might enhance skill learning. Isometric tasks that require pressure against immovable objects should benefit from kinetic KP because such tasks, which have many military and industrial applications, are defined by kinetic variables. The first evidence that kinetic KP improves performance in isometric tasks came from an experiment reported by English (1942). New military recruits were being taught to shoot a rifle. Good marksmanship requires that the stock of the rifle be squeezed simultaneously with the trigger. The soldiers were experiencing difficulty learning this technique. A new training method was implemented to provide kinetic feedback. The stock of the rifle was hollowed, and a fluid-filled bulb was placed within it. The bulb was attached to a fluid-filled tube that displayed the amount of force applied to the stock. The soldier could compare the level of the liquid in the tube when he shot the rifle to the level produced by an expert marksman. This method was remarkably effective, with even soldiers "given up as hopeless" achieving minimum standards quickly.

More recently, Newell, Sparrow, and Quinn (1985) examined kinetic KP in two experiments that had different criteria. In one, the task was to produce a peak force of 30 N against an immovable handle, whereas in the other it was to produce a specific force–time curve. Kinetic KP was provided in the form of the force–time curve for the trial that was just completed. This feedback improved both initial performance and retention for the task with the force–time criterion, but not for the task with the peak-force criterion.

Newell and Carlton (1987) evaluated whether generation of a force–time curve benefits from the superimposition of the desired curve on the feedback curve. For one experiment, the desired curve was a symmetric, normal curve. Superimposition of this curve on the feedback curve did not affect performance. However, in another

experiment, the desired curve was an asymmetric curve with which the performers would not be familiar. In this case, performance was improved by providing the curve with feedback.

There is some evidence that videotape replay can provide an effective medium for presentation of KP (Newell & Walter, 1981; Rothstein & Arnold, 1976). However, it is conceivable that the tape provides too much information, serving to confuse rather than clarify what is required for successful performance. One indication of such information overload is that videotape replay tends to be more effective when cues are provided to assist the learner in attending to specific aspects of his or her performance. The general principle emerging from the work of Newell and his colleagues is that the success of any type of augmented feedback depends on the extent to which it provides information that pertains to the task at hand. Hence, in deciding what types of KR or KP to provide, it is necessary to analyze in detail the requirements of the task.

Observational Learning

Another way to learn how to perform a motor task is to observe someone else (a model) performing it. Most research on *observational learning* has arisen from Bandura's (1986) social cognitive theory. According to this theory, the observer forms a cognitive representation of the required actions by attending to the salient features of the model's performance. This representation both guides the production of the action when the observer is asked to perform it and provides a referent against which feedback from the observer's own performance can be compared.

Partial learning of a movement sequence can occur through observation (Adams, 1984). The incompleteness of the learning is likely a function of such factors as the imprecision of the verbal representations of the movement, the lack of information about such nonvisual dimensions as static force and muscle tension, and the loss of those parts of the movement occurring outside the visual field. Presumably, if any of these factors could be improved, then performance might benefit. In fact, Carroll and Bandura (1982) showed that observational learning can be improved by using a television to present the normally unobservable sides of the movement to the observer.

The task examined by Carroll and Bandura (1982) was a complex pattern of manipulation of a paddle device (see Figure 15–8). The modeled display showed only the extreme right portion of the body from behind so that the orientation of the arm and hand would correspond to the observer's. A similar television display was used in some conditions to provide visual feedback when the observer performed the task. At various points during learning, the observer's cognitive representation of the actions was measured by

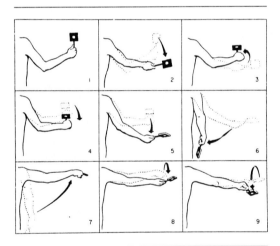

FIGURE 15–8 Reponse Components of the Action Pattern Investigated by Carroll and Bandura, with the Components Numbered in the Order in Which They Were Enacted.

From W. R. Carroll & A. Bandura (1982). The role of visual monitoring in observational learning of action patterns: Making the unobservable observable. *Journal of Motor Behavior, 14,* 153–167. Reprinted with permission of the Helen Dwight Reid Educational Foundation. Published by Heldref Publications, 1319 Eighteenth St., N. W., Washington, D.C. 20036–1802. Copyright © 1982.

having her or him order nine photographs representing components of the action sequence. Relatively accurate performance of the modeled patterns was obtained only after the observer had formed an accurate cognitive representation and if the observer's enactment could be seen.

Carroll and Bandura (1985, 1987) used the same task to examine in more detail the requirements of the visually guided enactments. Their experiments showed that, to be effective, the visual feedback had to be provided along with the enactment. When it was delayed by 75 s, performance was no better than when the visual feedback was not available. A similar high level of performance was obtained when the observer matched the modeled action pattern. In this case, it did not matter whether this was done concurrent with the modeled display or shortly thereafter. The high level of proficiency was retained when the modeling and visual feedback were removed.

When enactment of the learner's actions is not part of the procedure, both the accuracy of the cognitive representation and performance are greater with eight repetitions of the modeled performance than with only two (Carroll & Bandura, 1990). Moreover, concurrent verbal descriptions benefit the representation and performance, but only when repetitions are numerous.

To summarize, observational learning can be effective. It requires that an accurate cognitive representation be developed and that the learner be allowed to match the model's movements as they are viewed or to watch his or her own enactments. The relative effectiveness of observational learning for acquiring complex movement skills is still an open question. Newell, Morris, and Scully (1985) propose that observation is effective for learning the coarse aspects of tasks, such as the order and bounds of the movement components, but not the details.

TYPING

Typing is one of the most common perceptual–motor tasks in which humans interact with machines. Consequently, it is a topic of considerable interest to the field of human factors. Moreover, because typists across the entire range of skill are readily available for research, it is one perceptual–motor skill that can be easily investigated. For these reasons, there is a considerable body of research on typing (Salthouse, 1986).

The typewriter was first marketed in 1874 (Cooper, 1983). Initially, a "hunt-and-peck" method was used that involved only two fingers from each hand and required looking at the keyboard. Modern touch typing was first developed by Frank McGurrin. In 1888, he engaged in a contest with a typist who was skilled in the hunt-and-peck method. His well-publicized victory in that contest led to the gradual adoption of the touch-typing method over the next decade.

Salthouse (1984) proposed that typing is comprised of four subprocesses (see Figure 15–9). First, the text must be read and converted into chunks. These chunks are then decomposed into

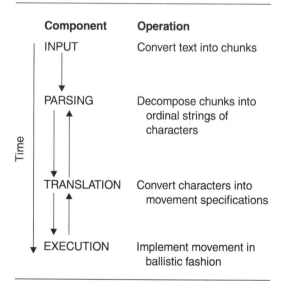

Component	Operation
INPUT	Convert text into chunks
PARSING	Decompose chunks into ordinal strings of characters
TRANSLATION	Convert characters into movement specifications
EXECUTION	Implement movement in ballistic fashion

FIGURE 15–9 The Four Component Processes of Typing.

After T. A. Salthouse (1986). Perceptual, cognitive, and motoric aspects of transcription typing. *Psychological Bulletin, 99,* 303–319. Copyright © 1986 by the American Psychological Association. Reprinted by permission.

strings of characters to be typed. The character representations must then be converted into movement specifications (motor programs), and finally the responses must be implemented ballistically. In short, skilled typing consists of perceptual, cognitive, and motor processes.

One basic characteristic of skilled typing is its speed. An average professional typist can type 60 words per minute, or approximately 5 keystrokes per second (a median interstroke interval of 200 ms). World champion typists can type as fast as 200 words per second, with a median interstroke interval of 60 ms. The durations of the interstroke intervals in skilled typists are well below the minimum time for a choice reaction. For example, Salthouse (1984) showed that individuals who typed at 177 ms per response showed a median interstroke interval of 560 ms in a serial, two-alternative, choice–reaction time task. Such results suggest that typing does not involve sequential key by key preparation of each letter, but rather that chunks of letters and their keystrokes are prepared together.

The basic unit for typing seems to be the word, rather than the individual letters. In support of this point, performance deteriorates when the material to be typed is changed from words to chunks of random letters (for example, Shaffer & Hardwick, 1968; West & Sabban, 1982). Moreover, unlike reading, typing speed is essentially the same for random words and meaningful text. The failure of the semantic and syntactic context provided by meaningful text to facilitate typing suggests that no cognitive processes beyond recognition of the word are involved. Each word may specify a motor program that controls the execution of the component keystrokes (Rumelhart & Norman, 1982).

Typing errors are made by both fast and slow typists. Most typing errors involve misspellings of words. Typing errors are predominantly of four types: substitutions (*work* for *word*), intrusions (*worrd* for *word*), omissions (*wrd* for *word*), and transpositions (*wrod* for *word*). All these apparently have their basis in the movement-related translation and execution processes

(Salthouse, 1986). Substitution errors tend to involve adjacent keys, as do intrusion errors, suggesting faulty movement specifications or mispositioning of the hands as the source. The interval between the keystroke preceding an omission error and the following keystroke is approximately twice the normal value, which suggests that the missing keystroke was attempted, but that the key was not pressed hard enough. Finally, most transposition errors occur between strokes on different hands, suggesting that they arise from timing errors.

Other than becoming faster, how does the performance of a typist change as skill is acquired? Perhaps the most significant change is that performance for digraphs (pairs of letters) typed with two hands or two fingers on the same hand improves greatly (Gentner, 1983). Initially, digraphs involving two fingers are slower than one-finger doubles, in which the same key is pressed twice in a row by the same finger. However, for skilled typists, this pattern is reversed. Moreover, for average typists, digraphs involving two fingers on different hands are slower than digraphs involving two fingers on the same hand, whereas unusually fast typists (above 90 words per minute) show extremely rapid two-finger digraphs. The differences in the ease with which these different types of digraphs are executed can be explained in terms of the physical difficulty of the movements. Much of the skill that is acquired involves coordinating rapid movements of fingers in parallel (for example, Rumelhart & Norman, 1982). Learning to coordinate rapid movements of fingers on the same hand seems to be particularly difficult.

Within digraph classes, there is still considerable variability in the interstroke intervals that cannot be accounted for by physical difficulty. Gentner, Larochelle, and Grudin (1988) examined different digraphs within the context of words and sentences and found that digraph frequency, word frequency, and syllable boundaries also affect the interstroke interval. Movement specification is facilitated for frequent digraphs, allowing the movements to be executed faster. In contrast, the advantage for high-frequency words and the syllable-boundary effects seem to be based in perceptual-memory processes.

To summarize, physical constraints are the primary limitations of typing speed. However, digraph frequency (whose basis is motoric), word frequency, and syllable boundaries (whose effects are on perception and/or memory) have a combined effect similar in magnitude to that of these physical constraints (Gentner, Larochelle, & Grudin, 1988). The most important changes that occur as typing skill is acquired involve a more efficient translation of characters to movements, and more efficient execution and coordination of the movements of successive keystrokes. These improvements in response selection and control are accompanied by perceptual changes that increase the span for encoding the written material.

SUMMARY

Motor skills are involved in the operation of many human–machine systems. The ease with which such skills are acquired varies greatly with the type of practice schedule that is used. A wide range of practice variability will lead to better performance of similar types of movements. Learning and performance will also benefit from the provision of augmented feedback. Knowledge of both results and performance is effective at enhancing learning when the information provided is consistent with the criterion for successful performance. The relation between the environment in which practice occurs and that in which the acquired skill must be performed will determine whether positive or negative transfer occurs. Through careful structuring of the training situation, the human factors specialist can facilitate an operator's progress through the phases of skill acquisition.

RECOMMENDED READING

Adams, J. A. (1987). Historical review and appraisal of research on the learning, retention, and transfer of human motor skills. *Psychological Bulletin, 101*, 41–74.

Fitts, P. M., & Posner, M. I. (1967). *Human Performance*. Belmont, CA: Brooks/Cole.

Holding, D. H. (ed.) (1989). *Human Skills,* 2nd ed. New York: Wiley.

Magill, R. A. (1989). *Motor Learning: Concepts and Applications,* 3rd ed. Dubuque, IA: W. C. Brown.

Schmidt, R. A. (1988). *Motor Control and Learning: A Behavioral Emphasis,* 2nd ed. Champaign, IL: Human Kinetics.

CHAPTER 16

CONTROLS AND CONTROLLING ACTIONS

How do the operators avoid the occasional mistake, confusion, or accidental bumping against the wrong control? Or misaim? They don't. Fortunately, airplanes and power plants are pretty robust. A few errors every hour is not important—usually.

—D. A. Norman, 1988

INTRODUCTION

Just as machines communicate to humans through displays, humans communicate to machines through controls. Controls require the execution of coordinated actions to effectively communicate the desired system changes to the machine. A wide variety of physical devices are available for use as controls, including push buttons, toggle switches, joysticks, and knobs. Different controls require different types of actions, which make them suited to different applications. One purpose of human factors is to specify the particular controls and layouts of control panels that will optimize both operator and system performance.

Individual controls must be designed so that they can be operated easily by the users for whom they are intended. Biomechanic and anthropometric factors, as well as population stereotypes, must be taken into account in determining the size and shape of a control. The designer must also consider the nature of the control task, for which the most important parameters are the muscle force required and the speed and accuracy with which the control can be manipulated (Bullinger, Kern, & Muntzinger, 1987). When several controls are arranged on a panel, their identities and functions must be easily distinguishable. Also, it should be possible for the operator to reach all the controls and apply the forces necessary for their operation. Performance can vary widely as a function of the specific controls and their arrangements.

CONTROL FEATURES

The properties of individual controls are diverse. Some require considerable force to operate, perhaps to avoid accidental activation, whereas others require little force. Some are pushed, some pulled, and some turned. The relation of controlling actions to system response can also vary greatly. A single controlling action may produce a major change in the system or only a small change. Applying the brake pedal in a moving car produces a large system change, whereas pulling the turn-signal lever produces a small system change. In the present section, we discuss the features of controls that should be considered when selecting one for a particular application.

Basic Dimensions

The most basic distinction between control types is whether information is transmitted discretely or continuously. *Discrete controls* can be set to one of a fixed number of states. For example, a light switch has two settings, one for light off and

another for light on. Alternatively, *continuous controls* transmit information from any value along a continuum of states. A dimmer switch is the continuous analog to a light switch. Discrete controls should be used when there is a small number of discrete control states, whereas continuous controls are best when there is a continuum of control states or a large number of discrete control states.

Controls can be linear or rotary. A light switch is both discrete and linear, because its movement is along a single axis. Stereo equalizers often use continuous linear controls to select the output level of different frequency bands. The dimmer switch typically is a knob that must be turned and, hence, is a rotary control. Controls can also be classified as unidimensional or multidimensional. Both the light switch and the dimmer switch are unidimensional, because they adjust the single dimension of lighting level. In contrast, a joystick is two dimensional, because it controls position in two-dimensional space. In a few cases, such as a joystick or a pressure plate, the control may be fixed and responsive to force (*isometric control*), rather than movable and responsive to displacement (*isotonic control*).

Other control features include mass, shape, range of motion, and resistance to movement. The usefulness of a particular control and the relative ease with which a human can operate it are functions of these and other factors. Figure 16–1 gives examples of some of the common control types. Tables 16–1 and 16–2 summarize the uses of the various types of discrete and continuous controls, respectively.

Control Resistance

Any control will have at least some resistance to movement. This means that force must be applied to operate a control. When designing an interface, the designer can modify (to some degree) the type and amount of resistance that are present. These characteristics affect the force that must be applied to initiate a change in the position of the control, the feel of the control, the speed and

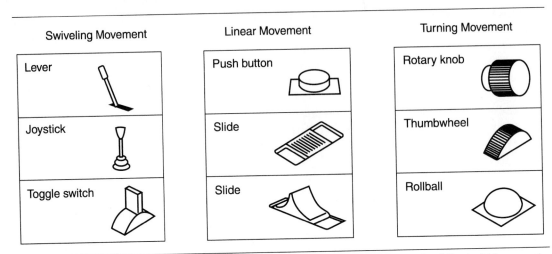

FIGURE 16–1 Examples of Control Types, Categorized According to the Path of Control Movement.

TABLE 16–1 Uses for Discrete Controls

TYPE	USES
Linear	
Push button	When a control or an array of controls is needed for momentary contact or for activating a locking circuit
Legend	When an integral legend is required for push button applications
Slide	When two or more positions are required
Toggle	When two positions are required or space limitations are severe; three-position toggles are used only as spring-loaded, center-off type or when rotary or legend controls are not feasible
Rocker	In place of toggles when toggles may cause snagging problems or scarcity of panel space precludes separate labeling of switch positions; three-position rockers are used only as spring-loaded, center-off type or when rotary or legend controls are not feasible
Push-pull	When two positions are required and such configuration is expected (for example, auto headlights) or when panel space is scarce and related functions can be combined (for example, ON–OFF/volume control); three-position push–pulls are used only when inadvertent positioning is not critical
Rotary	
Selector	When three or more positions are required; in two-position applications when swift visual identification is more important than positioning speed
Key operated	In two-position applications to prevent unauthorized operation
Thumbwheel	When a compact digital control-input device with readout is required

Table from K. R. Boff & J. E. Lincoln (Eds.), *Engineering Data Compendium: Human Perception and Performance,* 1988. Reprinted with permission.

TABLE 16–2   Uses for Continuous Controls

TYPE	USES
Linear	
Lever	When large amounts of force or displacement are involved or when multidimensional control movements are required
Isotonic (displacement) joystick	When precise or continuous control in two or more related dimensions is required
	When positioning accuracy is more important than positioning speed
	Data pickoff from CRT or free-drawn graphics
Isometric (force) joystick	When a return to center after each entry or readout is required, operator feedback is primarily visual from system response rather than kinesthetic from the stick, and there is minimal delay and tight coupling between control and input and system response
Track ball	Data pickoff from CRT; when there may be cumulative travel in a given direction; zero-order control only
Mouse	Data pickoff or entry of coordinate values on a CRT; zero-order control only
Light pen	Track-oriented readout device; data pickoff, data entry on CRT
Rotary	
Continuous rotary	When low forces and precision are required
Ganged	Used in limited applications where scarce panel space precludes the use of single, continuous rotary controls
Thumbwheel	Used as an alternative to continuous rotary controls when a compact control device is required

Table from K. R. Boff & J. E. Lincoln (Eds.), *Engineering Data Compendium: Human Perception and Performance,* 1988. Reprinted with permission.

accuracy of operation, and the smoothness with which a continuous control movement can be made.

Types of Resistance.   Four distinct kinds of resistance (elastic, frictional, viscous, and inertial) have different effects that must be considered when designing a control (Chapanis & Kinkade, 1972). Spring-loaded controls have *elastic resistance.* The primary characteristic of elastic resistance is that it increases as the control is displaced farther from the neutral position. This direct relation between resistance and position provides intrinsic proprioceptive feedback about the amount of displacement. Such feedback can enhance performance when the position of the control is directly related to the position of the machine or display element that it controls. Another property

of elastic resistance is that the control will return to the neutral position when released. Because of this property, controls with elastic resistance are often called *deadman switches.* If something happens to the operator, deadman switches ensure that the machine will not continue out of control.

Frictional resistance provides a second type. Static friction is highest for a resting control and decreases once motion begins. Sliding friction, produced by movement of the control, is not influenced by the velocity or position of the control. In contrast to elastic resistance, frictional resistance does not assist movement control because the amount of friction is independent of control displacement. In other words, the amount of resistance encountered at any point in the movement provides no information about the positioning of the control.

Viscous resistance is an increasing function of the velocity with which the control is moved. As when moving a spoon in a thick liquid, the faster the movement is, the greater the resistance. Because viscous resistance is a direct function of control velocity, it can provide useful proprioceptive feedback for tasks in which velocity is critical. Viscous resistance also opposes abrupt changes in velocity and promotes smooth control movements.

Inertial resistance varies as a direct function of movement acceleration. Large forces must be applied to start control movement, but the forces can be reduced as acceleration increases. After the control begins to move, the inertia tends to keep the control moving and oppose stopping it. This means that large forces are required to stop the control. Revolving doors typically have high inertial resistance. Due to their mass, considerable force must be applied to initiate movement, but movement tends to continue once the force is removed. Inertial resistance creates a tendency for the operator to overshoot the target setting.

Performance and Resistance. Knowles and Sheridan (1966) investigated frictional and inertial resistance for rotary controls. Their first experiments determined operators' sensitivities to changes in friction and inertia using the method of limits. For both friction and inertia, the just noticeable difference was a 10% to 20% change relative to the standard. In their final experiment, operators rated controls of different weights under different levels of frictional, viscous, and inertial resistance. Lighter controls were preferred over heavier controls, and viscous resistance was preferred to frictional resistance. Controls with some inertial resistance were preferred over those with none.

Although operators tended to prefer rotary knobs with some degree of inertia, inertia impedes performance in continuous tasks. Howland and Noble (1953) had people perform a task during which a cursor was to follow a target moving in a sine-wave pattern. A rotary control determined the position of the cursor, and in different

conditions, the control was loaded with all combinations of elastic, viscous, and inertial resistance. Relative to a free control with no resistance, inertial resistance alone or in combination with the other types of resistance decreased performance (see Figure 16–2). The best performance was obtained with elastic resistance alone, probably because of the proprioceptive feedback about location that it provided. An important point for control design is that the various types of resistance produced interactive effects when combined within a single control. These effects were not predictable from performance with controls that had only a single type of resistance.

Manipulation–Outcome Relations

When a control is manipulated by an operator, the operator's intent is to produce a system response. With a continuous control, the speed and accuracy of control actions will be a function of several factors. We have discussed some effects of the resistance that is built into the control. Other factors include deadspace and backlash, the control–display ratio, and control order. The influence of these factors on continuous control is often investigated in *tracking tasks.*

Tracking.   A tracking task is characterized by a path and a device used to follow the path. In driving, the road is the path and the task is to keep the car on the road. According to Adams (1961, p. 55), three features define a tracking task:

1. A paced (i.e., time function) externally programmed input or command signal defines a motor response for the operator, which he performs by manipulating a control mechanism.
2. The control mechanism generates an output signal.
3. The input signal minus the output signal is the tracking error quantity, and the operator's requirement is to null this error.

There are two kinds of tracking tasks (Hammerton, 1989), pursuit and compensatory (see

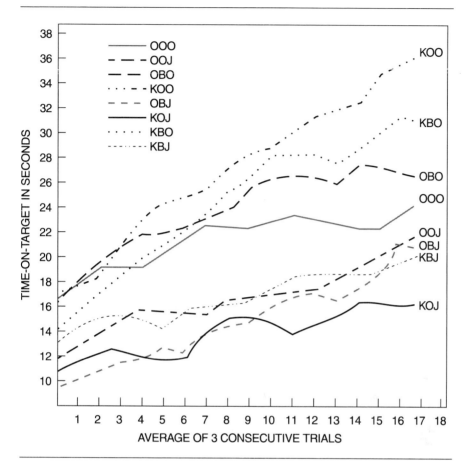

FIGURE 16–2   Mean Time-on-target for the Eight Experimental Conditions, as a Function of Practice, Examined by Howland and Noble (1953). For the Labels, the Letter K in the First Column Indicates Elastic Resistance, the Letter B in the Second Column Indicates Viscous Resistance, and the Letter J in the Third Column Indicates Inertial Resistance. An O in any Column Indicates the Absence of the Corresponding Type of Resistance.

From D. Howland & M. E. Noble (1953). The effect of physical constants of a control on tracking performance. *Journal of Experimental Psychology, 46,* 353–360.

Figure 16–3). In a pursuit task, the track and the person's output are visible simultaneously. For example, one version of a pursuit task involves a moving dot on a display screen, sometimes called a track marker. The person has control of a cursor that is to be kept on top of the track marker. Information about error is available to the person through the discrepancy between the positions for the two dots. In compensatory tracking, only the difference between the track and the current state is presented. In this example, the position of a single dot around a zero point would be shown that displays the distance between the cursor and the track marker of the pursuit display.

A pursuit display has several advantages over a compensatory display (Poulton, 1969).

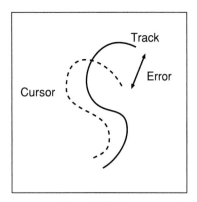

Pursuit Display

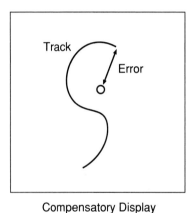

Compensatory Display

FIGURE 16–3 Pursuit and Compensatory Tracking Displays.

The movement of the track marker is separate from the response movements, so any sequential or statistical characteristics of the track are readily apparent. Once these characteristics have been learned, the location and rate of movement of the track marker in the near future can be predicted with better accuracy. The separate representation of response movements provides immediate feedback about the effects of the control movements, which leads to faster learning of the control-display relationship. When an error occurs, it is possible to tell whether it was due to an inaccurate control movement or to an unexpected movement of the track marker.

Finally, in pursuit tracking the relation between the control movements and the controlled element is spatially compatible, whereas for compensatory tracking the relationship is reversed. For example, in a vertical track, if the track is too high, the cursor will move upward and so require a downward response. Because a pursuit display provides more information than a compensatory display in a form that is more compatible with the desired control action, it is not surprising that performance with pursuit tracking is superior to that with compensatory tracking (Poulton, 1974).

Given that tracking occurs across a relatively long period of time and requires continual comparisons of a current state to a goal state, performance can be described as closed loop. In principle, closed-loop control models can be applied to tracking performance. Similarly, because the track and controlling actions can be conceived as information input to and output by the operator, information theory can also be used to model tracking performance. Researchers once hoped that quantitative closed-loop or information-theoretic models could be developed that would adequately explain tracking performance, but such models have not been very successful (Hammerton, 1989).

Deadspace and Backlash. The *deadspace* for a control is the amount of control movement around the null position that can occur with no effect on the system. For example, the steering wheel of an automobile must be turned more than some minimum amount before the automobile will start to turn. *Backlash* refers to deadspace that is present at any control position. For the automobile, after turning the wheel clockwise, some minimum amount of turn in the counterclockwise direction must be exceeded before the wheels will start to turn back. Backlash can be understood by placing a hollow cylinder over a joystick control (Poulton, 1974). When the cylinder is moved to the left, the joystick does not start moving until the cylinder comes into contact with it on the right side. When the direction in which the cylinder is moving is reversed, the joystick will not begin movement back to the right until the cylinder comes into contact with it on the left side.

Deadspace and backlash decrease the accuracy of control actions, particularly with sensitive control systems (Rockway & Franks, 1959; Rogers, 1970). Gibbs (1962) tested joysticks under a variety of conditions and found that performance was always hindered when backlash was present. Performance was best with joysticks of intermediate sensitivity that had no backlash.

Control-display Ratio. Control sensitivity can be characterized by the *control-display ratio,* which is the ratio of the magnitude of control adjustment to the magnitude of the change in a display indicator (see Figure 16–4). When referring more generally to the relation between the control movement and the response of the sys-

tem, the term control–response ratio is used. A low control–display ratio indicates high gain, whereas a high ratio indicates low gain. Generally, *gain* is a measure of the responsiveness of a control.

Movement of the control and system response can be described in terms of linear distance or in terms of radial angle or revolutions. The former is most appropriate for levers, whereas the latter is used for wheels and cranks. For a linear lever paired with a linear display, the control–display ratio (*C/D*) is the linear displacement of the lever (*C*) divided by the corresponding displacement of the display element (*D*). For a joystick control,

$$C = \frac{a}{360} \times 2\pi L$$

where *a* is angular movement in degrees and *L* is the length of the joystick. For a rotary control paired with a linear display, the control–display ratio is the reciprocal of the display movement produced by one revolution of the control.

In positioning a control, the *travel time* refers to the time to move the control into the vicinity of the desired setting, whereas the *fine adjust time* refers to the additional time required to arrive at the precise setting. As shown in Figure 16–5, a high control–display ratio minimizes travel time, whereas a low ratio minimizes fine adjust time. In other words, with a highly sensitive tuning knob for a radio, you can quickly move the indicator from one end of the dial to the other, but it is difficult to home in on the intended station when you get there. The reverse relation holds with a control of low sensitivity.

The optimum control–display ratio for situations in which both travel time and adjustment time are critical will be an intermediate value. This will allow relatively fast travel time coupled with relatively fast fine adjust time. Alternatively, a control with high gain can be used for coarse adjustments and one with low gain for fine adjustments. Hammerton (1989) notes that for any real system the limited range of travel for a control puts a lower limit on the sensitivity of the

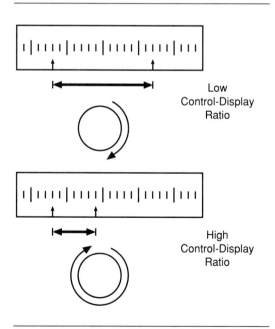

FIGURE 16–4 Illustrations of Low and High Control–Display Ratios.

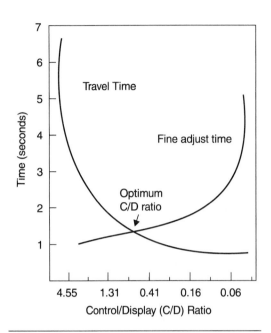

FIGURE 16–5   Travel Time and Fine Adjust Time, as a Function of Control–Display Ratio.

control. For example, a joystick can only reach about 40° from vertical, so a high control–display ratio is not possible. When the range is limited in this manner, the optimum control–display ratio is usually the one with the lowest sensitivity. Because many other variables influence the optimum ratio, it is best to test a number of possible ratios for an intended application with a representative sample of users.

Arnaut and Greenstein (1990) have questioned whether the control–display ratio adequately characterizes the performance of a control. They distinguished four components of the control and its output: display and control amplitude (or movement distance) and display and control target width (the range of positions that will be on target). Gain typically is specified by the ratio of the display and control amplitudes. However, Arnaut and Greenstein found that performance in cursor positioning with a mouse was

not adequately predicted by gain alone. Performance was also affected by display target width, as would be expected from Fitts's law. Consequently, they proposed that performance might be best predicted by a combination of gain and Fitts's index of difficulty. Apparently, performance will be optimized by a combination of gain and difficulty, and this optimal level cannot be predicted from either alone.

Control Order.   The discussion of control–display ratios focused on tasks for which control position determined the position of the display element. However, other relations between control changes and system responses affect performance. The term *control order* refers to the changes in a display or other system response that occur as derivatives of control position with respect to time. For a zero-order control, such as those discussed to this point, a direct relation holds between the displacement of the control and the position of the display element. A mouse control for a computer cursor is typically of this type. A first-order control determines velocity. That is, a particular displacement controls the rate at which the display changes. Examples include the system composed of the automobile gas pedal, engine, and brake pedal (Poulton, 1974) and a joystick that, when held at a specific position, causes the cursor to move in a particular direction at a constant velocity.

A second-order control determines the acceleration of the display. This would be the case if the cursor kept accelerating at a constant amount when the joystick was held in a specific position. Some processes in nuclear reactor control rooms and chemical plants use second-order controls. Even higher-order controls are used in other complex systems. For example, the steering mechanism of a ship or submarine is best characterized as third order, with considerable lag between the controlling action and the system response.

Typically, performance is better with lower-order controls than with higher-order controls. The reason for this can be illustrated by the actions required to move a cursor from the center of the screen to a target location on the left and then back to center. With a zero-order control, the joystick is moved left to the position that corresponds to the target location and then held in that position. To return to center, the joystick is moved back to the neutral position. For a first-order control, at least two movements are required for each segment of the task. Positioning the joystick to the left imparts leftward velocity to the cursor. To stop the cursor at the target location (that is, to impart zero velocity), the joystick must be returned to the neutral setting. Similar actions in the opposite direction are required to return the cursor to center. For a second-order control, a minimum of three movements is required for each segment. Deflection of the joystick to the left produces a constant rate of acceleration toward the target location. To decelerate, the joystick must be moved to the corresponding position on the right and then returned to center just as the cursor reaches the target. With higher-order systems, the relation between control actions and the changes of the system becomes even more complex and obscure. A general human factors principle is to use the lowest possible order of control.

Order of control also plays a role in determining optimal control gain. Kantowitz and Elvers (1988) compared performance with zero-order positional and first-order velocity controls using an isometric joystick. Performance was considerably better overall with the positional control. Moreover, high gain improved performance with the velocity control but hindered it with the positional control. Thus, order of control is another factor that influences the optimal gain for a control.

Anzai (1984) used simulated ship steering to examine how people learn to perform in a complex system with a high order of control. The task was to steer a ship through a series of gates as fast as possible, much like a large tanker would be steered into a narrow harbor. The system used a second-order control. With such a control, the history of control actions must be taken into account to determine future control actions. Other factors that made control of the ship difficult were its inertia, the lag between when a particular control action was taken and when the ship started responding, and the differences between the perspective for the displayed direction angle of the ship and the corresponding steering angle.

Verbal protocols showed that novice operators spent a large portion of their time engaged in acquiring causal knowledge of the relations between control actions and changes in the ship's trajectory. Their attention was devoted primarily to the immediate results of control actions rather than to predicting the future or to selecting strategies. Experienced operators focused instead on making predictions and using strategies based on more distant subgoals. According to Anzai (1984), a novice operator uses general heuristics such as "The ship is going straight, but the next gate is at the right, so I turn the control dial to the right." The course of the ship is monitored to detect errors, which in turn leads to the development of more refined heuristics and strategies. In short, control of a complex system involves extensive use of cognitive strategies that ultimately lead to an accurate mental model of the manipulation–outcome relationships.

Performance with higher-order control systems can be improved by using augmented displays that provide visual feedback in a form consistent with the display–control relationship (Hammerton, 1989). A rate-augmented display provides both the current state of the system and the rate at which it is changing. So, for example, an aircraft pilot may be provided information about altitude and rate of change in altitude. The rate information is useful during approach and leveling out at a desired altitude.

A predictor display shows both the current status of the system and the way in which it is likely to change in the immediate future. The amount of future time incorporated into the display will be a function of the speed at which the system responds. This display presents what the state of the system will be if the operator keeps the control at its current setting. Figure 16–6 shows a predictor display that is used to assist a

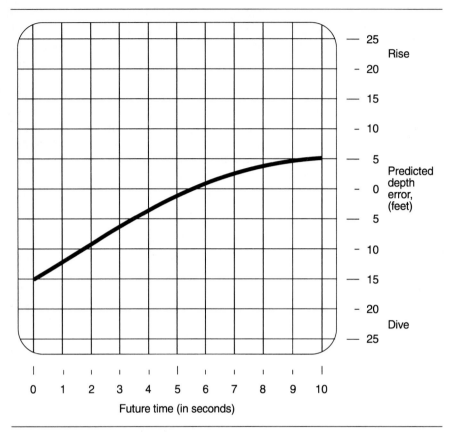

FIGURE 16–6   A Predictive Display to Assist a Submariner in Leveling Off at an
Intended Depth.

From C. R. Kelley (1962). Predictor instruments look into the future. *Control Engineering, 9,*
March, 86–90. Reprinted by permission of Cahners Publishing.

submariner in leveling off at an intended depth
(Kelley, 1962).

Augmented displays may also facilitate the
acquisition of appropriate mental models of the
system. Eberts and Schneider (1985) had people
learn to perform a second-order tracking task,
some with an augmented parabola display that
indicated the required control positions for a
given acceleration (see Figure 16–7) and some
without. The parabola demonstrated to the operator the relation between the position of the joystick and the acceleration of the cursor. Those who

performed with this parabola-augmented display
during acquisition were able to perform the tracking task accurately after the display was removed.
It seems that the augmented display not only
aided performance, but it also provided the operators with the knowledge of results necessary to
learn the second-order relationship.

Many systems have become increasingly
automated, with the role of the operator shifting
from one of continuous manual control to one of
supervisory control. Such is the case with process
control systems. The operator primarily monitors

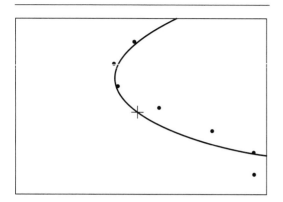

FIGURE 16–7 A Parabola Display Indicating the Required Positions for a Given Acceleration.

From R. E. Eberts & W. Schneider, Internalizing the system dynamics for a second-order system. Reprinted with permission from *Human Factors,* Vol. 27, No. 4, pp. 371–393. Copyright © 1985 by The Human Factors Society. All rights reserved.

the performance of semiautomated subsystems, taking action when an emergency is detected. Because complex problem solving often is required, the cognitive processes of the operator are even more important than in difficult manual control tasks. The performance of the operator will depend heavily on the content of his or her mental model.

Moray (1987) noted that, because the operator has had experience with only a limited range of states of the system, the operator's mental model will be a reduced version of the complete model that characterizes the system. This reduced mental model will consist of subsystems in which some states are relabeled and combined. The reduced mental model has the virtues of being simpler and less capacity demanding than the complete version. However, it does not allow the true state of the system to be deduced unambiguously.

The reduced model will be sufficient during normal operating conditions. Moray (1987) suggests that decision aids and displays for normal operation will be most useful if they are based on analyses of the subsystems contained in the op-

erators' mental models. However, solutions to emergencies typically require consideration of the complete system model. Support systems for emergencies should assist the operator in "breaking the cognitive set" imposed by the restricted mental model and encourage the operator to think in terms of the complete model. Decision-support tools based on expert knowledge provide a promising means for assisting both the normal and emergency procedures in supervisory control (Zimolong et al., 1987).

CONTROL PANELS

In most situations, a control is not placed in isolation but is included among other controls on a panel. Usually, there is also a visual display that indicates the state of the system. The operator must select the appropriate control in response to displayed information and avoid operating inappropriate controls. Several factors influence performance in such situations.

Coding of Controls

When a control panel contains more than one control, the issue of control identifiability becomes important. The appropriate control action will not be performed if the wrong control is operated, and the resulting change in the system may cause the system to fail. It is important that the operator be able to identify the appropriate control quickly and accurately. To minimize confusions in identification, controls must be coded so that they can be easily distinguished. Several coding methods can be used in a particular situation, depending on (1) the demands on the operator, (2) the coding methods already being used, (3) the illumination level, (4) the speed and accuracy required for control identification, (5) the available space, and (6) the number of controls that must be coded (Hunt, 1953).

Location Coding. In most applications, controls are distinguished by their locations. Location coding can be used as the primary distinction among controls if the separation between them is sufficient. Such is the case for the accelerator and brake pedals in automobiles, which are distinguished by having the brake situated to the left of the accelerator. Location coding is only effective if the operator can reliably distinguish the different control locations. There are no detailed guidelines for the separation of controls to ensure accurate location coding. A laboratory study of limb positioning by Magill and Parks (1983) suggests that in some circumstances the final spatial positions of continuous movements can be reliably discriminated if the positions are as little as 1.25 cm apart. However, for most situations, controls must be separated considerably farther apart than this.

Many airplane accidents in World War II were attributed to pilots who failed to discriminate between flaps and landing-gear controls (Fitts & Jones, 1947). The two controls were situated in close proximity, with no other distinguishing features besides their different locations. Consequently, when the flaps were to be adjusted during landing, the landing gear was often raised instead. Despite the fact that it has been known for many years that this problem can be alleviated by using other forms of control coding, the National Transportation Safety Board recently reported that control misidentification, due to the exclusive use of location coding, was the major source of accidents in one popular small aircraft (Norman, 1988).

Localizing controls is more accurate along a vertical dimension than along a horizontal dimension. Fitts and Crannell (1953) had blindfolded individuals reach to and activate one of nine toggle switches arrayed in a vertical column or horizontal row. The reaches were more accurate with the vertical arrangement than with the horizontal arrangement. Few errors were made when vertically arranged controls were separated by 6.3 cm or more and when horizontally arranged controls were separated by 10.2 cm or more.

Because of the relative imprecision of location coding, it alone is not sufficient for most applications. Typically, location coding is augmented with some other form of coding. In fact, when other forms of coding are not provided by system designers, operators often institute their own augmented coding systems (see Figure 16–8).

Labels.   Either alphanumeric or symbolic labels can be used to identify controls. However, the use of labels as the sole indicators of control functions is not encouraged for several reasons. For one, the operator must be able to see the label, which is not possible if the level of illumination is low or if the operator is unable to look at the control. Another reason is that the operator must be literate if the label is alphanumeric or must be able to identify the symbol if it is not. Also, when there is a large number of similar controls distinguished only by labels, responding tends to be slow and inaccurate. Finally, adequate space for the labels is not always available. The following general principles should be adhered to when labeling controls (Chapanis & Kinkade, 1972):

> Locate labels systematically relative to the controls.
> Make labels brief, without using technical terms.
> Avoid using abstract symbols that may require special training, and use common symbols in a conventional manner.
> Use standard, easily readable fonts for alphanumeric characters.
> Position labels so that they can be referred to while the operator engages the control.

Color Coding.   Color provides another means for coding visible controls. Recall from Chapter 8 that an operator's capacity to make absolute judgments is limited to about five categories along a single dimension. Thus, for most situations, no more than five colors should be used. However, this number can be larger when the controls are close enough to allow comparisons between them. The primary disadvantage of color coding is that perceived color will vary as a function of the illumination. Psychophysical experiments can be used to determine the dis-

FIGURE 16–8   The Control-room Operators in a Nuclear Power Plant Placed Beer-tap Handles Over Knobs to Distinguish Them.
From J. L. Seminara, W. R. Gonzalez, & S. O. Parsons (1977). *Human Factors Review of Nuclear Power Plant Control Room Design.* Reprinted by permission.

criminability of the desired set of colors under all possible levels of illumination.

One use of color coding is to enhance performance when the displayed signals are also colored. Poock (1969) examined a situation in which a two by two display of four stimulus lights was paired with a similar arrangement of four toggle switches. In a control condition, all the lights were red and the switches white, whereas in a color-coding situation, the lights were of four different colors and the assigned responses were the same color. When the assignment was spatially compatible so that the toggle switch was in the same relative position as the light to which it was assigned, the control and color-coded conditions yielded equivalent performance. However, when the assignment was spatially incompatible, reaction time was facilitated greatly by correspondence between the stimulus color and the response color.

Shape Coding.   Shape coding of controls is particularly useful. The shape provides both a visual feature for distinguishing controls and a tactile feature that can be used if the viewing conditions are poor or the operator's gaze needs to be directed elsewhere. Operators can accurately distinguish a large number of shapes (between eight and ten carefully selected shapes) through touch. The principal drawbacks of shape coding are that it may alter the ease with which a control can be manipulated and increase the difficulty of monitoring its setting.

An early study on shape coding was performed by Jenkins (1946). Blindfolded persons felt a knob and attempted to identify it from a set of 25 shapes. Based on the error patterns, Jenkins identified two groups of knobs for which the within-group confusions were minimal (see Figure 16–9). Other similar sets have been proposed (Hunt, 1953).

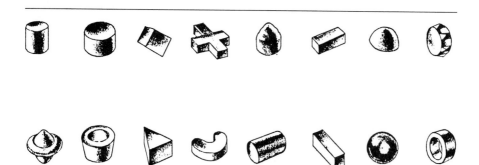

FIGURE 16–9 Two Sets of Eight Knobs for Which Within-group Confusions Are Minimal.

From D. P. Hunt (1953). The coding of aircraft controls. (Report No. 53-221). Wright Air Development Center, U.S. Air Force. Public domain.

Size Coding. Size coding can also be used for situations in which vision is restricted. However, people can accurately discriminate only a few different sizes. The range of sizes needed for more than two controls will make the controls difficult to operate. Very large or very small controls may be difficult to grasp and manipulate. Hence, size coding is best used in conjunction with other coding methods.

Size coding can involve both the diameter of the control knob and its thickness. Bradley (1967) found that knobs were not confused when they differed by 1.27 cm in diameter or 0.93 cm in thickness. By combining diameter and thickness

differences, a larger set of discriminable controls can be created.

Texture Coding. Another dimension on which controls can vary is their surface texture. Bradley (1967) also investigated the ability to tactually discriminate the knobs shown in Figure 16–10. People were asked to identify which of two knobs was being felt by indicating the correct one from a picture. Three classes of textures, smooth, fluted, and knurled, could be identified reliably. That is, the smooth knob was never confused with any other knob, and the fluted knobs were rarely confused with the knurled knobs. However,

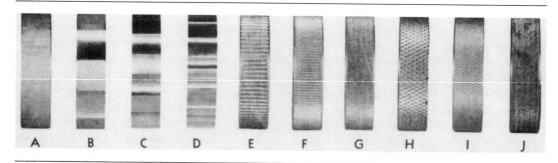

FIGURE 16–10 Examples of Smooth (A), Fluted (B, C, D), and Knurled (E, F, G, H, I, J), Knobs.

From J. V. Bradley, Tactual coding of cylindrical knobs. Reprinted with permission from *Human Factors,* Vol. 9, No. 5, pp. 483–496, 1967. Copyright © 1967 by The Human Factors Society. All rights reserved.

within the categories of knurled and fluted knobs, there was considerable confusion. Bradley proposed that these three texture classes can be used for the coding of controls. When coupled with size coding by diameter and thickness, a large set of tactually identifiable knobs can be constructed.

Other Codes.   In addition to the common coding dimensions, coding can be based on the type of control operation. For example, a rotary control for amplitude is not likely to be confused with a push button on-off switch. However, coding by mode of operation will not be an effective way to prevent selection errors in most situations because the control has to be selected before it can be operated. Redundant coding using two or more dimensions can be particularly effective. By combining some type of visual coding in the form of labels or colors together with some type of tactual coding, the designer can ensure that the information specifying a control is available to more than one sensory modality. Given these alternative coding schemes, it should be possible for the designer to choose an optimal coding system for any system environment.

Control Arrangements

When discussing visual displays in Chapter 8, we stressed the importance of the functional grouping of displays by spatial proximity and similarity. Functional grouping is also an effective means for organizing control panels. It is particularly beneficial when the groupings of the controls correspond with those of the display.

In addition to preferred spatial relations, there are population stereotypes about the locations of controls. Casey and Kiso (1990) evaluated the position of three critical controls (throttle, range shift, and remote hydraulic) on 69 different tractors and obtained subjective ratings of these positions from many tractor drivers. Across the different tractors, there was high variability in the location of each control. These locations had a strong influence on the users' acceptability ratings, and the users' preferred locations for each

control depended on their functions. Similar stereotypes are involved for other machines.

When control panels contain many controls, it is important to ensure that the controls be within the reach of the majority of operators who will be using the machine and that the most frequently used controls be easily accessible. To ensure that 95% of the users will be able to reach the controls, a *reach envelope* can be established based on the fifth percentile of the population's reach distance. Figure 16–11 shows two such reach envelopes for seated male operators. The immediate reach envelope specifies the region within which controls can be reached without bending, whereas the maximum reach envelope specifies the controls that can be reached with bending. Frequently used controls should be located within the immediate reach envelope, whereas rarely used controls should be within the maximum reach boundary.

An index for specifying the degree of accessibility for a control panel was developed by Banks and Boone (1981). This *index of accessibility* (IA) is based on the immediate reach envelope, the frequencies with which individual controls are used, and the relative physical positions of the controls with respect to the operator. The index is defined as

$$IA = r_{yx} - \frac{1}{s} \sum_{i=1}^{s} \left(\frac{\sum_{j=1}^{n} \hat{f}_{ij}}{\sum_{j=1}^{N} f_{ij}} \right)$$

where r_{xy} is the Pearson correlation coefficient between ranked frequency of use and the distance of each control from the operator, s is the number of people tested, f_{ij} is the rank of the jth control in terms of relative frequency of use, $\hat{f}_{ij}$ is the rank of the jth control outside the ith operator's immediate reach envelope, N is the total number of controls, and n_i is the number of controls outside the ith operator's immediate reach envelope. The index is the correlation between frequency of use

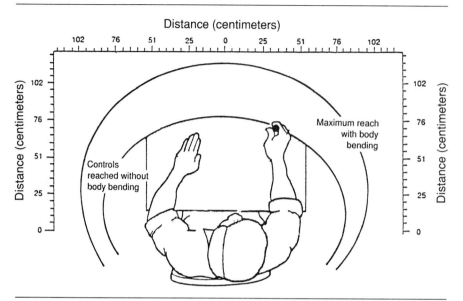

FIGURE 16–11 Immediate and Maximum Reach Envelopes, Based on the 5th Percentile for Adult Males.

and distance, adjusted to account for the frequency with which the operator uses controls outside the immediate reach envelope. This index can range from 1.0 (best accessibility) to −2.0 (worst accessibility). An example calculation of this index is presented in Table 16–3. The primary limitation of the accessibility index is that it does not take into account grouping by function, sequence, or spacing.

Preventing Accidental Operation

Inadvertent operation of a control on a panel can be the cause of system failure. When the consequences of accidental activation are serious, steps should be taken to ensure that the control cannot be unintentionally activated. However, because each of these steps makes it more difficult to access or activate the control, they will also make intentional activation more difficult.

There are several ways to minimize the likelihood of accidental activation (Chapanis & Kinkade, 1972). The control can be located where the operator is unlikely to come into accidental

contact with it. It can also be recessed or have barriers placed around it. Similarly, if the control is not used frequently, a protective cover can be placed over it, or it can be locked into position. Another option is to require a sequence of actions to activate the control. Finally, most types of resistance can be used to increase the force required to activate the control and, hence, decrease the probability of accidental activation.

SPECIFIC CONTROLS

To this point, we have discussed general principles about controls that can be applied to design decisions. However, because each type of control is unique, specific features must also be considered when deciding whether to use a particular control. Consequently, several types of controls and their applications will now be considered.

Hand-operated Controls

Most controls are hand operated. As indicated at the beginning of the chapter, such controls come

TABLE 16–3   Calculation of the Index of Accessibility

RANKED FREQUENCY OF CONTROL, x	DISTANCE, y (cm)	IMMEDIATE REACH ENVELOPE (cm)
1	65	Operator 1: 68
2	72	Operator 2: 76
3	65	Operator 3: 88
4	87	
5	87	

$$r_{xy} = \frac{N\left(\sum xy\right) - \left(\sum x\right)\left(\sum y\right)}{\sqrt{[N\left(\sum x^2\right) - \left(\sum x\right)^2][N\left(\sum y^2\right) - \left(\sum y\right)^2]}}$$

$$= \frac{5(1187) - (15)(376)}{\sqrt{[5(55) - 15^2][5(28{,}772) - 376^2]}}$$

$$= \frac{295}{\sqrt{(50)(2487)}} = 0.837$$

$$IA = r_{xy} - \left(\frac{1}{s}\right)\sum_{i=1}^{s}\left(\frac{\sum_{j=1}^{n}\hat{f}_{ij}}{\sum_{j=1}^{N}f_{ij}}\right) \qquad \sum_{j=1}^{N}f_{ij} = 15$$

$$= 0.837 - \left(\frac{1}{3}\right)\left(\frac{2+4+5}{15} + \frac{4+5}{15} + \frac{0}{15}\right)$$

$$= 0.393$$

in various shapes and sizes. Among the most widely used are push buttons, toggle switches, rotary selector switches, and rotary knobs. Table 16–4 summarizes the characteristics of each of these four types of controls.

Push-button and Toggle Switches. Push buttons are used as controls on a range of devices from calculators to industrial control panels. They are used for stopping and starting machines, for engaging and disengaging particular operating modes, and for discrete increments of continuous dimensions (such as loudness). As with all controls, push buttons must be designed and placed so that they can be reached and operated.

When using push buttons their resistance, displacement, diameter, and separation from each other are of most concern. Recommended physical dimensions as a function of operation by finger or thumb and application are shown in Table 16–5 (Moore, 1975). The optimal resistance depends on factors such as the extent to which accidental activation must be avoided and the strength of the user population. For many situations, feedback that the button has been pushed should be provided in the form of a click.

Because of Fitts's law, the size of the button should increase with the distance that the finger must be moved to reach the button and the speed required for the response. Bradley and Wallis (1958) conducted a systematic examination of spacing and size of push buttons on performance. They found that when the spacing between centers is held constant a decrease in the diameters of

TABLE 16–4   Comparison of Common Control Types

CHARACTERISTIC	PUSH BUTTON	TOGGLE SWITCH	ROTARY SELECTOR SWITCH	CONTINUOUS KNOB
Time required to make control setting	Very quick	Very quick	Medium to quick	—
Recommended number of control positions (settings)	2	2 to 3	3 to 24	—
Likelihood of accidental activation	Medium	Medium	Low	Medium
Effectiveness of coding	Fair	Fair	Good	Good
Effectiveness of visually identifying control position	Poor	Good	Fair	Fair
Effectiveness of check-reading to determine control position when part of a group of like controls	Poor	Good	Good	Good

From A. Chapanis & R. G. Kinkade (1972). Design of controls. In H. P. Van Cott & R. G. Kinkade (Eds.), *Human Engineering Guide to Equipment Design* (pp. 465–584). U.S. Government Printing Office.

the buttons reduces errors with little effect on response time. With spacing between edges held constant, the accuracy and speed of responding are a positive function of the diameter of the buttons. Thus, as the separation between buttons decreases, performance will suffer. This decrease in performance will be even more dramatic if visual feedback is not available. When visual feedback is not available, the buttons should be more widely spaced.

Any of the means of coding can be used to assist push-button identification. If labels are used, they should be mounted above the buttons so that they can be seen while the button is being depressed. If the buttons are mounted closely together, the labels can be placed on the buttons to avoid confusion about which label goes with which button. Indicator lights can also be used if they will be visible to the operator. Tactile coding can be used, but to be effective the shapes must be distinguishable by fingertip.

Moore (1974) conducted an experiment to determine a set of six discriminable push-button shapes that could be assigned to the control functions Start, Stop, Slow, Delayed Stop, Inch, and Reverse. Twenty-five shapes were designed on a 2-cm diameter button (see Figure 16–12). People touched each shape through a hole in a curtain

with the tip of the forefinger and were asked to identify the shape. The shapes 1, 4, 21, 22, 23, and 24 were seldom confused and provided an easily discriminable set.

After Moore (1974) determined the set of six discriminable controls, he still faced the problem of which control to assign to which function. Accordingly, he conducted another experiment in which blindfolded individuals ranked each of the six buttons in terms of their suitability for each control function. These rankings were then used to determine the final assignments. In other words, Moore determined the stereotypic function for each push button so that their functions could be assigned consistently. Theise (1989) has shown that optimization algorithms can be easily applied to Moore's and other confusability data to select optimal sets of any size.

Many of these same factors are pertinent to toggle switches. However, the direction in which the switch is to be flipped must be considered. Moreover, their positions should be such that the same orientation of the hand can be used to flip all switches. Bradley and Wallis (1960) found that the fastest responses occurred when toggle switches were arranged horizontally and were to be switched in a downward direction. A vertical orientation of the array was best when a right or

TABLE 16–5 Recommended Minimum (Min), Maximum (Max), and Preferred Physical Dimensions of Pushbuttons for Operations by Finger or Thumb

	DIAMETER (MM)	DISPLACEMENT (MM)		RESISTANCE (G)		CONTROL SEPARATION (MM)	
	Min	*Min*	*Max*	*Min*	*Max*	*Min*	*Preferred*
Type of Operations							
Fingertip							
One finger—randomly	13	3	6	283	1133	13	50
One finger—sequentially	13	3	6	283	1133	6	13
Different fingers—randomly or sequentially	13	3	6	140	560	6	13
Thumb (or palm)	19	3	38	283	2272	25	150
Applications							
Heavy industrial push-button	19	6	38	283	2272	25	50
Car dashboard switch	13	6	13	283	1133	13	25
Calculating machine keys	13	3		100	200	3	
Typewriter	13	0.75	4.75	26	152	6	6

From T. G. Moore (1975). Industrial push-buttons. *Applied Ergonomics, 6,* 33–38. Reprinted by permission of the publishers, Butterworth-Heinemann Ltd. (c).

FIGURE 16–12   Push Button Shapes Examined by Moore.

From T. G. Moore (1975). Industrial push-buttons. *Applied Ergonomics, 6,* 33–38. Reprinted by permission of the publishers, Butterworth-Heinemann, Ltd. (c)

left movement was required. Inadvertent activation occurred much less often with the toggle switches than with push buttons, particularly when the spacing was small, leading Bradley and Wallis to recommend that toggle switches be used over push buttons when avoidance of inadvertent activation is a primary consideration and the spacing between centers is less than 2.54 cm. However, the time to activate toggle switches increases as the density of controls increases (that is, separation decreases) and the number of controls increases (Siegel, Schultz, & Lanterman, 1963).

Rotary Selector Switches and Controls. Rotary selector switches can accommodate up to 24 discriminable settings. The primary drawback is that

these switches cannot be operated as quickly as toggle switches or push buttons. Figure 16–13 shows recommended dimensions for rotary switches. The pointer should be obvious and mounted close to the scale. The beginning and end of the ranges should have stops, and the switch should click into each setting.

Plath and Kolesnik (1966) compared performance on a data-entry task using rotary selectors, thumbwheels, and push buttons. Three-digit numbers were presented that had to be entered by setting 10-position rotary or thumbwheel controls or by operating a panel of 10 push buttons. Positioning time was significantly less with the rotary switch, but more errors occurred in which the wrong number was read from the control.

Rotary controls can also be continuous. Continuous rotary knobs are used for such things as increasing the output of an amplifier. Many of the same considerations that apply to other controls apply to continuous rotary knobs. For instance, it is important to have adequate spacing between knobs. Bradley (1969b) examined performance as a function of spacing between knobs, knob diameter, and knob configuration. He found that performance improved as the distance between knob edges was increased up to 2.54 cm, with only slight improvements at larger separations beyond this. Similarly, with the distance between knob centers held constant, fewer errors were made with smaller-diameter controls. However, for equal distances between knob edges, performance was a positive function of knob diameter. It is best to array the knobs vertically, because contact errors occur less frequently than for horizontal arrays. When size coding is used, the control knobs need to differ by at least 1.27 cm in diameter or 0.95 cm in thickness to minimize confusion (Bradley, 1967).

When space behind the control panel is limited, it is sometimes convenient to use concentrically mounted rotary knobs. Such controls are useful when the control functions are related, when the controls must be operated in sequence, when some knobs of necessity must be large, and if inadvertent activation of one of the ganged

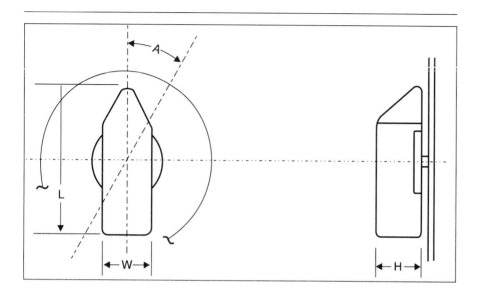

	Dimensions			
	Length **L**	**Width** **W**	**Depth** **H**	**Resistance**
Minimum	25 mm (1 in.)		16 mm (0.625 in.)	113 mN-m (1in.-lb)
Maximum	100 mm (4 in.)	25 mm (7 in.)	75 mm (3 in.)	678 mN-m (6 in.-lb)

	Displacement A		Separation	
	Regular*	**Large****	**One-Hand** **Random**	**Two-Hand** **Operation**
Minimum	15 deg	30 deg	25 mm (1 in.)	75 mm (3 in.)
Maximum	40 deg	90 deg		
Preferred	—	—	50 mm (2 in.)	125 mm (5 in.)

*For facilitating performance.
**When special engineering requirements demand large separation.

FIGURE 16–13 Recommended Dimensions for Rotary Switches.
Figure from K. R. Boff & J. E. Lincoln (Eds.), *Engineering Data Compendium: Human Perception and Performance,* 1988. Reprinted with permission.

knobs is not critical. Bradley (1969a) examined the desired dimensions for concentric controls. He determined that, if the middle of three concentrically ganged knobs is 4.08 cm in diameter, the diameter of the smaller knob should be at least 2.54 cm less and that of the larger knob should be 3.17 cm greater. His more general recommendations are shown in Figure 16–14. Unfortunately, due to the large differences in size necessary to distinguish the controls, little reduction of panel space will result from concentric mounting.

As is the general case in human factors, controls must be designed with the intended user population in mind. For example, individuals with arthritis or muscular dystrophy may have difficulty with certain rotary controls. Arthritic individuals are not able to apply as much torque to rotary controls as individuals with no known or

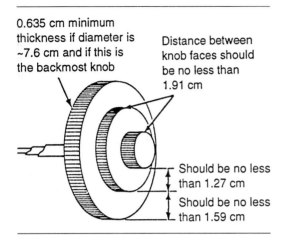

0.635 cm minimum thickness if diameter is ~7.6 cm and if this is the backmost knob

Distance between knob faces should be no less than 1.91 cm

Should be no less than 1.27 cm

Should be no less than 1.59 cm

FIGURE 16–14 Recommended Dimensions for Concentric Controls.

From J. V. Bradley, Desirable dimensions for concentric controls. Reprinted from *Human Factors,* Vol. 11, No. 3, pp. 213–226, 1969. Copyright © 1969 by The Human Factors Society. All rights reserved.

apparent arthritis (Metz et al., 1990). Similarly, peak torque exertion for females is only 66% of that for males (Mital & Sanghavi, 1986). Consequently, the minimum force necessary to turn a rotary control will depend on the population of users.

Multifunction Controls. As systems have become more complex, the number of control functions has increased. This problem can be addressed through the use of multifunction controls (Wierwille, 1984). One type of multifunction control consists of a joystick that includes additional switches. The F-18 aircraft has two multifunction controls, one for the left hand and one for the right. These controls are shown in Figure 16–15. They are used with head-up displays to allow the pilot to maintain visual contact with the target. Thus, the controls must be operable without being viewed directly.

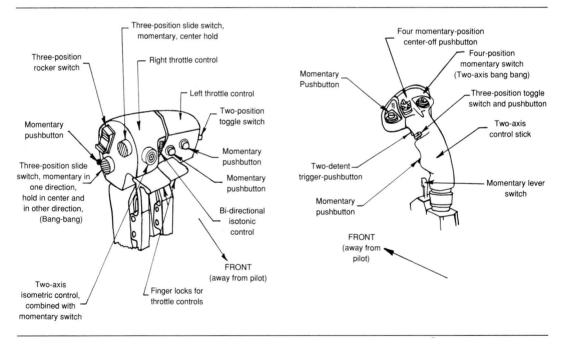

FIGURE 16–15 Left- and Right-hand Multifunctional Controls for the F-18 Aircraft.

From W. Wierville (1984). The design and location of control: A brief review and introduction to new problems. In H. Schmidtke (Ed.), *Ergonomic Data for Equipment Design* (pp. 179–194). Copyright © 1984 by Plenum Press. Reprinted by permission.

As Wierwille (1984) stresses, the use of multifunction controls represents a distinct change in design philosophy. Most of the basic design principles discussed earlier, such as display–control compatibility, minimization of accidental activation, and functional grouping, must be compromised. The new principles are that the controls must be designed so that (1) they need not be observed, (2) the hands remain in contact with the control, and (3) auxiliary controls can be easily activated by the thumb and fingers.

Foot-operated Controls

Foot controls are used in automobiles and airplanes. They are also used to power vehicles, such as bicycles, and to operate some musical instruments (for example, pianos) and electrical machinery (for example, sewing machines). As a general rule, foot controls provide a viable option for situations in which the hands are occupied or considerable force must be exerted.

Of primary concern is the speed and accuracy with which foot controls can be activated. Kroemer (1971) required seated people to move their right feet 150 mm to a 60-mm target. He found that, after several sessions of practice, movements in all directions (front, back, left, right) could be made very quickly (in approximately 100 ms).

Fitts's law states that movement time is a function of the width and distance of the target. Drury (1975) evaluated Fitts's law for repetitive foot movements. He noted that the effective target width is determined by both the actual target width and shoe size. He modified the index of difficulty (I) to account for shoe width:

$$I = \log_2 \left(\frac{D}{W + S} + 0.5 \right)$$

where D is target size, W is target width, and S is shoe sole width. In two experiments, this modified version of Fitts's law accurately described movement time for foot movements. Drury emphasized that, when the separation between coplanar pedals is set at a minimum safe separation of 130 mm (which is the 99th percentile shoe size), pedal width has relatively little influence on movement time.

Probably the most research on foot controls has involved brake and accelerator pedals in automobiles. Typically, the accelerator is mounted lower than the brake. However, responses are considerably slower with this configuration than when the pedals are coplanar (Davies & Watt, 1969; Snyder, 1976). Moreover, movement time is even faster when the brake pedal is placed 2.5 to 5.1 cm lower than the accelerator (Glass & Suggs, 1977). The apparent reason for this improvement is that the accelerator typically is depressed at the time that a braking action must be taken. The heights of the depressed accelerator and the brake will be more comparable if the resting position of the brake is lower.

Incidents are reported every year in which an automobile appears to have accelerated out of control, even though the operator claims to have had his or her foot on the brake and not the accelerator. Schmidt (1989) has noted that these unintended acceleration incidents are probably not due to mechanical failure because such episodes have been reported for a wide variety of automatic transmission designs. Instead, unintended acceleration seems to be caused by foot-placement errors. That is, the driver inadvertently depresses the accelerator when intending to depress the brake. Errors of this type have been observed in a variety of experimental tasks. The Texas Transportation Institute recently reported that vehicle to vehicle variation in placement of the brake and accelerator pedals in different car models is sufficiently large that the probability of pedal errors is increased when driving an unfamiliar car. Schmidt proposes that such errors may be due to variability in nerve impulses at the levels of the muscles and spinal cord, which may explain why drivers are unaware of the error. This unawareness of the error in foot placement is the major factor in being unable to stop the car.

Specialized Controls

For certain applications, it is desirable to have controls that do not require limb movements. Such controls are particularly useful for individuals who have limited use of their limbs, but, more generally, they may be beneficial for situations in which the limbs are otherwise engaged.

Speech Controls. Automated speech technology has progressed to the point where it is now possible to use speech-activated controls for computers and other systems (Simpson et al., 1985). A speech-recognition system includes a recognition algorithm and a device that responds to the recognized speech. One basic distinction can be made between speaker-dependent and speaker-independent systems. The dependent systems, which are most common, require examples of the user's own speech, whereas the independent systems are intended to recognize speech spoken by virtually anyone. Speaker-independent recognition systems work best with a small vocabulary (less than 20 utterances) and a relatively homogeneous population of speakers.

A second basic distinction is between isolated word, connected word, and continuous speech systems. Isolated-word systems, which are the most prevalent, respond to individual words and require the speaker to pause for at least 100 ms between words. Connected-word systems do not require artificial pauses, but the words must be spoken without inflection, as if they were being read from a list. Continuous-speech systems are intended for use with natural speech. The complexity of each system increases as the speech that they can recognize becomes more natural.

Recognition accuracy is the major limitation of any speech-recognition system. Conditions that produce variability in speech patterns, such as environmental stressors, will reduce the recognition accuracy. The successful implementation of a speech system requires that it be integrated with other equipment. Speech controls are likely to improve performance only for complex tasks in which the visual and manual demands are high.

Casali, Williges, and Dryden (1990) examined performance and user acceptability as a function of the accuracy of the speech recognizer and the size of its available vocabulary. People performed a data-entry task under three levels of accuracy and three sizes of vocabulary. The time to complete the task increased with decreases in accuracy and vocabulary, as did the number of uncorrected errors. However, user-acceptability ratings were affected only by the accuracy of the speech recognizer. Differences between older and younger people were apparent in slower task completion times for the elderly under conditions of low accuracy.

Automatic speech recognition is a particularly promising means of control for disabled individuals. Noyes, Haigh, and Starr (1989) reviewed the status of speech-recognizer technology and its applications, concluding that current speech-recognition systems have much to offer the physically challenged individual. Among other things, speech recognition can be used by disabled persons to control robotic arms, to interact with microcomputers, and to control their own medical environment. Noyes et al. cautioned that the recognition performance of speech-recognition systems must be improved before system control can be made completely dependent on speech. They targeted a lack of human factors work as impeding progress in this field.

Eye- and Head-movement Controls. Another way to control a system is through eye and head movements. Equipment for monitoring eye and head movements can be mounted on the head, and then the direction of gaze can be used to activate controls. Alternatively, a stick or pointing device can be attached to the head; this device can then be used to tap control input. Systems of these types have potential applications for the military and for disabled individuals.

One use of head-movement controls is to allow disabled individuals to enter information into a computer. In Chapter 14, we discussed the fact that Fitts's law applies to tapping that is controlled by the head. It also describes results that are obtained when the head movements directly control a cursor (Radwin, Vanderheiden, & Li, 1990; Spitz, 1990). The slope of the function relating movement time to the index of difficulty is substantially greater with head movements than it is with either a manually operated mouse or digitizing tablet. Because pointing with head movements is not as efficient as with manual input devices, head-movement control should be restricted to situations in which movement time is not a factor or in which the operator is physically handicapped.

Teleoperators.   *Teleoperators* are dextrous machines that perform as remote extensions of the operator's arms, hands, legs, and feet (Johnsen & Corliss, 1971). They can range from sophisticated robotic arms to tongs used to grasp objects and include prosthetics that can be used to enable a physically disabled person to perform more like someone who is not. Teleoperators enable such actions as picking up samples of the lunar surface from signals on earth and manipulating radioactive compounds.

Many traditional human factors issues must be confronted in the design of teleoperators. Designers must determine which control-oriented tasks to assign to the operator and which to the machine. Spatial correspondence should exist between the positions of the controls and those parts of the teleoperator that they control. Vision and other sensory feedback must be incorporated into the control. For the teleoperator itself, decisions must be made about which types of controls to use.

The control of teleoperators is subject to many of the same constraints as human motor control. Among other things, Fitts's law applies to the relation between speed and accuracy when making an aimed movement with a teleoperator arm, although the slope is much greater than for human arm movements (Draper, Handel, & Hood, 1990). Wallace and Carlson (1992) propose that the dynamics of teleoperator movement should be consistent with those of the operator for control to be optimal.

SUMMARY

Humans communicate with machines through the operation of controls. Controls come in a variety of types, shapes, and sizes. Their mechanical properties produce different feels that can be exploited to optimize performance in a variety of applications. Population stereotypes can also be exploited to ensure that the movements associated with a control function are the ones most natural for the operators involved. Performance will vary as a function of the relation between control displacement and system response.

Often, many controls are arranged on a single control panel. Panels must be designed to avoid confusion about which control to operate and about the relations among display elements and controls. Controls should be coded in such a way that they will be identifiable. Frequently used controls should be readily accessible, and controls critical to the integrity of the system should be designed to avoid accidental activation.

This chapter concludes our discussion of the ways that operators control their own movements and the movements of objects and machines in the environment around them. We have described the relationship between operators and machines from the perspective of information processing. The human and machine operate as a closed-loop system in which information is passed back and forth through the human–machine interface. It is important to recognize, however, that the human–machine system does not operate in isolation but in the context of the surrounding environment. Part 5 of this book will discuss the way in which the environment affects the performance of the operator, which in turn determines the performance of the entire system.

RECOMMENDED READING

Bullinger, H. J., Kern, P., & Muntzinger, W. F. (1987). Design of controls. In G. Salvendy (ed.), *Handbook of Human Factors* (pp. 577–600). New York: Wiley.

Chapanis, A., & Kinkade, R. G. (1972) Design of controls. In H. P. Van Cott & R. G. Kinkade (eds.), *Human Engineering Guide to Equipment Design* (pp. 345–379). Washington, DC: U.S. Superintendent of Documents.

Eastman Kodak Company (1983). *Ergonomic Design for People at Work,* Vol. 1. New York: Van Nostrand Reinhold.

Patrick, J., & Duncan, K. D. (eds.) (1988). *Training, Human Decision Making, and Control.* Amsterdam: North-Holland.

Poulton, E. C. (1974). *Tracking Skill and Manual Control.* New York: Academic Press.

ANTHROPOMETRICS AND WORKSPACE DESIGN

Designing workplaces, equipment, and the physical environment to fit the characteristics and capabilities of most people is a complex task.
—The Human Factors Section, Eastman Kodak Company

INTRODUCTION

The measurement of human physical characteristics is called *anthropometrics,* and *engineering anthropometry* refers to the design of equipment, tasks, and workspaces that ensures their compatibility with the anthropometric characteristics of the user population. The reach envelope discussed in Chapter 16 is an example of the use to which human factors specialists put anthropometric data. By designing the envelope around the 5th percentile for reach distance, 95% of the users should be able to reach the controls within the envelope.

It is not enough just to know whether controls or other objects can be reached. In addition, the motions of the joints of the body and the range of these motions need to be considered. *Biomechanics* involves the motions of the body. Human factors specialists apply biomechanical data to equipment design. As with anthropometrics, the basic idea is that equipment and tasks should be designed to accommodate the biomechanics of the user population.

One major use of anthropometric data is in the design of workspaces. A workspace is any area in which a person works for an extended period of time. Workspaces are desks, control panels, computer work stations, assembly-line stations, truck cabs, and so on. Working in a poorly designed workspace for long amounts of time can be physically and psychologically damaging to the operator, as well as detrimental to the operation of the system. Several aspects of workspace design, such as the display of information and the organization of control panels, have been discussed in previous chapters. More broadly, the ensemble of equipment that makes up the workspace must be designed and arranged to be compatible with the operator's physical capabilities (see Figure 17–1).

In the present chapter we summarize the principles of engineering anthropometry and biomechanics. Violations of these principles can result in painful and debilitating injuries. Anthropometrics and biomechanics play an important role in hand-tool design and manual materials handling. Because tool usage and manual materials handling are involved in many jobs and are the sources of many work-related injuries, factors that influence the efficiency and safety of tools and materials handling are evaluated. The way in which anthropometric and biomechanical factors are incorporated into workspace design is then considered.

ENGINEERING ANTHROPOMETRY

The term *anthropometry* means "to measure man." Anthropometrics thus refers to measurement of the dimensions of the human body. Measurements of particular body dimensions will be made for many individuals within a population of interest, with the purpose of accurately describing the anthropometric characteristics of that population. The resulting distributions of measurements are normally distributed. Measures of central tendency (mean or median) and variability (standard deviation) published in tables allow the design engineer to reconstruct the distributions. Often the tables also include values for commonly used percentile ranks.

The most commonly used percentile ranks are the 5th, 50th, and 95th percentiles, below which 5%, 50%, and 95% of the population fall.

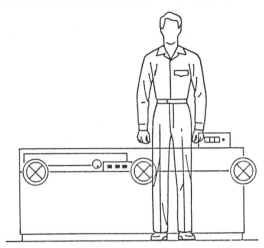

(a) Most people look like this, but ...

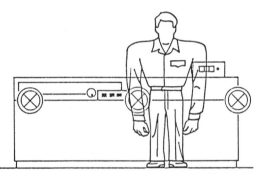

(b) Some designers think that people are shaped like this

FIGURE 17–1   A Designer's Conception of the Ideal Lathe Operator, as Compared to the Average Operator.

From *Ergonomic Design for People at Work* (Vol. 1). Published by Van Nostrand Reinhold, 1983. Copyright © 1983 by Eastman Kodak Company. Reprinted courtesy of Eastman Kodak Company.

For example, Table 17–1 lists the body dimensions for females and males in the United States. The purpose of the respective percentiles is to represent minimal, average, and maximum values of the measurement. These data are used to establish design criteria for equipment that is intended for human use. They are also used to provide criteria for evaluating existing equipment and for selecting operators to fit the work-

TABLE 17–1 U.S. Civilian Body Dimensions, Female/Male, in Centimeters for Ages 20 to 60 Years[a]

	PERCENTILES			
	5th	*50th*	*95th*	*Standard Deviation*
Heights[(f above floor, s above seat)]				
Stature (height)[f]	149.5 / 161.8	160.5 / 173.6	171.3 / 184.4	6.6 / 6.9
Eye height[f]	138.3 / 151.1	148.9 / 162.4	159.3 / 172.7	6.4 / 6.6[b]
Shoulder (acromion) height[f]	121.1 / 132.3	131.1 / 142.8	141.9 / 152.4	6.1 / 6.1[b]
Elbow height[f]	93.6 / 100.0	101.2 / 109.9	108.8 / 119.0	4.6 / 5.8
Knuckle height[f]	64.3 / 69.8	70.2 / 75.4	75.9 / 80.4	3.5 / 3.2
Height, sitting[s]	78.6 / 84.2	85.0 / 90.6	90.7 / 96.7	3.5 / 3.7
Eye height, sitting[s]	67.5 / 72.6	73.3 / 78.6	78.5 / 84.4	3.3 / 3.6[b]
Shoulder height, sitting[s]	49.2 / 52.7	55.7 / 59.4	61.7 / 65.8	3.8 / 4.0[b]
Elbow rest height, sitting[s]	18.1 / 19.0	23.3 / 24.3	28.1 / 29.4	2.9 / 3.0
Knee height, sitting[f]	45.2 / 49.3	49.8 / 54.3	54.5 / 59.3	2.7 / 2.9
Popliteal height, sitting[f]	35.5 / 39.2	39.8 / 44.2	44.3 / 48.8	2.6 / 2.8
Thigh clearance height[f]	10.6 / 11.4	13.7 / 14.4	17.5 / 17.7	1.8 / 1.7
Depths				
Chest depth	21.4 / 21.4	24.2 / 24.2	29.7 / 27.6	2.5 / 1.9[b]
Elbow–fingertip distance	38.5 / 44.1	42.1 / 47.9	56.0 / 51.4	2.2 / 2.2
Buttock–knee distance, sitting	51.8 / 54.0	56.9 / 59.4	62.5 / 64.2	3.1 / 3.0
Buttock–popliteal distance, sitting	43.0 / 44.2	48.1 / 49.5	53.5 / 54.8	3.1 / 3.0
Forward reach, functional	64.0 / 76.3	71.0 / 82.5	79.0 / 88.3	4.5 / 5.0
Breadths				
Elbow to elbow breadth	31.5 / 35.0	38.4 / 41.7	49.1 / 50.6	5.4 / 4.6
Hip breadth, sitting	31.2 / 30.8	36.4 / 35.4	43.7 / 40.6	3.7 / 2.8
Head dimensions				
Head breadth	13.6 / 14.4	14.54 / 15.42	15.5 / 16.4	0.57 / 0.59
Head circumference	52.3 / 53.8	54.9 / 56.8	57.7 / 59.3	1.63 / 1.68
Interpupillary distance	5.1 / 5.5	5.83 / 6.20	6.5 / 6.8	0.44 / 0.39
Foot dimensions				
Foot length	22.3 / 24.8	24.1 / 26.9	26.2 / 29.0	1.19 / 1.28
Foot breadth	8.1 / 9.0	8.84 / 9.79	9.7 / 10.7	0.50 / 0.53
Lateral malleolus height	5.8 / 6.2	6.78 / 7.03	7.8 / 8.0	0.59 / 0.54
Hand dimensions				
Hand length	16.4 / 17.6	17.95 / 19.05	19.8 / 20.6	1.04 / 0.93
Breadth, metacarpal	7.0 / 8.2	7.66 / 8.88	8.4 / 9.8	0.41 / 0.47
Circumference, metacarpal	16.9 / 19.9	18.36 / 21.55	19.9 / 23.5	0.89 / 1.09
Thickness, meta III	2.5 / 2.4	2.77 / 2.76	3.1 / 3.1	0.18 / 0.21
Digit 1: Breadth of interphalangeal	1.7 / 2.1	1.98 / 2.29	2.1 / 2.5	0.12 / 0.21
Crotch-tip length	4.7 / 5.1	5.36 / 5.88	6.1 / 6.6	0.44 / 0.45

TABLE 17–1 Continued

	PERCENTILES			
	5th	50th	95th	Standard Deviation
Digit 2: Breadth of				
distal joint	1.4 / 1.7	1.55 / 1.85	1.7 / 2.0	0.10 / 0.12
Crotch-tip length	6.1 / 6.8	6.88 / 7.52	7.8 / 8.2	0.52 / 0.46
Digit 3: Breadth of				
distal joint	1.4 / 1.7	1.53 / 1.85	1.7 / 2.0	0.09 / 0.12
Crotch-tip length	7.0 / 7.8	7.77 / 8.53	8.7 / 9.5	0.51 / 0.51
Digit 4: Breadth of				
distal joint	1.3 / 1.6	1.42 / 1.70	1.6 / 1.9	0.09 / 0.11
Crotch-tip length	6.5 / 7.4	7.29 / 7.99	8.2 / 8.9	0.53 / 0.47
Digit 5: Breadth of				
distal joint	1.2 / 1.4	1.32 / 1.57	1.5 / 1.8	0.09 / 0.12
Crotch-tip length	4.8 / 5.4	5.44 / 6.08	6.2 / 6.99	0.44 / 0.47
Weight (in kg)	46.2 / 56.2	61.1 / 74.0	89.9 / 97.1	13.8 / 12.6

From K. H. E. Kroemer, H. J. Kroemer, & K. E. Kroemer-Elbert, *Engineering Physiology* (2nd ed.). Copyright © 1990 by Van Nostrand Reinhold. Reprinted by permission.
[a]Courtesy of Dr. J. T. McConville, Anthropology Research Project, Yellow Springs OH 45387 and Dr. K. W. Kennedy, then USAF-AAMRL-HEG, OH 45433.
[b]Estimated by K.H.E. Kroemer.

space dimensions (Kroemer, 1983a). For example, the Apollo Command Module was designed to accommodate up to the 90th percentile for standing height (among other measurements), so astronaut recruits could not exceed 1.83 m (approximately 6 ft).

Anthropometric Measurement

In classical anthropometry, the concern has been with static measures obtained while the body is in a particular posture. Standing height would be an example of a static measure. Static measures are the core of the anthropometric data base. Functional measurements, which incorporate biomechanical constraints, are also needed to indicate whether the operator can execute a particular function. The reach envelope is an example of a functional measurement, because reaching will

differ for various grasps that must be used and tasks that must be performed with an object. Functional anthropometry is used to specify the workspace dimensions needed for the operator.

Measurements can be made with instruments such as measuring tapes, calipers, and weight scales, as well as more sophisticated photographic, electronic, and sonic systems that can measure the static positions of body joints and their motions (Hsiao & Keyserling, 1990). The following terms are basic in anthropometry (Kroemer, Kroemer, & Kroemer-Elbert, 1990, pp. 2–3):

> *Height* is a straight-line, point-to-point vertical measurement.
> *Breadth* is a straight-line, point-to-point horizontal measurement running across the body or a body segment.
> *Depth* is a straight-line, point-to-point horizontal measurement running fore–aft the body.

Distance is a straight-line, point-to-point measurement between landmarks on the body.

Curvature is a point-to-point measurement following a body contour; this measurement is neither closed nor usually circular.

Circumference is a closed measurement that follows a body contour; hence this measurement usually is not circular.

Reach is a point-to-point measurement following the long axis of the arm or leg.

Anthropometric measures usually are described in terms of the position of the body, the part of the body being measured, and the direction of the dimension being measured. The measurements often are with reference to the measuring planes and descriptive terms shown in Figure 17–2, with the person standing or seated, as in Figure 17–3.

Biomechanical measurements typically are more complex. The muscle force generated by a

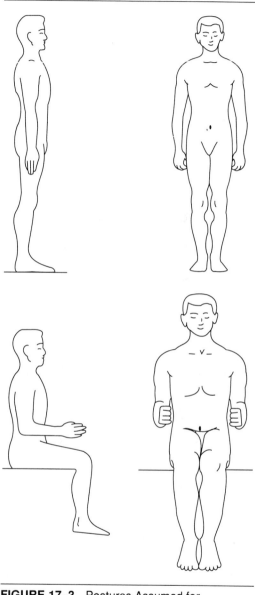

FIGURE 17–3 Postures Assumed for Anthropometric Measurements.

person, which is of particular interest in engineering anthropometry, can be measured directly. Static strength can be defined as the maximal force that muscles can exert isometrically in a single effort (Roebuck, Kroemer, & Thomson,

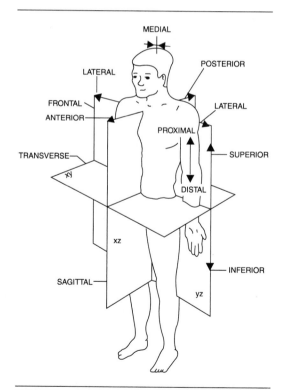

FIGURE 17–2 Descriptive Terms and Measuring Planes Used in Anthropometry.

1975) and dynamic strength as the amount of force that can be applied throughout the range of motion (Ayoub, 1982). However, most applications of biomechanical data must rely on models of the musculoskeletal system to estimate the range of motion and stress for particular body segments (Kroemer et al., 1988). Anthropometric data are used together with these models to evaluate particular designs.

Engineering anthropometry provides important data for the design of equipment to ensure that it will be usable by all but the extreme members of a population. For clearance problems, which include head room, knee room, elbow room, and access to passageways and equipment, the largest or tallest individuals should be considered. Most often the 95th percentile value for height or breadth will be used. For reach problems, which involve the locations of controls and objects, as well as seat height when the feet must reach the floor, the design should be based on the lower extreme, or the 5th percentile value for arm length and popliteal (knee) height. If an object is intended to be out of reach, such as a control that should not be unintentionally activated, then this criterion is reversed.

For problems of work-surface height, such as kitchen-counter or desk height, the design should be for the average individual, or the 50th percentile. However, even when designing for the 50th percentile, the work surface will be too high or too low for most individuals. When possible, it is best to allow adjustment of such things as seat height and work-surface height so that the arrangement can be optimized for each individual. Posture problems that arise because a work surface is too high or too low or because a chair is at the wrong height can be prevented by adjustability.

Sources of Anthropometric Data

There are several sources of anthropometric data. Among these are the NASA *Anthropometric Source Book* (1978) and the *USAF Anthropometric Data Bank,* which include the results of many separate surveys. As with the use of any tabled data source, caution should be exercised in using anthropometric data. The population for which the measures were made must correspond with the population of intended users if the tabled values are to be applied meaningfully. For example, the height of Taiwanese and Japanese populations is considerably less than that of U.S. and European populations (Li, Hwang, & Wang, 1990). Consequently, designs based on the anthropometric data for the former will not be appropriate for the latter, and vice versa.

Data for civilian populations are somewhat limited, because most available data were obtained from military populations (Van Cott, 1980). Military and civilian populations are similar in terms of head, hand, and foot size, but differ on most other dimensions (Kroemer, Kroemer, & Kroemer-Elbert, 1990). One possible way to use the military data for civilian populations is to adjust the tabled values to take into account the population differences. McConville, Robinette, and Churchill (1981) have shown that, if civilian males are matched with the military samples on height and weight, the military data are adequate for many design purposes. However, such is not the case for females, where the matched sample of military women differs substantially from civilian women. The lack of civilian anthropometric data stems in part from the nonexistence of a central agency devoted to the collection of such data.

Anthropometric data obtained from the civilian population of adults cannot generally be applied to specific subpopulations. For example, the median weight for farm equipment operators is about 14% greater than for the general population (Casey, 1989). As a consequence, seats designed to satisfy anthropometric criteria for the general population will not be appropriate for the greater weight of many farm equipment operators. The dimensions of the equipment need to be increased to accommodate the larger size of the operators. As another example, the girth of a pregnant woman is larger than that of a nonpregnant woman. Culver and Viano (1990) have collected anthropometric data for women in all stages of pregnancy. These data can be used to design automobile interiors and restraints, among other things, so that the increased girth of a pregnant woman can be accommodated.

Insufficient anthropometric data are available for people over age 65 (Kroemer et al., 1988). Kelly and Kroemer (1990) have tabulated anthropometric data from the existing studies of the elderly. They note that most of these studies have been conducted with healthy white males. Consequently, much information of importance regarding elderly females is missing, as are data classified according to health status and other characteristics. More generally, because variance increases with age, the elderly population is very heterogeneous, although they are often treated as a homogeneous group. Not only does physical size change, but many people over age 65 have chronic health conditions and diminished functional capabilities that restrict their mobility. These restrictions are not represented in the anthropometric data.

Similarly, although the pertinent anthropometric measurements for mentally and physically challenged persons differ from those of the general population, relatively few data are available for designing workspaces and tools that are ergonomically acceptable for these special populations (Deivanayagam, 1982). A study by Hobson and Molenbroek (1990) obtained anthropometric data to be used in designing seats for people with cerebral palsy. Hobson and Molenbroek emphasized the importance of delineating

differences within disabled populations, because even persons with the same disability will show differences in posture, muscle development and bone structure. For anthropometric data from these populations to be useful, such differences must be noted.

Biomechanical Factors

Equipment within a workspace is often used for extended periods of time. Therefore, the equipment must not only be designed to be accessible but also to be used for prolonged periods. With extended use, many actions are performed, some repetitively and some infrequently. Consequently, biomechanical constraints become major factors in the design and evaluation of tasks and workspaces. By considering these biomechanical factors, as well as anthropometric factors, conditions that promote injury and discomfort can be eliminated early in the design of a workspace. Modification of a poorly designed workspace after it has been implemented is always expensive.

Tichauer (1978, p. 32) defined *work tolerance* as "a state in which the individual worker performs at economically acceptable rates, while enjoying high levels of emotional and physiological well-being." This means that an operator should be both productive and healthy. The level of work tolerance depends on three categories of biomechanical factors (see Table 17–2).

The first category involves factors that influence aspects of posture. Good posture minimizes

TABLE 17–2   Factors to Maximize Biomechanical Work Tolerance

POSTURAL		ENGINEERING		KINESIOLOGICAL	
P1	Keep elbows down.	E1	Avoid compression ischemia.	K1	Keep forward reaches short.
P2	Minimize moments on spine.	E2	Avoid critical vibrations.	K2	Avoid muscular insufficiency.
P3	Consider sex differences.	E3	Individualize chair design.	K3	Avoid straight-line motions.
P4	Optimize skeletal configuration.	E4	Avoid stress concentration.	K4	Consider working gloves.
P5	Avoid head movement.	E5	Keep wrist straight.	K5	Avoid antagonist fatigue.

From E. Tichauer (1978). *The Biomechanical Basis of Ergonomics.* Copyright © 1978 by John Wiley & Sons, Inc. Reprinted by permission of John Wiley & Sons, Inc.

skeletal and muscular stress. Such stress can be prevented by designing the workspace so that elbows can be close to the body and so that forces (moments) acting on the spine are small. Tasks must be structured to allow both men and women to maintain good posture. For example, differences between the center of mass in males and females can result in a 15% increase in lifting stress for a woman over that experienced by a man while lifting the same object. Head movements should be minimized because they are both time consuming and physically stressful when performed repeatedly.

Engineering considerations are those that refer to the design of the system interface. Compression ischemia, or obstruction of the blood flow, can be caused by improperly designed or misused equipment. Exposure to vibrations, discussed in Chapter 18, can cause tissue damage and psychological stress. It is important that chairs occupied by operators for long periods of time be designed to provide proper support. Often, stress can be concentrated on particular tissues during repetitive work. Specialized equipment, such as tools that allow the wrist to be kept straight, can be used to prevent injuries.

Kinesiological factors are those regarding the type and range of movements that are performed. Long, forward reaches produce stress on the spinal column and so should be avoided. The term muscular insufficiency is used to describe the decreased range of movement due to overextended antagonist muscles or to completely contracted agonist muscles. It can be prevented by designing the workspace so that controls, tools, and other objects do not require manipulation at the extremes of muscular contraction. Curved movements are more natural than straight movements, and they are easier to learn and produce less fatigue. Movements can be obstructed by protective clothing, such as gloves and chemical suits, so the operator's restricted range of movement while wearing such clothing must be taken into consideration. Antagonist muscles are smaller than agonist muscles, and smaller mus-

cles fatigue more quickly than larger muscles. Consequently, tasks should be designed to prevent fatigue of the smallest muscles involved.

CUMULATIVE TRAUMA DISORDERS

When certain types of manual actions are performed repetitively, they lead to *cumulative trauma disorders*. Such disorders are a collection of "syndromes characterized by discomfort, impairment, disability or persistent pain in joints, muscles, tendons and other soft tissues, with or without physical manifestations" (Kroemer, 1989, p. 274). Cumulative trauma disorders are associated with many work activities, including manual assembly, packing, and typing, as well as with leisure activities such as sports and playing video games. The disorders arise from repeated physical stress at the joints, which in turn causes damage to the tissues and/or to the associated nerve fibers. These disorders can cause extreme pain and physical impairment to a worker, as well as reduced productivity and increased medical costs and disability compensation for an industry.

The symptoms of cumulative trauma disorders include pain, swelling, weakness, and numbness in the affected region. The onset of the symptoms usually occurs in three stages (Chatterjee, 1987). In the first stage, pain and weakness may occur during work but subside during off hours. During the second stage, the symptoms are evident between work shifts and the ability to perform repetitive work is diminished. Finally, in the third stage, pain is persistent even when at rest. Sleep may be disrupted, and performance of a range of tasks may be difficult. Each of the first two stages usually lasts for weeks or months, while the third stage may last for years. It is important to detect the disorder at the first stage, because it is completely reversible at that point if the source of the physical stress is removed or brought within acceptable limits.

Cumulative trauma disorders can occur at any joint and associated body region. However, most occur in the upper extremity of the body, with 60% of all cases involving the wrist and hand. Table 17–3 lists several of the disorders for the hand and wrist and their associated risk factors. The most widely publicized of these disorders is carpal tunnel syndrome. This syndrome arises when large intrawrist forces produce inflammation and swelling of the ligaments and tendons in the carpal tunnel of the wrist (see Figure 17–4). This swelling puts pressure on the median nerve, which delivers neural signals to and from the thumb and index and middle fingers.

Pain, numbness, and tingling of the fingers are early symptoms of carpal tunnel syndrome, with atrophy of the muscles and significant reduction in use of the fingers occurring at more advanced stages. Similar symptoms occur for the ring and little fingers when the ulnar nerve that innervates them is entrapped in the Guyon tunnel. Guyon tunnel syndrome is less common and less disabling than carpal tunnel syndrome.

Tendonitus is a disorder associated with inflammation of a tendon that is tensed or moved

TABLE 17–3   Some Reported Occupational Risk Factors for Cumulative Trauma Disorders of the Upper Extremity

DISORDER	REPORTED OCCUPATIONAL RISK FACTORS
Carpal tunnel syndrome	1. Accustomed and unaccustomed repetitive work with the hands 2. Work that involves repeated wrist flexion or extreme extension, particularly in combination with forceful pinching 3. Repeated forces on the base of the palm and wrist
Tenosynovitis and peritendonitis crepitans of the abductor and extensor pollicus tendons of the radial styloid (DeQuervain's disease)	1. More than 2,000 manipulations per hour 2. Performance of unaccustomed work 3. Single or repetitive local strain 4. Direct local blunt trauma 5. Simple repetitive movement that is forceful and fast 6. Repeated radial deviation of the wrist, particularly in combination with forceful exertions of the thumb 7. Repeated ulnar deviation of the wrist, particularly in combination with forceful exertions of the thumb
Tenosynovitis of finger flexor tendons	Exertions with a flexed wrist
Tenosynovitis of finger extensor tendons	Ulnar deviation of the wrist outward rotation
Epicondylitis	Radial deviation of the wrist with inward wrist rotation
Ganglionic cysts	1. Sudden or hard, unaccustomed use of tendon or joint 2. Repeated manipulations with extended wrist 3. Repeated twisting of the wrist
Neuritis in the fingers	Contact with hand tools over a nerve in the palm of sides or fingers

From T. J. Armstrong et al. (1982). Investigation of cumulative trauma disorders in a poultry processing plant. *American Industrial Hygiene Association Journal, 43,* 103–116. Reprinted by permission.

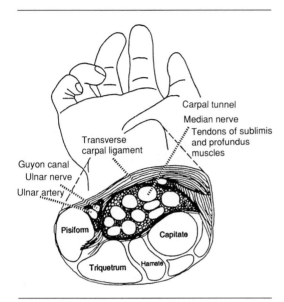

FIGURE 17–4   The Carpal Tunnel and Associated Ligaments, Tendons and Nerve.

repetitively. Tendons are usually protected by a sheath that contains lubricating fluid. Teno-synovitus and ganglionic cysts arise from swelling of the sheath due to excess fluid. In the case of cysts, this leads to visible bumps on the skin. Disorders of tendons and nerve entrapment are not restricted to the wrist and hand. Such disorders also occur in the elbow and arm and the neck and shoulder.

Three factors contribute to the occurrence of cumulative trauma disorders (Ayoub & Wittels, 1989): individual risk factors, ergonomic deficiencies of the workspace or the job, and management practices. Many individual risk factors are associated with the disorders. More women than men develop the disorders, and the incidence increases with age. Diseases that reduce circulation, as well as past injuries and other traumatic conditions, increase the risk. Physically fit individuals have less incidence of cumulative trauma disorders than do unfit individuals.

However, fitting the person to the job is not a solution. A tool, workstation, or job should be designed to fit an operator's physical capabilities. Activities should be avoided that require highly repetitive movements, prolonged exertion of force involving more than 30% of a person's muscle strength, awkward or extreme positions for the body segments, or a single body posture to be maintained for long time periods (Kroemer, 1989). The incidence of cumulative trauma disorders can be minimized through proper tool design and through proper workspace design and work allocation.

Management practices can also affect the incidence of cumulative trauma disorders. By analyzing tasks and jobs for their potential to produce disorders, the jobs can be designed to minimize the risk. Moreover, if workers and medical personnel are aware of the early symptoms associated with the disorders, diagnosis and treatment of a disorder can be made at an early, easily reversible stage. Procedures should be instituted for reassigning a worker diagnosed with a cumulative trauma disorder to a different job with different postural and movement characteristics. The problem will likely recur or even be aggravated if the worker is returned to the same job unless the underlying cause of the disorder can be identified and eliminated.

HAND TOOLS

Manual hand tools enable the performance of tasks that would be difficult or impossible to perform without the tools. Power hand tools provide the additional benefit of replacing the operator's strength with a different primary energy source, thereby reducing the amount of physical exertion for the operator and increasing the amount of force that can be generated. To be efficient, a tool must fulfill several requirements (Drillis, 1963). The tool should (1) perform well the function for which it is intended, (2) be properly proportioned to the operator's body dimensions, (3) be adjusted to the strength and work capacity of the operator, (4) not cause premature fatigue, (5) be adapted to the operator's sensory capacities, and (6) be inexpensive to purchase and maintain.

Hand tools are simple relative to complex systems such as manufacturing plants and aircraft, so there is a tendency to underestimate the importance of human factors considerations in tool design. Yet, as should be apparent from the requirements listed above, a tool must be designed to be compatible with human physical and psychological capabilities if it is to be used efficiently and safely. Because most hand tools do not conform to human factors specifications, the proportion of work-related injuries attributable to hand-tool use is between 9% and 10% (Mital, 1986). Problems that occur when human factors are not considered in tool design include the following (Greenberg & Chaffin, 1977, p. 7):

a. Pinching, crushing and amputation of the finger tips or of entire fingers;
b. Entry of foreign objects into the eyes, with possible loss of vision;
c. Straining or "tearing" of muscle tendons, causing acute and chronic pain with reduced function;
d. Inflammation of the wrist/hand tendon sheaths and nerves, making finger and wrist motion very painful and limited;
e. Back pains, with resulting difficulty of torso motion and lifting;
f. Muscle fatigue, causing decreased capability for performing manual work;
g. Mental fatigue, producing slow and error-prone work;
h. Prolonged operator learning times.

Tool Handles

The design goal for many hand tools is to maximize the forces produced with the tool while minimizing the physical stress to which the body is subjected. When the wrist deviates from its neutral posture, the amount of stress on the supporting tissues and the median nerve increases significantly. Consequently, to minimize cumulative trauma disorders, tools should be shaped to avoid bending of the wrist. Figure 17–5 shows a bent-handled soldering iron that reduces wrist deviation relative to a straight-handled iron. Tichauer (1978) compared two groups of trainees

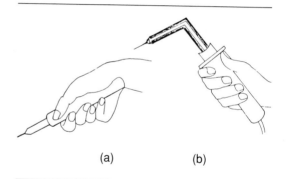

(a)   (b)

FIGURE 17–5   Straight-handled (a) and Bent-handled (b) Soldering Irons Held in the Posture for Soldering on a Horizontal Surface. The Forearm is in a More Natural Posture with the Bent-handled Iron.

From D. B. Chaffin & G. B. J. Andersson (1984). *Occupational Biomechanics.* Copyright © 1984 by John Wiley & Sons, Inc. Reprinted by permission of John Wiley & Sons, Inc.

on an electronics assembly line using either bent-handled or straight-handled pliers (see Figure 17–6). After 12 weeks on the job, 60% of the trainees using the straight-handled pliers had developed some type of wrist-related disorder, compared to only 10% of those using the bent-handled pliers.

Schoenmarklin and Marras (1989a & b) investigated the effects of handle angle for two hammering tasks. People hammered either a horizontal surface (a bench) or a vertical surface (a wall) using a hammer with a handle that was angled 0°, 20°, or 40° from its center of mass (see Figure 17–7). The amount of wrist flexion at impact was least for the 40° handle and greatest for the 0° handle. This reduced wrist deviation using angled hammers suggests that they would reduce hand–wrist disorders.

No differences in accuracy as a function of handle angle were observed when hammering the horizontal surface, although accuracy was slightly reduced for the 20° and 40° handles than for the 0° handle when hammering the vertical surface. Measures of fatigue and subjective ratings of discomfort revealed no benefits or costs

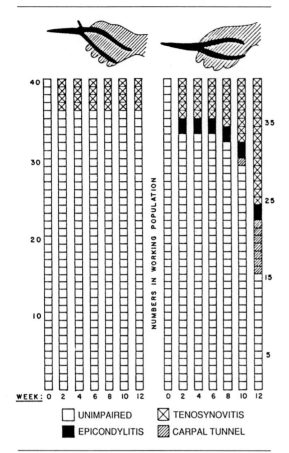

FIGURE 17–6 Percentages of Electronics Trainees Showing Cumulative Trauma Disorders After Using Either Bent or Straight Pliers for 0–12 Weeks.

From E. R. Tichauer (1976). Biomechanics sustains occupational health and safety. Reprinted from *Industrial Engineering* magazine, February 1976. Copyright 1976, Institute of Industrial Engineers, 25 Technology Park/Atlanta, Norcross, Georgia 30092.

When a tool requires bending the wrist, the user will often compensate by raising the arm (abduction). Chaffin (1973) showed that the time for muscle fatigue to occur is an increasing function of the amount of abduction. Thus, another possible contribution of bent-handled tools is to reduce the muscle fatigue associated with abduction.

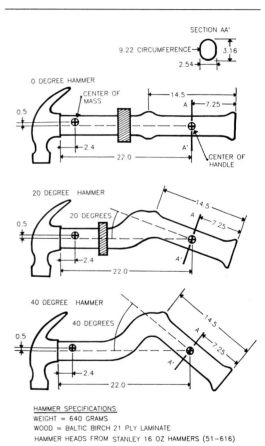

FIGURE 17–7   Hammers with Handles Angled 0°, 20° and 40°.

From R. W. Schoenmarklin & W. S. Marras, Effects of handle angle and work orientation on hammering: I. Wrist motion and hammering performance. Reprinted with permission from *Human Factors*, Vol. 31, No. 4, pp. 397–411, 1989. Copyright © by The Human Factors Society, Inc. All rights reserved.

associated with the angled handles, but all persons reported less discomfort for the horizontal hammering position. Schoenmarklin and Marras (1989b) recommend the use of bent-handled hammers, because the reduction of wrist deviation has relatively little effect on performance, muscle fatigue, and subjective discomfort.

Tool Grips

Tools should be designed to accommodate hand grips that are appropriate for the task. In the power grip, the four fingers of the hand wrap around the tool grip, with the thumb reaching around the other side and touching the index finger. The power grip allows force to be applied parallel to the forearm (as in sawing), at an angle (as in hammering), and about the forearm (as in turning a screwdriver). In precision grips, the thumb opposes the fingertips. Precision grips allow much finer control than the power grip. An internal precision grip is used for such things as table knives, whereas an external precision grip is used for things such as pencils. Fatigue will be accelerated if a tool requires both the use of a power grip and precise control.

The optimal thickness for the diameter of a power grip is 3.8 cm (Ayoub & Lo Presti, 1971). Precision grips are smaller, but should not be less than 0.63 cm. A tool intended for use with a power grip must have room for all four fingers, and a tool manipulated by a precision grip must be sufficiently long that the handle rests against the base of the thumb, which provides support. An ideal grip surface will be compressible, with a high friction coefficient (Konz, 1974). It should have a smooth surface and should conduct neither heat nor electricity.

Kroemer (1986) has noted that the distinction between power and precision grips is not sufficient to describe the wide range of possible hand–handle couplings. Consequently, he developed a taxonomy of 10 hand–handle couplings based on the geometric interactions between anatomic sections of the hand and handle surfaces. This taxonomy, shown in Figure 17–8, provides functional descriptions of two types of touches (1 and 2), five types of grips (3 to 7), and three types of grasps (8 to 10).

Manual or Power Tools

Whenever possible, the use of power tools should be considered (Konz, 1974). They can generate more power than human muscles and, hence, perform tasks that could not be accomplished otherwise. Moreover, power tools can perform tasks faster, and the operator suffers much less from fatigue.

Power tools may be an effective means for minimizing the potential for cumulative trauma disorders associated with repetitive movements. For example, the twisting or racheting motion required to operate a manual screwdriver is largely eliminated by a power screwdriver. Although this may not be of much consequence if a screwdriver is used only occasionally, it is a major concern for a worker who must use the screwdriver repetitively. Use of a racheting screwdriver to insert 1,000 screws a day may result in 5,000 exertions, which can be reduced to 1,000 exertions when an electric screwdriver is used (Armstrong, Ulin, & Ways, 1990). Moreover, the load on the forearm muscles is reduced when an electric screwdriver is used (Cederqvist et al., 1990).

It cannot be assumed that switching to a power tool will automatically reduce the risk of cumulative trauma disorders. Significantly higher gripping forces may be required by the operator to control the power tool. Also, the benefit due to reduced repetitive movements can be negated if the power tool requires the operator to adopt a more stressful working posture. For example, an electrical screwdriver may require the operator to exert more force on the screw against the workpiece, possible using both arms rather than one. There is also a family of trauma disorders related to vibration of the tool, which will be discussed in Chapter 18. Careful analysis of all the pertinent factors involved in the performance of a task is necessary before deciding what type of tool will be best for repetitive use.

Additional Principles

Several additional principles apply to hand-tool design (Konz, 1974). The first is to use special-purpose tools instead of general-purpose tools.

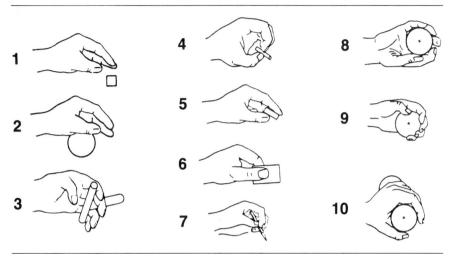

FIGURE 17–8 Ten Hand-handle Couplings 1. *Finger Touch:* One Finger Touches an Object Without Holding It. 2. *Palm Touch:* Some Part of the Inner Surface of the Hand Touches the Object Without Holding It. 3. *Finger Palmar Grip (Hook Grip):* One Finger or Several Fingers Hook(s) Onto a Ridge or Handle. 4. *Thumb-Fingertip Grip (Tip Grip):* The Thumb Opposes One Fingertip. 5. *Thumb-Finger Palmar Grip (Pinch or Plier Grip):* Thumb Pad Opposes the Palmar Pad of One Finger (or the Pads of Several Fingers) Near the Tips. 6. *Thumb-Forefinger Side Grip:* Thumb Opposes the (Radial) Side of the Forefinger. 7. *Thumb-Two Finger Grip (Writing Grip):* Thumb and Two Fingers (Often Forefinger and Index Finger) Oppose Each Other at or Near the Tips. 8. *Thumb-Fingertips Enclosure (Disk Grip):* Thumb Pad and The Pads of Three or Four Fingers Oppose Each Other Near the Tips. 9. *Finger-Palm Enclosure (Collett Enclosure):* Most, or All, of the Inner Surface of the Hand is in Contact with the Object While Enclosing It. 10. *Power Grasp.* The Total Inner Hand Surface is Grasping the Handle Which Runs Parallel to the Knuckles and Generally Protrudes on One or Both Sides from the Hand.

From K. H. E. Kroemer, Coupling the hand with the handle: An improved notation of touch, grip, and grasp. Reprinted with permission from *Human Factors,* Vol. 28, No. 3, pp. 337–339, 1986. Copyright © 1986 by The Human Factors Society, Inc. All rights reserved.

General-purpose tools have the benefit of being useful for a variety of tasks. Thus, initial capital costs will be less for such tools. However, the assets of general-purpose tools are offset by the fact that additional time will be required to perform most tasks. If the tool is used often, the costs accrued by longer delays will typically exceed the initial savings. Special-purpose tools will also be more capable of performing the specific tasks for which they were developed than will general-purpose tools.

A second principle is to design tools to be used by either hand. When tools are designed for either hand, left-handed people can use them as effectively as can right-handed people. Moreover, performance of most tasks produces muscle fatigue, and it is often beneficial to switch hands.

Third, the appropriate muscle group should be used. The forearm muscles are stronger than finger muscles and, hence, should be used when considerable force is needed. Also, the hand is stronger when closing than when opening. This suggests that tools such as scissors should normally be held open by a spring so that force is not required to open them.

MANUAL MATERIALS HANDLING

In the industrial environment, many workers are required to handle materials, such as packaged products. In such tasks, the possibility of injury is significant. Manual materials handling accounts for approximately 25% to 30% of all overexertion injuries (Mital, 1983). To reduce the number of such injuries, workers must not only be taught appropriate handling methods, but the entire work system must be structured with the goal of injury reduction in mind. The factors that affect the likelihood of manual handling injuries fall into four distinct groups (Chaffin & Andersson, 1984): worker characteristics (for example, physical, training); material and container characteristics (for example, load, dimensions); task characteristics (for example, workspace geometry, pace); and work practices (for example, administrative safety incentives, work shifts).

The various operations performed in manual materials handling include lifting and lowering, pushing and pulling, and carrying. Associated with each of these operations are factors that influence the likelihood of physical injury, such as the direction, speed, and frequency of the movement. The container or load being handled affects the risk of injury directly through its bulk, shape, and weight and indirectly through the limitations that it imposes on the way in which it can be held and carried (Drury & Coury, 1982).

Lifting and Lowering

Three static force components are important to lifting and lowering (Tichauer, 1978). The first of these is called the sagittal moment and refers to a weighted average of the forces acting downward in the sagittal plane (see Figure 17–2). The magnitude of the sagittal moment depends on the weight of the body segments, work-surface height, position (seated or standing), and so on.

Lateral moments arise when weight is shifted from one foot to another and refer to the sum of the forces acting downward in the lateral plane. Torsional moments arise when twisting at the waist. All such forces produce stress on the spine and other joints of the body and thus should be minimized.

The forces operating on the spine during lifting increase as the weight of the load being lifted increases. An inability to get a good purchase on the object, asymmetric weight distribution in the object, and unusual shapes are factors that all act to require lifting postures that increase the forces operating on the spine. These effects also increase with increasing distance, speed, and frequency of lifts.

Guidelines for manual lifting have been established by the National Institute for Occupational Safety and Health and have been published in the *Work Practices Guide for Manual Lifting* (NIOSH, 1981). These guidelines distinguish among jobs that require infrequent lifts, frequent lifts for less than an hour, and frequent lifts for an entire workday. A distinction is also made between the *action limit* (AL), which is an upper bound for acceptable lifting conditions when no other intervention is required, and the *maximum permissible limit* (MPL), which is a higher bound that should not be exceeded under any circumstance. Loads that fall between these two limits require administrative controls, that is, special training and recruitment of workers and mechanical aids.

Table 17–4 contains the formulas to determine AL and MPL, which are functions of the lifting variables discussed earlier. Figure 17–9 shows the value of AL and MPL as a function of the distance of the weight load from the body.

The NIOSH guidelines are based on models of the human being that assume no variation in time. That is, they are static. Mirka and Marras (1990) have argued that these static forces are insufficient to determine safe limits. They obtained velocity and acceleration profiles for the trunk during low- and high-velocity lifts. The forces produced by the muscles in the trunk dur-

TABLE 17–4   Equations for Computing AL and MPL from the NIOSH Guidelines

$$AL = 392 \left(\frac{15}{H}\right) [1 - (0.004 \mid V - 175 \mid)] \left(0.7 + \frac{7.5}{D}\right) \left(1 - \frac{F}{F_{max}}\right)$$

and for the MPL,

$$MPL = 3AL$$

where

AL and MPL are the maximum weight-lifting values (in newtons) for the given job conditions.

H is the horizontal distance (cm) from the load center of mass at the origin of the vertical lift to the midpoint between the ankles, with a minimum value of 15 cm (body interference) and a maximum value of 80 cm (reach distance for most people).

V is the vertical distance (cm) from the load center of mass at the origin of the vertical lift measured from the floor, with no minimum value and a maximum of 175 cm (upward reach for most people).

D is the vertical travel distance (cm) of the object assuming a minimum value of 25 cm and a maximum of 200 cm minus the vertical origin height V. Note: If the distance moved is small (D less than 25 cm), the effect is nominal, so D is set equal to 25 cm.

F is the average frequency of lifting (lifts per minute) with a minimum value for occasional lifts of 0.2 (once every 5 min) and a maximum value F_{max} defined by both the period of lifting (less than 1 hr or for 8 hr) and whether the lifting involves only arm work or significant body stabilization of movement.

From D. B. Chaffin & G. B. J. Andersson (1984), *Occupational Biomechanics*. Copyright © 1984 by John Wiley & Sons, Inc. Reprinted by permission of John Wiley & Sons, Inc.

ing such lifts can eventually lead to damage of the spinal discs. Smooth, controlled lifting motions have been thought to minimize these forces. For symmetric and asymmetric lifting postures, Mirka and Marras found that trunk acceleration peaked at a much higher level for fast lifts than for slow lifts. However, for slow lifts, trunk acceleration peaked more often. The forces on the spine for the slow lifts were sometimes greater overall than for the fast lifts. Because current guidelines assume a constant force throughout the lift, they may underestimate the load on the spine during slow lifts. These data suggest that many other variables, such as external forces and the cumulative effects of trauma, must be considered before determining the best velocity for a lift. Marras and Sommerich (1991) propose a dynamic model that considers these and other variables as an alternative to models based on constant force.

The NIOSH guidelines are also based on forces exerted during symmetric lifts in the sagittal plane. Yet in many industrial situations, lifting is asymmetric and the center of gravity is not centered (see Figure 17–10). Mital and Manivasigan (1983) investigated the effects of center of gravity and hand preference on a person's willingness to lift an object. They found that people would lift more when the load's center of gravity was at the body midline. If the center of gravity was offset toward either the left or right hand, the maximum weight that people would lift decreased by as much as 2 kg. This drop was greatest when the center of gravity was shifted toward the nonpreferred hand. Thus, the location of center of gravity affects the maximum weight that people find acceptable.

Marras and Mirka (1989) showed that the force generated during a lift varies systematically with lift asymmetry and lift angle. Lifting force decreased with increasing twist around the waist and with increasing lift velocity. However, lowering force increased when lowering velocity increased. This means that strength was greatest for low lifting velocities and high lowering velocities. Lifting strength was greater than low-

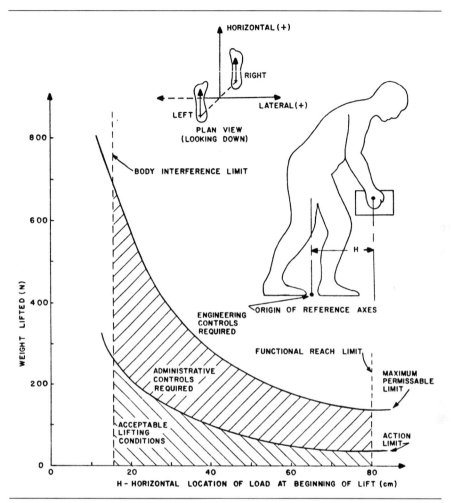

FIGURE 17–9   Action Limit and Maximum Permissible Limit for Different Horizontal Locations of Loads Lifted from the Floor to Knuckle Height on an Infrequent Basis.

From D. B. Chaffin & G. B. J. Andersson (1984). *Occupational Biomechanics.* Copyright © 1984 by John Wiley & Sons, Inc. Reprinted by permission of John Wiley & Sons, Inc.

ering strength, except when the person was twisted at the waist. Above all, Marras and Mirka emphasize that, because strength varies with lift velocity, it cannot be measured statically.

One task that involves large forces exerted during high levels of activity is garbage collecting. Kemper et al. (1990) reported the results from an extensive study conducted in the Nether-

lands on garbage collectors. They compared the workers' ability to handle (carry, lift, and throw) trash cans and plastic bags. The movements required to handle the bag were more efficient than those required for the trash can. That is, workers could carry more weight with the bags and could throw the bags with more force. Using the bags, the garbage collectors gathered 70% more gar-

FIGURE 17–10 A Person Engaged in an Asymmetric Lift.

Adapted from C. T. Morgan et al. (Eds.) (1963). *Human Engineering Guide to Equipment Design.* Copyright © 1963 by McGraw-Hill.

and isoinertial testing, which measures the maximum mass that a person can handle. Isometric and isokinetic strength testing require limited movement of the person being tested. Isoinertial testing measures force dynamically. Just as Marras and Mirka discouraged the use of static strength measures, Kroemer (1983b) concluded that such measures are often inappropriate for screening a person's handling capability. He demonstrated that the measures under dynamic tests, such as the isoinertial testing methods, were more reliable than those made under static tests.

Carrying and Pushing–Pulling

Many tasks require that an object be carried. Such is the case for package delivery, mail delivery, warehouse loading operations, and many other jobs. Carrying requires that the worker exert the force needed to lift an object and that this force be maintained until the destination is reached. Consequently, the maximum weight that can be carried will be less than the weight that can be lifted.

Carrying often involves one hand, as is the case for carrying a suitcase. With one-handed carrying, less force can be generated than with two-handed carrying and, moreover, the harmful stresses associated with lifting asymmetric loads come into play. Figure 17–11 shows the maximum weights that are recommended when an object is carried with one or two hands for varying distances.

Other industrial tasks, such as tool operation, require that pushing or pulling forces be exerted. Large forces of this type are required if a hand truck or hand cart is used. The force that can be applied varies as a function of body weight, the height at which force is applied, the distance of force application from the body, the frictional coefficient of the floor and shoes, and the duration of force application (Eastman Kodak Company, 1986).

Chaffin, Andres, and Garg (1983) recorded the postures assumed by men and women of vary-

bage than when garbage cans were used. As a result, the city of Haarlem replaced garbage cans with plastic garbage bags and changed from twice- to once-a-week collection.

Even though the garbage collectors were performing more efficiently, they still were working over acceptable limits of workload tolerance and, therefore, were risking back injuries. One way to reduce back injuries is to screen workers for lifting capabilities. Only those people whose physical strength is sufficient to handle the materials safely would be assigned to the job. Three screening techniques are used: isometric strength testing, which measures the force exerted on a stationary object; isokinetic testing, which measures strength while moving at a constant speed;

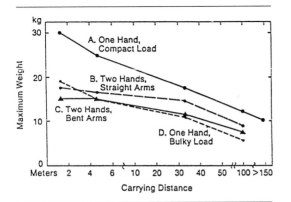

FIGURE 17–11   Maximum Load Weight as a Function of Carrying Distance and Carrying Posture.

From *Ergonomic Design For People at Work* (Vol. 2). Published by Van Nostrand Reinhold, 1986. Copyright © 1986 by Eastman Kodak Company. Reprinted courtesy of Eastman Kodak Company.

ing sizes when they were asked to exert push and pull forces. When the feet were required to be side by side, there was no difference between pushing and pulling strength. When the feet were staggered, men showed greater pushing than pulling strength. When the height of the handle was raised, strength was diminished. Strength was much greater overall when the feet were staggered, because the back foot allowed more forward or backward lean.

Similar factors affect vertical pushing or pulling and the application of lateral forces. For vertical pushing and pulling, the height at which the force must be exerted is critical. Also, less force can be generated when sitting than when standing. The maximum lateral forces that can be generated are approximately half those that can be generated for horizontal pushes and pulls. As with manual lifting, task considerations should determine the way that a workspace is structured for pushing or pulling.

When trying to improve conditions for jobs that require lifting, carrying, and pushing, the entire system in which the tasks are performed must be taken into account. This point is illus-

trated in a study by Nygard and Ilmarinen (1990). Dairy truck drivers must load and unload large volumes of dairy products daily. In Finland, a rolling delivery system was instituted with the intent of lowering the physical workload imposed on the truck drivers. This system allowed the products to be moved from the dairy to the truck and from the truck to the store on transport dollies. With this method, the amount of carrying was decreased, whereas more pushing was required.

Measures of physiological strain showed only a slight improvement with the rolling delivery system, and this improvement was evident at the dairy but not at the store. The apparent reason was that the dairies were built to accommodate dollies, whereas many of the stores were not. Some of the stores had no platform for loading and unloading, and steps or stairs often had to be negotiated. The authors conclude that ergonomic improvements must be made throughout the entire delivery system for a marked decrease in physical strain to occur.

WORKSPACE DESIGN

The design of a workspace depends on the hardware that is to be operated, how displays and controls are located, the seating for the operator, the computer software available to the operator (if any), the physical environment, and the organization and scheduling of work (see Figure 17–12). The design of a workspace will influence the efficiency with which the work can be performed and the well-being of the operator. The basic goal for workspace design is to ensure that most people can perform the required tasks safely and efficiently. The workspace should be arranged to minimize extraneous motions, the time to reach controls and other equipment, as well as biomechanical stresses that can cause fatigue and injury (Chaffin, 1987). Factors to be considered include (1) whether the work position is sitting or standing, (2) the layout and height of the work surface, (3) chair design and height, and (4) the location of visual displays.

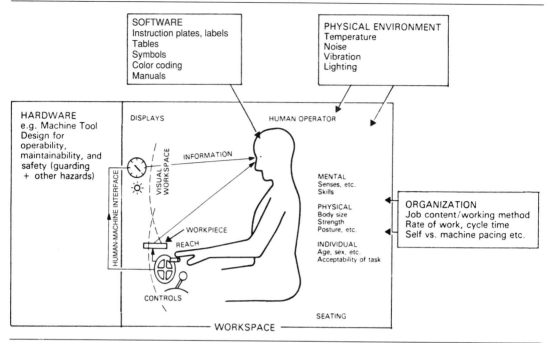

FIGURE 17–12   Ergonomic Considerations in Workspace Design.
From *The Ergonomics of Workspaces and Machines: A Design Manual,* T. S. Clark & E. N.
Corlett (1984), Taylor & Francis, London. Reproduced with permission.

Working Position

The first decision to be made in workspace design is the working position (Clark & Corlett, 1984; Eastman Kodak Company, 1983). The workspace can be built for use while standing, sitting, or both. For each type, the work surface should allow activities to be performed easily. Items that are handled frequently should be situated within the normal area, which can be reached while the upper arm is hanging at the person's side. Less frequently used items should be within the maximum area, which can be reached by extending the arm (Barnes, 1963). The work surface height should permit the arms to hang in a relaxed manner from the shoulder, with the forearm placed nearly horizontal.

Because standing postures allow more mobility, a standing position is preferred if the op-

erator must move about frequently. Similarly, more force can be exerted from a standing position; hence, standing is preferred when heavy objects must be handled or large downward forces exerted (as in packaging). A standing position is also useful if the space necessary for knee clearance is not available.

The optimal height of the work surface for a standing workspace varies as a function of the type of task performed. For tasks such as writing and light assembly, the optimal working height is 107 cm (see Figure 17–13). Because greater force can be generated at lower heights, the optimal height for tasks requiring large downward or sideward forces is less (91 cm). In both cases, the height of the objects being handled must be taken into account in determining the height of the work surface. An adjustable work-surface level allows different users to select an optimal height

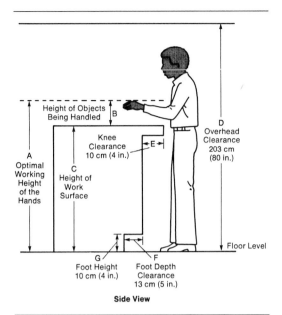

Side View

FIGURE 17–13 Recommended Standing Workspace Dimensions.

From *Ergonomic Design for People at Work* (Vol. 1). Published by Van Nostrand Reinhold, 1983. Copyright © 1983 by Eastman Kodak Company. Reprinted courtesy of Eastman Kodak Company.

and permits the height of the surface to be adjusted for different types of manual activity.

Activities that require fine control are best performed at sitting work stations, because it is easier to maintain stability of the body while sitting. They are also best for close visual work, when large forces are not required and when all items are reachable from the seated position. As with standing workspaces, the optimal working height varies as a function of the tasks that the operator must perform. For most tasks, such as writing, the surface should be at elbow height when seated. However, for fine detail work, in which greater stability is required and detail must be discriminated, it may be higher. For example, Delleman and Dul (1990) recommend that table height for sewing machine operators be at least 5 cm above elbow height. The range of adjustment for such a table should be from 5 cm above the

5th percentile seated elbow height of the user population to 15 cm above the 95th percentile height.

Sit–stand workspaces are useful when the operator needs to be mobile and there are multiple tasks, some of which are performed best while seated and some while standing. The primary consideration involves designing the workspace so that it can be used effectively in both sitting and standing postures. One possibility is to situate the work-surface height at the lowest possible level for standing tasks, with a high seat provided for sitting. A drawback of this approach is that the seat may be unsafe at this height and not amenable to repositioning.

Seating

The design of seats used by the operators at seated work-stations is a major factor in the operators' comfort and, hence, performance. As with any other equipment, a seat can have a good or poor ergonomic design (Corlett, 1990). Table 17–5 lists some of the functional factors for a work seat. The optimal seat design will depend on the tasks to be performed and the individual characteristics of the users.

When an operator sits, the weight of the body is transferred primarily to the seat (see Figure 17–14). Some part of the weight may also be transferred to the backrests and armrests, as well as to the floor and work surface. Of most concern is the posture adopted by the operator, which is directly influenced by the chair design and the task that is performed (Andersson, 1986; Chaffin & Andersson, 1984). Sitting increases pressure on the lumbar discs of the spine (see Figure 17–15), and good posture is necessary to minimize this pressure. During sitting, the motion of the spine is restricted, lumbar bending occurs when forward and backward movement of the torso is performed during the task, and the flow of spinal fluid can be impaired (Serber, 1990). If the seat induces poor posture, these factors can lead to chronic back pain, herniated discs, and pinched nerves.

TABLE 17–5   Functional Factors in Sitting

Task	Sitter	Seat
Seeing	Support weight	Seat height
Reaching	Resist accelerations	Seat shape
	Under-thigh clearance	Backrest shape
	Trunk-thigh angle	Stability
	Leg loading	Lumbar support
	Spinal loading	Adjustment range
	Neck–arms loading	Ingress–egress
	Abdominal discomforts	
	Stability	
	Postural changes	
	Long-term use	
	Acceptability	
	Comfort	

From E. N. Corlett (1990). The evaluation of industrial seating. In J. R. Wilson & E. N. Corlett (Eds.), *Evaluation of Human Work* (pp. 500–515). Reprinted by permission of Taylor & Francis, Inc.

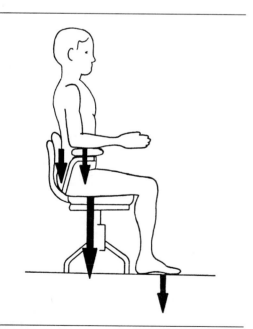

FIGURE 17–14   Transfer of Body Weight When Sitting.

From D. B. Chaffin & G. B. J. Andersson (1984). *Occupational Biomechanics.* Copyright © 1984 by John Wiley & Sons, Inc. Reprinted by permission of John Wiley & Sons, Inc.

One requirement for a good seat design is that the seat height be such that little bending of the spine is necessary. Moreover, the seat should be designed to provide appropriate support and encourage a good posture (Pile, 1979). Increasing backrest inclination places more load on the backrest and reduces pressure on the spinal discs (Andersson, 1986). Pressure can also be reduced by providing support for the lumbar portion of the back and by using armrests to support the weight of the arms. The thighs should exert as little pressure as possible on the seat, to prevent compression ischemia, which could result in swelling of the legs. The weight of the body should be supported primarily by the buttocks, and the feet should rest on the floor or a footstool. Failure to design the seat appropriately can lead to pain in both the upper and lower parts of the body (Hunting & Grandjean, 1976).

Seats should be adjustable in height, when possible, and they must be stable. Adjustability will allow operators of different sizes to select an appropriate height, and it also allows changes relative to the work-surface height as a function of the type of task being performed. The elderly and other special populations have distinct physical limitations that need to be accommodated in seat design. The ease of ingress (getting in) and

Posterior   Anterior

←   →

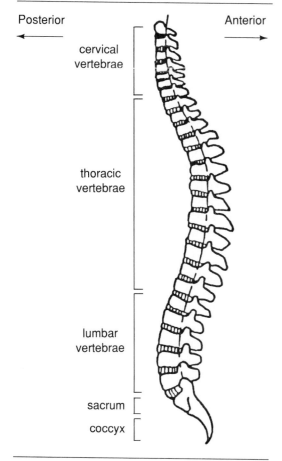

cervical
vertebrae

thoracic
vertebrae

lumbar
vertebrae

sacrum

coccyx

FIGURE 17–15 The Human Spinal Column.

stricted knee space. The high backrest was found to produce better performance for the forward-pushing task, the low backrest for sideways viewing, and the sit–stand seat for the assembly task. In other words, body loads can be reduced and comfort increased by selecting a chair that is appropriate for the task demands.

A new work seat appropriate for the tasks performed by sewing operators in an industrial setting was designed and evaluated by Yu and Keyserling (1989). The new seat was devised to allow workers to maintain the low sit–stand posture that they preferred. This involved redesigning the backrest to give thoracic and lumbar support and redesigning the seat pan to give more pelvic and thigh support. Workers reported significantly less discomfort when sitting on the new chair, and 41 of 50 workers preferred it over the old chair. This demonstrates that something as basic as seat redesign may be a first step toward enhancing the work environment and increasing work tolerance.

Positioning of Visual Displays

Regardless of whether the operator is sitting or standing, it is important that visual displays be

egress (getting out) is one major factor for these populations (Munton, Chamberlain, & Wright, 1981).

Eklund and Corlett (1986) evaluated three chair designs for use with three types of tasks (see Figure 17–16). One design had a high backrest, another had a low backrest that provided lumbar support, and the final design was a sit–stand seat. People performed each of three tasks. In the forward-pushing task (c), a handle was gripped with both hands and pushed forward to produce a force. In the sideways viewing task (b), people viewed a television set placed 90° to the left. Finally, an assembly task (a), which involved screwing nuts on bolts, was performed with re-

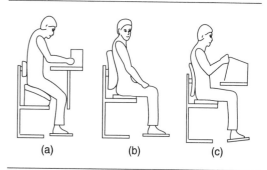

(a)   (b)   (c)

FIGURE 17–16 Postures for the Assembly Task (a), the Sideways-viewing Task (b), and the Pushing Task (c).

From Experimental and biomechanical analysis of seating, E. N. Eklund & E. N. Corlett (1986). In *The Ergonomics of Working Postures* (pp. 319–330), E. N. Corlett, J. W. Wilson, & I. Manenica (Eds.), Taylor & Francis, London. Reproduced with permission.

viewed easily and without excessive stress on the musculoskeletal system. For visual positioning, the line of sight and field of view are critical (Rühmann, 1984). The line of sight refers to the direction in which the eye is fixated. The horizontal line of sight is that obtained when the head and eyes are maintained in a straight position (see Figure 17–17). For a relaxed, comfortable head posture, with the eyes straight ahead, the head is inclined forward approximately 10° to 15°. So the line of sight relative to the head is 10° to 15° below the horizontal line of sight. Finally, the normal line of sight, for which the eyes are also relaxed, is 25° to 30° below horizontal. Displays positioned so that the normal line of sight is maintained most of the time will minimize fatigue.

The maximum direct field of view is that part of the environment that can stimulate sensory receptors when fixation is held constant. It is a region extending 45° above and below the line of sight and 95° to either side when viewing is binocular. The functional field of view is not usually as large and decreases still further when viewing is monocular, when colors must be distinguished, and so on. The functional field becomes larger than the direct field of view when the eyes are allowed to change fixation, and larger still when the head can move. High-priority displays should be within the direct field of view when the head is in a relaxed position. Medium-priority visual information should be accessible with eye movements alone, and low-priority information should be visible with head and/or trunk rotation.

Positioning of Controls and Objects

The two-dimensional reach envelope was introduced in Chapter 16 when we discussed the positioning of controls. The reach envelope can be expanded into a three-dimensional surface that partly surrounds the body (see Figure 17–18). The normal reach surface involves locations that can be reached without leaning or stretching. All controls or objects that are used regularly should be located within this normal reach surface. Objects that are used occasionally can be located outside this area, but within the maximum reach surface, where they can be reached with some stretching and leaning.

The dimensions of the three-dimensional reach envelope depend on whether the workspace requires sitting or standing. They are also affected by other factors that influence the operator's mobility, such as table height, whether one or two arms must be used, clothing, and physical restraints. Forward reach is impaired by increased table height (see Figure 17–19) and for tasks that require the use of both arms. Similarly, bulky clothing and safety restraints (see Figure 17–20), such as seatbelts, restrict movement and so decrease the range of the three-dimensional reach envelope.

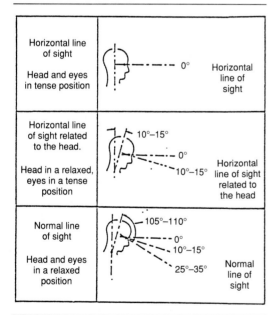

FIGURE 17–17   Lines of Sight.
From H. P. Rühmann (1984). Basic data for the design of consoles. In H. Schmidtke (Ed.), *Ergonomic Data for Equipment Design* (pp. 15–144). Reprinted by permission of Plenum Publishing Corporation.

FIGURE 17–18 The Normal, Seated Reach Surface.

From *Ergonomic Design for People at Work* (Vol. 1). Published by Van Nostrand Reinhold, 1983. Copyright © 1983 by Eastman Kodak Company. Reprinted courtesy of Eastman Kodak Company.

Steps in Workspace Design

Although anthropometric and biomechanical data provide the foundation for effective workspace design, the design process itself involves many steps of development and evaluation. This process relies on converting tabled data into concrete drawings, scale models, mock-ups and prototypes. Roebuck, Kroemer, and Thomson (1975) summarize these steps as follows:

1. *Establish requirements.* Determine the goals of the system and other pertinent requirements.
2. *Define and describe the population.* Appropriate use of anthropometric data involves definition of the user population and corresponding anthropometric values. If available tables do not fit the population or measurements of interest, new measurements may be necessary.
3. *Select design limits.* A design criterion population is specified by determining the range of percentiles for which the workspace is designed.
4. *Prepare basic body dimension drawings.* The pertinent anthropometric data are used to design an "individual" who corresponds to the desired percentile.
5. *Prepare drafting aids.* Plastic overlays of the individual are prepared, sometimes along with two-dimensional mannequins.
6. *Prepare workspace layout.* In this step, the designer uses the anthropometric data to construct the functional layout. The layout should accommodate individuals at the intended percentile.
7. *Mathematical analysis.* Mathematical calculations of geometric interrelationships between the human and the workspace are computed.
8. *Develop a small-scale model.* Scale models are constructed to determine whether obvious design flaws exist.
9. *Prepare test requirements.* Explicit experimental tests are developed to verify that the system criteria have been met.
10. *Prepare mock-ups and prototypes.* Full size mock-ups are built for use in evaluating the design adequacy with real users.
11. *Prepare reach and clearance envelopes.* Humans are used in the mock-up, positioned as they would be in actual operation, to determine the functional envelopes.
12. *Prepare special measuring devices.* New measuring devices may need to be built to evaluate the workspace.
13. *Test the mock-up and prototype.* Batteries of tests are conducted with appropriate test subjects.
14. *Communicate the results.* Based on the results of the workspace evaluation, documented recommendations for design are made. The expected consequences and costs of following or not following the recommendations must be conveyed clearly.

Some variation of these steps should be followed in the design and evaluation of any work-

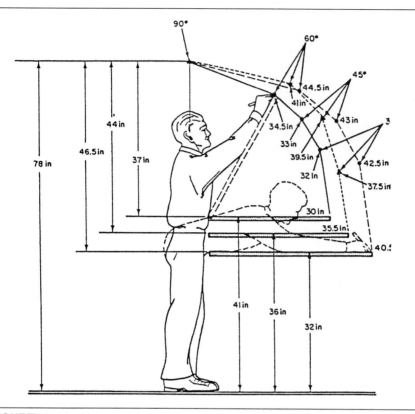

FIGURE 17–19   Maximum Reach for a 5th-Percentile Operator at Drafting Tables of Different Lengths.

From Design of individual workplaces (1972). In H. P. Van Cott & R. G. Kinkade (Eds.). *Human Engineering Guide to Equipment Design,* pp. 381–418. U.S. Government Printing Office.

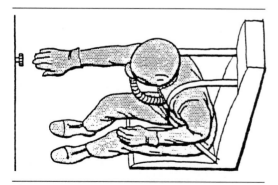

FIGURE 17–20   Maximum Reach for a 5th-Percentile Operator Wearing Protective Clothing and Safety Restraints.

Adapted from C. T. Morgan et al. (Eds.) (1963). *Human Engineering Guide to Equipment Design.* Copyright © 1963 by McGraw-Hill.

space. While doing so, the designer should adhere to the general principles shown in Table 17–6. This procedure will maximize the likelihood that the workspace will be suited to both the task and the user.

SUMMARY

Anthropometric measures provide indications of the dimensions of the human body that must be accommodated when designing for human use. A good design will allow most of the intended user population to operate the equipment and manipulate objects effectively. Cumulative trauma disorders can occur when a person must make movements that are repetitive and/or that require considerable force. Tools should be designed to

TABLE 17–6   The General Principles for Workspace Design

Avoid static work.
Avoid extreme position of the joints.
Avoid overloading the muscular system.
Aim at best mechanical advantage.
Avoid unnatural postures.
Maintain a proper sitting position.
Permit change of posture.
Allow the small operator to reach and the large operator to fit.
Train the operator to use the physical facility.
Match the job demands to operator capacity.
Allow the operator to maintain an upright and forward-facing posture during work.
When vision is a requirement of the task, permit the necessary work points to be adequately visible
    with the head and trunk upright or with just the head inclined slightly forward.
Avoid work performed at or above the level of the heart.

From M. M. Ayoub & M. Miller (1991). Industrial workplace design. In A. Mital & W. Karwowski
(Eds.), *Workspace, Equipment and Tool Design* (pp. 67–92). Reprinted by permission of Elsevier
Science Publishers BV.

minimize such disorders by not requiring the operator to adopt extreme joint angles and/or generate large forces.

Because handling of heavy or bulky objects can cause profound injuries, tasks that involve lifting should be structured to minimize injuries. Psychological and biomechanical factors, as well as anthropometric factors, must be given consideration when designing a workspace. Necessary equipment must be within reach and operable within the physical constraints of the environment. Displays must be visible, repetitive movements that stress the musculoskeletal system should be avoided, and it should be possible for the operator to maintain a good posture.

RECOMMENDED READING

Chaffin, D. B., & Andersson, G. B. J. (1984). *Occupational Biomechanics*. New York: Wiley.

Clark, T. S., & Corlett, E. N. (1984). *The Ergonomics of Workspaces and Machines: A Design Manual*. London: Taylor & Francis.

Greenberg, L., & Chaffin, D. (1977). *Workers and Their Tools: A Guide to the Ergonomic Design of Handtools and Small Presses*. Midland, MI: Pendell.

Kroemer, K. H. E., et al. (1988). *Ergonomic Models of Anthropometry, Human Biomechanics, and Operator–Equipment Interfaces*. Washington, DC: National Academy Press.

Tichauer, E. (1978). *The Biomechanical Basis of Ergonomics*. New York: Wiley.

THE PHYSICAL ENVIRONMENT

> *The physical environment is all around us; it constantly affects our behavior. If it is cold outside, we put on extra clothes; if it rains we carry an umbrella; in strong sunlight we wear sunglasses; and if we get too close to a road drill we cover our ears. Just as it affects our daily living, aspects of the environment at work are also able to influence our working behavior and efficiency to a greater or lesser extent.*
>
> —D. J. Oborne and M. M. Gruneberg, 1983

INTRODUCTION

Previously, we talked about issues involving workspace design, controls, and tools that have an obvious, direct influence on human performance. Performance is also influenced by the physical environment. Anyone who has tried to mow a lawn in the heat of a summer afternoon or balance a checkbook while a baby is crying can appreciate the influence of these sometimes subtle environmental variables. Often, the effect of the environment is not obvious during the design of a workspace. Physical factors become evident when the workspace is implemented within the larger work environment.

By anticipating possible problem areas, such as glare on a visual display screen, tasks and workspaces can be designed to minimize the consequences of noxious environmental variables. Despite all attempts to reduce the impact of deleterious factors, some issues may arise only through the synergy of the workplace. Action often must be taken "on the spot" to remedy problems as they are detected. In this chapter, we will examine four powerful environmental variables: lighting, noise, vibration, and climate. These variables are often compounded within larger environments, such as offices, buildings, and other contained environments. They are also sources of stress, which can have harmful physiological and psychological consequences.

LIGHTING

One of the most noticeable environmental variables is lighting, which can affect the performance of tasks by restricting visual perception. Poor lighting has been held responsible for several health problems and adverse effects on mood. There are four issues to consider when selecting lighting (Megaw & Bellamy, 1983). The first of these is the importance of lighting level to the performance of the task. The second is the speed and accuracy with which the task must be performed. The third issue is observer comfort. Finally, the subjective impression of the quality of the illuminated environment must be considered. Megaw and Bellamy point out that good lighting produces the best visual conditions for the least cost.

Light Measurement

The evaluation of lighting begins with the measurement of light intensity. The units of light intensity change depending on whether the light measured is reflected from or generated by the surface on which the measurement is made. *Illuminance* refers to the amount of light falling on a surface, and *luminance* refers to the light generated by a surface. Central to the concepts of luminance and illuminance is luminous flux, which is measured in lumens. This measure represents the power of the light source corrected for the sensitivity of the visual system. Illuminance is the density of luminous flux per unit area, and luminance is the luminous flux emitted from a point source in a given direction. Luminance is a func-

tion of the illuminance and the reflectance of a surface.

Both luminance and illuminance can be measured with a device called a photometer. The sensitivity of the photometer parallels that of the human spectral sensitivity curve under photopic viewing conditions. To measure luminance, a lens with a small aperture is coupled with the photometer. The lens is focused on the surface of interest from any distance. If the light energy within the focused region is not uniform, the photometer integrates over the focused area to give an average luminance. The photometer gives the measure of luminance in candelas per square meter (cd/m^2).

To measure illuminance, an illuminance probe is coupled with the photometer and placed on the illuminated surface. Illuminance also can be measured with a hand-held illumination meter. Unlike luminance, the amount of illuminance will vary with the distance from the light source. The photometer gives the measure of illuminance in lumens per square meter (lm/m^2), or lux (lx).

Light Sources

Illuminance will vary with the kind of light source, as will lighting costs and the accuracy of color perception (color rendering). The most basic distinction is made between natural and artificial lighting. Sunlight contains energy across the entire spectrum, with relatively more energy devoted to the long wavelengths. Natural lighting is inexpensive and its color rendering is very good, but the level of illumination will vary as a function of such factors as time of day and the degree of cloudiness. Moreover, the distribution of natural light cannot be easily controlled. With natural lighting the costs of electricity and lighting fixtures are avoided, but there is the cost of heating and cooling associated with the windows.

Most offices are constructed without regard to the presence of natural lighting, so the distribution of light is not always uniform throughout an office. A desk near a window will receive more illumination than one farther away. One alternative to this design practice is called the PSALI (Permanent Supplementary Artificial Lighting Installation) approach. With this approach, the availability of natural light throughout the office is first considered. Then artificial lighting is added to create a uniform light distribution over all areas (Hopkinson & Longmore, 1959). So additional light fixtures would be installed to illuminate desks farthest from the window. Despite the apparent usefulness of the PSALI approach, it has rarely been used.

The two most common types of artificial light use incandescent or fluorescent bulbs. Incandescent lamps are the most widely used but are the least efficient in terms of lumens per watt. Incandescent light is produced by current flowing through a filament that becomes heated and glows. Very little of the energy used to heat the filament results in visible light. Fluorescent lamps can be as much as four times as efficient as incandescent lamps, but fluorescent fixtures are more expensive. The fluorescent bulb is a gas-discharge bulb in which electric current is alternated through an inert gas. The energy produced by the current is nonvisible ultraviolet light, which excites phosphors coating the inside of the bulb. Although the light appears steady, it actually flickers at a high frequency.

Incandescent and fluorescent lamps are the least efficient of the available artificial light sources. Other gas-discharge lamps, such as metal halide and sodium lamps, are far more efficient. However, these other lamps are costly and their color-rendering capabilities are very poor. Poor color rendering arises from peaks in the spectral frequency distribution of a lamp. Figure 18–1 shows the spectra for four types of lamps. The incandescent and fluorescent spectra are much smoother than those of the metal halide and sodium lamps. The extreme peaks in the metal halide and sodium spectra provide large amounts of light from few wavelengths. The predominance of these few wavelengths can "wash" the work area with the hues of those wavelengths, making color perception inaccurate.

Another major distinction between light sources is whether the lighting is direct or indirect. Direct lighting generally refers to light that falls on a surface directly from the light source. In contrast, for indirect lighting the light from the source has been reflected from other surfaces before falling on the work surface. Technically, if 90% of the light from the source is directed toward the work surface (downward), the lighting is classified as direct. If 90% of the light is directed away from the work surface (upward), the lighting is classified as indirect. In selecting between direct and indirect lighting, it is important to keep in mind that direct lighting is usually associated with glare and that indirect lighting is not usually appropriate for work requiring close visual inspection. These issues will be discussed in more detail later in this section.

Illumination and Performance

Tasks differ in their degree of visual difficulty. Visual difficulty is a function of the size of the smallest critical details or items with which the operator works and their contrast with the background. Often, simply increasing illumination does not make a visually difficult task easy. Figure 18–2 shows the relation between size, illuminance, and contrast observed by Weston (1945). Performance is an increasing function of each of these variables. Although performance for small, low-contrast items improves with increased illumination, performance is always much poorer than that for larger, higher-contrast items.

Human factors specialists are concerned specifically with the effects of illumination on performance. Consequently, many field studies are conducted to directly evaluate performance under different levels of illumination and types of lighting. For example, Stenzel (1962) measured productivity under changes of lighting in a leather factory over a four-year period. The workers' tasks involved cutting shapes from skins to make leathergoods such as purses and wallets. For the first two years of the study, work was performed in daylight with additional fluorescent fixtures,

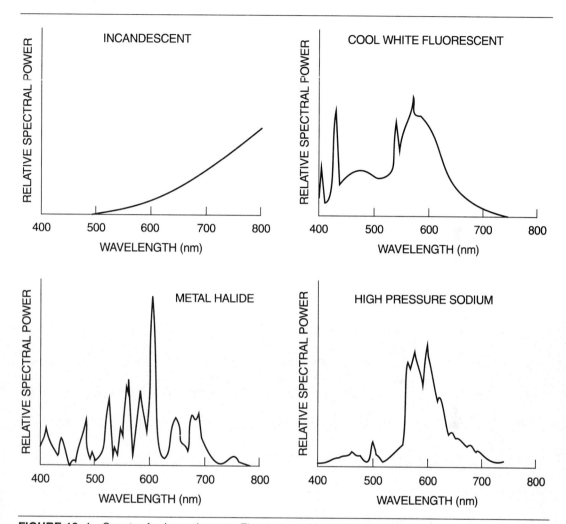

FIGURE 18–1   Spectra for Incandescent, Fluorescent, Metal Halide, and Sodium Lamps.

From W. H. Cushman & B. Crist (1987). Illumination. In G. Salvendy (Ed.), *Handbook of Human Factors* (pp. 670–695). Copyright © 1987 by John Wiley & Sons, Inc. Reprinted by permission of John Wiley & Sons, Inc.

which gave an overall illuminance, of 350 lx. Before the third year, the daylight was eliminated and fluorescent lighting was installed that provided a uniform 1,000-lx illumination. As shown in Figure 18–3, performance was clearly improved after the installation of the lighting. Although this suggests that the new illumination level caused the increase in productivity, the

change in performance could be due to other factors. Such factors may include the uniformity of illumination, color modifications, or unrelated variables (such as pay raises or different work schedules) that may have been altered at about the same time as the change in lighting.

The difficulty of controlling extraneous variables in the work environment is apparent in the

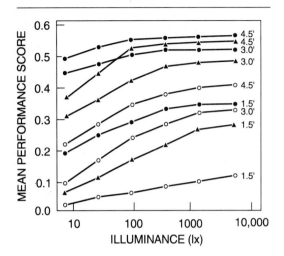

FIGURE 18–2 The Effects of Size (in Minutes of Visual Angle), Illuminance, and Contrast on Performance. (● = High, ▲ = Medium, ○ = Low.)

From W. H. Cushman & B. Crist (1987). Illumination. In G. Salvendy (Ed.), *Handbook of Human Factors* (pp.

Hawthorne lighting experiments, which were introduced in Chapter 1. Three experiments were conducted from 1924 to 1927 at the Hawthorne Plant of the Western Electric Company to assess the effects of lighting on productivity (Gillespie, 1991). The impetus for the experiments came from the electrical industry, which claimed that good lighting would increase productivity significantly. The workers were informed about the nature of the study in order to obtain their cooperation.

In the initial experiment, three test groups of workers involved in the assembly of telephone parts performed under higher than normal lighting levels, while a control group performed under normal lighting. Production increased dramatically in the three test groups relative to the level of productivity before the experiment, but it also increased a similar amount for the control group. Also, within each experimental group, there was no correlation between productivity

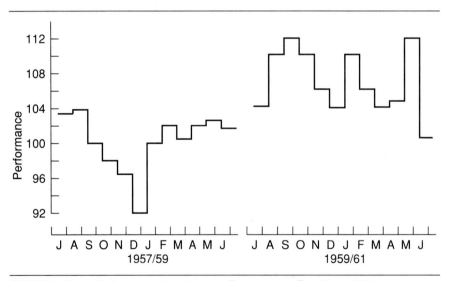

FIGURE 18–3 Performance in a Leather Factory as a Function of Lighting Conditions (Left Panel Is Old Lighting; Right Panel Is New Lighting) and Month (July Through June).

From P. R. Boyce (1981). *Human factors in lighting.* Reprinted with permission of McGraw-Hill, Inc.

and the lighting level that was in effect across different work periods. Apparently, the increased productivity was due to an increase in management involvement required for measuring lighting levels and productivity, rather than to the lighting level itself.

In the two remaining experiments, explicit attempts were made to control these supervisory factors. Again, there was little influence of lighting except at very low illumination levels. However, the possibility exists that the workers may have expended more effort under conditions of low illumination to compensate for any increased difficulty. The Hawthorne experiments illustrate that it is difficult to draw definite conclusions about the effects of lighting from studies conducted in the work environment.

To study the effects of lighting under conditions that enable more definite conclusions, it is necessary to move the task environment into the laboratory. This also requires that the task be simulated, preserving its critical elements while eliminating those that would make a causal relationship difficult to establish. Stenzel and Sommer (1969) performed such a laboratory experiment in which people either sorted screws or crocheted stoles. They varied illuminance from 100 to 1,700 lx. The number of errors that were observed decreased with increasing illuminance for crocheting but not for sorting. For the sorting task, errors decreased as illuminance increased to 700 lx, but then increased as illuminance rose to 1,700 lx. Therefore, the effect of increasing illumination depended on the specific task that was performed.

Illumination and contrast are particularly critical in designing workplaces appropriate for older adults, because visual acuity declines rapidly with age. Smith and Rea (1978) had young (18 to 22 years) and older (49 to 62 years) adults proofread paragraphs for misspelled words. Paragraphs were presented as good, fair, or poor quality text on white or blue paper, and illumination was varied from 10 to 4,900 lx. Performance increased as the copy quality increased and also

as the illumination increased. However, the young adults showed very little improvement with increased illumination, whereas the older adults showed marked improvement (see Figure 18–4). Smith and Rea conclude that illumination and print quality are more important for older than for younger people.

In addition to being concerned about performance, the human factors specialist must take into account the comfort of the worker. A visual environment is comfortable when required perceptual tasks can be performed with little effort or distraction and without causing stress. The results of several studies suggest that the luminance ratio of the task to its surroundings should not exceed 5:1 (Cushman & Crist, 1987). However, a study by Cushman, Dunn, and Peters (1984) indicates that comfort and performance do not decrease significantly with luminance ratios even as large as 110:1. They had people make prints of negatives under luminance ratios ranging from 3.4:1 to 110:1. As the luminance ratio decreased, printing rate declined slightly, but so did the error rate. The participants reported less ocular discomfort and overall fatigue when they were allowed to adjust the luminance ratio.

Flynn (1977) has published the results from studies in which workers gave subjective ratings of different types of lighting. Workers rated their impressions of lighting qualities, such as visual clarity, pleasantness, spaciousness, and how relaxing it was. The lighting used in these studies was adjusted along several dimensions. An overhead versus peripheral dimension involved whether the lights were mounted on the ceiling or on the wall. A nonuniform versus uniform distinction referred to the distribution of light in the room as a function of the distribution of objects and surfaces. Lighting was also adjusted to be either bright or dim and either warm or cool. The results of these studies are shown in Table 18–1. The values of different lighting dimensions are presented with the positive qualities of, for example, spaciousness and privacy that they evoke. Some of these qualities will be more important

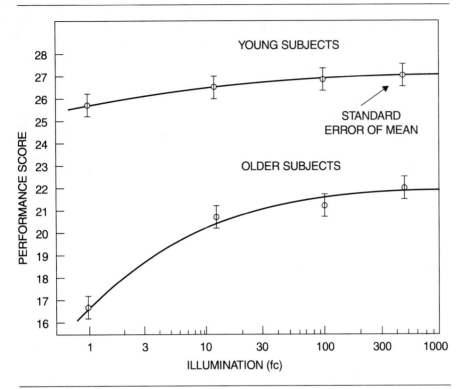

FIGURE 18–4 Proofreading Performance by Young and Old Subjects as a Function of Illumination Level.

Reprinted with permission from S. W. Smith and M. S. Rea (1978). Proofreading under different levels of illumination. *Journal of the Illuminating Engineering Society, 8,* 47–52.

than others, depending on the task. A consideration of subjective effects can ensure that the worker is both productive and comfortable in the work environment.

Hedge (1991) conducted a field study investigating productivity and comfort with two lighting systems installed in a large, windowless office building. These were lensed-indirect uplighting (LIL) and direct parabolic lighting (DPL). The LIL was provided by lighting fixtures (luminaires) suspended from the ceiling, which projected light upward to be reflected from the walls and ceiling. The DPL was provided by luminaires recessed into the ceiling and shielded by parabolic louvers. Workers in the offices in which these lighting systems were installed re-

sponded to a questionnaire that asked them about their satisfaction with the lighting. The DPL system generated significantly more complaints than the LIL system about such problems as glare and harshness, and workers estimated up to four times more productivity loss because of such lighting problems. Workers in the DPL group also reported three to four times more productivity loss due to visual health problems, such as focusing problems, watery eyes, or tiredness.

Glare

Glare refers to high-intensity light that can cause discomfort and interfere with the perception of objects of lower intensity. The effect of a higher-

TABLE 18–1   Lighting Reinforcement of Subjective Effects

SUBJECTIVE IMPRESSION	REINFORCING LIGHTING MODES
Visual clarity	Bright, uniform lighting mode
	Some peripheral emphasis, such as with high-reflectance walls or wall lighting
Spaciousness	Uniform, peripheral (wall) lighting
	Brightness is a reinforcing factor, but not a decisive one
Relaxation	Nonuniform lighting mode
	Peripheral (wall) emphasis, rather than overhead lighting
Privacy or *intimacy*	Nonuniform lighting mode
	Tendency toward low light intensities in the immediate locale of the user, with higher brightnesses remote from the user
	Peripheral (wall) emphasis is a reinforcing factor, but not a decisive one
Pleasantness and *preference*	Nonuniform lighting mode
	Peripheral (wall) emphasis

Reprinted from J. E. Flynn (1977). A study of subjective responses to low energy and nonuniform lighting systems. *Lighting Design and Application, 7,* 6–15. Published by the Illuminating Engineering Society of North America.

intensity glare source is to make the distribution of light on the retina uneven, and the highly excited areas of the retina tend to inhibit those areas not as excited. This impairs perception of lower-intensity detail.

Several distinctions between types of glare can be made. Light sources within the visual field, such as windows and luminaires, can produce direct glare. Reflected glare can be produced by objects and surfaces that reflect light. A light source is said to be in an offending zone if light reflects from the work surface into the eyes (see Figure 18–5). One type of reflected glare is specular reflection, which produces images of objects in the room on the viewing surface. A veiling reflection is one that results in a complete reduction of contrast over parts of the viewing surface. Direct and reflected glare can be particularly debilitating for workstations with visual display units (VDUs).

Glare can also be classified according to its severity. *Disability glare* reduces the contrast ratio of display characters by increasing the luminance of both the display background and the characters; this reduces the detectability, legibil-

ity, and readability of the display characters. *Discomfort glare,* which may or may not be accompanied by disability glare, will cause the operator discomfort when the work surface is viewed for a period of time.

Because discomfort is a subjective experience, it will be affected by many factors other than intensity. Sivak, Olson, and Zeltner (1989) reasoned that European drivers, because of their experience with low-intensity amber headlights, may be more subject to discomfort glare than U.S. drivers when driving on U.S. roadways. This was the case; West German drivers rated filtered and unfiltered headlights of different brightnesses higher in discomfort than did U.S. drivers. The drivers' past experience helped determine the degree of discomfort.

The potential for discomfort glare can be assessed by the visual comfort probability (VCP) method (Guth, 1963). The VCP method relies on the calculation of a glare sensation index (M):

$$M = \frac{L_S Q}{2PF^{0.44}}$$

OFFENDING ZONE

FIGURE 18–5 The Offending Zone for Glare.

From W. H. Cushman & B. Crist (1987). Illumination. In G. Salvendy (Ed.), *Handbook of Human Factors* (pp. 670–695). Copyright © 1987 by John Wiley & Sons, Inc. Reprinted by permission of John Wiley & Sons, Inc.

In this equation L_S is the luminance of the glare source, P is an index of the position of the glare source from the line of sight, F is the luminance of the entire field of view including the glare source, and

$$Q = 20.4\,W_S + 1.52\,W_S^{0.2} - 0.075$$

where W_S is the (solid) visual angle of the glare source. When several glare sources must be considered at one location, the glare sensation for each source at that position can be calculated and the results compounded into the single discomfort glare rating (DGR) by the formula

$$DGR = \left(\sum_{i=1}^{n} M_i \right)^a$$

where n is the number of glare sources and

$$a = n^{-0.0914}$$

The VCP is defined as the percentage of people who would find the given level of glare acceptable.

There are many procedures for reducing glare. Window luminance can be controlled by using blinds or shades. Similarly, glare from luminaires can be reduced by using shades and baffles to cut the amount of light coming directly from the source. VDUs or other displays can be located so that bright sources of light are not in the field of view and reflections are not seen on the screen. The display can be positioned to avoid glare by tilting or swiveling the screen. Antiglare devices, such as screen filters, can be used for VDUs, but they reduce contrast and so may degrade visibility.

The console used by air-traffic controllers has several characteristics that make lighting particularly difficult (see Figure 18–6). There are several VDUs in a single console tilted at different angles toward the air-traffic controller. Yet, it is important to maintain high levels of illumination behind the console for maintenance pur-

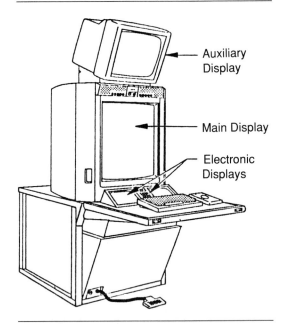

Auxiliary Display

Main Display

Electronic Displays

FIGURE 18–6 An Air Traffic Controller's Console.

From P. A. Krois et al., Air traffic control facility lighting. Reprinted with permission from *Proceedings of the Human Factors Society 35th Annual Meeting*, pp. 551–555, 1991. Copyright 1991 by The Human Factors Society, Inc. All rights reserved.

poses. Krois et al. (1991) proposed a combination of direct and indirect lighting to satisfy both of these requirements (see Figure 18–7). They recommend that indirect lighting luminaires be used in the area for operations, whereas direct lighting luminaires protected by baffles be used in the area for maintenance. The use of baffling prevents glare on the VDUs from the direct lighting.

NOISE

Noise usually refers to background sound that is irrelevant to the tasks that are to be performed. It is present to some extent in any work environment, as well as in all other settings. Noise can be generated by office equipment, machinery, conversation, and ventilation systems, among other things. High levels of noise can result in worker discomfort, reducing performance and producing hearing loss that may be permanent. An evaluation of noise from a human factors perspective must determine whether the noise is within acceptable limits and, as with lighting, must establish suitable esthetic criteria for the well-being of the workers.

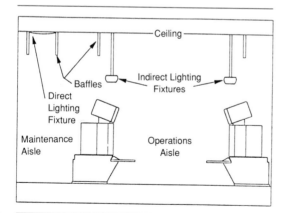

FIGURE 18–7   Lighting for an Air Traffic Control Workplace.

From P. A. Krois et al., Air traffic control facility lighting. Reprinted with permission from *Proceedings of the Human Factors Society 35th Annual Meeting*, pp. 551–555, 1991. Copyright 1991 by The Human Factors Society, Inc. All rights reserved.

Noise Measurement

Sound is measured with reference to its intensity and its frequency composition. A sound-level meter (see Figure 18–8) provides a single measure of amplitude averaged over the auditory spectrum. Just as the photometer is calibrated for the human's sensitivity to light of different wavelengths, the sound-level meter is calibrated according to the human's sensitivity to tones of

FIGURE 18-8   Model 2700 Impulse Sound Level Meter Provided by Quest Electronics, Oconomowoc, Wisconsin.

different frequencies. Because relative sensitivity is a function of the amplitude of a tone, a different calibration must be used to measure noise at different intensity levels.

A sound-level meter usually has three scales, one appropriate for low intensities (the A scale), one for intermediate intensities (the B scale), and one for high intensities (the C scale). As shown in Figure 18–9, the scales differ primarily in the weighting of frequencies below 500 Hz. If the same sound is measured using both the A and C scales, a comparison between these measurements gives an indication of the intensity of low-frequency components in the sound. If the two measures are very similar, the sound energy contains components that are mostly above 500 Hz, whereas if the C measure is much higher than the A measure, a substantial portion of the sound energy is below 500 Hz. Some sophisticated meters include band-pass filters to allow measurements of sound energy within specified frequency regions.

In most circumstances, noise levels will not be constant over extended periods of time. Rather, the noise will fluctuate, either quite rapidly or more gradually. Most sound-level meters are equipped with slow and fast settings that differ in the length of the time interval in which the noise is sampled. For relatively stable noise levels, either setting can be used. If the noise level changes rapidly, the slow setting will allow the observer to take a reading of the meter. Some meters are equipped with hold buttons that allow the maximum or minimum reading to be displayed when the meter is set for fast sampling.

Total noise exposure across the course of a day is often a concern in the work environment. This exposure can be measured using a device called a dosemeter, which is worn by the worker for an entire day. These meters are small and inexpensive, but their measurements can be inaccurate. This is because the meter will register high noise levels that arise because the noise source is close to the microphone. Although some of these sounds may be of concern, others, such as the worker's own voice, may not.

Noise Level and Performance

High noise levels can be detrimental to performance. As discussed in Chapter 8, noise can mask speech and nonspeech sounds. This masking can directly interfere with a worker's attempt to communicate and to perceive auditory displays. Communication can also suffer from the changes in speech patterns that occur when a speaker shouts to overcome a high background noise level. One problem that arises in office environments is noise from background conversation, which can disrupt a worker's ability to concentrate on reading or listening to other verbal material.

Noise can often produce highly emotional responses, such as the startle reflex. Anyone who has been exposed to the sound of fingernails scraped over a blackboard can appreciate how compelling some sounds can be. Fortunately, such responses are usually very brief and rapidly diminish with repeated exposure. Not all emotional responses are detrimental to performance, however. McGrath (1963) demonstrated that background noise producing a higher level of arousal also produced better performance on a

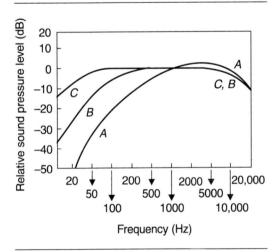

FIGURE 18–9 The Spectral Weightings for the A, B, and C Scales on a Sound-Level Meter.

vigilance task, in which performance tends to decline as arousal decreases. In short, monotonous tasks may benefit from the presence of noise.

Laboratory studies have shown that noise levels as low as 80 dB(C) can have a detrimental effect on performance. Jones and Broadbent (1987) suggest that performance of the following activities may be adversely affected by noise: (1) tasks of extended duration, if the background noise is continuous; (2) tasks that require a steady gaze or fixed posture, which can be disrupted if a person is startled by sudden noise; (3) unimportant or infrequent tasks; (4) tasks that require comprehension of verbal material; and (5) open

tasks, in which a rapid change of response may be required.

Hearing Loss

Exposure to high noise levels can lead to either temporary or permanent decreases in auditory sensitivity. Such decreases are called *threshold shifts*. A temporary threshold shift is defined as an elevation in the auditory threshold measured 2 min after exposure. The magnitude of the temporary threshold shift is a function of the noise level and frequency and the length of exposure time (see Figure 18–10). A permanent threshold shift

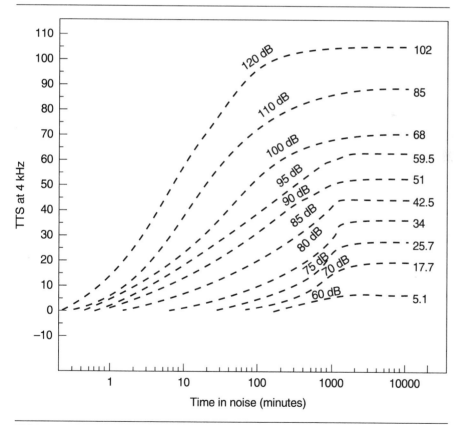

FIGURE 18–10   Temporary Threshold Shift as a Function of Noise Level, Frequency, and Exposure Time.

From J. D. Miller (1974). Effects of noise on people. *Journal of the Acoustical Society of America, 56,* 729–764. Reprinted by permission.

is defined as an elevation in the auditory threshold that is irreversible, that is, permanent damage. The magnitude of a permanent threshold shift also varies with the exposure duration and noise frequency (see Figure 18–11). The accumulated effects of exposure to 80-dB(A) noise for 10 years of 8-hr shifts appears to be negligible (Passchier-Vermeer, 1974), but these effects increase dramatically for noise levels of 85 dB(A) and above (see Figure 18–12). The amount of time that a worker can be exposed to potentially damaging noise levels without producing a permanent threshold shift declines with increasing decibels. The maximum exposure duration to high-level noise is presented in Figure 18–13.

The anatomy of the inner ear consists of several very delicate structures. Because the nature of sound energy is air pressure, rapid intense sounds can deliver extremely high pressures that may result in acoustic trauma, by which the structures of the inner ear are permanently damaged.

Such sounds include those produced by gunshots and claxons, in which the onset of the sound is rapid or stepped. Sounds that have more gradual or ramped onsets allow the acoustic reflex to protect the inner ear.

Noise Reduction

Because the effects of noise can have such profound physical consequences, reduction of noise is a fundamental concern in human factors. A goal of machinery and equipment designers should be to minimize the noise output of their products. When engineering efforts have been exhausted, the worker can be protected from noisy equipment by baffles, which provide a physical sound absorbing barrier between the worker and the source of the noise.

One of the simplest resources available for noise control is ear-protection devices, which fall into two categories: ear plugs and earmuffs. Sev-

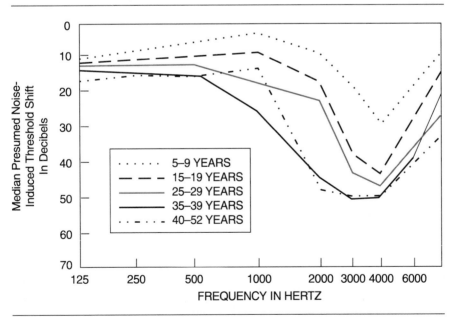

FIGURE 18–11 Permanent Threshold Shift as a Function of Exposure Duration and Noise Frequency.

From W. Taylor et al. (1965). Study of noise and hearing in jute weaving. *Journal of the Acoustical Society of America*, 38, 113–120. Reprinted by permission.

One advantage of earmuffs is that, when combined with earphones, they can provide both a source of protection against external noise and a means to deliver acoustic information in a noisy environment. Ultimate protection is afforded by the use of earplugs together with earmuffs. Park and Casali's (1991) results indicate that, whichever hearing protection device is chosen, the worker needs to be trained in its use. Because of the discrepancy between manufacturers' noise-

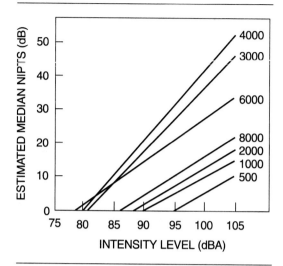

FIGURE 18–12   Accumulated Effects of Exposure to Noise (Noise-Induced Permanent Threshold Shifts) of Different Intensity Levels for 10 Years.

From W. D. Ward (1983). Noise-induced hearing loss. In D. M. Jones & A. J. Chapman (Eds.), *Noise & Society.* Reprinted by permission of John Wiley & Sons, Ltd.

eral types of ear plugs and earmuffs are readily available over the counter, and the degree of sound reduction that they are supposed to provide is usually clearly marked on the packaging. However, the degree of attenuation actually provided seems to be less than the manufacturers' ratings (Park & Casali, 1991). Earmuffs are more expensive, but they have been found to be more effective than ear plugs in field studies. Park and Casali reported that this finding is probably due to the lack of training provided to users on how to fit ear plugs. They investigated three types of ear plugs and a popular earmuff. Their results are shown in Figure 18–14. The earmuff provided more protection for untrained users, probably because the earmuff is easy to fit. For users trained on its fit, however, a malleable foam plug, the E-A-R plug, provided maximum noise reduction. Note that for both trained and untrained users the noise-reduction ratings were less than those claimed by the manufacturers.

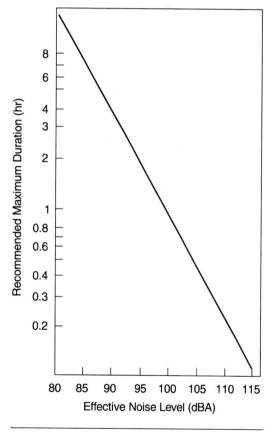

FIGURE 18–13   The Maximum Acceptable Exposure Duration to High-level Noise.

From *Ergonomic Design for People at Work* (Vol. 1). Published by Van Nostrand Reinhold, 1983. Copyright © 1983 by Eastman Kodak Company. Reprinted courtesy of Eastman Kodak Company.

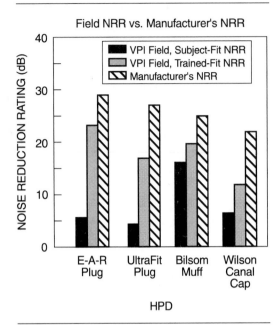

FIGURE 18–14 Noise-reduction Ratings for Four Hearing Protection Devices for Trained and Untrained Subjects and as Provided by the Manufacturer.

From M. Y. Park & J. G. Casali, A controlled investigation of infiled attenuation performance of selected insert, earmuff, and canal cap hearing protectors. Reprinted with permission from *Human Factors*, Vol. 33, No. 6, pp. 693–714, 1991. Copyright © 1991 by The Human Factors Society, Inc. All rights reserved.

reduction ratings and the attenuation actually provided, a large safety margin between the actual noise level and the noise-reduction rating should be allowed.

Criteria for the acceptability of different noise levels should be consulted when evaluating the noise level of a workplace. Beranek, Blazier, and Figwer (1971) compiled the results of many studies that used subjective ratings of office workers and speech communication requirements, among other things, to generate *preferred noise criterion* (PNC) curves (see Figure 18–15). These curves show the relationship between in-

tensity and frequency on the PNC for different task environments. The lower the frequency of the noise is, the higher its intensity must be to achieve any PNC level. To use the curves, a decision must first be made about the appropriate PNC level for the environment in question (see Table 18–2). Then sound levels are measured for each octave frequency band. If the intensity in any band exceeds the chosen PNC value, the environment is too noisy and measures to reduce noise in the offending bands should be taken.

VIBRATION

Auditory noise is often accompanied by mechanical vibration that can cause vibration of the operator. The term *vibration* refers to any oscillatory motion around a central point and is usually described in three dimensions. As with sound waves, vibration can be characterized in terms of amplitude and frequency. Most vibration with which a person would come into contact is irregular. Complex patterns of vibration can be broken into a weighted sum of sinusoidal vibrations, just as a complex tone can be broken into a weighted sum of pure tones.

Vibration is typically measured with an accelerometer, an electrical device that measures displacement acceleration in one or more dimensions. From the acceleration data, the velocity and displacement data can be derived. The accelerometer can be attached either to the vibration source or to bony sites on the body. An accelerometer should be as small as possible and be sensitive to the ranges of acceleration and frequencies expected. The most common descriptive measure of vibration is the root-mean- square (rms) value:

$$X_{rms} = \sqrt{\frac{1}{T}\int_0^T x^2(t)\, dt}$$

where $x(t)$ is displacement along a particular dimension as a function of time.

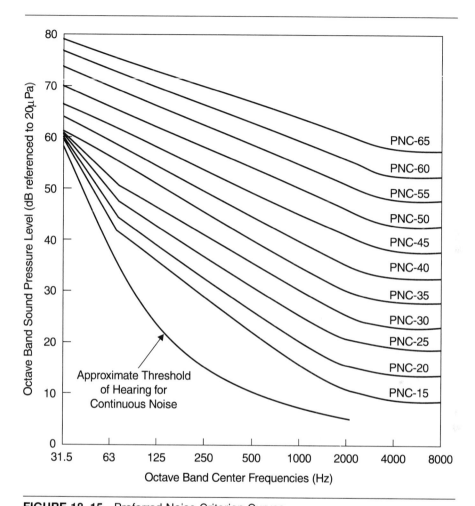

FIGURE 18–15 Preferred Noise Criterion Curves.

From L. L. Beranek, W. E. Blazier, & J. J. Figwer (1971). Preferred noise criterion (PNC) curves and their application to rooms. *Journal of the Acoustical Society of America, 50*, 1223–1228. Reprinted by permission.

Operators who work with powered equipment, such as heavy vehicles or hydraulic devices, experience body vibrations for extended periods of time. As with any repetitive motion, this extended exposure can be detrimental to the health of the operator. The presence of vibration also has the more immediate effect of degrading performance by interfering with motor control. A distinction can be made between whole-body vibration and segmental vibration applied to particular body parts (Wasserman, 1987).

Whole-body Vibration

Whole-body vibration is transmitted to an operator through supports, such as floors, seats, and backrests. One concern is the frequency of the vibration. Every object, even the human body,

TABLE 18–2 Recommended PNC Curves and Sound Pressure Levels for Several Categories of Activity

ACOUSTICAL REQUIREMENTS	PNC CURVE	APPROXIMATE[a] L_A, dB(A)
Listening to faint music or distant microphone pickup used	10–20	21–30
Excellent listening conditions	Not to exceed 20	Not to exceed 30
Close microphone pickup only	Not to exceed 25	Not to exceed 34
Good listening conditions	Not to exceed 35	Not to exceed 42
Sleeping, resting, and relaxing	25–40	34–47
Conversing or listening to radio and TV	30–40	38–47
Moderately good listening conditions	35–45	42–52
Fair listening conditions	40–50	47–56
Moderately fair listening conditions	45–55	52–61
Just acceptable speech and telephone communication	50–60	56–66
Speech not required but no risk of hearing damage	60–75	66–80

From L. L. Beranek, W. E. Blazier, & J. J. Figwer (1971). Preferred noise criterion (PNC) curves and their application to rooms. *Journal of the Acoustical Society of America, 50,* 1223–1228. Reprinted by permission.

[a]These levels (L_A) are to be used only for approximate estimates, since the overall sound pressure level does not give an indication of the spectrum.

has a resonant frequency. If vibration is transmitted to an object at a frequency near the object's resonant frequency, the object will vibrate with an amplitude higher than that of the vibration source. For the human body, the resonant frequency is approximately 5 Hz. This means that frequencies in the neighborhood of 5 Hz can have an even greater damaging effect on the body than frequencies outside this neighborhood.

Mistrot et al. (1990) attempted to determine the best method for predicting discomfort caused by whole-body vibration. Their study took place in both the laboratory and field. In the lab, people experienced vibration either in one or two axes of motion and had to judge their discomfort. In the field, several professional truck drivers drove a truck with different loads at different speeds over good or poor sections of road. Accelerometers were placed in the driver's chair to measure vibration in all three dimensions, and the drivers estimated their degree of discomfort. Comparing the field study with the laboratory study, Mistrot et al. conclude that discomfort is best predicted by calculating the rms of the displacement in each axis and taking the square root of a weighted sum of these values.

Bongers et al. (1990) compared the prevalence of back pain in helicopter pilots versus nonflying air force officers. Helicopter pilots experience considerable vibration that is transmitted primarily through the seat. Bongers et al. measured the prevalence of transient and chronic back pain. They found that helicopter pilots are more prone to both transient and chronic pain. The prevalence of transient back pain was greatest for pilots who received smaller doses of vibration than for those who received more. However, chronic back pain was less frequent in this group, and pilots that experienced the greatest vibration doses had the highest incidence of chronic back pain. As the age of the pilot increased, so did the incidence of chronic back pain.

Segmental Vibration

Segmental vibration usually occurs while using power tools. This results in vibration of the hand–arm segment, to which we will limit our discussion. Other types include head–shoulder and head–eye vibrations. The arm shows very little resonance; most vibrations are absorbed into the hand. As vibration frequency increases, less of the vibration is transmitted up the arm (Reynolds & Angevine, 1977). For vibrations of approximately 100 Hz, the entire vibration is absorbed by the hand.

One immediate consequence of segmental vibration may be to cause misperception of the movement and location of the vibrated segment, which in turn can lead to inaccurate aimed movements and possibly accidents. Evidence for such misperception comes from a study by Goodwin, McCloskey, and Matthews (1972). In their experiments, blindfolded participants received vibratory stimulation to the tendon of one of the major elbow muscles, either the biceps or triceps. This was accomplished by placing a vibrator on the skin overlying the tendon for one arm. Such vibration induces a reflexive movement of the arm, which the participant was to match by voluntarily moving the other arm.

The vibration resulted in an illusion of movement and location, as shown by mismatches between the positions of each arm, in the direction that would occur if the vibrated muscle were being stretched. Vibration apparently activated intramuscular receptors that are also sensitive to muscle stretch. The resulting neural activity was then interpreted by the brain as attributable to muscle stretch, rather than vibration, which resulted in misperception of the movement at the joint. Similar results have been found for other joints, as well, suggesting that vibration could severely hamper motor performance, particularly when visual feedback about the position of the vibrated segment is not available.

A common complaint from the use of vibrating power tools is vibration-induced white finger (VWF), a cumulative trauma disorder that is also known as Raynaud's disease. VWF arises from stuctural damage to blood vessels and nerves and is characterized by extreme numbness and intermittent tingling. In later stages of the disease, the finger alternates between blanching (or whiteness) and cyanosis (or blueness), which is symptomatic of interruptions in the blood supply to the finger. The amount of exposure that can be tolerated is a decreasing function of the intensity of the vibration. Figure 18–16 shows the percentages of people who will develop blanching systems after exposure to different magnitudes of vibrations for extended periods of time. VWF can be aggravated by a tight grip and working in the cold, which are factors that cause closure of the arteries. In particular, vibrations between 40 and

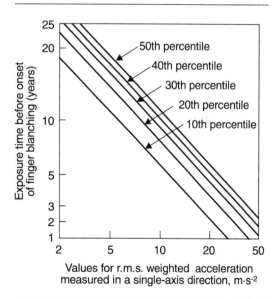

FIGURE 18–16   Years of Exposure Before Developing Symptoms of Advanced Stages of VWF, as a Function of the Intensity of Vibration.

Extracts of ISO 5349:1986 are reproduced with the permission of the International Organization for Standardization (ISO). Copies of the complete standard may be obtained from ISO, C.P. 56, 1211 Geneva 20, Switzerland or, in the USA, from ANSI, 11 West 42nd Street, 13th Floor, New York, NY 10036.

125 Hz increase the likelihood of VWF (Kroemer, 1989).

THERMAL COMFORT AND AIR QUALITY

The climate of a working environment usually refers to the temperature and relative humidity of the workers' surroundings. In some workplaces, normal temperature and humidity can be maintained. In other instances, it is not possible to do so. Extremes of temperature and humidity can severely restrict the capabilities of the worker in terms of stamina, motor function, and overall performance.

Fanger (1977) established the concept of a *comfort zone* (see Figure 18–17). This is a range of temperatures and humidities (combined with air speed) that most people would find comfortable while performing tasks that require low levels of physical activity. For moderate air speeds, the acceptable range of temperatures varies from 19° C to 26° C (66° F to 79° F), and relative humidity varies from 35% to 65% but humidity can range as low as 20% and as high as 85% in some circumstances (Eastman Kodak Company, 1983).

An individual's impression of comfort will be influenced by several factors. Predictably, heavy workloads shift the comfort zone to lower temperatures. Workers do not often perform heavy work continuously throughout a shift, and not all workers on a shift will be performing heavy work. Thus, the temperature selected must be a compromise between the comfort zone for sedentary work and that for heavy work. One way around this potential problem is to provide those workers that perform less strenuous tasks with warmer clothing, such as sweaters or jackets.

Analogous to the comfort zone is the discomfort zone. Discomfort arises when the body's thermal regulatory system is strained beyond its normal bounds. This can be brought on by some combinations of temperature, humidity, and workload. One concern involves excessive sweating. Sweating is usually associated with

some degree of overall discomfort. It can also result in slipperiness when handling tools and controls and restricted body movements when clothing becomes wet. When the environment is hot, several work practices can alleviate the problems associated with heat. The workers should be provided with ample water and a cool area in which to rest. Workers must be trained to recognize the symptoms of hyperthermia, and they must be given enough time to acclimatize to the environment when they arrive as new employees or return after a leave.

Cold environments require additional clothing, which restricts movements. This means that tasks must be restructured to accommodate the decreased mobility of the workers. Also, the work environment must be screened for hazards that accompany the increased bulk of the clothing, such as open machinery in which the fabric can become entangled. Every effort should be made to eliminate drafts and to provide a source of radiant heat. Increased workloads will also make the cold environment more tolerable. Workers must be trained to recognize the symptoms of hypothermia.

Another important environmental consideration is air quality. The air must contain sufficient oxygen for breathing, but in most cases this is not a problem. Air quality issues usually focus on the presence of gaseous and particulate pollutants. Pollutants can be classified into three categories (ASHRAE, 1985):

1. Solid particulates, such as dust, fumes, and smoke.
2. Liquid particulates in the form of mists or fogs.
3. Nonparticulate gases.

When evaluating the air quality of an environment, each of these categories of pollutants can be measured. When their levels are high, the source of the pollutants must be determined.

Pollutants are spread from their sources by way of air movement, which is wind in the outdoor environment and the ventilation within an indoor environment. Because ventilation systems

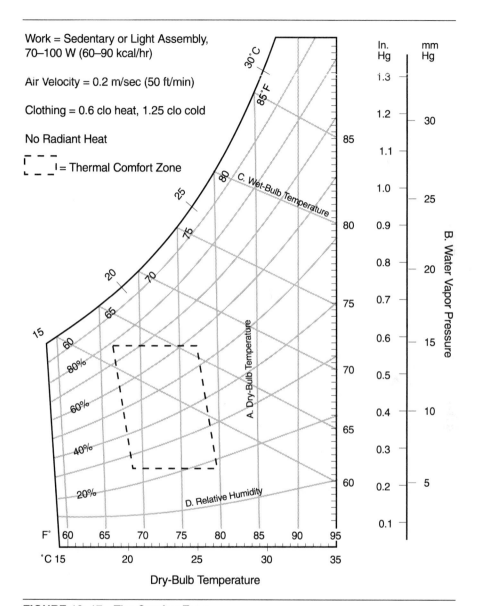

Work = Sedentary or Light Assembly, 70–100 W (60–90 kcal/hr)

Air Velocity = 0.2 m/sec (50 ft/min)

Clothing = 0.6 clo heat, 1.25 clo cold

No Radiant Heat

┌ ─ ─ ┐
│   │ = Thermal Comfort Zone
└ ─ ─ ┘

FIGURE 18–17   The Comfort Zone.

From *Ergonomic Design for People at Work* (Vol. 1). Published by Van Nostrand Reinhold, 1983. Copyright © 1983 by Eastman Kodak Company. Reprinted courtesy of Eastman Kodak Company.

bring in air from the outside, the source of an indoor pollutant can be from without or within. Air quality typically is improved by one of two methods. One method is to remove the pollutants using such devices as air filters. Alternatively, the contaminated air can be diluted with outdoor air (Cunningham, 1990), assuming that the outdoor air is not polluted. Building codes typically specify the amount of outdoor air required for specific applications.

INTERIOR ENVIRONMENTAL PROBLEMS

For buildings and rooms to be optimized for effective and safe human use, they must be designed to satisfy human factors criteria (Harrigan, 1987). The ambient environment in an office or other workplace contributes greatly to the productivity and health of the workers. Within a building, decisions have to be made about the environmental factors of lighting, noise, and climate discussed in this chapter.

Office Environment

All visual tasks will be affected by the quality of lighting. The lighting can also affect the incidence of headaches and eye strain, although there are few hard data on the characteristics of lighting that cause these problems (Hedge, 1988). One factor that can affect both performance and health is glare, discussed earlier in this chapter. Consequently, Grandjean (1987a) notes that offices should be designed to minimize glare. He gives several rules for providing sufficient illumination while minimizing the intensity and glare (see Table 18–3).

The amount of noise in an office is a direct function of its size and the number of occupants. Nemecek and Grandjean (1971; cited in Grandjean, 1987a) found that in large offices the most

disturbance comes from conversation. This is not because of the sound level, but because of the information content of the conversation. Grandjean (1987a) recommends that the equivalent noise level for large, open-plan offices fall between 54 and 59 dB(A), with peaks not exceeding 65 dB(A). When background noise exceeds this range, it will interfere with conversations and other activities. When background noise is below this range, background conversation may become distracting.

The temperature, humidity, and air quality of the office environment can affect productivity and health. For example, many people find cigarette smoke to be generally irritating. If the room is poorly ventilated, smoke can reach a degree of concentration that causes eye irritation and lung damage. Ventilation systems may also bring in polluted air from outside the building. The water used in humidifier and cooling systems can breed bacteria and fungi, which can then be spread through the ventilation.

These and other air quality problems, such as the spread of building particulates and solvents used in building construction materials, produce symptoms of building-related illness. In the case of such illnesses, a source within the building unrelated to human activity can be determined to be the problem. When a source of symptoms can-

---

TABLE 18–3   Rules for Lighting Offices

No light source should appear within the visual field of an office employee during his or her working activities.

All lights should be provided with shades or glare shields to prevent the luminance of the light source exceeding 200 cd/m^2.

The line from eye to light source must have an angle of more than 30° to the horizontal plane. If a smaller angle cannot be avoided, for example, in large offices, the lamps must be shaded more effectively.

Fluorescent tubes should be aligned at right angles to the line of sight.

It is better to use more lamps, each of lower power, than a few high-powered lamps.

To avoid annoying reflections from the desk surface, the line from eye to desk should not coincide with the line of reflected light.

The use of reflecting colors and materials on table-tops or office machines should be avoided.

From E. Grandjean (1987a). *Ergonomics in Computerized Offices.* Reprinted by permission of Taylor & Francis.

not be located, a building is said to suffer from sick building syndrome. This syndrome has become prominent since energy conservation began to be incorporated into building design in the 1970s. The tightly sealed buildings that were constructed minimized ventilation, resulting in a buildup of pollutants generated within the building. To relieve the syndrome, better ventilation and more efficient filtration systems are recommended.

A recent development in office design is that of environmentally responsive workstations (Reese, 1992). At each workstation, the employee can control lighting, background sound, temperature, and the amount of filtered fresh air. It is even possible for the employee to use a panel under the desk to provide additional warmth from the waist down. The workstation is also equipped with a sensor that automatically shuts off the equipment when the station is unoccupied for 10 minutes. To determine whether the increased control over personal comfort enhanced performance, a study was conducted in which half of the workstations in a company had their controls disabled on a random schedule. The results showed that productivity was increased by 2% at those workstations that were not disabled.

Hostile Environments

As technology has progressed, humans have moved into more and more hostile environments. People now take jet flights across continents, live underwater in submarines for extended durations, and travel in space. All such exotic settings require contained environments in which the atmosphere, lighting, and heat are provided artificially. They also possess unique properties enforced by the external environment that must be accommodated in designing for the human.

Most notable is the extension of human life to outer space. The space environment has many unique characteristics. A breathable atmosphere must be provided to support life. Resources, such as food and water, must be supplied. The lack of gravity adds a new perspective to the design of the workplace. In the absence of gravity, the human body increases in height by up to 5 cm (Louviere & Jackson, 1982) and the natural body posture changes (see Figure 18–18).

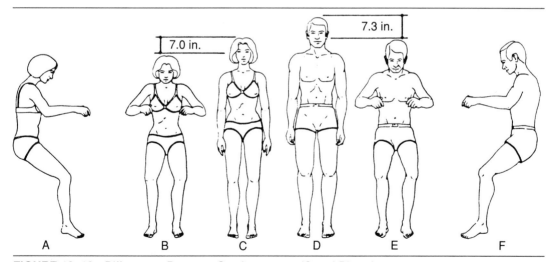

FIGURE 18–18   Differences Between Gravity-present (C and D) and Gravity-absent (A, B, E, and F) Neutral Body Positions.

From A. J. Louviere & J. T. Jackson (1982). Man-machine design for space flight. In T. S. Cheston & D. L. Winter (Eds.), *Human Factors of Outer Space Production*. Westview Press.

The first spaceflight by Yuri Gagarin was less than a day long. Since such early brief excursions into space, the durations of space voyages have increased greatly. For example, the NASA space shuttle program requires astronauts to live outside the earth's atmosphere for as long as several weeks. It is not sufficient just to keep the astronauts alive; they also must function well for the entire flight.

In the future, entire colonies of people will be living and working in space for much longer periods of time. The range of people that must be accommodated and the tasks that they perform will be much more varied. Issues in the design of work and living spaces thus will become more prominent, with the specific characteristics of the extraterrestrial environment taken into account. The best place for studying the effects of containment on groups of people for extended durations is thought to be the winter research stations in Antarctica (Harrison, Clearwater, & McKay, 1991). With the exception of the absence of gravity and lack of oxygen, these stations exist in a hostile environment and have most of the characteristics that would be associated with space colonies.

STRESS

Stress refers to a physiological response to unpleasant or unusual conditions. These conditions may be imposed by the physical environment, the task performed, one's personality and social interactions, among other things. Although specific demands, such as temperature extremes and digestion, produce specific physiological responses, they all cause the same nonspecific demand on the body to adapt itself. This demand for adaptation is called stress.

General Adaptation Syndrome and Stressors

The characterization of stress as a physiological response was originated by Hans Selye in 1936. He noticed that rats injected with different toxic drugs exhibited many of the same symptoms. He also discovered a characteristic pattern of tissue changes in the adrenal and thymus glands and in the lining of the stomach wall taken from sick rats. Sick rats, or stressed rats, had swollen adrenal glands, atrophied thymus glands, and stomach ulcers. These three symptoms are now known as the *general adaptation syndrome* (Selye, 1973). This syndrome is characterized by stages of physiological responses of increasing intensity.

The first stage in the syndrome is the *alarm* reaction, which is the initial response to a change in the state of the body. It is characterized by discharge of adrenalin into the bloodstream. If the stressor inducing the alarm reaction is not so strong that the animal dies, then the second, *resistance* stage of the syndrome is entered. In this stage, adrenalin is no longer secreted, and the body acts to adapt to the presence of the stressor. As exposure to the stressor continues, the final *exhaustion* stage is entered when the body's resources are depleted and tissue begins to break down.

Stress is not simply a function of physiological factors; it is also determined by psychological factors. Of most importance is the way that an individual appraises or construes his or her situation (Lazarus & Folkman, 1984). This cognitive appraisal determines whether the environment is perceived as merely pleasant or intolerable. The appraisal can be affected by such things as the reasons provided to the individual about situations as they stand and the degree of control that the individual has over the situation.

When stress becomes extremely high, it can severely impair a person's ability to make decisions, particularly if the time to consider the alternatives is perceived to be insufficient. In such situations, a pattern of responses may be induced that is called *hypervigilance* (Janis & Mann, 1977). This is a panic state in which memory span is reduced and thinking becomes overly simplistic. The person in a state of hypervigilance searches frantically for a solution to the problem, failing to consider all the possible alternative choices. In an attempt to beat the decision deadline, a hasty decision is often made that has some promise for immediate relief, but with negative longer-term consequences. Hypervigilance likely contributes to many human errors that occur in emergency situations, which are characterized by sudden stimuli indicating a situation that may be life threatening and for which a solution must be found quickly.

Hockey (1986) distinguishes three classes of stressors: physical stressors, social stressors, and drugs. He further distinguishes between external versus internal sources of stress and transient versus sustained stress. External stressors arise from changes in the environment, such as heat, lighting level, or noise, whereas internal stressors arise from the natural dynamics of the body. Transient stressors are temporary, whereas sustained sources are of longer duration.

Figure 18–19 shows the relationship between different stressors and the internal cognitive states. The human is designated by the larger broken box, and the human's internal cognitive states by the smaller broken box within it. Drugs and physical and social factors provide external stress, whereas cyclical changes (such as a woman's menstrual cycle) and fatigue provide internal stress. Physical stress is caused by annoying and uncomfortable environmental conditions of the type discussed in this chapter. Physical stressors have their primary influence directly on the stress state of the individual, although their effects are mediated to some extent by the person's cognitive appraisal of the situation. Physical stressors can also produce fatigue. The influence of social stressors, by which

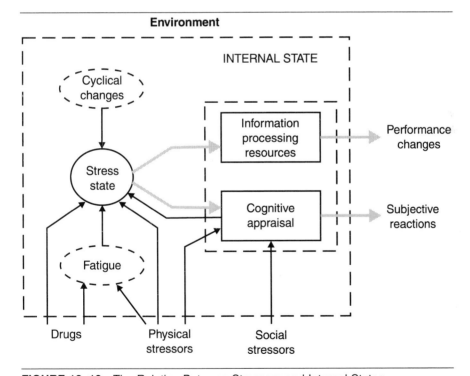

FIGURE 18–19 The Relation Between Stressors and Internal States.

From G. R. J. Hockey (1986). Changes in operational efficiency as a function of environmental stress, fatigue, and circadian rhythms. In K. R. Boff, L. Kaufman, & J. P. Thomas (Eds.), *Handbook of Perception and Human Performance, Vol. II: Cognitive Processes and Performance* (pp.44-1–44-49). Copyright © 1986 by John Wiley & Sons, Inc. Reprinted by permission of John Wiley & Sons, Inc.

Hockey means such things as anxiety about evaluations of one's performance and incentives, is mediated by cognitive appraisal. Drugs are often taken in response to stress in an attempt to regulate the body state. Thus, drugs have their primary effect on the stress state. They can also influence the person's level of fatigue, which in turn affects the stress state.

Fatigue refers to the wide range of situations in which an individual feels tired. It can be caused by excessive physical and mental workloads and loss or disruption of sleep. It includes not only feelings of tiredness but also boredom. Cyclical stressors are those involving natural, physiological rhythms. These stressors are usually studied by investigating performance when they are disrupted, for example, by shift work or jet flight. High fatigue and disruptions of circadian rhythms (see Chapter 19) increase stress.

Table 18–4 gives a summary of the different classes of stressors and the locus of their effects. Large differences exist between people in their susceptibility to stress. The same stressor applied to two different people may have different effects. Moreover, the effect of a given stressor may vary depending on the task at hand. The level of stress induced by a particular variable (for example, cold temperature) may not be as great with an undemanding task as with a demanding task. The effect of a particular stressor on the stress state will tend to be larger in the presence of other stressors.

Occupational Stress

The term *occupational stress* refers specifically to stress associated with a person's job. Stress in the work environment can arise from four

TABLE 18–4   Classes of stressors

CLASS OF STRESSOR	EXAMPLES	MODE OF EFFECT	INTERACTING VARIABLE
Physical	Heat–cold, noise–vibration, lighting conditions, atmospheric conditions	Direct effect on central nervous system via changes in sensory receptors	Individual differences, task, possibility of control, other stressors
Social	Anxiety, incentives	Cognitive mediation	Individual differences, type of task, presence of other stressors
Drug	Medical (tranquilizers), social (caffeine, nicotine, alcohol)	Direct effect on central nervous system	Individual differences, task, other stressors
Fatigue	Boredom, fatigue, sleep deprivation	Both direct physiological and cognitive mediation	Individual differences, type of task, time of day, other stressors
Cyclical	Sleep–wake cycle, body-temperature rhythm, other physiological rhythms; usually studied are disruptions of the rhythms by shift work or transzonal flight	Some are dependent on environmental changes; others seem internally driven	Individual differences, task, form of the disruption

Table from K. R. Boff & J. E. Lincoln, *Engineering Data Compendium: Human Perception and Performance,* 1988. Reprinted with permission.

sources: the physical and social environment, organizational factors, the task, and the individual's personality attributes and skills (Smith, 1987). The environmental sources are climate, lighting, and so on. Physical environmental stressors are more of a factor for blue-collar jobs than for white-collar jobs. Organizational factors can be broken down into those of job involvement and organizational support. An autocratic supervisory style usually leads to dissatisfaction and, hence, increased stress. Lack of performance feedback or continually negative feedback can also be stressful. Workers in an organization that allows employees to participate in decisions that affect their jobs will experience less stress than workers in an organization that does not. Opportunities for career development also lessen occupational stress.

Job task factors include mental and physical workload, shift work, deadlines, and variety. Other factors such as role conflict and ambiguity contribute as well. To some extent, an individual must be matched to the job. Training must be appropriate, the job must be acceptable to the individual, and the individual must possess the physical and mental capabilities to perform the job. The degree to which a worker is not well matched to her or his job in part determines the level of stress that the worker will experience.

In a contained environment, such as a space station or Antarctic research station, it is not possible to temporarily withdraw because the environment is hostile to life. Forced containment thus restricts the actions that a person can take to reduce stress. Moreover, additional stressors associated with confinement are introduced. These include (1) the surrounding hostile environment, (2) a limited supply of life-supporting resources, (3) cramped living spaces and enforced intimacy, (4) the absence of friends and family, (5) few recreational activities, (6) artificial atmosphere, and (7) an inability to leave the contained environment (Blair, 1991).

The stress of a contained environment manifests itself in several ways. Changes in appetite and sleep patterns are most common. Food becomes very important as a source of stimulation, leading to increased appetite and weight gain. Sleep patterns are disrupted, perhaps from decreased activity and the loss of light and dark cycles. Because of the enforced proximity with other people in contained environments, one person's sleep–wake cycle can be very disruptive if it differs from the sleep–wake cycle of others. Anxiety and depression are common, and an individual's sense of time can be distorted.

Because these stressors are continuously present in contained environments, the best way to control stress is through careful screening of the applicants. Individuals should be selected who adapt well and are not unduly affected by the stressors induced by the contained environment. Blair (1991) describes a good candidate as one whose predominant interest is in work and who is comfortable in, but has no great need for, socializing. He describes the best candidates as "often not very interesting people."

SUMMARY

Human performance, health, and safety are not determined solely by the design of displays, controls, and the immediate work station. Additionally, the larger environment in which the human lives and works makes a difference between tolerable and intolerable working conditions. Appropriate illumination must be provided, noise levels need to be within tolerable ranges, protection against extreme noise and vibration should be provided, the climate should be adjusted to the demands of the task, and high air quality should be maintained.

Inadequate environmental conditions are major contributors to stress. Stress is also produced by a variety of other factors, including such things as the social environment, task demands, and long-term confinement. High levels of stress can result in illness and decreased levels of performance. Through selecting candidates using appropriate screening methods and designing the environment and tasks to minimize stress, it is possible to keep stress within acceptable limits.

RECOMMENDED READING _____

Boyce, P. R. (1981). *Human Factors in Lighting*. New York: Macmillan.

Galitz, W. O. (1984). *Humanizing Office Automation: The Impact of Ergonomics on Productivity.* Wellesley, MA: QED Information Sciences.

Griffin, M. J. (1990). *Handbook of Human Vibration.* New York: Academic Press.

Oborne, D. J., & Gruneberg, M. M. (eds.) (1983). *The Physical Environment at Work.* New York: Wiley.

Singleton, W. T. (ed.) (1982). *The Body at Work.* New York: Cambridge University Press.

Tempest, W. (ed.) (1985). *The Noise Handbook.* New York: Academic Press.

CHAPTER 19

HUMAN RESOURCE MANAGEMENT

A growing movement within the field of ergonomics has emerged which brings into focus the interactions between the social and organizational context of a system and the design, implementation, and use of technology within that system.

—O. Brown, Jr., 1990

INTRODUCTION

In addition to the influence of the physical design of workspaces and the larger work environment, the performance and well-being of a worker are influenced by many nonphysical factors. Worker satisfaction is a function of the job that a worker must perform, work schedules, and whether the worker's skills are adequate for the job. The degree of participation that the workers have in policy decisions, the avenues of communication available within an organization, and the social interactions experienced everyday with coworkers and supervisors also play a major role in determining job satisfaction. This in turn affects the

physical and psychological health of a worker, as well as her or his level of productivity.

Productivity bears directly on an organization's bottom line, its profits, as well as on other measures of organizational success. The recognition of the fact that organizational performance is determined by the productivity of individual employees has drawn the human factors expert into areas traditionally left to management. The problems associated with job and organizational design, employee selection and evaluation, and management issues form the basis of the field of industrial–organizational psychology. However, such organizational design and management problems are also of concern in human factors,

423

because an employee must perform within the context of specific job expectations and the organizational structure.

The organization can be regarded as a sociotechnical system that transforms inputs into outputs (Emery & Trist, 1960). The structure of the organization sets limits on the extent to which the organizational goals can be achieved. Hence, *macroergonomics* is an approach to the "human–organization–environment–machine interface" that begins with the organization and then considers "microergonomic" issues of environment and workspace design in the context of the organizational goals (Hendrick, 1991).

The unique perspective that the human factors specialist brings to organizational design and management is that of optimizing human and system performance within the overall system context, which in this case is the organization. Of most concern for human factors are issues of employee selection, training, work schedules, and the influence of organizational structure on decisions. In the present chapter, we will examine the social and organizational factors that affect the performance of the organizational system and the individual employee within it. We begin with the individual employee, discussing job-related factors such as employee recruitment and job design. We then move to employee interactions and some of the ways that social psychology can be exploited to the benefit of the organizational group. We will conclude with issues pertaining to the organizational structure, such as how groups interact, employee participation in decision making, and the process of organizational change.

THE INDIVIDUAL EMPLOYEE

We have already discussed many factors that influence worker performance and satisfaction. These involved the physical aspects of the human–machine interface and the surrounding environment, as well as task demands. The core of human factors involves analysis of the psychological and physical requirements for performing specific tasks. Because a job usually involves performance of many tasks, the human factors expert may be called upon to perform a job analysis.

The broad range of activities demanded by most jobs usually means that employees must possess many different skills. A *job analysis* is a well-defined and rigorous procedure that provides information about the tasks and requirements of a job. The job analysis is used to design appropriate selection criteria for prospective employees, to determine the amount and type of training that is required for employees to perform the job satisfactorily, and to provide a basis for the evaluation of employee performance. It is also used to determine whether jobs are well designed from a human factors perspective and to redesign jobs that are not. A job analysis, then, has perhaps the most profound effect on an employee's activities.

Job Analysis and Design

The job analysis is performed to determine the work that must be done. As Jewell and Siegall (1990, p. 86) note, "By itself, job analysis has nothing to say about the best way to do a job (job design), how well it is being done currently (performance appraisal), or what it is worth to the organization to have this job done (job evaluation)." The purpose of a job analysis is to provide a job description that lists the tasks that must be performed, the responsibilities that a worker in that position holds, and the conditions under which the tasks and responsibilities are carried out. A job analysis also provides as an end result a job specification, which deals entirely with the skills, training, and individual characteristics required of a person holding that job. Table 19–1 provides an outline of the information that might be collected in a job analysis.

Information may be collected from several sources (Jewell & Siegall, 1990). Records provided by supervisory evaluations, company files, and the U.S. Department of Labor Employment and Training Administration's *Dictionary of Occupational Titles* can serve as starting points. The

TABLE 19–1 Information That May Be Collected in Job Analysis

I. Information about the job itself
  A. Work tasks
  B. Work procedures
  C. Machines, tools, equipment, and materials used
  D. Responsibilities involved
II. Information about the outcome of worker activities
  A. Products made or services performed
  B. Work standards (time limits, quality, and so on)
III. Information about work conditions
  A. Place of job in organization structure
  B. Work schedule
  C. Physical working conditions
  D. Incentives (financial and other)
IV. Information about human requirements for job
  A. Physical requirements
  B. Work experience
  C. Education and training
  D. Personal characteristics, such as interests

bulk of it can be collected from those actually employed at the job. Interviews and questionnaires may be administered to job incumbents to determine not only the actual tasks involved, but also the employees' perceptions about the task requirements and the necessary skills. Job incumbents may also be observed by staff trained to perform job analysis. Finally, other people who know the job, such as supervisors, managers, and outside experts, may contribute their knowledge to the job analysis data base.

Clearly, the most valuable source of information is the job incumbent. One way to gather this information is by using interviews and questionnaires. In an open interview, unstructured questions are asked of the incumbent. Large amounts of data are collected by this method, but it may be difficult to organize and analyze them. An alternative to the open interview is the use of a structured questionnaire. A structured questionnaire is a set of standard questions that can be used to elicit the same information as might be obtained in an open interview. One of the most popular

structured questionnaires used to conduct job analyses is the Position Analysis Questionnaire (PAQ; McCormick, Jeanneret, & Mecham, 1972). The PAQ contains approximately 200 questions covering six major subdivisions of a job (see Table 19–2). These subdivisions are (1) information input, (2) mediation processes, (3) work output, (4) interpersonal activities, (5) work situation and job context, and (6) all other miscellaneous aspects. Each major subdivision has a number of job elements associated with it. For each job element, the PAQ has an appropriate response scale. So, for example, the interviewer may ask the interviewee to rate the "extent of use" of keyboard devices on a scale from 0 (not applicable) to 5 (constant use).

For some jobs, structured questionnaires such as the PAQ may not be appropriate. For instance, administering the PAQ may yield a large number of "not applicable" responses. In these circumstances, an open interview, an alternative questionnaire, or even a different source of information may need to be considered. Several

TABLE 19–2   Position Analysis Questionnaire: The Six Major Subdivisions with Examples

---

Information Input (35)
    Sources of job information (20): Use of written materials
    Discrimination and perceptual activities (15): Estimating speed of moving objects
Mediation Processes (14)
    Decision making and reasoning (2): Reasoning in problem solving
    Information processing (6): Encoding and decoding
    Use of stored information (6): Using mathematics
Work Output (50)
    Use of physical devices (29): Use of keyboard devices
    Integrative manual activities (8): Handling objects or materials
    General body activities (7): Climbing
    Manipulation and coordination activities (6): Hand–arm manipulation
Interpersonal Activities (36)
    Communications (10): Instructing
    Interpersonal relationships (3): Serving or catering
    Personal contact (15): Personal contact with public customers
    Supervision and coordination (8): Level of supervision received
Work Situation and Job Context (18)
    Physical working conditions (12): low temperature
    Psychological and sociological aspects (6): Civic obligations
Miscellaneous Aspects (36)
    Work schedule, method of pay, and apparel (21): Irregular hours
    Job demands (12): Specified (controlled) work pace
    Responsibility (3): Responsibility for safety of others

From E. J. McCormick, P. R. Jeanneret, & R. C. Mecham (1972). A study of job characteristics and job dimensions as based on the Position Analysis Questionnaire (PAQ). *Journal of Applied Psychology, 56,* 347–368.

Numbers in parentheses refer to the number of items on the questionnaire dealing with the topic.

---

job analysis techniques exist that focus on the individual elements of specific jobs (for example, Functional Job Analysis, Fine, 1974, and the Critical Incident Technique, Flanagan, 1954), rather than on categories common to all jobs, as does the PAQ. Also, Fleishman and Quaintance (1984) provide an alternative taxonomy of physical and cognitive abilities that is intended to describe the performance requirements of any job. They present 50 ability dimensions on which all jobs can be rated. The Fleishman and Quaintance taxonomy is particularly useful for analyzing the physical requirements of jobs. Regardless of what technique is used to collect the information on a job analysis, when the data are com-

piled, job descriptions and specifications can be written that capture the features of the jobs.

In some situations, the purpose of a job analysis is to design or redesign jobs to eliminate problems and maximize efficiency. *Job design* involves decisions about the tasks that will be performed by the workers and how these tasks are to be grouped together and assigned to individual jobs (Davis & Wacker, 1987). Many issues of job design are of concern for job redesign.

The tasks involved in a job can be classified as technical or organizational. Technical tasks are those that contribute directly to the production of products or services, whereas organizational tasks are those regarding the organizational structure and procedures. Within both of these realms, job design determines who shall perform which tasks. For technical tasks, this often involves consideration of how various tools, displays, and controls will be situated in the workplace. Job design also considers the manner in which individuals within the organization will relate to each other and how individuals will be compensated and rewarded (Davis & Wacker, 1987). The human factors specialist formulates job design criteria, performs task analyses, and devises alternative design plans with their associated costs and benefits.

Employee Selection

Few brain surgeons possess the technical skills to fly a Boeing 747, although their level of training is extensive. The most basic goal of an employer is to select individuals whose training is appropriate for the work that a job requires. How does an employer decide on the minimum requirements for employment and select the most highly qualified personnel from a pool of applicants? Many of these decisions are made on the basis of a job analysis. The job specification resulting from a job analysis can be used to develop employment criteria, training programs, and employee evaluations.

To fill a position, an employer must generate a suitable pool of applicants and narrow this pool down to the most qualified individuals. Recruitment often involves the development of a job description so that the job can be advertised and communicated to qualified individuals. It is important that the job description be such that the desired pool of applicants is clearly targeted and becomes aware of the position. Internal recruiting refers to generating a pool of applicants already employed by the organization. Internal recruiting has a number of advantages, including reduced expenses and the psychological benefits provided to employees by the opportunity for job advancement. External recruiting refers to the activities directed toward the employment of persons not already associated with the organization. Its benefits include a larger pool of applicants, which allows the employer more selectivity.

After recruitment, the applicants must be screened to determine those who are most likely to be successful at the job. The initial screening device is often an application form, which can be used to elicit pertinent information such as an applicant's educational background. The most widely used screening device is the personal interview. Often the interview may take place after one or more of the other screening methods have been used. Despite its wide use, the personal interview is neither a reliable nor valid indicator of future job performance. As with any other subjective measure, the evaluation of the applicant is affected by decision biases of the interviewer. Additional screening devices include standardized tests, which may measure ability and personality, and tests that provide a prospective employer with a work sample.

All screening methods are regarded as tests, because the applicants' responses to several critical items determine whether they will be considered further. By law, application questions and tests that are used as screening criteria must be shown to be valid indicators of future job performance. In the United States, employers are bound by Title VII of the Civil Rights Act of 1964. The purpose of Title VII is to prohibit unfair hiring practices. An unfair hiring practice is one in which screening of potential employees occurs on the basis of race, color, sex, religion or nationality. Based on Title VII, the Equal Employment Opportunity Commission (EEOC) established the first guidelines for fair hiring practices in 1966. However, the EEOC was not legally empowered until 1972. The EEOC can now bring suit against employers for violating EEO laws.

A selection procedure is said to have adverse impact if the four-fifths rule is violated. This rule is a general guideline which states that any selection procedure resulting in a hiring rate (of some percentage) for a majority group, such as white males, must result in a hiring rate that is no less than four-fifths of that percentage for a protected minority group. If a selection procedure has adverse impact, the employer is required to show that the procedure is valid, that is, that it has "job relatedness." Furthermore, the law requires an affirmative action plan for larger organizations involving not only hiring but the recruiting of underrepresented minorities.

Training

Rarely do new employees come to work completely trained. Usually, the employer will need to provide a training program to ensure that the employees will become equipped with all necessary skills. The employer must decide how much and what type of training to provide. This decision usually rests on a comparison between the new employees' level of skill and the outcome of a job analysis. In most cases, the amount of training required can be reduced by hiring more highly skilled applicants. However, highly skilled applicants require higher salaries and so increase cost.

Many factors can influence the effectiveness of a training program. These factors include the variability of the conditions under which training occurs, the schedule with which training is administered, and the feedback that is provided, as discussed in Chapters 12 and 15. Also of importance is the ability of the trainer to convey the important information, to motivate the employee, and to convince the employee that he or she will be successful at the job.

Training can occur on the job, on site, or off site. The benefits of on-the-job training are that the employee is immediately productive and no special training facilities are needed. Because on-the-job training is often informal, one potential drawback is whether correct and safe procedures are being taught. Another drawback is that mistakes made on the job by a trainee may have serious consequences.

Related to on-the-job training is job rotation, in which an employee is moved from one work station or job to another on a periodic basis. Job rotation is often used in industry as a way to teach employees a range of tasks. By training employees at more than one job, operations will not be disrupted if a worker is absent or suddenly quits. For example, the U.S. military employs a form of job rotation in which each soldier receives a new assignment every two or three years. Job rotation helps develop a flexible work force that is familiar with may of the jobs critical to the functioning of the organization. However, it is generally inappropriate when a high degree of skill is necessary to perform a specific job proficiently.

On-site training occurs within a special facility at the job site. The advantage relative to on-the-job training is that the training is more controlled and systematic. However, the worker is not immediately contributing to productivity, and there is a cost associated with furnishing the training facility. Off-site training is often provided by an outside organization, such as a technical school or university. In one form, workshops of short duration are offered in which employees can learn skills that should be beneficial to their job performance. When more extended training is needed, many companies encourage employees to return to school to become certified or to receive advanced degrees.

Performance Appraisal

Employee performance in any organization is evaluated both informally and formally. Informal evaluations occur continuously, forming the basis of an employee's acceptance by his or her peers, the impression of the employee held by the boss, and the employee's own perception of belonging to the organization. The process of formally evaluating employee performance is called *performance appraisal,* and it is usually conducted in a structured and systematic way to provide feedback to both the employee and management. A performance appraisal gives an employee the information needed to improve performance, and it gives management the information necessary for administrative decisions, such as promotion.

A performance appraisal can have several positive results, such as motivating the employee to perform better, providing a better understanding of the employee, clarifying job and performance expectancies, and enabling a fair determination of rewards (Mohrman, Resnick-West, & Lawler, 1989). However, if the appraisal is perceived as unfair, the employee may become less motivated or even quit, relationships among employees may worsen, and lawsuits may be filed. Because performance appraisal can have devastating effects on an employee's position within an organization and because an organization needs to have the best work force possible, it is important that performance appraisal be done well. However, development of an effective performance appraisal procedure is not an easy matter.

An effective performance appraisal begins with an understanding of what it is that must be evaluated. Many times an employee may be evaluated on the basis of personal traits or characteristics, such as appearance, that may or may not be relevant to the job. An employee may also be evaluated based on the results of performance, such as the number of sales accomplished or the number of accidents in which he or she was involved. Although evaluation on the basis of results may sound attractive, the results of an employee's performance are subject to many factors outside the employee's control. For example, a salesperson's poor sales record could be due to an impoverished local economy.

It is universally agreed that performance evaluation should be based on the job description. An accurate job description gives a list of critical behaviors that can be used to determine if an employee is functioning well. In other words, the description distinguishes employee behaviors that are relevant to the job from ones that are not. It also provides a way to give specific suggestions on areas where performance might be improved or where additional training may be needed.

Once the basis on which an employee is to be evaluated has been established, who is to appraise the employee's performance and how the evaluation is to be made must be determined. Both decisions depend on the organizational design and the purpose of the evaluation (Mohrman,

Resnick-West, & Lawler, 1989). Appraisers can be immediate supervisors, higher-level managers, the appraisees themselves, subordinates, or independent observers. Each appraiser brings a unique perspective that tends to emphasize certain types of performance information over other types. The choice of appraisal method depends on the reason for the evaluation. If the purpose is to select from a group of employees only a few to receive incentives or to be laid off, then a comparative evaluation scheme must be used in which employees are rank ordered. Usually, however, evaluations are individual and designed to provide feedback that can be used for improvement of performance.

The most common method of individual evaluation is the use of rating scales (Landy & Farr, 1980). The two most popular types of scales are the behaviorally anchored rating scale (BARS) and the behavior observation scale (BOS). Associated with each point on a BARS is a specific anchor behavior (see Figure 19–1). The BOS requires the rater to give a frequency associated with the performance of each behavior. Both of these scales represent significant improvements over evaluation methods that have been used in the past, in large part due to their dependence on job descriptions and their decreased susceptibility to rater bias.

It is the specter of appraisal error, particularly rater bias, that haunts the process of performance appraisal. One source of error is inherent in the rating instrument itself. A rating scale may be ambiguous; for example, the words *average* and *satisfactory* may mean different things to different raters. A scale may be deficient in that it does not accommodate all aspects of performance relevant to a job. Conversely, a scale may be contaminated by forcing the evaluation of irrelevant aspects of performance. Finally, a scale may be invalid in that it does not measure what it was intended to measure.

By far the most pervasive type of appraisal error is due to the rater. The rater brings a host of misperceptions, biases and prejudices to the performance appraisal setting. The rater does not do this intentionally, but because he or she is subject

Cooperative Behavior: Willingness to help others to get a job done.

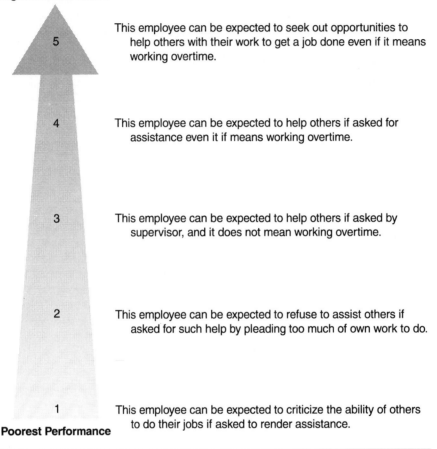

Highest Performance

5   This employee can be expected to seek out opportunities to help others with their work to get a job done even if it means working overtime.

4   This employee can be expected to help others if asked for assistance even it if means working overtime.

3   This employee can be expected to help others if asked by supervisor, and it does not mean working overtime.

2   This employee can be expected to refuse to assist others if asked for such help by pleading too much of own work to do.

1   This employee can be expected to criticize the ability of others to do their jobs if asked to render assistance.

Poorest Performance

FIGURE 19–1   An Item from a Behaviorally Anchored Rating Scale.

to the same information-processing limitations that arise in every other situation requiring cognition and decision making. Bias can operate to reduce the load on rater memory; categorizing an employee as "bad" has the benefit that specific behaviors do not have to be evaluated each time an employee is brought to mind. This most pervasive bias is called halo error, which refers to the tendency to evaluate mediocre behavior by bad and good employees as bad or good, respectively. Although rater bias cannot be eliminated, it can

be reduced by extensive training (Landy & Farr, 1980).

Schedules and Rhythms

Circadian Rhythms. One concern associated with job design is the development of effective work schedules. Issues regarding work schedules are closely related to issues about biological rhythms. Biological rhythms are the natural oscillations of the human body. Of primary concern are *circadian rhythms,* which are oscillations with periods of approximately 24 hr. Circadian rhythms are traced by sleep–wake cycles and body temperature. Some circadian rhythms are endogenous, which means that they are internally driven, and others are exogenous, which means that they are externally driven.

Body temperature typically is used to measure the status of the endogenous part of the circadian rhythms, because it is easy to track and is reliable. The circadian rhythm for body temperature drops steadily from midnight until early morning. It then rises throughout the day until late evening, when it begins to drop again (see Figure 19–2). Performance on many tasks, such as simple dexterity, inspection, and monitoring, is

positively correlated with the cyclical change in body temperature, showing a similar pattern that lags slightly behind the temperature cycle (Colquhoun, 1971). For example, Browne (1949) investigated the performance of switchboard operators over the course of 24 hr and found that it paralleled the circadian temperature rhythm (see Figure 19–3). Because the trough of the circadian temperature rhythm occurs at night, performance will tend to be poorer for nightwork than for daywork.

Performance is only partly a function of the endogenous rhythms, and performance of more complicated tasks that involve reasoning or decision making does not seem to follow the rhythm of body temperature. Folkard (1975) measured performance on tests of logical reasoning and demonstrated that speed increased from 8:00 A.M. to 5:00 P.M. and then dropped. Although speed of performance increased as body temperature increased, it peaked much sooner. Moreover, accuracy of performance was little influenced by the time of day.

Circadian rhythms make it difficult for a person to sleep during the day when the normal nighttime sleep pattern is disrupted. For a person accustomed to sleeping at night, endogenous rhythms are in phases during the day that promote alertness rather than drowsiness, and so they

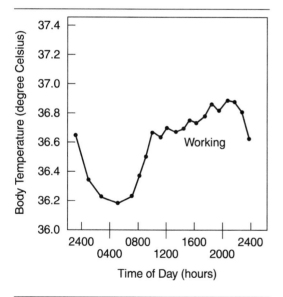

FIGURE 19–2   Body Temperature Throughout the Day.

From G. R. J. Hockey (1986). Changes in operational efficiency as a function of environmental stress, fatigue, and circadian rhythms. In K. R. Boff, L. Kaufman, & J. P. Thomas (Eds.), *Handbook of Perception and Human Performance, Vol. II: Cognitive Processes and Performance.* (pp. 44-1–44-49). Copyright © 1986 by John Wiley & Sons, Inc. Reprinted by permission of John Wiley & Sons, Inc.

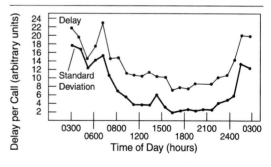

FIGURE 19–3   Time to Make a Telephone Connection, as a Function of Time of Day.

From R. C. Browne (1949). The Day and Night Performance of Teleprinter Switchboard Operators. *Journal of Occupational Psychology, 23,* 121–126.

make sleep difficult. Moreover, many exogenous factors, such as sunlight and increased noise can contribute to sleep disturbance. Akerstedt and Gillberg (1982) examined sleep in a laboratory study for volunteers whose normal sleeping period was delayed. They found that morning sleeps were only 60% of the duration of normal night sleep, even though the person had been deprived of sleep the night before and the influence of exogenous factors was minimized. For a person to sleep well, the time when a person tries to sleep must be aligned with the sleep phase of the circadian wake–sleep cycle.

When the standard day–night, wake–sleep cycle is disrupted, the circadian rhythms will start to adjust. Exogenous rhythms adapt quickly and completely to the changes in the external stimuli, whereas endogenous rhythms do not. However, because few rhythms are completely exogenous, adaptation to altered environmental conditions is usually gradual. For example, it takes at least a week for the circadian temperature rhythm to adjust to an 8-hr phase delay of the type that occurs when a person starts working at night. Moreover, because the different rhythms adjust at different rates, the body is out of synch during the adjustment period.

Work Schedules. The standard work schedule in the United States is five days a week for 40 hr, with the work performed during the daytime. Schedules can deviate from this standard in terms of the amount of work time and/or the hours of the day during which the work is performed. When the amount of work exceeds 40 hr, the schedule is called overtime. Overtime can be in the form of an increased number of hours worked on each day or working more days each week. In both cases, the fatigue associated with working additional hours usually results in a decreased rate of productivity relative to that shown for the standard 40-hr week. Moreover, when extra hours are worked on a given day, these hours will typically be during a phase of the circadian cycle in which alertness and performance are depressed. Thus, although the absolute amount of

productivity may be increased with an overtime schedule, this occurs at a cost that may not justify the overtime.

Shift workers are employed by organizations that must be in operation for longer than 8 hr per day. Approximately 20% of the U.S. work force currently engages in shift work, and this percentage will likely increase due to the cost associated with leaving expensive machinery idle and to an increasing demand for services that are available throughout the entire day (Monk, 1989). If an organization is in operation continuously, that is, 24 hr a day, usually three shifts of workers are employed. The day typically is broken up into daytime, evening, and night shifts. There is little evidence to suggest that all employees prefer, say, daytime shifts over evening or night shifts.

Horne, Brass, and Pettitt (1980) demonstrated clear individual performance differences for people who preferred morning versus evening work. Persons classified as morning types and evening types performed a vigilance task. Performance steadily increased throughout the day for evening types and decreased throughout the day for morning types (see Figure 19–4). Moreover, the peaks of the endogenous circadian rhythms, such as body temperature, occurred earlier in the day for morning types than for evening types. Morning types appear to be less suited to shift work than evening types, because their rhythms do not adjust as readily as those of evening types (Dahlgren, 1988).

Few employees prefer rotating shift schedules in which days off are followed by a change to a different shift; most prefer fixed shift assignments that do not change. Hughes and Folkard (1976) studied the performance of various simple tasks by six people working in an Antarctic research station. They showed that even 10 days after an 8-hr change in the schedule, the participants' performance rhythms had not yet adapted to that of the prechange rhythms. Other studies have indicated that complete adaptation usually does not occur until approximately 21 days after changing to the new shift (Colquhoun, Blake, &

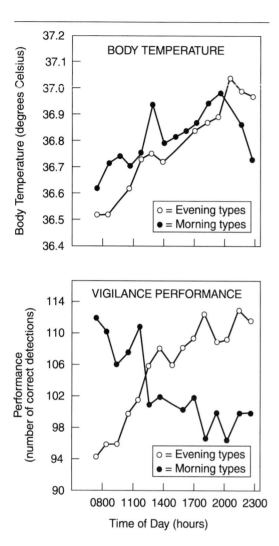

FIGURE 19–4   Body Temperature and Performance, as a Function of the Time of Day, for Subjects Preferring Morning or Evening Work.

From G. R. J. Hockey (1983). *Stress and Fatigue in Human Performance.* Copyright © 1983 by John Wiley & Sons, Inc. Reprinted with permission of John Wiley & Sons, Inc.

Edwards, 1968). One benefit of fixed schedules is that eventually there is a relatively complete adaptation of the circadian system for working the evening or night shift.

The most widely used shift rotation cycle is one week. The employee works for four to seven days on one shift and then switches to another. From the standpoint of circadian rhythms, this is the worst possible rotation cycle. Endogenous rhythms will always be in the process of adapting, and sleep deprivation will be chronic. Two alternatives to this schedule are a faster rotation rate of one to two days per shift or a slower rate of three to four weeks per shift. A rapid rotation schedule will maintain the normal circadian cycle. Sleep deprivation will be minimal because the worker should be able to maintain a normal sleeping schedule on those days for which he or she is not working the night shift and on days off. A slower rotation schedule allows the circadian rhythm to adapt to the particular shift that is in effect, optimizing performance efficiency during the work period and preventing extreme sleep deprivation. Although there is widespread agreement that either of these rotation rates is better than the one-week rotation, there is little evidence to suggest that either the fast or slow schedule is preferable.

Aside from the standard 8-hr shift, other shift schedules have been developed, each with its own costs and benefits. When shift work must be implemented, these alternatives should be considered. Because different people prefer different work schedules, one alternative that may be optimal for some situations is flextime (Ralston, Anthony, & Gustafson, 1985). Flextime refers to a schedule in which a significant amount of variability in an individual's working hours is acceptable. An employee is required to be on the job for some predetermined amount of time each day, for example, 8 hr, and must be on the job during some predesignated interval, for example, 10:00 A.M. to 2:00 P.M. This interval is called core time. The employee has control over all work time outside core time. Flextime has the benefit of allowing the employee to coordinate her or his personal needs with work responsibilities. By allowing the employee to structure the work schedule so that he or she feels best, productivity may also increase.

Another alternative to the 8-hr schedule is the compressed work week in which employees work four days a week for 10 hr a day. There are advantages to compressed schedules, such as the large block of leisure time that they provide, but fatigue is a major problem. However, productivity may be greater if the last 8 hr are contained in a fifth day rather than distributed at the end of four work days. Also, for workers on rotating shifts, three days off may disrupt the adaptation of circadian rhythms to the current shift.

Shift work introduces numerous other problems that may affect worker performance (Monk, 1989). Workers on a fixed night shift are much more likely to try to work a second job than are day workers. Clearly, performance will suffer in such situations. Shift schedules also introduce domestic and social problems. Shift workers may go for days without seeing their children for any substantial period of time. They may feel isolated from their families and community. If these domestic and social factors are not addressed by the employer, they can have a significant adverse impact on productivity.

One way to combat the problems that arise from shift work is to provide adequate employee education and counseling (Monk, 1989). Workers should be instructed about circadian rhythms and actions that they may take to facilitate the intended alignment of the rhythms. For example, a worker who is working nights on a fixed or slowly rotating schedule should identify and strengthen habits that will enable rapid change to and maintenance of a nocturnal orientation. The worker should maintain a regular schedule of sleep, eating, and physical and social activity, but sleeping during the day and being active at night. The importance of taking actions to maximize the amount of sleep that occurs during sleep time should be stressed. Such actions include installing heavy curtains to block out sunlight, unplugging the telephone, and avoiding the use of caffeine during the hours before bedtime. Finally, the entire family should be made aware of the potential domestic difficulties that accompany shift work and possible ways to cope with them.

INTERACTIONS AMONG EMPLOYEES

The most basic interactions among employees take place on an individual level. The type of relationship two people share is often reflected in the distance that they preserve between them. This management of space is called *proxemics* (Hall, 1959). The study of proxemics emphasizes on how people use the spaces around them and their distances from other people to convey social messages. Issues involving proxemics are of importance to human factors, because proximity to other people affects a person's level of stress and aggression and so a person's performance.

Personal Space

Central to the study of proxemics is the concept of *personal space*. Personal space is an area surrounding the body that, when entered by another, gives rise to strong emotions. The size of the personal space varies as a function of the type of social interaction and the nature of the relationship between the people involved. Hall (1966) distinguished four levels of personal space, each having a near and far phase. Intimate distance varies from 0 to 45 cm. The near phase of intimate distance is from 0 to 15 cm and involves body contact. The far phase is from 15 to 45 cm and is used by close friends. Personal distance varies from 45 to 120 cm. Personal interactions take place within arms' length. The near phase is from 45 to 75 cm and is the distance at which good friends converse. The far phase varies from 75 to 120 cm and is used for interactions between friends and acquaintances.

The third level of personal space is social distance. It varies between 1.2 and 3.5 m. At this distance, no one expects to be touched. In the near phase, from 1.2 to 2.0 m, business transactions or interactions between unacquainted persons occur. In the far phase, from 2.0 to 3.5 m, there is no sense of friendship and interactions are more formal. The last level is public distance, which is 3.5 m or more separation. This distance is characteristic of public speakers and their audience. It requires that voices be raised for communication. The near phase, from 3.5 to 7.0 m, would be used perhaps by an instructor in the classroom, whereas the far phase, beyond 7.0 m, would be used by important public figures.

When the near boundary of a person's space is violated by someone who is excluded from that space (by the nature of the relationship), the person experiences arousal and discomfort. One consequence of the personal space construct is that the distance at which anxiety will first be experienced varies as a function of the nature of the interaction. Although not emphasized by the personal space construct, the distance between people also serves a communicative role. So, for example, if two people are almost touching, a third person who is watching them receives the message that they are on intimate terms.

Individual performance in groups is best when the distance between group members is appropriate to the required interactions. If a competitive situation exists, the optimal separation should be greater than when cooperation is required. Seta, Paulus, and Schkade (1976) varied proximity under conditions in which group members were either to cooperate or to compete in solving a maze. Groups were composed of four members spaced 1.5 m apart in the far condition and 0.6 m apart in the close condition. When members were seated close together, performance was best if they were required to cooperate. When seated far apart, performance was best if they were required to compete. In other words, cooperation was best when the proximity was within the distance for personal relationships, whereas competition was best when proximity was outside this range.

Gardin et al. (1973) investigated cooperative behavior as a function of proximity and eye contact. People participated in a game called the prisoner's dilemma, in which two people play the role of prisoners. In the prisoner's dilemma, each prisoner is given the choice of either remaining silent or confessing. The utility of either choice depends on what both prisoners do (see Figure 19–5). The prisoner's dilemma configuration is

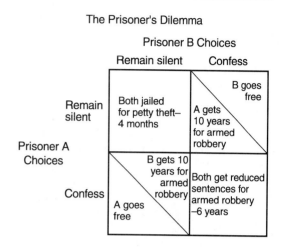

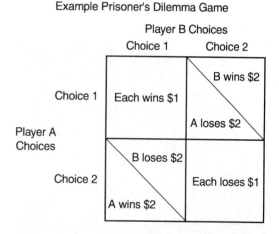

FIGURE 19–5   The Prisoner's Dilemma.

used as a tool to observe the dynamics of cooperative and competitive behavior between two people. The game can be structured so that each player must make a sequence of choices and so establish a pattern of cooperation or competition between the two players. Gardin et al. placed the players close together (side by side seating) or far apart (across the table seating), with eye contact either available or blocked by physical barriers. When eye contact was not available, cooperation tended to be better in the close condition. However, when eye contact was available, considerably more cooperation was evident in the far condition. Thus, when interpersonal separation exceeds the personal distance, cooperation can be mediated by eye contact.

Territoriality

Territoriality refers to behavior patterns oriented toward occupying and controlling a defined physical space. The definition of territoriality can also be extended to ideas and objects. Territorial behavior involves personalization or marking of property, the habitual occupation of a space, and, in some circumstances, the defense of the space or objects.

Altman and Chemers (1980) classified territories into primary, secondary, and public territories. These territories differ in terms of the privacy or accessibility allowed by each. Primary territories, such as homes, are owned and controlled on a permanent basis. They are central to the daily life of the occupants. Secondary territories are more shared than primary territories, but access is nonetheless controlled to some extent. A person's desk at work could be an example of either a primary or secondary territory. Public territories are open to everyone, although access can be limited by unacceptable behavior or discrimination. Public territories are characterized by rapid turnover of the people that use them. Territorial behavior can also be observed with objects and ideas, since objects are often marked, defended, and controlled, and ideas are also defended through patents and copyright.

Territory can be infringed through invasion, violation, or contamination (Lyman & Scott, 1967). Invasion occurs when an outsider enters a territory for the purpose of controlling it. Violation, which may be deliberate or accidental, occurs when a territory is entered temporarily. Contamination occurs when an outsider enters an area temporarily and leaves something unpleasant behind. Intruders differ in their styles of approach. A distinction can be made between avoidant and offensive styles of intrusion (Som-

mer, 1967). An avoidant style is deferential and nonconfrontational, whereas an offensive style is confrontational and direct.

Knapp (1978) distinguished between prevention and reaction defenses. Prevention defenses, such as marking behavior, take place before any violation of territory. Reactions are defenses that occur after an infringement and are usually physical. For example, the posting of a no trespassing sign is preventive, whereas ordering an intruder to leave your land at gunpoint is reactive. The intensity of the reaction depends on the territory that is violated; it is strongest for infringements of primary territory and least for infringements of public territory. In the latter case, the most common response to infringement is abandonment.

The perception of a primary territory allows its occupant a feeling of security and control. We might conclude, therefore, that designs fostering the perception of primary territory would be more comfortable than designs that do not. Architectural features that demarcate distinct territories for individuals and groups can be built into work places and public places. Personalizations of the environment should be encouraged for further marking of territorial distinctions and for encouraging self- and group identities.

Crowding and Privacy

Crowding has a profound effect on human behavior, particularly because of territorial limitations and continuous, unavoidable violations of personal space. Crime, poverty, and other societal problems have been linked to crowding. *Crowding* is an experience associated with the density of people within a given area. Whereas density is a measure of the number of people in the area, crowding is the perception of that density. As shown in Figure 19–6, the perception of crowding is also based on personal characteristics, characteristics of the physical and social settings, and an evaluation of coping assets. The same density may lead to different perceptions of crowding in different settings and may vary across individuals.

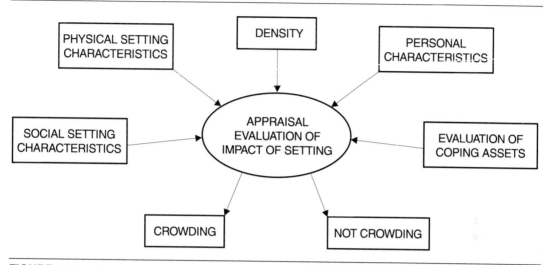

FIGURE 19–6   Determinants of Crowding.

From A. Baum & P. B. Paulus (1987). Crowding. In D. Stokols & I. Altman (Eds.), *Handbook of Environmental Psychology* (Vol. 1, pp. 533–570). Copyright © 1987 John Wiley & Sons, Inc. Reprinted by permission of John Wiley & Sons, Inc.

There are two types of density. When density is changed by adding new people to a group, social density is increased. When the same group of people is moved into a smaller space, spatial density is increased. Density must also be distinguished from proximity, which refers to the distance between people. Knowles (1983) proposed a model of crowding that states that crowding is directly related to the number of people and inversely related to their distance. He asked observers to rate impressions of crowding as depicted in slides of groups that varied in size and distance. He found that, as predicted, estimates of crowding increased with the number of people in a slide and decreased with their distance (see Figure 19–7). Knowles proposed the following proximity index:

$$E_i = k \sqrt{\frac{N}{D}}$$

where E_i is the total energy of interaction at point i, or impression of crowding, D is the distance of each person from point i, N is the size of the group, and k is a constant.

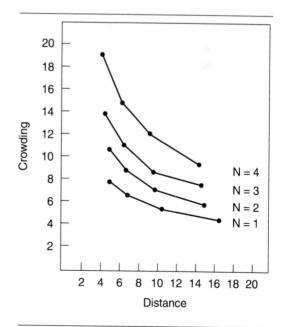

FIGURE 19–7   Estimates of Crowding as a Function of Number of People (*N*) and Their Distance.

Based on data from Knowles (1983).

High levels of stress and arousal can result from high densities. Stress and arousal have been measured using blood pressure, the galvanic skin response, and sweating. The level of stress experienced in high-density situations is a function of the size of an individual's personal space. Aiello et al. (1977) showed that individuals who preferred large separations between themselves and others were more susceptible to stress in high-density situations than those who preferred small separations (see Figure 19–8). This means that individual factors are important in determining whether high density will produce physiological arousal.

Seta, Paulus, and Schkade (1976), who conducted the experiment on interpersonal distance discussed earlier, also conducted an experiment in which group size was either two or four members. The groups were instructed either to compete or cooperate during a memorization task. Seta et al. found that, when members were required to cooperate, performance was better in the larger group. However, when members were required to compete, performance was better in the smaller group.

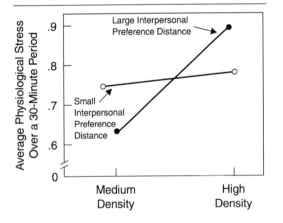

FIGURE 19–8 Physiological Stress as a Function of Preferred Distance and Crowding.

From R. G. Gifford (1987). *Environmental Psychology: Principles and Practice.* Copyright © 1987 Allyn and Bacon. Reprinted by permission.

The Yerkes–Dodson law, discussed in Chapter 9, states that performance is an inverted, U-shaped function of arousal. Thus, as would be expected by any independent variable that influences arousal, crowding can impair performance. Such impairment is most evident for complex tasks (Baum & Paulus, 1987), since the performance of complex tasks suffers more than the performance of simpler tasks at high levels of arousal. Aftereffects of crowding are evident in that the performance of a task can be impaired immediately after being in a crowded environment.

Behavioral responses to crowding can be classified as withdrawal or aggression. If the option is available, individuals will tend to avoid crowding by escaping from crowded areas. When escape is impossible, an individual may withdraw by ignoring others or attacking those perceived as responsible for their stress. In these circumstances, aggression is seen as a means to establish control. Gang violence is one example of this type of behavior.

Many accounts of crowding emphasize the perceived loss of control in high-density situations. Baron and Rodin (1978) distinguish four types of such control. Decision control is the person's ability to choose his or her own goals, and outcome control is the extent to which the attainment of these goals can be determined by the person's actions. Onset control refers to the extent to which exposure to the crowded situation is determined by the individual, and offset control refers to the ability to remove oneself from the crowded situation. When there is a perceived lack of control over such factors, an individual often stops trying to cope with the environment and passively accepts the conditions. This reaction is called learned helplessness.

Office Space and Arrangement

Social factors, such as territoriality and crowding, are prominent in the workplace. Through appropriate design, it is possible to take advantage of the benefits of these factors and to avoid their negative consequences. Social factors can be considered by systematically evaluating a room or office design from the perspective of those people who will be using it (Harrigan, 1987). Such a program requires answering questions about the purpose of the room or building, the characteristics of the operations that will take place there, and the nature and frequency of information exchange between people and groups. Who will be using the facility, and what are their characteristics? How many people must it accommodate, and what circulation patterns will facilitate their flow?

After acquiring information about the purpose of the structure, the tasks to be performed, and the users, this information is used to determine design criteria and objectives. Space planning should determine the spaces needed, their size, and how they are arranged. Within the rooms and offices of the building, furniture and appropriate equipment must be provided along with the utilities that maintain an acceptable ambient environment.

The office is one such environment where concepts of social interaction can be applied. The human factors evaluation must begin with consideration of the office's purpose, the workers and other users, and the tasks to be performed in the office. The activities of office workers can be classified into four broad categories (Bennett, 1971; Galitz, 1984): cognitive, communicative,

procedural, and physical (see Table 19–3). Cognitive activities require judgment and decision making, whereas communicative activities involve both direct and indirect communication with coworkers and other people. Procedural and physical activities involve routinized work that is not intellectually demanding.

Helander (1985) distinguished four frequent types of cognitive and communicative office interactions: transacting, documenting, telephoning, and meeting. Transacting refers to data manipulations such as those that might be performed at a VDU. Documenting is the creation of documents such as text and mail. Telephoning involves communication with another person, and a meeting involves communication with a group of people. Helander notes that office automation should be implemented in such a way that these interactions are facilitated. For example, speech-recognition systems can be incorporated into VDUs to improve the performance of transactional tasks in which the hands are otherwise occupied. Similarly, teleconferencing and audio conferencing may reduce the time and cost associated with trips to meetings. Electronic and voice mail, in which messages are held for the intended party, can reduce the time devoted to unsuccessful phone calls.

Traditional offices have fixed walls and typically hold only a small number of workers. Such offices provide privacy and relatively low

TABLE 19–3   Human Office Activities

COGNITIVE	COMMUNICATIVE	PROCEDURAL	PHYSICAL
Information gathering	Conferring and meeting	Completing forms	Travel
Data analysis and calculating	Telephoning	Checking documents	Typing and keying
Planning and scheduling	Writing		Filing and retrieval
Reading and proofreading	Dictating		Mail handling
Decision making			Copying and reproducing
Information storage and retrieval			Collating and sorting
			Pickup and delivery
			Using equipment

Reprinted by permission from the QED Publishing Group. Excerpted from *Humanizing Office Automation: The Impact of Ergonomics on Productivity*, by W. O. Galitz (1984).

noise levels. The primary human factors consideration in the design of traditional offices is the selection and placement of the furnishings. Propst (1966) reported the results of several years' investigation into the design and arrangement of office equipment. He obtained information from experts in several disciplines, studied the office patterns of workers that were considered exceptional, experimented with prototype offices, and tested several different office environments. He emphasized the need for flexibility, while pointing out that most office plans rely on oversimplified and restrictive concepts. The office needs to be organized around an active individual, rather than the stereotypic sedentary desk worker. The furniture and layouts that Propst designed have come to be known collectively as the action office (see Figure 19–9).

The purpose of the action office is not to improve creativity and decision making, but rather to facilitate fact gathering and information-processing activities and so make performance more efficient. Fucigna (1967) evaluated the action office by surveying workers who were switched from a standard office to the action office. The workers indicated that the action office was far superior to the standard office. The workers felt that they were better organized and more efficient, that they could make more use of information, and that they were less likely to forget important things. Thus, the action office served the needs of its occupants better than the standard office.

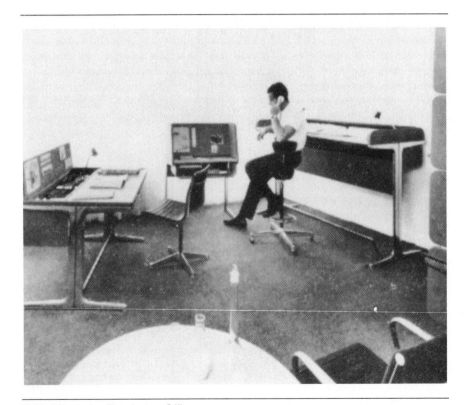

FIGURE 19–9 The Action Office.

From R. L. Propst, The action office. Reprinted with permission from *Human Factors,* Vol. 8, No. 4, pp. 299–306. Copyright 1966 by The Human Factors Society. All rights reserved.

An alternative to the traditional closed office is the open office. One type, sometimes called a bullpen office, has many desks arranged in rows and columns. This arrangement allows a large number of people to occupy a limited space, while still allowing for traffic flow and maintenance. However, most workers find a bullpen-style office dehumanizing. An alternative style of open office is the landscaped design (see Figure 19–10), in which desks and private offices are grouped together according to their functions and the interactions of the employees. The landscaped design uses movable barriers to provide greater privacy than in the bullpen design.

Brookes and Kaplan (1972) investigated the efficiency of the landscaped-style office. Employees who worked in a rectilinear, bullpen office were surveyed about the productivity, group interaction, the esthetics and environmental description of the office. The office was then redesigned using a landscape plan, eliminating private offices and the linear flow between desks. Nine months after the office redesign, workers were again surveyed with the same questionnaire. There was no increase in productivity, and the workers disliked the noise, lack of privacy, and visual distractions associated with the landscape plan. Although the workers agreed that the new office looked much better

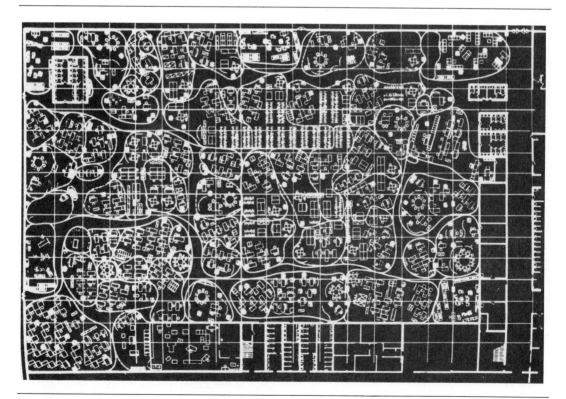

FIGURE 19–10 Blueprint of a Landscaped Office.

From M. J. Brookes & A. Kaplan, The office environment: Space planning and affective behavior. Reprinted with permission from *Human Factors,* Vol. 14, No. 5, pp. 373—391, 1972. Copyright © 1972 by The Human Factors Society. All rights reserved.

than the old one, they did not judge it to work better.

This study illustrates that the major problem in any open office is the presence of visual and auditory distractions. Table 19–4 gives several means to control the influence of these distractions. Visual distractions are easily prevented by using barriers. Auditory distractions pose a more serious problem, and Turley (1978) has suggested that when open office plans fail, as in the study of Brookes and Kaplan (1972), it is because of noise reflected from hard ceilings.

Another style of open office is the nonterritorial office. In this type of office, the workers are not assigned their own spaces. All work is performed at benches or tables, and a worker may decide to work anywhere that suits him or her. Allen and Gerstberger (1973) studied the effects of this layout on performance and communication within a product-engineering department. A questionnaire was administered to product engineers before and after the removal of office walls and permanently assigned workstations. Communication rate among department members increased over 50% in the nonterritorial office. Although performance did not change, the engineers preferred the nonterritorial office over the traditional office arrangement. This preference for the nonterritorial office seems contradictory

to the implications of territoriality research discussed earlier. It likely arises from the collaborative nature of the research group and would not be found for settings in which a high degree of interaction was not required.

The value of systematic consideration of the users in office design is illustrated by a case study reported by Dumesnil (1987). A small office housing two separate work activities, commercial designing and political consulting, needed to be redesigned. Four people worked in the office, three in commercial design and one in consulting, which was small and had ground and main levels (see Figure 19–11, left panel). The options for remodeling were restricted by a limited budget, the fact that no architectural changes could be made, and a desire to use most of the existing office furniture.

Dumesnil (1987) used the techniques of unobtrusive observation and focused interviewing at various times throughout the work schedule to determine social–behavioral problems with the existing office. The problems identified were (1) territorial confusion, (2) lack of privacy, leading to many nonwork-related distractions and difficulty in protecting the privacy of communications, (3) lack of definition of public and private territory, and (4) lack of personal space to maintain the appropriate interpersonal distances. The

TABLE 19–4   Controlling Visual and Acoustic Distractions

Use barriers to block sound transmissions and prevent visual distractions. Barriers should be at least 5 ft (preferably 6 ft) high and should go to the floor.

Use efficient sound-absorbent materials with high absorption coefficients for ceilings (most important) and for barriers and walls. For walls, the most important area is from desk-top height to 6 ft above the floor.

Position overhead lights so as to minimize sound reflected from the lens material to workstations.

Angle windows slightly outward at the top so that sound energy is reflected toward the sound-absorbent ceiling.

Consider using supplemental sound-absorbing baffles.

Use a noise-masking system so that there is a continuous, unobtrusive, and indistinguishable murmur throughout the work space.

MAIN LEVEL—*BEFORE*

MAIN LEVEL—*AFTER*

GROUND LEVEL—*BEFORE*

GROUND LEVEL—*AFTER*

FIGURE 19–11   Office Arrangements for the Main and Ground Levels, Before and After Redesign.

From C. D. Dumesnil, Office case study: Social behavior in relation to the design of the environment. Reprinted with permission from the *Journal of Architectural and Planning Research, 4:* 11, 1987, pp. 7–13.

solutions to these problems involved moving the political consultant from the reception desk on the main level to the ground level, installing tall modular cabinets as barriers between workstations, designating a new waiting area and placing the reception area between it and the workstations (this provided a visual cue that kept visitors from entering the work or conference areas uninvited), and separate, distinct conference areas for the designers and the political consultant. These changes eliminated conflicts over space, resulted in more task-oriented verbal interactions, and, most importantly, increased productivity and user satisfaction.

INTERACTION BETWEEN ORGANIZATIONAL GROUPS

Employee performance is not only influenced by the design of jobs and the office environment, but also by the organizational environment. Such things as management style, benefit packages, and the opportunity for advancement all affect an employee's feelings of well-being, company loyalty, and willingness to perform. The organizational system can be analyzed in terms of goals and subsystems, in much the same manner as jobs are analyzed, to maximize the possibility of attaining organizational goals.

The organizational system consists of two major subsystems (Hendrick, 1991). The technical subsystem involves the tasks that are to be performed, whereas the personnel subsystem defines the ways in which the tasks will be performed and by whom. The technical subsystem is relatively fixed after its implementation, so the personnel subsystem is primarily responsible for adapting to changing circumstances. Our discussion focuses on the psychosocial aspects of the personnel subsystem.

Communication in Organizations

Organizational communication refers to the transmission of information between two or more individuals or groups. Aside from compensation, communication probably has the greatest impact on job satisfaction. It is fundamental to all organizational operations. It is how organizations achieve their goals. The transmission of information can take place through formal or informal channels, and the information may or may not be work related.

To understand how information flows in an organization, it is important to understand the organizational hierarchy (see Figure 19–12). The topmost level of the hierarchy is the president or chief executive officer (CEO) of the company. The hierarchy proceeds through the levels of management down to the rank and file employees. Communication can take three directions in this hierarchy: up, down, or horizontal. Upward communications are from subordinates to superiors and are used to inform or persuade. Downward communications take place from superiors to subordinates and are also used to inform, as well as to command. Horizontal communication occurs across a single level in the hierarchy and is a means to influence coworkers and integrate information.

Informal communications are communications that circumvent the organization's official communication protocols. This information often comes through the grapevine (for example, Sutton & Porter, 1968). Manifestations and uses of the grapevine are classes of phenomena that receive a great deal of attention from social psychologists. However, our concern is with the formal flow of information through an organization, that is, the communication network.

The communication network can be either centralized or decentralized. In a centralized network, information moves from a single source to subgroups in the hierarchy, and little communication occurs across those subgroups. In a decentralized network, no single information source can be pinpointed; subgroups communicate among each other and superiors.

Generally, knowledge is power. The dissemination of information in a network is a way to convey social messages. That is, individuals who are selected to receive information can be

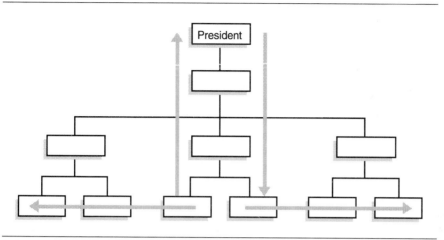

FIGURE 19–12   An Organizational Hierarchy, with Arrows Indicating Upward, Downward, and Horizontal Communication.

viewed as more important than those who are not selected. A superior may choose to reward particular subordinates by making them the recipients of information. O'Reilly (1980) reported that job satisfaction was directly related to the amount of information that an employee is receiving relative to that which he or she believes is needed to perform the job. Thus, information dissemination should be done with care.

As information flows through a communication network, the information changes. Nichols (1962) determined that the way that information changes is a function of its direction through the communication network. Information that flows downward from superiors to subordinates is often subjected to filtering, in which parts of the message are lost. In contrast, information that flows upward through the network is often subjected to distortions in which parts of the message are changed. Information that flows horizontally through the network is often exaggerated. The general point is that a message will not be transmitted through the organizational hierarchy with perfect fidelity.

Shaw (1981) has determined that job performance and satisfaction are correlated with the communication network. Higher job performance

is associated with centralized networks when the tasks making up the job are simple. In contrast, when the tasks making up the job are complicated, a decentralized network leads to higher performance. Overall, decentralized communication networks lead to better job satisfaction, but the highest job satisfaction for both types of networks is reported by the individual who is the source of the information.

Employee Involvement

The communication network used in an organization depends on the managerial style. Likert (1961) distinguished four styles: exploitative authoritative, benevolent authoritative, consultative, and participative. For the authoritative styles, organizational decisions are made at the higher levels of the hierarchy, and information flow is downward. Whereas an exploitative authority generally disregards suggestions from the lower levels of the hierarchy and uses fear to motivate employees, a benevolent authority takes into account suggestions of subordinates and uses both rewards and punishments for motivation. The consultative style allows for some decision making to be lower in the hierarchy and uses rewards as the primary source of motivation. The participative style allows for decision making throughout the organization and motivates through economic rewards derived from organizational change through participation.

It has generally been accepted that employee satisfaction will be highest and performance best with the participative style of management, because people show more approval of a decision when they have been involved in the decision-making process. However, in a recent review of studies on employee participation, Cotton et al. (1988) determined that only certain forms of participation reliably produced better performance. The first of these is employee ownership, in which each employee is a shareholder in the organization. The second is informal participation, and the third is participation in specific decisions. Informal participation merely refers to the interpersonal relationships between superiors and subordinates.

In recent years, some form of employee participation in organizational decision making has been instituted in many companies as part of a *quality of work life program* (Brown, 1986). An additional component of such programs is a concern with the impact of the organization on the individual workers and the relation of this impact to organizational effectiveness. Quality of work life programs often include job enrichment opportunities, job redesign, and ongoing feedback from the employees about the program and other organizational issues. The general idea is that workers will be happier and more productive when the organization is responsive to their personal needs.

Organizational Development

In the course of normal operations, organizational managers often discover flaws in policy that adversely affect their bottom line. Keeping the profit margin in mind, every organization has a structure and a set of goals. Associated with its structure and goals is the organization's effec-

tiveness, or how well it achieves its goals. There are many measures of organizational effectiveness, such as the aforementioned profitability, and others such as stability. Organizational development is the improvement of organizational effectiveness through the deliberate change of structure and goals.

Organizational structure has three components (Hendrick, 1991; Robbins, 1983). The first of these is complexity, which is the level of differentiation of the organization's activities, for example, the number of divisions and the way that information is passed from one division to another. Vertical differentiation is the number of levels in the hierarchy between the chief executive and the workers involved directly in output from the organization. Horizontal differentiation is the degree of specialization and departmentalization. Increases in differentiation produce increases in organizational complexity. It is important for an organization to include appropriate means for integrating across the different elements in the system structure.

The second component is formalization, which refers to the rules and procedures that guide the behavior of the people in the organization. The more formalized an organization is, the more standardized are its procedures. Generally, the higher the level of professionalism in the jobs is, the less formalized the organizational structures should be.

The third component is centralization, which is the degree to which authority is distributed at one level or downward in the organizational hierarchy. The degree of centralization that is optimal varies as a function of things such as the predictability of the organizational environment and the amount of coordinated, strategic planning that is needed.

Whereas the structure of an organization defines its rules of operation, the goals define what the organization is trying to achieve. Goals differ according to their time frame, focus, and criteria (Szilagyi & Wallace, 1983). Goals may be short, intermediate, or long term, and the action taken to achieve a goal may be one of maintenance, improvement, or development. Goals may include such things as productivity, resources and innovation, and profitability.

Organizational development is a change in structure and goals to improve organizational effectiveness. The process of change involves

1. identifying the system's purpose or goals;
2. making explicit the relevant measures of organizational effectiveness; weighting them, and subsequently utilizing these organizational effectiveness measures as criteria for evaluating feasible alternative structures;
3. systematically developing the design of the three major components of organizational structure;
4. systematically considering the system's *technology, psychosocial,* and relevant *external environment* variables as moderators of organizational structure; and
5. deciding on the general *type* of organizational structure for the system. (Hendrick, 1987, p. 472)

Although organizational development is usually initiated by top-level management, the agent of change is very often an outside management consultant, usually an industrial–organizational psychologist. The immediate stimulus for change is often a problem, such as high turnover rates among employees or poor labor–management relations. However, in some cases it may arise from the success of the organization, say, through the need to reorganize as the organization grows and expands.

Organizational development proceeds in much the same manner as the development and evaluation of any other system. A series of steps is followed from the initial perception of a problem or opportunity to the implementation and assessment of change. Figure 19–13 shows an ideal model of organizational development proposed by Lewin (1951). After the perception and diagnosis of a problem, a plan for implementing specific changes is developed. This plan is then implemented and, after implementation, more data are collected to evaluate the impact of the changes. This information is then used for further planning. As Jewell and Siegall (1990) note, this model requires a great many resources that many organizations may lack. It also fosters a dependency of the organization on the change agent. Thus, in many cases, this model may not be adhered to rigidly.

SUMMARY

The performance and productivity of any organization are functions of how well human resources are managed. In this chapter, we have discussed social and managerial issues that bear either directly or indirectly on employee well-being. Employee well-being in turn influences productivity, which determines whether or not an organization will effectively achieve its goals. A job analysis provides a description of the tasks that a worker must perform. It can serve as the basis for job design, employee selection, and training, among other things. Work schedules also interact with performance and job satisfaction. A variety of schedules can be considered for use in specific situations and, when possible, adjusted to fit worker preferences.

Social influences play an important role in job satisfaction and performance. A workplace should be designed to accommodate the types of social interactions that will occur in it. It is also important to consider the organizational structure. The way that information is transmitted to individuals in the organization and the extent to which employees are involved in organizational decisions have a direct impact on organizational effectiveness. To ensure that these macroergonomic factors are given appropriate consideration, as well as such microergonomic factors as workspace design, it is necessary to regard the organization as the overall system of interest. The human factors expert, who possesses sophisticated knowledge about human–machine systems, is in a unique position to aid in organizational development and job design.

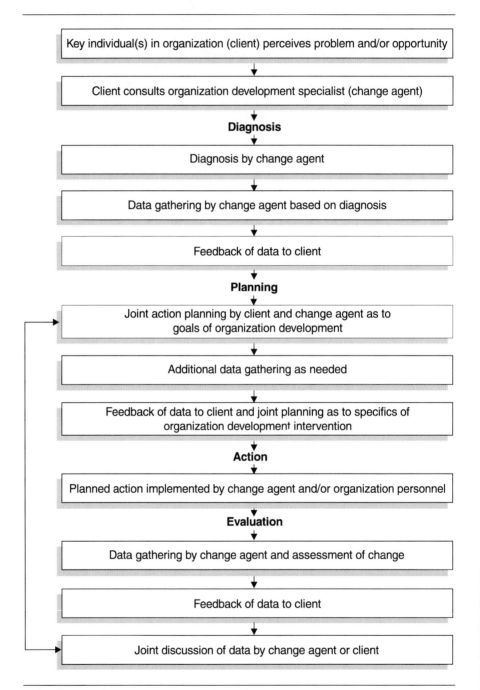

FIGURE 19–13   Stages in Organizational Development.

RECOMMENDED READING

Bennis, W. G., Benne, K. D., & Chin, R. (1976). *The Planning of Change,* 3rd ed. New York: Holt, Rinehart & Winston.

Gifford, R. (1987). *Environmental Psychology: Principles and Practice.* Boston: Allyn and Bacon.

Grandjean, E. (1987). *Ergonomics in Computerized Offices.* London: Taylor & Francis.

Noro, K., & Brown, O., Jr. (eds.) (1990). *Human Factors in Organizational Design and Management—III.* Amsterdam: North-Holland.

Smither, R. D. (1988). *The Psychology of Work and Human Performance.* New York: Harper & Row.

HUMAN-COMPUTER INTERACTION

Computers and the types of information systems that computers make possible represent new challenges to those who wish to find ways to ensure that the machines we build are well suited to human use.

—R. S. Nickerson, 1986

INTRODUCTION

The greatest technological change to occur in the home and work environment in the last half of the twentieth century has been the computer. Among other things, computers have revolutionized the ways in which manufacturing processes are controlled, provided immense computational power for solving complex problems, and significantly enhanced the availability of all types of information. Without leaving the office, a researcher can now perform sophisticated data analyses; access electronic indexes by subject, author, title and keyword to find journal articles and books in specific domains; construct documents in a form suitable for publication; communicate rapidly through electronic mail with colleagues; and engage in broad discussions of research issues with authorities spread throughout the world. The range of computer applications will only increase in the future.

The earliest computers were available only for limited use by select populations of relatively sophisticated users. These users knew a great deal about the computer hardware and programmed their own software. However, with the advent of the microcomputer, powerful computers are now available to virtually everyone, and many users have little or no familiarity with the operation of computers or programming. Software packages for specific applications have become widely available, which also broadens the range of people who use computers. Designing computers to be used comfortably and effectively by all users is an ergonomic challenge of unsurpassed magnitude.

Throughout the book, we have discussed studies that involved various aspects of computer use. Some aspects, such as the acquisition of programming skill and the use of expert systems, were covered in detail, whereas others were mentioned in the context of broader issues. Given the prominent role that research on *human–computer interaction* plays in contemporary human factors, it is important to integrate the most fundamental aspects of human–computer interaction within a single chapter.

Computer usage represents a microcosm to which virtually all of the human factors issues surveyed in this book can be applied. Sensory and perceptual factors enter into the best ways to display information. Motoric factors must be considered to develop appropriate input devices for the user to communicate with the computer. Because the computer is a "thinking machine," cognitive factors are even more crucial than for many other human factors applications. Interfaces that are compatible with characteristics of attention, memory, and thought will be much easier to use than ones that are not.

A microcomputer or computer terminal is part of a computer workstation. The workstation also includes the work surface on which the display unit and data-entry devices are placed, chairs, and other ancillary devices. The workstation itself is situated within a larger physical environment, which in most cases is an office. Anthropometric factors of the type involved in the design of any workspace need to be taken into account, as do the characteristics of the physical environment in which the computer workstation is embedded. Social and organizational factors, such as the way in which computerization will alter a person's job, come into play as well. Be-

cause the ergonomic problems encountered in human–computer interaction span the full range of human factors issues, this chapter will also provide an overview of many of the factors discussed earlier in the book and how these factors can be addressed in this particular application.

COMPUTER WORKSTATIONS

An increasing number of workers spend significant amounts of time at computer workstations. Consequently, poorly designed workstations can induce fatigue, restrict the performance of the operator, and create health problems. To minimize these hazards, anthropometric, biomechanical, and psychological factors must be considered in the design of the computer workstation, just as they must for workspaces in which more physically demanding work is required. In 1988, guidelines for computer workstations in the office environment were developed by the Human Factors Society (HFS) for the American National Standards Institute (ANSI). Our discussion of computer workstations is based in part on these ANSI/HFS guidelines.

Visual Display Units

The form of visual display that has come to be used most widely in recent years is the VDU. Displays are typically presented on a cathode-ray tube, which consists of an electron gun that projects a beam of electrons at a phosphor-coated glass panel. When the electrons strike the phosphor particles, they become momentarily illuminated and light is emitted. The light is emitted in rapid flashes, typically at a refresh rate of 50 or 60 Hz. It is seen as continuous as long as the critical flicker frequency for fusion is exceeded (see Chapter 5). Similar to the structure of human color vision, a color display has three types of phosphors, corresponding to the primary colors of red, blue, and green, whereas a monochromatic display has one type.

Many factors pertaining to perceptibility and comfort must be considered in the use of VDUs.

Because the images are displayed in series of rapid light flashes, the images may have a noticeable and annoying flicker. The critical flicker frequency is a function of many factors, but the most important in this context are the refresh rate and phosphor persistence (how long the phosphor emits light after being struck by the electron beam). Brauninger et al. (1984) evaluated the degree of luminance oscillation exhibited by 33 VDU models and found that only 11 of them had a sufficiently high refresh rate to be free of perceptible flicker. The characters on a VDU can also show *jitter,* or slight horizontal or vertical displacements in location. Jitter causes characters on the same line to run together, degrading performance and causing visual discomfort.

Character legibility is a function of luminance, contrast with the background, and sharpness of the boundaries. The characters or the background, whichever is of higher luminance, should have a luminance of at least 35 cd/m^2. Increases in intensity past 35 cd/m^2 do not appreciably improve perception, which is why this value was chosen for the ANSI/HFS standard. The contrast ratio between the luminance of the character and the luminance of the background should be at least 3:1. Any ratio less than this will make the characters less legible. Contrast ratios higher than 3:1 will result in better perceptibility, and so the highest possible contrast ratio is preferred. Characters with sharp boundaries will be more legible than characters with fuzzy boundaries. Over half of the VDUs examined by Brauninger et al. (1984) had fuzzy character boundaries.

For alphanumeric displays to be legible and readable, they must be sufficiently large. The same is true of the characters displayed on a VDU. The ANSI/HFS standard recommends a minimum character height of 16 minutes of visual angle at the intended viewing distance, with a height of 20 to 22 minutes preferred. So, for a viewing distance of 60 cm, characters should be no smaller than 0.28 cm tall. Legibility will be even better for characters 0.35 cm tall. The height to width ratio and the stroke width also influence legibility. Because different characters have different widths, the height to width ratio is based on the modal width for a particular character set. A height to width ratio between 1 to 0.7 and 1 to 0.9 and a stroke width greater than one-twelfth of the character height are recommended. Between-character spacing of at least 10% of the height is necessary to minimize lateral masking, and between-line spacing should be a minimum of two stroke widths or 15% of character height, whichever is greater.

Displays can have either light characters against a dark background (positive contrast polarity) or dark characters against a light background (negative contrast polarity). The ANSI/HFS guidelines do not specify either polarity. However, findings suggest that performance is better with negative contrast polarity displays. Depth of focus is greater with negative displays, as indicated by the fact that pupil size and accommodation do not vary as much as they do with a positive display (Taptagaporn & Saito, 1990). Users generally indicate a preference for and show better performance with negative displays.

Bauer and Cavonius (1980) found that users recognized 23% more nonsense words and responded 8% faster when the symbols were dark on light than when they were light on dark. Similarly, Snyder et al. (1990) and Sanders and Bernecker (1990) showed that less time was required to read text or to search for a letter target in a display when the contrast polarity was negative than when it was positive. Several factors could contribute to the superior performance with dark characters. As indicated in Chapter 6, it is easier to distinguish detail for dark figures against light backgrounds. Moreover, the presence of high-intensity light across a large area of the screen would tend to minimize glare from outside sources. Finally, it may be easier to shift attention from the VDU to nearby printed material (which is usually black on white) when the contrast relations are the same (Radl, 1980). The only drawback to negative polarity displays is that flicker is more noticeable when the background is light than when it is dark.

Monochromatic visual displays are usually white, green, or amber. For color displays, the characters and background may be of different hues. Radl (1980) found that operators preferred and performed better with monochromatic displays using a yellow phosphor or a yellow filter. Different symbol–background color combinations were examined for color displays. Performance was poorer when the background and symbols were of similar color (for example, yellow on green). However, Pastoor (1990) found no evidence that color combinations influenced legibility as long as luminance contrast was sufficiently high. Although short-wavelength, desaturated colors tended to be preferred for light text on a dark background, performance was not affected. Not only does color show little influence on initial performance, but there is also no interaction across time when a task is performed for 4 hr (Mathews, Lovasik, & Mertins, 1989).

The ANSI/HFS standard recommends a minimum viewing distance from a VDU of at least 30 cm. Preferred viewing distance from a VDU shows considerable variability, although most people prefer a distance greater than 50 cm (Brown & Schaum, 1980; Gratton et al., 1990). Moreover, people tend to shift to even longer viewing distances during extended sessions (Gratton et al., 1990). The preference for distances greater than 50 cm likely is due to eye strain being greater at viewing distances of 50 cm or less (Jaschinski-Kruza, 1988). The longer viewing distances are preferred even when gaze must be shifted frequently to a document located 50 cm away, and the additional changes in accommodation and vergence required do not increase eye strain (Jaschinski-Kruza, 1990).

Finally, there have been concerns about potential health hazards associated with the use of VDUs. It has been speculated that radiation from VDUs might cause health problems, such as cataracts, miscarriages, and birth defects. However, the evidence suggests that the danger from emissions from VDUs is inconsequential (Ong, Koh, & Phoon, 1988).

Controls for Data Entry

Computer workstations include controls that allow the user to enter information into the computer. The controls should be designed and selected to be physiologically and psychologically compatible with the computing environment.

Keyboards. Keyboard devices have emerged as the most typical means for data entry because of the ease with which alphanumeric information can be entered. With few exceptions, alphabetic keyboards use the standard typewriter keyboard usually referred to as the QWERTY keyboard (QWERTY comes from the first six letters along the top line; see Figure 20–1a) or the Sholes keyboard, after its designer. The QWERTY keyboard was designed before the advent of human factors. Consequently, it deviates from optimality in several respects. Five problems associated with the QWERTY keyboard that directly influence typing performance (for example, Griffith, 1949) are that

1. almost half of the hand positioning between consecutive key strokes requires within-hand movements, which are more difficult than between-hand movements,
2. more than two-thirds of key strokes require movement from the "home row" to another row,
3. approximately 10% of the key strokes require the most difficult action, moving a single hand two rows from the home row,
4. more than half of all key strokes are executed by the left hand,
5. several fingers are overloaded because total key stroke assignments are not evenly distributed among the fingers.

These somewhat clumsy characteristics of the QWERTY keyboard conceivably could both hamper performance and increase the likelihood of repetitive stress injuries. As a result, alternatives to it have been devised.

Most notable of the alternative keyboards is the Dvorak (1943) arrangement (see Figure 20–

Qwerty Keyboard

(a)

FIGURE 20–2   Alphabetic Keyboard.

Dvorak Keyboard

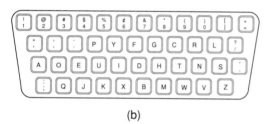

(b)

FIGURE 20–1   QWERTY (a) and Dvorak (b) Keyboards.

1b). The Dvorak keyboard was designed to alleviate most of the problems associated with the QWERTY arrangement. Evidence indicates that the key arrangement of the Dvorak system can yield improvements in speed ranging from 5% to 20% over the QWERTY keyboard, with reduced hand and finger fatigue. However, it is questionable whether performance improvements of such magnitude are really worth the cost and effort of retraining the population (Norman, 1983). A number of computer systems now offer both keyboard arrangements, either in the form of a new keyboard or in the form of software that modifies the key assignment of the existing keyboard.

Another keyboard arrangement that has been examined is alphabetic (see Figure 20–2). Alphabetic keyboards begin with the letter A at the top row of alphabetic characters and then proceed in a left to right manner through the alphabet. This relation is continued on the next two rows. The

general idea behind such keyboards seems to be that typists might benefit from their knowledge of the alphabet. However, studies have shown that both skilled typists and nontypists perform better with the QWERTY keyboard (Michaels, 1971; Norman & Fisher, 1982).

Numeric keyboards are used to enter numeric data and perform simple calculations. The most common physical arrangement of numeric keyboards for the digits 0 through 9 is three rows of three keys, with the zero key centered below. For computer number pads and calculators, the bottom row is 1 to 3 and the top row is 7 to 9 (see Figure 20–3b). Most people can become highly skilled at keying numbers using this arrangement. However, the keys on a push-button telephone

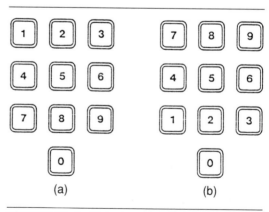

(a)   (b)

FIGURE 20–3   Telephone (a) and Calculator (b) Keyboards.

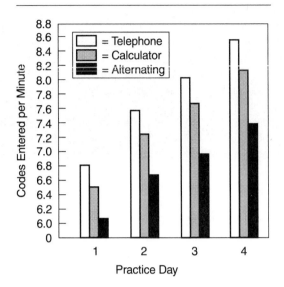

FIGURE 20–4 Numeric Entry Speed as a Function of Practice for People Using a Telephone Arrangement, a Calculator Arrangement, or Alternating Between Them.
Based on Conrad & Hull, 1968.

are arranged so that the bottom row is 7 to 9 and the top row is 1 to 3 (see Figure 20–3a). Conrad and Hull (1968) found that data-entry speed was slightly faster with the telephone arrangement than with the calculator arrangement. More importantly, alternation between the two arrangements produced the poorest performance (see Figure 20–4). Switching between the two keypads is essentially a varied mapping task; per-

formance is usually poor when the stimulus–response mapping is changed from trial to trial. This suggests that people who frequently alternate between use of telephones and numeric entry pads may experience difficulty, which likely could be alleviated by structuring the task environment so that alternations are infrequent or by modifying one of the keypads to be consistent with the other.

A keyboard often includes cursor keys that allow the movement of the cursor over the screen. These keys should be arranged in a two-dimensional layout that maintains spatial compatibility between the location of each key and the corresponding direction of cursor movement. Any of the three arrangements shown in Figure 20–5 is acceptable.

Keyboard Design. In addition to keyboard layout, the physical aspects of the keyboard design can influence performance. Several features of the keys must be considered, including size, spacing, and displacement. Keying is faster and more accurate with 1.2-cm-diameter keys than with smaller ones (Deininger, 1960; Hufford & Coburn, 1961). Keys larger than 1.2 cm will result in a much larger keyboard and keying will become more difficult. Keying performance is also poorer if the distance between the centers of the keys is less than 19 mm (Alden, Daniels, & Kanarick, 1972; Deininger, 1960). If the keys are closer than 19 mm, it is hard to distiguish them by touch alone, and keying errors are more frequent.

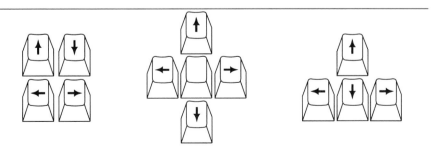

FIGURE 20–5 Three Layouts of Cursor Keys.

To actuate a key, some amount of force must be applied to the key surface to move the key downward some distance. Generally, small amounts of force and small displacements are preferred, although, within limits, force and displacement do not have much effect on performance. The recommended range for displacement is 1.5 to 6.0 mm (Kinkead & Gonzalez, 1969), and for force it is 0.30 to 0.75 N. More important than the actual displacement and force required is the variability of force and displacement for all the different keys. All keys must be uniform across the keyboard for smooth and efficient keying.

Feedback that a key has been actuated will enhance performance. For example, touch typists can type faster with a conventional keyboard that provides ample proprioceptive feedback about the downward stroke than with a membrane keyboard, which provides almost none (Loeb, 1983). Another source of proprioceptive feedback is the resistance provided by the key, which should have a sharp breakaway point to inform the operator that the keystroke has been registered. Many computer keyboards also provide auditory feedback in the form of soft tones or clicks. Appropriate proprioceptive feedback is apparently more important than auditory feedback, however. Auditory feedback coinciding with key actuation has not been found to significantly improve performance (Monty, Snyder, & Birdwell, 1983; Pollard & Cooper, 1979), as long as sufficient proprioceptive information is available without clicks.

Several other mechanical factors also affect keying performance. One of these is keyset interlocks that prevent actuation of more than one key at a time. Another is the point during displacement where the key is actuated. Performance improves when the key is not engaged until the final 25% of its displacement (Alden, Daniels, and Kanarick, 1972). The final mechanical factor is system response time, which should be about 0.08 s. This allows high keying speed and prevents bounce, or multiple activations with the same key press.

Continuous use of keyboards for extended periods of times can induce carpal tunnel syndrome. Keyboards, along with the surface on which they are placed and the accompanying chair, should allow users to adopt and maintain comfortable arm positions that involve minimal bending of the wrists. The primary keyboard characteristic to consider is slope, which should be adjustable to accommodate individual preferences. A range of possible slopes from 0° to 25° will usually be adequate (Miller & Suther, 1983).

The typical keyboard has rows of keys that require the two hands to be placed side by side. Such placement involves considerable ulnar abduction (sideward twisting of the hands), as well as inward bending of the wrists. More ergonomically sound keyboards (see Figure 20–6) allow the hands to be angled inward, eliminating ulnar abduction, and placed on a lateral slope, to minimize bending. Despite their potential for reducing cumulative trauma disorders, such keyboards have yet to gain wide acceptance.

Other Data Entry Devices.   As graphics and software packages become increasingly sophisticated, new devices for data entry and general computer interaction are being developed. For example, touch screens allow an operator to touch locations on a screen to engage particular functions. Touch screens operate by outputting a position in X and Y coordinates corresponding to wherever a touch is detected. A device called a light pen operates a screen entry tool in much the same way. Touch pads and digitizing tablets are comparable to touch screens and light pens, except that the entry is made on an external surface that corresponds to the screen area. The mouse is another external data-entry tool that is rolled over a flat surface to control cursor positions.

Each of these devices is used for pointing. Their primary purposes are to select an option from a menu, to move a cursor in two-dimensional space, or to enter analog data, all by specifying locations on the screen. Each carries with it specific advantages and disadvantages. For example, touch screens allow visual input and mo-

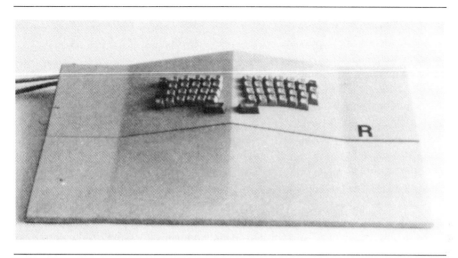

FIGURE 20–6   An Ergonomically Sound Keyboard.

From M. Nakaseko et al., Studies on ergonomically designed alphanumeric keyboards. Reprinted by permission from *Human Factors,* Vol. 27, No. 2, pp. 175–187, 1985. Copyright © 1985 by The Human Factors Society.

tor output to occur at the same location, require minimal training, and do not require good eye–hand coordination (Pfauth & Priest, 1981). However, they are not appropriate for some types of input, the finger can block the screen, the screen soils quickly, and physical fatigue can arise from reaching for the screen. In short, the specific advantages and disadvantages of the different data-entry devices need to be considered relative to the intended use of the device.

Card, English, and Burr (1978) evaluated cursor-positioning performance with four pointing devices. Two of these were a mouse and an isometric joystick. The other two were keypads, one using four directional arrow keys and a home key, and the other using keys designed to indicate text landmarks, such as paragraph beginnings or the next word. The mouse far outperformed the other pointing devices. It was faster and less prone to error and demonstrated maximal compatibility between hand and cursor movement. Although the specific equipment used in this study is now obsolete, the mouse is still the preferred positioning tool (see also Albert, 1982).

The default gain (sensitivity) of a standard mouse is 2 (a control–display ratio of $\frac{1}{2}$). Most support software for the standard mouse allows this gain to be adjusted, but this involves a reconfiguration of the system parameters. In recent years, several versions of "powermice" have been marketed that allow gain to be adjusted on line. A powermouse may include a higher gain that is either triggered by the operator or automatically when the mouse's velocity exceeds a threshold value. For another type of powermouse, the gain varies as a continuous, positive function of velocity. Manufacturers claim that powermice increase positioning speed relative to a standard mouse.

Jellinek and Card (1990) questioned this claim, noting that gain would not be expected to have much influence on positioning time, except at extreme values, because Fitts's law does not include a term for gain. They tested this proposition by having operators perform a tapping task in which a cursor was moved back and forth between two vertical strip targets. For mice with fixed gain, doubling the gain from 2 to 4 made little difference in movement time, but further doublings progressively slowed movement time. When the standard mouse with gain 2 was compared to a mouse that automatically switched to a higher gain at higher velocities and to a mouse that had a continuously variable gain, the standard mouse again produced movement times at least as fast as those of the other mice. Although powermice do not seem to improve performance, one possible benefit of the higher gains is that the footprint of the area in which the mouse moves is smaller. Thus, less of the work surface is devoted to the mouse and shorter movements are required when using it.

The Workstation

Furniture. The furniture used for the computer workstation and the way in which the computer is situated with respect to the furniture can significantly affect performance, comfort, and safety. Physical discomfort increases the likelihood of injury when:

1. The keyboard level above the floor is too low.
2. Forearms and wrists cannot rest on adequate support.
3. The keyboard level above the desk is too high.
4. Operators have a marked head inclination.
5. Operators adopt a slanting position of the thighs under the table due to insufficient space for the legs.

6. Operators disclose a marked sideward twisting of hands while operating the keyboard. (Grandjean, 1987b, pp. 1380–1381)

Appropriate workstation furniture can help alleviate these problems.

As with any workspace, the lower and upper extremes of the user population should be accommodated by the workstation. The ANSI/HFS standard recommends using the 5th percentile for females as the lower extreme and the 95th percentile for males as the upper extreme, in most situations. The amount of clearance for the legs, the height of support surfaces for the display unit and keyboard, and the type of seating must be considered. A computer workstation can be designed for sitting or standing, although the latter is typically used only when there are many additional tasks away from the VDU or a user's time at the station is relatively brief. Hence, we consider only seated workstations, for which the relevant anthropometric data are shown in Table 20–1.

The work surface must allow for ample leg clearance underneath. If it does not, users will have to adopt awkward postures that may cause discomfort and musculoskeletal injury. The depth, width, and height of the region underneath the surface must be sufficient to accommodate most users. Figure 20–7 shows the resulting clearance envelopes for the 5th percentile female and 95th percentile male populations in the

TABLE 20–1 Seated Male and Female Dimensions in Centimeters

DESCRIPTION OF MEASUREMENT	5% FEMALE	95% MALE
Seated eye height (erect)	67.5	84.4
Functional reach	67.7	87.0
Knee height	45.2	59.3
Buttock–knee length	51.8	64.2
Popliteal (inner knee) height	35.5	48.8
Elbow–elbow breadth	31.5	50.6

From *Engineering Physiology: Bases of Human Factors/Ergonomics,* 2nd ed. by K. H. E. Kroemer, H. J. Kroemer & K. E. Kroemer-Elbert. Copyright © 1990 by Van Nostrand-Reinhold. Reprinted by permission.

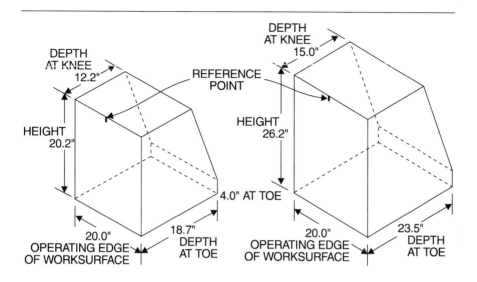

FIGURE 20–7   Minimum Clearance Envelopes for 5th Percentile Female (a) and a 5th Percentile Male (b) Populations.

Reprinted with permission from *American National Standard for Human Factors Engineering of Visual Display Terminal Workstations* (ANSI/HFS 100-1988). Copyright © 1988 by The Human Factors Society, Inc. All rights reserved.

United States. It is best if the work surface height is adjustable between these extremes. Otherwise, the dimensions should accommodate the upper extreme, that is, the 95th percentile male user.

The keyboard surface should allow the user to place the keyboard at a height at which the forearm makes an angle of 70° to 90° with the superior frontal plane. For adjustable surfaces, a range of heights from 58 to 71 cm is adequate. For nonadjustable surfaces, the upper extreme height is desirable, with footrests and adjustable chairs used to accommodate smaller users. An additional wrist support could be provided to further prevent bending of the wrist.

An appropriate display height will prevent the user from having to assume awkward postures and reduce the physical stress associated with having to look up. If the display support surface is adjustable, it should allow the top of the display to be aligned with the horizontal line of sight, with the primary viewing area falling between this line and 60° below it. If the height is not adjustable, it should be set so that the lines of sight to the top of the display for all users are below the horizontal plane. The recommended dimensions for height are summarized in Figure 20–8. Document holders can also prevent awkward inclinations of the neck and head while entering information into the computer. The document holder should be positioned so that the frequency and extent of the head movements that must be made between the screen and the document are minimized.

The seat is an important part of a computer workstation. Because the user may spend many hours at the workstation, a seat that provides appropriate support and stability is necessary for user comfort and optimal productivity. Most of the general recommendations for seating discussed in Chapter 17 apply to computer workstations. A seat should have an adjustable height, with footrests provided if the range of adjustabil-

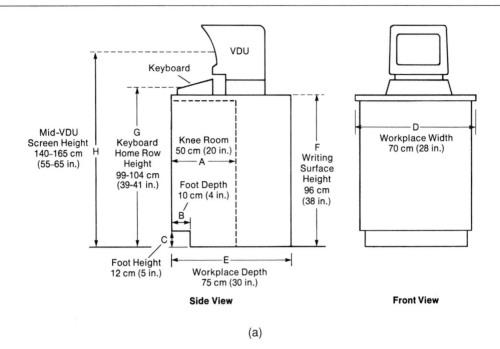

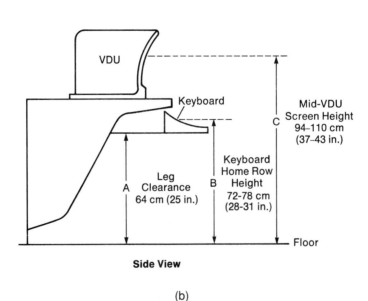

FIGURE 20–8 Standing (a) and Seated (b) VDU Workstations.

From *Ergnomic Design for People at Work* (Vol. 1). Published by Van Nostrand Reinhold, 1983. Copyright © 1983 by Eastman Kodak Company. Reprinted courtesy of Eastman Kodak Company.

ity does not permit a person's feet to be placed on the floor. The seat should also have a backrest that provides support to the lumbar region of the spine. The inclination of the backrest should be adjustable between 90° and 120° (Grandjean, 1987).

Grandjean, Hunting, and Pidermann (1983) conducted a field study to determine workers' preferences for an adjustable VDU station and their preferred postures. They found that workers preferred to lean backward regardless of orthopedic recommendations and the suitability of the chair. The preferred settings for the adjustable workstation deviated from the recommended norms. For viewing angle, the workers preferred smaller viewing angles than those typically prescribed. They also preferred greater viewing distances.

Sauter, Schleifer, and Knutson (1991) examined the effects of posture and workstation design on reports of discomfort by VDU users. Seat height, softness, the height of the seat back, the height of the keyboard, trunk angle, upper-arm angle, and other factors were measured in a correlational study. Leg discomfort increased with low, soft seats. Arm discomfort increased with increases in keyboard height above elbow level. Sauter et al. target the neck, shoulder, and wrist as problem areas, even for a good design in which all other factors are accommodated. They recommend frequent rest breaks or physical exercises to relieve the fatigue arising from continuous use of the workstation.

Physical Environment.   The level of ambient illumination and placement of light sources is particularly important for use of VDUs. Light energy is projected from VDUs rather than reflected. Because the glass surface of the screen also reflects light, high levels of illumination can cause disabling glare that masks the displayed characters. For example, Sanders and Bernecker (1990) found that the ability of observers to detect a target letter within text decreased as the intensity of a veiling luminance on the screen increased. In general, the amount of glare on a surface is a positive function of the luminance, size, and proximity of a light source to the line of sight.

Because the VDU is its own light source, reading the characters it projects is best under relatively low levels of illumination. However, many tasks require reading from printed material as well as the screen, and higher levels of ambient illumination or a source of local lighting is needed to perform those tasks. Glare can be minimized in such situations by locating light sources so that they do not reflect directly off the screen and are not in the visual field when the screen is viewed. It is also possible to shield luminaires or use indirect lighting, to cover windows with drapes or shades, to position the screen to avoid glare, or to use an antiglare treatment for the display screen. Some antiglare methods reduce the contrast and sharpness of the characters on the screen, which may offset at least some of the benefit obtained from reducing glare.

Noise levels also need to be considered in workstation design. Noise that is emitted from such things as the cooling fan inside the computer, actuation of keys on the keyboard, tones or speech displays generated by the computer, and operation of the printer may be substantial. Even the VDU itself may emit an audible high-pitched squeal. Prior to the advent of laser printers, letter-quality copy was made using daisy-wheel, impact printers. These printers were exceedingly noisy and had to be placed away from the immediate workplaces or within sound-attenuating enclosures. In general, acoustical control can be achieved by using sound-absorbing materials, such as carpeting, and by space planning that situates workstations in appropriate locations and at proper distances from each other. The goal is to have the total noise level at the workstation be of a magnitude that masks sounds from the surrounding environment while not interfering with the user's performance.

HUMAN–COMPUTER DIALOGUE

The complexity of the information that must be transmitted between the computer and the user can be great, and there is considerable flexibility in the ways that this information can be presented. The range of sophistication of computer users varies from nonprogrammers who use the computer for specific tasks (for example, word processing) to computer scientists familiar with the computer hardware and many programming languages. These individual differences reduce the problem of human–computer interaction to one of interfacing the computer process with the appropriate level of human thought (Carroll, 1987). With the advent of the microcomputer, many software packages for a range of activities have become widely available. Consequently, a concern in human–computer interaction involves the design of software interfaces to make the dialogue between the user and the computer as efficient as possible.

Computer software designs are often less than optimal because of the complexity of the information that must be transmitted, the numerous ways it can be done, and the distinct skill levels of the various users. One goal of research in human–computer interaction is to understand the nature of the dialogue between the operator and the computer so that it can be optimized in software design. A great deal of emphasis has been placed on determining what the users of a software system know and what additional information they need in order to use the system effectively.

Mental Representations

When a user starts to learn a specific software system, he or she must begin at the initial, cognitive phase of skill acquisition. The user acquires knowledge about the system by reading instructions, performing training tutorials, imitating described routines, and practicing with the system. As the user gains experience with the software, her or his performance becomes progressively more skilled. If the software is similar to other systems with which the user is familiar, positive transfer may occur to the new system, depending on the extent that the structures and functions of

the two systems are consistent. Negative transfer may also occur depending on the extent that the systems are inconsistent. Regrettably, inconsistency across user interfaces is the rule rather than the exception (Polson, 1988).

One major concern is how to characterize what a user knows about a software system (Carroll & Olson, 1987). Accurate characterization of the user's knowledge at various stages of experience with the software is important for designing interfaces that will facilitate performance and training methods that will enhance learning. It has been suggested that a user's knowledge may include one or more of the following (Carroll & Olson, 1987, p. xv):

1. simple rules that prescribe a sequence of actions that apply under certain conditions;
2. general methods that fit certain general situations and goals; and
3. mental models, knowledge of the components of a system, their interconnection, and the processes that change the components; knowledge that forms the basis for users being able to construct reasonable actions; and explanations about why a set of actions is appropriate.

Three different types of representational techniques, corresponding to simple rules, general methods, and mental models, have been developed to characterize each of these forms of knowledge.

Simple Rules. The most basic representational technique analyzes communication at the interface in terms of simple sequences of actions. The general methods used to perform tasks and the knowledge of the underlying system are not considered. Because general methods and system knowledge are not considered, rule-based representations capture the difficulties encountered when someone learns the steps by rote. This most closely resembles the way that novices learn software. That is, the sequences of actions necessary to perform common tasks are learned with no deeper understanding of why those sequences work.

By estimating the amount of time that is needed to perform each act within the sequences, it is possible to predict the design alternative and user method that should result in the fastest performance. Card, Moran, and Newell (1983) formulated a keystroke-level model that analyzes only observable keystroke and mouse-movement behaviors. The keystroke model was shown to be effective at estimating the relative execution times for different software systems. Similarly, Reisner (1984) correctly predicted which of two interactive drawing programs would be easier to use, learn, and remember based on an analysis of the sequences of physical and mental actions within each program.

General Methods. Another form of representation is the knowledge of general methods, including goals, subgoals, the methods that can accomplish the subgoals, and sequences of operations to execute these methods. This form of representation is used in the goals, operators, methods, and selection rules (GOMS) model developed by Card, Moran and Newell (1983). With this approach, the use of a software system to perform a specific task is viewed as a problem-solving process. As in any problem-solving situation, the structure of the task is crucial to performance. In the GOMS model, the task structure is specified in terms of goals and subgoals, with methods being steps consisting of basic perceptual, cognitive, and motor operators that can be used to accomplish the goals. Selection rules specify which method will be used when more than one method is available for accomplishing a goal.

As one example, consider the task of editing text, in which the goal of the task might be to make changes with the word processor that correspond to those marked on a printed version of the manuscript (Carroll & Olson, 1987). This primary goal is broken into subgoals, such as finding each string of characters that needs changing and making the changes. The subgoals are partitioned into lower-level subgoals, which are then partitioned into further subgoals, with the process

stopping when a method is found that specifies a sequence of operations that will achieve a subgoal. When more than one method will achieve a subgoal, the user selects among the methods by using general rules. A user may decide to go through the text line by line or page by page, or to use a search function, based on factors such as the distance in the text to the next string that needs changing. The GOMS model will be discussed further in Chapter 21.

One advantage of the methods approach over the simple rules approach is that it can capture the way that more advanced users choose between various methods in specific situations. The chunking and higher-level organizational capabilities of experts can be incorporated into methods representations. This approach has proved to be useful for estimating performance times of alternative interfaces, but not for predicting errors.

Mental Models. The third type of representation is the mental model, introduced more generally in Chapter 10. Here, this term is used to describe the users' conception of the software being implemented. According to Smith et al. (1992 p. 3), "Generally, a mental model can be conceived as the user's understanding of the relationship between the input and output so that a user can predict, after the development of a mental model, the output which would be produced for the possible inputs." The mental model specifies how and why the software system works the way it does. This model can be used to mentally simulate the outcome of a specific action. A key point regarding mental models is that the accuracy of the model, and hence the accuracy of its predictions, can vary greatly.

The mental models formed by novice users are often erroneous, inefficient, and adequate only for simple cases. This is illustrated by studies investigating users' often erroneous understanding of calculators (for example, Mayer & Bayman, 1981). Other studies have shown that even experienced users of a text-editing system use only a few of the available commands and employ inefficient general methods (Rosson, 1983), indicating that experience alone is not sufficient for the development of an efficient mental model.

One implication of the preceding discussion is that the design of a software interface and the accompanying instructional material should suggest an appropriate conceptual model of the way the software operates, thus allowing the user to easily develop an accurate mental model that corresponds to the system. Engineers often design interfaces to reflect the system's underlying mechanisms. However, the engineering model is usually not the best one for a user, whose primary goal is to complete a specific task (Gentner & Grudin, 1990). An interface that is based on a conceptual model of the task is often more appropriate.

One possible approach to presenting an appropriate conceptual model is to design software interfaces that correspond to the mental models of naive users. However, this approach has not been shown to be effective (Carroll & Olson, 1987). A second design approach is to simplify the system and its interface so that a more adequate conceptual model can be communicated to the user. This approach has had some success, with Carroll and Carrithers (1984) showing that a system was learned faster when initial training was given with a subset of basic commands, with the remaining commands then introduced gradually. Rather than focusing on the user's mental model, a third approach focuses on the methods learned by the user, that is, the grammar of the interface language. This approach has also met with some success in determining the best interface.

The mental model concept suggests that interfaces and training methods should use metaphors and analogies that enable users to bring their preexisting knowledge to bear on understanding and learning the new interface. Mayer (1975) demonstrated the value of analogies for novices who were learning computer programming skills. The analogies that he used were that computer input was like a ticket window, computer memory like a blackboard, control struc-

tures like shopping lists, and computer output like a message pad. These analogies facilitated learning, particularly for persons with low scores on the Scholastic Aptitude Test. Commonly used metaphors include a desk-top metaphor for file management, a ledger metaphor for spreadsheets, a typewriter and paper metaphor for word processing, and a cut-and-paste metaphor for desktop publishing (Carroll, Mack, & Kellogg, 1988). When choosing an analogy to demonstrate some aspect of an interface, it is important to select an appropriate one. Inappropriate analogies may mislead the user.

A field study by van der Veer and Felt (1988) illustrates the use of metaphor and analogy to convey an appropriate conceptual model. They organized a three-day course for managers of an insurance company. The course was designed to teach the managers the general principles of a new computerized office system, composed of a set of subsystems for a variety of office management tasks. Because all the managers were familiar with office environments, the training procedure was based on metaphors that appealed to this knowledge.

Two metaphors were used. One was intended to induce a mental model of the interaction with the computer at the task level (that is, the tasks, subtasks, and their interrelations). It was developed in terms of delegation of subtasks to different "persons." The second metaphor was used to induce an image representing the functional structure of the system during interaction with the user. For this metaphor, a picture was drawn that depicted the parts of the system and the communication channels between the parts (see Figure 20–9). The channels were shown as tubes, with valves depicting points at which there was a choice of destination. To facilitate comprehension, four subpictures were developed, each of which represented a view of the system with reference to one of the tools (see Figure 20–10).

Following the course, the managers completed a questionnaire that, among other things, obtained information about the type of representations used for their mental models of the

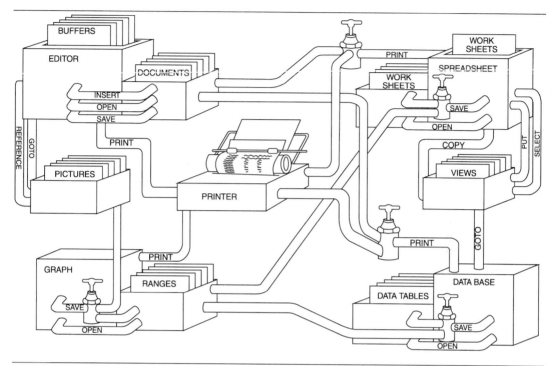

FIGURE 20–9 Visual–Spatial Metaphor of the Semantics of the Office-management System.

From G. C. van der Veer & M. A. M. Felt (1988). Development of mental models of an office system. In G. C. van der Veer & G. Mulder (Eds.), *Human–Computer Interaction: Psychonomic Aspects* (pp. 250–272). Copyright © 1988 Springer-Verlag, Inc. Reprinted by permission.

system. A variety of representations, from command listings to spatial representations were reported. The spatial model described by one manager is shown in Figure 20–11. Van der Veer and Felt (1988) concluded that the use of the two metaphors was effective for persons who rely on imagery, but that other conceptual models might be better for people who are not good imagers. The findings from this preliminary field study are not definitive, but indicate how the mental model approach can be applied to developing instructional methods.

User Interfaces and Dialogue Design

A human–computer dialogue has many aspects (Murray, 1991). The dialogue structure determines the way in which needed information is requested by the user, when that information is required, and the form in which it is presented to the user. The dialogue structure also determines how the style of interaction between the user and computer is managed, as well as how input–output requests and displays are controlled by the software.

There is little agreement on what distinguishes a good interface from a poor one, but some basic principles can be followed (Jones, 1989). First, the interface must be designed for the intended user population. If the users' level of computer sophistication is low, then the design must accommodate it. Second, the symbols and terms used in the interface should be familiar. Third, the type of interface selected should be appropriate for the particular application. Fourth, graphics should be used only when they can be of some value, and, related to this point, clutter or unnecessary information on the screen should be avoided.

All human–computer dialogues have several major characteristics (see Table 20–2). A distinction can be made between whether the dialogue is initiated by the computer in the form of prompts or initiated by the user. Computer-initiated dialogues lead the user through the appropriate steps, but this can be time consuming. Such dialogues may be more appropriate for naive users. Flexibility refers to the number of different ways in which a given task can be accomplished. Low flexibility is best for novice users because it minimizes sources of confusion.

Complexity refers to the number of options available to the user at any given time. One way to achieve low complexity is to partition the possible commands so that at each step the user selects from only a small set. The power of a system refers to the amount of work that can be accomplished in response to a single command. Although high power generally is good, it has the possible drawbacks of decreasing system generality and increasing complexity. Information load reflects the extent to which the limited-capacity resources of the operator are being depleted. For best performance, information load needs to be kept within an intermediate range.

Menus.   One decision that must be made when designing an interface is whether to use com-

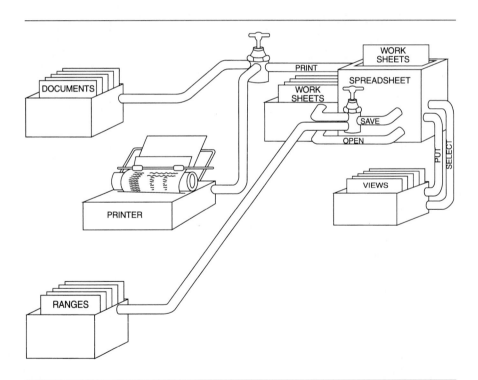

FIGURE 20–10   Visual–Spatial Metaphor of the Semantics of a Single Tool in the Office-management System.

From G. C. van der Veer & M. A. M. Felt (1988). Development of mental models of an office system. In G. C. van der Veer & G. Mulder (Eds.), *Human–Computer Interaction: Psychonomic Aspects* (pp. 250–272). Copyright © 1988 Springer-Verlag, Inc. Reprinted by permission.

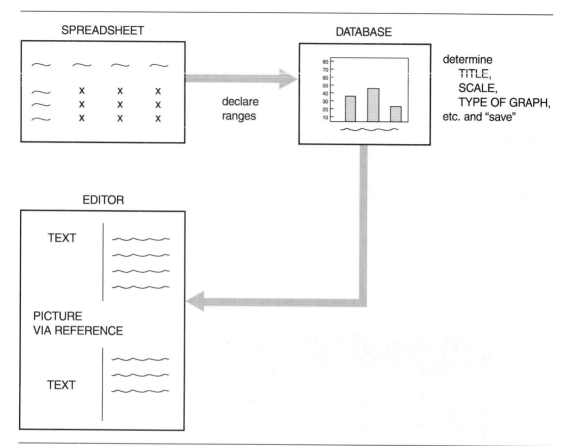

FIGURE 20–11   A User's Image Representation at the Task Level.
From G. C. van der Veer & M. A. M. Felt (1988). Development of mental models of an office system. In G. C. van der Veer & G. Mulder (Eds.), *Human–Computer Interaction: Psychonomic Aspects* (pp. 250–272). Copyright © 1988 Springer-Verlag, Inc. Reprinted by permission.

mands or menus. With a command interface, the user must enter the commands using the proper syntax. In contrast, a menu presents a list of possible actions that are appropriate at that time. The trade-offs that must be considered when deciding between command or menu interfaces are shown in Table 20–3 (Paap & Roské-Hofstrand, 1988). Basically, menus provide structure and minimize memory load, but at the cost of speed and flexibility. Hence, menus are generally considered to be best for novices, whereas commands are best for experienced users.

Most menu systems have a hierarchical structure. A selection from the initial menu in the hierarchy produces a second menu, and so on. When designing a menu, the designer is faced with a depth–breadth trade-off. That is, the menu system can be organized into several levels with a few choices at each level or a few levels with many choices. More depth enables funneling of the user through a series of simple decisions. However, because each additional menu requires a transaction with the computer, a cost is associated with depth. One alternative that may be pref-

TABLE 20–2   Basic Dialogue Properties and Considerations

PROPERTY	DESIGN CONSIDERATIONS
Initiative	*Computer initiated:*
	For naive or casual users
	Relies on passive rather than active vocabulary
	Can teach a system model to unfamiliar users
	Satisfactory for experienced users if system response is fast
	Can constrain the amount of information in a transaction
	User initiated:
	For experienced users
	For frequently used actions or rapid interchanges
Flexibility	For experienced or sophisticated users
	Increases error rate of inexperienced users
	Results in use of known problem-solving solutions rather than unlearned alternatives that are less cumbersome
Complexity	Optimal level is a function of task and user type
	Deviation from optimal complexity results in degraded performance
	Redundant or irrelevant commands impair performance
Power	Must correspond to user's needs, which may change over time
	System generality decreases with use of powerful (rather than less powerful) basic commands
	Powerful commands (in conjunction with basic commands) increase complexity
Information load	Performance degrades if load is too high or too low
	Load can be empirically measured or estimated
	Load is a major success factor, but not often a formal design consideration

Table from K. R. Boff & J. E. Lincoln (Eds.), *Engineering Data Compendium: Human perception and performance,* 1988. Reprinted with permission.

erable is to group the items on a menu into categories. This organization shares some of the benefits of funneling, but without the time penalty associated with a series of transactions.

One problem that novice users have with menus is that they tend to make errors at the higher hierarchical levels, in part because the category labels are often more ambiguous at the higher levels (Lee et al., 1986; Whiteside et al., 1985). Such errors are particularly costly, because they may not be discovered until the user has proceeded through additional levels of the menu system. Lee et al. propose that one solution to this problem is to provide menu keyword indexes that allow the lower levels to be accessed directly. Menu keywords minimize the number of levels through which the user has to proceed, as well as bypass those levels that give the users the most difficulty.

Lee and MacGregor (1985), Paap and Roské-Hofstrand (1986), and Fisher, Yungkurth, and Moss (1990) have provided quantitative methods for determining the optimal breadth and depth in specific situations. These methods are based in part on models of visual search, which are used to estimate the search time within menus. Because of the range of individual differences in a typical user population, the best option may be to provide flexibility in alternative interface formats. That is, it may be best to provide the user with a choice between menu and command interfaces if possible.

TABLE 20–3   Assumed Trade-offs between Menus and Commands

Menus simply require that the user be able to understand or recognize the options, whereas *commands* require the user to learn and recall the command names and argument structure.

Menus guide the user step by step, suggesting viable options and hiding inappropriate actions, whereas *commands* must be learned and cannot prevent the user from trying options in incorrect contexts.

Commands are highly flexible, permitting the user to reorder the actions into procedures never anticipated by the designer, whereas *menus* need to be organized into structures that can limit their flexibility.

Commands require very little screen space, whereas *menus* can be very demanding of space and may require the user to navigate through several panels.

From K. R. Paap & R. J. Roské-Hofstrand (1988). Design of menus. In M. Helander (Ed.), *Handbook of Human–Computer Interaction* (pp. 205–235). Reprinted by permission of Elsevier Science Publishers BV.

Online Aiding.   Most computer users need assistance on some occasions, and on-line aiding is one way to provide such assistance. The goals of on-line aiding are to provide information for the present situation and to enhance future performance. A distinction can be made between on-line assistance dialogues and on-line instructional dialogues (Elkerton, 1988). The former is a help system that provides information when requested. The latter involves tutorials intended to provide general-purpose instructions and practice on the use of the software system. One problem with help systems is that users tend not to use them. Magers (1983) found that user attitudes toward the use of the help system, as well as their performance, benefited from an enhanced interface that had a special help key, provided more examples, was task oriented, provided command synonyms, suggested specific corrections, minimized the length of time to obtain help, and provided feedback. Thus, with care, an effective help system can be designed.

With tutorials, issues of skill transfer to the real system become important. Research has indicated that tutorials can decrease training time and support successful transfer to the operational system (for example, Carroll & Carrithers, 1984; Catrambone & Carroll, 1987). In general, the research indicates that the initial training interface should be of reduced complexity, with the alternative interface methods introduced progressively.

Recent Advances.   One of the most important advances for the presentation of textual material in recent years is hypertext. Hypertext stores information in a multilayered environment, rather than in a single spatially organized layer. Hypertext consists of two basic elements: chunks of textual information and links between the chunks (Hashim, 1990). The major difference from standard text documents is that in a hypertext document it is possible to move directly to any place by following a link. This is because the document is organized like a library card catalog. Text is stored at connected nodes of a network. One use of hypertext is to improve the accessibility of information for crew system designers and users (Glushko, 1991). Handbooks, standards documents, software manuals, and maintenance aids can be made available on line in a format that allows rapid accessibility of the relevant information.

Another advance in interface design has been the use of visual icons to present information. The typical recommendation is that icons be used to communicate the functions performed by the computer (for example, Rubinstein & Hersh, 1984), because icons can directly depict these functions. It also is agreed that, if icons are poorly designed, they can impair performance (Potosnak, 1988). Displays that use well-designed icons along with text are judged to be more meaningful than icons or text presented alone (Guastello, Traut, & Korienek, 1989).

Merwin et al. (1990) investigated the combined use of icons and visual effects (that is, types of screen transitions) on the ability of users to traverse a complex data base. Users were required to navigate through a data base for the purpose of purchasing a specified tonnage of a fruit from a given country. Items were displayed in menu form as either text alone or as text with an icon. Selection of the correct item resulted in the screen changing to the next menu through either instantaneous change, gradual dissolving into the new menu, or zooming of the new menu outward. The time to select an item was unaffected by the presence of icons and the particular visual effect used. However, recall of the data base was significantly improved by icons and significantly impaired by dissolving screens when text alone was used. Merwin et al. suggest that icons could aid performance with large, complex data bases and that novel visual effects should be implemented cautiously.

A range of other types of interfaces has been developed (Smith et al., 1992). Graphical interfaces present information spatially. For example, the U.S. Navy designed a computer-based instructional program to teach students how to control the steam engine of a ship (Stevens, Roberts, & Stead, 1983). A graphics interface was incorporated into the program, because experts reported that they used a spatial representation of the engine to assist them in problem solving. Speech interfaces are also being developed for use in certain situations.

Given the wide range of skill possessed by software users, individual differences in preferred modes of interaction, and the various applications for which a particular software

package may be used, it is clear that the interface should be adaptable. Most software packages include at least some facilities for tailoring the interface by doing such things as changing default options and defining individualized command sets. The drawbacks to adaptable software are that the range of customizing is usually limited and that the user must learn the procedures for tailoring the software to her or his needs.

MacLean et al. (1990) stress that significant effort is required to acquire the skills necessary for tailoring software. Consequently, customizing is most likely to be done by skilled programmers and least likely by casual users. MacLean et al. show that nonprogramming users can learn to tailor their own working environment if the architecture supports a large number of tailoring techniques. They also emphasize the importance of an organization that promotes tailoring by encouraging users to think about improving their interfaces and sharing their insights and expertise.

An even better alternative to tailoring is to have interfaces automatically adjust to the requirements of their users. Consequently, steps are already being taken toward the development of self-adaptive interfaces that will automatically accommodate an individual's abilities, current level of skill, and the application for which the software is being used. Murray (1991) describes a possible architecture for an adaptive system (see Figure 20–12). The architecture consists of three main subsystems: the user modeler, the domain modeler, and the interaction modeler.

The user modeler, composed of two components, is an explicit representation of the user. One component, the user profile, holds details about the user that can be updated at the end of a session. The other component, the embedded user model, is similar to the inference engine of an expert system. It uses the profile information to drive and alter the interaction and the interface features presented to the user. The domain modeler is a representation of the software system itself. Its purpose is to adapt the interface to the particular task at hand. In addition to a task model, the domain modeler includes an expert

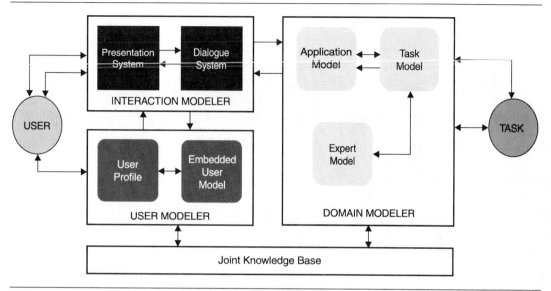

FIGURE 20–12   A Possible Architecture for an Adaptive System.

From D. Murray (1991). Modeling for adaptivity. In M. J. Tauber & D. Ackermann (Eds.), *Mental Models and Human–Computer Interaction 2* (pp. 81–93). Reprinted by permission of Elsevier Science Publishers BV.

model, possibly derived from the system designer, "which is based upon the user's view of the semantics of the application" (Murray, 1991, p. 88), and an application model, which makes decisions about specific task characteristics. The domain modeler and the user modeler have input to the interaction modeler, which is concerned directly with the presentation of information and control of the dialogue.

Stages of Software Interface Design

The design of human–computer interfaces occurs in three stages (Williges, Williges, & Elkerton, 1987). As illustrated in Figure 20–13, these stages are initial design, formative evaluation, and summative evaluation. The first stage involves development of an initial configuration. In this stage, clear objectives must be specified, an analysis of the tasks and functions of the interface should be performed, the intended user population needs to be considered and consulted, and design guidelines should be examined. The final

step is to combine the obtained information into a form that enables walking through the control structure.

In the formative evaluation stage, the interface developed in initial design is implemented and evaluated to determine whether the design objectives have been met. If not, the interface is redesigned. Rapid prototyping refers to tools that allow rapid implementation and redesign of interface prototypes. Also, user-defined interfaces, or facade configurations, may be helpful if the technology for implementation of the interface is not yet available. Finally, user-acceptance testing is conducted on the intended population of users to determine whether the design goals have been met. Usability testing at this stage, before marketing the software system, has come to be increasingly emphasized because users strenuously objected to buying systems that were not user friendly (Schell, 1987).

Summative evaluation is performed on the final, operational software interface. This design is compared with competing designs and earlier

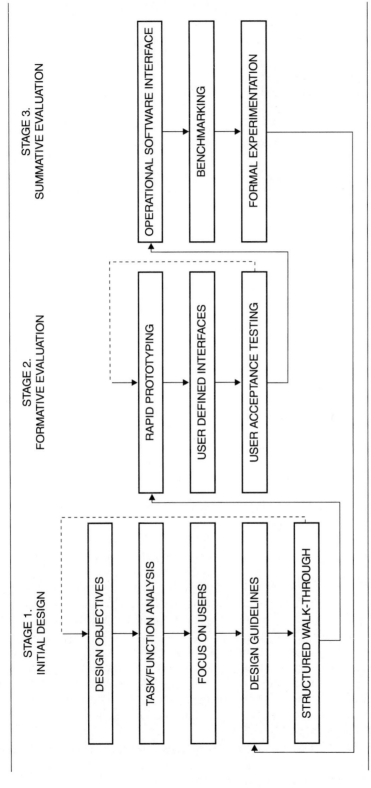

FIGURE 20–13 Flow Diagram of the Three Stages in the Design of Human–Computer Software Interfaces.
From R. C. Williges, B. H. Williges, & J. Elkerton (1987). Software interface design. In G. Salvendy (Ed.),
Handbook of Human Factors (pp. 1416–1449). Copyright © 1987 by John Wiley & Sons, Inc. Reprinted by
permission of John Wiley & Sons, Inc.

versions to evaluate its effectiveness. Benchmarking refers to the use of standardized tests to evaluate how performance with the interface compares to that with competing designs. Formal experimentation is also performed to evaluate specific aspects of the software system.

Two features of the interface-design process should be emphasized. First, the intended population of users should be considered and involved in all stages of the design process. This feature, sometimes called participatory design, is more difficult to implement than it might seem. Organizational policies may act to discourage the design team from involving users in the process. Moreover, an appropriate group of users must be identified, and the design team must gain access to them. Even when users are involved in the design process, the preferences of this small, often nonrandom sample of users must not be inappropriately overgeneralized to the entire population of potential users.

The second feature of the design process is its iterative nature, as indicated by the feedback loops within the initial design and formative evaluation stages, as well as between the summative evaluation stage and the initial design stage. This means that, as knowledge is gained through testing and evaluation, it becomes incorporated into the redesign of the software package. The redesign based on summative evaluation is directly evident in the evolution of most software packages from the initial operational system to subsequent, more refined versions.

THE WORK ENVIRONMENT

The introduction of computer technology into the work environment is designed to positively affect employees' attitudes and job satisfaction, as well as to increase productivity. However, this is often not the case. Employees may resist the new technology and may feel that their workload has increased after it is introduced. The major point of macroergonomics is that human factors must be implemented within the context of the organizational environment. This point is particularly

relevant to computer technology, because its introduction affects social interactions among employees, the way that jobs are performed, and the structure of the organization itself. If the larger context surrounding the introduction of the new technology is not considered, it may have undesired consequences.

The introduction of computer technology will directly affect the jobs of the employees who use the technology. In some cases, jobs may be eliminated. In such situations, the technology will be more acceptable if employees can be given the opportunity to transfer to jobs of equal merit within the organization. There may be an increase or decrease in workload and job pressure, job control and autonomy, and the way that a variety of tasks are structured (Smith et al., 1992). These and other possible changes are complex functions of the capabilities of the new technology for performing its intended task, the physical and organizational environment in which it is introduced, and management objectives and practices (Buchanan & Boddy, 1983). The implementation of new computer technology requires coordination of the technical and organizational plans (Robey, 1987). Job analyses for new jobs and job redesign for existing jobs will probable be necessary to accommodate the changes. Participation from the employees can be used to assist in the redesign and to ensure successful implementation.

Computer technologies can also have complex effects on the social and organizational environments. The quantity and quality of communications between employees may change, as may the structure and mode of operation of the organization. New staff and changing roles may lead to employee morale problems. Table 20–4 summarizes guidelines for social and organizational change to accommodate computer technology.

Some specific types of changes that may occur with the introduction of computer technologies are as follows (Smith et al., 1992). The amount of face to face interaction among employees tends to decrease, whereas communications

TABLE 20–4   Guidelines for Designing Social, Organizational and Management Factors in Human–Computer Interaction Environments

Helpful and supportive supervision
Flexibility of hardware and software design
Employee involvement and participation in decision making (design, purchasing, and implementation of hardware and software)
Design of reward system (administrative, social, and monetary rewards)
Setup of workload standards (scientific basis, fairness, employee involvement and acceptance)
Job enlargement and enrichment
Electronic monitoring of worker performance (fairness, feedback to employees, supervisory style, privacy)
Continuous communication between employees and management
Implementation of change
Development of career paths

Adapted from M. J. Smith et al. (1992). Human–computer interaction. In G. Salvendy (Ed.), *Handbook of Industrial Engineering* (2nd ed.). Copyright © 1992 John Wiley & Sons, Inc. Adapted by permission of John Wiley & Sons, Inc.

by means of the computer (such as sending memos through electronic mail) tend to increase. Employees throughout the organization may receive more memos and so be more fully informed about the activities of the organization. Communications through electronic mail tend to be informal and thus tend to break down barriers in communication between levels of the organizational hierarchy. Moreover, computer networks open the possibility to increased cooperation and interdependence among departments within the organization. One consequence of these changes is to decentralize decision making.

One possibility opened up by the computer age is that of home-based work, in which the employee works at home with the aid of telecommunications (Nickerson, 1986). The positive aspects of home-based work are that the time spent commuting to work is saved, the employee has more flexibility in working hours, and the work is performed in the comfortable environment of the home. However, there are many potential drawbacks to such a work arrangement. There are many distractions around the home that may result in decreased productivity. More importantly, the employee is isolated from the rest of the employees, which decreases group interactions and cohesion. The isolation of the employee

from superiors may also reduce the chances for promotion.

SUMMARY

The application of human factors to human–computer interaction involves all the topic areas discussed in this book. Perceptual factors must be considered in determining the design of visual display units. Motoric factors must be considered in the design of effective input devices. Such devices must be compatible with the spatial properties of displays and with the users' past experiences with keyboards and other controlling devices. The display and keyboard, together with the accompanying furniture, must be arranged so that the computer workstation is compatible with the anthropometric characteristics of the user population. The physical aspects of the environment in which the workstation is placed must also be considered.

Cognitive factors are of major concern in computer usage, because the interactions between humans and computers involve communication of information. By considering the knowledge possessed by users, it is possible to design software programs and accompanying training materials that can be used effectively and efficiently. It should even be possible in the near future to have the computer interface self-adapt as the user's representation of the system changes with practice. By considering the user from the outset of the software design process, the likelihood that the resulting product will be user friendly can be maximized.

Introduction of computer technologies into an organization can have complex effects. Jobs may change, new personnel may be needed, training programs for existing personnel may be required, the nature and number of communications may change, and the organizational management and decision-making structure may be altered. Macroergonomic analyses must be performed if the benefits of the new technologies are to be fully realized.

RECOMMENDED READING

Carroll, J. M. (ed.) (1991). *Designing Interaction: Psychology at the Human–Computer Interface*. New York: Cambridge University Press.

———— (ed.) (1987). *Interfacing Thought: Cognitive Aspects of Human–Computer Interaction*. Cambridge, MA: MIT Press.

Guindon, R. (ed.) (1988). *Cognitive Science and Its Applications for Human–Computer Interaction*. Hillsdale, NJ: Lawrence Erlbaum.

Helander, M. (ed.) (1988). *Handbook of Human–Computer Interaction*. Amsterdam: North-Holland.

Nickerson, R. S. (1986). *Using Computers*. Cambridge, MA: MIT Press.

CHAPTER 21

THE PRACTICE OF HUMAN FACTORS

We do not have to experience confusion or suffer from undiscovered errors. Proper design can make a difference in our quality of life. . . . Now you are on your own. If you are a designer, help fight the battle for usability. If you are a user, then join your voice with those who cry for usable products.

—D. Norman, 1988

INTRODUCTION

The fundamental premise of human factors is that system performance can be improved by designing for human use. Things that are as simple as a hammer or as complex as a tractor, on up to the complicated interactions arising between humans and machines on a factory floor, can benefit from a human factors analysis. Armchair evaluations or "common sense" approaches to most of the design issues discussed in this book are insufficient and inappropriate. If common sense was all that was necessary to design safe and usable products, then everyone would be able to use their VCRs, pilot error would not be the cause of

many air-traffic accidents, secretaries would not complain about their VDU workstations, and there would be no human factors profession.

The physical and psychological aspects of human performance have been studied for over a century. Consequently, we know a lot about factors that influence human performance and methods for evaluating performance under many different conditions. This accumulation of human factors data and the methods used to gather them can be applied by the human factors expert to resolve a wide range of design issues. In this book, we have examined perceptual, cognitive, and motoric aspects of performance, retaining throughout the conception of the human as an information-processing system. The value of this viewpoint is that both the human and machine components within the larger system can be evaluated using similar criteria.

The system concept has been presented as a framework for studying the influence of design variables in which the performance of the components, as well as overall system performance, is evaluated relative to the goals of the system. Without such a framework, human factors would consist of an uncountable number of unrelated facts, and the way in which these facts should be applied to specific design problems would be unclear. We would know that operators prefer entering data with one software interface rather than another or that operators of a control panel respond faster and more accurately when a critical switch is located on the left rather than the right. However, we would be unable to use this information to generalize to novel tasks or environments. Each time a new design problem surfaced, the human factors expert would have to begin from scratch.

This final chapter will examine several issues pertaining to the practice of human factors. The human factors specialist must play an active role in many stages of the development process for systems and products. The first step in this process is convincing management that the benefits of human factors analyses outweigh their costs. When such analyses are performed, the human factors expert needs to provide the designer with quantitative predictions of performance for different design alternatives, rather than with vague prescriptions. Models of human performance that are not intended for application can be difficult to implement. Consequently, engineering models have been developed to produce ballpark predictions for specific situations. After products have been designed, the organizations that provide them have to be concerned with safety and liability. Litigation may arise over issues of usability engineering, such as whether the product presented an unreasonable hazard to the user while performing the task for which it was intended. We will examine each of these issues in turn in this chapter.

SYSTEM DEVELOPMENT

Making the Case for Human Factors

One problem faced by human factors specialists is that of convincing managers, engineers, and other organizational authorities that the money invested in a human factors program is well spent. One reason for this problem is that the costs of human factors analyses in both time and resources are readily apparent to management, but the benefits are not as immediate. It should be obvious by now that there are many benefits provided by human factors analyses that improve safety and performance, which in turn translate into financial gains (Karat, 1990). These benefits arise from both in-house improvements in equipment, facilities and procedures and improved usability of consumer products.

One way to convince management of the need to support ergonomics programs and usability engineering is to perform a cost–benefit analysis and to present the results of this analysis in terms of the amount of money that the company will save through supporting such programs (Simpson, 1990). An ergonomics program within an organization can increase productivity and decrease overhead, as well as improve employees' work satisfaction (Smith, 1985). In product design, cost reduction can occur by identifying design problems in the early development stages, before a product is developed and tested. Long-term benefits include reduced training expenses, greater user productivity and acceptance, fewer faulty products, and decreased maintenance costs.

By performing cost–benefit analyses, human factors specialists not only justify their own funding, but also

1. Educate themselves and others about the financial contribution of human factors. . . .

2. Support product management decisions about the allocation of resources to groups competing for resources on a product.
3. Communicate with product managers and senior management about shared fiscal and organizational goals.
4. Support other groups within the organization (e.g., marketing, education, maintenance), and
5. Gain feedback about how to improve the use of human factors resource from individual to organization-wide levels. (Karat, 1992, p. 1)

There are three steps to a cost–benefit analysis (Burrill & Ellsworth, 1980, as cited in Karat, 1992): (1) The variables associated with costs and benefits for a project are identified, along with their associated values. (2) The relationship between the costs and benefits is analyzed. (3) A decision is made about the amount of money and resources to be invested in the human factors analysis. Estimating the costs and benefits associated with a human factors program is difficult, because human performance and productivity are influenced by many interacting variables (Corlett, 1988). However, several studies have demonstrated that such analyses can be performed effectively.

Occupational Ergonomics Programs. Macy and Mirvis (1976) identified 12 cost outcomes that need to be assessed when implementing ergonomics programs for redesigning work. These are absenteeism, labor turnover, tardiness, human error, accidents, grievances and disputes, learning rate, productivity rate, theft and sabotage, inefficiency or yields, cooperative activities, and maintenance. Corlett (1988) emphasizes that good work conditions also provide commercial and personal benefits through promoting increased comfort, satisfaction, and positive attitudes toward work.

A study by Spilling, Eitrheim, and Aaras (1986) illustrates the benefits derived from improving the work environment. In a plant where telephone switching equipment is made, the employees assemble and wire electromechanical components. Prior to 1975, all workstations had a fixed height, requiring many workers to assume awkward postures and so work under high levels of muscular stress. In 1975, new ergonomically sound workstations were introduced that had adjustable surface heights and allowed the employees to work either sitting or standing. In addition, an improved ventilation system and better lighting were installed later. The costs associated with these changes were determined and compared to the benefits derived from dramatic reductions in labor turnover (reduced costs of recruitment, training, and salaries for instructors) and sick leave (reduction in sick payments). The total financial benefit was approximately nine times greater than the cost of the improvements.

Similar benefits were apparent in a program instituted at a shop for repairing railroad cars (Research Pays Off, 1989). Many of the jobs at the shop involved the lifting of heavy objects. As a consequence, the incidence of accidents resulting in time off work was high, with many involving back injuries. An ergonomics program was introduced, resulting in the redesign of equipment to minimize bending and lifting. As part of the program, employees were taught to bend and lift safely, and regular meetings between management and the employees were instituted to convey increased organizational concern about safety. The lost days due to injuries dropped from 579 in 1985 before introduction of the ergonomics program to 0 in 1987 and 1988, and absenteeism dropped from 4.0% to 1.0%. Moreover, without any increase in the work force, productivity increased from approximately 1,564 cars repaired in 1985 to an estimate of 2,900 cars for 1988. The cost–benefit ratio was estimated to be at least 1 to 10.

Because many companies may not have the resources for an occupational ergonomics program, some providers of office equipment supply their customers with such services at the time that the equipment is purchased. One leading supplier of information-processing equipment in the United States offers retailers several ergonomic services (Sluchak, 1990). These include consultation about workstation design, assistance in conducting in-store evaluations of equipment, assistance in implementing employee training programs, recommendations for interface design, and briefings on topics such as cumulative trauma disorders.

System and Product Development.   The costs associated with the incorporation of human factors into the system development process include wages for the human factors personnel. In addition, several distinct costs are associated specifically with the human factors process (Mantei & Teorey, 1988, p. 430). These include expenses involved with evaluating the concerns of the intended user population in preliminary focus groups, constructing product or system mockups, designing and modifying prototypes, creating a laboratory and conducting user studies, and conducting user surveys.

The cost–benefit ratio will depend on the number of users affected by the ergonomic changes. Karat (1990) performed cost–benefit analyses for two software development projects that had incorporated human factors concerns. One of these projects was small scale and the other was large scale. She estimated the savings to cost ratio to be 2:1 for the small project and 100:1 for the large project. The savings that arise from human factors testing increase dramatically as the size of the user population increases (Mantei & Teorey, 1988). For smaller projects, it will not be cost effective to have a complete human factors testing program. A cost–benefit analysis can be useful not only to justify the human factors research but also to make the investment in such research commensurate with the expected savings to cost ratio.

System Development Process

Phases.   Once a human factors program is supported, the application of human factors principles to system development proceeds in two phases: (1) the design of the system and its support subsystems and (2) the testing and evaluation of the system (Meister, 1989). Human factors specialists should participate in both phases of system development by applying human performance data, principles, and methods.

The development of a system is driven by the system requirements (Meister, 1989). System development begins with a broadly defined goal and proceeds to more molecular tasks and subtasks. Most system requirements do not include human performance objectives; only physical performance is specified. Consequently, the human factors specialist must deduce the operator requirements from the physical requirements of the system.

It is important that human factors specialists be involved from the outset, because design decisions made at the broader molar levels of system development have consequences for the molecular levels. From the initial decisions onward, human factors criteria, as well as physical performance criteria, must be met if the system is to perform optimally. The U.S. military has initiated programs, such as MANPRINT (see Chapter 1), that require that human factors concerns be considered from the outset of the system-development process. These programs were necessary because failures to consider such concerns before initial design decisions were made had resulted in the production of equipment that could not be used effectively.

System development proceeds in a series of phases (Meister, 1989). The first phase is *system planning*. During this phase, the need for the system is identified. During the second phase, *preliminary design,* alternative designs for the system are considered, developmental tests are begun, prototypes are constructed, and a plan for testing and evaluating is created. In *detail design,* development of the system is performed and plans are made for production. Following this phase, a *production and development* phase results in the production of the system, which then receives operational testing and evaluation.

Several distinct questions regarding human performance arise at each of the phases of system development. These questions are shown in Table 21–1. At the system planning phase, the human factors specialist evaluates the changes in the task requirements, the personnel that will be required, and the nature and amount of training needed for the new system relative to its predecessor. During preliminary design, the concern is primarily with judging the alternative design options in terms of their usability. Options should be chosen that minimize the probability of human error. Similar questions must be answered in the detail design phase, where the goal is a final system design that is adequately engineered to accommodate human performance limitations. In the production and development phase, the operational system is evaluated to determine whether any deficiencies still exist.

The inputs from the human factors specialist regarding human performance during system development consist of four types: (1) The first type involves the design of the system hardware, software, and operating procedures. (2) The specialist may provide inputs regarding the selection and acquisition of system personnel. (3) The third type of input pertains to the type and amount of training to be provided to personnel. (4) Input is provided for evaluating the operational effectiveness of personnel.

Through the systematic application of human performance data, principles, and methods at all phases of system development, the design of the system will be optimized for human use. This

---

TABLE 21–1   Behavioral Questions Arising in System Development

---

System Planning

1. Assuming a predecessor system, what changes in the new system from the configuration of the predecessor system mandate changes in numbers and types of personnel, their selection, their training, and methods of system operation?

Preliminary Design

2. Which of the various design options available at this time is more effective from a behavioral standpoint?
3. Will system personnel in these options be able to perform all required functions effectively without excessive workload?
4. What factors are potential sources of difficulty or error, and can these be eliminated or modified in the design?

Detail Design

5. Which is the better or best of the design options proposed?
6. What level of personnel performance can one achieve with each design configuration, and does this level satisfy system requirements?
7. Will personnel encounter excessive workload, and what can be done about it?
8. What training should be provided to personnel to achieve a specified level of performance?
9. Are (a) hardware–software, (b) procedures, (c) technical data, and (d) total job design adequately engineered from the human point of view?

Testing and Evaluation

10. Are system personnel able to do their jobs effectively?
11. Does the system satisfy its personnel requirements?
12. Have all system dimensions affected by behavioral variables been properly engineered from the human point of view?
13. What design inadequacies must be rectified?

From D. Meister (1989). *Conceptual Aspects of Human Factors.* The Johns Hopkins University Press, Baltimore/London, 1989.

optimization results in increased safety, utility, and productivity, thus benefiting the system managers, operators, and, ultimately, consumers.

Facilitating Human Factors Inputs. When an organization implements a human factors program, it usually will be best if the human factors specialists are in a single, centralized group or department under a manager who is sensitive to human factors organizational issues (Hawkins, 1990; Hendrick, 1990). Such an arrangement has several advantages that allow the human factors specialists to maximize their contributions to projects. The manager can champion human factors concerns in the higher organizational levels, which is essential for creating an environment in which human factors will flourish. By establishing a rapport with persons in authority and increasing their awareness about the role of human factors in system design, the manager and group can ensure that their efforts will be supported within the organization. Also, financial support for laboratories and research facilities is more likely if there is a human factors group or department, rather than individuals scattered throughout departments. A stable human factors group also helps to establish credibility with the system designers and engineers. Project managers are more likely to seek advice from the human factors specialists because of their credibility and visibility. Finally, the group will foster a sense of professional identity that will assist morale and help in the recruitment of human factors specialists.

One problem faced by human factors specialists is that most designers have at best a neutral opinion of human factors. Designers rank human factors concerns as their least important criteria for evaluating the design of a product (Meister, 1987). Moreover, all persons involved in the design of a system will view the problem from the standpoint of their disciplines. Each will discuss the problem using the vocabulary with which they are familiar and attempt solutions to the problem using discipline-specific methods (Rouse, Cody, & Boff, 1991). Because of the difficulty of communication, the information pro-

vided by the human factors specialist may become lost and, hence, have little impact on the system development process.

This problem is acute in the early planning and design phases of system development. Rouse and Cody (1988) indicate that concern with human factors issues typically arises only late in the detail design phase, well after many crucial decisions have been made. Consequently, the contribution of the human factors specialist is diminished by the necessity of working around the established features of the system. One solution to this problem involves the implementation of models that enable the human factors specialist and the designer to collaborate in evaluating alternative designs before prototypes have been developed. The purpose of engineering models of human performance is to bring existing knowledge to bear on the initial design decisions.

ENGINEERING MODELS OF HUMAN PERFORMANCE

Our discussions of the various aspects of human information processing in the earlier chapters provided insight into many important characteristics of human performance. Basic principles have been covered, such as that performance deteriorates when working memory is overloaded and that movement time is a linear function of movement difficulty (Fitts's law). We have also presented many alternative theoretical models to explain these phenomena. This foundation, formed from data and theory, is necessary for anyone who wishes to incorporate human factors into design decisions.

When faced with a specific design problem, a variety of sources can be consulted (Rouse & Cody, 1989). These include textbooks, handbooks that prescribe specifications, and journal articles. Unfortunately, there is no easy way to specify exactly those human limitations that will be critical in the situation of interest and the ways in which they may interact with each other. There are many precise models of human information processing. However, these models have been developed with the goal of providing the best account of the detailed body of data that exists on a narrow topic. Consequently, a given model typically is restricted in the tasks and phenomena that it addresses and is at a level of detail that may not be appropriate for design problems. Considerable effort is thus being devoted to developing engineering models that a designer can use to predict human performance (Elkind et al., 1989; McMillan et al., 1989).

Engineering models give several benefits to the design engineer (Rouse & Cody, 1989). A model forces rigor and consistency in the analyses. It also serves as a framework for organizing information and indicating what additional information is needed. Moreover, the quantitative predictions provided by engineering models are more likely to be incorporated into design decisions than are vague recommendations. The primary drawback associated with the use of engineering models of human performance is that their predictions will be only as reliable as the accuracy of the model and the data that are entered into it. Thus, it is important to put the model in perspective and to remember the maxim "garbage in, garbage out."

Card, Moran, and Newell (1983) proposed that engineering models of human performance should satisfy three criteria: (1) The models should be based on the view of the human as an information processor. (2) Emphasis should be placed on approximate calculations based on a task analysis; from this analysis, the information-processing operations for achieving these goals can be modeled. (3) The model should allow prediction for systems during the design phase of development, before they have been built. The model should make it easy for a designer to provide approximate quantitative predictions of performance for design alternatives. We will describe two types of engineering models of human performance that satisfy these criteria, cognitive models developed primarily from research in cognitive psychology and control theory models developed primarily from research in industrial engineering.

Cognitive Models

Comprehensive cognitive models are intended to provide complete accounts of the information subprocesses that underlie the performance of a range of tasks. Such models are exemplified by a comprehensive framework for application to the domain of human–computer interaction developed by Card, Moran, and Newell (1983). This framework has two components. The first is a general model of the human information processing system called the *model human processor*. It consists of a perceptual processor, a cognitive processor, and a motor processor, as well as a working memory (with separate visual and auditory image stores) and a long-term memory (see Figure 21–1). Each processor has one quantitative parameter, the cycle time (time to process the smallest unit of information), and each memory has three parameters (the storage capacity, decay constant, and the code type). These parameters are presumed to be context free; consequently, estimates of their values determined from basic human performance research can be plugged in when modeling the performance of tasks with specific software interfaces.

The principles of operation of the model human processor are summarized in Table 21–2. Many of these principles are based on fundamental laws of human performance that were covered in earlier chapters. The major contribution of the model human processor is that it provides a complete model of human information processing, from perception to action, that can be used to predict human behavior in real-world tasks.

The rationality principle is most fundamental to the model human processor. This is the assumption that the user acts rationally to attain goals. If an individual acts irrationally, an analysis of the goal structure of the task would not serve a useful purpose. The rationality principle justifies the second major component of the framework, a task analysis in terms of the goals and requirements. In the model human processor, the task analysis determines the goals, operators, methods, and selection rules (GOMS) that char-

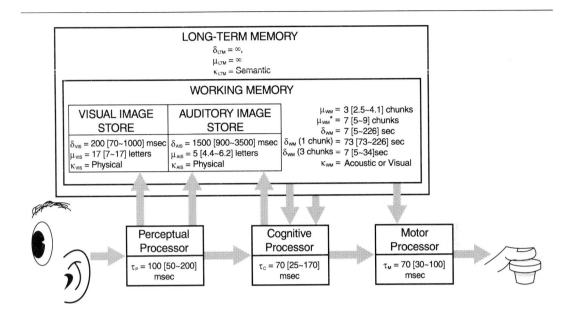

FIGURE 21–1   The Model Human Processor.

acterize a task, as was described in Chapter 20. After first determining the goal structure, the information-processing sequence is specified by defining the methods for achieving the goals, the elementary operations from which the methods are composed, and the selection rules for choosing between alternative methods. The end result is an information-processing model that describes the sequence of operations executed to achieve goals persuant to performance of the task. Table 21–3 shows an algorithm for determining the abbreviation of a computer command using a vowel deletion rule. By specifying cycle times for the execution of the elementary operations, a prediction can be generated for the time to perform the task of generating an abbreviation.

Card, Moran, and Newell (1983) conducted numerous experiments on various aspects of a text editing task. These experiments were used to provide the elements of task analyses, that is, how methods are selected and the order of operations.

Four different levels of analysis were considered. The most basic was the unit-task level, for which there is only one operator that is assumed to take a constant amount of time per unit task. The functional level of analysis was more detailed and decomposed the unit task into subgoals and operators for each functional step in the edit sequence. Even more detailed was the argument level of analysis, in which the methods of the functional level were decomposed into the steps of specifying commands and arguments. Finally, the keystroke level specified the elemental perceptual, cognitive, and motor actions that comprised performance of the tasks. Card et al. found that predictions regarding choice of methods, the sequence of arguments, and editing time were relatively good, with the functional level of analysis providing the best predictor.

GOMS analyses within the context of the model human processor have met with considerable success in a variety of tasks involving hu-

TABLE 21–2   The Model Human Processor—Principles of Operation

P0. *Recognize-act cycle of the cognitive processor.* On each cycle of the cognitive processor, the contents of working memory initiate actions associatively linked to them in long-term memory; these actions in turn modify the contents of working memory.

P1. *Variable perceptual processor rate principle.* The perceptual processor cycle time τ_p varies inversely with stimulus intensity.

P2. *Encoding specificity principle.* Specific encoding operations performed on what is perceived determine what is stored, and what is stored determines what retrieval cues are effective in providing access to what is stored.

P3. *Discrimination principle.* The difficulty of memory retrieval is determined by the candidates that exist in the memory, relative to the retrieval cues.

P4. *Variable cognitive processor rate principle.* The cognitive processor cycle time τ_c is shorter when greater effort is induced by increased task demands or information loads; it also diminishes with practice.

P5. *Fitts's law.* The time T_{pos} to move the hand to a target of size S that lies a distance D away is given by

$$T_{pos} = I_M \log_2 \frac{2D}{S} + 0.5$$

where $70 < I_M < 120$ ms/bit.

P6. *Power law of practice.* The time T_n to perform a task on the nth trial follows a power law:

$$T_n = T_1 n^{-\alpha}$$

where $0.2 < \alpha x < 0.6$.

P7. *Information Theory principle.* Decision time T increases with uncertainty about the judgment or decision to be made:

$$T = I_C H$$

where H is bits of information and $0 < I_C < 157$ ms/bit. For n equally probable alternatives,

$$H = \log_2 (n + 1)$$

For n alternatives with different probabilities, p_i, of occurrence,

$$H = \sum_i p_i \log_2 \left(\frac{1}{p_i} + 1\right)$$

P8. *Rationality principle.* A person acts so as to attain his goals through rational action, given the structure of the task and their inputs of information and bounded by limitations on their knowledge and processing abilities:

$$\text{goals} + \text{task} + \text{operators} + \text{inputs}$$
$$+ \text{knowledge} + \text{processing limits} \rightarrow \text{behavior}$$

P9. *Problem space principle.* The rational activity in which people engage to solve a problem can be described in terms of (1) a set of states of knowledge, (2) operators for changing one state into another, (3) constraints on applying operators, and (4) control knowledge for deciding which operator to apply next.

From S. K. Card, P. P. Moran, & A. P. Newell, The model human processor. In. K. R. Boff, L. Kaufman, & J. P. Thomas (Eds.). *Handbook of Perception and Human Performance* (pp. 45-1–45-35). Copyright © 1986 by John Wiley and Sons, Inc. Adapted with permission.

TABLE 21–3   GOMS Algorithm for Figuring out Vowel-deletion Abbreviations

---

Algorithm	Operator Type
BEGIN	
Stimulus ← Get-Stimulus("Command")	Perceptual
Spelling ← Get-Spelling(Stimulus)	Cognitive
Initiate-Response(Spelling[First-Letter])	Cognitive
Execute-Response(Spelling[First-Letter])	Motor
Next-Letter ← Get-Next-Letter(Spelling)	Cognitive
REPEAT BEGIN	
IF-SUCCEEDED Is-Consonant?(Next-Letter)	Cognitive
THEN BEGIN	
Initiate-Response(Next-Letter)	Cognitive
Execute-Response(Next-Letter)	Motor
Next-Letter ← Get-Next-Letter(Spelling)	Cognitive
END	
ELSE IF-SUCCEEDED Is-Vowel?(Next-Letter)	Cognitive
THEN Next-Letter ← Get-Next-Letter(Spelling)	Cognitive
END	
UNTIL Null?(Next-Letter)	
IF-SUCCEEDED Null?(Next-Letter)	Cognitive
THEN BEGIN	
Initiate-Response("Return")	Cognitive
Execute-Response("Return")	Motor
END	
END	

From B. E. John & A. Newell (1990). Toward an engineering model of stimulus–response compatability. In R. W. Proctor & T. G. Reeve (Eds.), *Stimulus–Response Compatibility: An Integrated Perspective*. Copyright © 1990 by Elsevier Science Publishers, BV. Reprinted by permission.

man-computer interaction (Olson & Olson, 1990). These tasks include the use of text editors, graphics programs, and spreadsheet programs; entering different kinds of keyboard commands, and manipulating files. Such analyses have also been used to generate a range of stimulus–response compatibility effects (Laird, Rosenbloom, & Newell, 1986) and to describe routine cockpit tasks (Hulme & Hamilton, 1989). However, the original framework does not give an account of changes that occur as skill is acquired, does not predict errors, assumes strictly serial processing, and does not address mental workload (Olson & Olson, 1990). More recent extensions of the framework have addressed issues of learning and errors (for example, Lerch, Mantei, & Olson, 1989; Polson, 1988).

To simulate human performance in complex human–machine systems, a cognitive model called the *human operator simulator* has been developed (Harris, Iavecchia, & Dick, 1989). It is a software system consisting of a resident human operator model and a language for specifying the equipment characteristics and operator procedures. Much like the model human processor, the human operator model contains information-processing submodels for different microactions that must be performed. The major process submodels are shown in Figure 21–2.

For simulating performance in a variety of weapons and flight systems, three major components (see Figure 21–3) must be specified (Harris, Iavecchia, & Dick, 1989, p. 286):

1. environment (e.g., number, location, speed, and bearing of targets)
2. hardware system (e.g., sensors, signal processors, displays, and controls)

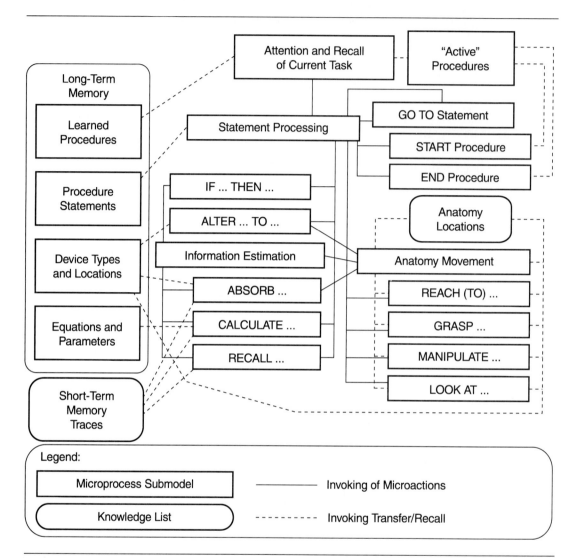

FIGURE 21–2 Major Submodels and Knowledge Lists in the Human Operator Simulator.

From S. Baron, D. S. Kruser, & B. M. Huey (Eds.) (1990), *Quantitative Modeling of Human Performance in Complex, Dynamic Systems,* National Academy Press.

3. operator procedures and tactics for interacting with the system and for accomplishing mission goals

The interfaces between the three components must also be specified. These interfaces deter-

mine such things as the capabilities of the hardware for detecting environmental events, the effects of heat and other environmental stressors on performance, and how difficult it will be for the operator to perform the required tasks. The exe-

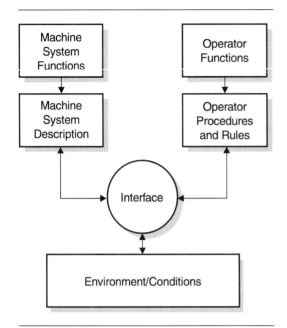

FIGURE 21–3   The Three Major HOS Simulation Components That Are Connected Through the Interface.

From R. Harris, H. P. Iavecchia, and A. O. Dick (1989). The human operator simulator (HOS-LV). In G. R. McMillan et al. (Eds.), *Applications of Human Performance Models to System Design* (pp. 275–280). Copyright © 1989 by Plenum Press. Reprinted by permission.

cution of the simulation produces a time-based analysis of operator and system performance. The human operator simulator is well suited for analyzing the effects of control–display design, workstation layout, and allocation of tasks. However, there has been little empirical validation of the quantitative accuracy of the predictions made for complex systems.

Control Theory Models

Control theory models are specialized for tasks, such as piloting an aircraft, that require monitoring and controlling of operations of complex systems. Control theory models view the operator as a control element in a closed-loop system (see Figure 21–4). It is assumed that operators approximate the characteristics of good electromechanical control systems, subject to the limitations inherent in human information processing. Initial models were restricted to dynamic systems involving one or more manual control tasks, but more recent comprehensive models cover the range of supervisory activities engaged in by the operators of a complex system.

Several fundamental requirements have driven the development of the comprehensive, multitask models (Baron & Corker, 1989). A system model must represent the operators together with all the nonhuman aspects of the system. The cognitive and decision processes that characterize human performance in the complex system environment must be articulated clearly. Communication among crew members and between operator and machine must be modeled, as should each crew member's mental model about the state of the system, goals, and so on.

The most comprehensive model of this type is the procedure-oriented crew model (PROCRU), which was developed to evaluate changes in system design and procedures on the safety of landing approaches of aircraft (Baron & Corker, 1989). The model is a closed-loop system that has separate components for the air-traffic controller, landing aids provided by the air-traffic control system, the aircraft, and both pilots (the one who is flying and the one who is not).

The pilot models are based on variations of the information- processing structure of the control theoretic models. Additional mechanisms allow for selection among tasks and performance of discrete tasks. Both continuous and discrete procedures consist of several elements: an enabling event, a function that determines the urgency for executing the procedure, and a prescription for executing the procedure.

PROCRU and other comprehensive control theory models produce dynamic output that varies as the representation of the situation evolves (Baron, Kruser, & Huey, 1990). Although the

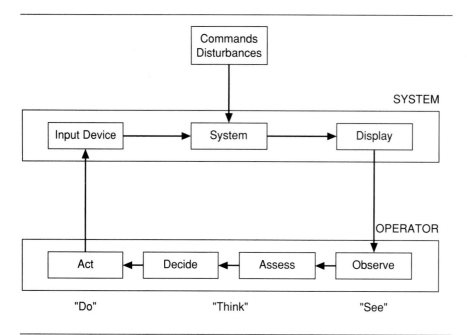

FIGURE 21–4   Closed-loop, Control Theory View of a Human–Machine System.

basics of control theory models have been validated in many contexts, there has been little empirical validation for comprehensive models such as PROCRU.

Toolboxes

An alternative approach to comprehensive models is to develop specialized models that focus on particular aspects of human information processing. Many models are available for simulating numerous features of perceptual, cognitive, motor, and biomechanical performance. One example is the set of models for predicting mental workload that was described in Chapter 9. It may be possible to develop software toolboxes that contain the models most relevant to the design of a specific system, such as a helicopter (Elkind et al., 1989). The primary benefit of the toolbox approach relative to comprehensive models is that the specific models in the toolbox will be more precise for the particular situations to

which they apply. Major drawbacks in the preparation of these toolboxes include the lack of models that are sufficiently easy to use and the difficulty of integrating information across the different models.

FORENSIC HUMAN FACTORS

Design decisions, whether made on a systematic basis or not, determine the usability and safety of the final product. When something goes wrong, such as when the use of the product results in injury, and if the human factors expert has been involved in the product design, then he or she must share the responsibility for design imperfections. Moreover, human factors experts who were not involved in the development of a product may be called on to evaluate the product and its development process to determine what went wrong. The involvement of human factors considerations in the legal system is called forensic human factors.

Liability

An organization is responsible for the safety of many people. Primarily, these are the people who use the products or services produced by the organization and the workers are employed by the organization. If an organization fails to meet this responsibility, it can be held liable in a court of law. Thus, it is important for an organization to maintain safe practices and to ensure that these practices can be justified if called into question.

In the United States, safety in the workplace is governed by the directives of the Occupational Safety and Health Administration (OSHA) and the National Institute for Occupational Safety and Health (NIOSH). OSHA was created by the passage of the Occupational Safety and Health Act of 1970 to ensure a safe work environment. It requires employers to reduce workplace hazards and to implement safety and health programs that inform and train the employees (OSHA, 1989). Violations of the standards may result in citations being issued and fines being leveled by OSHA. Human factors specialists contribute to the development and evaluation of the standards and can devise programs that verify that the employer is in compliance and that employees will follow the safety procedures.

When injury or death occurs in the workplace, the employer can be held legally liable. Liability also applies to products or services sold to people outside the organization. The law distinguishes between product liability and service liability cases; both arise from the failure of performance, in the first case of a product and in the second case of a person. When someone is injured as a result of such failures, litigation may be undertaken to determine negligence and, if necessary, how the injured party should be compensated.

Safe operation of a product by a population of users requires a match between the design of the product and the users' capabilities. During the design phase, the human factors specialist assists in the identification and evaluation of hazards, risks, and danger. A hazard is a situation for which there is the potential for injury or death. The degree of risk is the probability of injury or death occurring. Danger refers to the combination of hazard and risk. For danger to exist, there must be a hazard for which the risk probability is not insignificant.

It is very difficult to determine if a product is unreasonably dangerous. For example, chain saws are dangerous, but any reduction in the danger would make them less useful. Wade (1965) provided seven criteria that form the basis of the "unreasonable danger" test:

1. The usefulness and desirability of the product.
2. The availability of other and safer products to meet the same needs.
3. The likelihood of injury and its probable seriousness.
4. The obviousness of the danger.
5. Common knowledge and normal public expectation of the danger (particularly for established products).
6. The avoidability of injury by care in use of the product (including the effect of instructions or warnings).
7. The ability to eliminate the danger without seriously impairing the usefulness of the product or making it unduly expensive. (quoted in Weinstein et al., 1978, p. 47)

Standards, such as those published by the American National Standards Institute (ANSI), make contractual agreements about and identification of mass-produced products possible; standards are intended to guarantee uniformity in mass-produced goods. Safety is only one of many concerns that published standards are intended to address. Adherence to published safety standards is not sufficient to ensure a safe product and does not absolve a manufacturer of liability. The courts regard standards as only the minimum requirements of a reasonable product. The criteria for the standards may be outdated, standards published by different institutions may be inconsistent, the risk allowed by the standards may still be significant, and many aspects of product design will not be covered by standards. Generally, standards may not be good enough, and the time and money spent trying to meet minimum requirements set forth in the standards could be better spent in research and design (Peters, 1977).

Weinstein et al. (1978, p. 148) have recast the reasonable danger test into a set of criteria that can be applied to a design that meets the appropriate standards:

1. Delineate the scope of product uses.
2. Identify the environments within which the product will be used.
3. Describe the user population.
4. Postulate all possible hazards, including estimates of probability of occurrence and seriousness of resulting harm.
5. Delineate all alternative design features or production techniques, including warnings and instructions, that can be expected to effectively mitigate or eliminate the hazards.
6. Evaluate such alternatives relative to the expected performance standards of the product, including the following:
   a. Other hazards that may be introduced by the alternatives.
   b. Their effect on the subsequent usefulness of the product.
   c. Their effect on the ultimate cost of the product.
   d. A comparison to similar products.
7. Decide which features to include in the final design.

When an injury occurs for which a product is implicated as a possible cause, a legal complaint may be filed in civil court. It is not sufficient simply to show that the product was the likely cause, but it must also be established that a legal responsibility to the consumer was not met by the manufacturer of the product. A manufacturer may fail to meet its legal responsibilities in one of four ways. *Negligence* and *gross negligence* are focused on the behavior of the defendant, in that the defendant failed to engage in reasonable actions that would have prevented the accident. Gross negligence differs from negligence in that the defendant engaged in reckless and wanton misconduct.

Strict liability focuses on the product and not the defendant. Although the manufacturer need not have been in any way negligent, the manufacturer can be held liable for any product defect if that defect was the cause of the injury. Under strict liability, it is not only the manufacturer that can be held liable. The manufacturer must have sold the product either to the plaintiff or to one of many members of a distributive chain, all of whom may be named as defendants in the trial (Weinstein et al., 1978): (1) the producer of the raw material; (2) the maker of a component part; (3) the assembler or subassembler; (4) the packager of the final product; (5) the wholesaler, distributor, or middleman; (6) one who holds the product out to be his or her own; (7) the retailer. Any or all of these members can be held liable if it can be proved that a product was defective when it left their possession.

The last way in which a defendant can fail to meet his or her responsibilities is through *breach of express warranty,* which occurs when a product fails to function as the defendant stated it would. Such statements can be oral or written and can be contained in advertising or in the name of the product. For example, the drug Rogaine, marketed as a baldness cure in the United States, is sold under the name Regain in Europe. Under U.S. product liability law, the name Regain provides an express warranty that the product will cure baldness.

It is important to remember that, even though a product may be designed well, liability concerns may arise from the nature of the product itself. For example, John Gatzemeyer designed a safety rail that attaches to bannisters to help small children climb up and down stairs (Pierson, 1990). Although the design won several prizes, as of September 1990 no industry was willing to manufacture the product. The threat of liability was enough to discourage potential manufacturers, even though the product would reduce the danger associated with children and stairs. It does not take much imagination to think of many ways that the manufacturer could be held liable for such a product, including warning labels, installation instructions, unforeseen breakage, and so on.

Expert Testimony

Human factors specialists are called on in the development of a product or system to reduce a manufacturer's risk of liability, as well as during litigation to provide expert testimony concerning human limitations and the product in question. An example case involved incidents of unintended acceleration of the Audi 5000 automobile. As discussed in Chapter 16, unintended acceleration incidents in vehicles with automatic transmissions have been reported since the 1940s (Schmidt, 1989). Such incidents are relatively rare and are not limited to any particular make or model. However, in the late 1980s, charges were made that the Audi 5000 was involved in an unusually high number of unintended acceleration accidents.

The charges against the Audi 5000 arose from a case in February 1986 in which a woman driving an Audi struck and killed her 6-year-old son when the car accelerated out of control. A lawsuit was filed in April of that year claiming that a design defect in the Audi transmission was the cause of the unintended acceleration. The case received considerable media coverage, culminating in November with an exposé on the CBS investigative reporting program, "60 Minutes." Following this program, a flood of claims were made alleging incidents of unintended acceleration involving the Audi 5000.

The litigation against Audi's parent company, Volkswagen of America, proceeded in two phases (Huber, 1991). In the first phase, the plaintiffs insisted that there was a flaw in the Audi transmission, as in the initial case described above. However, the evidence overwhelmingly indicated that the unintended acceleration was due to foot placement errors and not mechanical failure, leading the jury in the initial case to return a verdict in favor of the defendants in June 1988 (Baker, 1989). At that point, at least one plaintiff returned to court charging that the sudden acceleration was in fact due to foot placement errors that would not have occurred if the pedals had been designed differently.

Issues regarding human performance capabilities and design are crucial to many product liability cases, and this is apparent in the case of the Audi 5000. In the first phase of Audi's litigation, the human factors expert could have testified regarding the likelihood that an instance of unintended acceleration was due to an undetected foot placement error. This same testimony, together with information regarding the sizes and locations of the pedals, could have been used by opposing council during the second phase of Audi's litigation. However, to make such a case against Audi, it would have to be shown that unintended acceleration incidents were in fact greater for the Audi than for other automobiles and that the pedals were placed in such a manner to increase the likelihood of foot placement errors. Because neither of these claims is true, the defense could use the testimony of a human factors specialist to prevent Audi from being unjustly found negligent.

These issues are illustrative of the types of questions that arise in legal proceedings for which the testimony of a human factors specialist may be of value. During litigation, a human factors specialist can provide information pertinent to the following questions:

1. Was the product design, service, or process appropriate for the knowledge, skills, and abilities (KSAs) to be expected of normally functioning users (or clients) in the expected operational environment?
2. If not, could the service or the product design have been modified so that it would have been appropriate to the KSA of the anticipated user population?
3. If there was less than an optimal match between product design and the KSA of the expected user population, was an attempt made to modify the user population KSA by adequate selection procedures and/or by providing appropriate information by means of adequate training, instructions, and warnings?
4. If not, was it technically feasible to have provided such selection procedures and/or information transfer?

5. If [testimony indicates] that the information provided was not appropriate to the idiosyncrasies of the injured party, was it technically possible for the design of the product, selection, and/or information exchange to have been altered to accommodate those idiosyncrasies? (Kurke, 1986, p. 13)

The human factors expert participates in two stages of litigation (Robinson, 1989). The first stage is the taking of a deposition. During a deposition, the opposing attorney asks the expert witness a list of questions. The witness answers these questions under oath. The questions, answers, and any objections raised by the attorney soliciting the testimony are recorded and transcribed for the record. The deposition serves two purposes. The first is to provide opposing counsel with the facts, expert opinions, and qualifications of the expert needed to make a case for his or her client. The second is to evaluate the effectiveness of the expert as a witness. If the deposition is strong, the case may be settled before the second stage of litigation, the trial.

During a trial, the expert witness will testify in response to direct examination by the attorney by whom she or he was hired and then in response to cross examination by the opposing attorney. The purpose of trial testimony is to present the facts of the case to the judge and jury in a way that they will understand and believe. It is important to remember that the nature of litigation is adversarial. Attorneys for both the defendant and the plaintiff are legally obligated to use any (ethical) means possible to win the case for their clients. Because of this, rendering expert opinion is rarely a pleasant experience. During cross examination, the human factors expert may be subjected to what is essentially a personal attack. The witness will be called on to defend his or her credentials and the basis of his or her opinion. The witness will be asked misleading questions and may have his or her testimony restricted to exclude possibly relevant information on the basis of opposing counsel's objections.

The expert witness is in a position of authority regarding the issues on which he or she testifies. The expert witness is also paid for her or his time by one of the interested parties. The combination of unquestioned authority and monetary compensation puts the expert witness, as well as the field of human factors, in a position where professional and scientific integrity come into question. Money and power can be overwhelmingly seductive, but until recently there has been no documented code of ethics for forensic human factors. Rudov (1988) drafted an article to be appended to the Ethical Code for the Human Factors Society concerning expert witness conduct. This article outlines behaviors that ensure that the witness is unbiased and not motivated by personal gain, that the witness adheres to a high scientific standard, and that the witness not abuse his or her position of authority and so damage the reputation of the human factors profession.

HUMAN FACTORS AND SOCIETY

Human factors is a vital profession that has much to contribute to society. As the profession emerged from World War II, its emphasis was one of "lights and buttons" in military systems. Since that time, the profession has rapidly expanded. It now includes a wide range of domains covering both the military and the private sectors. Many forces have led to the rise of human factors, the most compelling being the rapid growth of high-technology systems in which human performance is often the variable that limits the performance of the system. Others include increased concern with workers' health and safety, demands from consumers for products that are easier to use, and the financial benefits that arise from improvements in the match between the human and the machine.

As the human factors profession has grown, the range of disciplines that interact to form its knowledge base has also grown. For example, the National Research Council Committee on Human Factors includes "specialists in such fields as psychology, engineering, biomechanics, physiology, medicine, cognitive sciences, machine intelligence, computer sciences, sociology, education, and human factors engineering" (Elkind et al., 1989, p. xiii). The highly interdisciplinary nature of the profession encourages communication across area boundaries with the specific goal of solving applied problems. Such interdisciplinary communication provides a basis for fundamental advances in understanding that contribute to society through more usable, safer products and services.

An immediate application of human factors research is toward the design of equipment and environments for the very young, the aged, and the handicapped. In recent years, society has become more aware of the challenges that face such special populations. One challenge to human fac-

tors is to improve the quality of life for these populations through designs that allow them to attain personal goals and fulfillment with the same ease as those not so challenged. Human factors has a responsibility to see that products intended for use by special populations are more than just modifications of products designed for the population at large.

Because the forces that led to the founding and expansion of the human factors profession continue to exert their influence, humans factors will continue to grow. Current efforts to provide a better integration of the basic information regarding human performance and the applied concerns of system and product designers should enable usability engineering to be a fundamental component of any design process.

RECOMMENDED READING

Card, S. K., Moran, T. P, & Newell, A. (1983). *The Psychology of Human–Computer Interaction.* Hillsdale, NJ: Lawrence Erlbaum.

Christensen, J. M. (1987). The human factors profession. In G. Salvendy (ed.), *Handbook of Human Factors* (pp. 1–16). New York: Wiley.

Kurke, M. I., & Meyer, R. G. (eds.) (1986). *Psychology in Product Liability and Personal Injury Litigation.* Washington, DC: Hemisphere Publishing.

McMillan, G. R., et al. (eds.) (1989). *Applications of Human Performance Models to System Design.* New York: Plenum.

Rouse, W. B., & Boff, K. R. (eds.) (1987). *System Design: Behavioral Perspectives on Designers, Tools, and Organizations.* Amsterdam: North-Holland.

Areas Under the Standard Normal Curve from the z to Infinity

z	0	0.01	0.02	0.03	0.04	0.05	0.06	0.07	0.08	0.09
0	0.5000	0.5040	0.5080	0.5120	0.5160	0.5199	0.5239	0.5279	0.5319	0.5359
0.1	0.5398	0.5438	0.5478	0.5517	0.5557	0.5596	0.5636	0.5675	0.5714	0.5753
0.2	0.5793	0.5832	0.5871	0.5910	0.5948	0.5987	0.6026	0.6064	0.6103	0.6141
0.3	0.6179	0.6217	0.6255	0.6293	0.6331	0.6368	0.6406	0.6443	0.6480	0.6517
0.4	0.6554	0.6591	0.6628	0.6664	0.6700	0.6736	0.6772	0.6808	0.6844	0.6879
0.5	0.6915	0.6950	0.6985	0.7019	0.7054	0.7088	0.7123	0.7157	0.7190	0.7224
0.6	0.7257	0.7291	0.7324	0.7357	0.7389	0.7422	0.7454	0.7486	0.7517	0.7549
0.7	0.7580	0.7611	0.7642	0.7673	0.7704	0.7734	0.7764	0.7794	0.7823	0.7852
0.8	0.7881	0.7910	0.7939	0.7967	0.7995	0.8023	0.8051	0.8079	0.8106	0.8133
0.9	0.8159	0.8186	0.8212	0.8238	0.8264	0.8289	0.8315	0.8340	0.8365	0.8389
1.0	0.8413	0.8438	0.8461	0.8485	0.8508	0.8531	0.8554	0.8577	0.8599	0.8621
1.1	0.8643	0.8665	0.8686	0.8708	0.8729	0.8749	0.8770	0.8790	0.8810	0.8830
1.2	0.8849	0.8869	0.8888	0.8907	0.8925	0.8944	0.8962	0.8980	0.8997	0.9015
1.3	0.9032	0.9049	0.9066	0.9082	0.9099	0.9115	0.9131	0.9147	0.9162	0.9177
1.4	0.9192	0.9207	0.9222	0.9236	0.9251	0.9265	0.9279	0.9292	0.9306	0.9319
1.5	0.9332	0.9345	0.9357	0.9370	0.9382	0.9394	0.9406	0.9418	0.9429	0.9441
1.6	0.9452	0.9463	0.9474	0.9484	0.9495	0.9505	0.9515	0.9525	0.9535	0.9545
1.7	0.9554	0.9564	0.9573	0.9582	0.9591	0.9599	0.9608	0.9616	0.9625	0.9633
1.8	0.9641	0.9649	0.9656	0.9664	0.9671	0.9678	0.9686	0.9693	0.9699	0.9706
1.9	0.9713	0.9719	0.9726	0.9732	0.9738	0.9744	0.9750	0.9756	0.9761	0.9767
2.0	0.9773	0.9778	0.9783	0.9788	0.9793	0.9798	0.9803	0.9808	0.9812	0.9817
2.1	0.9821	0.9826	0.9830	0.9834	0.9838	0.9842	0.9846	0.9850	0.9854	0.9857
2.2	0.9861	0.9864	0.9868	0.9871	0.9875	0.9878	0.9881	0.9884	0.9887	0.9890
2.3	0.9893	0.9896	0.9898	0.9901	0.9904	0.9906	0.9909	0.9911	0.9913	0.9916
2.4	0.9918	0.9920	0.9922	0.9925	0.9927	0.9929	0.9931	0.9932	0.9934	0.9936
2.5	0.9938	0.9940	0.9941	0.9943	0.9945	0.9946	0.9948	0.9949	0.9951	0.9952
2.6	0.9953	0.9955	0.9956	0.9957	0.9959	0.9960	0.9961	0.9962	0.9963	0.9964
2.7	0.9965	0.9966	0.9967	0.9968	0.9969	0.9970	0.9971	0.9972	0.9973	0.9974
2.8	0.9974	0.9975	0.9976	0.9977	0.9977	0.9978	0.9979	0.9979	0.9980	0.9981
2.9	0.9981	0.9982	0.9983	0.9983	0.9984	0.9984	0.9985	0.9985	0.9986	0.9986
3.0	0.9987	0.9987	0.9987	0.9988	0.9988	0.9989	0.9989	0.9989	0.9990	0.9990
3.1	0.9990	0.9991	0.9991	0.9991	0.9992	0.9992	0.9992	0.9992	0.9993	0.9993
3.2	0.9993	0.9993	0.9994	0.9994	0.9994	0.9994	0.9994	0.9995	0.9995	0.9995
3.3	0.9995	0.9995	0.9996	0.9996	0.9996	0.9996	0.9996	0.9996	0.9996	0.9997
3.4	0.9997	0.9997	0.9997	0.9997	0.9997	0.9997	0.9997	0.9997	0.9997	0.9998
3.5	0.9998	0.9998	0.9998	0.9998	0.9998	0.9998	0.9998	0.9998	0.9998	0.9998
3.6	0.9998	0.9998	0.9999	0.9999	0.9999	0.9999	0.9999	0.9999	0.9999	0.9999
3.7	0.9999	0.9999	0.9999	0.9999	0.9999	0.9999	0.9999	0.9999	0.9999	0.9999

Area computed using *Mathematica,* Wolfram Research, Inc.

Values of $\log_2 n$ and $-p \log_2 p$

n or p	$\log_2 n$	$-p \log_2 p$	n or p	$\log_2 n$	$-p \log_2 p$	n or p	$\log_2 n$	$-p \log_2 p$
1	0.000	0.0664	35	5.129	0.5301	68	6.087	0.3784
2	1.000	0.1129	36	5.170	0.5306	69	6.109	0.3694
3	1.585	0.1518	37	5.209	0.5307	70	6.129	0.3602
4	2.000	0.1858	38	5.248	0.5304	71	6.150	0.3508
5	2.322	0.2161	39	5.285	0.5298	72	6.170	0.3412
6	2.585	0.2435	40	5.322	0.5288	73	6.190	0.3314
7	2.807	0.2686	41	5.358	0.5274	74	6.209	0.3215
8	3.000	0.2915	42	5.392	0.5256	75	6.229	0.3113
9	3.170	0.3127	43	5.426	0.5236	76	6.248	0.3009
10	3.322	0.3322	44	5.459	0.5211	77	6.267	0.2903
11	3.459	0.3503	45	5.492	0.5184	78	6.285	0.2796
12	3.585	0.3671	46	5.524	0.5153	79	6.304	0.2687
13	3.700	0.3826	47	5.555	0.5120	80	6.322	0.2575
14	3.807	0.3971	48	5.585	0.5083	81	6.340	0.2462
15	3.907	0.4105	49	5.615	0.5043	82	6.358	0.2348
16	4.000	0.4230	50	5.644	0.5000	83	6.375	0.2231
17	4.087	0.4346	51	5.672	0.4954	84	6.392	0.2113
18	4.170	0.4453	52	5.700	0.4906	85	6.409	0.1993
19	4.248	0.4552	53	5.728	0.4854	86	6.426	0.1871
20	4.322	0.4644	54	5.755	0.4800	87	6.443	0.1748
21	4.392	0.4728	55	5.781	0.4744	88	6.459	0.1623
22	4.459	0.4806	56	5.807	0.4684	89	6.476	0.1496
23	4.524	0.4877	57	5.833	0.4623	90	6.492	0.1368
24	4.585	0.4941	58	5.858	0.4558	91	6.508	0.1238
25	4.644	0.5000	59	5.883	0.4491	92	6.524	0.1107
26	4.700	0.5053	60	5.907	0.4422	93	6.539	0.0974
27	4.755	0.5100	61	5.931	0.4350	94	6.555	0.0839
28	4.807	0.5142	62	5.954	0.4276	95	6.570	0.0703
29	4.858	0.5179	63	5.977	0.4199	96	6.585	0.0565
30	4.907	0.5211	64	6.000	0.4121	97	6.600	0.0426
32	4.954	0.5238	65	6.022	0.4040	98	6.615	0.0286
32	5.000	0.5260	66	6.044	0.3957	99	6.629	0.0140
33	5.044	0.5278	67	6.066	0.3871	100	6.644	0.0000
34	5.087	0.5292						

GLOSSARY

Absolute threshold (4) The minimum amount of physical energy in a stimulus necessary for the detection of that stimulus.

Accommodation (5) The process by which the lens changes shape to keep images in focus on the retina.

Acoustic reflex (5) The muscular reflex within the middle ear that restricts the movement of the ossicles, protecting the inner ear from loud sounds.

Action limit (17) The maximum acceptable load that can be lifted with no other equipment or intervention.

Action potential (5) The movement of an electric charge down the axon of a neuron.

Active touch (7) The perception of an object through manipulation.

Acuity (5) The ability to perceive fine detail.

Additive-factors logic (4) The notion that, if the effect of two variables on reaction time is additive (that is, the effect of both variables together is equal to the sum of the effects of both variables alone), then the variables must influence different stages of information processing. Systematic application of additive-factors logic can give some idea of the stages of processing required for a task and how these stages are arranged.

Analogy (11) A problem-solving heuristic that relies on a comparison between an unfamiliar problem and a well-known problem.

Anchoring heuristic (11) An inductive heuristic from which the estimated frequency of an event is determined by the initial evidence presented about the event.

Anthropometrics (17) The measurement of human bodily characteristics.

Apparent motion (7) Perceived motion produced by discrete changes in location of stimulation.

Arithmetic mean (2) The sum of all values of a dependent variable divided by the number of such values.

Articulation index (8) A measure of speech intelligibility, used especially for situations with background noise.

Assembly error (3) See *manufacturing error*.

Associative phase (12) The intermediate phase of skill acquisition in which associations between task elements are being formed.

Astigmatism (5) Irregularities in the shape of the cornea that blur contours of the image that are in certain orientations.

Auditory canal (5) The canal of the outer ear that is located between the pinna and the tympanic membrane.

Autonomous phase (12) The final phase of skill acquisition in which task execution becomes automatic.

Availability heuristic (11) An inductive heuristic used to estimate probabilities of events according to the ease with which the events can be remembered.

Backlash (16) Insensitivity to control movement that is present at any control position.

Basilar membrane (5) An organ in the inner ear that contains the auditory sensory receptors.

Behavioral variables (2) Variables that involve human action.

Binocular depth cues (7) Cues to the depth of an object in an image based on slight differences in the two images that each eye receives.

Binocular disparity (7) The retinal distance between corresponding points in the images received by each eye.

Biomechanics (17) The mechanical properties of the moving body.

Blind spot (5) The location on the retina where the optic nerve leaves the eye and, hence, there are no sensory receptors.

Breach of express warranty (21) The failure of a product to function as its manufacturer stated or implied that it would.

Brightness (6) The sensation corresponding to the intensity of light waves.

Carryover effects (2) A problem that arises in a within-subject design where performance in one treatment condition is affected by previously received treatments.

Categorical perception (7) The tendency to perceive stimuli in discrete categories, rather than as varying along continua.

Numbers in parentheses refer to the chapter in which a term is first defined.

Central tendency (2)   A value around which a distribution of numbers (scores or measurements, for example) tends to cluster.

Certainty effect (11)   Gambles with highly probable outcomes tend to be selected over gambles with improbable outcomes of higher value.

Check reading (7)   A systematic inspection of each of several dials to verify that all register normal operating values.

Choice reaction time (4)   The amount of time required to execute an appropriate response to the onset of a stimulus from two or more alternative responses.

Circadian rhythms (19)   Biological oscillations of the body with periods of approximately 24 hours.

Closed-loop systems (3)   Systems that make use of feedback.

Closed-loop theory (15)   A theory of motor skill acquisition that assumes that movement control can be represented by a closed-loop system in which sensory feedback is compared to an internal referent acquired through practice.

Cochlea (5)   A bony, fluid-filled coiled cavity in the inner ear that contains the basilar membrane.

Cognitive phase (12)   The initial phase of skill acquisition in which performance of a task relies on rules and instructions.

Color circle (6)   The color appearance system created by connecting the short- and long-wavelength ends of the visual spectrum with nonspectral purple.

Comfort zone (18)   The temperature and humidity combinations that are comfortable for most people.

Communication error (3)   Inaccurate transmission of information between members of a team.

Computational method (3)   A method of human reliability analysis that calculates the probability of system success from tabled data giving the probabilities of relevant human and machine errors.

Cones (5)   The sensory receptors responsible for color vision and perception of detail.

Connectionist models (12)   Models of cognitive function that store information as connections between "nodes" which represent cognitive or neural structures that may be found in the brain.

Conspicuity (8)   The ability of a display to attract attention, or how conspicuous it is.

Contextual interference (15)   Difficulty in remembering an item due to the context in which it is presented.

Continuous controls (16)   Controls that can be set to any value along a continuum.

Contrast sensitivity function (6)   A graph expressing sensitivity to contrast as a function of the spatial frequency of a sine-wave grating.

Control–display ratio (16)   The ratio of the magnitude of control adjustment to the magnitude of the change in a display indicator.

Control knowledge (11)   Knowledge of how to structure and coordinate a problem to achieve a solution.

Control order (16)   The relationship between the position of a control and the position, velocity, or acceleration of a display or system.

Control procedures (2)   Systematic methods used to reduce the influence of extraneous variables in a study. Control procedures help ensure that the effects observed on the dependent variables are due to the independent variables and nothing else.

Control structure (11)   The collection of programs that drive a knowledge-based software system.

Cooperative principle (10)   The assumption that a speaker is being cooperative and sincere to further the purpose of a conversation.

Correct rejection (4)   Correctly responding that a signal is not present.

Cost of concurrence (9)   The difference between the performance level on a task when it is performed alone versus when it is performed with another task to which no attentional resources are devoted.

Counterbalancing procedures (2)   Procedures used in within-subjects designs to minimize the effects of practice and fatigue, involving the presentation of treatment conditions in different orders.

Critical bandwidth (6)   The range of frequencies contained in a complex tone outside which inclusion of additional frequencies increases the loudness.

Critical flicker frequency (6)   The highest rate of flicker at which a stimulus can still be perceived as flickering. Flicker frequencies higher than this critical frequency result in the perception of a continuous stimulus.

Crowding (19)   A psychological experience associated with a high population density.

Cumulative distribution function (3)   The function describing the probability that a dependent variable is less than or equal to some value.

Cumulative trauma disorders (17)   A family of syndromes arising from repeated physical stress on a joint.

Dark adaptation (6)   The process of improvement in sensitivity to light energy under conditions of low illumination.

Data-limited processing (4)   Limitations of human information processing attributable to impoverished input.

Deadspace (16)   The amount of control movement around a neutral position that can occur with no effect on the system.

Decision analysis (11)   The reduction of a complex decision problem into a series of smaller, simpler component problems.

Decision-support system (11)   A computer program that guides the decision-making process.

Declarative knowledge (11)   Knowledge that is available for verbalization.

Deduction (11)   Reasoning about the solution to a problem based on formal logic applied to conditions of the problem.

Dependent variable (2)   A variable representing the phenomenon of interest that is measured as a function of the independent variables.

Depth of field (5)   The extent of the area before and beyond a fixated object in which other objects are also in focus.

Descriptive models (11)   Models of decision making that capture the ways that people think and decide.

Descriptive statistics (2)   Methods of condensing data to allow the description or summary of research results.

Design error (3)   An error in machine design that makes operation difficult or error prone.

Detail design (21)   The third phase of system development, in which the initial preliminary design is developed further and plans are made for production.

Detectability (4)   The degree to which the presence or absence of a stimulus can be determined.

Dichromatic vision (6)   Color blindness in which one of the three types of cone photopigments is missing.

Difference threshold (4)   The minimum amount of difference between the physical energies in two stimuli necessary to detect a difference between the stimuli.

Differential research (2)   Experiments that use subject variables as independent variables to evaluate the effects of individual differences on other variables of interest.

Disability glare (18)   Glare that reduces the detectability, legibility, and readability of display characters, which in turn impairs performance.

Discomfort glare (18)   Glare that causes visual discomfort when a work surface is viewed for a period of time.

Discrete controls (16)   Controls that can be set to one of a fixed number of states.

Discriminability (4)   The degree to which a difference between two stimuli can be detected.

Distinctiveness (10)   The degree to which one remembered item stands apart from other remembered items.

Distributed practice (15)   Performance of a task for periods interspersed with periods of rest.

Divided attention (9)   The act of focusing attention on several sources of input at once.

Dynamic acuity (6)   The ability to resolve detail for moving stimuli.

Dynamic displays (8)   Displays that change over time, such as altimeters.

Echoic memory (10)   The sensory store for the auditory system.

Ecological validity (2)   The extent to which the effects observed in a research setting can be applied to a real-world setting.

Elaborative rehearsal (10)   Constructing relationships among items in short-term memory to enhance long-term retention.

Elastic resistance (16)   The resistance felt in a spring-loaded control, which causes the control to return to a neutral position when released.

Elimination by aspects (11)   A descriptive decision-making heuristic by which the decision-making process occurs through a systematic elimination of features for comparison.

Empiricism (2)   Evaluating scientific hypotheses through the collection of data based on controlled observations.

Encoding specificity principle (10)   The ability to remember an item will depend on the match between the context in which it is retrieved and the context in which it is encoded.

Engineering anthropometry (17)   The use of anthropometric data in the design of equipment.

Engineering psychology (1)   See *human factors*.

Episodic memory (10)   Memory for specific events.

Equal loudness contours (6)   The intensity levels across tones of varying frequencies that result in equal perceived loudness.

Equal pitch contours (6)   The frequencies across tones of varying intensity levels that result in equal perceived pitch.

Ergonomics (1) See *human factors.*

Error of commission (3) The performance of an incorrect action.

Error of omission (3) The failure to perform a necessary action.

Expected-utility theory (11) A normative theory of decision making in which choices are based on the average utility of different objects or outcomes.

Expert system (12) A knowlege-based software system intended to perform as an expert consultant.

Fact base (11) The data base and models used by a knowledge-based software system.

False alarm (4) Incorrectly responding that a signal was present.

Far point (5) The point beyond which increasing the distance of a fixated object requires no further change in accommodation to keep its image in focus.

Fatigue effects (2) Decrements in performance attributable only to the amount of time spent at a task.

Feature-comparison models (10) Models of memory that assume concepts are stored as lists of features.

Fechner's law (1) The magnitude of a sensation is proportional to the logarithm of the physical intensity of a stimulus.

Figure–ground organization (7) The segregation of parts of an image into objects against a background.

Filter-attenuation model (9) A model of attention similar to filter theory that presumes that several sources of input are differentially weighted, which allows some information from unattended sources to enter the central processing channel.

Filter theory (9) A model of attention that presumes the existence of a central processing channel that can act on input from only a single source at one time.

Fine adjust time (16) After the travel time, the time required to adjust the position of a control precisely.

Fitts's law (14) Movement time is a linear function of the index of difficulty.

Fourier analysis (5) A method of decomposing a complex waveform into its component sinusoids.

Fovea (5) That region on the retina containing only cone receptors. Acuity is highest in this region.

Framing (11) How a decision-making problem is presented.

Frequency distribution (2) A plot of the number of times each value of a dependent variable was observed.

Frequency of use (8) A design principle that the most frequently used and important displays or controls should be located in the central visual field.

Frequency theory (6) A theory of pitch perception suggesting that the frequency of vibration of the basilar membrane is represented by a pattern of neural firing that occurs at the same frequency.

Frictional resistance (16) Resistance encountered at any point during the movement of a control due to the mechanical properties of the control.

Functional equivalence (15) The extent to which the tasks performed in a simulated environment mimic those of the real world.

Gain (16) A measure of the responsiveness of a control, inversely related to the control–display ratio.

General adaptation syndrome (18) A physiological response to stress characterized by swollen adrenal glands, atrophied thymus glands, and stomach ulcers when exposure to stress has been prolonged and severe.

Gestalt grouping (7) The tendency for elements to be grouped into wholes on the basis of proximity, similarity, and so on.

Given-new strategy (10) The fact that sentences in a meaningful conversation contain both old and new information.

Glare (18) A high-intensity light that interferes with the perception of objects of lower intensity.

Go–no go reaction time (4) The amount of time required to execute a single response to the onset of a particular subset of the possible stimuli.

Gross negligence (21) Reckless and wanton disregard by the manufacturer of a product of the manufacturer's legal responsibilities.

Harmonics (5) Integer multiples of the fundamental frequency of a complex tone.

Hawthorne effect (1) Changes in performance or productivity that can be traced to any alteration of the workplace environment and not to any specific variable that was manipulated to effect the alteration.

Hazard function (3) The function describing the probability that a system component fails in a given instant, given that it has operated successfully up to that point.

Hick–Hyman law (13) Choice reaction time is a linear function of the amount of information transmitted.

Hit (4) Correctly responding that a signal is present.

Human-computer interaction (20) That area of human factors concerned with the design of computer workstations and software interfaces to optimize performance of computer-based tasks.

Human factors (1)   The study of human behavioral and biological characteristics that influence the efficiency with which a human can interact with the inanimate components of a human–machine system.

Human information processing (1)   The view that human perception, cognition, and action are based on a systematic processing of information from the environment.

Human–machine system (1)   An entity consisting of a human operator and a machine that work together to achieve some goal.

Human reliability (3)   The probability that an operator makes no errors while interacting as part of a human–machine system.

Hyperopia (5)   Farsightedness, or the inability to see close objects.

Hypervigilance (18)   A state of panic in which thinking becomes overly simplistic, resulting in hasty, poor decision making.

Hypothesis (2)   A tentative and experimentally testable statement about the cause of some phenomenon.

Iconic memory (10)   The sensory store for the visual system.

Identification acuity (6)   Acuity as measured by a Snellen eye chart; the distance at which an observer could identify letters that an observer with normal vision could identify at a standard distance.

Illuminance (18)   The amount of light falling on a surface.

Impulse variability model (14)   A model of timed movement control that assumes an initial burst of force, followed by the damping of the resulting movement.

Independence point (9)   The point in the performance operating characteristic space indicated by the performance level of each task when performed alone.

Independent variable (2)   A variable that is overtly changed in an experiment to determine whether it affects a dependent variable.

Index of accessibility (16)   A measure of the ease with which frequently used controls on a panel can be reached.

Index of difficulty (14)   A measure of the difficulty of an aimed movement, given by the logarithm to the base 2 of the ratio of twice the distance to the target divided by the target width.

Induced motion (7)   Perceived movement of a stationary element induced by motion of its frame of reference.

Induction (11)   Reasoning in which a general solution to a problem is generated from the particular conditions of the problem.

Inertial resistance (16)   A control resistance that decreases as control acceleration increases.

Information theory (4)   Quantifying the information in a set of events by the average minimum number of binary questions required to determine the identity of an item in the set.

Input error (3)   An error that occurs during the perception of a stimulus.

Installation error (3)   An error in the installation of a machine that leads to system failure.

Interaural intensity differences (7)   Differences in the intensity of a sound at each ear, due to a sound shadow created by the head, that provide cues to position.

Interaural time differences (7)   Differences in the time at which a tone reaches each ear that provide cues to positions.

Internal validity (2)   The degree to which effects observed in a study can be attributed to the variables of interest.

Inverse square law (5)   The intensity of an auditory signal is inversely related to the squared distance of the sound source.

Isolation effect (11)   More attention is focused on features that are unique to different choices rather than on features that the choices have in common.

Isometric control (16)   A fixed control that responds according to the amount of force exerted on it.

Isotonic control (16)   A movable control that responds according to its amount of displacement.

Iterative corrections model (14)   A theory of movement control that assumes that an aimed movement is composed of a series of discrete submovements, each traversing a fixed proportion of the distance to the target.

Job analysis (19)   An analysis of a position (job) to determine the tasks and responsibilities of a worker in that position, the conditions under which that worker must perform, and the skills and training that the position requires.

Job design (19)   The act of structuring tasks and assigning them to positions.

Kinesthesis (5)   Sensory information about the location of the limbs during movement.

Knowledge of performance (15)   Detailed feedback concerning the performance of a movement.

Knowledge of results (15) Feedback concerning the success or failure of a movement.

Lateral inhibition (6) The inhibition of a cell's firing rate due to the activity of neighboring cells.

Late-selection model (9) A model of attention that presumes that information from all input channels is identified, but that only the information from the attended input source is acted on.

Legibility (8) The ease with which symbols and letters can be discerned.

Level of processing (10) The degree of elaborative or semantic processing performed on information in short-term memory.

Lightness (6) The perceived reflectance of an object, or how dark or light the object appears on a scale from black to white.

Lightness constancy (6) Maintenance of perceived relative lightness under different levels of illumination.

Lightness contrast (6) Changes in the lightness of an object with changes in the intensity of the surrounding area.

Likelihood alarm (8) A warning, caution, or advisory signal that also presents information about the likelihood of an event.

Link analysis (8) An analysis of display panel design based on connections between displays, defined in terms of frequency and sequence of use. Link analysis can also be used to analyze control panels and to aid in the design of workstations.

Loading task paradigm (9) A method of measuring mental workload in a dual-task situation in which the emphasis is placed on the secondary task, and mental workload is estimated from performance on the primary task.

Long-term store (10) An unlimited-capacity memory system that retains information for an indefinite period of time.

Luminance (18) The amount of light generated by a surface.

Macroergonomics (19) An approach to human factors that stresses the organizational and social environment in which the human–machine system functions.

Maintenance error (3) An error during routine maintenance of a machine that leads to system failure.

Maintenance rehearsal (10) Covert repetition of material held in short-term memory.

Manufacturing error (3) An error in the fabrication of a machine that leads to system failure.

Masked threshold (8) The amount of physical energy in a stimulus necessary to detect that stimulus when it is presented in a noisy background.

Masking (6) The interference between the presentation of one stimulus and the perception of another presented in close spatial and/or temporal proximity.

Massed practice (15) Continuous performance of a task for an extended period of time.

Maximum permissible limit (17) The highest limit for lifting that should not be exceeded under any circumstances.

Median (2) That value of a dependent variable below which and above which 50% of all values fall; the value with a percentile rank of 50%.

Mediation error (3) An error that occurs during cognition that is not attributable to misperception of a stimulus or incorrect execution of an intended action.

Mental model (10) A dynamic representation or simulation of a problem held in working memory.

Mental workload (9) An estimate of the attentional demands of a task.

Method of constant stimuli (4) A method to determine a threshold that presents a large number of stimulus intensities in random order.

Method of limits (4) A method to determine a threshold that presents stimulus intensities in increasing or decreasing increments.

Miss (4) Incorrectly responding that a signal was not present.

Mistakes (4) Errors that arise in the planning of an action.

Mnemonics (10) Mental strategies used to organize and aid memory for information.

Mode (2) The most frequently occurring value of a dependent variable.

Monochromatic vision (6) A kind of color blindness in which an individual has either no cones or only one type of cone.

Monocular depth cues (7) Cues to the depth of an object in an image that are available to a monocular viewer. Stationary monocular cues are those used to portray depth in still paintings. Additional monocular cues are provided when an observer moves.

Monte Carlo method (3) A method of human reliability analysis in which system performance is predicted by simulating a model system.

Motion contrast (7)   Apparent motion of a stationary texture induced by motion of a surrounding texture.

Motor program (14)   An abstract plan thought to control specific classes of movements.

Motor unit (14)   A small group of muscle fibers innervated by a single motor neuron.

Multiple-resource model (9)   A model of attention that presumes the existence of several pools of mental resources, each appropriate to different kinds of stimuli, processing, and response modalities.

Myopia (5)   Nearsightedness, or the inability to see distant objects.

Naturalistic research (2)   The observation of behavior in real-world settings without manipulation of any independent variables.

Near point (5)   The point at which moving an object closer produces no further accommodation.

Negligence (21)   The failure of a manufacturer to engage in reasonable actions to meet his or her legal responsibilities.

Network models (10)   Models of memory in which concepts are represented as connections between functionally related neural units.

Neuron (5)   A cell that transmits an electrochemical signal within the nervous system.

Normative models (11)   Models of decision making that predict the choices that would be made by an optimal decision maker.

Null hypothesis (2)   The proposal that a treatment had no effect on the dependent variable.

Observational learning (15)   Learning to perform a task by watching another performer.

Occupational stress (18)   Stress that arises from the work environment.

Oculomotor depth cues (7)   Cues to the depth of an object in an image based on proprioceptive feedback from the muscles in the eye.

Olfactory cilia (5)   The likely sensory receptors for olfaction.

Olfactory epithelium (5)   That area of the nasal cavity that contains the olfactory sensory receptors.

Open-loop systems (3)   Systems that do not make use of feedback.

Operating error (3)   An inappropriate use or operation of a machine.

Operational definition (2)   The definition of an object or concept in terms of its actions or behavior.

Opponent process theory (6)   A theory of color vision that proposes neural mechanisms code blue and yellow together and red and green together so that one color of a pair can be signaled, but not both.

Optimized initial impulse model (14)   A model of movement control that combines elements of the iterative corrections and impulse variability models.

Organizational development (19)   Changes in the structure and goals of an organization, designed to improve organizational effectiveness.

Ossicles (5)   The three small bones in the inner ear that transmit pressure changes from the tympanic membrane to the oval window.

Output error (3)   The selection and execution of an inappropriate action.

Oval window (5)   A membrane that receives vibrations from the ossicles and produces waves in the fluid around the basilar membrane.

Parallel components (3)   System components that receive input and commence operation simultaneously.

Part–whole transfer (15)   The extent to which practice with the components of a task improves performance of the entire task.

Passive touch (7)   The perception of a texture pressed against the skin.

Pay for performance (19)   A pay schedule in which salary depends on a worker's level of productivity.

Percentile rank (2)   A measurement given to a particular value of a dependent variable that specifies the percentage of scores that fall below it.

Perceptual organization (7)   The way that relationships are formed among the different elements of an image to produce a percept.

Performance appraisal (19)   The formal evaluation of an employee's performance.

Performance efficiency (9)   A measure of how efficiently two tasks can be performed together, defined as the smallest distance between the performance operating characteristic curve and the independence point.

Performance operating characteristic (9)   A plot of performance for a divided-attention situation, by which the performance of one task is plotted as a function of the performance on another task under several levels of relative task emphasis.

Personal space (19)   The area immediately surrounding one's body.

Personnel selection (1)   Choosing employees for a job on the basis of the match between their characteristics or qualifications and the job requirements

Phoneme (7)   The smallest unit of speech that, when changed, changes the meaning of an utterance.

Photometry (6)   Measurement of the functional amount of light energy for human vision.

Photopic vision (5)   Vision under conditions of bright light, controlled primarily by cones.

Pinna (5)   The outer, visible part of the ear.

Place theory (6)   A theory of pitch perception that proposes that the perception of pitch is determined by the location of the active receptors on the basilar membrane and the neurons that they innervate.

Population stereotype (13)   An intuitive association between a control motion and its associated effect.

Positive misaccommodation (8)   A problem that arises in the use of head-up displays in which an observer's eyes accommodate for a distance closer than the far point. This results in poor size and depth perception.

Power law of practice (12)   The empirical finding that performance (as measured by response time or accuracy) improves as a power function of the amount of time spent practicing a task.

Practice effects (2)   Improvements in performance attributable only to the amount of time spent performing a task.

Preference reversals (11)   A change in the most preferred object under changes in the context in which the choice is presented.

Preferred noise criterion (18)   A level of background noise intensity and frequency that is optimal for a given task environment.

Preliminary design (21)   The second phase of system development, in which alternative designs are considered, resulting in an initial, tentative design.

Presbyopia (5)   A loss of accommodative ability that comes with age.

Proactive interference (10)   Forgetting of information that occurs because of the memory of previously presented information.

Probability (2)   A number from 0 to 1 that indicates the likelihood of a random event. Usually, the number of times that an event of interest is observed divided by the total number of observations made.

Probability density function (2)   The continuous analogue to the probability distribution; used to assign probabilities to continuous events (for example, time).

Probability distribution (2)   A relative frequency distribution over an entire set of discrete events, describing the proportion of times that each event occurs relative to all other events.

Procedural knowledge (11)   Knowledge of how tasks are performed that is not available for verbalization.

Production and development phase (21)   The final phase of system development, in which the system is actually built, tested, and evaluated.

Production system (11)   A data base, control system and set of if-then rules that can be used to solve simple or complex problems.

Proprioception (5)   Sensory information about the position of the limbs.

Proxemics (19)   The way that people manage the space around them and their distances from other people.

Psychological refractory period (13)   Increases in response time when two responses must be executed in rapid succession.

Psychophysical scaling (4)   A mathematical expression relating the physical intensity of a stimulus to its perceived magnitude.

Psychophysics (1)   The study of the relation between physical stimulus properties and psychological experience.

Pupillometry (9)   The measurement of the diameter of the pupil.

Purkinje shift (6)   The relatively greater perceived brightness of objects of short wavelength under scotopic viewing conditions.

Quantitative error (3)   An action that fails by being either insufficient or excessive.

Radiometry (6)   Measurement of light energy.

Random walk (4)   A continuous model of information processing that assumes that evidence is accumulated over time toward alternative responses.

Reach envelope (16)   An area in which controls and other objects should be located to ensure that some large percentage of the population will be able to reach them.

Reactivity (11)   Changes in a mental process due to concurrent verbalization of that process.

Readability (8)   The degree to which a display of letters or characters allows fast and accurate recognition of information.

Receiver operating characteristic (4)   A plot of the proportion of hits as a function of the proportion of false alarms under several levels of response bias.

Receptive field (5)   The area of sensory receptors that, when stimulated, affects the firing rate of a particular neuron.

Reflection effect (11) When expected utilities are positive, the high probability outcomes are preferred even when their expected utility is low. When expected utilities are negative, low probability outcomes are preferred.

Relative frequency distribution (2) A plot of the proportion of times that a value of a dependent variable was observed.

Reliability (3) The probability that a system, subsystem, or component does not fail.

Representativeness heuristic (11) An inductive heuristic used to assign probabilities to events according to their perceived similarity between some representative outcome.

Resolution acuity (6) The ability to distinguish between a field of varying contrast and a field of uniform intensity.

Resource-limited processing (4) Limitations in human information processing attributable to a lack of cognitive resources, for example, attention or working memory.

Response bias (4) A tendency to prefer one response over others, regardless of the stimulus conditions.

Retina (5) A two-dimensional grid of sensory receptors and associated neurons lining the back wall of the eye.

Risk analysis (3) A comprehensive analysis of the costs of system failure, taking into account system and human reliability and the risks that accompany specific failures.

Rods (5) The sensory receptors responsible for vision under conditions of low illumination.

Schema (10) An abstract mental representation, similar to a mental model, for organizing sequences of events.

Schema theory (15) A theory of motor skill that assumes the existence of a generalized motor program, the parameters of which are determined by schemas acquired through practice.

Scientific method (2) The process by which alternative hypotheses concerning the cause of some phenomenon are evaluated. This evaluation is based on the outcomes of controlled observations.

Scotopic vision (5) Vision under conditions of low illumination, primarily controlled by the rods.

Selection error (3) An action performed with the wrong control.

Selective attention (9) The act of focusing on one source of information and ignoring all others.

Semantic context (7) The effect of the meaning of a context on the perception of a stimulus.

Semantic memory (10) Long-term memory for general knowledge.

Sensory receptors (5) Specialized cells in a sensory system that convert physical energy into nervous impulses.

Sensory store (10) A buffer that retains sensory information briefly.

Sequence error (3) The performance of an action at the wrong position within a sequence of actions.

Sequence of use (8) A design principle that states that, if displays must be scanned in a fixed sequence, the displays should be arranged in that sequence.

Serial components (3) An arrangement of system components in which each component receives as input the output of a previous component and delivers its output as input to the following component.

Shape constancy (7) The tendency to perceive an object as having the same shape regardless of its slant or tilt.

Short-term store (10) A limited-capacity memory system in which information is retained through rehearsal.

Simple reaction time (4) The amount of time required to react with a single response to the onset of any stimulus event.

Size constancy (7) The tendency to perceive an object as having the same size regardless of its visual angle.

Skill-rule-knowledge framework (3) A framework of cognitive behavior in which behaviors are classified according to the level of skill involved.

Slips (3) Errors arising in the execution of an action.

Somesthetic senses (5) Those senses associated with skin, joints, muscles, and tendons, including touch, pressure, temperature, pain, vibration, and proprioception.

Span of apprehension (10) The number of briefly displayed visual stimuli that can be reported without error.

Speech spectrogram (7) A plot of the frequencies that appear in a speech signal over time.

Spinal reflex (14) Simple actions controlled by the spinal cord.

Standard deviation (2) The square root of the variance of a dependent variable.

Static displays (8) Displays that do not change over time, such as road signs.

Stevens's law (4) The magnitude of sensation provided by a stimulus is directly proportional to some power of the physical intensity of the stimulus when sensation is scaled using magnitude estimation procedures.

Stimulus–response compatibility (13) The ease with which a response to a stimulus can be selected based on the assignment of stimuli to responses.

Stimulus variables (2) Environmental factors that affect behavior.

Strict liability (21) A manufacturer's responsibility for any product defect.

Stroboscopic motion (7) The perception of movement arising from the sequential illumination of two or more spatially separated lights in close succession.

Strong methods (11) Methods of problem solving based on an expert's knowledge of a domain.

Structurally limited processing (4) Limitations in human information processing that arise when one structure is called on to perform more than one task.

Subject variables (2) Individual differences such as physical characteristics, mental abilities, and training.

Subjective assessment techniques (9) Measurements obtained through an operator's evaluation of some aspect of a task or procedure. These techniques are commonly used to measure mental workload.

Subsidiary task paradigm (9) A method of measuring mental workload using a dual-task situation in which emphasis is placed on the primary task and mental workload is estimated from performance on the secondary task.

Subtractive logic (4) The notion that the time to perform a mental event can be found by measuring the reaction time in a task that requires that event and in a task that requires everything except that event and then subtracting the two.

Survivor function (3) The function describing a component's reliability over time, or the probability that some event (for example, failure) does not occur before a given time.

Syllogism (11) A list of premises and a conclusion drawn from them.

Synapse (5) The narrow gap between two connected neurons through which transmitter substances flow.

Syntactic context (7) The effect of grammatical context on the perception of a stimulus.

System (3) A collection of components that act together to achieve a goal that could not be achieved by any single component alone.

System planning (21) The first phase of system development, in which the need for a system is identified.

Task analysis (1) The analysis of a task in terms of its perceptual, cognitive, and motor components.

Task environment (11) The objects and allowable actions that may be used to achieve a solution to a problem.

Taste buds (5) Groups of sensory receptors on the tongue.

Teleoperators (16) General-purpose, dextrous human-machine systems that augment the physical skills of the operator.

Territoriality (19) Behavior patterns oriented toward occupying and controlling physical spaces.

Theory (2) An organized framework of causal statements that allows the understanding, prediction, and control of some phenomena.

Threshold shift (18) A decrease in auditory sensitivity due to exposure to high noise levels.

Timbre (6) The texture of a complex tone, which is determined by such factors as the relative intensities of its harmonics.

Time-and-motion study (1) An analysis of the movements required to perform a job and the time required for each movement.

Timing error (3) The performance of an action at the wrong time.

Tracking task (16) A task that requires matching a dynamic stimulus signal with an identical output signal.

Transfer-appropriate processing (10) The ability to remember an item encoded in a particular way depends on the way in which the item is tested.

Transmitted information (4) The amount of information (in bits) passing through a communication channel, as derived from the amount of information in the input and the amount of information in the output.

Travel time (16) The time required to move a control into the vicinity of a desired position.

Trichromatic color theory (6) A theory of color vision that proposes that color is perceived as a function of the relative activity in the blue, green, and red color systems.

Two-point thresholds (6) The minimum distance between two points of stimulation on the skin that allows the perception of two distinct stimuli.

Tympanic membrane (5) A delicate membrane that vibrates with changes in air pressure created by an auditory stimulus. It is also called the eardrum.

Unitary-resource model (9) A model of attention that views attention as a single pool of resources reserved for mental activities.

User interface (11) The component of a software system responsible for presenting output to and receiving input from the user.

Utility (11) The subjective worth of an object or event.

Validity (2) The degree to which a test or some other measurement device measures what it is supposed to measure.

Variability (2) A measure that indicates the degree of "spread" in a distribution of numbers from a central point. Usually, the variance.

Variability of practice (15) The extent to which the specific movements executed during practice of a motor skill differ from each other.

Variables (2) Critical events or objects that change or can be changed.

Variance (2) The sum of all squared differences between the values of a dependent variable and their mean, divided by the total number of such values minus 1.

Vergence (5) Rotations of the eyes inward or outward with changes in the point of fixation.

Vernier acuity (6) The ability to discriminate between a broken and unbroken line.

Vestibular sense (5) The sense associated with the perception of bodily motion and balance.

Vigilance task (9) A task characterized by the requirement of detecting small, infrequent changes in the environment over long periods of time.

Vigilance decrement (9) A decline in the hit rate over time in the performance of a vigilance task.

Viscous resistance (16) Control resistance that increases with control velocity.

Visibility (8) How well a display can be seen, or how visible it is.

Visual angle (6) A measure of the size of the retinal image of an object.

Visual cortex (5) The primary receiving area of the cortex in which visual signals are processed and recombined.

Visual dominance (8) The priority that visual information receives when information arrives from the visual and other systems simultaneously.

Weak methods (11) Methods of problem solving of broad applicability used to solve unfamiliar problems when the correct way to proceed is unknown.

Weber's law (1) The smallest detectable change in the magnitude of a stimulus is a constant proportion of the magnitude of the original stimulus.

Work tolerance (17) The ability of an operator to perform well while maintaining physical and emotional health.

Working memory (10) Another name for short-term memory that emphasizes the operations that occur on information in short-term memory.

Yerkes–Dodson law (9) Performance is an inverted U-shaped function of arousal, with best performance at intermediate levels of arousal.

REFERENCES

Aaronson, D., & Scarborough, H. (1976). Performance theories for sentence coding: Some qualitative evidence. *Journal of Experimental Psychology: Human Perception and Performance, 2,* 56–70.

Abrams, R. A., Meyer, D. E., & Kornblum, S. (1989). Speed and accuracy of saccadic eye movements: Characteristics of impulse variability in the oculomotor system *Journal of Experimental Psychology: Human Perception and Performance, 15,* 529–543.

Adams, J. A. (1961). Human tracking behavior. *Psychological Bulletin, 58,* 55–79.

Adams, J. A. (1967). Engineering psychology. In H. Helson & W. Bevan (eds.), *Contemporary Approaches to Psychology* (pp. 345–383). New York: Van Nostrand Reinhold.

Adams, J. A. (1971). A closed-loop theory of motor learning. *Journal of Motor Behavior, 3,* 111–150.

Adams, J. A. (1972). Research and the future of engineering psychology. *American Psychologist, 27,* 615–622.

Adams, J. A. (1984). Learning of movement sequences. *Psychological Bulletin, 96,* 3–28.

Adams, J. A. (1987). Historical review and appraisal of research on the learning, retention, and transfer of human motor skills. *Psychological Bulletin, 101,* 41–74.

Adams, J. A., & Dijkstra, S. (1966). Short-term memory for motor responses. *Journal of Experimental Psychology, 71,* 314–318.

Adams, J. A., & Hufford, L. E. (1962). Contributions of a part-task trainer to the learning and relearning of a time-shared flight-maneuver. *Human Factors, 4,* 159–170.

Adelson, B. (1981). Problem solving and the development of abstract categories in programming languages. *Memory & Cognition, 9,* 422–433.

Aiello, J. R., DeRisi, D. T., Epstein, Y. M., & Karlin, R. A. (1977). Crowding and the role of interpersonal distance preference. *Sociometry, 40,* 271–282.

Akerstedt, T., & Gillberg, M. (1982). Displacement of the sleep period and sleep deprivation: Implications for shift work. *Human Neurobiology, 1,* 163–171.

Albert, A. (1982). The effect of graphic input devices on performance in a cursor positioning task. In *Proceedings of the Human Factors Society 26th Annual Meeting* (pp. 54–58). Santa Monica, CA: Human Factors Society.

Alden, D. G., Daniels, R. W., & Kanarick, A. F. (1972). Keyboard design and operation: A review of the major issues. *Human Factors, 14,* 275–293.

Aldrich, F. K., & Parkin, A. J. (1987). Tangible line graphs: An experimental investigation of three formats using capsule paper. *Human Factors, 20,* 301–309.

Aldrich, T. B., & Szabo, S. M. (1986). A methodology for predicting crew workload in new weapon systems. In *Proceedings of the Human Factors Society 30th Annual Meeting* (pp. 633–637). Santa Monica, CA: Human Factors Society.

Allen, T. J., & Gerstberger, P. G. (1973). A field experiment to improve communications in a product engineering department: The nonterritorial office. *Human Factors, 15,* 487–498.

Allport, D. A. (1989). Visual attention. In M. I. Posner (ed.), *Foundations of Cognitive Science* (pp. 631–682). Cambridge, MA: MIT Press.

Allport, D. A., Antonis, B., & Reynolds, P. (1972). On the division of attention: A disproof of the single channel hypothesis. *Quarterly Journal of Experimental Psychology, 24,* 225–235.

Alluisi, E. A., & Warm, J. S. (1990). Things that go together: A review of stimulus–response compatibility effects. In R. W. Proctor & T. G. Reeve (eds.), *Stimulus-response Compatibility: An Integrated Perspective* (pp. 3–30). Amsterdam: North-Holland.

Altman, I., & Chemers, M. (1980). *Culture and Environment.* Monterey, CA: Brooks/Cole.

Amar, J. (1920). *The Human Motor.* New York: E. P. Dutton.

ASHRAE. (American Society of Heating, Refrigerating, and Air Conditioning Engineers). (1985). *ASHRAE Handbook 1985: Fundamentals.* Atlanta, GA: ASHRAE.

Ammons, R. B. (1958). Le mouvement. In G. H. Steward & J. P. Steward (eds.), *Current Psychological Issues* (pp. 146–183). New York: Holt, Rinehart and Winston.

Anderson, J. R. (1983). *The Architecture of Cognition.* Cambridge, MA: Harvard University Press.

Anderson, J. R. (1990). *Cognitive Psychology and Its Implications* (3rd ed.). San Francisco: W. H. Freeman.

Anderson, J. R., Conrad, F. G., & Corbett, A. T. (1989). Skill acquisition and the LISP tutor. *Cognitive Science, 13,* 467–505.

Anderson, J. R., Farell, R., & Sauers, R. (1984). Learning to program in LISP. *Cognitive Science, 8,* 87–129.

Andersson, G. B. J. (1986). Loads on the spine during sitting. In N. Corlett, J. Wilson, & I. Manenica (eds.), *The Ergonomics of Working Postures* (pp. 309–318). London: Taylor & Francis.

Andres, R. O., & Hartung, K. J. (1989). Prediction of head movement time using Fitts' law. *Human Factors, 31,* 703–713.

Annett, J. (1985). Motor learning: A review. In H. Heuer, & U. Kleinbeck, & K. H. Schmidt (eds.), *Motor Behavior: Programming, Control, and Acquisition* (pp. 189–212). New York: Springer-Verlag.

ANSI/HFS. (American National Standards Institute/Human Factors Society) (1988). *American National Standard for Human Factors Engineering of Visual Display Terminal Workstations.* Santa Monica, CA: Human Factors Society.

Anstis, S. (1986). Motion perception in the frontal plane: Sensory aspects. In K. R. Boff, L. Kaufman, & J. P. Thomas (eds.), *Handbook of Perception and Human Performance, Vol. I: Sensory Processes and Perception* (pp. 16-1 to 16-27). New York: Wiley.

Anthony, W. P., & Harrison, C. W. (1972). Tympanic membrane perforations: Effect on audiograms. *Archives of Otolaryngology, 95,* 506–510.

Antin, J. F., Lauretta, D. J., & Wolf, L. D. (1991). The intensity of auditory warning tones in the automobile environment: Detection and preference evaluations. *Applied Ergonomics, 22,* 13–19.

Anzai, Y. (1984). Cognitive control of real-time event-driven systems. *Cognitive Science, 8,* 221–254.

Anzola, G. P., Bertoloni, G., Buchtel, H. A., & Rizzolatti, G. (1977). Spatial compatibility and anatomical factors in simple and choice reaction time. *Neuropsychologia, 15,* 295–302.

Appelle, S. (1972). Perception and discrimination as a function of stimulus orientation: The oblique effect in man and animals. *Psychological Bulletin, 78,* 266–278.

Armstrong, E. (1989). A comparative review of the primate motor system. *Journal of Motor Behavior, 21,* 493–517.

Armstrong, T. J., Foulke, J. A., Joseph, B. S., & Goldstein, S. A. (1982). Investigation of cumulative trauma disorders in a poultry processing plant. *American Industrial Hygiene Association Journal, 43* (2), 103–116.

Armstrong, T. J., Ulin, S., & Ways, C. (1990). Hand tools and control of cumulative trauma disorders of the upper limb. In C. M. Haselgrave, J. R. Wilson, E. N. Corlett, & I. Manenica (eds.), *Work Design in Practice* (pp. 43–50). London: Taylor & Francis.

Arnaut, L. Y., & Greenstein, J. S. (1990). Is display/control gain a useful metric for optimizing an interference? *Human Factors, 32,* 651–663.

Associated Press wire story (1990a). Drinking on the job. April 29, 1990.

Associated Press wire story (1990b). Failure to enunciate causes bus chaos. July 31, 1990.

Atkinson, R. C., Holmgren, J. E., & Juola, J. F. (1969). Processing time as influenced by the number of elements in a visual display. *Perception & Psychophysics, 6,* 321–326.

Atkinson, R. C., & Shiffrin, R. M. (1968). Human memory: A proposed system and its control processes. In K. W. Spence (ed.), *The Psychology of Learning and Motivation* (Vol. 2, pp. 89–195). New York: Academic Press.

Averbach, E., & Coriell, A. S. (1961). Short-term memory in vision. *Bell Systems Technical Journal, 40,* 309–328.

Ayoub, M. M. (1982). Overview of methods to assess voluntary exertions. In R. Easterby, K. H. E. Kroemer, & D. B. Chaffin (eds.), *Anthropometry and Biomechanics: Theory and Application* (pp. 127–133). New York: Plenum.

Ayoub, M., & Lo Presti, P. (1971). The determination of an optimum size cylindrical handle by use of electromyography. *Ergonomics, 4,* 503–518.

Ayoub, M. M., & Miller, M. (1991). Industrial workplace design. In A. Mital & W. Karwowski (eds.), *Workspace, Equipment and Tool Design* (pp. 67–92). Amsterdam: Elsevier.

Ayoub, M. A., & Wittels, N. E. (1989). Cumulative trauma disorders. In D. J. Oborne (ed.), *International Reviews of Ergonomics* (Vol. 3, pp. 217–272). London: Taylor & Francis.

Babbage, C. (1832). *On the Economy of Machinery and Manufactures.* Philadelphia: Carey & Lea.

Baddeley, A. (1986). *Working Memory.* New York: Oxford University Press.

Baddeley, A. (1990). *Human Memory: Theory and Practice.* Boston: Allyn and Bacon.

Baddeley, A. D., & Ecob, J. R. (1973). Reaction time and short-term memory: A trace strength alternative to the high-speed scanning hypothesis. *Quarterly Journal of Experimental Psychology, 25,* 229–240.

Baddeley, A. D., Logie, R. H., Nimmo-Smith, M. I., & Brereton, N. (1985). Components of fluent reading, *Journal of Memory and Language, 24,* 119–131.

Bailey, R. W. (1982). *Human Performance Engineering: A Guide for System Designers.* Englewood Cliffs, NJ: Prentice Hall.

Bakan, P. (ed.) (1966). *Attention.* New York: Van Nostrand.

Baker, C. H. (1963). Signal duration as a factor in vigilance tasks. *Science, 141,* 1196–1197.

Baker, C. L., & Braddick, O. J. (1985). Temporal properties of the short-range process in apparent motion. *Perception, 14,* 181–192.

Baker, D. S. (1989). Major defense verdicts of 1988. *ABA Journal,* November, 82–86.

Bandura, A. (1986). *Social Foundations of Thought and Action: A Social Cognitive Theory.* Englewood Cliffs, NJ: Prentice Hall.

Banks, W. P., & Prinzmetal, W. (1976). Configurational effects in visual information processing. *Perception & Psychophysics, 19,* 361–367.

Banks, W. W., & Boone, M. P. (1981). A method for quantifying control accessibility. *Human Factors, 23,* 299–303.

Barber, A. V. (1990). Visual mechanisms and predictors of far field visual task performance. *Human Factors, 32,* 217–234.

Barlow, H. B., & Mollon, J. D. (eds.) (1982). *The Senses.* New York: Cambridge University Press.

Barlow, R. E., & Proschan, F. (1965). *Mathematical Theory of Reliability.* New York: Wiley.

Barnes, R. M. (1963). *Motion and Time Study,* 5th ed. New York: Wiley.

Baron, J. (1988). *Thinking and Deciding.* New York: Cambridge University Press.

Baron, R. M., & Rodin, J. (1978). Personal control as a mediator of crowding. In A. Baum, J. E. Singer, & S. Valins (eds.), *Advances in Environmental Psychology, Vol. 1, The Urban Environment* (pp. 145–190). Hillsdale, NJ: Lawrence Erlbaum.

Baron, S., & Corker, K. (1989). Engineering-based approaches to human performance modeling. In G. R. McMillan, et al. (eds.), *Applications of Human Performance Models to System Design* (pp. 203–217). New York: Plenum.

Baron, S., Kruser, D. S., & Huey, B. M. (eds.) (1990). *Quantitative Modeling of Human Performance in Complex, Dynamic Systems.* Washington, DC: National Academy Press.

Barrett, H. H., & Swindell, W. (1981). *Radiological Imaging: The Theory of Image Formation, Detection and Processing.* New York: Academic Press.

Bartleson, C. J. (1968). Pupil diameters and retinal illuminances in interocular brightness matching. *Journal of the Optical Society of America, 58,* 853–855.

Bashford, J. A., Jr., Riener, K. R., & Warren, R. M. (1992). Increasing the intelligibilty of speech through multiple phonemic restorations. *Perception & Psychophysics, 51,* 211–217.

Bashore, T. R. (1990). Stimulus–response compatibility viewed from a cognitive psychophysiological perspective. In R. W. Proctor & T. G. Reeve (eds.), *Stimulus–Response Compatibility: An Integrated Perspective* (pp. 183–223). Amsterdam: North-Holland.

Battacchi, M. W., Pelamatti, G. M., & Umiltà, C. (1990). Is there a modality effect? Evidence for visual recency and suffix effects. *Memory & Cognition, 18,* 651–658.

Battig, W. F. (1979). The flexibility of human memory. In L. S. Cermak & F. I. M. Craik (eds.), *Levels of Processing in Human Memory* (pp. 23–44). Hillsdale, NJ: Lawrence Erlbaum.

Baudhuin, E. A. (1987). The design of industrial and flight simulators. In S. M. Cormier & J. D. Hagman (eds.), *Transfer of Learning* (pp. 217–237). New York: Academic Press.

Bauer, D., & Cavonius, C. R. (1980). Improving the legibility of visual display units through contrast reversal. In E. Grandjean & E. Vigliani (eds.), *Ergonomic Aspects of Visual Display Terminals* (pp. 137–142). London: Taylor and Francis.

Bauer, D. W., & Eddy, J. K. (1986). The representation of command language syntax. *Human Factors, 28,* 1–10.

Baum, A., & Paulus, P. B. (1987). Crowding. In D. Stokols & I. Altman (eds.), *Handbook of Environmental Psychology* (Vol. 1, pp. 533–570). New York: Wiley.

Bazovsky, I. (1961). *Reliability: Theory and Practice.* Englewood Cliffs, NJ: Prentice Hall.

Beatty, J. (1982). Task-evoked pupillary responses, processing load, and the structure of processing resources. *Psychological Bulletin, 91,* 276–292.

Beck, J. (1966). Effects of orientation and of shape similarity on perceptual grouping. *Perception & Psychophysics, 1,* 300–302.

Becker, A. B., Warm, J. S., Dember, W. N., & Hancock, P. A. (1991). Effects of feedback on perceived workload in vigilance performance. In *Proceedings of the Human Factors Society 35th Annual Meeting* (Vol. 2, pp. 1491–1494). Santa Monica, CA: Human Factors Society.

Békésy, G., von (1960). *Experiments in Hearing.* New York: McGraw-Hill.

Bell, P. A. (1978). Effects of heat and noise stress on primary and subsidiary task performance. *Human Factors, 20,* 749–752.

Bennett, C. A. (1971). Toward empirical, practicable, comprehensive task taxonomy. *Human Factors, 13,* 229–235.

Beranek, L. L., Blazier, W. E., & Figwer, J. J. (1971). Preferred noise criterion (PNC) curves and their application to rooms. *Journal of the Acoustical Society of America, 50,* 1223–1228.

Berglund, M. B. (1991). Quality assurance in environmental psychophysics. In S. J. Bolanowski, Jr., & G. A. Gescheider (eds.), *Ratio Scaling of Psychological Magnitude* (pp. 140–162). Hillsdale, NJ: Lawrence Erlbaum.

Berglund, B., Berglund, U., & Lindvall, T. (1974). A psychological detection method in environmental research. *Environmental Research, 1,* 342–352.

Bergman, M., Blumenfeld, V. G., Cascardo, D., Dash, B., Levitt, H., & Margulies, M. K. (1976). Age-related decrement in hearing for speech: Sampling and longitudinal studies. *Journal of Gerontology, 31,* 533–538.

Beringer, D. B., Williges, R. C., & Roscoe, S. N. (1975). The transition of experienced pilots to a frequency-separated aircraft attitude display. *Human Factors, 17,* 401–414.

Berkowitz, P., & Casali, S. P. (1990). Influence of age on the ability to hear telephone ringers of different spectral content. In *Proceedings of the Human Factors Society 34th Annual Meeting* (Vol. 1, pp. 132–136). Santa Monica, CA: Human Factors Society.

Berliner, C., Angell, D., & Shearer, J. (1964). Behaviors, measures and instruments for performance evaluation in simulated environments. Paper presented at a Symposium and Workshop on Quantification of Human Performance, Albuquerque, NM.

Berlyne, D. E. (1957). Conflict and choice time. *British Journal of Psychology, 48,* 106–118.

Bernstein, I. H., Proctor, J. D., Proctor, R. W., & Schurman, D. L. (1973). Metacontrast and brightness discrimination. *Perception & Psychophysics, 14,* 293–297.

Bernstein, N. (1967). *The Coordination and Regulation of Movements.* Elmsford, NY: Pergamon Press.

Beveridge, M., & Parkins, E. (1987). Visual representation in analogical problem solving. *Memory & Cognition, 15,* 230–234.

Biederman, I., Glass, A. L., & Stacy, E. W., Jr. (1973). Searching for objects in real-world scenes. *Journal of Experimental Psychology, 97,* 22–27.

Biederman, I., Mezzanotte, R. J., Rabinowitz, J. C., Francolini, C. M., & Plude, D. (1981). Detecting the unexpected in photo interpretation. *Human Factors, 23,* 153–164.

Biehal, G., & Chakravarti, D. (1989). The effects of concurrent verbalization on choice processing. *Journal of Marketing Research, 26,* 84–96.

Bizzi, E., & Abend, W. (1983). Posture control and trajectory formation in single- and multi-joint arm movements. In J. E. Desmedt (ed.), *Motor Control Mechanisms in Health and Disease* (pp. 31–45). New York: Raven Press. Cambridge, MA: MIT Press.

Bizzi, E., & Mussa-Ivaldi, F. A. (1989). Geometrical and mechanical issues in movement planning and control. In M. I. Posner (ed.), *Foundations of Cognitive Science* (pp. 769–792). Cambridge, MA: MIT Press.

Blair, S. M. (1991). The Antarctic experience. In A. A. Harrison, Y. A. Clearwater, & C. P. McKay (eds.), *From Anatarctica to Outer Space: Life in Isolation and Confinement* (pp. 57–64). New York: Springer-Verlag.

Bliss, J. C., Crane, H. D., Mansfield, P. K., & Townsend, J. T. (1966). Information available in brief tactile presentations. *Perception & Psychophysics, 1,* 273–283.

Boersema, T., Zwaga, H. J. G., & Adams, A. S. (1989). Conspicuity in realistic scenes: An eye-movement measure. *Applied Ergonomics, 20,* 267–273.

Boff, K. R., & Lincoln, J. E. (1988). *Engineering Data Compendium: Human Perception and Performance.* Wright-Patterson AFB, OH: Harry G. Armstrong Medical Research Laboratory.

Boles, D. B., & Wickens, C. D. (1987). Display formatting in information integration and nonintegration tasks. *Human Factors, 29,* 395–496.

Bongers, P. M., Hulshof, C. T. J., Dijkstra, L., Boshuizen, H. C., Groenhout, H. J. M., Valken, E. (1990). Back pain and exposure to whole body vibration in helicopter pilots. *Ergonomics, 33,* 1007–1026.

Borelli, G. A. (1679/1989). *On the Movement of Animals* (P. Maquet, trans.). New York: Springer-Verlag.

Boring, E. G. (1942). *Sensation and Perception in the History of Experimental Psychology.* New York: Appleton-Century-Crofts.

Bousfield, W. A. (1953). The occurrence of clustering in recall of randomly arranged associates. *Journal of General Psychology, 49,* 229–240.

Bower, G. H., Clark, M. C., Lesgold, A. M., & Winzenz, D. (1969). Hierarchical retrieval schemes in recall of categorized word lists. *Journal of Verbal Learning and Verbal Behavior, 8,* 323–343.

Bower, G. H., & Hilgard, E. R. (1981). *Theories of Learning,* 5th ed. Englewood Cliffs, NJ: Prentice Hall.

Boyce, P. R. (1981). *Human Factors in Lighting.* New York: Macmillan.

Bradley, J. V. (1967). Tactual coding of cylindrical knobs. *Human Factors, 9,* 483–496.

Bradley, J. V. (1969a). Desirable dimensions for concentric controls. *Human Factors, 11,* 213–226.

Bradley, J. V. (1969b). Optimum knob crowding. *Human Factors, 11,* 227–238.

Bradley, J. V., & Wallis, R. A. (1958). Spacing of on–off controls. 1: Pushbuttons (WADC-TR 58-2). Wright-Patterson AFB, OH: Wright Air Development Center.

Bradley, J. V., & Wallis, R. A. (1960). Spacing of toggle switch on–off controls. *Engineering Psychology and Industrial Psychology, 2,* 8–19.

Bramel, D., & Friend, R. (1981). Hawthorne, the myth of the docile worker, and class bias in psychology. *American Psychologist, 36,* 867–878.

Bransford, J. D., Barclay, J. R., & Franks, J. J. (1972). Sentence memory: A constructive versus interpretive approach. *Cognitive Psychology, 3,* 193–209.

Bransford, J. D., & Johnson, M. K. (1972). Contextual prerequisites for understanding: Some investigations of comprehension and recall. *Journal of Verbal Learning and Verbal Behavior, 11,* 717–726.

Brauninger, U., Grandjean, E., van der Heiden, G, Nishiyama, K., & Gierer, R. (1984). Lighting characteristics of VDTs from an ergonomic point of view. In E. Grandjean (ed.), *Ergonomics and Health in Modern Offices* (pp. 383–390). London: Taylor & Francis.

Brebner, J., Shephard, M., & Cairney, P. T. (1972). Spatial relationships and S–R compatibility, *Acta Psychologica, 36,* 1–15.

Bregman, A. S., & Rudnicky, A. I. (1975). Auditory segregation: Stream or streams? *Journal of Experimental Psychology: Human Perception and Performance, 1,* 263–267.

Breitmeyer, B. G., & Ganz, L. (1976). Implications of sustained and transient channels for theories of visual pattern masking, saccadic suppression, and information processing. *Psychological Review, 83,* 1–36.

Brenner, M., & Cash, J. R. (1991). Speech analysis as an index of alcohol intoxication—The Exxon Valdez accident. *Aviation, Space, and Environmental Medicine, 20,* 893–898

Brewer, W. F., & Lichtenstein, E. H. (1981). Event schemas, story schemas, and story grammars. In J. L. Long & A. Baddeley (eds.), *Attention and Performance IX* (pp. 363–379). Hillsdale, NJ: Lawrence Erlbaum.

Bridgeman, B. (1988). *The Biology of Behavior and Mind.* New York: Wiley.

Bridgeman, B., & Delgado, D. (1984). Sensory effects of eyepress are due to efference. *Perception & Psychophysics, 36,* 482–484.

Brinkman, C., & Porter, R. (1983). Supplementary motor area and premotor area of monkey cerebral cortex: Functional organization and activities of single neurons during performance of a learned movement. In J. E. Desmedt (ed.), *Motor Control Mechanisms in Health and Disease* (pp. 393–420). New York: Raven Press.

Broadbent, D. E. (1958). *Perception and Communication.* Elmsford, NY: Pergamon Press.

Broadbent, D. E., & Gregory, M. (1965). Effects of noise and of signal rate upon vigilance analyzed by means of decision theory. *Human Factors, 7,* 155–162.

Brookes, M. J., & Kaplan, A. (1972). The office environment: Space planning and affective behavior. *Human Factors, 14,* 373–391.

Brooks, L. R. (1968). Spatial and verbal components of the act of recall. *Canadian Journal of Psychology, 22,* 349–368.

Brown, C. R., & Schaum, D. L. (1980). User-adjusted VDU parameters. In E. Grandjean & F. Vigliani (eds.), *Ergonomic Aspects of Visual Display Terminals* (pp. 195–200). London: Taylor & Francis.

Brown, J. (1958). Some tests of the decay theory of immediate memory. *Quarterly Journal of Experimental Psychology, 10,* 12–21.

Brown, J. L. (1965). Flicker and intermittent stimulation. In C. H. Graham (ed.), *Vision and Visual Perception* (pp. 251–320). New York: Wiley.

Brown, O., Jr. (1986). Participatory ergonomics: Historical perspectives, trends and effectiveness of QWL programs. In O. Brown, Jr., & H. W. Hendrick (eds.), *Human Factors in Organizational Design and Management II* (pp. 433–437). Amsterdam: North-Holland.

Brown, O., Jr. (1990). Macroergonomics: A review. In K. Noro & O. Brown, Jr. (eds.), *Human Factors in Organizational Design and Management III* (pp. 15–20). Amsterdam: North-Holland.

Browne, R. C. (1949). The day and night performance of teleprinter switchboard operators. *Journal of Occupational Psychology, 23,* 121–126.

Bryan, W. L. (1892). On the development of voluntary motor ability. *American Journal of Psychology, 5,* 125–204.

Bryan, W. L., & Harter, N. (1899). Studies of the telegraphic language. The acquisition of a hierarchy of habits. *Psychological Review, 6,* 345–375.

Buchanan, D., & Boddy, D. (1983). Advanced technology and the quality of working life: The effects of computerized controls on biscuit-making operators. *Journal of Occupational Psychology, 56,* 109–119.

Bullinger, H.-J., Kern, P., & Muntzinger, W. F. (1987). Design of controls. In G. Salvendy (ed.), *Handbook of Human Factors* (pp. 577–600). New York: Wiley.

Burrill, C., & Ellsworth, L. (1980). *Modern Project Management: Foundations for Quality and Productivity.* Tenafly, NJ: Burrill-Ellsworth.

Caelli, T., & Porter, D. (1980). On difficulties in localizing ambulance sirens. *Human Factors, 22,* 719–724.

Campbell, F. W., & Robson, J. G. (1968). Application of Fourier analysis to the visibility of gratings. *Journal of Physiology, 197,* 551–566.

Campbell, F. W., & Westheimer, G. (1960). Dynamics of accommodation responses in the human eye. *Journal of Physiology, 151,* 285–295.

Card, S. K., English, W., & Burr, B. (1978). Evaluation of mouse, rate-controlled isometric joystick, step keys, and text keys for text selection on a CRT. *Ergonomics, 21,* 601–613.

Card, S. K., Moran, T. P., & Newell, A. (1983). *The Psychology of Human–Computer Interaction.* Hillsdale, NJ: Lawrence Erlbaum.

Carlton, L. G. (1992). Visual processing in aimed movements. In D. Elliott & L. Proteau (eds.), *Vision and Motor Control* (pp. 3–31). Amsterdam: North-Holland.

Carpenter, R. H. S., & Blakemore, C. (1973). Interactions between orientations in human vision. *Experimental Brain Research, 18,* 287–303.

Carroll, J. M. (ed.) (1987). *Interfacing Thought: Cognitive Aspects of Human–Computer Interaction.* Cambridge, MA: MIT Press.

Carroll, J. M., & Carrithers, C. (1984). Training wheels in a user interface. *Communications of the ACM, 27,* 800–806.

Carroll, J. M., Mack, R. L., & Kellog, W. A. (1988). Interface metaphors and the user interface design. In M. Helander (ed.), *Handbook of Human–Computer Interaction* (pp. 67–85). Amsterdam: North-Holland.

Carroll, J. M., & Olson, J. R. (eds.) (1987). *Mental Models in Human–Computer Interaction: Research Issues about What the User of Software Knows.* Washington, DC: National Academy Press.

Carroll, W. R., & Bandura, A. (1982). The role of visual monitoring in observational learning of action patterns: Making the unobservable observable. *Journal of Motor Behavior, 14,* 153–167.

Carroll, W. R., & Bandura, A. (1985). Role of timing of visual monitoring and motor rehearsal in observational learning of action patterns. *Journal of Motor Behavior, 17,* 269–281.

Carroll, W. R., & Bandura, A. (1987). Translating cognition into action: The role of visual guidance in observational learning of action patterns. *Journal of Motor Behavior, 19,* 385–398.

Carroll, W. R., & Bandura, A. (1990). Representational guidance of action production in observational learning: A causal analysis. *Journal of Motor Behavior, 22,* 85–97.

Carron, A. V. (1969). Performance and learning in a discrete motor task under massed versus distributed practice. *Research Quarterly, 40,* 481–489.

Carron, A. V. (1972). Motor performance and learning under physical fatigue. *Medicine and Science in Sports, 4,* 101–106.

Casali, S. P., Williges, B. H., & Dryden, R. D. (1990). Effects of recognition accuracy and vocabulary size of a speech recognition system on task performance and user acceptance. *Human Factors, 32,* 183–196.

Casey, S. M. (1989). Anthropometry of farm equipment operators. *Human Factors Society Bulletin, 32* (7), 1–3.

Casey, S. M., & Kiso, J. L. (1990). The acceptability of control locations and related features in agricultural tractor cabs. In *Proceedings of the Human Factors Society 34th Annual Meeting* (pp. 743–747). Santa Monica, CA: Human Factors Society.

Catrambone, R., & Carroll, J. M. (1987). Learning a word-processing system with training wheels and guided exploration. In *Proceedings of CHI+GI 1987* (pp. 169–174). New York: Association for Computing Machinery.

Cattell, J. M. (1886). The time it takes to see and name objects. *Mind, 11,* 63–65.

Cavallo, V., & Laurent, M. (1988). Visual information and skill level in time-to-collision estimation. *Perception, 17,* 622–632.

Cavanagh, J. P. (1972). Relation between immediate memory span and the memory search rate. *Psychological Review, 79,* 525–530.

Cederqvist, T., Lindberg, M., Magnussen, B., & Ortengren, R. (1990). Influence of cordless rechargeable screwdrivers on upper extremity work load in electrical installation work. In C. M. Haselgrave, J. R. Wilson, E. N. Corlett, & I. Manenica (eds.), *Work Design in Practice* (pp. 51–59). London: Taylor & Francis.

Chaffin, D. B. (1973). Localized muscle fatigue—definition and measurement. *Journal of Occupational Measurement, 15,* 346–334.

Chaffin, D. B. (1987). Biomechanical aspects of workplace design. In G. Salvendy (ed.), *Handbook of Human Factors* (pp. 601–619). New York: Wiley.

Chaffin, D. B., & Andersson, G. B. J. (1984). *Occupational Biomechanics.* New York: Wiley.

Chaffin, D. B., Andres, R. O., & Garg, A. (1983). Volitional postures during maximal push/pull exertions in the sagittal plane. *Human Factors, 25,* 541–550.

Chapanis, A., Garner, W. R., & Morgan, C. T. (1949). *Applied Experimental Psychology: Human Factors in Engineering Design.* New York: Wiley.

Chapanis, A., & Kinkade, R. G. (1972). Design of controls. In H. P. Van Cott & R. G. Kinkade (eds.), *Human Engineering Guide to Equipment Design* (pp. 345–379). Washington, DC: U.S. Superintendent of Documents.

Chapanis, A., & Lindenbaum, L. E. (1959). A reaction time study of four control-display linkages. *Human Factors, 1,* 1–7.

Chapanis, A., & Moulden, J. V. (1990). Short-term memory for numbers. *Human Factors, 32,* 123–138.

Chapanis, A., Parrish, R. N., Ochsman, R. B., & Weeks, G. D. (1977). Studies in interactive communication: II. The effects of four communication modes on the linguistic performance of teams during cooperative problem solving. *Human Factors, 19,* 101–126.

Chase, W. G. (1983). Spatial representations of taxi drivers. In D. R. Rogers & J. H. Sloboda (eds.), *Acquisition of Symbolic Skills* (pp. 391–405). New York: Plenum.

Chase, W. G., & Ericsson, K. A. (1981). Skilled memory. In J. R. Anderson (ed.), *Cognitive Skills and Their Acquisition* (pp. 141–189). Hillsdale, NJ: Lawrence Erlbaum.

Chase, W. G., & Simon, H. A. (1973). Perception in chess. *Cognitive Psychology, 4,* 55–81.

Chatterjee, D. S. (1987). Repetition strain injury—A recent review. *Journal of the Society of Occupational Medicine, 37,* 100–105.

Cheng, P. W., & Holyoak, K. J. (1985). Pragmatic reasoning schemas. *Cognitive Psychology, 17,* 391–416.

Cheng, P. W., Holyoak, K. J., Nisbett, R. E., & Oliver, L. M. (1986). Pragmatic versus syntactic approaches to training deductive reasoning. *Cognitive Psychology, 18,* 293–328.

Cherry, E. C. (1953). Some experiments on the recognition of speech, with one and with two ears. *Journal of the Acoustical Society of America, 25,* 975–979.

Cherry, E. C., & Taylor, W. K. (1954). Some further experiments on the recognition of speech with one and two ears. *Journal of the Acoustical Society of America, 26,* 554–559.

Cheung, B. S. K., Howard, I. P., & Money, K. E. (1991). Visually induced sickness in normal and bilaterally labyrinthine-defective subjects. *Aviation, Space, and Environmental Medicine, 62,* 527–531.

Chi, M. T. H., Feltovich, P. J., & Glaser, R. (1981). Categorization and representation of physics problems by experts and novices. *Cognitive Science, 5,* 121–125.

Chignell, M. H., & Peterson, J. G. (1988). Strategic issues in knowledge engineering. *Human Factors, 30,* 381–394.

Christ, R. E. (1975). Review and analysis of color coding research for visual displays. *Human Factors, 17,* 542–570.

Christ, R. E., & Corso, G. M. (1983). The effects of extended practice on the evaluation of visual display codes. *Human Factors, 25,* 71–84.

Christensen, J. M., Topmiller, D. A., & Gill, R. T. (1988). Human factors definitions revisited. *Human Factors Society Bulletin, 31* (10), 7–8.

Cicerone, C. M., & Nerger, J. L. (1989). The density of cones in the fovea centralis of the human dichromat. *Vision Research, 24,* 1587–1595.

Clark, C. D., & Hogben, J. H. (1991). Visible persistence following a brief increment in stimulus luminance. *Perception & Psychophysics, 49,* 212–226.

Clark, H. H., & Clark, E. V. (1968). Semantic distinctions and memory for complex sentences. *Quarterly Journal of Experimental Psychology, 20,* 129–138.

Clark, T. S., & Corlett, E. N. (1984). *The Ergonomics of Workspaces and Machines: A Design Manual.* London: Taylor & Francis.

Cline, D., Hofstetter, H. W., & Griffin, J. R. (1989). *Dictionary of Visual Science,* 4th ed. Radnor, PA: Chilton.

Cohen, J. D., Dunbar, K., & McClelland, J. L. (1990). On the control of automatic processes: A parallel distributed processing account of the Stroop effect. *Psychological Review, 97,* 332–361.

Colavita, F. B. (1974). Human sensory dominance. *Perception & Psychophysics, 16,* 409–412.

Coles, M. G. H., Gratton, G., Bashore, T. R., Eriksen, C. W., & Donchin, E. (1985). A psychophysiological investigation of the continuous flow model of human information processing. *Journal of Experimental Psychology: Human Perception and Performance, 11,* 529–553.

Colley, A. M., & Beech, J. R. (1989). Acquiring and performing cognitive skills. In A. M. Colley & J. R. Beech (eds.), *Acquisition and Performance of Cognitive Skills* (pp. 1–16). New York: Wiley.

Collins, A. M., & Loftus, E. F. (1975). A spreading-activation theory of semantic memory. *Psychological Review, 82,* 407–428.

Colquhoun, W. P. (1971). *Biological Rhythms and Human Performance.* New York: Academic Press.

Colquhoun, W. P., Blake, M. J. F., & Edwards, R. S. (1968). Experimental studies of shift-work II: Stabilized eight-hour shift systems. *Ergonomics, 11,* 527–546.

Coltheart, M. (1980). Iconic memory and visible persistence. *Perception & Psychophysics, 27,* 183–228.

Coltheart, M., & Freeman, R. (1974). Case alternation impairs word recognition. *Bulletin of the Psychonomic Society, 3,* 102–104.

Connelly, E. M. (1984). Transformations of software and code may lead to reduced errors. *Interact '84: First IFIP conference on human–computer interaction.* Amsterdam: Elsevier.

Conrad, R. (1964). Acoustic confusion in immediate memory. *British Journal of Psychology, 55,* 75–84.

Conrad, R., & Hull, A. J. (1968). The preferred layout for numerical data-entry keysets. *Ergonomics, 11,* 165–173.

Cook, N. L. (1989). The applicability of verbal mnemonics for different populations: A review. *Applied Cognitive Psychology, 3,* 3–22.

Cooper, G. E., & Harper, R. P., Jr. (1969). *The Use of Pilot Rating in the Evaluation of Aircraft Handling Qualities* (NASA TN-D-5153). Washington, DC: National Aeronautics and Space Administration.

Cooper, J. M., & Glassow, R. B. (1972). *Kinesiology,* 3rd ed. St. Louis, MO: C. V. Mosby.

Cooper, W. E. (1983). Introduction. In W. E. Cooper (ed.), *Cognitive Aspects of Skilled Typewriting* (pp. 1–38). New York: Springer-Verlag.

Corballis, M. C., Kirby, J., & Miller, A. (1972). Access to elements of a memorized list. *Journal of Experimental Psychology, 94,* 185–190.

Coren, S., & Girgus, J. S. (1978). *Seeing is Deceiving: The Psychology of Visual Illusions.* Hillsdale, NJ: Lawrence Erlbaum.

Coren, S., Porac, C., & Ward, L. M. (1984). *Sensation and Perception,* 2nd ed. New York: Academic Press.

Coren, S., & Ward, L. M. (1989). *Sensation and Perception,* 3rd ed. New York: Harcourt Brace Jovanovich.

Corlett, E. N. (1988). Cost–benefit analysis of ergonomic and work design changes. In D. J. Oborne (ed.), *International Reviews of Ergonomics* (Vol. 2, pp. 85–104). London: Taylor & Francis.

Corlett, E. N. (1990). The evaluation of industrial seating. In J. R. Wilson & E. N. Corlett (eds.), *Evaluation of Human Work* (pp. 500–515). London: Taylor & Francis.

Corlett, J. (1992). The role of vision in the planning, guidance and adaptation of locomotion through the environment. In D. Elliott & L. Proteau (eds.), *Vision and Motor Control* (pp. 375–397). Amsterdam: North-Holland.

Cormier, S. M., & Hagman, J. D. (eds.) (1987). *Transfer of Learning: Contemporary Research and Applications.* New York: Academic Press.

Cotten, D. J., Thomas, J. R., Spieth, W. R., & Biasiotto, J. (1972). Temporary fatigue effects in a gross motor skill. *Journal of Motor Behavior, 4,* 217–222.

Cotton, J. L., Vollrath, D.A., Froggatt, K. L., Lengnick-Hall, M. L., & Jennings, K. R. (1988). Employee participation: Diverse forms and different outcomes. *Academy of Management Review, 13,* 8–22.

Cowan, N. (1984). On short and long auditory stores. *Psychological Bulletin, 96,* 341–370.

Craig, A. (1991). Vigilance and monitoring for multiple signals. In D. L. Damos (ed.), *Multiple-task Performance* (pp. 153–171). London: Taylor & Francis.

Craig, J. (1980). *Designing with Type,* rev. ed. New York: Watson-Guptill Publications.

Craik, F. I. M., & Lockhart, R. S. (1972). Levels of processing: A framework for memory research. *Journal of Verbal Learning and Verbal Behavior, 11,* 671–684.

Craik, F. I. M., & Tulving, E. (1975). Depth of processing and the retention of words in episodic memory. *Journal of Experimental Psychology: General, 104,* 268–294.

Crossman, E. R. F. W. (1959). A theory of the acquisition of speed-skill. *Ergonomics, 2,* 153–156.

Crossman, E. R. F. W., & Goodeve, P. J. (1983). Feedback control of hand-movement and Fitts' law. *Quarterly Journal of Experimental Psychology, 35A,* 251–278. (Originally presented at a meeting of the Experimental Psychology Society, Oxford, England, 1963)

Crowder, R. G., & Morton, J. (1969). Precategorical acoustic store (PAS). *Perception & Psychophysics, 5,* 365–373.

Cullinane, T. P. (1977). Minimizing cost and effort in performing a link analysis. *Human Factors, 19,* 151–156.

Culver, C. C., & Viano, D. C. (1990). Anthropometry of seated women during pregnancy: Defining a fetal region for crash protection research. *Human Factors, 32,* 625–636.

Cung, L. D., & Ng, T. S. (1989). DESPLATE: A diagnostic expert system for faulty plan views shapes of steel plates. In J. R. Quinlan (ed.), *Applications of Expert Systems* (Vol. 2, pp. 156–169). Reading, MA: Addison-Wesley.

Cunningham, G. (1990). Air quality. In N. C. Ruck (ed.), *Building Design and Human Performance* (pp. 29–39). New York: Van Nostrand Reinhold.

Cushman, W. H., & Crist, B. (1987). Illumination. In G. Salvendy (ed.), *Handbook of Human Factors* (pp. 670–695). New York: Wiley.

Cushman, W. H., Dunn, J. E., & Peters, K. A. (1984). Workplace luminance ratios: Do they affect subjective fatigue and performance? In *Proceedings of the Human Factors Society 28th Annual Meeting* (p. 991). Santa Monica, CA: Human Factors Society.

Cutting, J. E. (1978). Generation of synthetic male and female walkers through manipulation of a biomechanical invariant. *Perception, 7,* 393–405.

Dahlgren, K. (1988). Shiftwork scheduling and their impact upon operators in nuclear power plants. *IEEE Fourth Conference on Human Factors in Power Plants* (pp. 517–521). Piscataway, NJ: Institute of Electrical and Electronics Engineers.

Daneman, M., & Carpenter, P. A. (1980). Individual differences in working memory and reading. *Journal of Verbal Learning and Verbal Behavior, 19,* 450–466.

Darwin, C. J., Turvey, M. T., & Crowder, R. G. (1972). An auditory analogue of the Sperling partial report procedure: Evidence for brief auditory storage. *Cognitive Psychology, 3,* 255–267.

Davies, B. T., & Watt, J. M., Jr. (1969). Preliminary investigation of movement time between brake and accelerator pedals in automobiles. *Human Factors, 11,* 407–410.

Davies, D. R., & Tune, G. S. (1969). *Human Vigilance Performance.* New York: Elsevier.

Davis, L. E., & Wacker, G. J. (1987). Job design. In G. Salvendy (ed.), *Handbook of Human Factors* (pp. 431–452). New York: Wiley.

Deatherage, B. H. (1972). Auditory and other sensory forms of information presentation. In H. P. Van Cott & R. G. Kinkade (eds.), *Human Engineering Guide to Equipment Design,* rev. ed. (pp. 123–

160). Washington, DC: U.S. Government Printing Office.

Deecke, L., Scheid, P., & Kornhuber, H. H. (1969). Distribution of readiness potential, premotion positivity, and motor potential of the human cerebral cortex preceding voluntary finger movements. *Experimental Brain Research, 7,* 158–168.

de Groot, A. (1966). Perception and memory versus thought: Some old ideas and recent findings. In B. Kleinmuntz (ed.), *Problem Solving* (pp. 19–50). New York: Wiley.

Deininger, R. L. (1960). Human factors engineering studies for the design and use of pushbutton telephone sets. *Bell Systems Technical Journal, 39,* 995–1012.

Deivanayagam, S. (1982). Anthropometry of mentally and physically handicapped persons employed in productive occupations. In R. Easterby, K. H. E. Kroemer, & D. B. Chaffin (eds.), *Anthropometry and Biomechanics: Theory and Application* (pp. 67–70). New York: Plenum.

De Jong, R., Coles, M. G. H., Logan, G. D., & Gratton, G. (1990). In search of the point of no return: The control of response processes. *Journal of Experimental Psychology: Human Perception and Performance, 16,* 164–182.

de Lange, H. (1958). Research into the dynamic nature of human fovea–cortex systems with intermittent and modulated light. I. Attenuation characteristics with white and colored light. *Journal of the Optical Society of America, 48,* 777–784.

Delleman, N. J., & Dul, J. (1990). Ergonomic guidelines for adjustment and redesign of sewing machine workplaces. In C. M. Haslegrave, J. R. Wilson, E. N. Corlett, & I. Manenica (eds.), *Work Design in Practice* (pp. 155–160). London: Taylor & Francis.

Dellis, E. (1988). Automotive head-up displays: Just around the corner. *Automotive Engineering, 96,* 107–110.

DeMonasterio, F. M. (1978). Center and surround mechanisms of opponent-color X and Y ganglion cells of retina of macaques. *Journal of Neurophysiology, 41,* 1418–1434.

Deutsch, J. A., & Deutsch, D. (1963). Attention: Some theoretical considerations. *Psychological Review, 70,* 80–90.

De Valois, R. L., & De Valois, K. K. (1980). Spatial vision. *Annual Review of Psychology, 31,* 309–341.

Dixon, P. (1982). Plans and written directions for complex tasks. *Journal of Verbal Learning and Verbal Behavior, 21,* 70–84.

Dixon, P., & Gabrys, G. (1991). Learning to operate complex devices: Effects of conceptual and operational similarity. *Human Factors, 33,* 103–120.

Donchin, E. (1981). Event-related brain potentials: A tool in the study of human information processing. In H. Begleiter (ed.), *Evoked Potentials in Psychiatry.* New York: Plenum.

Donders, F. C. (1868/1969). On the speed of mental processes (W. G. Koster, trans.). *Acta Psychologica, 30,* 412–431.

Dougherty, D. J., Emery, J. H., & Curtin, J. G. (1964). *Comparison of Perceptual Workload in Flying Standard Instrumentation and the Contact Analogy Vertical Display* (JANAIR-D278–421–019). Fort Worth, TX: Bell Helicopter Co. (DTIC NO. 610617).

Dougherty, E. M., & Fragola, J. R. (1988). *Human Reliability Analysis.* New York: Wiley.

Dowling, J. E., & Boycott, B. B. (1966). Organization of the primate retina: Electron microscopy. *Proceedings of the Royal Society (London), Series B, 166,* 80–111.

Draper, J. V., Handel, S., & Hood, C. C. (1990). Fitts' task by teleoperator: Movement time, velocity, and acceleration. In *Proceedings of the Human Factors Society 34th Annual Meeting* (pp. 127–131). Santa Monica, CA: Human Factors Society.

Drillis, R. J. (1963). Folk norms and biomechanics. *Human Factors, 5,* 427–441.

Druckman, D., & Bjork, R. A. (eds.) (1991). *In the Mind's Eye: Enhancing Human Performance.* Washington, DC: National Academy Press.

Druckman, D., & Swets, J. A. (eds.) (1988). *Enhancing Human Performance: Issues, Theories, and Techniques.* Washington, DC: National Academy Press.

Drury, C. (1975). Application of Fitts' law to foot-pedal design. *Human Factors, 17,* 368–373.

Drury, C. G., & Coury, B. G. (1982). Container and handle design for manual handling. In R. Easterby, K. H. E. Kroemer, & D. B. Chaffin (eds.), *Anthropometry and Biomechanics: Theory and Application* (pp. 259–268). New York: Plenum.

Dumesnil, C. D. (1987). Office case study: Social behavior in relation to the design of the environment. *Journal of Architectural and Planning Research, 4,* 7–13.

Duncan, J. (1977). Response selection rules in spatial choice reaction tasks. In S. Dornic (ed.), *Attention and Performance IV* (pp. 49–61). Hillsdale, NJ: Erlbaum.

Duncan, J. (1980). The locus of interference in the perception of simultaneous stimuli. *Psychological Review, 87,* 272–300.

Duncan-Johnson, C. C., & Donchin, E. (1977). On quantifying surprise: The variation in event-related potentials with subjective probability. *Psychophysiology, 14,* 456–467.

Duncker, K. (1945). On problem solving. *Psychological Monographs, 58* (whole No. 270).

Dutta, A., & Proctor, R. W. (1992). Persistence of stimulus–response compatibility effects with extended practice. *Journal of Experimental Psychology: Learning, Memory, and Cognition, 18,* 801–809.

Dvorak, A. (1943). There is a better typewriter keyboard. *National Business Education Quarterly, 12,* 51–58.

Easterbrook, J. A. (1959). The effect of emotion on cue utilization and the organization of behavior. *Psychological Review, 66,* 183–201.

Easterby, R. S. (1967). Perceptual organization in static displays for man/machine systems. *Ergonomics, 10,* 193–205.

Easterby, R. S. (1970). The perception of symbols for machine displays. *Ergonomics, 13,* 149–158.

Eastman Kodak Company (1983). *Ergonomic Design for People at Work,* Vol. 1. New York: Van Nostrand Reinhold.

Eastman Kodak Company (1986). *Ergonomic Design for People at Work,* Vol. 2. New York: Van Nostrand Reinhold.

Ebbinghaus, H. (1885/1964). *Memory* (H. A. Ruger & C. E. Bussenius, trans.). New York: Dover.

Eberts, R., Lang, G. T., & Gabel, M. (1987). Expert/novice differences in designing with a CAD system. *Proceedings of 1987 IEEE Conference on Systems, Man, and Cybernetics* (pp. 985–989). New York: Institute of Electrical and Electronics Engineers.

Eberts, R. E., & MacMillan, A. G. (1985). Misperception of small cars. In R. E. Eberts & C. G. Eberts (eds.), *Trends in Ergonomics/Human Factors II* (pp. 33–39). Amsterdam: North-Holland.

Eberts, R. E., & Posey, J. W. (1990). The mental model in stimulus-response compatibility. In R. W. Proctor & T. G. Reeve (eds.), *Stimulus–Response Compatibility: An Integrated Perspective* (pp. 389–425). Amsterdam: North-Holland.

Eberts, R. E., & Schneider, W. (1985). Internalizing the system dynamics for a second order system. *Human Factors, 27,* 371–393.

Egan, J. P., Carterette, E. C., & Thwing, E. J. (1954). Some factors affecting multichannel listening. *Journal of the Acoustical Society of America, 26,* 774–782.

Eggemeier, F. T. (1988). Properties of workload assessment techniques. In P. A. Hancock & N. Meshkati (eds.), *Human Mental Workload* (pp. 41–62). Amsterdam: North-Holland.

Eggleston, R. G., & Quinn, T. J. (1984). A preliminary evaluation of a projective workload assessment procedure. In *Proceedings of the Human Factors Society 28th Annual Meeting* (pp. 695–699). Santa Monica, CA: Human Factors Society.

Ehrlich, K., & Soloway, E. (1984). An empirical investigation of the tacit plan knowledge in programming. In J. C. Thomas & M. Schneider (eds.), *Human Factors in Computer Systems* (pp. 113–133). Norwood, NJ: Ablex.

Eimas, P. D., & Corbit, J. D. (1973). Selective adaptation of linguistic feature detectors. *Cognitive Psychology, 4,* 99–109.

Einstein, G. O., & Hunt, R. R. (1980). Levels of processing and organization: Additive effects of individual-item and relational processing. *Journal of Experimental Psychology: Human Learning and Memory, 6,* 588–598.

Eklund, J. A. E., & Corlett, E. N. (1986). Experimental and biomechical analysis of seating. In N. Corlett, J. W. Wilson, & I. Manenica (eds.), *The Ergonomics of Working Postures* (pp. 319–330). London: Taylor & Francis.

Elkerton, J. (1988). Online aiding for human–computer interfaces. In M. Helander (ed.), *Handbook of Human–Computer Interaction* (pp. 354–364). Amsterdam: North-Holland.

Elkind, J. I., Card, S. K., Hochberg, J., & Huey, B. M. (eds.) (1989). *Human Performance Models for Computer-aided Engineering.* Washington, DC: National Academy Press.

Ells, J. G., & Dewar, R. E. (1979). Rapid comprehension of verbal and symbolic traffic sign messages. *Human Factors, 21,* 161–168.

Emery, F. E., & Trist, E. L. (1960). Sociotechnical systems. In C. W. Churchman & M. Verhulst (eds.), *Management Science: Models and Techniques II*. Elmsford, NY: Pergamon Press.

English, H. B. (1942). How psychology can facilitate military training—A concrete example. *Journal of Applied Psychology, 26*, 3–7.

Epstein, W., Park, J., & Casey, A. (1961). The current status of the size–distance hypothesis. *Psychological Bulletin, 58*, 491–514.

Ericsson, K. A., & Polson, P. G. (1988). A cognitive analysis of exceptional memory for restaurant orders. In M. T. H. Chi, R. Glaser, & M. J. Farr (eds.), *The Nature of Expertise* (pp. 23–70). Hillsdale, NJ: Lawrence Erlbaum.

Ericsson, K. A., & Simon, H. A. (1980). Verbal reports as data. *Psychological Review, 87*, 215–251.

Ericsson, K. A., & Simon, H. A. (1984). *Protocol Analysis: Verbal Reports as Data*. Cambridge, MA: MIT Press.

Eriksen, B. A., & Eriksen, C. W. (1974). Effects of noise letters upon the identification of a target letter in a nonsearch task. *Perception & Psychophysics, 16*, 143–149.

Eriksen, C. W., & Schultz, D. W. (1978). Temporal factors in visual information processing: A tutorial review. In J. Requin (ed.), *Attention and Performance VII* (pp. 3–23). Hillsdale, NJ: Lawrence Erlbaum.

Eriksen, C. W., & Schultz, D. W. (1979). Information processing in visual search: A continous flow conception and experimental results. *Perception & Psychophysics, 25*, 249–263.

Eriksen, C. W., & St. James, J. D. (1986). Visual attention within and around the field of focal attention: A zoom lens model. *Perception & Psychophysics, 40*, 225–240.

Estes, W. K. (1972). An associative basis for coding and organization in memory. In A. W. Melton & E. Martin (eds.), *Coding Processes in Human Memory* (pp. 161–190). Washington, DC: Winston.

Estes, W. K. (1986). Array models for category learning. *Cognitive Psychology, 18*, 500–549.

Evans, D. W., & Ginsburg, A. P. (1982). Predicting age-related differences in discriminating road signs using contrast sensitivity. *Journal of the Optical Society of America, 72*, 1785–1786.

Evans, J. St. B. T. (1989). *Bias in Human Reasoning: Causes and Consequences*. Hillsdale, NJ: Lawrence Erlbaum.

Eysenck, M. W. (1979). Depth, elaboration, and distinctiveness. In L. S. Cermak & F. I. M. Craik (eds.), *Levels of Processing in Human Memory* (pp. 89–118). Hillsdale, NJ: Lawrence Erlbaum.

Fanger, P. O. (1977). Local discomfort to the human body caused by nonuniform thermal environments. *Annals of Occupational Hygiene, 20*, 285–291.

Fechner, G. T. (1860/1966). *Elements of Psychophysics*, Vol. 1 (E. G. Boring & D. H. Howes, eds.; H. E. Adler, trans.). New York: Holt, Rinehart and Winston.

Fein, A., & Szuts, E. Z. (1982). *Photoreceptors: Their Role in Vision*. New York: Cambridge University Press.

Fel'dman, A. G. (1966). Functional tuning of the nervous system during control of movement or maintenance of steady posture. III. Mechanographic analysis of the execution by man of the simplest motor task. *Biophysics, 11*, 766–775.

Feltz, D., & Landers, D. M. (1983). The effects of mental practice on motor skill learning and performance: A meta-analysis. *Journal of Sport Psychology, 5*, 25–57.

Fenn, W. D. (1938). The mechanics of muscular contraction in man. *Journal of Applied Physics, 9*, 165–177.

Fine, S. A. (1974). Functional job analysis: An approach to a technology for manpower planning. *Personnel Journal, 53*, 813–818.

Fischman, M. G., & Schneider, T. (1985). Skill level, vision, and proprioception in simple one-hand catching. *Journal of Motor Behavior, 18*, 497–501.

Fisher, D. L., Coury, B. G., Tengs, T. O., & Duffy, S. A. (1989). Minimizing the time to search visual displays: The role of highlighting. *Human Factors, 31*, 167–182.

Fisher, D. L., & Tan, K. C. (1989). Visual displays: The highlighting paradox. *Human Factors, 31*, 17–30.

Fisher, D. L., Yungkurth, E. J., & Moss, S. M. (1990). Optimal menu hierarchy design: Syntax and semantics. *Human Factors, 32*, 665–683.

Fitts, P. M. (1954). The information capacity of the human motor system in controlling the amplitude of movement. *Journal of Experimental Psychology, 47*, 381–391.

Fitts, P. M. (1964). Perceptual–motor skill learning. In A. W. Melton (ed.), *Categories of Human Learning* (pp. 243–285). New York: Academic Press.

Fitts, P. M., & Crannell, C. W. (1953). *Studies in Location Discrimination*. Wright Air Development

Center Technical Report. Wright–Patterson Air Force Base, OH: U.S. Air Force.

Fitts, P. M., & Deininger, R. L. (1954). S–R compatibility: Correspondence among paired elements within stimulus and response codes. *Journal of Experimental Psychology, 48,* 483–491.

Fitts, P. M., & Jones, R. E. (1947). *Analysis of Factors Contributing to 460 "Pilot-Error" Experiences in Operating Aircraft Controls.* Report TSEAA-694-12, Air Materiel Command, Wright Patterson Air Force Base. Reprinted in H. W. Sinaiko (ed.) (1961), *Selected Papers on Human Factors in the Design and Use of Control Systems* (pp. 332–358). New York: Dover.

Fitts, P. M., Jones, R. E., & Milton, J. L. (1950). Eye movements of aircraft pilots during instrument-landing approaches. *Aeronautical Engineering Review, 9,* 1–16.

Fitts, P. M., & Posner, M. I. (1967). *Human Performance.* Monterey, CA: Brooks/Cole.

Fitts, P. M., & Seeger, C. M. (1953). S–R compatibility: Spatial characteristics of stimulus and response codes. *Journal of Experimental Psychology, 46,* 199–210.

Fitzgerald, K. (1989). Probing Boeing's crossed connections. *IEEE Spectrum,* May, 30–35.

Flanagan, J. C. (1954). The critical incident technique. *Psychological Bulletin, 51,* 327–358.

Fleishman, E. A., & Quaintance, M. K. (1984). *Taxonomies of Human Performance: The Description of Human Tasks.* New York: Academic Press.

Fleming, R. A. (1970). The processing of conflicting information in a simulated tactical decision-making task. *Human Factors, 12,* 375–385.

Fletcher, H., & Munson, W. A. (1933). Loudness, its definition, measurement and calculation. *Journal of the Acoustical Society of America, 5,* 82–108.

Fletcher, J. L., & Riopelle, A. J. (1960). Protective effect of the acoustic reflex for impulsive noises. *Journal of the Acoustical Society of America, 32,* 401–404.

Flynn, J. E. (1977). A study of subjective responses to low energy and nonuniform lighting systems. *Lighting Design and Application, 7(2),* 6–15.

Fodor, J. A., & Garrett, M. (1967). Some syntactic determinants of sentential complexity. *Perception & Psychophysics, 2,* 289–296.

Folkard, S. (1975). Diurnal variation in logical reasoning. *British Journal of Psychology, 66,* 1–8.

Fong, G. T., Krantz, D. H., & Nisbett, R. E. (1986). The effects of statistical training on thinking about everyday problems. *Cognitive Psychology, 18,* 253–292.

Fox, R. (1978). In R. Held, H. W. Leibowitz, & H. L. Teuber (eds.), *Handbook of Sensory Physiology, Vol. 8: Perception* (pp. 629–653). New York: Springer-Verlag.

Frost, N. (1972). Encoding and retrieval in visual memory tasks. *Journal of Experimental Psychology, 95,* 317–326.

Fucigna, J. T. (1967). The ergonomics of offices. *Ergonomics, 10,* 589–604.

Galinsky, T. L., Warm, J. S., Dember, W. N., Weiler, E. M., & Scerbo, M. W. (1990). Sensory alternation and vigilance performance: The role of pathway inhibition. *Human Factors, 32,* 717–728.

Galitz, W. O. (1984). *Humanizing Office Automation: The Impact of Ergonomics on Productivity.* Wellesley, MA: QED Information Sciences.

Gallant, S. I. (1988). Connectionist expert systems. *Communications of the ACM, 31,* 152–169.

Gardin, H., Kaplan, K. J., Firestone, I., & Cowan, G. (1973). Proxemic effects on cooperation, attitude, and approach avoidance in a prisoner's dilemma game. *Journal of Personality and Social Psychology, 27,* 13–18.

Gardiner, P. C., & Edwards, W. (1975). Public values: Multiattribute utility measurement for social decision-making. In M. F. Kaplan & S. Schwartz (eds.), *Human Judgment and Decision Processes* (pp. 1–37). New York: Academic Press.

Garner, W. R. (1962). *Uncertainty and Structure as Psychological Concepts.* New York: Wiley.

Garner, W. R. (1974). *The Processing of Information and Structure.* Hillsdale, NJ: Lawrence Erlbaum.

Garner, W. R., & Clement, D. E. (1963). Goodness of pattern and pattern uncertainty. *Journal of Verbal Learning and Verbal Behavior, 2,* 446–452.

Gebotys, R. J., & Claxton-Oldfield, S. P. (1989). Errors in the quantification of uncertainty: A product of heuristics or minimal probability knowledge. *Applied Cognitive Psychology, 3,* 237–250.

Geiselman, R. E., McCloskey, B. P., Mossler, R. A., & Zielan, D. S. (1984). An empirical evaluation of mnemonic instruction for remembering names. *Human Learning, 3,* 1–7.

Gelb, A. (1929). Die "Farbenkonstanz" der Sehding. *Handbook of Normal and Pathological Physiology, 12,* 594–678.

Gentile, A. M. (1972). A working model of skill acquisition with application to teaching. *Quest, 17,* 3–23.

Gentner, D., & Stevens, A. L. (eds.) (1983). *Mental Models*. Hillsdale, NJ: Lawrence Erlbaum.

Gentner, D. R. (1983). Keystroke timing in transcription typing. In W. E. Cooper (ed.), *Cognitive Aspects of Skilled Typewriting* (pp. 95–120). New York: Springer-Verlag.

Gentner, D. R., & Grudin, J. (1990). Why good engineers (sometimes) create bad interfaces. In *Human Factors in Computing Systems: CHI '90 Conference Proceedings* (pp. 277–282). Reading, MA: Addison-Wesley.

Gentner, D. R., Larochelle, S., & Grudin, J. (1988). Lexical, sublexical, and peripheral effects in skilled typewriting. *Cognitive Psychology, 20,* 524–548.

Georgopoulos, A. P. (1990). Neurophysiology of reaching. In M. Jeannerod (ed.), *Attention and Performance XIII: Motor Representation and Control* (pp. 227–263). Hillsdale, NJ: Lawrence Erlbaum.

Gescheider, G. A. (1985). *Psychophysics: Method, Theory, and Application,* 2nd ed. Hillsdale, NJ: Lawrence Erlbaum.

Gibbs, C. B. (1962). Controller design: Interactions of controlling limbs, time-lags, and gains in positional and velocity systems. *Ergonomics, 5,* 385–402.

Gibson, J. J. (1950). *The Perception of the Visual World.* Boston: Houghton Mifflin.

Gibson, J. J. (1979). *The Ecological Approach to Visual Perception.* Boston: Houghton Mifflin.

Gick, M. L., & Holyoak, K. J. (1980). Analogical problem solving. *Cognitive Psychology, 12,* 306–355.

Gick, M. L., & Holyoak, K. J. (1983). Schema induction and analogical transfer. *Cognitive Psychology, 15,* 1–38.

Gies, J. (1991). Automating the worker. *American Heritage of Invention and Technology, 6* (3), 56–63.

Gifford, R. (1987). *Environmental Psychology: Principles and Practice.* Boston: Allyn and Bacon.

Gilbreth, F. B. (1909). *Bricklaying System.* New York: Clark.

Gilchrist, A. L. (1977). Perceived lightness depends on perceived spatial arrangement. *Science, 195,* 185–187.

Gill, N. F., & Dallenbach, K. M. (1926). A preliminary study of the range of attention. *American Journal of Psychology, 37,* 247–256.

Gillan, D. J., Burns, M. J., Nicodemus, C. L., & Smith, R. L. (1986). The space station: Human factors and productivity. *Human Factors Society Bulletin, 29* (11), 1–3.

Gillespie, R. (1991). *Manufacturing Knowledge: A History of the Hawthorne Experiments.* New York: Cambridge University Press.

Gilmore, G. C., Hersh, A., Caramazza, A., & Griffin, J. (1979). Multidimensional letter similarity derived from recognition errors. *Perception & Psychophysics, 25,* 425–431.

Ginsburg, A. P., Evans, D. W., Sekuler, R., & Harp, S. A. (1982). Contrast sensitivity predicts pilots' performance in aircraft simulators. *American Journal of Optometry and Physiological Optics, 59,* 105–108.

Glaser, R., & Chi, M. T. H. (1988). Overview. In M. T. H. Chi, R. Glaser, & M. J. Farr (eds.), *The Nature of Expertise* (pp. xv–xxviii). Hillsdale, NJ: Lawrence Erlbaum.

Glass, J. T., Zaloom, V., & Gates, D. (1991). Computer-aided link analysis (CALA). *Computers in Industry, 16,* 179–187.

Glass, S., & Suggs, C. (1977). Optimization of vehicle-brake foot pedal travel time. *Applied Ergonomics, 8,* 215–218.

Gluck, M. A., & Bower, G. H. (1988). Evaluating an adaptive network model of human learning. *Journal of Memory and Language, 27,* 166–195.

Glushko, R. J. (1991). *Hypertext: Prospects and problems for Crew System Design.* Wright-Patterson AFB, OH: Crew System Ergonomics Information Analysis Center.

Godwin, M. A., & Schmidt, R. A. (1971). Muscular fatigue and discrete motor learning. *Research Quarterly, 42,* 374–383.

Goldstein, E. B. (1989). *Sensation and Perception,* 3rd ed. Belmont, CA: Wadsworth.

Goodwin, G. M., McCloskey, D. J., & Matthews, P. B. C. (1972). The contribution of muscle afferents to kinaesthesia shown by vibration-induced illusions of movement and by the effect of paralysing joint afferents. *Brain, 95,* 705–748.

Gopher, D., & Donchin, E. (1986). Workload: An examination of the concept. In K. R. Boff, L. Kaufman, & J. P. Thomas (eds.), *Handbook of Perception and Human Performance Vol. II: Cognitive Processes and Performance* (pp. 41-1 to 41-49). New York: Wiley.

Gopher, D., & Kahneman, D. (1971). Individual differences in attention and the prediction of flight criteria. *Perceptual and Motor Skills, 33,* 1335–1342.

Gopher, D., Karis, D. & Koenig, W. (1985). The representation of movement schemas in long-term memory: Lessons from the acquisition of a transcription skill. *Acta Psychologica, 60,* 105–134.

Gordon, P. C., & Meyer, D. E. (1987). Control of serial order in rapidly spoken syllable sequences. *Journal of Memory and Language, 26,* 300–321.

Gottlieb, M. D., Kietzman, M. L., & Berenhaus, I. J. (1985). Two-pulse measures of temporal integration in the fovea and peripheral retina. *Perception & Psychophysics, 37,* 135–138.

Gottsdanker, R. (1980). The ubiquitous role of preparation. In G. E. Stelmach & J. Requin (eds.), *Tutorials in Motor Behavior* (pp. 355–371). Amsterdam: North-Holland.

Grandjean, E. (1987a). *Ergonomics in Computerized Offices.* London: Taylor & Francis.

Grandjean, E. (1987b). Design of VDT workstations. In G. Salvendy (ed.), *Handbook of Human Factors* (pp. 1361–1397). New York: Wiley.

Grandjean, E., Hunting, W., & Pidermann, M. (1983). VDT workstation design: Preferred settings and their effects. *Human Factors, 25,* 161–175.

Gratton, I., Piccoli, B., Zaniboni, A., Meroni, M., & Grieco, A. (1990). Change in visual function and viewing distance during work with VDTs. *Ergonomics, 33,* 1433–1441.

Green, D. M., & Swets, J. A. (1966). *Signal Detection Theory and Psychophysics.* New York: Wiley.

Greenberg, L., & Chaffin, D. (1977). *Workers and Their Tools: A Guide to the Ergonomic Design of Handtools and Small Presses.* Midland, MI: Pendell Publishing.

Gregory, R. L. (1966). *Eye and Brain: The Psychology of Seeing.* New York: McGraw-Hill.

Grether, W. F., & Baker, C. A. (1972). Visual presentation of information. In H. A. Van Cott & R. G. Kinkade (eds.), *Human Engineering Guide to Equipment Design,* rev. ed. (pp. 41–121). Washington, DC: U.S. Government Printing Office.

Grice, G. R. (1968). Stimulus intensity and response evocation. *Psychological Review, 75,* 359–373.

Grice, H. P. (1975). Logic and conversation. In P. Cole & J. L. Morgan (eds.), *Syntax and Semantics, Vol. 3: Speech Acts* (pp. 41–58). New York: Seminar Press.

Griffin, M. J. (1990). *Handbook of Human Vibration.* New York: Academic Press.

Griffith, R. T. (1949). The minimotion typewriter keyboard. *Journal of Franklin Institute, 248,* 399–436.

Griggs, R. A., & Cox, J. R. (1982). The elusive thematic-materials effect in Wason's selection task. *British Journal of Psychology, 73,* 407–420.

Griggs, R. A., & Newstead, S. E. (1982). The role of problem structure in deductive reasoning. *Journal of Experimental Psychology: Learning, Memory, and Cognition, 8,* 297–307.

Grillner, S. (1975). Locomotion in vertebrates: Central mechanisms and reflex interaction. *Physiological Reviews, 55,* 247–304.

Grosslight, J. H., Fletcher, H. J., Masterton, R. B., & Hagen, R. (1978). Monocular vision and landing performance in general aviation pilots: Cyclops revisited. *Human Factors, 20,* 27–33.

Grossman, L., & Eagle, M. (1970). Synonymity, antonymity, and association in false recognition responses. *Journal of Experimental Psychology, 83,* 244–248.

Guastello, S. J., Traut, M., & Korienek, G. (1989). Verbal versus pictorial representations of objects in a human–computer interface. *International Journal of Man–Machine Studies, 31,* 99–120.

Guth, S. K. (1963). A method for the evaluation of discomfort glare. *Illumination Engineering, 58,* 351.

Hall, E. T. (1959). *The Silent Language.* Garden City, NY: Doubleday.

Hall, E. T. (1966). *The Hidden Dimension.* Garden City, NY: Doubleday.

Hamburger, H., & Booker, L. D. (1989). Managing uncertainty in expert systems: Rationale, theory, and techniques. In J. Liebowitz & D. A. De Salvo (eds.), *Structuring Expert Systems: Domain Design and Development* (pp. 241–271). Englewood Cliffs, NJ: Prentice Hall (Yourdon Press).

Hammerton, M. (1989). Tracking. In D. H. Holding (ed.), *Human Skills,* 2nd ed. (pp. 171–195). New York: Wiley.

Hanisch, K. A., Kramer, A. F., & Hulin, C. L. (1991). Cognitive representations, control, and understanding of complex systems: A field study focusing on components of users' mental models and expert/novice differences. *Ergonomics, 34,* 1129–1145.

Hankey, J. M., & Dingus, T. A. (1990). A validation of SWAT as a measure of workload induced by changes in operator capacity. In *Proceedings of the Human Factors Society 34th Annual Meeting* (pp. 112–115). Santa Monica, CA: Human Factors Society.

Hannaman, G. W., Spurgin, A. J., & Lukic, Y. (1985). A model for assessing human cognitive reliability in PRA studies. In *1985 IEEE Third Conference on Human Factors and Nuclear Safety* (pp. 343–353). New York: Institute of Electrical and Electronics Engineers.

Hanne, K.-H., & Hoepelman, J. (1990). Natural language and direct manipulation interfaces for expert systems (multimodal communication). In D. Berry & A. Hart (eds.), *Expert Systems: Human Issues* (pp. 156–168). Cambridge, MA: MIT Press.

Hardiman, P. T., Dufresne, R., & Mestre, J. P. (1989). The relation between problem categorization and problem solving among experts and novices. *Memory & Cognition, 17,* 627–638.

Harmon, L. D., & Julesz, B. (1973). Masking in visual recognition: Effects of two-dimensional filtered noise. *Science, 180,* 1194–1197.

Harrigan, J. E. (1987). Architecture and interior design. In G. Salvendy (ed.), *Handbook of Human Factors* (pp. 742–764). New York: Wiley.

Harris, R., Iavecchia, H. P., & Dick, A. O. (1989). The human operator simulator (HOS-IV). In G. R. McMillan, D. Beevis, E. Salas, M. H. Strub, R. Sutton, & L. Van Breda (eds.), *Applications of Human Performance Models to System Design* (pp. 275–280). New York: Plenum.

Harrison, A. A., Clearwater, Y. A., & McKay, C. P. (eds.) (1991). *From Anatarctica to Outer Space: Life in Isolation and Confinement.* New York: Springer-Verlag.

Hart, S. G., & Staveland, L. E. (1988). Development of NASA-TLX (Task Load Index): Results of empirical and theoretical research. In P. A. Hancock & N. Meshkati (eds.), *Human Mental Workload* (pp. 139–183). Amsterdam: North-Holland.

Hasbroucq, T., & Guiard, Y. (1991). Stimulus–response compatability and the Simon effect: Toward a conceptual clarification. *Journal of Experimental Psychology: Human Perception and Performance, 17,* 246–266.

Hashim, S. H. (1990). *Exploring Hypertext Programming: Writing Knowledge Representation and Problem-solving Programs.* Blue Ridge Summit, PA: Windcrest.

Haviland, S., & Clark, H. H. (1974). What's new? Acquiring new information as a process in comprehension. *Journal of Verbal Learning and Verbal Behavior, 13,* 512–521.

Hawkins, W. H. (1990). Where does human factors fit in R&D organizations? *IEEE Aerospace and Electronic Systems Magazine, 5* (9), 31–33.

Hebb, D. O. (1961). Distinctive features of learning in the higher animal. In J. F. Delafresnaye (ed.), *Brain Mechanisms and Learning* (pp. 37–46). New York: Oxford University Press.

Hedge, A. (1988). Environmental conditions and health in offices. *International Reviews of Ergonomics, 2,* 87–110.

Hedge, A. (1991). The effects of direct and indirect office lighting on VDT workers. In *Proceedings of the Human Factors Society 35th Annual Meeting* (pp. 536–540). Santa Monica, CA: Human Factors Society.

Heise, G. A., & Miller, G. A. (1951). An experimental study of auditory patterns. *American Journal of Psychology, 64,* 68–77.

Heister, G., Schroeder-Heister, P. & Ehrenstein, W. H. (1990). Spatial coding and spatio-anatomical mapping: Evidence for a hierarchical model of spatial stimulus–response compatibility. In R. W. Proctor & T. G. Reeve (eds.), *Stimulus–Response Compatibility: An Integrated Perspective* (pp. 117–143). Amsterdam: North-Holland.

Heitman, R. J., Stockton, C. A., & Lambert, C. (1987). The effects of fatigue on motor performance and learning in mentally retarded individuals. *American Corrective Therapy Journal, 41,* 40–43.

Helander, M. G. (1985). Emerging office automation systems. *Human Factors, 27,* 3–20.

Helander, M. G. (1987). Design of visual displays. In G. Salvendy (ed.), *Handbook of Human Factors* (pp. 507–549). New York: Wiley.

Helmholtz, H. von (1852). On the theory of compound colors. *Philosophical Magazine, 4,* 519–534.

Helmholtz, H. von (1867). *Handbook of Physiological Optics,* Vol. 3. Leipzig: Voss.

Hendrick, H. W. (1987). Organizational design. In G. Salvendy (ed.), *Handbook of Human Factors* (pp. 470–494). New York: Wiley.

Hendrick, H. W. (1990). Factors affecting the adequacy of ergonomic efforts on large-scale-system development programs. *Ergonomics, 33,* 639–642.

Hendrick, H. W. (1991). Ergonomics in organizational design and management. *Ergonomics, 34,* 743–756.

Henry, F. M., & Rogers, D. E. (1960). Increased response latency for complicated movements and a "memory drum" theory of neuromotor reaction. *Research Quarterly, 31,* 448–458.

Herbart, J. F. (1816/1891). *A Textbook in Psychology: An Attempt to Found the Science of Psychology on Experience, Metaphysics, and Mathematics,* 2nd ed. (W. T. Harris, ed.; M. K. Smith, trans.). New York: Appleton.

Herman, L. M., & Kantowitz, B. H. (1970). The psychological refractory period: Only half of the double stimulation story? *Psychological Bulletin, 73,* 74–86.

Herrmann, D. J., & Petros, S. J. (1990). Commercial memory aids. *Applied Cognitive Psychology, 4,* 439–450.

Hertzberg, H. T. E. (1972). Engineering anthropology. In H. P. Van Cott & R. G. Kinkade (eds.), *Human Engineering Guide to Equipment Design* (pp. 467–584). Washington, DC: U.S. Government Printing Office.

Heuer, H. (1990). Rapid responses with the left or right hand: Response–response compatibility effects due to intermanual interactions. In R. W. Proctor & T. G. Reeve (eds.), *Stimulus–Response Compatibility: An Integrated Perspective* (pp. 311–342). Amsterdam: North-Holland.

Heuer, H., Hollendiek, G., Kroger, H., & Romer, T. (1989). The resting position of the eyes and the influence of observation distance and visual fatigue on VDT work. *Zeitschrift fur Experimentelle und Angewandte Psychologie, 36,* 538–566.

Hick, W. E. (1952). On the rate of gain of information. *Quarterly Journal of Experimental Psychology, 4,* 11–26.

Higginson, G. (1931). *Fields of psychology: A Study of Man and His Environment.* New York: Holt.

Hitt, J. D. (1961). An evaluation of five different abstract coding methods—Experiment IV. *Human Factors, 3,* 120–130.

Hobson, D. A., & Molenbroek, J. F. M. (1990). Anthropometry and design for the disabled: Experience with seating design for the cerebral palsy population. *Applied Ergonomics, 21,* 43–54.

Hochberg, J. E. (1978). *Perception,* 2nd ed. Englewood Cliffs, NJ: Prentice Hall.

Hockey, G. R. J. (1986). Changes in operational efficiency as a function of environmental stress, fatigue, and circadian rhythms. In K. R. Boff, L. Kaufman, & J. P. Thomas (eds.), *Handbook of Perception and Human Performance, Vol. II: Cognitive Processes and Performance* (pp. 44-1 to 44-49). New York: Wiley.

Hoffman, E. R. (1990). Strength of component principles determining direction-of-turn stereotypes for horizontally moving displays. In *Proceedings of the Human Factors Society 34th Annual Meeting* (pp. 457–461). Santa Monica, CA: Human Factors Society.

Holahan, C. J., Culler, R. E., & Wilcox, B. L. (1978). Effects of visual distraction on reaction time in a simulated traffic environment. *Human Factors, 20,* 409–413.

Holland, J. H., Holyoak, K. J., Nisbett, R. E., & Thagard, P. R. (1986). *Induction: Processes of Inference, Learning, and Discovery.* Cambridge, MA: MIT Press.

Holt, R. W., Boehm-Davis, D. A., & Schultz, A. C. (1987). Mental representations of programs for student and professional programmers. In G. M. Olson, S. Sheppard, & E. Soloway (eds.), *Empirical Studies of Programmers: Second Workshop.* Norwood, NJ: Ablex.

Holway, A. H., & Boring, E. G. (1941). Determinants of apparent visual size with distance variant. *American Journal of Psychology, 54,* 21–37.

Holyoak, K. J., & Koh, K. (1987). Surface and structural similarity in analogical transfer. *Memory & Cognition, 15,* 332–340.

Holyoak, K. J., & Nisbett, R. E. (1988). Induction. In R J. Sternberg & E. E. Smith (eds.), *The Psychology of Human Thought* (pp. 50–91). New York: Cambridge University Press.

Hood, P. C., & Finkelstein, M. A. (1986). Sensitivity to light. In K. R. Boff, L. Kaufman, & J. P. Thomas (eds.), *Handbook of Perception and Human Performance, Vol. I: Sensory Processes and Perception,* (pp. 5-1 to 5-66). New York: Wiley.

Hopkinson, R. G., & Longmore, J. (1959). Attention and distraction in the lighting of work places. *Ergonomics, 2,* 321–333.

Horne, J. A., Brass, C. G., & Pettitt, A. N. (1980). Circadian performance differences between morning and evening "types." *Ergonomics, 23,* 29–36.

Hotta, A., Takahashi, T., Takahashi, K., & Kogi, K. (1981). Relations between direction-of-motion stereotypes for controls in living space. *Journal of Human Ergology, 10,* 73–82.

Houck, D. (1991) Fighter pilot display requirements for post-stall maneuvers. *Visual Performance Group Technical Newsletter, 13* (1), 1–4.

Howland, D., & Noble, M. E. (1953). The effect of physical constants of a control on tracking performance. *Journal of Experimental Psychology, 46,* 353–360.

Hsiao, H., & Keyserling, W. M. (1990). A three-dimensional ultrasonic system for posture measurement. *Ergonomics, 33,* 1089–1114.

Hubel, D. H., & Wiesel, T. N. (1979). Brain mechanisms of vision. *Scientific American, 241,* 150–163.

Huber, P. W. (1991). *Galileo's Revenge: Junk Science in the Courtroom.* New York: Basic Books.

Hufford, L. E., & Coburn, R. (1961). *Operator Performance on Miniaturized Decolmantery Keysets.* NEL Report No. 1083. San Diego, CA: U. S. Naval Electronics Laboratory.

Hughes, D. G., & Folkard, S. (1976). Adaptation to an 8-hr shift in living routine by members of a socially isolated community. *Nature, 264,* 432–434.

Hulme, A. J., & Hamilton, G. R. (1989). Human engineering models: A user's perspective. In G. R. McMillan, D. Beevis, E. Salas, M. H. Strub, R. Sutton, & L. Van Breda (eds.), *Applications of Human Performance Models to System Design* (pp. 487–500). New York: Plenum.

Human Factors Society Directory and Yearbook (1992). Santa Monica, CA: Human Factors Society.

Humphreys, P. (1988). Human reliability assessors guide: An overview. In B. A. Sayers (ed.), *Human Factors and Decision Making* (pp. 71–86). New York: Elsevier Applied Sciences.

Humphreys, P. C., & McFadden, W. (1980). Experiences with MAUD: Aiding decision structuring versus bootstrapping the decision maker. *Acta Psychologica, 45,* 51–69.

Hunt, D. P. (1953). *The Coding of Aircraft Controls* (Report No. 53-221). Wright Air Development Center. Wright-Patterson Air Force Base, OH: U.S. Air Force.

Hunt, E. (1989). Connectionist and rule-based representations of expert knowledge. *Behavior Research Methods, Instruments, & Computers, 21,* 88–95.

Hunting, W., & Grandjean, E. (1976). Hunting and Grandjean high back. *Design, 333,* 34–35.

Hyde, T. S., & Jenkins, J. J. (1973). Recall for words as a function of semantic, graphic, and syntactic orienting tasks. *Journal of Verbal Learning and Verbal Behavior, 12,* 471–480.

Hyman, R. (1953). Stimulus information as a determinant of reaction time. *Journal of Experimental Psychology, 45,* 188–196.

Intons-Peterson, M. J., & Fournier, J. (1986). External and internal memory aids: When and how often do we use them? *Journal of Experimental Psychology: General, 115,* 267–280.

Isreal, J. B., Wickens, C. D., Chesney, G. L., & Donchin, E. (1980). The event-related brain potential as an index of display-monitoring workload. *Human Factors, 22,* 211–224.

Jacobsen, A., & Gilchrist, A. L. (1988). The ratio principle holds over a million-to-one range of illumination. *Perception & Psychophysics, 43,* 1–6.

Jacobson, E. (1932). Electrophysiology mental activities. *American Journal of Psychology, 44,* 677–694.

Jacoby, L. L., & Craik, F. I. M. (1979). Effects of elaboration of processing at encoding and retrieval: Trace distinctiveness and recovery of initial context. In L. S. Cermak & F. I. M. Craik (eds.), *Levels of Processing in Human Memory* (pp. 1–21). Hillsdale, NJ: Lawrence Erlbaum.

Jagacinski, R., Miller, D., & Gilson, R. (1979). A comparison of kinesthetic-tactual displays via a critical tracking task. *Human Factors, 21,* 79–86.

Jagacinski, R. J., & Monk, D. L. (1985). Fitts' law in two dimensions with hand and head movements. *Journal of Motor Behavior, 17,* 77–95.

James, W. (1890/1950). *The Principles of Psychology,* Vol. 1. New York: Dover Press.

Janis, I. L., & Mann, L. (1977). *Decision Making: A Psychological Analysis of Conflict, Choice, and Commitment.* New York: Free Press.

Jaschinski-Kruza, W. (1988). Visual strain during VDU work: The effect of viewing distance and dark focus. *Ergonomics, 31,* 1449–1465.

Jaschinski-Kruza, W. (1990). On the preferred viewing distances to screen and document at VDU workplaces. *Ergonomics, 33,* 1055–1063.

Jaschinski-Kruza, W. (1991). Eyestrain in VDU users: Viewing distance and the resting position of ocular muscles. *Human Factors, 33,* 69–83.

Jeannerod, M. (1981). Intersegmental coordination during reaching at natural objects. In J. L. Long & A. Baddeley (eds.), *Attention and Performance X* (pp. 153–169). Hillsdale, NJ: Lawrence Erlbaum.

Jeannerod, M. (1984). The timing of natural prehension movement. *Journal of Motor Behavior, 26,* 235–254.

Jeannerod, M., & Marteniuk, R. G. (1992). Functional characteristics of prehension: From data to artificial networks. In D. Elliott & L. Proteau (eds.), *Vision and Motor Control* (pp. 197–232). Amsterdam: North-Holland.

Jellinek, H. D., & Card, S. K. (1990). Powermice and user performance. In *Human Factors in Computing Systems: CHI '90 Conference Proceedings* (pp. 213–220). Reading, MA: Addison-Wesley.

Jenkins, W. O. (1946). *Investigation of Shapes for Use in Coding Aircraft Control Knobs.* Air Materiel Command Memorandum Report No. TSEAA-694-4. Dayton, OH: U.S. Air Force.

Jensen, R. S. (1982). Pilot judgment: Training and evaluation. *Human Factors, 34,* 61–73.

Jewell, L. N., & Siegall, M. (1990). *Contemporary Industrial/Organizational Psychology,* 2nd ed. St. Paul, MN: West.

Johannson, G. (1975). Visual motion perception. *Scientific American, 232,* 76–89.

John, B. E., & Newell, A. (1990). Toward an engineering model of stimulus–response compatibility. In R. W. Proctor & T. G. Reeve (eds.), *Stimulus–Response Compatibility: An Integrated Perspective* (pp. 427–479). Amsterdam: North-Holland.

Johnsen, E. G., & Corliss, W. R. (1971). *Human Factors Applications in Teleoperator Design and Operation.* New York: Wiley.

Johnson, M. K., Bransford, J. D., & Solomon, S. K. (1973). Memory for tacit implications of sentences. *Journal of Experimental Psychology, 98,* 203–205.

Johnson, P. J., Forester, J. A., Calderwood, R., & Weisgerber, S. A. (1983). Resource allocation and the attentional demands of letter encoding. *Journal of Experimental Psychology: General, 112,* 616–638.

Johnson-Laird, P. N. (1983). *Mental Models.* Cambridge, MA: Harvard University Press.

Johnson-Laird, P. N. (1989). Mental models. In M. I. Posner (ed.), *Foundations of Cognitive Science* (pp. 469–499). Cambridge, MA: MIT Press.

Johnson-Laird, P. N., Legrenzi, P., & Legrenzi, M. S. (1972). Reasoning and a sense of reality. *British Journal of Psychology, 63,* 395–400.

Johnston, W. A., & Heinz, S. P. (1978). Flexibility and capacity demands of attention. *Journal of Experimental Psychology: General, 107,* 420–435.

Jones, D. M., & Broadbent, D. E. (1987). Noise. In G. Salvendy (ed.), *Handbook of Human Factors* (pp. 623–649). New York: Wiley.

Jones, D. M., Morris, N., & Quayle, A. J. (1987). The psychology of briefing. *Applied Ergonomics, 18,* 335–339.

Jones, M. (1989). Man–machine interface design for expert systems. In J. Liebowitz & D. A. De Salvo (eds.), *Structuring Expert Systems: Domain, Design, and Development* (pp. 87–124). Englewood Cliffs, NJ: Prentice Hall (Yourdon Press).

Julesz, B. (1971). *Foundations of Cyclopean Perception.* Chicago: University of Chicago Press.

Just, M. A., & Carpenter, P. A. (1980). A theory of reading: From eye fixations to comprehension. *Psychological Review, 87,* 329–354.

Kahneman, D. (1973). *Attention and Effort.* Englewood Cliffs, NJ: Prentice Hall.

Kahneman, D., Ben-Ishai, R., & Lotan, M. (1973). Relation of a test of attention to road accidents, *Journal of Applied Psychology, 58,* 113–1155.

Kahneman, D., Norman, J., & Kubovy, M. (1967). Critical duration for the resolution of form: Centrally or peripherally determined? *Journal of Experimental Psychology, 73,* 323–327.

Kahneman, D., Slovic, P., & Tversky, A. (1982). *Judgment under uncertainty: Heuristics and Biases.* New York: Cambridge University Press.

Kahneman, D., & Tversky, A. (1972). Subjective probability: A judgment of representativeness. *Cognitive Psychology, 3,* 430–454.

Kahneman, D., & Tversky, A. (1973). On the psychology of prediction. *Psychological Review, 80,* 237–251.

Kahneman, D., & Tversky, A. (1979). Prospect theory. *Econometrika, 47,* 263–292.

Kaminaka, M. S., & Egli, E. A. (1984). Determination of stereotypes for lever control of object motions using computer generated graphics. *Ergonomics, 27,* 918–995.

Kantowitz, B. H. (1982). Interfacing human information processing and engineering psychology. In W. C. Howell and E. A. Fleishman (eds.), *Human Performance and Productivity, Vol. 2: Information Processing and Decision Making* (pp. 31–81). Hillsdale, NJ: Lawrence Erlbaum.

Kantowitz, B. H. (1987). Mental workload. In P. A. Hancock (ed.), *Human factors psychology* (pp. 81–121). Amsterdam: North-Holland.

Kantowitz, B. H. (1989). The role of human information processing models in system development. In *Proceedings of the Human Factors Society 33rd Annual Meeting* (pp. 1059–1063). Santa Monica, CA: Human Factors Society.

Kantowitz, B. H., & Elvers, G. C. (1988). Fitts' law with an isometric controller: Effects of order of control and control-display gain. *Journal of Motor Behavior, 20,* 53–66.

Kantowitz, B. H., Triggs, T. J., & Barnes, V. E. (1990). Stimulus–response compatibility and human factors. In R. W. Proctor & T. G. Reeve (eds.), *Stimulus–Response Compatibility: An Integrated Perspective* (pp. 365–388). Amsterdam: North-Holland.

Karat, C.-M. (1990). Cost–benefit analyses of usability engineering techniques. In *Proceedings of the Human Factors Society 34th Annual Meeting* (pp. 839–843). Santa Monica, CA: Human Factors Society.

Karat, C.-M. (1992). Cost-justifying human factors support on software development projects. *Human Factors Society Bulletin, 35* (No. 11), 1–4.

Karlin, S., & Taylor, H. M. (1975). *A First Course in Stochastic Processes.* New York: Academic Press.

Kassab, S. J. (1974). Research note: Reduction of muscular fatigue associated with repetitive light assembly operations by means of arm counterbalancing. *Human Factors, 16,* 323–326.

Kawabata, N. (1984). Perception at the blind spot and similiarity grouping. *Perception & Psychophysics, 36,* 151–158.

Kawabata, N. (1990). Structural information processing in peripheral vision. *Perception, 19,* 631–636.

Keele, S. W. (1968). Movement control in skilled motor performance. *Psychological Bulletin, 70,* 387–403.

Keele, S. W. (1986). Motor control. In K. R. Boff, L, Kaufman, & J. P. Thomas (eds.), *Handbook of Perception and Human Performance Vol. II* (pp. 30-1 to 30-60). New York: Wiley.

Keele, S. W., Cohen, A., & Ivry, R. (1990). Motor programs: concepts and issues. In M. Jeannerod (ed.), *Attention and Performance XIII* (pp. 77–110). Hillsdale, NJ: Lawrence Erlbaum.

Keele, S. W., & Hawkins, H. L. (1982). Explorations of individual differences relevant to high skill level. *Journal of Motor Behavior, 14,* 3–23.

Keele, S. W., & Posner, M. I. (1968). Processing of visual feedback in rapid movements. *Journal of Experimental Psychology, 77,* 155–158.

Keen, P. G. W., & Scott-Morton, M. S. (1978). *Decision Support Systems: An Organizational Perspective.* Reading, MA: Addison-Wesley.

Kelley, C. R. (1962). Predictor instruments look into the future. *Control Engineering, 9,* May, 86–90.

Kelly, P. L., & Kroemer, K. H. E. (1990). Anthropometry of the elderly: Status and recommendations. *Human Factors, 32,* 571–595.

Kelso, J. A. S., Putnam, C. A., & Goodman, D. (1983). On the space–time structure of human interlimb coordination. *Quarterly Journal of Experimental Psychology, 35A,* 347–375.

Kelso, J. A. S., Southard, D. L., & Goodman, D. (1979). On the nature of human interlimb coordination. *Science, 203,* 1029–1031.

Kemper, H. C. G., van Aalst, R., Leegwater, A., Maas, S., & Knibbe, J. J. (1990). The physical and physiological workload of refuse collectors. *Ergonomics, 33,* 1471–1486.

Kenshalo, D. R. (1972). The cutaneous senses. In J. W. Kling & L. A. Riggs (eds.), *Woodworth & Schlosberg's Experimental Psychology,* 3rd ed. (pp. 117–168). New York: Holt, Rinehart & Winston.

Keppel, G., & Underwood, B. J. (1962). Proactive inhibition in short-term retention of single items. *Journal of Verbal Learning and Verbal Behavior, 1,* 153–161.

Kerlinger, F. N. (1973). *Foundations of Behavioral Research,* 2nd ed. New York: Holt, Rinehart and Winston.

Kerr, B. A., & Langolf, G. D. (1977). Speed of aiming movements. *Quarterly Journal of Experimental Psychology, 29,* 475–481.

Kerr, R. (1973). Movement time in an underwater environment. *Journal of Motor Behavior, 5,* 175–178.

Kewley-Port, D., & Luce, P. A. (1984). Time-varying features of initial stop consonants in auditory running spectra: A first report. *Perception & Psychophysics, 35,* 353–360.

Kieras, D. E., & Bovair, S. (1984). The role of a mental model in learning to operate a device. *Cognitive Science, 8,* 255–273.

Kieras, D. E., & Bovair, S. (1986). The acquisition of procedures from text: A production-system analysis of transfer of training. *Journal of Memory and Language, 25,* 507–524.

Kieras, D., & Polson, P. G. (1985). An approach to the formal analysis of user complexity. *International Journal of Man–Machine Studies, 22,* 365–394.

Kinkead, R. D., & Gonzalez, B. K. (1969). *Human Factors Design Recommendations for Touch-operated Keyboards—Final Report.* Document 12091-fr. Minneapolis, MN: Honeywell.

Kintsch, W., & Keenan, J. (1973). Reading rate and retention as a function of the number of propositions in the base structure of sentences. *Cognitive Psychology, 5,* 257–274.

Kintsch, W., & van Dijk, T. A. (1978). Toward a model of text comprehension and production. *Psychological Review, 85,* 363–394.

Kirwan, B. (1988). A comparative evaluation of five human reliability assessment techniques. In B. A. Sayers (ed.), *Human Factors and Decision Making* (pp. 87–109). New York: Elsevier Applied Sciences.

Klapp, S. T. (1977). Reaction time analysis of programmed control. *Exercise and Sport Science Reviews, 5,* 231–253.

Klapp, S. T. (1979). Doing two things at once: The role of temporal compatibility. *Memory & Cognition, 7,* 375–381.

Klapp, S. T. (1988). Short-term memory limits in human performance. In P. A. Hancock (ed.), *Human Factors Psychology* (pp. 1–27). Amsterdam: North-Holland.

Kleffner, D. A., & Ramachandran, V. S. (1992). On the perception of shape from shading. *Perception & Psychophysics, 52,* 18–36.

Klein, G. A. (1989). Recognition-primed decisions. In W. B. Rouse (ed.), *Advances in Man–Machine Systems Research,* Vol. 5 (pp. 47–92). Greenwich, CT: JAI Press.

Klein, R. M., & Posner, M. I. (1974). Attention to visual and kinesthetic components of skill. *Brain Research, 71,* 401–411.

Kleiner, B. M., Drury, C. G., & Christopher, C. L. (1987). Sensitivity of human tactile inspection. *Human Factors, 29,* 1–7.

Knapp, M. L. (1978). *Nonverbal Communication in Human Interaction.* New York: Holt, Rinehart, and Winston.

Knowles, E. S. (1983). Social physics and the effects of others: Tests of the effects of audience size and distance on social judgments and behavior. *Journal of Personality and Social Psychology, 45,* 1263–1279.

Knowles, W. B., & Sheridan, T. B. (1966). The "feel" of rotary controls: Friction and inertia. *Human Factors, 8,* 209–216.

Koffka, K. (1935). *Principles of Gestalt Psychology.* New York: Harcourt, Brace, & World.

Kohfeld, D. L. (1969). Effects of the intensity of auditory and visual ready signals on simple reaction time. *Journal of Experimental Psychology, 82,* 88–95.

Kolodner, J. L. (1991). Improving human decision making through case-based decision aiding. *AI Magazine, 12* (2), 52–68.

Konz, S. (1974). Design of hand tools. In *Proceedings of the Human Factors Society 18th Annual Meeting* (pp. 292–300). Santa Monica, CA: Human Factors Society.

Kornblum, S. (1973). Sequential effects in choice reaction time: A tutorial review. In S. Kornblum (ed.), *Attention and Performance IV* (pp. 259–288). New York: Academic Press.

Kornblum, S., Hasbroucq, T., & Osman, A. (1990). Dimensional overlap: Cognitive basis for stimulus–response compatability—A model and taxonomy. *Psychological Review, 97,* 253–270.

Kosnik, W. D., Sekuler, R., & Kline, D. W. (1990). Self-reported visual problems of older drivers. *Human Factors, 5,* 597–608.

Kosslyn, S. M. (1975). Information representation in visual images. *Cognitive Psychology, 7,* 341–370.

Kosslyn, S. M. (1980). *Image and Mind.* Cambridge, MA: Harvard University Press.

Kosslyn, S. M., Ball, T. M., & Reiser, B. J. (1978). Visual images preserve metric spatial information: Evidence from studies of image scanning. *Journal of Experimental Psychology: Human Perception and Performance, 4,* 47–60.

Kramer, A. F., Sirevaag, E. J., & Braune, R. (1987). A psychophysiological assessment of operator workload during simulated flight missions. *Human Factors, 29,* 145–160.

Kreifeldt, J., Parkin, L., Rothschild, P., & Wempe, T. (1976, May). Implications of a mixture of aircraft with and without traffic situation displays for air traffic management. In *Twelfth Annual Conference on Manual Control* (pp. 179–200). Washington, DC: National Aeronautics and Space Administration.

Kristofferson, M. W. (1972). When item recognition and visual search functions are similar. *Perception & Psychophysics, 12,* 379–384.

Kroemer, K. H. E. (1971). Foot operation of controls. *Ergonomics, 14,* 333–361.

Kroemer, K. H. E. (1983a). Engineering anthropometry: Workspace and equipment to fit the user. In D. J. Oborne & M. M. Gruneberg (eds.), *The Physical Environment at Work* (pp. 39–68). New York: Wiley.

Kroemer, K. H. E. (1983b). Isoinertial technique to assess individual lifting capability. *Human Factors, 25,* 493–506.

Kroemer, K. H. E. (1986). Coupling the hand with the handle: An improved notation of touch, grip, and grasp. *Human Factors, 28,* 337–339.

Kroemer, K. H. E. (1989). Cumulative trauma disorders: Their recognition and ergonomics measures to avoid them. *Applied Ergonomics, 20,* 274–280.

Kroemer, K. H. E., Kroemer, H. J., & Kroemer-Elbert, K. E. (1990). *Engineering physiology: Bases of Human Factors/Ergonomics,* 2nd ed. New York: Van Nostrand Reinhold.

Kroemer, K. H. E., & Marras, W. S. (1981). Evaluation of maximal and submaximal static muscle exertions. *Human Factors, 23,* 643–653.

Kroemer, K. H. E., Snook, S. H., Meadows, S. K., & Deutsch, S. (1988). *Ergonomic Models of Anthropometry, Human Biomechanics, and Operator–Equipment Interfaces.* Washington, DC: National Academy Press.

Krois, P. A., Lenorovitz, D. R., McKeon, P. S., Snyder, C. A., Tobey, W. K., & Bashinski, H. S. (1991). Air traffic control facility lighting. In Proceedings of the *Human Factors Society 35th Annual Meeting* (pp. 551–555). Santa Monica, CA: Human Factors Society.

Krueger, L. E. (1989). Reconciling Fechner and Stevens: Toward a unified psychophysical law. *Behavioral and Brain Sciences, 12,* 251–267.

Kryter, K. D. (1972). Speech communication. In H. P. Van Cott & R. G. Kinkade (eds.), *Human Engineering Guide to Equipment Design,* rev. ed. (pp. 161–226). Washington, DC: U.S. Government Printing Office.

Kryter, K. D., & Williams, C. E. (1965). Masking of speech by aircraft noise. *Journal of the Acoustical Society of America, 37,* 138–150.

Kurke, M. I. (1986). Anatomy of product liability/personal injury litigation. In Kurke, M. I., & Meyer, R. G. (eds.), *Psychology in Product Liability and Personal Injury Litigation* (pp. 3–15). Washington, DC: Hemisphere Publishing.

Laabs, G. J. (1973). Retention characteristics of different reproduction cues in motor short-term memory. *Journal of Experimental Psychology, 100,* 168–177.

Lackner, J. R. (1990). Sensory–motor adaptation to high force levels in parabolic flight maneuvers. In M. Jeannerod (ed.), *Attention and Performance XIII: Motor Representation and Control* (pp. 527–548). Hillsdale, NJ: Lawrence Erlbaum.

Laird, J., Rosenbloom, P., & Newell, A. (1986). *Universal Subgoaling and Chunking.* Boston: Kluwer.

Landis, C. (1954). Determinants of the critical flicker fusion threshold. *Psychological Review, 34,* 259–286.

Landy, F. J., & Farr, J. L. (1980). Performance rating. *Psychological Bulletin, 87,* 72–107.

Lane, N. E. (1987). *Skill Acquisition Rates and Patterns: Issues and Training Implications.* New York: Springer-Verlag.

Langolf, G., & Hancock, W. M. (1975). Human performance times in microscope work. *AIEE Transactions, 7,* 110–117.

Lashley, K. S. (1951). The problem of serial order in behavior. In L. A. Jefress (ed.), *Cerebral Mechanisms in Behavior* (pp. 112–136). New York: Wiley.

Laughery, K. R., Sr. (1992). Should HFS change its name? *Human Factors Society Bulletin, 35* (1), 1–2.

Lavery, J. J. (1962). Retention of simple motor skills as a function of type of knowledge of results. *Canadian Journal of Psychology, 16,* 300–311.

Lazarus, R. S., & Folkman, S. (1984). *Stress, Appraisal, and Coping.* New York: Springer-Verlag.

Leavitt, J. L., Lee, T. D., & Romanow, S. K. E. (1980). Proactive interference and movement attribute change in motor short-term memory. In C. H. Nadeau, W. R. Halliwell, K. M. Newell, & G. C. Roberts (eds.), *Psychology of Motor Behavior and Sport—1979* (pp. 585–593). Champaign, IL: Human Kinetics.

Lederman, S. J., & Campbell, J. I. (1982). Tangible graphs for the blind. *Human Factors, 24,* 85–100.

Lee, D. N. (1976). A theory of visual control of braking based on information about time-to-collision. *Perception, 5,* 437–459.

Lee, D. N., & Lishman, J. R. (1975). Visual proprioceptive control of stance. *Journal of Human Movement Studies, 1,* 87–95.

Lee, D. N., Lishman, J. R., & Thomson, J. A. (1982). Regulation of gait in long jumping. *Journal of Experimental Psychology: Human Perception and Performance, 8,* 448–459.

Lee, D. N., Young, D. S., Reddish, P. E., Lough, S., & Clayton, T. M. H. (1983). Visual timing in hitting an accelerating ball. *Quarterly Journal of Experimental Psychology, 35A,* 333–346.

Lee, E., & MacGregor, J. (1985). Minimizing user search time in menu retrieval systems. *Human Factors, 27,* 157–162.

Lee, E., MacGregor, J., Lam, N., & Chao, G. (1986). Keyboard retrieval: An effective alternative to menu indexes. *Ergonomics, 29,* 115–130.

Lee, T. D., & Genovese, E. D. (1988). Distribution of practice in motor skill acquisition: Learning and performance effects reconsidered. *Research Quarterly for Exercise and Sport, 59,* 277–287.

Lee, T. D., & Genovese, E. D. (1989). Distribution of motor skill acquisition: Different effects for discrete and continuous tasks. *Research Quarterly for Exercise and Sport, 70,* 59–65.

Lee, T. D., & Magill, R. A. (1983). Activity during the post-KR interval: Effects upon performance or learning? *Research Quarterly for Exercise and Sport, 54,* 340–354.

Lee, T. D., & Magill, R. A. (1985). Can forgetting facilitate skill acquision. In D. Goodman, R. B. Wilberg, & I. M. Franks (eds.), *Differing Perspective in Motor Learning, Memory, and Control* (pp. 3–22). Amsterdam: North Holland.

Lee, T. D., Magill, R. A., & Weeks, D. J. (1985). Influence of practice schedule on testing schema theory predictions in adults. *Journal of Motor Behavior, 17,* 283–299.

Leibowitz, H. W., & Owens, D. A. (1975). Anomalous myopias and the intermediate dark focus of accommodation. *Science, 189,* 646–648.

Leibowitz, H. W., & Owens, D. A. (1986). We drive by night. *Psychology Today,* January, 55–58.

Leibowitz, H. W., & Post, R. B. (1982). The two modes of processing concept and some implications. In J. Beck (ed.), *Organization and Representation in Perception* (pp. 343–363). Hillsdale, NJ: Lawrence Erlbaum.

Leibowitz, H. W., Post, R. B., Brandt, T., & Dichgans, J. (1982). Implications of recent developments in dynamic spatial orientation and visual resolution for vehicle guidance. In A. H. Wertheim, W. A. Wagenaar, & H. W. Leibowitz (eds.), *Tutorials on Motion Perception* (pp. 231–260). New York: Plenum.

Leonard, J. A. (1958). Partial advance information in a choice reaction task. *British Journal of Psychology, 49,* 89–96.

Leonard, J. A. (1959). Tactual choice reactions: I. *Quarterly Journal of Experimental Psychology, 11,* 76–83.

Lerch, F. J., Mantei, M. M., & Olson, J. R. (1989). Translating ideas into action: Cognitive analysis of errors in spreadsheet formulas. In *Proceedings of the CHI '89 Conference on Human Factors in Computing Systems* (pp. 121–126). New York: Van Nostrand Reinhold.

Lewin, K. (1951). *Field Theory in Social Science.* New York: Harper & Row.

Lewis, D., McAllister, D. E., & Adams, J. A. (1951). Facilitation and interference in performance on the Modified Mashburn Apparatus: I. The effects of varying the amount of original learning. *Journal of Experimental Psychology, 41,* 247–260.

Lewis, J. L. (1970). Semantic processing of unattended messages using dichotic listening. *Journal of Experimental Psychology, 85,* 225–228.

Lewis, R. (1990). Design economy in the creation of manned space systems. *Human Factors Society Bulletin, 32* (3), 5–6.

Li, C.-C., Hwang, S.-L., & Wang, M.-Y. (1990). Static anthropometry of civilian Chinese in Taiwan using computer-analyzed photography. *Human Factors, 32,* 359–370.

Lichtenstein, S., & Slovic, P. (1971). Reversal of preferences between bids and choices in gambling decision. *Journal of Experimental Psychology, 89,* 46–55.

Lichtenstein, S., Slovic, P., Fischoff, B., Layman, M., Combs, B. (1978). Judged frequency of lethal events. *Journal of Experimental Psychology: Human Learning and Memory, 4,* 551–578.

Lie, I. (1980). Visual detection and resolution as a function of retinal locus. *Vision Research, 20,* 967–974.

Liebowitz, J. (1990). *The Dynamics of Decision Support Systems and Expert Systems.* Chicago: Dryden Press.

Likert, R. (1961). *New Patterns of Management.* New York: McGraw-Hill.

Lindahl, L. G. (1945). Movement analysis as an industrial training method. *Journal of Applied Psychology, 29,* 420–436.

Livingston, M. S., & Hubel, D. H. (1987). Psychophysical evidence for separate channels for the perception of form, color, movement, and depth. *Journal of Neuroscience, 7,* 3416–3468.

Loeb, K. M. C. (1983). Membrane keyboards and human performance. *Bell System Technical Journal, 62,* 1733–1749.

Loftus, E. F., & Loftus, G. R. (1980). On the permanence of stored information in the human brain. *American Psychologist, 35,* 409–420.

Loftus, G. R., Dark, V. J., & Williams, D. (1979). Short-term memory factors in ground controller/pilot communication. *Human Factors, 21,* 169–181.

Logan, G. D., & Cowan, W. B. (1984). On the ability to inhibit thought and action: A theory of an act of control. *Psychological Review, 91,* 295–327.

Lorge, I. (1930). *Influence of Regularly Interpolated Time Intervals Upon Subsequent Learning* (Teacher College Contributions to Education, No. 438). New York: Columbia University, Teachers College.

Louviere, A. J., & Jackson, J. T. (1982). Man–machine design for spaceflight. In T. S. Cheston & D. L. Winter (eds.), *Human Factors of Outer Space Production* (pp. 97–112). Boulder, CO: Westview Press.

Lovasik, J. V., Matthews, S. M. L., & Kergoat, H. (1989). Neural, optical, and search performance in prolonged viewing of chromatic displays. *Human Factors, 31,* 273–289.

Loveless, N. E. (1962). Direction-of-motion stereotypes: A review. *Ergonomics, 5,* 357–383.

Luce, P. A., Feustal, T. C., & Pisoni, D. B. (1983). Capacity demands in short-term memory for synthetic and natural speech. *Human Factors, 25,* 17–32.

Luce, R. D. (1986). *Response Times: Their Role in Inferring Elementary Mental Organization.* New York: Oxford University Press.

Lusted, L. B. (1971). Signal detectability and medical decision-making. *Science, 171,* 1217–1219.

Lyman, S. L., & Scott, M. B. (1967). Territoriality: A neglected sociological dimension. *Social Problems, 15,* 235–249.

Lynch, M. P., Oller, D. K., & Eilers, R. E. (1989). Portable tactile aids for speech perception. *Volta Review, 91* (5), 113–126.

Lysaght, R. S., Hill, S. G., Dick, A. O., Plamondon, B. D., Wherry, R. J., Zaklad, A. L., & Bittner, A. C. (1989). *Operator Workload: A Comprehensive Review of Operator Workload Methodologies.* Technical Report 851. Alexandria, VA: U.S. Army Research Institute for the Social Sciences.

Mack, A. (1986). Perceptual aspects of motion in the frontal plane. In K. R. Boff, L. Kaufman, & J. P. Thomas (eds.), *Handbook of Perception and Human Performance, Vol I: Sensory Processes and Perception* (pp. 17-1 to 17-38). New York: Wiley.

MacKay, D. G. (1981). The problem of rehearsal or mental practice. *Journal of Motor Behavior, 13,* 274–285.

Mackett-Stout, J., & Dewar, R. (1981). Evaluation of symbolic public information signs. *Human Factors, 23,* 139–151.

Mackworth, N. H. (1950). *Researches on the Measurement of Human Performance* (Special Report No. 268). London: Medical Research Council, Her Majesty's Stationary Office.

Mackworth, N. H. (1965). Visual noise causes tunnel vision. *Psychonomic Science, 3,* 67–68.

MacLean, A., Carter, K., Lovstrand, L., & Moran, T. (1990). User-tailorable systems: Pressing the issues with buttons. In *Human Factors in Computing Systems: CHI '90 Conference Proceedings* (pp. 213–220). Reading, MA: Addison-Wesley.

MacLeod, C. M. (1991). Half a century of research on the Stroop effect: An integrative review. *Psychological Review, 109,* 163–203.

Macy, B. A., & Mirvis, P. H. (1976). A methodology for assessment of quality of work life and organizational effectiveness in behavioural-economic terms. *Administrative Science Quarterly, 21,* 212–216.

Madni, A. M. (1988). The role of human factors in expert systems design and acceptance. *Human Factors, 30,* 395–414.

Magers, C. S. (1983). An experimental evaluation of on-line HELP for non-programmers. In *Proceedings of CHI 83: Human Factors in Computing Systems* (pp. 277–281). New York: ACM.

Magill, R. A. (1989). *Motor Learning: Concepts and Applications,* 3rd ed. Dubuque, IA: W. C. Brown.

Magill, R. A., & Parks, P. F. (1983). The psychophysics of kinesthesis for positioning responses: The physical stimulus–psychological response relationship. *Research Quarterly for Exercise and Sport, 54,* 346–351.

Magill, R. A., & Wood, C. A. (1986). Knowledge of results precision as a learning variable in motor skill acquisition. *Research Quarterly for Exercise and Sport, 57,* 170–173.

Magliero, A., Bashore, T. R., Coles, M. G. H., & Donchin, E. (1984). On the dependence of P300 latency on stimulus evaluation processes. *Psychophysiology, 21,* 171–186.

Magnussen, S., & Kurtenbach, W. (1980). Linear summation of tilt illusion and tilt aftereffect. *Vision Research, 20,* 39–42.

Makous, J. C., & Middlebrooks, J. C. (1990). Two-dimensional sound localization by human listeners. *Journal of the Acoustical Society of America, 87,* 2188–2200.

Malone, T. B. (1986). The centered high-mounted brakelight: A human factors success story. *Human Factors Society Bulletin, 29* (10), 1–3.

Mansfield, R. (1974). Neural basis of orientation perception in primate vision. *Science, 186,* 1133–1135.

Mansfield, R. J. W. (1973). Latency functions in human vision. *Vision Research, 13,* 2219–2234.

Man–Systems Integration Standards (1987). Lockheed Missiles and Space Company, Inc., Man–Systems Division, NASA, Lyndon B. Johnson Space Center, Houston, TX.

Mantei, M. M., & Teorey, T. J. (1988). Cost/benefit analysis for incorporating human factors in the software cycle. *Communications of the ACM, 31,* 428–439.

Marey, E.-J. (1902). *The History of Chronophotography.* Washington, DC: Smithsonian Institution.

Marics, M. A., & Williges, B. H. (1988). The intelligibility of synthesized speech in data inquiry systems. *Human Factors, 30,* 719–732.

Marras, W. S., & Kroemer, K. H. E. (1980). A method to evaluate human factors/ergonomics design variables of distress signals. *Human Factors, 22,* 389–399.

Marras, W. S., & Mirka, G. A. (1989). Trunk strength during asymmetric trunk motion. *Human Factors, 31,* 667–677.

Marras, W. S., & Sommerich, C. M. (1991). A three-dimensional motion model of loads on the lumbar spine: I. Model structure. *Human Factors, 33,* 123–137.

Marslen-Wilson, W. D. (1975). Sentence perception as an interactive parallel process. *Science, 189,* 226–228.

Marteniuk, R. G. (1976). Cognitive information processes in motor short-term memory and movement production. In G. E. Stelmach (ed.), *Motor Control: Issues and Trends* (pp. 175–186). New York: Academic Press.

Marteniuk, R. G. (1986). Information processes in movement learning: Capacity and structural interference effects. *Journal of Motor Behavior, 18,* 55–75.

Marteniuk, R. G., MacKenzie, C. L., Jeannerod, M., Athenes, S., & Dugas, C. (1987). Constraints on human arm movement trajectories. *Canadian Journal of Psychology, 41,* 365–378.

Mathews, M. L., Lovasik, J. V., & Mertins, K. (1989). Visual performance and subjective discomfort in prolonged viewing of chromatic displays. *Human Factors, 31,* 259–272.

Matin, L., Picoult, E., Stevens, J., Edwards, M., & MacArthur, R. (1982). Oculoparalytic illusion: Visual-field dependent spatial mislocations by humans partially paralyzed with curare. *Science, 216,* 198–201.

Matlin, M. W. (1988). *Sensation and Perception,* 2nd ed. Boston: Allyn and Bacon.

Mattingly, I. G., & Studdert-Kennedy, M. (eds.) (1991). *Modularity and the Motor Theory of Speech Perception.* Hillsdale, NJ: Lawrence Erlbaum.

Mayer, R. E. (1975). Different problem solving competencies established in learning computer programming with and without meaningful models. *Journal of Educational Psychology, 67,* 725–734.

Mayer, R. E. (1988). From novice to expert. In M. Helander (ed.), *Handbook of Human–Computer Interaction* (pp. 569–580). Amsterdam: North-Holland.

Mayer, R. E., & Bayman, P. (1981). Psychology of calculator languages: A framework for describing differences in users' knowledge. *Communications of the ACM, 24,* 511–520.

Mazur, K. M., & Reising, J. M. (1990). The relative effectiveness of three visual depth cues in a dynamic air situation display. In *Proceedings of the*

Human Factors Society 34th Annual Meeting (pp. 16–19). Santa Monica, CA: Human Factors Society.

McCabe, P. A., & Dey, F. L. (1965). The effect of aspirin upon auditory sensitivity. *Annals of Otology, Rhinology, and Laryngology, 74,* 312–325.

McCarthy, G., & Donchin, E. (1981). A metric for thought: A comparison of P300 latency and reaction time. *Science, 211,* 77–80.

McClelland, J. L. (1979). On the time relations of mental processes: An examination of systems of processes in cascade. *Psychological Review, 86,* 287–330.

McCloskey, M. (1983). Naive theories of motion. In D. Gentner & A. L. Stevens (eds.), *Mental models* (pp. 299–324). Hillsdale, NJ: Lawrence Erlbaum.

McCollough, C. (1965). Color adaptation of edge-detectors in the human visual system. *Science, 149,* 115–116.

McConville, J. T., Robinette, K. M., & Churchill, T. D. (1981). *An Anthropometric Data Base for Commercial Design Applications, Phase I.* Final Report NSF/BNS-81001 (PB 81–211070). Washington, DC: National Science Foundation.

McCormick, E. J., Jeanneret, P. R., & Mecham, R. C. (1972). A study of job characteristics and job dimensions as based on the Position Analysis Questionnaire (PAQ). *Journal of Applied Psychology, 56,* 347–368.

McCracken, J. H., & Aldrich, T. B. (1984). *Analysis of Selected LHX Mission Functions: Implications for Operator Workload and System Automation Goals* (TNA AS1479-24-84). Fort Rucker, AL: Anacapa Sciences.

McDowd, J. M. (1986). The effects of age and extended practice on divided attention performance. *Journal of Gerontology, 41,* 764–769.

McGrath, J. J. (1963). Irrelevant stimulation and vigilance performance. In D. N. Buckner and J. J. McGrath (eds.), *Vigilance: A Symposium* (pp. 3–19). New York: McGraw-Hill.

McKeithen, K. B., Reitman, J. S., Rueter, H. H., & Hirtle, S. C. (1981). Knowledge organization and skill differences in computer programmers. *Cognitive Psychology, 13,* 307–325.

McKnight, A. J., Shinar, D., & Hilburn, B. (1991). The visual and driving performance of monocular and binocular heavy-duty truck drivers. *Accident Analysis & Prevention, 23,* 225–237.

McMillan, G. R., Beevis, D., Salas, E., Strub, M. H., Sutton, R., & Van Breda, L. (eds.) (1989). *Applications of Human Performance Models to System Design.* New York: Plenum.

McNaughton, G. B. (1985, October). The problem. Presented at a workshop on flight attitude awareness. Wright-Patterson Air Force Base, OH: Wright Aeronautical Laboratories and Life Support System Program Office.

Megaw, E. D., & Bellamy, L. J. (1983). Illumination at work. In D. J. Oborne & M. M. Gruneberg (eds.), *The Physical Environment at Work* (pp. 109–141). New York: Wiley.

Meister, D. (1971). *Human Factors: Theory and Practice.* New York: Wiley.

Meister, D. (1985). *Behavioral Analysis and Measurement Methods.* New York: Wiley.

Meister, D. (1987). Systems design, development, and testing. In G. Salvendy (ed.), *Handbook of Human Factors* (pp. 17–42). New York: Wiley.

Meister, D. (1989). *Conceptual Aspects of Human Factors.* Baltimore, MD: Johns Hopkins University Press.

Meister, D. (1991). The definition and measurement of systems. *Human Factors Society Bulletin, 34(2),* 3–5.

Meister, D., & Rabideau, G. (1965). *Human Factors Evaluation in System Development.* New York: Wiley.

Mertens, H. W., & Lewis, M. F. (1981). Effect of different runway size on pilot performance during simulated night landing approaches. U.S. Federal Aviation Administration Office of Aviation Medicine Technical Report (FAA-AH-81-6). Washington, DC: Federal Aviation Administration.

Mertens, H. W., & Lewis, M. F. (1982). Effects of approach lighting and visible runway length on perception of approach angle in simulated night landings. U.S. Federal Aviation Administration Office of Aviation Technical Report (FAA-AM-82-6). Washington, DC: Federal Aviation Administration.

Merton, P. A. (1972). How we control the contraction of our muscles. *Scientific American, 226,* 30–37.

Merwin, D. H., Dyer, B. P., Humphrey, D. G., Grimes, J., & Larish, J. F. (1990). The impact of icons and visual effects on learning computer databases. In *Proceedings of the Human Factors Society 34th Annual Meeting* (pp. 424–428). Santa Monica, CA: Human Factors Society.

Meshkati, N. (1988). Heart rate variability and mental workload assessment. In P. A. Hancock & N. Meshkati (eds.), *Human Mental Workload* (pp. 101–115). Amsterdam: North-Holland.

Metz, S., Isle, B., Denno, S., Li, W. (1990). Small rotary controls: Limitations for people with arthritis. In *Proceedings of the Human Factors Society 34th Annual Meeting* (pp. 137–140). Santa Monica, CA: Human Factors Society.

Meyer, D. E., Abrams, R. A., Kornblum, S., Wright, C. W., & Smith, J. E. K. (1988). Optimality in human motor performance: Ideal control of rapid aimed movements. *Psychological Review, 95,* 340–370.

Meyer, D. E., Smith, J. E. K., Kornblum, S., Abrams, R. A., & Wright, C. E. (1990). Speed–accuracy tradeoffs in aimed movements: Toward a theory of rapid voluntary action. In M. Jeannerod (ed.), *Attention and Performance XIII* (pp. 173–226). Hillsdale, NJ: Lawrence Erlbaum.

Michaels, S. E. (1971). QWERTY versus alphabetic keyboards as a function of typing skill. *Human Factors, 13,* 419–426.

Miller, D. P., & Swain, A. D. (1987). Human error and human reliability. In G. Salvendy (ed.), *Handbook of Human Factors* (pp. 219–250). New York: Wiley.

Miller, G. A. (1956). The magical number seven, plus or minus two: Some limits on our capacity for processing information. *Psychological Review, 63,* 81–97.

Miller, G. A., & Glucksberg, S. (1988). Psycholinguistic aspects of pragmatics and semantics. In R. C. Atkinson, R. J. Herrnstein, G. Lindzey, & R. D. Luce (eds.), *Stevens' Handbook of Experimental Psychology,* 2nd ed. (pp. 417–472). New York: Wiley.

Miller, G. A., & Isard, S. (1963). Some perceptual consequences of linguistic rules. *Journal of Verbal Learning and Verbal Behavior, 2,* 212–228.

Miller, J. (1988). Discrete and continuous models of human information processing: Theoretical distinctions and empirical results. *Acta Psychologica, 67,* 191–257.

Miller, R. J. (1990). Pitfalls in the conception, manipulation, and measurement of visual accommodation. *Human Factors, 32,* 27–44.

Miller, W., & Suther, T. W., III. (1983). Display station anthropometrics: Preferred height and angle settings of CRT and keyboard. *Human Factors, 25,* 401–408.

Mirka, G. A., & Marras, W. S. (1990). Lumbar motion response to a constant load velocity lift. *Human Factors, 32,* 493–501.

Mistrot, P., Donati, P., Galimore, J. P., & Florentin, D. (1990). Assessing the discomfort of the whole-body multi-axis vibration: laboratory and field experiments. *Ergonomics, 33,* 1523–1536.

Mital, A. (1983). Special issue preface. *Human Factors, 25,* 471–472.

Mital, A. (1986). Special-issue preface. *Human Factors, 28,* 251.

Mital, A., & Manivasigan, I. (1983). Maximum acceptable weight of lift as a function of material density, center of gravity location, hand preference, and frequency. *Human Factors, 25,* 33–42.

Mital, A., & Ramanan, S. (1985). Accuracy of check-reading dials. In R. E. Eberts & C. G. Eberts (eds.), *Trends in Ergonomics/Human Factors II* (pp. 105–113). Amsterdam: North-Holland.

Mital, A., & Sanghavi, N. (1986). Comparison of maximum volitional torque exertion capabilities of males and females using common hand tools. *Human Factors, 28,* 283–294.

Mohrman, A. M., Jr., Resnick-West, S. M., & Lawler, E. E., II (1989). *Designing Performance Appraisal Systems.* San Francisco: Jossey-Bass.

Monk, T. H. (1989). Human factors implications of shiftwork. *International Reviews of Ergonomics, 2,* 111–128.

Monty, R. W., Snyder, H. L., & Birdwell, G. G. (1983). Evaluation of several keyboard design paramaters. In *Proceedings of the Human Factors Society 27th Annual Meeting* (pp. 201–205). Santa Monica, CA: Human Factors Society.

Moore, T. G. (1974). Tactile and kinesthetic aspects of pushbuttons. *Applied Ergonomics, 52,* 66–71.

Moore, T. G. (1975). Industrial push-buttons. *Applied Ergonomics, 6,* 33–38.

Moray, N. (1959). Attention in dichotic listening: Affective cues and the influence of instructions. *Quarterly Journal of Experimental Psychology, 11,* 56–60.

Moray, N. (1982). Subjective mental workload. *Human Factors, 24,* 25–40.

Moray, N. (1987). Intelligent aids, mental models, and the theory of machines. *International Journal of Man–Machine Studies, 27,* 619–629.

Morgan, M. J., Watt, R. J., & McKee, S. P. (1983). Exposure duration affects the sensitivity of vernier acuity to target motion. *Vision Research, 23,* 541–546.

Morin, R. E., & Grant, D. A. (1955). Learning and performance on a key-pressing task as a function of the degree of spatial stimulus–response correspondence. *Journal of Experimental Psychology, 49,* 39–47.

Morris, C. D., Bransford, J. D., & Franks, J. J. (1977). Levels of processing versus transfer appropriate processing. *Journal of Verbal Learning and Verbal Behavior, 16,* 519–533.

Morrison, J. D., & Whiteside, T. C. D. (1984). Binocular cues in the perception of distance of a point source of light. *Perception, 13,* 555–566.

Morton, J. A. (1969). Interaction of information in word recognition. *Psychological Review, 76,* 165–178.

Mowbray, G. H. (1960). Choice reaction time for skilled responses. *Quarterly Journal of Experimental Psychology, 12,* 193–202.

Mowbray, G. H., & Rhoades, M. U. (1959). On the reduction of choice-reaction times with practice. *Quarterly Journal of Experimental Psychology, 11,* 16–23.

Mulder, T., & Hulstijn, W. (1985). Sensory feedback in the learning of a novel motor task. *Journal of Motor Behavior, 17,* 110–128.

Munton, J. S., Chamberlain, N. A., & Wright, V. (1981). An investigation into the problems of easy chairs used by the arthritic and the elderly. *Rheumatology and Rehabilitation, 20,* 164–173.

Murray, D. (1991). Modelling for adaptivity. In M. J. Tauber & D. Ackermann (eds.), *Mental Models and Human–Computer Interaction, 2* (pp. 81–93). Amsterdam: North-Holland.

Murrell, G. A. (1975). A reappraisal of artificial signals as an aid to a visual monitoring task. *Ergonomics, 18,* 693–700.

Muybridge, E. (1955). *The Human Figure in Motion.* New York: Dover.

Näätänen, R. (1973). The inverted-U relationship between activation and performance. In S. Kornblum (ed.), *Attention and Performance IV* (pp. 155–174). New York: Academic Press.

Nakaseko, M., Grandjean, E., Hunting, W., & Grier, R. (1985). Studies on ergonomically designed alphanumeric keyboards. *Human Factors, 27,* 175–187.

Nanda, R., & Adler, G. L. (eds.) (1977). *Learning Curves: Theory and Application.* Atlanta, GA: American Institute of Industrial Engineers.

Naruo, N., Lehto, M., & Salvendy, G. (1990). Development of a knowledge-based decision support system for diagnosing malfunctions of advanced production equipment. *International Journal of Production Research, 28,* 2259–2276.

NASA (National Aeronautics and Space Administration) (1978). *Anthropometric Source Book.* NASA Reference Publication 1024. Springfield, VA: National Technical Information Service.

Navon, D., & Gopher, D. (1979). On the economy of the human information processing system. *Psychological Review, 86,* 214–255.

Neely, J. H. (1977). Semantic priming and retrieval from lexical memory: Roles of inhibitionless spreading activation and limited-capacity attention. *Journal of Experimental Psychology: General, 106,* 226–254.

Neill, W. T., Lissner, L. S., & Beck, J. L. (1990). Negative priming in same–different matching: Further evidence for a central locus of inhibition. *Perception & Psychophysics, 48,* 398–400.

Nelson, T. O., & Rothbart, R. (1972). Acoustic savings for items forgotten from long-term memory. *Journal of Experimental Psychology, 93,* 357–360.

Nelson, W. R. (1988). Human factors considerations for expert systems in the nuclear industry. - *Proceedings of the IEEE Conference on Human Factors and Power Plants* (pp. 109–114). New York: Institute of Electrical and Electronics Engineers.

Nelson, W. R., & Blackman, H. S. (1987). Experimental evaluation of expert systems for nuclear reactor operators: Human factors considerations. *International Journal of Industrial Ergonomics, 2,* 91–100.

Nemecek, J., & Grandjean, E. (1971). Das Gressraumbüro in arbeits physiologischer Sicht. *Industrielle Organisation, 40,* 233–243.

Neumann, O. (1987). Beyond capacity: A functional view of attention. In H. Heuer & A. F. Sanders (eds.), *Perspectives on Perception and Action* (pp. 361–394). Hillsdale, NJ: Lawrence Erlbaum.

Neves, D. M., & Anderson, J. R. (1981). Knowledge compilation: Mechanisms for the automatization of cognitive skills. In J. R. Anderson (ed.), *Cognitive Skills and Their Acquisition* (pp. 57–84). Hillsdale, NJ: Lawrence Erlbaum.

Newell, A. (1990). *Unified theories of cognition.* Cambridge, MA: Harvard University Press.

Newell, A., & Rosenbloom, P. S. (1981). Mechanisms of skill acquisition and the law of practice. In J. R. Anderson (eds.), *Cognitive Skills and Their Acquisition* (pp. 1–55). Hillsdale, NJ: Lawrence Erlbaum.

Newell, A., & Simon, H. A. (1972). *Human Problem Solving.* Englewood Cliffs, NJ: Prentice Hall.

Newell, K. M. (1976). Knowledge of results and motor learning. *Exercise and Sport Sciences Reviews, 4,* 195–227.

Newell, K. M., & Carlton, M. J. (1987). Augmented information and the acquisition of isometric tasks. *Journal of Motor Behavior, 19,* 4–12.

Newell, K. M., Morris, L. R., & Scully, D. M. (1985). Augmented information and the acquisition of skill in physical activity. In R. L. Terjung (ed.), *Exercise and Sport Sciences Reviews* (pp. 235–261). New York: Macmillan.

Newell, K. M., Sparrow, W. A., & Quinn, J. T. (1985). Kinetic information feedback for learning isometric tasks. *Journal of Human Movement Studies, 11,* 113–123.

Newell, K. M., & Walter, C. B. (1981). Kinematic and kinetic parameters as information feedback in motor skill acquisition. *Journal of Human Movement Studies, 7,* 235–254.

Newman, R. L. (1987). Responses to Roscoe, "The trouble with HUDS and HMDS." *Human Factors Society Bulletin, 30* (10), 3–5.

Nichols, R. G. (1962). Listening is good business. *Management of Personnel Quarterly, 4,* 4.

Nickerson, R. S. (1986). *Using Computers.* Cambridge, MA: MIT Press.

Nicoletti, R., Anzola, G. P., Luppino, G., Rizzolatti, G., & Umiltà, C. (1982). Spatial compatibility effects on the same side of the body midline. *Journal of Experimental Psychology: Human Perception and Performance, 8,* 664–673.

Nilsson, N. J. (1980). *Principles of Artificial Intelligence.* Los Altos, CA: Morgan Kaufmann.

NIOSH (National Institute for Occupational Safety and Health) (1981). *Work Practices Guide for Manual Lifting.* DHHS/NIOSH Publication No. 81–122. Washington, DC: U.S. Government Printing Office.

Norman, D. A. (1968). Toward a theory of memory and attention. *Psychological Review, 75,* 522–536.

Norman, D. A. (1981). Categorization of action slips. *Psychological Review, 88,* 1–15.

Norman, D. (1983). *The DVORAK revival: Is it really worth the cost?* La Jolla, CA: Institute for Cognitive Science, University of California, San Diego.

Norman, D. A. (1988). *The Psychology of Everyday Things.* New York: Basic Books.

Norman, D. A., & Bobrow, D. (1978). On data-limited and resource-limited processing. *Cognitive Psychology, 7,* 44–60.

Norman, D., & Fisher, D. (1982). Why alphabetic keyboards are not easy to use: Keyboard layout doesn't much matter. *Human Factors, 24,* 509–519.

Nosofsky, R. M. (1987). Attention, similarity, and the identification–categorization relationship. *Journal of Experimental Psychology: General, 115,* 39–57.

Noyes, J. M., Haigh, R., & Starr, A. F. (1989). Automatic speech recognition for disabled people. *Applied Ergonomics, 20,* 293–298.

Nygard, C.-H., & Ilmarinen, J. (1990). Effects of changes in delivery of dairy products on physical strain of truck drivers. In C. M. Haslegrave, J. R. Wilson, E. N. Corlett, & I. Manenica (eds.), *Work Design in Practice* (pp. 142–148). London: Taylor & Francis.

Nygren, T. E. (1991). Psychometric properties of subjective workload measurement techniques: Implications for their use in the assessment of perceived mental workload. *Human Factors, 33,* 17–34.

Oborne, D. J., & Gruneberg, M. M. (1983). The environment and productivity. In D. J. Oborne & M. M. Gruneberg (eds.), *The Physical Environment at Work* (pp. 1–9). New York: Wiley.

Ogden, G. D., Levine, J. M., & Eisner, E. J. (1979). Measurement of workload by secondary tasks. *Human Factors, 21,* 529–548.

Olson, H. F. (1967). *Music, Physics and Engineering,* 2nd ed. New York: Dover.

Olson, J. R., & Olson, G. M. (1990). The growth of cognitive modeling in human–computer interaction since GOMS. *Human–Computer Interaction, 5,* 221–265.

O'Neil, W. M. (1957). *Introduction to Method in Psychology.* Carlton, Australia: Melbourne University Press.

Ong, C. N., Koh, D., & Phoon, W. O. (1988). Review and appraisal of health hazards of display terminals. *Displays: Technology and Applications, 9,* 3–13.

O'Reilly, C. A., III (1980). Individuals and information overload in organizations: Is more necessarily better? *Academy of Management Journal, 23,* 684–696.

OSHA (Occupational Safety and Health Administration) (1989). *OSHA: Employee Workplace Rights* (rev.). Washington, DC: Department of Labor.

Osherson, D. W., Smith, E. E., & Shafir, E. B. (1986). Some origins of belief. *Cognition, 24,* 197–224.

Ostry, D., Moray, N., & Marks, G. (1976). Attention, practice and semantic targets. *Journal of Experimental Psychology: Human Perception and Performance, 2,* 326–336.

Owens, D. A., & Leibowitz, H. W. (1980). Accommodation, convergence, and distance perception in low illumination. *American Journal of Optometry and Physiological Optics, 57,* 540–550.

Owens, D. A., & Leibowitz, H. W. (1983). Perceptual and motor consequences of tonic vergence. In C. M. Schor & K. J. Cuiffreda (eds.), *Vergence Eye Movements: Basic and Clinical Aspects* (pp. 23–97). Boston: Butterworth.

Owens, D. A., & Wolfe-Kelly, K. (1987). Nearwork, visual fatigue, and variations of oculomotor tonus. *Investigative Ophthalmology and Visual Science, 28,* 745–749.

Oyama, T. (1987). Perception studies and their applications to environmental design. *International Journal of Psychology, 22,* 447–451.

Paap, K. R., & Ogden, W. G. (1981). Letter encoding is an obligatory but capacity-demanding operation. *Journal of Experimental Psychology: Human Perception and Performance, 7,* 518–528.

Paap, K. R., & Roské-Hofstrand, R. J. (1986). The optimal number of menu options per panel. *Human Factors, 28,* 377–385.

Paap, K. R., & Roské-Hofstrand, R. J. (1988). Design of menus. In M. Helander (ed.), *Handbook of Human–Computer Interaction* (pp. 205–235). Amsterdam: North-Holland.

Pachella, R. G. (1974). The interpretation of reaction time in information-processing research. In B. H. Kantowitz (ed.), *Human Information Processing: Tutorials in Performance and Cognition* (pp. 41–82). Hillsdale, NJ: Lawrence Erlbaum.

Pack, M., Cotten, D. J., & Biasiotto, J. (1974). Effect of four fatigue levels on performance and learning of a novel dynamic balance skill. *Journal of Motor Behavior, 6,* 191–197.

Paivio, A. (1986). *Mental Representations: A Dual Coding Approach.* New York: Oxford University Press.

Palmer, J. (1986). Mechanisms of displacement discrimination with and without perceived movement. *Journal of Experimental Psychology: Human Perception and Performance, 12,* 411–421.

Parasuraman, R. (1979). Memory load and event rate control sensitivity decrements in sustained attention. *Science, 205,* 924–927.

Parasuraman, R., & Davies, D. R. (1976). Decision theory analysis of response latencies in vigilance. *Journal of Experimental Psychology: Human Perception and Performance, 2,* 569–582.

Parasuraman, R., & Mouloua, M. (1987). Interaction of signal discriminability and task type in vigilance decrement. *Perception & Psychophysics, 41,* 17–22.

Parasuraman, R., & Nestor, P. G. (1991). Attention and driving skills in aging and Alzheimer's disease. *Human Factors, 33,* 539–557.

Park, K. S. (1987). *Human Reliability: Analysis, Prediction, and Prevention of Human Errors.* Amsterdam: Elsevier.

Park, M.-Y., & Casali, J. G. (1991). A controlled investigation of in-field attenuation performance of selected insert, earmuff, and canal cap hearing protectors. *Human Factors, 33,* 693–714.

Parsaye, K., & Chignell, M. (1987). *Expert systems for experts.* New York: Wiley.

Pashler, H. (1984). Processing stages in overlapping tasks: Evidence for a central bottleneck. *Journal of Experimental Psychology: Human Perception and Performance, 10,* 358–377.

Pashler, H. (1989). Dissociations and dependencies between speed and accuracy: Evidence for a two-component theory of divided attention in simple tasks. *Cognitive Psychology, 21,* 469–514.

Pashler, H., & Baylis, G. (1991). Procedural learning: 2. Intertrial repetition effects in speeded choice tasks. *Journal of Experimental Psychology: Learning, Memory, and Cognition, 17,* 33–48.

Passchier-Vermeer, W. (1974). Hearing loss due to continuous exposure to steady state broad-band noise. *Journal of the Acoustical Society of America, 56,* 1585–1593.

Pastoor, S. (1990). Legibility and subjective preference for color combinations in text. *Human Factors, 32,* 157–171.

Patterson, R. D. (1982). *Guidelines for Auditory Warning Systems on Civil Aircraft: The Learning and Retention of Warnings*. CAA Paper 82017. London: Civil Aviation Authority.

Paulignan, Y., MacKenzie, C., Marteniuk, R., & Jeannerod, M. (1990). The coupling of arm and finger movements during prehension. *Experimental Brain Research, 79*, 431–436.

Payne, D., & Altman, J. (1962). *An Index of Electronic Equipment Operability: Report of Development*. Report AIR-C-43–1/62. Pittsburgh, PA: American Institutes of Research.

Penfield, W., & Rasmussen, T. (1950). *The Cerebral Cortex of Man: A Clinical Study of Localization of Function*. New York: Macmillan.

Pepper, R. L., & Herman, L. M. (1970). Decay and interference effects in the short-term retention of a discrete motor act. *Journal of Experimental Psychology, 83* (Monograph Supplement 2), 1–18.

Peters, G. A. (1977). Why only a fool relies on safety standards. *Hazard Prevention, 14* (2).

Peterson, L. R., & Gentile, A. (1963). Proactive interference as a function of time between tests. *Journal of Experimental Psychology, 70*, 473–478.

Peterson, L. R., & Peterson, M. J. (1959). Short-term retention of individual verbal items. *Journal of Experimental Psychology, 58*, 193–198.

Petre, M. (1991). What experts want from programming languages. *Ergonomics, 34*, 1113–1127.

Petros, T. V., Bentz, B., Hammes, K., & Zehr, H. D. (1990). The components of text that influence reading times and recall in skilled and less skilled college readers. *Discourse Processes, 13*, 387–400.

Pfauth, M., & Priest, J. (1981). Person–computer interface using touch screen devices. In *Proceedings of the Human Factors Society 25th Annual Meeting* (pp. 500–504). Santa Monica, CA: Human Factors Society.

Philp, R. B., Fields, G. N., & Roberts, W. A. (1989). Memory deficit caused by compressed air equivalent to 36 meters of seawater. *Journal of Applied Psychology, 74*, 443–446.

Pickles, J. O. (1988). *An Introduction to the Physiology of Hearing*, 2nd ed. New York: Academic Press.

Pierson, J. (1990). Form and function: Children's handrail hasn't found a home. *Wall Street Journal*, September 6.

Pile, J. F. (1979). *Modern Furniture*. New York: Wiley.

Pisoni, D. B. (1982). Perceptual evaluation of voice response systems: Intelligibility, recognition, and understanding. *Workshop of Standardization for Speech I/O Technology* (pp. 183–192). Gaithersburg, MD: National Bureau of Standards.

Plant, G. (1988). Speech reading with tactile supplements. *Volta Review, 90* (5), 149–160.

Plateau, J. A. F. (1872). Sur la mesure des sensations physiques, et sur la loi que lie l'intensité de ces sensations à l'intensité de la cause excitante. *Bulletins de l'Academie Royal des Sciences, des Lettres, et des Beaux-Arts de Belgique, 33*, 376–388.

Plath, D. W., & Kolesnik, P. E. (1966). Readability and operability of three types of digital switches. *Journal of Engineering Psychology, 5*, 47–53.

Pohlman, L. D., & Sorkin, R. D. (1976). Simultaneous three-channel signal detection: Performance and criterion as a function of order of report. *Perception & Psychophysics, 20*, 179–186.

Pollack, I. (1952). The information of elementary and auditory displays. *Journal of the Acoustical Society of America, 24*, 745–749.

Pollack, S. R. (1990). Tech wrecks. *Detroit Free Press*, Sept. 1, p. 1C.

Pollard, D., & Cooper, M. M. (1979). The effect of feedback on keying performance. *Applied Ergonomics, 10*, 194–200.

Pollatsek, A., & Rayner, K. (1989). Reading. In M. I. Posner (ed.), *Handbook of Cognitive Science* (pp. 401–436). Cambridge, MA: MIT Press.

Polson, P. G. (1988). The consequence of consistent and inconsistent user interfaces. In R. G. Guindon (ed.), *Cognitive Science and Its Applications for Human–Computer Interaction* (pp. 59–108). Hillsdale, NJ: Lawrence Erlbaum.

Pomerantz, J. R. (1981). Perceptual organization in information processing. In M. Kubovy & J. R. Pomerantz (eds.), *Perceptual organization* (pp. 141–180). Hillsdale, NJ: Lawrence Erlbaum.

Pomerantz, J. R., & Kubovy, M. (1986). Theoretical approaches to perceptual organization. In K. R. Boff, L. Kaufman, & J. P. Thomas (eds.), *Handbook of Human Perception and Performance, Vol. II: Cognitive Processes and Performance* (pp. 36-1 to 36-46). New York: Wiley.

Ponds, R. W. H. N., Brouwer, W. B., & van Wolffelaar, P. C. (1988). Age differences in divided attention in a simulated driving task. *Journal of Gerontology, 43*, P151–P156.

Poock, G. K. (1969). Color coding effects in compatible and noncompatible display-control arrangements. *Journal of Applied Psychology, 53,* 301–303.

Poon, L. W., Walsh-Sweeney, L., & Fozard, J. L. (1980). Memory skill training for the elderly: Salient issues on the use of imagery mnemonics. In L. W. Poon, J. L. Fozard, L. S. Cermak (eds.), *New Directions in Memory and Aging* (pp. 461–484). Hillsdale, NJ: Lawrence Erlbaum.

Posner, M. I. (1986). Overview. In K. R. Boff, L. Kaufman, & J. P. Thomas (eds.), *Handbook of Perception and Human Performance, Vol. II: Cognitive Processes and Performance* (pp. V-3 to V-10). New York: Wiley.

Posner, M. I., & Boies, S. J. (1971). Components of attention. *Psychological Review, 78,* 391–408.

Posner, M. I., Klein, R., Summers, J., & Buggie, S. C. (1973). On the selection of signals. *Memory & Cognition, 1,* 2–12.

Posner, M. I., Nissen, M. J., & Klein, R. (1976). Visual dominance: An information processing account of its origins and significance. *Psychological Review, 83,* 157–171.

Posner, M. I., Nissen, M. J., & Ogden, W. C. (1978). Attended and unattended processing modes: The role of set for spatial location. In H. L. Pick & I. J. Saltzman (eds.), *Modes of Perceiving and Processing Information.* Hillsdale, NJ: Lawrence Erlbaum.

Post, T. R., & Brennan, M. L. (1976). An experimental study of the effectiveness of a formal vs. an informal presentation of a general heuristic process on problem solving in tenth grade geometry. *Journal for Research in Mathematics Education, 7,* 59–64.

Postman, L., & Underwood, B. J. (1973). Critical issues in interference theory. *Memory & Cognition, 1,* 19–40.

Potosnak, K. (1988). Do icons make user interfaces easier to use? *IEEE Software, May,* 97–99.

Poulton, E. C. (1957). On prediction in skilled movements. *Psychological Bulletin, 54,* 467–478.

Poulton, E. C. (1969). Tracking. In E. A. Bilodeau & I. M. Bilodeau (eds.), *Principles of Skill Acquisition* (pp. 287–318). New York: Academic Press.

Poulton, E. C. (1974). *Tracking Skill and Manual Control.* New York: Academic Press.

Povel, D.-J., & Collard, R. (1982). Structural factors in patterned finger tapping. *Acta Psychologica, 52,* 107–123.

Pratt, C. C. (1969). Introduction. In W. Kohler, *The Task of Gestalt Psychology.* Princeton, NJ: Princeton University Press.

Preczewski, S. C., & Fisher, D. L. (1990). The selection of alphanumeric code sequences. In *Proceedings of the Human Factors Society 34th Annual Meeting* (pp. 224–228). Santa Monica, CA: Human Factors Society.

Preece, A. D. (1990). DISPLAN: Designing a usable medical expert system. In D. Berry & A. Hart (eds.), *Expert Systems: Human Issues* (pp. 25–47). Cambridge, MA: MIT Press.

Prinzmetal, W., & Banks, W. P. (1977). Good continuation affects visual detection. *Perception & Psychophysics, 21,* 389–395.

Proctor, R. W., & Reeve, T. G. (1985). Compatibility effects in the assignment of symbolic stimuli to discrete finger responses. *Journal of Experimental Psychology: Human Perception and Performance, 11,* 623–639.

Proctor, R. W., & Reeve, T. G. (eds.) (1990). *Stimulus–response Compatibility: An Integrated Perspective.* Amsterdam: North-Holland.

Proctor, R. W., Reeve, T. G., & Weeks, D. J. (1990). A triphasic approach to the acquisition of response-selection skill. In G. H. Bower (ed.), *The Psychology of Learning and Motivation,* Vol. 26 (pp. 207–240). New York: Academic Press.

Propst, R. L. (1966). The action office. *Human Factors, 8,* 299–306.

Pulaski, P. D., Zee, D. S., & Robinson, D. A. (1981). The behavior of the vestibulo-ocular reflex at high velocities of head rotation. *Brain Research, 222,* 159–165.

Radl, G. W. (1980). Experimental investigations for optimal presentation-mode and colours of symbols on the CRT screen. In E. Grandjean & E. Vigliani (eds.), *Ergonomic Aspects of Visual Display Terminals* (pp. 127–135). London: Taylor & Francis.

Radwin, R. G., Vanderheiden, G. C., & Li, M.-L. (1990). A method for evaluating head-controlled computer input devices using Fitts' law. *Human Factors, 32,* 423–438.

Ralston, D. A., Anthony, W. P., & Gustafson, D. J. (1985). Employees may love flextime, but what does it do to the organization's performance. *Journal of Applied Psychology, 70,* 272–279.

Ramachandran, V. S. (1988). Perception of shape from shading. *Nature, 33,* 163–166.

Ramsey, C. L., & Schultz, A. C. (1989). Knowledge representation for expert systems development. In J. Liebowitz & D. A. De Salvo (eds.), *Structuring Expert Systems: Domain, Design, and Development* (pp. 273–301). Englewood Cliffs, NJ: Prentice Hall (Yourdon Press).

Randle, R. (1988). Visual accommodation: Mediated control and performance. In D. J. Oborne (ed.), *International Reviews of Ergonomics*, Vol. 2 (pp. 207–232). London: Taylor & Francis.

Rash, C. E., Verona, R. W., & Crowley, J. S. (1990). Night flight using thermal imaging systems. *Visual Performance Group Technical Newsletter, 12* (3), 1–7.

Rasmussen, J. (1986). *Information Processing and Human–Machine Interaction: An Approach to Cognitive Engineering*. Amsterdam: North-Holland.

Rasmussen, J. (1987). Cognitive control and human error mechanisms. In J. Rasmussen, K. Duncan, & J. Leplat (eds.), *New Technology and Human Error* (pp. 53–61). New York: Wiley.

Raugh, M. R., & Atkinson, R. C. (1975). A mnemonic method for learning a second-language vocabulary. *Journal of Educational Psychology, 67*, 1–16.

Reason, J. (1987). The psychology of mistakes: A brief review of planning failures. In J. Rasmussen, K. Duncan, & J. Leplat (eds.), *New Technology and Human Error* (pp. 45–52). New York: Wiley.

Reason, J. (1990). *Human Error*. Cambridge, MA: Cambridge University Press.

Reed, C. M., Durlach, N. I., Delhorne, L. A., Rabinowitz, W. M., & Grant, K. W. (1989). Research on tactual communication of speech: Ideas and findings. *Volta Review, 91* (5), 65–78.

Reed, C. M., Rabinowitz, W. M., Durlach, N. I., Braida, L. D., Conway-Fithian, S., & Schultz, M. C. (1985). Research on the Tadoma method in speech communication. *Journal of the Acoustical Society of America, 77*, 247–257.

Reese, K. M. (1992). Newscripts: Personal comfort control tied to productivity. *Chemical and Engineering News, 70* (20), 56.

Reeve, T. G., Dornier, L., & Weeks, D. J. (1990). Precision of knowledge of results: Consideration of the accuracy requirements imposed by the task. *Research Quarterly for Exercise and Sport, 61*, 284–291.

Reeve, T. G., & Proctor, R. W. (1984). On the advance preparation of discrete finger responses. *Journal of Experimental Psychology: Human Perception and Performance, 10*, 541–553.

Reeve, T. G., & Proctor, R. W. (1988). Determinants of two-choice reaction-time patterns for same-hand and different-hand finger pairings. *Journal of Motor Behavior, 20*, 317–340.

Reicher, G. M. (1969). Perceptual recognition as a function of meaningfulness of stimulus material. *Journal of Experimental Psychology, 81*, 275–280.

Reid, G. B., Shingledecker, C. A., & Eggemeier, F. T. (1981). Application of conjoint measurement to workload scale development. In *Proceedings of the Human Factors Society 25th Annual Meeting* (pp. 522–526). Santa Monica, CA: Human Factors Society.

Reisner, P. (1984). Formal grammar as a tool for analyzing ease of use: Some fundamental concepts. In J. Thomas & M. Schneider (eds.), *Human Factors in Computer Systems* (pp. 53–78). Norwood, NJ: Ablex.

Research Pays Off. (1989). Preventing back injuries: AAR program adopted at Union Pacific. *TR News, 140*, 16–17.

Reynolds, D. D., & Angevine, E. N. (1977). Hand–arm vibration. Part II: Vibration transmission and characteristics of the hand and arm. *Journal of Sound and Vibration, 51*, 255–265.

Richardson, A. (1967a). Mental practice: A review and discussion. Part I. *Research Quarterly, 38*, 95–107.

Richardson, A. (1967b). Mental practice: A review and discussion. Part II. *Research Quarterly, 38*, 263–273.

Rips, L. J. (1989). Similarity, typicality, and categorization. In S. Voisniadou & A. Ortony (eds.), *Similarity, Analogy, and Thought*. New York: Cambridge University Press.

Rips, L. J., & Marcus, S. L. (1977). Suppositions and the analysis of conditional sentences. In M. A. Just & P. A. Carpenter (eds.), *Cognitive Processes in Comprehension* (pp. 185–220). Hillsdale, NJ: Lawrence Erlbaum.

Robbins, S. R. (1983). *Organizational Theory: The Structure and Design of Organizations*. Englewood Cliffs, NJ: Prentice Hall.

Roberts, M., & Summerfield, Q. (1981). Audiovisual adaptation in speech perception. *Perception & Psychophysics, 30*, 309–314.

Robey, D. (1987). Implementation and the organizational impacts of information systems. *Interfaces, 17* (3), 72–84.

Robinson, C. P., & Eberts, R. E. (1987). Comparison of speech and pictorial displays in a cockpit environment. *Human Factors, 29*, 31–44.

Robinson, G. H. (1989). The practice of forensic human factors. *Human Factors Society Bulletin, 32* (4), 1–3.

Rock, I., & Palmer, S. (1990). The legacy of Gestalt psychology. *Scientific American, 263* (6), 84–90.

Rockway, M., & Franks, P. (1959). *Effects of Variations in Control Backlash and Gain on Tracking Performance* (Report No. 58–553). Wright Air Development Center, Wright–Patterson Air Force Base: U.S. Air Force.

Rockway, M. R., & Nullmeyer, R. T. (1984). Training effectiveness evaluations of the C-130 weapon system trainer wide-angle visual system. In *Annual Mini-symposium on Aerospace Science and Technology Conference Proceedings*. Wright–Patterson Air Force Base: U.S. Air Force.

Roebuck, J. A., Jr., Kroemer, K. H. E., & Thomson, W. G. (1975). *Engineering Anthropometry Methods*. New York: Wiley.

Rogers, J. (1970). Discrete tracking performance with limited velocity resolution. *Human Factors, 12, 331–339*.

Rogers, K. F. (1987). Ergonomics today: Interviews with Julien Christensen, Harry Davis, Kate Ehrlich, Karl Kroemer, Rani Lueder, and Gavriel Salvendy. In K. H. Pelsma (ed.), *Ergonomics Sourcebook: A Guide to Human Factors Information* (pp. 3–18). Lawrence, KS: Ergosyst Associates.

Roscoe, S. N. (1987). The trouble with HUDS and HMDS. *Human Factors Society Bulletin, 7*(10), 1–3.

Rosenbaum, D. A. (1983). The movement precuing technique: Assumptions, applications, and extensions. In R. A. Magill (ed.), *Memory and Control of Action* (pp. 231–274). Amsterdam: North-Holland.

Rosenbaum, D. A. (1991). *Human Motor Control*. New York: Academic Press.

Rosenbaum, D. A., Hindorff, V., & Munro, E. M. (1987). Scheduling and programming of rapid finger sequences: Tests and elaborations of the hierarchical editor model. *Journal of Experimental Psychology: Human Perception and Performance, 13*, 193–203.

Rosenbaum, D. A., Marchak, F., Barnes, H. J., Vaughan, J., Slotta, J. D., & Jorgensen, M. J. (1990). Constraints for action selection: Overhand versus underhand grips. In M. Jeannerod (ed.), *Attention and Performance XIII* (pp. 321–342). Hillsdale, NJ: Lawrence Erlbaum.

Rosenbloom, P. S., & Newell, A. (1987). An integrated computational model of stimulus–response compatibility and practice. In G. H. Bower (ed.), *The Psychology of Learning and Motivation*, Vol. 21 (pp. 1–52). New York: Academic Press.

Rosson, M. B. (1983). Patterns of experience in text editing. *Proceedings of the CHI 83 Conference on Human Factors in Computing* (pp. 171–175). New York: ACM.

Rosson, M. B., & Mellon, N. M. (1985). Behavioral issues in speech-based remote information retrieval. In L. Lerman (ed.), *Proceedings of the Voice I/O Systems Applications Conference '85*. San Francisco: AVIOS.

Rothstein, A. L., & Arnold, R. K. (1976). Bridging the gap: Application of research on videotape feedback and bowling. *Motor Skills: Theory into Practice, 1*, 35–62.

Rothwell, J. C., Traub, M. M., Day, B. L., Obeso, J. A., Thomas, P. K., & Marsden, D. (1982). Manual motor performance in a deafferented man. *Brain, 105*, 515–542.

Rouse, W. B. (1979). Problem solving performance of maintenance trainees in a fault diagnosis task. *Human Factors, 21*, 195–203.

Rouse, W. B., & Cody, W. J. (1988). On the design of man-machine systems: Principles, practices and prospects. *Automatica, 24*, 227–238.

Rouse, W. B., & Cody, W. J. (1989). Designers' criteria for choosing human performance models. In G. R. McMillan, D. Beevis, E. Salas, M. H. Strub, R. Sutton, & L. Van Breda (eds.), *Applications of Human Performance Models to System Design* (pp. 7–14). New York: Plenum.

Rouse, W. B., Cody, W. J., & Boff, K. R. (1991). The human factors of system design: Understanding and enhancing the role of human factors engineering. *International Journal of Human Factors in Manufacturing, 1*, 87–104.

Rubinstein, M. F. (1986). *Tools for Thinking and Problem Solving*. Englewood Cliffs, NJ: Prentice Hall.

Rubinstein, R., & Hersh, H. (1984). *The Human Factor*. Bedford, MA: Digital Press.

Rudov, M. H. (1988). Ethics for the forensic practitioner. *Human Factors Society Bulletin, 31* (6), 7–8.

Rühmann, H.-P. (1984). Basic data for the design of consoles. In H. Schmidtke (ed.), *Ergonomic Data for Equipment Design* (pp. 15–144). New York: Plenum.

Rumelhart, D. E. (1975). Notes on schema for stories. In D. G. Bobrow & A. M. Collins (eds.), *Representation and Understanding: Studies in Cognitive Science* (pp. 211–236). New York: Academic Press.

Rumelhart, D. E., & McClelland, J. L. (1986). *Parallel Distributed Processing: Explorations in the Microstructure of Cognition Volume 1: Foundations; Volume 2: Psychological and Biological Models.* Cambridge, MA: MIT Press.

Rumelhart, D. E., & Norman, D. A. (1982). Simulating a skilled typist: A study of skilled cognitive-motor performance. *Cognitive Science, 6,* 1–36.

Rumelhart, D. E., & Norman, D. A. (1988). Representation in memory. In R. C. Atkinson, R. J. Herrnstein, G. Lindzey, & R. D. Luce (eds.), *Stevens Handbook of Experimental Psychology,* 2nd ed. (pp. 511–587). New York: Wiley.

Rundell, O. H., & Williams, H. L. (1979). Alcohol and speed–accuracy tradeoff. *Human Factors, 21,* 433–443.

Runeson, S., & Frykholm, G. (1983). Kinematic specification of dynamics as an informational basis for person-and-action perception: Expectation, gender, recognition, and deceptive intention. *Journal of Experimental Psychology: General, 112,* 585–615.

Russo, J. E. (1977). The value of unit price information. *Journal of Marketing Research, 14,* 193–201.

Russo, J. E., Johnson, E. J., & Stephens, D. L. (1989). The validity of verbal protocols. *Memory & Cognition, 17,* 759–769.

Sackett, G. P., Ruppenthal, G. C., & Gluck, J. (1978). Introduction: An overview of methodological and statistical problems in observational research. In G. P. Sackett (ed.), *Observing Behavior, Vol. II: Data Collection and Analysis Methods (*pp. 1–14). Baltimore, MD: University Park Press.

Sackett, R. S. (1934). The influences of symbolic rehearsal upon the retention of a maze habit. *Journal of General Psychology, 10,* 376–395.

Sagan, C. (1990). Why we need to understand science. *Skeptical Inquirer, 14,* 263–269.

Sage, G. H. (1984). *Motor Learning and Control: A Neuropsychological Approach.* Dubuque, IA: W. C. Brown.

Salmoni, A. W. (1989). Motor skill learning. In D. H. Holding (ed.), *Human Skills,* 2nd ed., (pp. 197–227). New York: Wiley.

Salmoni, A. W., Schmidt, R. A., & Walter, C. B. (1984). Knowledge of results and motor learning: A review and critical reappraisal. *Psychological Bulletin, 95,* 355–386.

Salthouse, T. A. (1984). Effects of age and skill in typing. *Journal of Experimental Psychology: General, 113,* 345–371.

Salthouse, T. A. (1986). Perceptual, cognitive, and motoric aspects of transcription typing. *Psychological Bulletin, 99,* 303–319.

Salvendy, G. (ed.) (1987). *Handbook of Human Factors.* New York: Wiley.

Sanders, M. S., & McCormick, E. J. (1987). *Human Factors in Engineering and Design,* 6th ed. New York: McGraw-Hill.

Sanders, P. A., & Bernecker, C. A. (1990). Uniform veiling luminance and display polarity affect VDU user performance. *Journal of the Illuminating Engineering Society, 19*(2), 113–123.

Sauter, S. L., Schleifer, L. M., & Knutson, S. J. (1991). Work posture, workstation design, and musculoskeletal discomfort in a VDT data entry task. *Human Factors, 33,* 151–167.

Savage, J. A. (1991). Stuck between a VDT and a hard place. *Computerworld,* May 13, 63, 67.

Sayers, B. A. (ed.) (1988). *Human Factors and Decision Making.* New York: Elsevier Applied Science.

Scharf, B., Quigley, S., Aoki, C., Peachey, N., & Reeves, A. (1987). Focused auditory attention and frequency selectivity. *Perception & Psychophysics, 42,* 215–223.

Schell, D. A. (1987). Laboratory-based usability testing of on-line and printed computer information. *Human Factors Society Bulletin, 30* (3), 1–3.

Schendel, J. D., & Hagman, J. D. (1982). On sustaining procedural skills over a prolonged retention interval. *Journal of Applied Psychology, 67,* 605–610.

Schmidt, R. A. (1975). A schema theory of discrete motor skill learning. *Psychological Review, 82,* 225–260.

Schmidt, R. A. (1988). *Motor Control and Learning: A Behavioral Emphasis,* 2nd ed. Champaign, IL: Human Kinetics.

Schmidt, R. A. (1989). Unintended acceleration: A review of human factors contributions. *Human Factors, 31,* 345–364.

Schmidt, R. A., & Young, D. E. (1987). Transfer of movement control in motor skill learning. In S. M. Cormier & J. D. Hagman (eds.), *Transfer of*

Learning: Contemporary Research and Applications (pp. 47–79). New York: Academic Press.

Schmidt, R. A., & Young, D. E. (1991). Methodology for motor learning: A paradigm for kinematic feedback. *Journal of Motor Behavior, 23,* 13–24.

Schmidt, R. A., Young, D. E., Swinnen, S., & Shapiro, D. C. (1989). Summary knowledge of results for skill acquisition: Support for the guidance hypothesis. *Journal of Experimental Psychology: Learning, Memory, and Cognition, 15,* 352–359.

Schmidt, R. A., Zelaznik, H. N., Hawkins, B., Frank, J. S., & Quinn, J. T. (1979). Motor-output variability: A theory for the accuracy of rapid motor acts. *Psychological Review, 86,* 415–451.

Schneider, W., & Fisk, A. D. (1983). Attention theory and mechanisms of skilled performance. In R. A. Magill (ed.), *Memory and Control of Action* (pp. 119–143). Amsterdam: North-Holland.

Schneider, W., & Shiffrin, R. M. (1977). Controlled and automatic human information processing: I. Detection, search, and attention. *Psychological Review, 84,* 1–66.

Schoenmarklin, R. W., & Marras, W. S. (1989a). Effects of handle angle and work orientation on hammering: I. Wrist motion and hammering performance. *Human Factors, 31,* 397–412.

Schoenmarklin, R. W., & Marras, W. S. (1989b). Effects of handle angle and work orientation on hammering: II. Muscle fatigue and subjective ratings of body discomfort. *Human Factors, 31,* 413–420.

Schwartz, D. R., & Howell, W. C. (1985). Optional stopping performance under graphic and numeric CRT formatting. *Human Factors, 27,* 433–444.

Schwartz, D., Sparkman, J., & Deese, J. (1970). The process of understanding and judgment of comprehensibility. *Journal of Verbal Learning and Verbal Behavior, 9,* 87–93.

Scialfa, C. T., Garvey, P. M., Gish, K. W., Deering, L. M., Leibowitz, H. W., & Goebel, C. C. (1988). Relationships among measures of static and dynamic visual sensitivity. *Human Factors, 30,* 677–687.

Seibel, R. (1963). Discrimination reaction time for a 1,023 alternative task. *Journal of Experimental Psychology, 66,* 215–226.

Sekuler, R., & Blake, R. (1990). *Perception,* 2nd ed. New York: McGraw-Hill.

Selfridge, O. G. (1959). Pandemonium: A paradigm for learning. In D. B. Blake & A. M. Uttley (eds.), *Proceedings of the Symposium on the Mechanism of Thought Processes* (pp. 511–529). London: Her Majesty's Stationary Office.

Selye, H. (1973). The evolution of the stress concept. *American Scientist, 61,* 692–699.

Seminara, J. L., Gonzalez, W. R., & Parsons, S. O. (1977). *Human Factors Review of Nuclear Power Plant Control Room Design* (Technical report EPRI NP-309, Research project 501). Prepared by Lockheed Missiles and Space Co., Inc. (Sunnyvale, CA) for the Electric Power Research Institute (Palo Alto, CA).

Senders, J. W. (1964). The human operator as a monitor and controller of multi-degree of freedom systems. *IEEE Transactions on Human Factors and Electronics, HFE-5,* 2–5.

Senders, J. W., & Moray, N. P. (1991). *Human Error: Cause, Prediction, and Reduction.* Hillsdale, NJ: Lawrence Erlbaum.

Serber, H. (1990). New developments in the science of seating. *Human Factors Society Bulletin, 33* (2), 1–3.

Seta, J. J., Paulus, P. B., & Schkade, J. K. (1976). Effects of group size and proximity under cooperative and competitive conditions. *Journal of Personality and Social Psychology, 34,* 47–53.

Shaffer, L. H., & Hardwick, J. (1968). Typing performance as a function of text. *Quarterly Journal of Experimental Psychology, 20,* 360–369.

Shaffer, M. T., Shafer, J. B., & Kutch, G. B. (1986). Empirical workload and communication: Analysis of scout helicopter exercises. In *Proceedings of the Human Factors Society 30th Annual Meeting* (pp. 628–632). Santa Monica, CA: Human Factors Society.

Shafir, E. B., Smith, E. E., & Osherson, D. N. (1990). Typicality and reasoning fallacies. *Memory & Cognition, 18,* 229–239.

Shapiro, D. C., & Schmidt, R. A. (1982). The schema theory: Recent evidence and developmental implications. In J. A. S. Kelso & J. E. Clark (eds.), *The Development of Movement Control and Coordination* (pp. 113–150). New York: Wiley.

Shapiro, D. C., Zernicke, R. F., Gregor, R. J., & Diestel, J. D. (1981). Evidence for generalized motor programs using gait pattern analysis. *Journal of Motor Behavior, 13,* 33–47.

Sharp, R. H., & Whiting, H. T. A. (1974). Exposure and occluded duration effects in ball-catching skill. *Journal of Motor Behavior, 6,* 139–147.

Sharp, R. H., & Whiting, H. T. A. (1975). Information-processing and eye movement behavior in a ball catching skill. *Journal of Human Movement Studies, 1,* 124–131.

Shaughnessy, J. J., & Zechmeister, E. B. (1985). *Research Methods in Psychology.* New York: Knopf.

Shaw, M. E. (1981). *Group Dynamics: The Psychology of Small Group Behavior,* 3rd ed. New York: McGraw-Hill.

Shea, J. B., & Morgan, R. L. (1979). Contextual interference effects on acquisition, retention, and transfer of a motor skill. *Journal of Experimental Psychology: Human Learning and Memory, 5,* 179–187.

Sheedy, J. E., Bailey, I. L., Burl, M., & Bass, E. (1986). Binocular vs. monocular task performance. *American Journal of Optometry & Physiological Optics, 63,* 839–846.

Shepard, R. N., & Metzler, J. (1971). Mental rotation of three-dimensional objects. *Science, 171,* 701–703.

Sherrick, C. E., & Cholewiak, R. W. (1986). Cutaneous sensitivty. In K. R. Boff, L. Kaufman, & J. P. Thomas (eds.), *Handbook of Perception and Human Performance, Vol. I: Sensory Processes and Perception,* (pp. 12-1 to 12-58). New York: Wiley.

Sherrington, C. S. (1906). *Integrative Action of the Nervous System.* New Haven, CT: Yale University Press.

Shiffrin, R. M. (1988). Attention. In R. C. Atkinson, (eds.), *Stevens' Handbook of Experimental Psychology, Vol. 2* (pp. 739–811). New York: Wiley.

Shiffrin, R. M., & Schneider, W. (1977). Controlled and automatic human information processing: II. Perceptual learning, automatic attending, and a general theory. *Psychological Review, 84,* 127–190.

Shinar, D., & Acton, M. B. (1978). Control-display relationships on the four-burner range: Population stereotypes versus standards. *Human Factors, 20,* 13–17.

Shingledecker, C. A. (1980). Enhancing operator acceptance and noninterference in secondary task measures of workload. In *Proceedings of the 24th Annual Meeting of the Human Factors Society* (pp. 674–677). Santa Monica, CA: Human Factors Society.

Shoptaugh, C. F., & Whitaker, L. A. (1984). Verbal response times to directional traffic signs embedded in photographic street scenes. *Human Factors, 26,* 235–244.

Shulman, G. L., Remington, R. W., & McLean, J. P. (1979). Moving attention through visual space. *Journal of Experimental Psychology: Human Perception and Performance, 5,* 522–526.

Shulman, H. G. (1970). Encoding and retention of semantic and phonemic information in short-term memory. *Journal of Verbal Learning and Verbal Behavior, 9,* 499–508.

Siegel, A., & Wolf, J. (1969). *Man–Machine Simulation Models.* New York: Wiley.

Siegel, A. I., & Crain, K. (1960). Experimental investigations of cautionary signal presentations. *Ergonomics, 3,* 339–356.

Siegel, A. I., Schultz, D. G., & Lanterman, R. S. (1963). Factors affecting control activation time. *Human Factors, 5,* 71–80.

Simon, H. A. (1957). *Models of Man.* New York: Wiley.

Simon, H. A., & Gilmartin, K. (1973). A simulation of memory for chess positions. *Cognitive Psychology, 5,* 29–46.

Simon, J. R. (1969). Reactions toward the source of stimulation. *Journal of Experimental Psychology, 81,* 174–176.

Simon, J. R. (1990). The effects of an irrelevant directional cue on human information processing. In R. W. Proctor & T. G. Reeve (eds.), *Stimulus–Response Compatibility: An Integrated Perspective* (pp. 31–86). Amsterdam: North-Holland.

Simpson, C. A., McCauley, M. E., Roland, E. F., Ruth, J. C., & Williges, B. H. (1985). System design for speech recognition and generation. *Human Factors, 27,* 115–141.

Simpson, C. A., & Williams, D. H. (1980). Response time effects of alerting tone and semantic context for synthesized voice cockpit warnings. *Human Factors, 22,* 319–330.

Simpson, G. C. (1990). Costs and benefits in occupational ergonomics. *Ergonomics, 33,* 261–268.

Singleton, W. T. (ed.) (1978). *The Analysis of Practical Skills.* Baltimore, MD: University Park Press.

Singley, M. K., & Anderson, J. R. (1989). *The Transfer of Cognitive Skill.* Cambridge, MA: Harvard University Press.

Sivak, M. (1987). Human factors and road safety. *Applied Ergonomics, 18,* 289–296.

Sivak, M., & Olson, P. L. (1985). Optimal and minimal luminance characteristics for retro-reflective highway signs. *Transportation Research Record, 1027,* 53–57.

Sivak, M., Olson, P. L., & Zeltner, K. A. (1989). Effect of prior headlighting experience on ratings of discomfort glare. *Human Factors, 31,* 391–395.

Skipper, J. H., Rieger, C. A., & Wierwille, W. W. (1986). Evaluation of decision-tree rating scales for mental workload estimation. *Ergonomics, 29,* 383–399.

Slatter, P. E. (1987). *Building Expert Systems: Cognitive Emulation.* Chichester, England: Ellis Horwood.

Sluchak, T. J. (1990). Human factors: Added value to retail customers. In *Proceedings of the Human Factors Society 34th Annual Meeting* (pp. 752–756). Santa Monica, CA: Human Factors Society.

Smith, E. E. (1989). Concepts and induction. In M. I. Posner (ed.), *Foundations of Cognitive Science* (pp. 501–526). Cambridge, MA: MIT Press.

Smith, E. E., & Medin, D. L. (1981). *Categorization and Concepts.* Cambridge, MA: Harvard University Press.

Smith, E. E., Shoben, E. J., & Rips, L. J. (1974). Structure and process in semantic memory: A feature model for semantic decisions. *Psychological Review, 81,* 214–241.

Smith, L. A. (1985). Selling the idea to management. In D. C. Alexander & B. M. Pulat, *Industrial Ergonomics: A Practitioner's Guide.* Norcross, GA: Industrial Engineering and Management Press.

Smith, M. J. (1987). Occupational stress. In G. Salvendy (ed.), *Handbook of Human Factors* (pp. 844–860). New York: Wiley.

Smith, M. J., Carayon, P., Eberts, R., & Salvendy, G. (1992). Human–computer interaction. In G. Salvendy (ed.), *Handbook of Industrial Engineering,* 2nd ed. (pp. 1107–1144). New York: Wiley.

Smith, S. W., & Rea, M. S. (1978). Proofreading under different levels of illumination. *Journal of the Illuminating Engineering Society, 8,* 47–52.

Snyder, H. (1976). Braking movement time and accelerator-brake separation. *Human Factors, 18,* 201–204.

Snyder, H. L., Decker, J. J., Lloyd, C. J. C., & Dye, C. (1990). Effect of image polarity on VDT task performance. In *Proceedings of the Human Factors Society 34th Annual Meeting* (pp. 1447–1451). Santa Monica, CA: Human Factors Society.

Snyder, H. L., & Taylor, G. B. (1979). The sensitivity of response measures of alphanumeric legibility to variations in dot matrix display parameters. *Human Factors, 21,* 457–471.

Soechting, J. F., & Laquaniti, F. (1983). Modification of trajectory of a pointing movement in response to a change in target location. *Journal of Neurophysiology, 49,* 548–564.

Sojourner, R. J., & Antin, J. F. (1990). The effects of a simulated head-up display speedometer on perceptual task performance. *Human Factors, 32,* 329–339.

Soloway, E., Adelson, B., & Ehrlich, K. (1988). Knowledge and processes in the comprehension of computer programs. In M. T. H. Chi, R. Glaser, & M. J. Farr (eds.), *The Nature of Expertise* (pp. 129–152). Hillsdale, NJ: Lawrence Erlbaum.

Sommer, R. (1967). Sociofugal space. *American Journal of Sociology, 72,* 654–659.

Sorkin, R. D. (1987). Design of auditory and tactile displays. In G. Salvendy (ed.), *Handbook of Human Factors* (pp. 549–576). New York: Wiley.

Sorkin, R. D. (1989). Why are people turning off our alarms? *Human Factors Society Bulletin, 32* (4), 3–4.

Sorkin, R. D., Kantowitz, B. H., & Kantowitz, S. C. (1988). Likelihood alarm displays. *Human Factors, 30,* 445–459.

Sorkin, R. D., Wightman, F. L., Kistler, D. S., & Elvers, G. C. (1989). An exploratory study of the use of movement-correlated cues in an auditory head-up display. *Human Factors, 31,* 161–166.

Space-station Human Productivity Study: Volumes I–V (1985). Lockheed Missiles and Space Company, Inc., Man–Systems Division, NASA, Lyndon B. Johnson Space Center, Houston, TX.

Sparks, D. L. (1991). The neural encoding of the location of targets for saccadic eye movements. In J. Paillard (ed.), *Brain and Space* (pp. 3–19). New York: Oxford University Press.

Sperling, G. (1960). The information available in brief visual presentations. *Psychological Monographs, 74,* 1–29.

Spieth, W., Curtis, J. F., & Webster, J. C. (1954). Responding to one of two simultaneous messages. *Journal of the Acoustical Society of America, 26,* 391–396.

Spilling, S., Eitrheim, J., & Aaras, A. (1986). Cost–benefit analysis of work environment investment at STK's telephone plant at Kongsvinger. In N.

Corlett, J. Wilson, & I. Manenica (eds.), *The Ergonomics of Working Postures* (pp. 380–397). London: Taylor & Francis.

Spitz, G. (1990). Target acquisition performance using a head mounted cursor control device and a stylus with a digitizing table. In *Proceedings of the 34th Annual Meeting of the Human Factors Society* (pp. 405–409). Santa Monica, CA: Human Factors Society.

Stark, L., & Bridgeman, B. (1983). Role of corollary discharge in space constancy. *Perception & Psychophysics, 34,* 371–380.

Staszewski, J. J. (1988). Skilled memory and expert mental calculation. In M. T. H. Chi, R. Glaser, & M. J. Farr (eds.), *The Nature of Expertise* (pp. 71–128). Hillsdale, NJ: Lawrence Erlbaum.

Stelmach, G. E. (1974). Retention of motor skills. In J. R. Wilmore (ed.), *Exercise and Sport Sciences Review,* Vol. 2 (pp. 1–26). New York: Academic Press.

Stelmach, G. E. (1991). Basal ganglia impairment and force control. In J. Requin & G. E. Stelmach (eds.), *Tutorials in Motor Neuroscience* (pp. 137–148). Boston: Kluwer.

Stenzel, A. G. (1962). Experience with a 1000 lx leather factory. *Lichttechnik, 14,* 16.

Stenzel, A. G., & Sommer, J. (1969). The effect of illumination on tasks which are largely independent of vision. *Lichttechnik, 21,* 143.

Sternberg, S. (1966). High-speed scanning in human memory. *Science, 153,* 652–654.

Sternberg, S. (1969). The discovery of processing stages: Extensions of Donders' method. In W. G. Koster (ed.), *Attention and Performance II* (pp. 276–315). Amsterdam: North-Holland.

Sternberg, S., Monsell, S., Knoll, R. C., & Wright, C. E. (1978). The latency and duration of rapid movement sequences: Comparisons of speech and typewriting. In G. E. Stelmach (ed.), *Information Processing in Motor Control and Learning* (pp. 117–152). New York: Academic Press.

Stevens, A., Roberts, B., & Stead, L. (1983). The use of sophisticated graphics interface in computer-assisted instruction. *IEEE Computer Graphics and Applications, 3,* 25–31.

Stevens, J. C., Okulicz, W. C., & Marks, L. E. (1973). Temporal summation at the warmth threshold. *Perception & Psychophysics, 14,* 307–312.

Stevens, J. K., Emerson, R. C., Gerstein, G. L., Kallos, T., Neufeld, G. R., Nichols, C. W., & Rosenquist, A. C. (1976). Paralysis of the awake human: Visual perceptions. *Vision Research, 16,* 93–98.

Stevens, S. S. (1935). The relation of pitch to intensity. *Journal of the Acoustical Society of America, 6,* 150–154.

Stevens, S. S. (1951). Mathematics, measurement, and psychophysics. In S. S. Stevens (ed.), *Handbook of Experimental Psychology* (pp. 1–49). New York: Wiley.

Stevens, S. S. (1961). The psychophysics of sensory function. In W. A. Rosenblith (ed.), *Sensory Communication* (pp. 1–33). Cambridge, MA: MIT Press.

Stevens, S. S. (1975). *Psychophysics: Introduction to Its Perceptual, Neural, and Social Prospects.* New York: Wiley.

Stevens, S. S., & Galanter, E. H. (1957). Ratio scales and category scales for a dozen perceptual continua. *Journal of Experimental Psychology, 54,* 377–411.

Stroop, J. R. (1935/1992). Studies of interference in serial verbal reactions. *Journal of Experimental Psychology: General, 121,* 15–23.

Sturr, F., Kline, G. E., & Taub, H. A. (1990). Performance of young and older drivers on a static acuity test under photopic and mesopic luminance conditions. *Human Factors, 32,* 1–8.

Sutton, H., & Porter, L. W. (1968). A study of the grapevine in a governmental organization. *Personnel Psychology, 21,* 223–230.

Svaetchin, A. (1956). Spectral response curves of single cones. *Acta Psychologica, 1,* 93–101.

Swain, A. D., & Guttman, H. E. (1983). *Handbook of Human Reliability Analysis with Emphasis on Nuclear Power Plant Applications.* Albuquerque, NM: Sandia National Laboratories.

Swets, J. A., Green, D. M., Fay, T. H., Kryter, K. D., Nixon, C. M., Riney, J. S., Schultz, T. J., Tanner, W. P., Jr., & Whitcomb, M. A. (1975). A proposed standard fire alarm signal. *Journal of the Acoustical Society of America, 57,* 756–757.

Swets, J. A., & Pickett, R. M. (1982). *Evaluation of Diagnostic Systems: Methods from Signal Detection Theory.* New York: Academic Press.

Swinnen, S. P. (1990). Interpolated activities during the knowledge-of-results delay and post-knowledge-of-results interval: Effects on performance and learning. *Journal of Experimental Psychology: Learning, Memory, and Cognition, 16,* 692–705.

Swinnen, S. P., Schmidt, R. A., Nicholson, D. E., & Shapiro, D. C. (1990). Information feedback for skill acquisition: Instantaneous knowledge of results degrades learning. *Journal of Experimental Psychology: Learning, Memory, and Cognition, 16,* 706–716.

Szilagyi, A. D., Jr., & Wallace, M. J., Jr. (1983). *Organizational Behavior and Performance,* 3rd ed. Glenview, IL: Scott, Foresman.

Taptagaporn, S., & Saito, S. (1990). How display polarity and lighting conditions affect the pupil size of VDT operators. *Ergonomics, 33,* 201–208.

Taub, E., & Berman, A. J. (1968). Movement and learning in the absence of sensory feedback. In S. J. Freedman (ed.), *The Neuropsychology of Spatially Oriented Behavior* (pp. 173–192). Homewood, IL: Dorsey Press.

Taylor, F. W. (1911/1967). *The Principles of Scientific Management.* New York: W. W. Norton.

Teichner, W. H. (1962). Probability of detection and speed of response in simple monitoring. *Human Factors, 4,* 181–186.

Teichner, W. H., & Krebs, M. J. (1972). Laws of simple visual reaction time. *Psychological Review, 79,* 344–358.

Teichner, W. H., & Krebs, M. J. (1974). Laws of visual choice reaction time. *Psychological Review, 81,* 75–98.

Telford, C. W. (1931). Refractory phase of voluntary and associative resonses. *Journal of Experimental Psychology, 14,* 1–35.

Theise, E. S. (1989). Finding a subset of stimulus-response pairs with a minimum of total confusion: A binary integer programming approach. *Human Factors, 31,* 291–305.

Thomas, M., Gilson, R., Ziulkowski, S., & Gibbons, S. (1989). Short term memory demands in processing synthetic speech. In *Proceedings of the Human Factors Society 33rd Annual Meeting.* Santa Monica, CA: Human Factors Society.

Thorndike, E. L. (1906). *Principles of Teaching.* New York: A. G. Seiler.

Thorndyke, P. W. (1977). Cognitive structures in comprehension and memory of narrative discourse. *Cognitive Psychology, 13,* 526–550.

Thorndyke, P. W. (1984). Applications of schema theory in cognitive research. In J. R. Anderson & S. M. Kosslyn (eds.), *Tutorials in Learning and Memory* (pp. 167–191). San Francisco: W. H. Freeman.

Tichauer, E. (1978). *The Biomechanical Basis of Ergonomics.* New York: Wiley.

Tillman, B. (1987). Man–systems integration standards (NASA-STD-3000). *Human Factors Society Bulletin, 30* (6), 5–6.

Tipper, S. P. (1985). The negative priming effect: Inhibitory priming by ignored objects. *Quarterly Journal of Experimental Psychology, 37A,* 571–590.

Tolhurst, D. J., & Thompson, P. G. (1975). Orientation illusions and aftereffects: Inhibition between channels. *Vision Research, 15,* 967–972.

Tonndorf, J. (1960). Shearing motion in scala media of cochlear models. *Journal of Acoustical Society of America, 32,* 238–244.

Topmiller, D., Eckel, J., & Kozinsky, E. (1982). *Human Reliability Data Bank for Nuclear Power Plant Operators: Vol. 1, A Review of Existing Human Reliability Data Banks* (NUREG/CR-2744/1 of 2). Washington, DC: Nuclear Regulatory Commission.

Townsend, J. T. (1971). Theoretical analysis of an alphabetic confusion matrix. *Perception & Psychophysics, 9,* 40–50.

Townsend, J. T. (1974). Issues and models concerning the processing of a finite number of inputs. In B. H. Kantowitz (ed.), *Human Information Processing* (pp. 133–185). Hillsdale, NJ: Lawrence Erlbaum.

Townsend, J. T., & Roos, R. N. (1973). Search reaction time for single targets in multiletter stimuli with brief visual displays. *Memory & Cognition, 1,* 319–332.

Treisman, A. M. (1964a). The effect of irrelevant material on the efficiency of selective listening. *American Journal of Psychology, 77,* 533–546.

Treisman, A. M. (1964b). Verbal cues, language, and meaning in selective attention. *American Journal of Psychology, 77,* 206–219.

Treisman, A. M. (1986). Features and objects in visual processing. *Scientific American, 255,* 114–125.

Treisman, A. M., Squire, R., & Green, J. (1974). Semantic processing in dichotic listening? A replication. *Memory & Cognition, 2,* 641–646.

Treisman, A. M., Sykes, M., & Gelade, G. (1977). Selective attention and stimulus integration. In S. Dornic (ed.), *Attention and Performance VI* (pp. 333–361). Hillsdale, NJ: Lawrence Erlbaum.

Tseng, M. M., Law, P.-H., & Cerva, T. (1992). Knowledge-based systems. In G. Salvendy (ed.), *Handbook of Industrial Engineering,* 2nd ed. (pp. 184–210). New York: Wiley.

Tullis, T. S. (1983). The formatting of alphanumeric displays: A review and analysis. *Human Factors, 25,* 657–682.

Tullis, T. S. (1986). *Display Analysis Program* (Version 4.0). Lawrence, KS: The Report Store.

Tulving, E., & Donaldson, W. (eds.) (1972). *Organization of memory.* New York: Academic Press.

Tulving, E., & Pearlstone, Z. (1966). Availability versus accessibility of information in memory for words. *Journal of Verbal Learning and Verbal Behavior, 5,* 381–391.

Tulving, E., & Thomson, D. M. (1973). Encoding specificity and retrieval processes in episodic memory. *Psychological Review, 80,* 352–373.

Turley, A. M. (1978). Acoustical privacy for the open office. *The Office.* Report in *Space Planning,* Office of the Future. Pasadena, CA: Office Technology Research Group.

Tversky, A. (1969). Intransitivity of preferences. *Psychological Review, 76,* 31–48.

Tversky, A. (1972). Elimination by aspects: A theory of choice. *Psychological Review, 79,* 281–299.

Tversky, A., & Kahneman, D. (1973). Availability: A heuristic for judging frequency and probability. *Cognitive Psychology, 5,* 207–232.

Tversky, A., & Kahnemen, D. (1974). Judgment under uncertainty: Heuristics and biases. *Science, 211,* 453–458.

Tversky, A., & Kahneman, D. (1981). The framing of decisions and the psychology of choice. *Science, 211,* 453–458.

Tversky, A., Sattath, S., & Slovic, P. (1988). Contingent weighting in judgment and choice. *Psychological Review, 95,* 371–384.

Tversky, B. G. (1969). Pictorial and verbal encoding in a short-term memory task. *Perception & Psychophysics, 6,* 225–233.

Tyrrell, R. A., & Leibowitz, H. W. (1990). The relation of vergence effort to reports of visual fatigue following prolonged nearwork. *Human Factors, 32,* 341–357.

Umiltà, C., & Liotti, M. (1987). Egocentric and relative spatial codes in S–R compatibility. *Psychological Research, 49,* 81–90.

Umiltà, C., & Nicoletti, R. (1990). Spatial stimulus–response compatibility. In R. W. Proctor & T. G. Reeve (eds.), *Stimulus–Response Compatibility: An Integrated Perspective* (pp. 89–116). Amsterdam: North-Holland.

Uttal, W. R. (1973). *The Psychobiology of Sensory Coding.* New York: Harper & Row.

Uttal, W. R. (1990). On some two-way barriers between models and mechanisms. *Perception & Psychophysics, 48,* 188–203.

Valencia, G., & Agnew, J. R. (1990). Evaluation of a directional audio display synthesizer. In *Proceedings of the Human Factors Society* (pp. 6–10). Santa Monica, CA: Human Factors Society.

Van Cott, H. P. (1980). Civilian anthropometry data bases. In *Proceedings of the Human Factors Society 24th Annual Meeting* (pp. 34–36). Santa Monica, CA: Human Factors Society.

van der Veer, G. C., & Felt, M. A. M. (1988). Development of mental models of an office system. In G. C. van der Veer & G. Mulder (eds.), *Human–Computer Interaction: Psychonomic Aspects* (pp. 250–272). New York: Springer-Verlag.

Van Sonderen, J. F., Denier Van der Gon, J. J., & Gielen, S. C. A. M. (1988). Conditions determining early modification of motor programmes in response to changes in target location. *Experimental Brain Reserach, 71,* 320–328.

Verillo, T. R., Fraioli, A. J., & Smith, R. L. (1969). Sensation magnitude of vibrotactile stimuli. *Perception & Psychophysics, 6,* 366–372.

Vessey, I. (1986). Expertise in debugging computer programs: An analysis of the content of verbal protocols. *IEEE Transactions on Systems, Man, and Cybernetics, 16,* 621–637.

Vicente, K. J., Thornton, D. C., & Moray, N. (1987). Spectral analysis of sinus arrhythmia: A measure of mental effort. *Human Factors, 29,* 171–182.

Vidulich, M. A., Ward, G. F., & Schueren, J. (1991). Using the subjective workload dominance (SWORD) technique for projective workload assessment. *Human Factors, 33,* 677–691.

von Winterfeldt, D., & Edwards, W. (1986). *Decision Analysis and Behavioral Research.* New York: Cambridge University Press.

Voss, J. F., & Post, T. A. (1988). On the solving of ill-structured problems. In M. T. H. Chi, R. Glaser, & M. J. Farr (eds.), *The Nature of Expertise* (pp. 261–285). Hillsdale, NJ: Lawrence Erlbaum.

Wade, D. (1965). Strict liability of manufacturers. *Southwestern Law Journal, 19,* 5.

Wadman, W. J., Denier van der Gon, J. J., Geuze, R. H., & Mol, C. R. (1979). Control of fast goal-directed arm movements. *Journal of Human Movement Studies, 5,* 3–17.

Wallace, R. J. (1971). S–R compatibility and the idea of a response code. *Journal of Experimental Psychology, 88,* 354–360.

Wallace, S. A., & Carlson, L. E. (1992). Critical variables in the coordination of prosthetic and normal limbs. In G. E. Stelmach & J. Requin (eds.), *Tutorials in Motor Behavior II* (pp. 321–341). Amsterdam: North-Holland.

Wallace, S. A., & Newell, K. M. (1983). Visual control of discrete aiming movements. *Quarterly Journal of Experimental Psychology, 35A,* 311–321.

Wallach, H. (1972). The perception of neutral colors. In T. Held & W. Richards (eds.), *Perception: Mechanisms and Models: Readings from Scientific American* (pp. 278–285). San Francisco: W. H. Freeman.

Warm, J. S. (1984). An introduction to vigilance. In J. S. Warm (ed.), *Sustained Attention in Human Performance* (pp. 1–14). New York: Wiley.

Warren, R. M. (1970). Perceptual restoration of missing speech sounds. *Science, 167,* 392–393.

Warrick, M. J., Kibler, A. W., & Topmiller, D. A. (1965). Response time to unexpected stimuli. *Human Factors, 7,* 81–86.

Warrick, M. J., & Turner, L. (1963). *Simultaneous Activation of Bimanual Controls.* Aerospace Medical Research Laboratories Technical Documentary Report No. AMRL-TDR-63–6. Wright–Patterson Air Force Base, OH: U.S. Air Force.

Wason, P. (1969). Regression in reasoning. *British Journal of Psychology, 60,* 471–480.

Wasserman, D. E. (1987). Motion and vibration. In G. Salvendy (ed.), *Handbook of Human Factors* (pp. 650–669). New York: Wiley.

Watson, A. B. (1986). Temporal sensitivity. In K. R. Boff, L. Kaufman, & J. P. Thomas (eds.), *Handbook of Human Perception and Performance, Vol. I: Sensory Processes and Perception* (pp. 6-1 to 6-43). New York: Wiley.

Waugh, N. C., & Norman, D. A. (1965). Primary memory. *Psychological Review, 72,* 89–104.

Weber, E. H. (1846/1978). Per tastsinn und das gemeingefühl. In H. E. Ross & D. J. Murray (D. J. Murray, trans.), *E. H. Weber: The Sense of Touch.* New York: Academic Press.

Webster, J. C., & Klumpp, R. G. (1963). Articulation index and average curve-fitting methods of pre-dicting speech interference. *Journal of the Acoustical Society of America, 35,* 1339–1344.

Weeks, D. J., & Proctor, R. W. (1990). Compatibility effects for orthogonal stimulus–response dimensions. *Journal of Experimental Psychology: General, 119,* 355–366.

Weinberg, R. S. (1981). The relationship between mental preparation strategies and motor performance: A review and critique. *Quest, 33,* 195–213.

Weinstein, A. S., Twerski, A. D., Piehler, H. R., & Donaher, W. A. (1978). *Product Liability and the Reasonably Safe Product.* New York: Wiley.

Weinstein, S. (1968). Intensive and extensive aspects of tactile sensitivity as a function of body part, sex, and laterality. In D. R. Kenshalo (ed.), *The Skin Senses* (pp. 195–218). Springfield, IL: Charles C Thomas.

Weltman, G., & Egstrom, G. H. (1966). Perceptual narrowing in novice divers. *Human Factors, 8,* 499–505.

West, L. J., & Sabban, Y. (1982). Hierarchy of stroking habits at the typewriter. *Journal of Applied Psychology, 67,* 370–376.

Weston, H. C. (1945). The relationship between illuminance and visual efficiency—The effect of brightness and contrast. Industrial Health Research Board Report No. 87. London: Great Britain Medical Research Council.

Wever, E. G. (1970). *Theory of Hearing.* New York: Wiley.

Wheeler, J. (1989). More thoughts on the human factors of expert systems development. *Human Factors Society Bulletin, 32* (12), 1–4.

White, W. J., Warrick, M. J., & Grether, W. F. (1953). Instrument reading: III. Check reading of instrument groups. *Journal of Applied Psychology, 37,* 302–307.

Whitehurst, H. O. (1992). Screening designs used to estimate the relative effects of display factors on dial reading. *Human factors, 24,* 301–310.

Whiteside, J. Jones, S., Levy, P. S., & Wixon, D. (1985). User performance with command, menu, and iconic interfaces. *Proceedings of CHI 83* (pp. 144–148). New York: ACM.

Whiting, H. T. A. (1969). *Acquiring Ball Skill: A Psychological Interpretation.* London: G. Bell & Sons.

Whittingham, R. B. (1988). The application of the combined THERP/HCR model in human reliability assessment. In B. A. Sayers (ed.), *Human Factors and Decision Making* (pp. 126–138). New York: Elsevier Applied Science.

Wickelgren, W. A. (1964). Size of rehearsal group in short-term memory. *Journal of Experimental Psychology, 68,* 413–419.

Wickens, C. D. (1976). The effects of divided attention in information processing in tracking. *Journal of Experimental Psychology: Human Perception and Performance, 2,* 1–13.

Wickens, C. D. (1980). The structure of attentional resources. In R. S. Nickerson (ed.), *Attention and Performance VIII* (pp. 239–257). Hillsdale, NJ: Lawrence Erlbaum.

Wickens, C. D. (1984). Processing resources in attention. In R. Parasuraman & R. Davies (eds.), *Varieties of Attention* (pp. 63–102). New York: Academic Press.

Wickens, C. D., & Andre, A. D. (1990). Proximity compatibility and information display: Effects of color, space, and objectness on information integration. *Human Factors, 32,* 61–77.

Wickens, C. D., Hyman, F., Dellinger, J., Taylor, H., & Meador, M. (1986). The Sternberg memory search task as an index of pilot workload. *Ergonomics, 29,* 1371–1383.

Wickens, C. D., Sandry, D. L., & Vidulich, M. (1983). Compatibility and resource competition between modalities of input, central processing, and output. *Human Factors, 25,* 227–248.

Wickens, D. D. (1972). Characteristics of word encoding. In A. W. Melton & E. Martin (eds.), *Coding Processes in Human Memory* (pp. 191–215). Washington, DC: Winston.

Wicklund, M. E., & Loring, B. A. (1990). Human factors design of an AIDS prevention pamphlet. In *Proceedings of the Human Factors Society 34th Annual Meeting* (pp. 988–992). Santa Monica, CA: Human Factors Society.

Wiedenbeck, S. (1985). Novice/expert differences in programming skills. *International Journal of Man–Machine Studies, 23,* 383–390.

Wiener, E. L. (1964). Transfer of training in monitoring. *Perceptual and Motor Skills, 18,* 104.

Wiener, E. L. (1984). Vigilance and inspection. In J. S. Warm (ed.), *Sustained Attention in Human Performance* (pp. 207–246). New York: Wiley.

Wierwille, W. (1984). The design and location of controls: A brief review and introduction to new problems. In H. Schmidtke (ed.), *Ergonomic Data for Equipment Design* (pp. 179–194). New York: Plenum.

Wierwille, W. W., & Casali, J. G. (1983). A validated rating scale for global mental workload measurement applications. In *Proceedings of the Human Factors Society 27 Annual Meeting* (pp. 129–133). Santa Monica, CA: Human Factors Society.

Wiesendanger, M. (1990). The motor cortical areas and the problem of hierarchies. In M. Jeannerod (ed.), *Attention and Performance XIII* (pp. 59–75). Hillsdale, NJ: Lawrence Erlbaum.

Wightman, D. C., & Lintern, G. (1985). Part-task training for tracking and manual control. *Human Factors, 27,* 267–283.

Wiker, S. F., Langolf, G. D., & Chaffin, D. B. (1989). Arm posture and human movement capability. *Human Factors, 31,* 421–441.

Wilde, G., & Humes, L. E. (1990). Application of the articulation index to the speech recognition of normal and impaired listeners wearing hearing protection. *Journal of the Acoustical Society of America, 87,* 1192–1199.

Wilkinson, R. T. (1990). Response–stimulus interval in choice serial reaction time: Interaction with sleep deprivation, choice, and practice. *Quarterly Journal of Experimental Psychology, 42A,* 401–423.

Williams, J., & Singer, R. N. (1975). Muscular fatigue and the learning and performance of a motor control task. *Journal of Motor Behavior, 7,* 265–269.

Williams, L. J. (1985). Tunnel vision induced by a foveal load manipulation. *Human Factors, 27,* 221–227.

Williges, R. C., Williges, B. H., & Elkerton, J. (1987). Software interface design. In G. Salvendy (ed.), *Handbook of Human Factors* (pp. 1416–1449). New York: Wiley.

Wilson, G. F., & O'Donnell, R. D. (1988). Measurement of operator workload with the neuropsychological workload test battery. In P. A. Hancock & N. Meshkati (eds.), *Human Mental Workload* (pp. 63–100). Amsterdam: North-Holland.

Wing, A. M. (1980). The long and short of timing in response sequences. In G. E. Stelmach & J. Requin (eds.), *Tutorials in Motor Behavior* (pp. 469–486). Amsterdam: North-Holland.

Wing, A. M., & Kristofferson, A. B. (1973). Response delays and the discrete motor responses. *Perception & Psychophysics, 14,* 5–12.

Winstein, C. J., & Schmidt, R. (1989). Sensorimotor feedback. In D. H. Holding (ed.), *Human Skills,* 2nd ed. (pp. 17–47). New York: Wiley.

Winstein, C. J., & Schmidt, R. A. (1990). Reduced frequency of knowledge of results enhances motor skill learning. *Journal of Experimental Psychology: Learning, Memory, and Cognition, 16,* 677–691.

Wise, J. A. (1986). The space station: Human factors and habitability. *Human Factors Society Bulletin, 29* (5), 1–3.

Woodhouse, J. M., & Barlow, H. B. (1982). Spatial and temporal resolution and analysis. In H. B. Barlow & J. D. Mollon (eds.), *The Senses* (pp. 133–164). New York: Cambridge University Press.

Woodson, W. E. (1981). *Human Factors Design Handbook.* New York: McGraw-Hill.

Woodworth, R. S. (1899). The accuracy of voluntary movement. *Psychological Review Monograph Supplements, 3,* 1–119.

Woodworth, R. S., & Sells, S. B. (1935). An atmosphere effect in formal syllogistic reasoning. *Journal of Experimental Psychology, 18,* 451–460.

Worledge, D. H., Joksimovich, V., & Spurgin, A. J. (1988). Interim results and conclusions of the EPRI operator reliability experiments program. In E. W. Hagen (ed.), *1988 IEEE Fourth Conference on Human Factors and Power Plants* (pp. 315–322). New York: Institute of Electrical and Electronics Engineers.

Worringham, C. J., & Beringer, D. B. (1989). Operator orientation and compatibility in visual–motor task performance. *Ergonomics, 32,* 387–399.

Wright, C. E. (1990). Generalized motor programs: Reexamining claims of effector independence in writing. In M. Jeannerod (ed.), *Attention and Performance XIII: Motor Representation and Control* (pp. 294–320). Hillsdale, NJ: Lawrence Erlbaum.

Wright, G. (1984). *Behavioral Decision Theory.* Beverly Hills, CA: Sage Publications.

Wright, P. (1976). The harassed decision maker: Time pressures, distraction, and the use of evidence. *Journal of Applied Psychology, 59,* 555–561.

Wright, P. (1988). Functional literacy: Reading and writing at work. *Ergonomics, 31,* 265–290.

Wrisberg, C. A., & Winter, T. P. (1985). Reproducing the end location of a positioning movement: The long and short of it. *Journal of Motor Behavior, 17,* 242–254.

Wulf, G., & Schmidt, R. A. (1989). The learning of generalized motor programs: Reducing the relative frequency of knowledge of results enhances memory. *Journal of Experimental Psychology: Learning, Memory, and Cognition, 15,* 748–757.

Wyszecki, G. (1986). Color appearance. In K. R. Boff, L. Kaufman, & J. P. Thomas (eds.), *Handbook of Perception and Human Performance. Vol. I: Sensory Processes and Perception* (pp. 9-1 to 9-57). New York: Wiley.

Yerkes, R. M., & Dodson, J. D. (1908). The relation of strength of stimulus to rapidity of habit-formation. *Journal of Comparative Neurology of Psychology, 18,* 459–482.

Young, S. L., & Wogalter, M. S. (1990). Comprehension and memory of instruction manual warnings: Conspicuous print and pictorial icons. *Human Factors, 32,* 637–649.

Young, T. (1802). On the theory of light and colours. *Philosophical Transactions of the Royal Society of London, 92,* 12–48.

Yu, C.-Y., & Keyserling, W. M. (1989). Evaluation of a new workseat for industrial seating operations. *Applied Ergonomics, 20,* 17–25.

Zechmeister, E. B., & Nyberg, S. E. (1982). *Human Memory: An Introduction to Research and Theory.* Monterey, CA: Brooks/Cole.

Zelaznik, H. N., Hawkins, B., & Kisselburgh, L. (1983). Rapid visual feedback processing in single-aiming movements. *Journal of Motor Behavior, 15,* 217–236.

Zelman, S. (1973). Correlation of smoking history with hearing loss. *Journal of the American Medical Association, 223,* 920.

Zimolong, B., Nof, S. Y., Eberts, R. E., & Salvendy, G. (1987). On the limits of expert systems and engineering models in process control. *Behaviour and Information Technology, 6,* 15–36.

Zwaga, H. J. (1989). Comprehensibility estimates of public information symbols: Their validity and use. In *Proceedings of the Human Factors Society 33rd Annual Meeting,* Vol. 2 (pp. 979–983). Santa Monica, CA: Human Factors Society.

Zwicker, E. (1958). Uber psychologische und methodische Grundlagen der Lautheit. *Acustica, 8,* 237–258.

AUTHOR INDEX